Travels in
West Africa

Other Volumes in the Virago/Beacon Traveler Series

TRAVELS IN WEST AFRICA

Congo Français, Corisco and Cameroons

MARY H. KINGSLEY

*With a new Introduction
by Elizabeth Claridge*

FIFTH EDITION

Beacon Press   Boston

Beacon Press
25 Beacon Street
Boston, Massachusetts 02108

Beacon Press books
are published under the auspices of
the Unitarian Universalist Association of Congregations.

First published in 1897 by Macmillan & Co. Ltd.
Introduction ©1982 by Elizabeth Claridge
First published as a Beacon paperback in 1988
by arrangement with Virago Press Limited
All rights reserved
Printed in the United States of America

95 94 93 92 91 90 89 88   1 2 3 4 5 6 7 8

The Virago/Beacon Travelers edition of *Travels in West
Africa* has been reproduced from the unabridged 1897
Macmillan edition. Two full-page illustrations of fishes
(plate 1 showing *Ctenopoma kingsleyae*, *C. nanum*, and *C.
gabonense*; plate 2 showing *Mormyrus kingsleyae*, *Alestes
kingsleyae*, and *Barilius bibie*) have been omitted.

Library of Congress Cataloging-in-Publication Data

Kingsley, Mary Henrietta, 1862–1900.
Travels in West Africa.
(Virago/Beacon travelers)
Reprint. Originally published: London : Macmillan,
1897. With new introd.
Includes index.
1. Africa, West — Description and travel — 1851–1950.
2. Kingsley, Mary Henrietta, 1862–1900 — Journeys — Africa,
West. I. Title. II. Series.
DT472.K53   1988   916.6'0423   87-42856
ISBN 0-8070-7105-6 (pbk.)

CONTENTS

CHAPTER XXII

CHAPTER XXIII

CHAPTER XXIV

CHAPTER XXV

CHAPTER XXVI

CHAPTER XXVII

CHAPTER XXVIII

APPENDIX

TO MY BROTHER, C. G. KINGSLEY

THIS BOOK IS DEDICATED

INTRODUCTION TO THE FIFTH EDITION

In the summer of 1893 Mary Kingsley, aged thirty and unmarried, found herself for the first time in her life with 'five or six months which were not heavily forestalled'. Her parents, for whom she had kept house since childhood, had died within weeks of each other the previous year. Her brother, for whom she continued to keep house, had departed on a journey to the East. She decided to spend her respite from domesticity in West Africa, a region notorious for its deadly climate and diseases, its alarming wildlife, and its cannibals. Her object was to study native religion and law, and to collect zoological specimens, fresh-water fish in particular. In August, on a battered cargo-boat of the Royal African line, she sailed from Liverpool for Freetown in Sierra Leone, the first port of call on the West African coast for European shipping.

Few women of any period have stepped so abruptly from conventional circumstances into the unknown. Mary Kingsley is often compared to Marianne North, Constance Gordon Cumming, and Isabella Bird, those other redoubtable travellers who left the confines of Victorian England to explore remote and hazardous parts of the world, but they progressed to their more difficult journeys from preliminary excursions abroad. When Mary Kingsley boarded *S.S. Lagos*, the only woman apart from a stewardess among an assortment of 'old Coasters', her experience of foreign travel amounted to a week in Paris with a woman friend in 1888, and a trip to the Canaries by Castle liner to restore her spirits after her parents' deaths.

In the matter of dress suitable for a woman traveller, Mary Kingsley was of like mind with Miss North, Miss Gordon Cumming, and Miss Bird. Miss North made no particular issue of what she wore but it clearly never occurred to her to dress other than as a lady. Describing a trek across a sodden part of Brazil in 1872, she observed in *Recollections of a Happy Life*: 'My dress was as good as any could be for such riding, namely a short linsey petticoat and a long waterproof cloak with sleeves.' According to Miss Bird, Miss Gordon Cumming maintained a formidable elegance at all times. This failed to mollify Miss North on the occasions, as in Ceylon in 1876, she was mistaken for Miss Gordon Cumming: 'I got quite tired of her name, and heard far more about her than about the beautiful country with its orchids and elephants.' Isabella Bird thought her publisher, John Murray, should horsewhip the correspondent who had dared to suggest in *The Times* of November 22nd, 1879, that she had besported herself in the Rockies clad in 'masculine habilements for greater convenience'. Her actual attire, she asserted in a note to the second edition of *A Lady's Life in the Rocky Moutains* (a book Mary Kingsley thought 'charming'), had been a ladies riding-dress from Hawaii consisting of long Turkish trousers worn beneath an ankle-length skirt. Miss Kingsley had an equal, if more wry, aversion to 'masculine habilements'. For travelling in Africa, among tribes who tended to concentrate their adornments on their hair, she preferred a moleskin hat (now to be seen at the Royal Geographical Society), high-necked white blouse, cummerbund, long black skirt of stout material, and lace-up boots, with the occasional addition of a red silk tie.

The 'old Coasters' on the *Lagos*, deceived by her decorous appearance, assumed she must be a missionary or, more disconcerting still, a representative of the World's Women's Temperance Association. But Mary Kingsley had been brought up an agnostic, and remained 'a staunch Darwinian' to the end. Her evident unfamiliarity with the procedure of the Sunday Service, together with a certain robustness of speech and an unladylike curiosity about their work, relieved her companions of some anxiety but left them bewildered as to why she should be going somewhere so unsalubrious as

West Africa. She offered as explanation an interest in natural history. As she was to point out when she came to write *Travels in West Africa*, she was not given to discoursing on her psychological state. Had she been, she might have said she was going to West Africa because of her father.

Dr George Henry Kingsley — brother to Canon Charles (novelist, naturalist, and social reformer) and to Henry (author of *Ravenshoe*) — was an amateur naturalist and ethnologist, and an inveterate wanderer, usually as private physician to one aristocrat or another. On 9 October 1862 he married Mary Bailey; their first child, Mary Henrietta was born less than a week later, on 13 October. Throughout her childhood and youth, George Kingsley was at home at most two or three months in the year, and some years not at all. While he was amusing himself hunting, shooting, and fishing around the world, she was left with the care of an increasingly depressive mother, a 'delicate' younger brother, and the main responsibility for domestic matters, first at Highgate, then Bexley Heath, then Cambridge when brother Charles went up to the University. Into a life which rarely extended beyond the house and garden came letters describing hair-raising adventures in the South Seas, the Rocky Mountains (George Kingsley was the doctor who treated the fatal gunshot wounds of Isabella Bird's friend, 'Mountain Jim'), the Antipodes, South Africa, Japan.

While her ineffectual brother had £2,000 spent on his education, Mary Kingsley was obliged to learn what she could from books in her father's library, which included 'volume on volume of famous voyagers', and from any others she could scrounge, *The Pursuit of Knowledge Under Difficulties* being one. It may be imagined with what irritation she read a reference to herself as 'the learned one' in one of her father's letters from the Rockies. When George Kingsley began to study primitive societies with some seriousness, with particular reference to sacrificial rites, his daughter became 'his underworker on that subject, collecting accounts given by travellers'. To be able to read 'views taken on the question by

German authors', she was allowed tuition in the language, her only 'paid-for education'. Against the odds, and in the shadow of her father, she made herself into an erudite ethnologist and informed naturalist.

Her ruthlessly circumscribed upbringing left Mary Kingsley with a pronounced sense of duty to others, an attitude reinforced by her agnosticism in a way that George Eliot summarised: 'God is inconceivable, immortality is unbelievable, but duty is peremptory and absolute.' It also left her with the conviction that she had no individuality and no right to a life of her own. Florence Nightingale used the same terms in 'Cassandra', her bitter diatribe against the constraints which crippled women. It forms part of her unpublished book, *Suggestions for Thought to Searchers after Religious Truth*, which she wrote when she was thirty-two in 1852, two years before the Crimean War broke out. In 1850 she had written in her diary: 'In my thirty-first year I see nothing but death.' In 1897 Mary Kingsley was to speak in a letter of 'the dreadful gloom of all my life before I went to West Africa'. Their stories have much in common: the despair they experienced as young women, the longing for proper training and worthwhile work, the dramatic exodus to find that work.

When Mary Kingsley's parents died she felt not only desolate with grief but bereft of purpose. With her brother Charles, who made a habit of denigrating her, she moved to a flat, and subsequently to a house, in Kensington. His disappearance to Burma confronted her with both vacuum and opportunity. In later years she gave as reason for going to West Africa a wish to continue her father's studies in one of the few parts of the world he had never visited. In a letter of 1899 she said that she had gone to West Africa to die, a remark which seems to indicate not so much a positive desire for death as guilt about wanting to live on her own terms. Perhaps her strongest impulse, shared by many women travellers, was that described by Ella Maillart in *Forbidden Journey*, her account of the journey she and Peter Fleming made across China in 1935: '. . . I could not help feeling that

danger, if it arose, would but allow of my drawing, at last, on
my dormant energies.'

To an extent that has to be inferred, Mary Kingsley's
choice of destination was influenced by the spirit of the times.
In the 1890s 'the dark continent', a phrase imprinted on the
popular imagination by the explorer Stanley, was the focus of
public curiosity and political machination. The last hundred
years had seen the map of Africa filled in by the great journeys
of Mungo Park, Hugh Clapperton, Richard Lander, Henry
Barth, David Livingstone, John Hanning Speke, Richard
Burton, Henry Morton Stanley, Pierre Savorgnan de Brazza,
and others. The last ten years had seen the European powers
jostling for territory and influence in the so-called 'Scramble
for Africa'. Nowhere was the scramble more piquant and
picaresque than in West Africa, 'the white man's grave'.

Mary Kingsley learnt something of its sepulchral fascination from returning traders she met in the Canaries in 1892.
She learnt very much more on the *Lagos*, particularly as to the
variety of deaths, insects, and trade products peculiar to the
place. She was to say in her second book, *West African Studies*:
'. . . to my listening to everything that was told me by my
first instructors, and believing in it, undoubtedly I have often
owed my life . . .'

The *Lagos* took her down the West African coast from
British Sierra Leone to Portuguese Angola. By the time she
left the boat at Loanda she had acquired a working knowledge
of 'trade English', the *lingua franca* of West Africa, which was
to be invaluable on her independent travels. From Loanda she
made her way, partly overland and partly by coastal steamer,
up the seaboard of Angola into the Congo Free State (that
grotesquely mis-named private empire of King Leopold II of
the Belgians), Portuguese Kacongo, the French Congo, the
German Cameroons, and finally to Old Calabar in the Niger
Coast Protectorate, British territory.

Her overriding impression was of 'the charm of West
Africa'. She discovered it in the forthright company of sailors
and traders; in treks into the bush with a few Africans as

carriers or crew; in the animistic minds of the Negro and the Bantu; in the heat and rains and mists and storms of a tropical climate; and, most intensely, in the forbidding beauty of the landscape: the line of luminous surf, the strip of white beach, the swathe of bronze mangrove-swamp, the wall of dark forest. Like Marianne North, she was happiest when alone among the 'non-human things' of nature. Her instinctive pantheism attuned her to the spirituality of Africa; her innate loneliness was consoled by its solitudes.

In January 1894 she returned to England with a collection of specimens which impressed her natural history mentor, Dr Günther of the British Museum; insights into 'the African mind-form' which breathed life into her years of ethnological reading; and the exhilarating sense of having found her *métier*. It was enough to decide her that 'there was any amount of work for me worth doing down there'; and in December, armed with a professional collector's outfit supplied by the British Museum, Mary Kingsley went back to West Africa.

Over the next eleven months she pursued 'beetles, fishes and fetish' still more purposefully, principally in the Niger Delta and Calabar districts of the Niger Coast Protectorate, and in the Gaboon region (Gabon) of the French Congo. Her expeditions in the latter took her into 'the wildest and most dangerous part of the West African regions': the terrain of dense rain forest intercut by the swift, sombre Ogowé river, 'the greatest strictly equatorial river in the world', and in-habited by 'a set of notoriously savage tribes, chief among which are the Fans'. She made the most exacting of her explorations through the forest with three Fans as guides, on a route north from the Ogowé to the Rembwe river which no white person had attempted before and, in its entirety, no black.

On such occasions she lived as her African companions did, eating native food and sleeping in village huts. To her men and to the village chiefs she presented herself 'in the guise of trader'. Her first journey to West Africa had introduced her to the skills and pleasures of trading. On her second she took it up in earnest, partly for the interest of it, partly to supplement the three hundred pounds she had allowed for her two journeys, but particularly for the entrée it gave her into the confidence and everyday life of African tribes. She was obliged in any case to pay her way in goods and had arranged credit with the firm of Hatton & Cookson. She never forgot the help its agents gave her, not the rough kindness of many others. They returned her respect and affection, calling her 'our own Only me' after her usual method of introducing herself as she emerged 'unheralded out of the bush in a dilapidated state'.

She was as enthusiastic a sailor as she was trader. Neither close encounters with man-eating crocodiles nor frequent duckings could deter her from paddling about stinking, fly-infested, leech-filled mangrove-swamps. With a crew of eight Igalwas and the cry 'Jump for bank, sar' ringing in her ears, she negotiated the formidable rapids of the Ogowé by canoe. In a calmer stretch of the river she mastered the art of single-canoeing. She took the helm of a ramshackle sailing-canoe down the Rembwe, and of 2,000-ton coastal steamers crossing the perilous Forcados Bar. She became expert on the depths of water available off the Coast and when necessary, as in Corisco Bay, took soundings with her umbrella. Normally self-deprecating, she would defend her navigational expertise vehemently.

As a final flourish to her West African travels, Mary Kingsley climbed the 13,760-foot Great Peak of the Cameroons by its south-east face. She learnt two years later that she had been the first person to reach the summit by that route. She knew at the time it was none of her business to go up mountains: 'There's next to no fish on them in West Africa, and precious little good rank fetish, as the population on them is sparse – the African, like myself, abhorring cool air.'

She returned to England on 30 November 1895, to cool air and a flurry in the Press about her exploits: 'I discovered, to my alarm, that I was, by freak of fate, the sea-serpent of the season.' Allusions to the dauntless lady traveller, as opposed to the ethnological and zoological work she had been doing, were inevitable. The previous decade Marianne North and Constance Gordon Cumming, friends by this time, had been embarassed into retreating from a party in Isabella Bird's honour by a Lady A. trilling triumphantly, 'three globe-trotteresses all at once!' Miss Bird, reported Marianne North with mixed feelings, remained 'unruffled and equal to the occasion'. Miss Kingsley enjoyed gatherings of that kind even less than Miss North and Miss Gordon Cumming.

She handed over her collection of specimens to the British Museum, insects to Mr W.F. Kirby, reptiles and fishes to Dr Günther, and was cheered by their findings. Kirby reported eight new species, two requiring new genera. Günther reported a new snake (according to Miss Kingsley, although not described by him), a rare lizard, eight new species of fresh-water fish and one exceptionally rare one. He named three of the new fish after her.

Meanwhile she began to refute publicly the prevailing view of the African as either inept child, or despicable brute (with, as the *Spectator* put it in December 1895, 'an apparently irredeemable proclivity to barbarism'), or a mixture of both, 'half-devil and half-child' to use Kipling's phrase of 1898. She found equally objectionable the notion current in philanthropic and temperance circles, and reflected in political ones, that this child or brute was 'led to good or bad respectively by the missionary and the trader'. She had seen for herself that all-too-often mission teaching corroded the morale and morals of the African by dividing him from his own culture and undermining its restraints. That government officials on the spot and the Colonial Office at home should sneer at the trader and do little to support England's trade interests in West Africa, seemed to Mary Kingsley absurdly wrong-headed. It was to substantiate her opinions that she wrote her great book, *Travels in West Africa*. The travels described belong to her second journey, although reference is made to the first.

It was Mary Kingsley's particular genius to be able to see

in what most Europeans of her day, including Joseph Conrad who spent five months in the Congo Free State in 1890, thought of as the darkness of Africa. At the heart of *Travels* is an account of her learning to see in the great rain forests, of the world which 'grows up gradually out of the gloom before your eyes'. (The Africans thought there were seven different types of rain forest but Mary Kingsley, a connoisseur of forests, decided there were nine.) The passage concludes with the words: 'As it is with the forest, so it is with the minds of the natives. Unless you live among the natives, you never get to know them. If you do this you gradually get a light into the true state of their mind-forest.' It is this quality of seeing, transmitted through vivid and witty prose, that gives *Travels in West Africa* its particular distinction.

Although she disliked the Crown Colony system by which England's West African possessions were governed, Mary Kingsley was an imperialist. She believed that England, historically a nation of merchant-adventurers, had every right to extend her trade across the globe and to protect it by the English flag, emblem of the highest form of justice. But she also believed that there could be no justice for the African under the English flag without a proper – she used the word 'scientific' – understanding of his native institutions and religion. In *Travels* she set against the imperial fiction of 'the dark continent', the scientific facts as she had seen them.

Few travellers have been so little weighed down by the presumptions of their own culture, or been so little protected on their journeys. Testimony to the dangers of West African travel can be seen in the writings of such as Du Chaillu, who scarified London society in 1861 with his melodramatic but accurate reports of cannibals and gorillas. Mary Kingsley was quick to refute the label of 'intrepid explorer', nor was she an explorer in the sense that the Royal Geographical Society would, or did, recognise. But she possessed in full measure that attribute which distinguishes the great traveller: presence of mind in the face of the alien or unexpected which amounts to a sort of grace. She never thought of it as courage herself, although others did. She preferred the word 'self-respect'. Her emphasis on it brings to mind Jane Eyre's remark: 'The more solitary, the more friendless, the more unsustained I am, the more I will respect myself.'

Mary Kingsley had many friends who loved her dearly, but West Africa was where she felt most herself and most at home. What she saw as her duty prevented her from returning there. She devoted the rest of her life to enlightening the English, in lectures and articles and political lobbying, as to West African affairs. In 1899 she published *West African Studies*, which she wrote to amplify her researches into fetish and to suggest a form of government better suited to West Africa than the Crown Colony system. Her chief recommendation was for the representation of traders, those 'palm-oil ruffians' she liked so well. Their 'enfranchisement' she considered of much more importance than women's suffrage: it was her nature to identify with outsiders and she was disinclined, 'owing to the morbid state of opinion regarding women's work' as she put it, to ally herself with feminist causes. She edited, and contributed a memoir to, a collection of her father's writings, published as *Notes on Sport and Travel* in 1900. Her *Story of West Africa*, a little volume in a popular series, was also published in 1900.

In March that year Mary Kingsley sailed for South Africa to nurse Boer prisoners of war, and perhaps to catch some fish from the Orange River for Dr Günther. On 12 February, she had concluded a lecture to the Imperial Institute in London with the words of an old sea-shanty: 'Goodbye and fare you well, for I am homeward bound.' In the course of her nursing duties at the hospital at Simonstown, she contracted enteric fever which led to heart failure. When she realised she was dying, she asked those around her to let her die alone. She died, aged thirty-seven, on 3 June. With full honours from the English naval and military stationed at Simonstown, and with a band playing, she was buried, as she had requested, at sea.   *Elizabeth Claridge, London 1982*

PREFACE TO THE FIRST EDITION

To the Reader.—What this book wants is not a simple Preface but an apology, and a very brilliant and convincing one at that. Recognising this fully, and feeling quite incompetent to write such a master-piece, I have asked several literary friends to write one for me, but they have kindly but firmly declined, stating that it is impossible satisfactorily to apologise for my liberties with Lindley Murray and the Queen's English. I am therefore left to make a feeble apology for this book myself, and all I can personally say is that it would have been much worse than it is had it not been for Dr. Henry Guillemard, who has not edited it, or of course the whole affair would have been better, but who has most kindly gone through the proof sheets, lassoing prepositions which were straying outside their sentence stockade, taking my eye off the water cask and fixing it on the scenery where I meant it to be, saying firmly in pencil on margins "No you don't," when I was committing some more than usually heinous literary crime, and so on.   In cases where his activities in these things may seem to the reader to have been wanting, I beg to state that they really were not.   It is I who have declined to ascend to a higher level of lucidity and correctness of diction than I am fitted for.   I cannot forbear from mentioning my gratitude to Mr. George Macmillan for his patience and kindness with me,—a mere jungle of information on West Africa.   Whether you my reader will share my gratitude is, I fear, doubtful, for if it had not been for him I should never have attempted to write a book at all, and in order to excuse his having induced me to try I beg to state that I have written only on things that I know from personal experience and very careful observation.   I have never accepted an explanation of a native custom from one person alone, nor have I set down things as being prevalent customs from having seen a single instance.   I have endeavoured to give you an honest account of the general state and manner of life in Lower Guinea and some description of the various types of country there.   In reading this section you must make allowances for my love of this sort of country, with its great forests and rivers and its animistic-minded inhabitants, and for my ability to be more comfortable there than in England. Your superior culture-instincts may militate against your enjoying West Africa, but if you go there you will find things as I have said.

LIST OF ILLUSTRATIONS

The illustrations to which asterisks are attached were first published by
kind permission of the Mission Évangélique of Paris

MAPS

FULL-PAGE ILLUSTRATIONS
Between pages 358 and 359

ILLUSTRATIONS IN TEXT

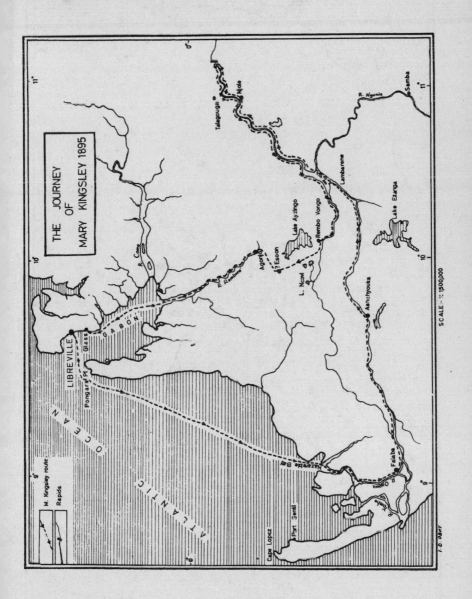

THE JOURNEY OF MARY KINGSLEY 1895

M. Kingsley route
Rapids

ATLANTIC OCEAN

LIBREVILLE
Glass
Pongara Pt
GABON
R. Como
R. Rembwe
Agonjo
Esoon
L. Ncovi
Lake Ayzingo
Rembo Vongo
Lambarene
Lake Ezanga
Talagouga
Njole
Samba
R. Ngunia
Arch. Yyouka
Falaba
R. Ogowé
Kembe
Port Gentil
Cape Lopez
Nazareth Bay

SCALE: 1:1,500,000

I. D. Obey

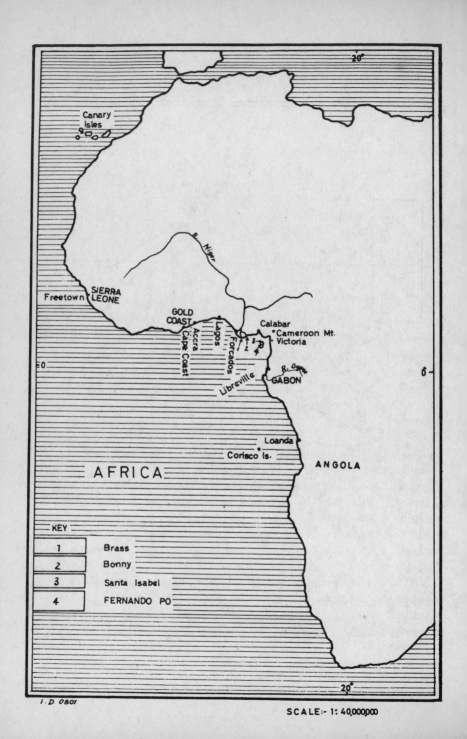

20°

Canary
Isles

R. Niger

SIERRA
Freetown LEONE

GOLD
COAST
Accra
Cape Coast
Lagos
Forcados
Libreville

Calabar
Cameroon Mt.
Victoria

R. Ogowe
GABON

E 0

6°

Loanda
Corisco Is.

ANGOLA

AFRICA

KEY

1	Brass
2	Bonny
3	Santa Isabel
4	FERNANDO PO

20°

I. D. OBOR

SCALE:- 1: 40,000,000

TRAVELS IN WEST AFRICA

INTRODUCTION

Relateth the various causes which impelled the author to embark upon the voyage.

IT was in 1893 that, for the first time in my life, I found myself in possession of five or six months which were not heavily forestalled, and feeling like a boy with a new half-crown, I lay about in my mind, as Mr. Bunyan would say, as to what to do with them. "Go and learn your tropics," said Science. Where on earth am I to go, I wondered, for tropics are tropics wherever found, so I got down an atlas and saw that either South America or West Africa must be my destination, for the Malayan region was too far off and too expensive. Then I got Wallace's *Geographical Distribution* and after reading that master's article on the Ethiopian region I hardened my heart and closed with West Africa. I did this the more readily because while I knew nothing of the practical condition of it, I knew a good deal both by tradition and report of South East America, and remembered that Yellow Jack was endemic, and that a certain naturalist, my superior physically and mentally, had come very near getting starved to death in the depressing society of an expedition slowly perishing of want and miscellaneous fevers up the Parana.

My ignorance regarding West Africa was soon removed. And although the vast cavity in my mind that it occupied is not even yet half filled up, there is a great deal of very curious information in its place. I use the word curious advisedly, for I think many seemed to translate my request for practical hints and advice into an advertisement that "Rubbish may be shot here." This same information is in a state of great confusion still, although I have made heroic efforts to codify it. I find, however, that it can almost all be got in under the following different headings, namely and to wit :—

The dangers of West Africa.
The disagreeables of West Africa.
The diseases of West Africa.
The things you must take to West Africa.
The things you find most handy in West Africa.
The worst possible things you can do in West Africa.

I inquired of all my friends as a beginning what they knew of West Africa. The majority knew nothing. A percentage said, "Oh, you can't possibly go there; that's where Sierra Leone is, the white man's grave, you know." If these were pressed further, one occasionally found that they had had relations who had gone out there after having been "sad trials," but, on consideration of their having left not only West Africa, but this world, were now forgiven and forgotten. One lady however kindly remembered a case of a gentleman who had resided some few years at Fernando Po, but when he returned an aged wreck of forty he shook so violently with ague as to dislodge a chandelier, thereby destroying a valuable tea-service and flattening the silver teapot in its midst.

No ; there was no doubt about it, the place was not healthy, and although I had not been "a sad trial," yet neither had the chandelier-dislodging Fernando Po gentleman. So I next turned my attention to cross-examining the doctors. "Deadliest spot on earth," they said cheerfully, and showed me maps of the geographical distribution of disease. Now I do not say that a country looks inviting when it is coloured in Scheele's green or a bilious yellow, but these colours may arise from lack of artistic gift in the cartographer. There is no mistaking what he means by black, however, and black you'll find they colour West Africa from above Sierra Leone to below the Congo. " I wouldn't go there if I were you," said my medical friends, " you'll catch something ; but if you must go, and you're as obstinate as a mule, just bring me——" and then followed a list of commissions from here to New York, any one of which——but I only found that out afterwards.

All my informants referred me to the missionaries. " There were," they said, in an airy way, " lots of them down there, and had been for years." So to missionary literature I addressed myself with great ardour ; alas ! only to find that these good people wrote their reports not to tell you how the country they resided in was, but how it was getting on towards being what it ought to be, and how necessary it was that their readers should subscribe more freely, and not get any foolishness into their heads about obtaining an inadequate supply of souls for their money. I also found fearful confirmation of my medical friends' statements about its unhealthiness, and various details of the distribution of cotton shirts over which I did not linger.

From the missionaries it was, however, that I got my first idea about the social condition of West Africa. I gathered that there existed there, firstly the native human beings—the raw material, as it were—and that these were led either to good or bad respectively by the missionary and the trader. There were also the Government representatives, whose chief business it was to strengthen and consolidate the missionary's work, a function they carried on but indifferently well. But as for those traders ! well, I put them down under the dangers of West Africa at once. Subsequently I came across the good old coast yarn of how, when a trader from that region went thence, it goes without saying where, the Fallen Angel without a moment's hesitation vacated the infernal throne (Milton) in his favour. This, I beg to note, is the marine form of the legend. When it occurs terrestrially the trader becomes a Liverpool mate. But of course no one need believe it either way—it is not a missionary's story.

Naturally, while my higher intelligence was taken up with attending to these statements, my mind got set on going, and I had to go. Fortunately I could number among my acquaintances one individual who had lived on the Coast for seven years. Not, it is true, on that part of it which I was bound for. Still his advice was pre-eminently worth attention, because, in spite of his long residence in the deadliest spot of the region, he was still in fair going order. I told him I intended going to West Africa, and he said, " When you have made up your mind to go to West Africa the very best thing you can do is to get it unmade again and go to Scotland instead ; but if your intelligence is not strong enough to do so, abstain from exposing yourself to the direct rays of the sun, take 4 grains of quinine every day for a fortnight before you reach the Rivers, and get some introductions to the Wesleyans ; they are the only people on the Coast who have got a hearse with feathers."

My attention was next turned to getting ready things to take with me. Having opened upon myself the sluice gates of advice, I rapidly became distracted. My friends and their friends alike seemed to labour under the delusion that I intended to charter a steamer and was a person of wealth beyond the dreams of avarice. The only thing to do in this state of affairs was to gratefully listen and let things drift. They showered on me various preparations of quinine and other so-called medical comforts, mustard leaves, a patent filter, a hot-water bottle, and last but not least a large square bottle purporting to be malt and cod-liver oil, which, rebelling against an African temperature, arose in its wrath, ejected its cork, and proclaimed itself an efficient but not too savoury glue.

Not only do the things you have got to take, but the things you have got to take them in, present a fine series of problems to the young traveller. Crowds of witnesses testified to the forms of baggage holders they had found invaluable, and these, it is unnecessary to say, were all different in form and material.

With all this *embarras de choix* I was too distracted to buy anything new in the way of baggage except a long waterproof sack neatly closed at the top with a bar and handle. Into this I put blankets, boots, books, in fact anything that would not go into my portmanteau or black bag. From the first I was haunted by a conviction that its bottom would come out, but it never did, and in spite of the fact that it had ideas of its own about the arrangement of its contents, it served me well throughout my voyage.

It was the beginning of August '93 when I first left England for " the Coast." Preparations of quinine with postage partially paid arrived up to the last moment, and a friend hastily sent two newspaper clippings, one entitled " A Week in a Palm-oil Tub," which was supposed to describe the sort of accommodation, companions, and fauna likely to be met with on a steamer going to West Africa, and on which I was to spend seven to *The Graphic* contributor's one; the other from *The Daily Telegraph*, reviewing a French book of " Phrases in common use " in Dahomey. The opening sentence in the latter was, " Help, I am drowning." Then came the inquiry, " If a man is not a thief? " and then another cry, " The boat is upset." " Get up, you lazy scamps," is the next exclamation, followed almost immediately by the question, " Why has not this man been buried? " " It is fetish that has killed him, and he must lie here exposed with nothing on him until only the bones remain," is the cheerful answer. This sounded discouraging to a person whose occupation would necessitate going about considerably in boats, and whose fixed desire was to study fetish. So with a feeling of foreboding gloom I left London for Liverpool—none the more cheerful for the matter-of-fact manner in which the steamboat agents had informed me that they did not issue return tickets by the West African lines of steamers.

I will not go into the details of that voyage here, much as I am given to discursiveness. They are more amusing than instructive, for on my first voyage out I did not know the Coast, and the Coast did not know me, and we mutually terrified each other. I fully expected to get killed by the local nobility and gentry; they thought I was connected with the World's Women's Temperance Association, and collecting shocking details for subsequent magic-lantern lectures on the liquor traffic ; so fearful misunderstandings

arose, but we gradually educated each other, and I had the
best of the affair ; for all I had got to teach them was that I
was only a beetle and fetish hunter, and so forth, while they
had to teach me a new world, and a very fascinating course of
study I found it. And whatever the Coast may have to say
against me—for my continual desire for hair-pins, and other
pins, my intolerable habit of getting into water, the abominations full of ants, that I brought into their houses, or things
emitting at unexpectedly short notice vivid and awful stenches
—they cannot but say that I was a diligent pupil, who honestly
tried to learn the lessons they taught me so kindly, though
some of those lessons were hard to a person who had never
previously been even in a tame bit of tropics, and whose life
for many years had been an entirely domestic one in a
University town.

One by one I took my old ideas derived from books and
thoughts based on imperfect knowledge and weighed them
against the real life around me, and found them either worthless or wanting. The greatest recantation I had to make
I made humbly before I had been three months on the Coast
in 1893. It was of my idea of the traders. What I had expected
to find them was a very different thing to what I did find
them ; and of their kindness to me I can never sufficiently
speak, for on that voyage I was utterly out of touch with the
governmental circles, and utterly dependent on the traders,
and the most useful lesson of all the lessons I learnt on the
West Coast in 1893 was that I could trust them. Had I not
learnt this very thoroughly I could never have gone out again
and carried out the voyage I give you a sketch of in this book.

Thanks to " the Agent," I have visited places I could never
otherwise have seen ; and to the respect and affection in which
he is held by the native, I owe it that I have done so in safety.
When I have arrived off his factory in a steamer or canoe,
unexpected, unintroduced, or turned up equally unheralded
out of the bush in a dilapidated state, he has always received
me with that gracious hospitality which must have given him,
under Coast conditions, very real trouble and inconvenience—
things he could have so readily found logical excuses against
entailing upon himself for the sake of an individual whom he

had never seen before—whom he most likely would never see again—and whom it was no earthly profit to him to see then. He has bestowed himself—Allah only knows where—on his small trading vessels so that I might have his one cabin. He has fished me out of sea and fresh water with boat-hooks ; he has continually given me good advice, which if I had only followed would have enabled me to keep out of water and any other sort of affliction ; and although he holds the meanest opinion of my intellect for going to such a place as West Africa for beetles, fishes and fetish, he has given me the greatest assistance in my work. The value of that work I pray you withhold judgment on, until I lay it before you in some ten volumes or so mostly in Latin. All I know that is true regarding West African facts, I owe to the traders ; the errors are my own.

To Dr. Günther, of the British Museum, I am deeply grateful for the kindness and interest he has always shown regarding all the specimens of natural history that I have been able to lay before him ; the majority of which must have had very old tales to tell him. Yet his courtesy and attention gave me the thing a worker in any work most wants— the sense that the work was worth doing—and sent me back to work again with the knowledge that if these things interested a man like him, it was a more than sufficient reason for me to go on collecting them. To Mr. W. H. F. Kirby I am much indebted for his working out my small collection of certain Orders of insects ; and to Mr. Thomas S. Forshaw, for the great help he has afforded me in revising my notes.

It is impossible for me even to catalogue my debts of gratitude still outstanding to the West Coast. Chiefly am I indebted to Mr. C. G. Hudson, whose kindness and influence enabled me to go up the Ogowé and to see as much of Congo Français as I have seen, and his efforts to take care of me were most ably seconded by Mr. Fildes. The French officials in " Congo Français " never hindered me, and always treated me with the greatest kindness. You may say there was no reason why they should not, for there is nothing in this fine colony of France that they need be ashamed of any one seeing ; but I find it is customary for travellers to say the French officials

throw obstacles in the way of any one visiting their possessions, so I merely beg to state this was decidedly not my
experience ; although my deplorable ignorance of French
prevented me from explaining my humble intentions to them.

The Rev. Dr. Nassau and Mr. R. E. Dennett have enabled
me, by placing at my disposal the rich funds of their knowledge of native life and idea, to amplify any deductions from
my own observation. Mr. Dennett's work I have not dealt
with in this work because it refers to tribes I was not
amongst on this journey, but to a tribe I made the acquaintance
with in my '93 voyage—the Fjort. Dr. Nassau's observations
I have referred to. Herr von Lucke, Vice-governor of
Cameroon, I am indebted to for not only allowing me, but
for assisting me by every means in his power, to go up
Cameroons Peak, and to the Governor of Cameroon, Herr
von Puttkamer, for his constant help and kindness. Indeed
so great has been the willingness to help me of all these
gentlemen, that it is a wonder to me, when I think of it, that
their efforts did not project me right across the continent and
out at Zanzibar. That this brilliant affair did not come off
is owing to my own lack of enterprise ; for I did not want
to go across the continent, and I do not hanker after Zanzibar,
but only to go puddling about obscure districts in West
Africa after raw fetish and fresh-water fishes.

I owe my ability to have profited by the kindness of these
gentlemen on land, to a gentleman of the sea—Captain
Murray. He was captain of the vessel I went out on in 1893,
and he saw then that my mind was full of errors that must
be eradicated if I was going to deal with the Coast successfully ; and so he eradicated those errors and replaced them
with sound knowledge from his own stores collected during
an acquaintance with the West Coast of over thirty years.
The education he has given me has been of the greatest value
to me, and I sincerely hope to make many more voyages
under him, for I well know he has still much to teach and
I to learn.

Last, but not least, I must chronicle my debts to the ladies.
First to those two courteous Portuguese ladies, Donna Anna
de Sousa Coutinho e Chichorro and her sister Donna Maria

de Sousa Coutinho, who did so much for me in Kacongo in 1893, and have remained, I am proud to say, my firm friends ever since. Lady MacDonald and Miss Mary Slessor I speak of in this book, but only faintly sketch the pleasure and help they have afforded me ; nor have I fully expressed my gratitude for the kindness of Madame Jacot of Lembarene, or Madame Forget of Talagouga. Then there are a whole list of nuns belonging to the Roman Catholic Missions on the South-West Coast, ever cheery and charming companions ; and Frau Plehn, whom it was ever a pleasure to see in Cameroons, and discourse with once again on things that seemed so far off then—art, science, and literature ; and Mrs. H. Duggan, of Cameroons too, who used, whenever I came into that port to rescue me from fearful states of starvation for toilet necessaries, and lend a sympathetic and intelligent ear to the "awful sufferings" I had gone through, until Cameroons became to me a thing to look forward to.

When in the Canaries in 1892, I used to smile, I regretfully own, at the conversation of a gentleman from the Gold Coast who was up there recruiting after a bad fever. His conversation consisted largely of anecdotes of friends of his, and nine times in ten he used to say, " He's dead now." Alas ! my own conversation may be smiled at now for the same cause. Many of my friends mentioned even in this very recent account of the Coast "are dead now." Most of those I learnt to know in 1893 ; chief among these is my old friend Captain Boler, of Bonny, from whom I first learnt a certain power of comprehending the African and his form of thought.

I have great reason to be grateful to the Africans themselves—to cultured men and women among them like Charles Owoo, Mbo, Sanga Glass, Jane Harrington and her sister at Gaboon, and to the bush natives ; but of my experience with them I give further details, so I need not dwell on them here.

I apologise to the general reader for giving so much detail on matters that really only affect myself, and I know that the indebtedness which all African travellers have to the white residents in Africa is a matter usually very lightly touched on. No doubt my voyage would seem a grander thing if I omitted mention of the help I received, but—well, there was a German gentleman once who evolved a camel out of his inner consciousness. It was a wonderful thing ; still, you know, it was not a good camel, only a thing which people personally unacquainted with camels could believe in. Now I am ambitious to make a picture, if I make one at all, that people who do know the original can believe in—even if they criticise its points—and so I give you details a more showy artist would omit.

CHAPTER I

LIVERPOOL TO SIERRA LEONE

Setting forth how the voyager departs from England in a stout vessel and in good company, and reaches in due course the Island of the Grand Canary, and then the Port of Sierra Leone : to which is added some account of this latter place and the comeliness of its women.

THE West Coast of Africa is like the Arctic regions in one particular, and that is that when you have once visited it you want to go back there again ; and, now I come to think of it, there is another particular in which it is like them, and that is that the chances you have of returning from it at all are small, for it is a *Belle Dame sans merci.*

I know that from many who know the Coast, there will be a chorus of dissent from the first part of my sentence, and a chorus of assent to the second. But if you were to take many of the men who most energetically assert that they wish they were home in England, "and see if they would ever come to the etc., etc., place again," and if you were to bring them home, and let them stay there a little while, I am pretty sure that—in the absence of attractions other than those of merely being home in England, notwithstanding its glorious joys of omnibuses, underground railways, and evening newspapers—these same men, in terms varying with individual cases, will be found sneaking back apologetically to the Coast.

I succumbed to the charm of the Coast as soon as I left Sierra Leone on my first voyage out, and I saw more than enough during that voyage to make me recognise that there was any amount of work for me worth doing down there. So I warned the Coast I was coming back again and the Coast did not believe me ; and on my return to it a second time displayed a genuine surprise, and formed an even higher opinion of my folly than it had formed on our first acquaintance, which is saying a good deal.

During this voyage in 1893, I had been to Old Calabar, and its Governor, Sir Claude MacDonald, had heard me expatiating on the absorbing interest of the Antarctic drift, and the importance of the collection of fresh-water fishes and so on.   So when Lady MacDonald heroically decided to go out to him in Calabar, they most kindly asked me if I would join her, and make my time fit hers for starting on my second journey.   This I most willingly did, but I fear that very sweet and gracious lady suffered a great deal of apprehension at the prospect of spending a month on board ship with a person so devoted to science as to go down the West Coast in its pursuit.   During the earlier days of our voyage she would attract my attention to all sorts of marine objects overboard, so as to amuse me.   I used to look at them, and think it would be the death of me if I had to work like this, explaining meanwhile aloud that " they were very interesting, but Haeckel had done them, and I was out after fresh-water fishes from a river north of the Congo this time," fearing all the while that she felt me unenthusiastic for not flying over into the ocean to secure the specimens.

However, my scientific qualities, whatever they may amount to, did not blind this lady long to the fact of my being after all a very ordinary individual, and she told me so—not in these crude words, indeed, but nicely and kindly—whereupon, in a burst of gratitude to her for understanding me, I appointed myself her honorary aide-de-camp on the spot, and her sincere admirer I shall remain for ever, fully recognising that her courage in going to the Coast was far greater than my own, for she had more to lose had fever claimed her, and she was in those days by no means under the spell of Africa.   But this is anticipating.

It was on the 23rd of December, 1894, that we left Liverpool in the *Batanga*, commanded by my old friend Captain Murray, under whose care I had made my first voyage. We ought to have left on the 22nd, but this we could not do, for it came on to blow a bit, such a considerable, bit indeed, that even the mighty Cunard liner *Lucania* could not leave the Mersey; moreover the *Batanga* could not have left even if she had wanted to, for the dock gates that shut her in could not be opened, so fierce was the gale. So it was Sunday the 23rd then, as I have said, that we got off, with no further misadventure save that, owing to the weather, the *Batanga* could not take her powder on board, a loss that nearly broke the carpenter's heart, as it robbed him of the pleasure of making that terrific bang with which a West Coaster salutes her ports of call.

On the 30th we sighted the Peak of Teneriffe early in the afternoon. It displayed itself, as usual, as an entirely celestial phenomenon. A great many people miss seeing it. Suffering under the delusion that El Pico is a terrestrial affair, they look in vain somewhere about the level of their own eyes, which are striving to penetrate the dense masses of mist that usually enshroud its slopes by day, and then a friend comes along, and gaily points out to the newcomer the glittering white triangle somewhere near the zenith. On some days the Peak stands out clear from ocean to summit, looking every inch and more of its 12,080 ft.; and this is said by the Canary fishermen to be a certain sign of rain, or fine weather, or a gale of wind; but whenever and however it may be seen, soft and dream-like in the sunshine, or melodramatic and bizarre in the moonlight, it is one of the most beautiful things the eye of man may see.

Soon after sighting Teneriffe, Lanzarote showed, and then the Grand Canary. Teneriffe is perhaps the most beautiful, but it is hard to judge between it and Grand Canary as seen from the sea. The superb cone this afternoon stood out a deep purple against a serpent-green sky, separated from the brilliant blue ocean by a girdle of pink and gold cumulus, while Grand Canary and Lanzarote looked as if they were formed from fantastic-shaped sunset cloud banks that by some spell had been solidified. The general colour of the mountains of Grand Canary, which rise peak after peak until they culminate in the Pico de las Nieves, some 6,000 feet high, is a yellowish red, and the air which lies among their rocky crevices and swathes their softer sides is a lovely lustrous blue. I used to fancy that if I could only have collected some of it in a bottle, and taken it home to show my friends, it would have come out as a fair blue-violet cloud in the gray air of Cambridge.

Just before the sudden dark came down, and when the sun was taking a curve out of the horizon of sea, all the clouds gathered round the three islands, leaving the sky a pure amethyst pink, and as a good-night to them the sun outlined them with rims of shining gold, and made the snow-clad Peak of Teneriffe blaze with star-white light. In a few minutes came the dusk, and as we neared Grand Canary, out of its cloud-bank gleamed the red flash of the lighthouse on the Isleta, and in a few more minutes, along the sea level, sparkled the five miles of irregularly distributed lights of Puerto de la Luz and the city of Las Palmas.

I will not here go into the subject of the Canary Islands, because it is one upon which I foresee a liability to become diffuse. I have visited them now five times; four times merely calling there on my way up and down to the Coast, but on the other occasion spending many weeks on them; and if I once start on the subject of their beauties, their trade, and their industries, why, who knows to what size this volume may not grow?

We reached Sierra Leone at 9 A.M. on the 7th of January, and as the place is hardly so much in touch with the general public as the Canaries are [1] I may perhaps venture to go more into details regarding it. The harbour is formed by the long low strip of land to the north called the Bullam shore, and to the south by the peninsula terminating in Cape Sierra Leone, a sandy promontory at the end of which is situated a lighthouse of irregular habits. Low hills covered with tropical forest growth rise from the sandy shores of the Cape, and along its face are three creeks or bays, deep inlets showing

---

[1] Sierra Leone has been known since the voyage of Hanno of Carthage in the sixth century B.C., but it has not got into general literature to any great extent since Pliny. The only later classic who has noticed it is Milton, who in a very suitable portion of *Paradise Lost* says of Notus and Afer, "black with thunderous clouds from Sierra Lona." Our occupation of it dates from 1787.

through their narrow entrances smooth beaches of yellow
sand, fenced inland by the forest of cotton-woods and palms,
with here and there an elephantine baobab.

The first of these bays is called Pirate Bay, the next
English Bay, and the third Kru Bay. The wooded hills of
the Cape rise after passing Kru Bay, and become spurs of
the mountain, 2,500 feet in height, which is the Sierra Leone
itself. There are, however, several mountains here besides
the Sierra Leone, the most conspicuous of them being the
peak known as Sugar Loaf, and when seen from the sea
they are very lovely, for their form is noble, and a wealth of
tropical vegetation covers them, which, unbroken in its con-
tinuity, but endless in its variety, seems to sweep over their
sides down to the shore like a sea, breaking here and there
into a surf of flowers.

It is the general opinion, indeed, of those who ought to know
that Sierra Leone appears at its best when seen from the sea,
particularly when you are leaving the harbour homeward
bound ; and that here its charms, artistic, moral, and residential,
end. But, from the experience I have gained of it, I have no
hesitation in saying that it is one of the best places for getting
luncheon in that I have ever happened on, and that a more
pleasant and varied way of spending an afternoon than going
about its capital, Free Town, with a certain Irish purser, who is
as well known as he is respected among the leviathan old
negro ladies, it would be hard to find. Still it must be
admitted it *is* rather hot.

Free Town is situated on the northern base of the mountain,
and extends along the sea-front with most business-like
wharves, quays, and warehouses. Viewed from the harbour,
" The Liverpool of West Africa,"[1] as it is called, looks as if it
were built of gray stone, which it is not. When you get ashore,
you will find that most of the stores and houses—the majority
of which, it may be remarked, are in a state of acute dilapidation—are of painted wood, with corrugated iron roofs. Here
and there, though, you will see a thatched house, its thatch

[1] Lagos also likes to bear this flattering appellation, and has now-a-
days more right to the title.

covered with creeping plants, and inhabited by colonies of creeping insects.

Some of the stores and churches are, it is true, built of stone, but this does not look like stone at a distance, being red in colour—unhewn blocks of the red stone of the locality. In the crannies of these buildings trailing plants covered with pretty mauve or yellow flowers take root, and everywhere, along the tops of the walls, and in the cracks of the houses, are ferns and flowering plants. They must get a good deal of their nourishment from the rich, thick air, which seems composed of 85 per cent. of warm water, and the remainder of the odours of Frangipani, orange flowers, magnolias, oleanders, and roses, combined with others that demonstrate that the inhabitants do not regard sanitary matters with the smallest degree of interest.

There is one central street, and the others are neatly planned out at right angles to it. None of them are in any way paved or metalled. They are covered in much prettier fashion, and in a way more suitable for naked feet, by green Bahama grass, save and except those which are so nearly perpendicular that they have got every bit of earth and grass cleared off them down to the red bed-rock, by the heavy rain of the wet season.

The shops, which fringe these streets in an uneven line, are like rooms with one side taken out, for shop-fronts, as we call them, are here unknown. Their floors are generally raised on a bed of stone a little above street level, but except when newly laid, these stones do not show, for the grass grows over them, making them into green banks. Inside, the shops are lined with shelves, on which are placed bundles of gay-coloured Manchester cottons and shawls, Swiss clocks, and rough but vividly coloured china ; or—what makes a brave show—brass, copper, and iron cooking-pots. Here and there you come across a baker's, with trays of banana fritters of tempting odour ; and there is no lack of barbers and chemists. Within all the shops are usually to be seen the proprietor and his family with a few friends, all exceedingly plump and happy, having a social shout together : a chat I cannot call it.

There is usually a counter across the middle, over which customers and casual callers alike love to loll. Some brutal tradesmen, notably chemists, who presumably regard this as unprofessional, affix tremendous nails, with their points outwards, to the fronts of their counter tops, in order to keep their visitors at a respectful distance.

In every direction natives are walking at a brisk pace, their naked feet making no sound on the springy turf of the streets, carrying on their heads huge burdens which are usually crowned by the hat of the bearer, a large limpet-shaped affair made of palm leaves. While some carry these enormous bundles, others bear logs or planks of wood, blocks of building stone, vessels containing palm-oil, baskets of vegetables, or tin tea-trays on which are folded shawls. As the great majority of the native inhabitants of Sierra Leone pay no attention whatever to where they are going, either in this world or the next, the confusion and noise are out of all proportion to the size of the town ; and when, as frequently happens, a section of actively perambulating burden-bearers charge recklessly into a sedentary section, the members of which have dismounted their loads and squatted themselves down beside them, right in the middle of the fair way, to have a friendly yell with some acquaintances, the row becomes terrific.

In among these crowds of country people walk stately Mohammedans, Mandingoes, Akers, and Fulahs of the Arabised tribes of the Western Soudan. These are lithe, well-made men, and walk with a peculiarly fine, elastic carriage. Their graceful garb consists of a long white loose-sleeved shirt, over which they wear either a long black mohair or silk gown, or a deep bright blue affair, not altogether unlike a University gown, only with more stuff in it and more folds. They are undoubtedly the gentlemen of the Sierra Leone native population, and they are becoming an increasing faction in the town, by no means to the pleasure of the Christians. For, although Bishop Ingram admits that they are always ready to side with the missionaries against the drink traffic, here their co-operation ceases, and he complains that they exercise a great influence over the native

Christian flock.   He says, " We are disposed to believe that
the words of their Koran are only a fetish and a charm to
the rank and file of their adherents, and that great superstition prevails among them, and is propagated by them," [1] but
how the Bishop can see a difference in this matter between
the use of the Koran and the Bible by the negro of Sierra
Leone, it is difficult to understand ; and judged by the
criterion of every-day conduct, the Mohammedan is in nine
cases in ten, the best man in West Africa.   But he is, I grieve
to say, not thoroughly orthodox.   The Koran I have seen
many of them using consists merely of extracts and prayers
written in Maghribi characters ; and I have grave doubts
whether they could read this any better than I could without
a dictionary.   I have also frequently seen them playing
warry, and another game, the name whereof I know not, but
it is played with little sticks of wood stuck in the ground, and
" something on the rub," or what corresponds to it ; although
they must be aware that, by this indulgence in the pleasures
of gambling, they will undoubtedly incur the penalty of
having donkeys graze upon their graves—yea, even on
the graves of their parents.   They should think of this, for
warry, when all's said and done, is a desperately dull game.

They are, moreover, by no means strict teetotallers, and
some individuals from Accra, whom I once met, shocked me
deeply by saying Mohammedans were divided into two
classes, Marabuts who do not drink, and Sonniki who do.   I
do not know where they can have picked up this idea ; but I
observed my acquaintances were "hard-shelled" Sonniki.
Again, the Sierra Leone and Lagos Mohammedans regard
working in leather and iron as quite respectable occupations,
which is not in accordance with views held in high
Mohammedan circles.   Very good leather-work they certainly turn out—bags, sheaths for daggers, and such like, to
say nothing of the quaint hats, made of the most brilliant
yellow, blue, and red leather strips plaited together : very
heavy, and very ugly, but useful.   Quite "rational dress"
hats in fact, for their broad brims hang down and shade the
neck, and they also shelter the eyes to such an extent that

[1] *Sierra Leone after a Hundred Years.*

the wearer can't see without bending up the front brim pretty frequently ;—but then I notice there always *is* something wrong with a rational article of dress. Then the bulbous dome top keeps off the sun from the head, rain runs off the whole affair easily, and bush does not catch in it. If I had sufficient strength of mind I would wear one myself, but even if I decorated it with cat-tails, or antelope hair, as is usually done, I do not feel I could face Piccadilly in one ; and you have no right to go about Africa in things you would be ashamed to be seen in at home.

The leather-work that meets with the severest criticism from the Christian party is the talisman or gri-gri bags, and it must be admitted that an immense number of them are sold. I have, however, opened at hazard some eighty-seven of these, and always found in them that which can do no man harm, be he black, white, or yellow, to wear over his heart; namely, the beautiful 113th *Sura* of the Koran, the "*Sura* of the Day-break," which says :—" I fly for refuge unto the Lord of the Day-break, that He may deliver me from the evil of those things which He has created ; from the evil of the night when it cometh on ; and from the evil of blowers upon knots, and from the evil of the envious when he envieth." This is written on a piece of paper, rolled or folded up tightly, and enclosed in a leathern case which is suspended round the neck. The talismans the Mohammedans make do not, how-ever, amount to a tenth part of those worn, the number whereof is enormous. I have never seen a negro in national costume without some, both round his neck, and round his leg, just under the knee ; and I dare say if the subject were gone into, and the clothes taken off the more fully-draped coloured gentlemen, you would hardly find one without an amulet of some kind. The great majority of these other charms are supplied by the ju-ju priests, or some enter-prising heathen who has a Suhman, or private devil, of his own.

But to the casual visitor at Sierra Leone the Mohammedan is a mere passing sensation. You neither feel a burning desire to laugh with, or at him, as in the case of the country folks, nor do you wish to punch his head, and split his coat

up his back—things you yearn to do to that perfect flower of
Sierra Leone culture, who yells your bald name across the
street at you, condescendingly informs you that you can go
and get letters that are waiting for you, while he smokes
his cigar and lolls in the shade, or in some similar way
displays his second-hand rubbishy white culture—a culture
far lower and less dignified than that of either the stately
Mandingo or the bush chief. I do not think that the Sierra
Leone dandy really means half as much insolence as he
shows ; but the truth is he feels too insecure of his own real
position, in spite of all the " side " he puts on, and so he dare
not be courteous like the Mandingo or the bush Fan.

It is the costume of the people in Free Town and its harbour
that will first attract the attention of the new-comer, notwithstanding the fact that the noise, the smell, and the heat are
simultaneously making desperate bids for that favour. The
ordinary man in the street wears anything he may have been
able to acquire, anyhow, and he does not fasten it on securely.
I fancy it must be capillary attraction, or some other par-
tially-understood force, that takes part in the matter. It is
certainly neither braces nor buttons. There are, of course,
some articles which from their very structure are fairly secure,
such as an umbrella with the stick and ribs removed, or a
shirt. This last-mentioned treasure, which usually becomes
the property of the ordinary man from a female relative or
admirer taking in white men's washing, is always worn flowing free, and has such a charm in itself that the happy possessor cares little what he continues his costume with—
trousers, loin cloth, red flannel petticoat, or rice-bag drawers,
being, as he would put it, " all same for one " to him.

I remember one day, when in the outskirts of the town, seeing
some country people coming in to market. It was during
the wet season, and when they hove in sight, they were, so to
speak, under bare poles, having nothing on worth mentioning.
But each carried a bundle done up in American cloth, with a
closed umbrella tucked into it. They pulled up as soon as
they thought it dangerous to proceed further, for fear of
meeting some of their town friends, and solemnly dressed,
holding umbrellas over each other the while. Then, dignified

and decorated, and each sporting his gingham, they marched into the town. Here and there in the street you come across a black man done up in a tweed suit, or in a black coat and tall hat ; and here and there a soldier of the West India regiment, smart and tidy-looking in his Zouave costume. These soldiers are said to be the cause of the many barbers' shops sprinkled about the town, as they are not allowed razors of their own, owing to their tendency to employ them too frequently in argument.

The ladies are divided into three classes ; the young girl you address as "tee-tee ;" the young person as "seester ;" the more mature charmer as "mammy ;" but I do not advise you to employ these terms when you are on your first visit, because you might get misunderstood. For, you see, by addressing a mammy as seester, she might think either that you were unconscious of her dignity as a married lady—a matter she would soon put you right on—or that you were flirting, which of course was totally foreign to your intention, and would make you uncomfortable. My advice is that you rigidly stick to missus or mammy. I have seen this done most successfully.

The ladies are almost as varied in their costume as the gentlemen, but always neater and cleaner ; and mighty picturesque they are too, and occasionally very pretty. A market-woman with her jolly brown face and laughing brown eyes—eyes all the softer for a touch of antimony—her ample form clothed in a lively print overall, made with a yoke at the shoulders, and a full long flounce which is gathered on to the yoke under the arms and falls fully to the feet ; with her head done up in a yellow or red handkerchief, and her snowy white teeth gleaming through her vast smiles, is a mighty pleasant thing to see, and to talk to. But, Allah ! the circumference of them !

The stone-built, whitewashed market buildings of Free Town have a creditably clean and tidy appearance considering the climate, and the quantity and variety of things exposed for sale—things one wants the pen of a Rabelais to catalogue. Here are all manner of fruits, some which are familiar to you in England ; others that soon become so to you in Africa. You take them as a matter of course if you are outward bound, but on your call homeward (if you make it) you will look on them as a blessing and a curiosity. For lower down, particularly in " the Rivers," these things are rarely to be had, and never in such perfection as here ; and to see again lettuces, yellow oranges, and tomatoes bigger than marbles is a sensation and a joy. Onions also there are, and if you are wise you will buy them when outward bound. If you are speculative in the bargain you will take as many as you can get, for here you may buy them from four to five shillings the box, and you can sell them below for any sum between twelve shillings and a sovereign.

Here, too, are beads, but for the most part of dull colour and cheap quality. Beans, too, are more than well represented. Horse-eye beans, used for playing warry ; vast, pantomime-sized beans, the insides of which being removed, and a few shot put in, make a pleasant rattle to hang at the wrist ; and evil Calabar beans, which can serve no good end at all here, and which it seems insolent to sell in open market, in a town where poisoning is said to be so prevalent that its own Bishop declares " small social gatherings are almost unknown from the fear of it." [1]

The piles of capsicums and chillies, the little heaps of Reckitt's Blue, vivid-coloured Berlin wools, pumpkins, pine-apples, and alligator pears, give rich and brilliant touches of colour, and relieve the more sombre tones of kola nuts, old iron, antelope horns, monkey skins, porcupine quills, and snails. These snails are a prominent feature in the market in a quiet way: they are used beaten up to help to make the sauce for palm oil chop ; and they are shot alive on to the floor in heaps, and are active and nomadic : whereby it falls out that people who buy other things such as vegetables, Berlin wool, or meat, are liable to find one of these massive gastropods mixed up in the affair. Treading on one of them is, for a nervous person, as alarming as the catastrophe of treading on one of the native black babies with which the market floor abounds. There are half a hundred other indescribabilia, and above all hovers the peculiar Sierra Leone smell and the peculiar Sierra Leone noise.

[1] *Sierra Leone after a Hundred Years.*

One of the chief features of Free Town are the jack crows.
Some writers say they are peculiar to Sierra Leone, others
that they are not, but both unite in calling them *Picathartes
gymnocephalus*. To the white people who live in daily contact
with them they are turkey-buzzards ; to the natives, Yubu.
Anyhow they are evil-looking fowl, and no ornament to the
roof-ridges they choose to sit on. The native Christians
ought to put a row of spikes along the top of their cathedral to
keep them off ; the beauty of that edifice is very far from great,
and it cannot carry off the effect produced by the row of these
noisome birds as they sit along its summit, with their wings
arranged at all manner of different angles in an " all gone "
way. One bird perhaps will have one straight out in front,
and the other casually disposed at right-angles, another both
straight out in front, and others again with both hanging
hopelessly down, but none with them neatly and tidily folded
up, as decent birds' wings should be. They all give the impression of having been extremely drunk the previous evening,
and of having subsequently fallen into some sticky abomination—into blood for choice. Being the scavengers of Free
Town, however, they are respected by the local authorities
and preserved ; and the natives tell me you never see either a
young or a dead one. The latter is a thing you would not
expect, for half of them look as if they could not live through
the afternoon. They also told me that when you got close to
them, they had a " 'trong, 'trong 'niff ; 'niff too much." I
did not try, but I am quite willing to believe this statement.

The other animals most in evidence in the streets are, first
and foremost, goats and sheep. I have to lump them together,
for it is exceedingly difficult to tell one from the other. All
along the Coast the empirical rule is that sheep carry their
tails down, and goats carry their tails up ; fortunately you
need not worry much anyway, for they both " taste rather
like the nothing that the world was made of," as Frau Buch-
holtz says, and own in addition a fibrous texture, and a certain twang. Small cinnamon-coloured cattle are to be got
here, but horses there are practically none. Now and again
some one who does not see why a horse should not live here
as well as at Accra or Lagos imports one, but it always

shortly dies. Some say it is because the natives who get their living by hammock-carrying poison them, others say the *tsetse* fly finishes them off ; and others, and these I believe are right, say that entozoa are the cause. Small, lean, lank, yellow dogs with very erect ears lead an awful existence, afflicted by many things, but beyond all others by the goats, who, rearing their families in the grassy streets choose to think the dogs intend attacking them. Last, but not least, there is the pig—a rich source of practice to the local lawyer.

The lawyer in Sierra Leone flourishes like the green bay-tree. All the West Coast natives, when the fear of the dangers of their own country-fashion law is off them, and they are under European institutions—I very nearly said control, but that would have been going too far—become exceedingly litigious, more litigious naturally in Sierra Leone because they have more European institutions there, among others trial by jury. Any law case, whether he wins it or not, is a pleasure to the African, because it gives him an opportunity of showing off his undoubted powers of rhetoric, and generally displaying himself. But there is no law case that gives the Sierra Leonean that joy that he gets out of summoning a white man, for he can get the white man before a jury of his fellow Sierra Leoneans—what they please to call in that benighted place a jury of his peers—and bully and insult him.

There is usually a summons or so awaiting a West Coast boat, and many a proud vessel has dropped anchor in Free Town harbour with one of her officers in a ventilator and another in a coal bunker. On one vessel by which I was a passenger, it was the second officer who was " wanted." Regaining the ship after a time on shore, we found the deck in an uproar. The centre of affairs was an enormous black lady, bearing a name honoured in English literature, and by profession a laundress, demanding that the body of the second mate in any condition should be rendered over to the hand of the law (represented by four Haussa policemen) on a warrant she held against him for not having discharged his washing-bill last time the steamer was in Sierra Leone. Now this worthy

man, tired by his morning labour, working cargo in the stewing heat, and strong in the virtue of an unblemished life here,
had gone to sleep in his cabin, out of which he was routed
and confronted with his accusatrix and the small frightened
man she had got with her, whom she kept on introducing as
"my brudah, sah." Unfortunately for the lady, it was not the
same gallant officer who held the post of second mate, but
another, and our injured innocent, joining in the chorus, returned thanks for his disturbance in language of singular
fluency. He is the only man I have ever met whose powers
of expression were equal to his feelings, and it is a merciful
providence for him it is so, for what that man feels sometimes
I think would burst a rock.

The lady and her brother went crestfallen ashore, but the
policemen stayed on board until we left, getting exceedingly
drunk the while. Looking over the side, I saw one of them
fold himself over the gunwale of the boat in which they were
going ashore with his head close to the water. His companions
heeded not, and I insisted on my friend the quartermaster
rescuing the sufferer, and arranging him in the bottom of the
boat, for not only was he in danger of drowning, but of acting
as an all too tempting live-bait for the sharks, which swarm
in the harbour. The quartermaster evidently thought this
was foolish weakness on my part, for it "was only a police-
man, and what are policemen but a kind of a sort of a custom
house officer, and what are custom house officers but the very
deuce?"

This, however, was not on the *Batanga*, but in the days
before I was an honorary aide-de-camp, remember. This
voyage out on the *Batanga* not even Sierra Leone could find
anything to summon us for.

CHAPTER II

THE GOLD COAST

Wherein some description of Cape Coast and Accra is given, to which are added divers observations on supplies to be obtained there.

CAPE COAST CASTLE and then Accra were the next places of general interest at which we stopped. The former looks well from 'the roadstead, and as if it had very recently been white-washed. It is surrounded by low, heavily-forested hills, which rise almost from the seashore, and the fine mass of its old castle does not display its dilapidation at a distance. More-over, the three stone forts of Victoria, William, and Macarthy, situated on separate hills commanding the town, add to the general appearance of permanent substantialness so different from the usual ramshackledom of West Coast settlements. Even when you go ashore and have had time to recover your senses, scattered by the surf experience, you find this substantialness a true one, not a mere visual delusion produced by painted wood as the seeming sub-stantialness of Sierra Leone turns out to be when you get to close quarters with it. It causes one some mental effort to grasp the fact that Cape Coast has been in European hands for centuries, but it requires a most un-modern power of credence to realise this of any other settle-ment on the whole western seaboard until you have the pleasure of seeing the beautiful city of San. Paul de Loanda, far away down south, past the Congo.

My experience of Cape Coast on this occasion was one of the hottest, but one of the pleasantest I have ever been through on the Gold Coast. The former attribute was due

to the climate, the latter to my kind friends, Mr. Batty, and
Mr. and Mrs. Dennis Kemp.   I was taken round the grand
stone-built houses with their high stone-walled yards and
sculpture-decorated gateways, built by the merchants of the
last century and of the century before, and through the great
rambling stone castle with its water-tanks cut in the solid
rock beneath it, and its commodious accommodation for
slaves awaiting shipment, now almost as obsolete as the guns
it mounts, but not quite so, for these cool and roomy chambers
serve to house the native constabulary and their extensive
families.

This being done, I was taken up an unmitigated hill, on
whose summit stands Fort William, a pepper-pot-like structure
now used as a lighthouse.   Our peregrinations having been
carried on under a fancy temperature, I was inclined to drink
in the beauty of this building from a position at its base, and
was looking round for a shady spot to sit down in, when my
intentions were ruthlessly frustrated by my companions, who
would stop at nothing short of its summit, where I eventually
found myself.   The view was exceedingly lovely and extensive.   Beneath, and between us and the sea, lay the
town in the blazing sun.   In among its solid stone buildings patches of native mud-built huts huddled together
as though they had been shaken down out of a sack into the
town to serve as dunnage.   Then came the snow-white
surf wall, and across it the blue sea with our steamer rolling
to and fro on the long, regular swell, impatiently waiting until
Sunday should be over and she could work cargo.   Round
us on all the other sides were wooded hills and valleys, and
away in the distance to the west showed the white town and
castle of Elmina and the nine-mile road thither, skirting
the surf-bound seashore, only broken on its level way by
the mouth of the Sweet River.   Over all was the brooding
silence of the noonday heat, broken only by the dulled
thunder of the surf.

After seeing these things we started down stairs, and on
reaching ground descended yet lower into a sort of stone-
walled dry moat, out of which opened clean, cool, cellar-like
chambers tunnelled into the earth.   These, I was informed,

had also been constructed to keep slaves in when they were the staple export of the Gold Coast. They were so refreshingly cool that I lingered looking at them and their massive doors, ere being marched up to ground level again, and down the hill through some singularly awful stenches, mostly arising from rubber, into the big Wesleyan church in the middle of the town. It is a building in the terrible Africo-Gothic style, but it compares most favourably with the cathedral at Sierra Leone, particularly internally, wherein, indeed, it far surpasses that structure. And then we returned to the Mission House and spent a very pleasant evening, save for the knowledge (which amounted in me to remorse) that, had it not been for my edification, not one of my friends would have spent the day toiling about the town they know only too well. Mr. Dennis Kemp was chairman and superintendent of the Wesleyan Mission on the Gold Coast when I was last there, and he had filled this important position for some time. This is the largest and most influential Protestant mission on the West Coast of Africa, and it is now, I am glad to say, adding a technical department to its scholastic and religious one. The Basel Mission has done a great deal of good work in giving technical instruction to the natives, and practically started this most important branch of their education. There is still an almost infinite amount of this work to be done, the African being so strangely deficient in mechanical culture ; infinitely more so, indeed, in this than in any other particular. All the other Protestant missions are following the Basel Mission's lead, and, recognising that a good deal of their failure arises from a want of this practical side in their instruction, are now starting technical schools :—the Church of England in Sierra Leone, the Wesleyans on the Gold Coast, and the Presbyterians in Calabar.

In some of these technical schools the sort of instruction given is, to my way of thinking, ill-advised ; arts of no immediate or great use in the present culture-condition of West Africa—such as printing, book-binding, and tailoring—being taught. But this is not the case under the Wesleyans, who also teach smith's work, carpentering, bricklaying, waggon-

building, &c.   Alas! none of the missions save the Roman
Catholic teach the thing that it is most important the natives
should learn, in the face of the conditions that European
government of the Coast has induced, namely, improved
methods of agriculture, and plantation work.

The Wesleyan Mission has only four white ministers here.
Native ministers there are seventeen, and the rest of the
staff is entirely native, consisting of 70 Catechists, 144 day
school teachers, 386 Sunday-school teachers, and 405 local
preachers.   The total number of fully accredited members of
this sect in 1893 was stated in the *Gold Coast Annual* to be
7,066.

The total amount of money raised by this mission on the
Gold Coast in 1893 was £5,338 14*s*. 9*d*.   This is a very
remarkable sum and most creditable to the native members
of the sect, for almost all the other native Christian bodies
are content to be in a state of pauperised dependency on
British subscriptions.   The headquarters of the Wesleyan
Mission were, up to last year, at Cape Coast, but now they
have been removed to Aburi on the hills some twenty-six
miles behind Accra, and Cape Coast is no longer the headquarters of any governmental or religious affair.   The
Government removed to Accra from Cape Coast several
years ago, on account of the great unhealthiness of the
latter place and in the hope that Accra would prove less
fatal.   Unfortunately this hope has not been realised ;
moreover the landing at Accra is worse than at Cape Coast,
and the supply of fresh water very poor.

Accra is one of the five West Coast towns that look well
from the sea.   The others don't look well from anywhere.   First
in order of beauty comes San. Paul de Loanda ; then Cape
Coast with its satellite Elmina, then Gaboon, then Accra with
its satellite Christiansborg, and lastly, Sierra Leone.

What there is of beauty in Accra is oriental in type.   Seen
from the sea, Fort St. James on the left and Christiansborg
Castle on the right, both almost on shore level, give, with an
outcrop of sandy dwarf cliffs, a certain air of balance and
strength to the town, though but for these and the two old
castles, Accra would be but a poor place and a flimsy, for the

rest of it is a mass of rubbishy mud and palm-leaf huts, and corrugated-iron dwellings for the Europeans.

Corrugated iron is my abomination. I quite understand it has points, and I do not attack from an æsthetic standpoint. It really looks well enough when it is painted white. There is, close to Christiansborg Castle, a patch of bungalows and offices for officialdom and wife that from a distance in the hard bright sunshine looks like an encampment of snow-white tents among the coco palms, and pretty enough withal. I am also aware that the corrugated-iron roof is an advantage in enabling you to collect and store rain-water, which is the safest kind of water you can get on the Coast, always supposing you have not painted the aforesaid roof with red oxide an hour or two before so collecting, as a friend of mine did once. But the heat inside those iron houses is far greater than inside mud-walled, brick, or wooden ones, and the alternations of temperature more sudden : mornings and evenings they are cold and clammy; draughty they are always, thereby giving you chill which means fever, and fever in West Africa means more than it does in most places.

Going on shore at Accra with Lady MacDonald gave me opportunities and advantages I should not otherwise have enjoyed, such as the hospitality of the Governor, luxurious transport from the landing place to Christiansborg Castle, a thorough inspection of the cathedral in course of erection, and the strange and highly interesting function of going to a tea-party at a police station to meet a king,—a real reigning king—who kindly attended with his suite and displayed an intelligent interest in photographs. Tackie (that is His Majesty's name) is an old, spare man, with a subdued manner. His sovereign rights are acknowledged by the Government so far as to hold him more or less responsible for any iniquity committed by his people ; and as the Government do not allow him to execute or flagellate the said people, earthly pomp is rather a hollow thing to Tackie.

On landing I was taken in charge by an Assistant Inspector of Police, and after a scrimmage for my chief's baggage and my own, which reminded me of a long ago landing on the distant island of Guernsey, the inspector and

I got into a 'rickshaw, locally called a go-cart. It was pulled in front by two government negroes and pushed behind by another pair, all neatly attired in white jackets and knee breeches, and crimson cummerbunds yards long, bound round their middles. Now it is an ingrained characteristic of the uneducated negro, that he cannot keep on a neat and complete garment of any kind. It does not matter what that garment may be ; so long as it is whole, off it comes. But as soon as that garment becomes a series of holes, held together by filaments of rag, he keeps it upon him in a manner that is marvellous, and you need have no further anxiety on its behalf. Therefore it was but natural that the governmental cummerbunds, being new, should come off their wearers several times in the course of our two mile trip, and as they wound riskily round the legs of their running wearers, we had to make halts while one end of the cummerbund was affixed to a tree-trunk and the other end to the man, who rapidly wound himself up in it again with a skill that spoke of constant practice.

The road to Christiansborg from Accra, which runs parallel to the sea and is broad and well-kept, is in places pleasantly shaded with pepper trees, eucalyptus, and palms. The first part of it, which forms the main street of Accra, is remarkable. The untidy, poverty-stricken native houses or huts are no credit to their owners, and a constant source of anxiety to a conscientious sanitary inspector. Almost every one of them is a shop, but this does not give rise to the animated commercial life one might imagine, owing, I presume, to the fact that every native inhabitant of Accra who has any money to get rid of is able recklessly to spend it in his own emporium. For these shops are of the store nature, each after his kind, and seem homogeneously stocked with tin pans, loud-patterned basins, iron pots, a few rolls of cloth and bottles of American rum. After passing these there are the Haussa lines, a few European houses, and the cathedral ; and when nearly into Christiansborg, a cemetery on either side of the road. That to the right is the old cemetery, now closed, and when I was there, in a disgracefully neglected state : a mere jungle of grass infested with snakes. Opposite to it is the cemetery now in use, and I remember well my first visit to it under the guidance of a gloomy Government official, who said he always walked there every afternoon, "so as to get used to the place before staying permanently in it,"—a rank waste of time and energy, by the way, as subsequent events proved, for he is now safe off the Gold Coast for good and all.

He took me across the well-kept grass to two newly dug graves, each covered with wooden hoods in a most business-like way. Evidently those hoods were regular parts of the cemetery's outfit. He said nothing, but waved his hand with a "take-your-choice,-they-are-both-quite-ready" style. "Why?" I queried laconically. "Oh! we always keep two graves ready dug for Europeans. We have to bury very quickly here, you know," he answered. I turned at bay. I had had already a very heavy dose of details of this sort that afternoon and was disinclined to believe another thing. So I said, "It's exceedingly wrong to do a thing like that, you only frighten people to death. You can't want new-dug graves daily. There are not enough white men in the whole place to keep the institution up." "We do," he replied, "at any rate at this season. Why, the other day we had two white men to bury before twelve o'clock, and at four, another dropped in on a steamer."

"At 4.30," said a companion, an exceedingly accurate member of the staff, "How you fellows *do* exaggerate!" Subsequent knowledge of the Gold Coast has convinced me fully that the extra funeral being placed half-an-hour sooner than it occurred is the usual percentage of exaggeration you will be able to find in stories relating to the local mortality. And at Accra, after I left it, and all along the Gold Coast, came one of those dreadful epidemic outbursts sweeping away more than half the white population in a few weeks. It is customary for the Government authorities to pooh-pooh the mortality, or to allege that it is owing to the bad habits of the white men; but this latter statement is far more untrue than any fever story an old coaster will tell you. The authorities at home, both of merchant firms and mission societies, follow suit and make the same statements. The true statistics are difficult to get at in English colonies, because the Government reports are as a general rule very badly prepared, and dodge giving important details like this with an almost diabolical ingenuity. And, added to this, they come out so long after the incidents referred to in them have taken place, that they are only fit for the early literature shelves of the British Museum.

But to return to our state journey along the Christiansborg road. We soon reached the castle, an exceedingly roomy and solid edifice built by the Danes, and far better fitted for the climate than our modern dwellings, in spite of our supposed advance in tropical hygiene. We entered by the sentry-guarded great gate into the courtyard; on the right hand were the rest of the guard; most of them asleep on their mats, but a few busy saying Dhikr, etc. towards Mecca, like the good Mohammedans these Haussas are, others winding themselves into their cummerbunds. On the left hand was Sir Brandford Griffiths' hobby—a choice and select little garden, of lovely eucharis lilies mostly in tubs, and rare and beautiful flowers brought by him from his Barbadian home; while shading it and the courtyard was a fine specimen of that superb thing of beauty—a flamboyant tree—glorious with its delicate-green acacia-like leaves and vermilion and yellow flowers, and astonishing with its vast beans. A flight of stone stairs leads from the courtyard to the upper part of the castle where the living rooms are, over the extensive series of cool tunnel-like slave barracoons, now used as store chambers. The upper rooms are high and large, and full of a soft pleasant light and the thunder of the everlasting surf breaking on the rocky spit on which the castle is built.

From the day the castle was built, now more than a hundred years ago, the surf spray has been swept by the on-shore evening breeze into every chink and cranny of the whole building, and hence the place is mouldy—mouldy to an extent I, with all my experience in that paradise for mould, West Africa, have never elsewhere seen. The matting on the floors took an impression of your foot as a light snowfall would. Beneath articles of furniture the cryptogams attained a size more in keeping with the coal period than with the nineteenth century. That unhappy furniture! How it suffers! From everything save one noble old gilt chair with the arms of Denmark embroidered on its throne-like form which is apparently acclimatised, the veneer hung in strips, as if each article had been trying to throw its clothes off to get cooler.

The looking-glasses, too, were in a sorry plight. You only saw yourself in sections in them. A dangerous thing, I should imagine, for shaving operations, just to be able to dimly catch sight of the top of your head, one eye, a portion of your nose, and a bit of shirt front. One member of the Government, I observed, was considerably done up with sticking-plaster round the jaw, which I mentally put down to a shaky hand, until I had trouble with my back hair with those governmental mirrors. One must never judge a fellow creature unkindly, especially on the Gold Coast.

Along the front of the living-rooms facing the sea is a single immense verandah. This is the place for social gatherings, and after dinner the ladies arrange themselves in a hard and fast row on chairs, while the gentlemen hang round about and talk. Conversation is carried on under difficulties, because of the ceaseless roar of the surf. In the middle of January I found conversation with a new-comer consisted of " You should have been here last week." " Eh ? " " You should have been here last week when we had the races (f)." " Oh ! you have a race-meeting ? ($m.f$)." " Yes, we have a regular race-course, you know ($f\!f$)." Then details regarding the races which you don't quite catch, but you say " Indeed," " Really though ! " " That must have been very nice," at random, and get regarded as being sympathetic, and are rewarded with more details. Another individual, whose name you do not catch, is introduced. He says something. You say " Eh ? " He says, " You should have been here last week when we had our races ($f\!f$)." Then come the details as before, and so on, *da capo*, throughout the evening. The other subjects of conversation with which one had to deal during meals relate to the new cathedral and Ashanti affairs. You of course know about the cathedral, and you ought to know about Ashanti affairs, and the real reason why King Kwoffe Karri Karri crossed the Prah in '74. But you usually don't, for both these subjects require sound previous education; superficial dealings with them are quite impossible, for the names of places and people in Ashanti are strange and choppy, and you will get mixed as to which is which if you don't take care.

Superficial things may have changed now Sir Brandford Griffiths has left the Gold Coast after his long term of service—the longest term, I think, ever served on the whole West Coast by a Governor. But they cannot have improved either in the way of courteous hospitality or in the thoughtful personal kindness which the late Governor gave his visitors.

For example, when we left the castle after receiving from him all manner of kind wishes, to say nothing of pipes and walking-sticks, he energetically went out of his way to save the life and reason of a young member of our party, a mere new-comer, who wore a light felt hat in the blazing mid-day sun. My chief and I went off respectively in go-carts to the landing-place at James Town, and the young man, who had also to return to the *Batanga*, followed not for some minutes. When he rejoined us we observed beautiful cool green leaves sticking out from under his hat in a wreath. The Governor had not done what many an old coaster would have done, namely, said: "There! that fellow will certainly peg out with that fool of a hat," and preserved a masterly inactivity. No, he had gathered with his own hands certain suitable herbs from his own garden, and filled the inadequate hat with them.

While we were waiting for the surf-boat, we had an object lesson in the surf trouble. Several stalwart negroes strolled to and fro along the sand in front of us, poking down iron bars into it ever and anon. Ever and anon they left these sticking in and strolled off, not as one might hastily have thought because they had had enough of the job, but to go and fetch a spade. What they were sounding for in the sand were the iron rails which had been capsized in coming ashore and which belong to a tramway in course of construction for running goods from the beach to the sheds. When we got on board the *Batanga*, we saw more of this tramway. A large surf-boat was being laden with its rails, and as it persisted, owing to the long heavy swell, in playing bob cherry with every bundle of them, the time came when the man at the winch "came back a bit" suddenly instead of "softly, softly" as he had been carefully ordered to do. This happened when the boat was nearly laden, and one of the bundles of rails hanging on the chain swung round and speared that lively surf-boat right through.

A scene of some excitement followed, accompanied by a perfect word-fog of directions and advice. The chain was hastily lowered into the boat and put round bundles of rails which were as hastily hauled back on to the *Batanga's* deck, but still the boat with the balance of the rails continued sinking, and her black crew when they realised this went "for water one time" and swam round at a respectful distance so as to avoid the coming down suck, in spite of being most distinctly requested to return to the boat and sling rails like fury. Then Captain Murray came upon the scene and rose to the occasion, ordering ropes to be passed bodily under the boat and round her in such a manner that she was held up, whether she would or no, until she was unloaded. Then she was hauled on deck and repaired during the rest of the voyage by my old friend the Portuguese carpenter, although he announced himself as "suffering from rheumatism under the influence of the doctor."

The Gold Coast is one of the few places in West Africa that I have never felt it my solemn duty to go and fish in. I really cannot say why. Seen from the sea it is a pleasant-looking land. The long lines of yellow, sandy beach backed by an almost continuous line of blue hills, which in some places come close to the beach, in other places show in the dim distance. It is hard to think that it is so unhealthy as it is, from just seeing it as you pass by. It has high land and has not those great masses of mangrove-swamp one usually, at first, associates with a bad fever district, but which prove on acquaintance to be at any rate no worse than this well-elevated open-forested Gold Coast land. There are many things to be had here and in Lagos which tend to make life more tolerable, that you cannot have elsewhere until you are south of the Congo. Horses, for example, do fairly well at Accra, though some twelve miles or so behind the town there is a belt of tsetse fly, specimens of which I have procured and had identified at the British Museum, and it is certain death to a horse, I am told, to take it to Aburi.

ON A GOLD COAST BEACH.

The food-supply, although bad and dear, is superior to that you get down south. Goats and sheep are fairly plentiful. In addition to fresh meat and tinned you are able to get a quantity of good sea fish, for the great West African Bank, which fringes the coast in the Bight of Benin, abounds in fish, although the native cook very rarely knows how to cook them. Then, too, you can get more fruit and

vegetables on the Gold Coast than at most places lower
down : the plantain,[1] not least among them—very good when
allowed to become ripe, and then cut into longitudinal strips,
and properly fried ; the banana, which surpasses it when
served in the same manner, or beaten up and mixed with rice,
butter, and eggs, and baked.   Eggs, by the way, according to
the great mass of native testimony, are laid in this country
in a state that makes them more fit for electioneering than
culinary purposes, and I shall never forget one tribe I was
once among, who, whenever I sat down on one of their
benches, used to smash eggs round me for ju-ju.   They
meant well.   But I will nobly resist the temptation to tell
egg stories and industriously catalogue the sour-sop, guava,
grenadilla, aubergine or garden-egg, yam, and sweet potato.

The sweet potato should be boiled, and then buttered and
browned in an oven, or fried.   When cooked in either way
I am devoted to them, but in the way I most frequently
come across them I abominate them, for they jeopardise
my existence both in this world and the next.   It is this
way : you are coming home from a long and dangerous
beetle-hunt in the forest ; you have battled with mighty
beetles the size of pie dishes, they have flown at your head,
got into your hair and then nipped you smartly.   You have
been also considerably stung and bitten by flies, ants, &c.,
and are most likely sopping wet with rain, or with the
wading of streams, and you are tired and your feet go low
along the ground, and it is getting, or has got, dark with
that ever-deluding tropical rapidity, and then you for your
sins get into a piece of ground which last year was a native's
farm, and, placing one foot under the tough vine of a surviving sweet potato, concealed by rank herbage, you plant
your other foot on another portion of the same vine.   Your
head you then deposit promptly in some prickly ground
crop or against a tree stump, and then, if there is human
blood in you, you say d—n !

Then there are also alligator-pears, limes, and oranges.

---

[1] Along the Coast, and in other parts of Africa, the coarser, flat-sided
kinds of banana are usually called plantains, the name banana being
reserved for the finer sorts, such as the little " silver banana."

There is something about those oranges I should like to have explained. They are usually green and sweetish in taste, nor have they much white pith, but now and again you get a big bright yellow one from those trees that have been imported, and these are very pithy and in full possession of the flavour of verjuice. They have also got the papaw on the Coast, the *Carica papaya* of botanists. It is an insipid fruit. To the newcomer it is a dreadful nuisance, for no sooner does an old coaster set eyes on it than he straightway says, " Paw-paws are awfully good for the digestion, and even if you just hang a tough fowl or a bit of goat in the tree among the leaves, it gets tender in no time, for there is an awful lot of pepsine in a paw-paw,"—which there is not, papaine being its active principle. After hearing this hymn of praise to the papaw some hundreds of times, it palls, and you usually arrive at this tired feeling about the thing by the time you reach the Gold Coast, for it is a most common object, and the same man will say the same thing about it a dozen times a day if he gets the chance. I got heartily sick of it on my first voyage out, and rashly determined to check the old coaster in this habit of his, preparatory to stamping the practice out. It was one of my many failures. I soon met an old coaster with a papaw fruit in sight, and before he had time to start, I boldly got away with—" The paw paw is awfully good for the digestion," hoping that this display of knowledge would impress him and exempt me from hearing the rest of the formula. But no. " Right you are," said he solemnly. " It's a powerful thing is the paw-paw. Why, the other day we had a sad case along here. You know what a nuisance young assistants are, bothering about their chop, and scorpions in their beds and boots, and what not and a half, and then, when you have pulled them through these, and often enough before, pegging out with fever, or going on the fly in the native town. Did you know poor B—? Well! he's dead now, had fever and went off like a babe in eight hours though he'd been out fourteen years for A — and D—. They sent him out a new book-keeper, a tender young thing with a dairymaid complexion and the notion that he'd got the indigestion. He fidgeted about it something awful. One

night there was a big paw-paw on the table for evening
chop, and so B—, who was an awfully good chap, told him
about how good it was for the digestion. The book-keeper
said his trouble always came on two hours after eating, and
asked if he might take a bit of the thing to his room.
' Certainly,' says B—, and as the paw-paw wasn't cut at that
meal the book-keeper quietly took it off whole with him.

"In the morning time he did not turn up. B—, just
before breakfast, went to his room and he wasn't there, but
he noticed the paw-paw was on the bed and that was all,
so he thought the book-keeper must have gone for a walk,
being, as it were, a bit too tender to have gone on the fly as
yet. So he just told the store clerk to tell the people to
return him to the firm when they found him straying around
lost, and thought no more about it, being, as it was, mail-day,
and him busy.

"Well! Fortunately the steward boy put that paw-paw on
the table again for twelve o'clock chop. If it hadn't been for
that, not a living soul would have known the going of the book-
keeper. For when B— cut it open, there, right inside it, were
nine steel trouser-buttons, a Waterbury watch, and the poor
young fellow's keys. For you see, instead of his digesting his
dinner with that paw-paw, the paw-paw took charge and
digested him, dinner and all, and when B. interrupted it, it
was just getting a grip on the steel things. There's an awful
lot of pepsine in a paw-paw, and if you hang, &c., &c."

I collapsed, feebly murmuring that it was very interesting,
but sad for the poor young fellow's friends.

"Not necessarily," said the old coaster. So he had the
last word, and never again will I attempt to alter the
ways of the genuine old coaster. What you have got to do
with him is to be very thankful you have had the honour of
knowing him.

Still I think we do over-estimate the value of the papaw,
although I certainly did once myself hang the leg of a goat no
mortal man could have got tooth into, on to a papaw tree
with a bit of string for the night. In the morning it was
clean gone, string and all ; but whether it was the pepsine,
the papaine, or a purloining pagan that was the cause of its

departure there was no evidence to show.   Yet I am myself, as Hans Breitmann says, "still skebdigal" as to the papaw, and I dare say you are too.

But I must forthwith stop writing about the Gold Coast, or I shall go on telling you stories and wasting your time, not to mention the danger of letting out those which would damage the nerves of the cultured of temperate climes, such as those relating to the youth who taught himself French from a six months' method book ; of the man who wore brass buttons ; the moving story of three leeches and two gentlemen ; the doctor up a creek ; and the reason why you should not eat pork along here because all the natives have either got the guinea-worm, or kraw-kraw or ulcers ; and then the pigs go and—dear me! it was a near thing that time.   I'll leave off at once.

CHAPTER III

FERNANDO PO AND THE BUBIS

Giving some account of the occupation of this island by the whites and the manners and customs of the blacks peculiar to it.

OUR outward voyage really terminated at Calabar, and it terminated gorgeously in fireworks and what not in honour of the coming of Lady MacDonald, the whole settlement, white and black, turning out to do her honour to the best of its ability; and its ability in this direction was far greater than, from my previous knowledge of coast conditions, I could have imagined possible.

Before Sir Claude MacDonald settled down again to local work, he and Lady MacDonald crossed to Fernando Po, still in the *Batanga*, and I accompanied them, thus getting an opportunity of seeing something of Spanish official circles. I have always been fascinated with the island, on account of its intense beauty and the high ethnological interest of its native inhabitants, and I have had during my previous voyage, and while staying in Cameroon, rather exceptional opportunities of studying both these subjects. I will therefore sketch the result of my observations here, doing so all the more readily, because this has no pretension to being a connected work,—a thing you possibly have already remarked.

I had heard sundry noble legends of Fernando Po, and seen the coast and a good deal of the island before, but although I had heard much of the Governor, I had never met him until I went up to his residence with Lady MacDonald and the Consul-General. He was a delightful person, who, as a Spanish naval officer, some time resident in Cuba, had picked up a lot of English, with a strong American accent clinging to it. He gave a most moving account of how, as soon as his appointment as Governor was announced, all his friends and acquaintances carefully explained to him that this appointment was equivalent to execution, only more

KING DUKE OF CALABAR IN FULL DRESS.

uncomfortable in the way it worked out. During the outward voyage this was daily confirmed by the stories told by the sailors and merchants personally acquainted with the place, who were able to support their information with dates and details of the decease of the victims to the climate.

Still he kept up a good heart, but when he arrived at the island he found his predecessor had died of fever ; and he himself, the day after landing, went down with a bad attack and he was placed in a bed—the same bed, he was mournfully informed, in which the last Governor had expired. Then he did believe, all in one awful lump, all the stories he had been told, and added to their horrors a few original conceptions of death and purgatory, and a lot of transparent semi-formed images of his own delirium. Fortunately both prophecy and personal conviction alike miscarried, and the Governor returned from the jaws of death. But without a moment's delay he withdrew from the Port of Clarence and went up the mountain to Basile, which is in the neighbourhood of the highest native village, where he built himself a house, and around it a little village of homes for the most unfortunate set of human beings I have ever laid eye on. They are the remnant of a set of Spanish colonists, who had been located at some spot in the Spanish possessions in Morocco, and finding that place unfit to support human life, petitioned the Government to remove them and let them try colonising elsewhere.

The Spanish Government just then had one of its occasional fits of interest in Fernando Po, and so shipped them here, and the Governor, a most kindly and generous man, who would have been a credit to any country, established them and their families around him at Basile, to share with him the advantages of the superior elevation ; advantages he profoundly believed in, and which he has always placed at the disposal of any sick white man on the island, of whatsoever nationality or religion. Undoubtedly the fever is not so severe at Basile as in the lowlands, but there are here the usual drawbacks to West African high land, namely an over supply of rain, and equally saturating mists, to say nothing of sudden and extreme alternations of temperature, and so the colonists still fall off, and their children die continuously from the various entozoa which abound upon the island.

When the Governor first settled upon the mountain he was very difficult to get at for business purposes, and a telephone was therefore run up to him from Clarence through the forest, and Spain at large felt proud at this dashing bit of enterprise in modern appliance. Alas! the primeval forests of Fernando Po were also charmed with the new toy, and they talked to each other on it with their leaves and branches to such an extent that a human being could not get a word in edgeways. So the Governor had to order the construction of a road along the course of the wire to keep the trees off it, but unfortunately the telephone is still an uncertain means of communication, because another interruption in its usefulness still afflicts it, namely the indigenous natives' habit of stealing bits out of its wire, for they are fully persuaded that they cannot be found out in their depredations provided they take sufficient care that they are not caught in the act. The Governor is thus liable to be cut off at any moment in the middle of a conversation with Clarence, and the amount of "Hellos" "Are you theres?" and "Speak louder, pleases" in Spanish that must at such times be poured out and wasted in the lonely forests before the break is realised and an unfortunate man sent off as a messenger, is terrible to think of.

But nothing would persuade the Governor to come a mile down towards Clarence until the day he should go there to join the vessel that was to take him home, and I am bound to say he looked as if the method was a sound one, for he was an exceedingly healthy, cheery-looking man. Possibly his abstinence from Fernando Po water—a dangerous beverage— and an adherence to a form of light sherry, had something to do with his immunity from fever, for his neighbours, the colonists and priests who are stationed near him, are by no means good advertisements for Basile as a health-resort.

Fernando Po is said to be a comparatively modern island, and not so very long ago to have been connected with the mainland, the strait between them being only nineteen miles across, and not having any deep soundings.[1] I fail to see what grounds there are for these ideas, for though Fernando Po's volcanoes are not yet extinct, but merely have their fires

[1] From Point Limbok, the seaward extremity of Cameroons mountain, to Cape Horatio, the most eastern extremity of Fernando Po, the soundings are, from the continent, 13, 17, 20, 23, 27, 29, 30, 34 fathoms; close on to the island, 35 and 29 fathoms.

banked, yet, on the other hand, the island has been in existence sufficiently long to get itself several peculiar species of
animals and plants, and that is a thing which takes time. I
myself do not believe that this island was ever connected with
the continent, but arose from the ocean as the result of a
terrific upheaval in the chain of volcanic activity which runs
across the Atlantic from the Cameroon Mountains in a SSW.
direction to Anno Bom island, and possibly even to the
Tristan da Cunha group midway between the Cape and South
America.

These volcanic islands are all of extreme beauty and
fertility. They consist of Fernando Po (10,190 ft.); Principe,
(3000 ft.); San Thomé (6,913 ft.); and Anno Bom, (1,350 ft.).
San Thomé and Principe are Portuguese possessions, Fernando
Po and Anno Bom Spanish, and they are all exceedingly
unhealthy. San Thomé is still called " The Dutchman's
Church-yard," on account of the devastation its climate
wrought among the Hollanders when they once occupied it ;
as they seem, at one time or another, to have occupied all
Portuguese possessions out here, during the long war these
two powers waged· with each other for supremacy in the
Bights, a supremacy that neither of them attained to. Principe is said to be the most unhealthy, and the reason of the
difference in this particular between Principe and Anno Bom
is said to arise from the fact that the former is on the Guinea
Current—a hot current—and Anno Bom on the Equatorial,
which averages 10° cooler than its neighbour.

The shores of San Thomé are washed by both currents,
and the currents round Fernando Po are in a mixed and
uncertain state. It is difficult, unless you have haunted
these seas, to realise the interest we take down there in
currents, particularly when you are navigating small sailing
boats, a pursuit I indulge in necessarily from my fishing
practices. Their effect on the climate too is very marked.
If we could only arrange for some terrific affair to take
place in the bed of the Atlantic, that would send that
precious Guinea current to the place it evidently comes
from, and get the cool Equatorial alongside the mainland
shore, West Africa would be quite another place.

Fernando Po is the most important island as regards size on the West African coast, and at the same time one of the most beautiful in the world. It is a great volcanic mass

THE MANGO AVENUE, FERNANDO PO.

with many craters, and culminates in the magnificent cone, Clarence Peak, called by the Spaniards, Pico de Santa Isabel, by the natives of the island O Wassa. Seen from the sea or from the continent it looks like an immense single mountain that has floated out to sea. It is visible during clear weather (and particularly sharply visible in the strange clearness you get after a tornado) from a hundred miles to seawards, and anything more perfect than Fernando Po when you sight it, as you occasionally do from far-away Bonny Bar, in the sunset, floating like a fairy island made of gold or of amethyst, I cannot conceive. It is almost equally lovely at close quarters, namely from the mainland at Victoria, nineteen miles distant. Its moods of beauty are infinite ; for the most part gentle and gorgeous, but I have seen it silhouetted hard against tornado-clouds, and grandly grim from the upper regions of its great brother Mungo. And as for Fernando Po in full moonlight—well there ! you had better go and see it yourself.

The whole island is, or rather I should say was, heavily forested almost to its peak, with a grand and varied type of forest, very rich in oil palms and tree-ferns, and having an undergrowth containing an immense variety and quantity of ferns and mosses. Sugar-cane also grows wild here, an uncommon thing in West Africa. The last botanical collection of any importance made from these forests was that of Herr Mann, and its examination showed that Abyssinian genera and species predominated, and that many species similar to those found in the mountains of Mauritius, the Isle de Bourbon, and Madagascar, were present. The number of European plants (forty-three genera, twenty-seven species) is strikingly large, most of the British forms being represented chiefly at the higher elevations. What was more striking was that it showed that South African forms were extremely rare, and not one of the characteristic types of St. Helena occurred.

Cocoa, coffee, and cinchona, alas ! flourish in Fernando Po, as the coffee suffers but little from the disease that harasses it on the mainland at Victoria, and this is the cause of the great destruction of the forest that is at present taking place. San Thomé, a few years ago, was discovered by its surprised neighbours to be amassing great wealth by growing coffee, and so Fernando Po and Principe immediately started to amass great wealth too, and are now hard at work with gangs of miscellaneous natives got from all parts of the Coast save the

Kru. For to the Kruboy, " Panier," as he calls " Spaniard," is a
name of horror worse even than Portuguee, although he holds
" God made white man and God made black man, but dem
debil make Portuguee," and he also remembers an unfortunate
affair that occurred some years ago now, in connection with
coffee-growing.

A number of Krumen engaged themselves for a two years'
term of labour on the Island of San Thomé, and when they
arrived there, were set to work on coffee plantations by the
Portuguese. Now agricultural work is "woman's palaver,"
but nevertheless the Krumen made shift to get through with
it, vowing the while no doubt, as they hopefully notched away
the moons on their tally-sticks, that they would never let the
girls at home know that they had been hoeing. But when
their moons were all complete, instead of being sent home
with their pay to " we country," they were put off from time
to time ; and month after month went by and they were still
on San Thomé, and still hoeing. At last the home-sick men,
in despair of ever getting free, started off secretly in ones and
twos to try and get to " we country " across hundreds of miles
of the storm-haunted Atlantic in small canoes, and with next
to no provisions. The result was a tragedy, but it might easily
have been worse ; for a few, a very few, were picked up alive
by English vessels and taken back to their beloved " we
country " to tell the tale. But many a canoe was found with
a dead Kruboy or so in it ; and many a one which, floating
bottom upwards, graphically spoke of madness caused by
hunger, thirst, and despair having driven its occupants overboard to the sharks.

My Portuguese friends assure me that there was never a
thought of permanently detaining the boys, and that they
were only just keeping them until other labourers arrived to
take their place on the plantations. I quite believe them, for I
have seen too much of the Portuguese in Africa to believe
that they would, in a wholesale way, be cruel to natives. But
I am not in the least surprised that the poor Krumen took
the Portuguese *logo* and *amanhã* for eternity itself, for I have
frequently done so.

The greatest length of the island lies N.E. and S.W., and

amounts to thirty-three miles ; the mean breadth is seventeen miles. The port, Clarence Cove, now called Santa Isabel by the Spaniards—who have been giving Spanish names to all the English-named places without any one taking much notice of them—is a very remarkable place, and except perhaps Gaboon the finest harbour on the West Coast. The point that brings Gaboon, anchorage up in line with Clarence Cove is its superior healthiness ; for Clarence is a section of a circle, and its shores are steep rocky cliffs from 100 to 200 feet high, and the place, to put it very mildly, exceedingly hot and stuffy. The cove is evidently a partly submerged crater, the submerged rim of the crater is almost a perfect semi-circle seawards—having on it 4, 5, 7, 8, and 10 fathoms of water save almost in the centre of the arc where there is a passage with 12 to 14 fathoms. Inside, in the crater, there is deeper water, running in places from 30 to 45 fathoms, and outside the submerged rim there is deeper water again, but rocky shoals abound. On the top of the shore cliffs stands the dilapidated little town of Clarence, on a plateau that falls away slightly towards the mountain for about a mile, when the ground commences to rise into the slopes of the Cordillera. On the narrow beach, tucked close against the cliffs, are a few stores belonging to the merchants, where goods are placed on landing, and there is a little pier too, but as it is usually having something done to its head, or else is closed by the authorities because they intend doing something by and by, the chances are against its being available for use. Hence it usually comes about that you have to land on the beach, and when you have done this you make your way up a very steep path, cut in the cliff-side, to the town. When you get there you find yourself in the very dullest town I know on the Coast. I remember when I first landed in Clarence I found its society in a flutter of expectation and alarm not untinged with horror. Clarence, nay, the whole of Fernando Po, was about to become so rackety and dissipated as to put Paris and Monte Carlo to the blush. Clarence was going to have a café ; and what was going to go on in that café I shrink from reciting.

I have little hesitation now in saying this alarm was a false one. When I next arrived in Clarence it was just as sound asleep and its streets as weed-grown as ever, although the café was open. My idea is the sleepiness of the place infected the café and took all the go out of it. But again it may have been that the inhabitants were too well guarded against its evil influence, for there are on the island fifty-two white lay-men, and fifty-four priests to take charge of them[1]—the extra two being, I presume, to look after the Governor's conduct, although this worthy man made a most spirited protest against this view when I suggested it to him ; and in addition to the priests there are several missionaries of the Methodist mission, and also a white gentleman who has invented a new religion. Anyhow, the café smoulders like a damp squib.

When you spend the day on shore and when, having ex-hausted the charms of the town,—a thing that usually takes from between ten minutes to a quarter of an hour,—you apply to an inhabitant for advice as to the disposal of the rest of your shore leave, you are told to "go and see the coals." You say you have not come to tropical islands to see a coal heap, and applying elsewhere for advice you probably get the same. So, as you were told to "go and see the coals" when you left your ship, you do as you are bid. These coals, the remnant of the store that was kept here for the English men-of-war, were left here when the naval station was removed. The Spaniards at first thought of using them, and ran a tram-way from Clarence to them. But when the tram-way was finished, their activity had run out too, and to this day there the coals remain. Now and again some one has the idea that they are quite good, and can be used for a steamer, and some people who have tried them say they are all right, and others say they are all wrong. And so the end of it will be that some few thousand years hence there will be a serious quarrel among geologists on the strange pocket of coal on Fernando Po, and they will run up continents, and raise and lower oceans to explain them, and they will doubtless get

[1] I am informed that the allowance made to these priests exceeds by some pounds the revenues Spain obtains from the Island. In Spanish possessions alone is a supporting allowance made to missionaries, though in all the other colonies they obtain a government grant.

more excitement and pleasure out of them than you can nowadays.

I am by no means a person who hungers for amusement—far from it ; but when I had been to see the coals I certainly felt as if I could cram another excitement into that afternoon without any great effort, and I cite this experience as a warning to others of the dangers of being unsatisfied ; for although I did discover a far superior and more thrilling thing, high up among the beautiful, blossoming shrubs that make a narrow fringe between the sea and the forest, namely, a large man-o'-war's pinnace, I could not find out how she got there, or why she stayed there. Flushed, however, with this discovery I must needs go on, still along the southern shore, with the grand, densely-forested mountains rising on my left, and the lovely Atlantic on my right,—now and then climbing over rocks, and then paddling across the bar of a tiny river (Munguba) which came creeping out from among the trees, smelling certainly unpleasant, but a joy to the eye. Then I struck a farm, where operations connected with preparing cocoa were proceeding, and the genial natives discoursed with me on the subject for a short time. Going on further I came to another farm, and had more discourse, and a lot of information about Liberia from a native of that country, and then on across other small rivers, the Burapulopu and the Bulabopi, up to a swampy forest, when I turned back at last well satisfied with my afternoon. Just as I passed my first farm I found that what I had regarded as a dry land shrub-belt was nothing of the kind. The tide had come in and taken full possession of it, running up to the forest wall. The forest was far too thick to get through, so there was nothing for it but a hurried waist-high wade. I went in for this remembering that I had been informed that there were very nasty crocodiles on the island, and that I had got to get past the mouth of that largest river—as crocodiley-looking a spot as you could wish for, if you had a gun. I saw none however, and so presume there are none there, for it is the habit of these animals, when they are handy to the sea, to lounge down and meet the in-coming tide. The worst part of the affair was getting round the projecting bits of rocky cliff where the sea was breaking ; not roughly, or I should not be writing this now.

The history of the English occupation of Fernando Po seems often misunderstood, and now and then one hears our Government reviled for handing it over to the Spaniards. But this was unavoidable, for we had it as a loan from Spain in 1827 as a naval station for our ships, at that time energetically commencing to suppress the slave trade in the Bights ; the idea being that this island would afford a more healthy and convenient spot for a naval depot than any port on the coast itself.

More convenient Fernando Po certainly was, but not more healthy, and ever since 1827 it has been accumulating for itself an evil reputation for unhealthiness which is only languishing just at present because there is an interval between its epidemics—fever in Fernando Po, even more than on the mainland, having periodic outbursts of a more serious type than the normal intermittent and remittent of the Coast. Moreover, Fernando Po shares with Senegal the undoubted yet doubtful honour of having had regular yellow fever. In 1862 and 1866 this disease was imported by a ship that had come from Havana. Since then it has not appeared in the definite South American form, and therefore does not seem to have obtained the foothold it has in Senegal, where a few years ago all the money voted for the keeping of the *Fête Nationale* was in one district devoted by public consent to the purchase of coffins, required by an overwhelming outbreak of Yellow Jack.

In 1858 the Spanish Government thinking, presumably, that the slave trade was suppressed enough, or at any rate to a sufficiently inconvenient extent, re-claimed Fernando Po, to the horror of the Baptist missionaries who had settled in Clarence apparently under the erroneous idea that the island had been definitely taken over by the English. This mission had received from the West African Company a large grant of land, and had collected round it a gathering of Sierra Leonians and other artisan and trading Africans who were attracted to Clarence by the work made by the naval station ; and these people, with the English traders who also settled

here for a like reason, were the founders of Clarence Town.
The declaration of the Spanish Government stating that
only Roman Catholic missions would be countenanced caused
the Baptists to abandon their possessions and withdraw to
the mainland in Ambas Bay, where they have since remained,
and nowadays Protestantism is represented by a Methodist
Mission which has a sub-branch on the mainland on the
Akwayafe River and one on the Qua Ibo.

The Spaniards, on resuming possession of the island, had
one of their attacks of activity regarding it, and sent out
with Don Carlos Chacon, who was to take over the command,
four Jesuit priests, a secretary, a commissariat officer, a
custom-house clerk, and a transport, the *Santa Maria*, with
a number of emigrant families. This attempt to colonise
Fernando Po should have at least done the good of
preventing such experiments ever being tried again with
women and children, for of these unfortunate creatures—for
whom, in spite of its being the wet season, no houses had
been provided—more than 20 per cent. died in the space
of five months. Mr. Hutchinson, who was English Consul
at the time, tells us that " In a very short time gaunt figures
of men, women, and children might be seen crawling through
the streets, with scarcely an evidence of life in their faces,
save the expression of a sort of torpid carelessness as to
how soon it might be their turn to drop off and die. The
Portino, a steamer, carried back fifty of them to Cadiz, who
looked when they embarked more like living skeletons of
skin and bone than animated human beings." [1] I quote this
not to cast reproach on the Spanish Government, but merely
to give a fact, a case in point, of the deadly failure of
endeavours to colonise on the West Coast, a thing which is
even now occasionally attempted, always with the same sad
results, though in most cases these attempts are now made
by religious and misinformed people under Bishop Taylor's
mission.

The Spaniards did not entirely confine their attention to
planting colonists in a ready-made state on the island. As
soon as they had settled themselves and built their barracks

[1] *Ten Years' Wanderings among the Ethiopians*, T. J. Hutchinson.

and Government House, they set to work and cleared away
the bush for an area of from four to six miles round the
town. The ground soon became overgrown again, but this
clearing is still perceptible in the different type of forest on
it, and has enabled the gardens and little plantations round
Clarence to be made more easily. My Spanish friends
assure me that the Portuguese, who discovered the island in
1471,[1] and who exchanged it and Anno Bom in 1778
to the Spaniards for the little island of Catalina and the

GOVERNOR'S PALACE, FERNANDO PO.

colony of Sacramento in South America, did not do anything to develop it. When they, the Spaniards, first entered
into possession they at once set to work to colonise and clear.
Then the colonisation scheme went to the bad, the natives
poisoned the wells, it is said, and the attention of the
Spaniards was in those days turned, for some inscrutable
reason, to the eastern shores of the island—a district now
quite abandoned by whites, on account of its unhealthiness

[1] There is difference of opinion among authorities as to whether
Fernando Po was discovered by Fernando Po or by Lopez Gonsalves.

—and they lost in addition to the colonists a terrible quantity of their sailors, in Concepcion Bay.[1] A lull then followed, and the Spaniards willingly lent the place to the English as aforesaid. They say we did nothing except establish Clarence as a headquarters, which they consider to have been a most excellent enterprise, and import the Baptist Mission, which they hold as a less estimable undertaking ; but there! that's nothing to what the Baptist Mission hold regarding the Spaniards. For my own part, I wish the Spaniards better luck this time in their activity, for in directing it to plantations they are on a truer and safer road to wealth than they have been with their previous importations of Cuban political prisoners and ready-made families of colonists, and I hope they will send home those unfortunate wretches they have there now, and commence, in their expected two years, to reap the profits of the coffee and cocoa. Certainly the chances are that they may, for the soil of Fernando Po is of exceeding fertility ; Mr. Hutchinson says he has known Indian corn planted here on a Monday evening make its appearance four inches above ground on the following Wednesday morning, within a period, he carefully says, of thirty-six hours. I have seen this sort of thing over in Victoria, but I like to get a grown strong man, and a Consul of Her Britannic Majesty, to say it for me.

Having discoursed at large on the various incomers to Fernando Po we may next turn to the natives, properly so-called, the Bubis. These people, although presenting a series of interesting problems to the ethnologist, both from their insular position, and their differentiation from any of the mainland peoples, are still but little known. To a great extent this has arisen from their exclusiveness, and their total lack of enthusiasm in trade matters, a thing that differentiates them more than any other characteristic from the mainlanders, who, young and old, men and women, regard trade as the great affair of life, take to it as soon as they can toddle, and don't even leave it off at death, according to their own accounts of

---

[1] From April 1777 till the end of 1782, 370 men out of the 547 died of fever.

the way the spirits of distinguished traders still dabble and interfere in market matters. But it is otherwise with the Bubi. A little rum, a few beads, and finish—then he will turn the rest of his attention to catching porcupines, or the beautiful little gazelles, gray on the back and white underneath, with which the island abounds. And what time he may have on hand after this, he spends in building houses and making himself hats. It is only his utterly spare moments that he employs in making just sufficient palm oil from the rich supply of nuts at his command to get that rum and those beads of his. Cloth he does not want; he utterly fails to see what good the stuff is, for he abhors clothes, and as a friend of mine observed :—" Señora, you'll see more bare skin on this island than in a regiment of grenadiers." He said this in Spanish, and I had to look it up in a dictionary and then think about it afterwards, so the statement irritated me, for I felt that the man knew enough English to be aware that it must work out as a bad pun. But nevertheless the truth was in it, for when you go outside Clarence you come across the Bubi ostentatiously unclothed—I say ostentatiously for the benefit of ethnologists—and this I have never elsewhere seen in West Africa. The Spanish authorities insist that the natives who come into the town should have something on, and so they array themselves in a bit of cotton cloth, which before they are out of sight of the town. on their homeward way, they strip off and stuff into their baskets, showing in this, as well as in all other particulars, how uninfluencible by white culture they are. For the Spaniards, like the Portuguese, are great sticklers for clothes, and insist on their natives wearing them—usually with only too much success. I shall never forget the yards and yards of cotton the ladies of Loanda wore ; and not content with making cocoons of their bodies, they wore over their heads, as a mantilla, some dozen yards or so of black cloth into the bargain. Moreover this insistence on drapery for the figure is not merely for towns ; a German officer told me the other day that when, a week or so before, his ship had called at Anno Bom, they were simply besieged for " clo', clo', clo' ;" the Anno Bomians explaining that they were all anxious to go across to Principe and get employment on coffee plantations, but that the Portuguese planters would not engage them in an unclothed state.

You must not, however, imagine that the Bubi is neglectful of his personal appearance.   In his way he is quite a dandy. But his idea of decoration goes in the direction of a plaster of " tola " pomatum over his body, and above all a hat.   This hat may be an antique European one, or a bound-round handkerchief, but it is more frequently a confection of native manufacture, and great taste and variety is displayed in its make. They are of plaited palm leaf—that's all you can safely generalise regarding them—for sometimes they have broad brims, sometimes narrow, sometimes no brims at all.   So, too, with the crown.   Sometimes it is thick and domed, sometimes non-existent, the wearer's hair aglow with red-tail parrots' feathers sticking up where the crown should be.   As a general rule these hats are much adorned with oddments of birds' plumes, and one chief I knew had quite a Regent-street Dolly Varden creation which he used to affix to his wool in a most intelligent way with bonnet-pins made of wood.   These hats are also a peculiarity of the Bubi, for none of the mainlanders care a row of pins for hats, except " for dandy," to wear occasionally, whereas the Bubi wears his perpetually, although he has by no means the same amount of sun to guard against owing to the glorious forests of his island.   I am told there is a certain sound reason in his devotion for his hat, and that is that it acts as a protection against a beautiful but poisonous green tree snake that abounds on Fernando Po, whose habit it is to hang, upside down, from the trees.   If the snake strikes the hat instead of the head when the wearer is out hunting, why so much the better for the wearer.

For earrings the Bubi wears pieces of wood stuck through the lobe of the ear, and although this is not a decorative habit still it is less undecorative than that of certain mainland friends of mine in this region, who wear large and necessarily dripping lumps of fat in their ears and in their hair.   His neck is hung round with jujus on strings—bits of the backbones of pythons, teeth, feathers, and antelope horns—and round his upper arm are bracelets, preferably made of ivory

got from the mainland, for celluloid bracelets carefully imported
for his 'benefit he refuses to look at. Often also these bracelets are made of beads, or a circlet of leaves, and when on
the war-path an armlet of twisted grass is always worn by the
men. Men and women alike wear armlets, and in the case of
the women they seem to be put on when young, for you see
puffs of flesh growing out from between them. They are also
not entirely for decoration, serving commonly as pockets, for
under them in the case of men is stuck a knife, and in the
case of women a tobacco pipe, a well-coloured clay. Leglets
of similar construction are worn just under the knee on the
right leg, while around the body you see belts of *tshibbu*, small
pieces cut from Achatectonia shells, which form the native
currency of the island. These shells are also made into veils
worn by the women at their wedding.

This native coinage-equivalent is very interesting, for such
things are exceedingly rare in West Africa. The only other
instance I personally know of a tribe in this part of the world
using a native-made coin is that of the Fans, who use little
bundles of imitation axe-heads. Dr. Oscar Baumann, who
knows more than any one else about these Bubis, thinks, I
believe, that these bits of Achatectonia shells may have been
introduced by the runaway Angola slaves in the old days, who
used to fly from their Portuguese owners on San Thomé to the
Spaniards on Fernando Po. The villages of the Bubis are in
the forest in the interior of the island, and they are fairly wide
apart. They are not a sea-beach folk, although each village
has its beach, which merely means the place to which it brings
its trade, these beaches being usually the dwelling places of
the so-called Portos,[1] negroes, who act as middle-men between
the Bubis and the whites.

You will often be told that the Bubis are singularly bad
house-builders, indeed that they make no definite houses at

[1] Porto is the Bubi name for black men who are not Bubis, these were
in old days Portuguese slaves, " Porto " being evidently a corruption of
"Portuguese," but it is used alike by the Bubi to designate Sierra
Leonian Accras, in fact, all the outer barbarian blacks. The name for
white men, Mandara, used by the Bubis, has a sort of resemblance to the
Effik name for whites, Makara, *i.e.*, the ruling one, but I do not know
whether these two words have any connection.

all, but only rough shelters of branches. This is, however, a
mistake. Shelters of this kind that you come across are
merely the rough huts put up by hunters, not true houses. The
village is usually fairly well built, and surrounded with a living
hedge of stakes. The houses inside this are four-cornered, the
walls made of logs of wood stuck in edgeways, and surmounted
by a roof of thatch pitched at an extremely stiff angle, and the
whole is usually surrounded with a dug-out drain to carry off
surface water. These houses, as usual on the West Coast, are
divisible into two classes—houses of assembly, and private
living houses. The first are much the larger. The latter are
very low, and sometimes ridiculously small, but still they are
houses and better than those awful Loango grass affairs you
get on the Congo.

Herr Baumann says that the houses high up on the mountain
have double walls between which there is a free space ; an
arrangement which may serve to minimise the extreme
draughtiness of an ordinary Bubi house—a very necessary thing
in these relatively chilly upper regions. I may remark on my
own account that the Bubi villages do not often lie right on
the path, but, like those you have to deal with up the Calabar,
some little way off it. This is no doubt for the purpose of
concealing their whereabouts from strangers, and it does it successfully too, for many a merry hour have I spent dodging
up and down a path trying to make out at what particular
point it was advisable to dive into the forest thicket to reach a
village. But this cultivates habits of observation, and a short
course of this work makes you recognise which tree is which
along miles of a bush path as easily as you would shops in
your own street at home.

The main interest of the Bubi's life lies in hunting, for
he is more of a sportsman than the majority of mainlanders.
He has not any big game to deal with, unless we except
pythons—which attain a great size on the island—and crocodiles. Elephants, though plentiful on the adjacent mainland,
are quite absent from Fernando Po, as are also hippos and the
great anthropoid apes ; but of the little gazelles, small
monkeys, porcupines, and squirrels he has a large supply, and
in the rivers a very pretty otter (*Lutra poensis*) with yellow

brown fur often quite golden underneath ; a creature which is,
I believe, identical with the Angola otter.

The Bubis use in their hunting flint-lock guns, but chiefly
traps and nets, and, I am told, slings. The advantage of these
latter methods are, I expect, the same as on the mainland,
where a distinguished sportsman once told me : " You go shoot
thing with gun. Berrah well—but you no get him thing for
sure. No sah. Dem gun make nize. Berrah well. You fren
hear dem nize and come look him, and you hab to go share
what you done kill. Or bad man hear him nize, and he come
look him, and you no fit to get share—you fit to get kill
yusself. Chii ! chii ! traps be best." I urged that the traps
might also be robbed. " No, sah," says he, " them bian (charm)
he look after them traps, he fit to make man who go tief swell
up and bust."

The Bubis also fish, mostly by basket traps, but they are
not experts either in this or in canoe management. Their
chief sea-shore sport is hunting for the eggs of the turtles who
lay in the sand from August to October. These eggs—about
200 in each nest—are about the size of a billiard-ball, with a
leathery envelope, and are much valued for food, as are also
the grubs of certain beetles got from the stems of the palm-
trees, and the honey of the wild bees which abound here.

Their domestic animals are the usual African list ; cats,
dogs, sheep, goats, and poultry. Pigs there are too, very
domestic in Clarence and in a wild state in the forest.
These pigs are the descendants of those imported by the
Spaniards, and not long ago became such an awful nuisance in Clarence that the Government issued instructions
that all pigs without rings in their noses—i.e. all in a condition to grub up back gardens—should be forthwith shot
if found abroad. This proclamation was issued by the
governmental bellman thus :—" I say—I say—I say –I say
Suppose pig walk—iron no live for him nose ! Gun shoot.
Kill him one time. Hear re ! hear re ! "

However a good many pigs with no iron living in their
noses got adrift and escaped into the interior, and have
flourished like the green bay-tree, destroying the Bubi's
plantation and eating his yams, while the Bubi retaliating

kills and eats them. So it's a drawn battle, for the Bubi enjoys the pig and the pig enjoys the yams, which are of singular excellence in this island and celebrated throughout the Bight. Now, I am told, the Government are firmly discouraging the export of these yams, which used to be quite a little branch of Fernando Po trade, in the hope, that this will induce the native to turn his attention to working in the coffee and cacao plantations. Hope springs eternal in the human breast, for the Bubi has shown continually since the 16th century that he takes no interest in these things whatsoever. Now and again a man or woman will come voluntarily and take service in Clarence, submit to clothes, and rapidly pick up the ways of a house or store. And just when their owner thinks he owns a treasure, and begins to boast that he has got an exception to all Bubidom, or else that he knows how to manage them better than other men, then a hole in that man's domestic arrangements suddenly appears. The Bubi has gone, without giving a moment's warning, and without stealing his master's property, but just softly and silently vanished away. And if hunted up the treasure will be found in his or her particular village — clothesless, comfortable, utterly unconcerned, and unaware that he or she has lost anything by leaving Clarence and civilisation. It is this conduct that gains for the Bubi the reputation of being a bigger idiot than he really is.

For West Africans their agriculture is of a fairly high description—the noteworthy point about it, however, is the absence of manioc. Manioc is grown on Fernando Po, but only by the Portos. The Bubi cultivated plants are yams (*Dioscorea alata*), koko (*Colocasia esculenta*)—the taro of the South Seas, and plantains. Their farms are well kept, particularly those in the grass districts by San Carlos Bay. The yams of the Cordillera districts are the best flavoured, but those of the east coast the largest. Palm-oil is used for domestic purposes in the usual ways, and palm wine both fresh and fermented is the ordinary native drink. Rum is held in high esteem, but used in a general way in moderation as a cordial and a treat, for the Bubi is, like the rest of the West

African natives, by no means an habitual drunkard. Gin he dislikes.[1]

And I may remark you will find the same opinion in regard to the Dualla in Cameroons river—on the undeniable authority of Dr. Buchner, and my own extensive experience of the West Coast bears it out.

Physically the Bubis are a fairly well-formed race of medium height; they are decidedly inferior to the Benga or the Krus, but quite on a level with the Effiks The women indeed are very comely: their colour is bronze and their skin the skin of the Bantu. Beards are not uncommon among the men, and these give their faces possibly more than anything else, a different look to the faces of the Effiks or the Duallas. Indeed the people physically most like the Bubis that I have

[1] I am glad to find that my own observations on the drink question entirely agree with those of Dr. Oscar Baumann, because he is an unprejudiced scientific observer, who has had great experience both in the Congo and Cameroon regions before he came to Fernando Po. In the support of my statement I may quote his own words :—" Die Bube trinken nämlich sehr gerne Rum ; Gin verschmähen sie vollständig, aber ausser Tabak und Salz gehört Rum zu den gesuchtesten europäischen Artikeln für sie. Wie bekannt hat sich in Europa ein heftiges Geschrei gegen die Vergiftung der Neger durch Alcohol erhoben. Wenn dasselbe schon für die meisten Stämme Westafrikas der Berechtigung fast vollständig entbehrt und in die Categorie verweisen worden muss die man mit dem nicht sehr schönen aber treffenden Ausdrucke " Humanitätsduselei" bezeichnet, so ist es den Bube gegenüber wohl mehr als zwecklos. Es mag ja vorkommen dass ein Bube wenn er sein Palmöl verkauft hat, sich ein oder zweimal im Jahre mit Rum ein Räuschlein antrinkt. Deshalb aber gleich von Alkohol-Vergiftung zu sprechen wäre mindestens lächerlich. Ich bin überzeugt dass mancher jener Herren die in Wort und Schrift so heftig gegen die Alkolismus der Neger zetern in ihren Studentenjahren allein mehr geistige Getränke genossen haben als zehn Bube während ihres ganzen Lebens. Der Handelsrum welcher wie ich mich öfters überzeugt zwar recht verwässert aber keineswegs abstossend schlecht schmeckt, ist den Bube gewöhnlich nur eine Delikatesse welche mit Andacht schluckweise genossen wird. Wenn ein Arbeiter bei uns einen Schluck Branntwein oder ein Glas Bier geniesst um sich zu stärken, so findet das Jeder in der Ordnung ; der Bube jedoch, welcher splitternackt tagelang in feuchten Bergwäldern umher klettern muss, soll beliebe nichts als Wasser trinken!" *Eine Africanische Tropen. insel Fernando Póo*, Dr. Oscar Baumann, Edward Hölzer, Wien, 1888.

ever seen, are undoubtedly the Bakwiri of Cameroons Mountain, who are also liable to be bearded, or possibly I should say more liable to wear beards, for a good deal of the African hairlessness you hear commented on—in the West African at any rate —arises from his deliberately pulling his hair out— his beard, moustache, whiskers, and occasionally, as among the Fans, his eyebrows.

Dr. Baumann, the great authority on the Bubi language says it is a Bantu stock.[1] I know nothing of it myself save that it is harsh in sound. Their method of counting is usually by fives but they are notably weak in arithmetical ability, differing in this particular from the mainlanders, and especially from their Negro neighbours, who are very good at figures, surpassing the Bantu in this, as indeed they do in most branches of intellectual activity.

But the most remarkable instance of inferiority the Bubis display is their ignorance regarding methods of working iron. I do not know that iron in a native state is found on Fernando Po, but scrap-iron they have been in touch with for some hundreds of years. The mainlanders are all cognisant of native methods of working iron, although many tribes of them now depend entirely on European trade for their supply of knives, &c., and this difference between them and the Bubis would seem to indicate that the migration of the latter to the island must have taken place at a fairly remote period, a period before the iron-working tribes came down to the coast. Of course, if you take the Bubi's usual explanation of his origin, namely that he came out of the crater on the top of Clarence Peak, this argument falls through ; but he has also another legend, one moreover which is likewise to be found upon the mainland, which says he was driven from the district north of the Gaboon estuary by the coming of the M'pongwe to the coast, and as this legend is the more likely of the two I think we may accept it as true, or nearly so. But what adds another difficulty to the matter is that the Bubi is not only unlearned in iron lore, but he was learned in stone, and up to the time of the youth of many

---

[1] "Beiträge zur Kenntniss der Bubisprache auf Fernando Póo," O. Baumann, *Zeitschrift für afrikanische Sprachen.* Berlin, 1888.

Porto-negroes on Fernando Po, he was making and using stone
implements, and none of the tribes within the memory of
man have done this on the mainland. It is true that up the
Niger and about Benin and Axim you get polished stone
celts, but these are regarded as weird affairs,—thunderbolts—
and suitable only for grinding up and making into medicine.
There is no trace in the traditions, as far as I have been able
to find, of any time at which stone implements were in common
use, and certainly the M'pongwe have not been a very long
time on the coast, for their coming is still remembered in their
traditions. The Bubi stone implements I have seen twice,
but on neither occasion could I secure one, and although
I have been long promised specimens from Fernando Po, I
have not yet received them. They are difficult to procure,
because none of the present towns are on really old sites, the
Bubi, like most Bantus, moving pretty frequently, either because the ground is witched, demonstrated by outbreaks of sickness, or because another village-full of his fellow creatures, or
a horrid white man plantation-making, has come too close to
him. A Roman Catholic priest in Ka Congo once told me a
legend he laughed much over, of how a fellow priest had
enterprisingly settled himself one night in the middle of a
Bubi village with intent to devote the remainder of his life to
quietly but thoroughly converting it. Next morning, when he
rose up, he found himself alone, the people having taken all
their portable possessions and vanished to build another
village elsewhere. The worthy Father spent some time chivying his flock about the forest, but in vain, and he returned
home disgusted, deciding that the Creator, for some wise
purpose, had dedicated the Bubis to the Devil.

The spears used by this interesting people are even to this
day made entirely of wood, and have such a Polynesian look
about them that I intend some time or other to bring some
home and experiment on that learned Polynesian-culture-ex-
pert, Baron von Hügel, with them :—intellectually experiment,
not physically, pray understand.

The pottery has a very early-man look about it, but in this
it does not differ much from that of the mainland, which is
quite as poor, and similarly made without a wheel, and sun-

baked. Those pots of the Bubis I have seen have, however, not had the pattern (any sort of pattern does, and it need not be carefully done) that runs round mainland pots to "keep their souls in"—*i.e.* to prevent their breaking up on their own account.

Their basket-work is of a superior order :· the baskets they make to hold the semi-fluid palm oil are excellent, and will hold water like a basin, but I am in doubt whether this art is original, or imported by the Portuguese runaway slaves, for they put me very much in mind of those made by my old friends the Kabinders, from whom a good many of those slaves were recruited. I think there is little doubt that several of the musical instruments own this origin, particularly their best beloved one, the elibo. This may be described as a wooden bell having inside it for clappers several (usually five) pieces of stick threaded on a bit of wood jammed into the dome of the bell and striking the rim, beyond which the clappers just protrude. These bells are very like those you meet with in Angola, but I have not seen on the island, nor does Dr. Baumann cite having seen, the peculiar double bell of Angola—the engongui. The Bubi bell is made out of one piece of wood and worked—or played—with both hands. Dr. Baumann says it is customary on bright moonlight nights for two lines of men to sit facing each other and to clap—one can hardly call it ring—these bells vigorously, but in good time, accompanying this performance with a monotonous song, while the delighted women and children dance round. The learned doctor evidently sees the picturesqueness of this practice, but notes that the words of the songs are not "tiefsinnige" (profound), as he has heard men for hours singing "The shark bites the Bubi's hand," only that over and over again and nothing more. This agrees with my own observations of all Bantu native songs. I have always found that the words of these songs were either the repetition of some such phrase as this, or a set of words referring to the recent adventures or experiences of the singer or the present company's little peculiarities ; with a very frequent chorus, old and conventional. I shall never forget a white man coming alongside a ship whereon I was once a passenger, quite unconscious that his

boatswain was singing as a solo : " Here we bring this wretched
creature : he's a very bad man : he does not give us any food,
or any money : he goes and gets drunk and——' but I forbear
repeating the text of the libel.   But after each statement the
rest of the crew joined in a chorus which was the native
equivalent of—" and so say all of us."

The native tunes used with these songs are far superior, and
I expect many of them are very old.   They are often full of
variety and beauty, particularly those of the M'pongwe and
Galwa, of which I will speak later.

The dances I have no personal knowledge of, but there is
othing in Baumann's description to make one think they are
distinct in themselves from the mainland dances.   I once saw
a dance at Fernando Po, but that was among Portos, and it
was my old friend the Batuco in all its beauty.   But there is
a distinct peculiarity about the places the dances are held on,
every village having a kept piece of ground outside it
which is the dancing place for the village—the ball-room as
it were ; and exceedingly picturesque these dances must be,
for they are mostly held during the nights of full moon.
These kept grounds remind one very much of the similar
looking patches of kept grass one sees in villages in Ka
Congo, but there is no similarity in their use, for the Ka Congo
lawns are of fetish, not frivolous, import.

The Bubis have an instrument I have never seen in an
identical form on the mainland.   It is made like a bow, with
a tense string of fibre.   One end of the bow is placed against
the mouth, and the string is then struck by the right hand
with a small round stick, while with the left it is scraped with
a piece of shell or a knife-blade.   This excruciating instrument, I warn any one who may think of living among the
Bubis, is very popular.   The drums used are both the Dualla
form—all wood—and the ordinary skin-covered drum, and I
think if I catalogue fifes made of wood, I shall have nearly
finished the Bubi orchestra.   I have doubts on this point because I rather question whether I may be allowed to refer to
a very old bullock hide—unmounted—as a musical instrument
without bringing down the wrath of musicians on my head.
These stiff, dry pelts are much thought of, and played by the

artistes by being shaken as accompaniments to other instruments—they make a noise, and that is after all the soul of
most African instrumental music. These instruments are all
that is left of certain bullocks which many years ago the
Spaniards introduced, hoping to improve the food supply.
They seemed as if they would have flourished well on the
island, on the stretches of grass land in the Cordillera and
the East, but the Bubis, being great sportsmen, killed them
all off.

The festivities of the Bubis—dances, weddings, feasts, &c.,
—at which this miscellaneous collection of instruments are
used in concert, usually take place in November, the dry
season ; but the Bubi is liable to pour forth his soul in the
bosom of his family at any time of the day or night, from
June to January, and when he pours it forth on that bow affair
it makes the lonely European long for home.

Divisions of time the Bubi can hardly be said to have, but
this is a point upon which all West Africans are rather weak,
particularly the Bantu.   He has, however, a definite name for
November, December, and January—the dry season months
—calling them Lobos.

The fetish of these people, although agreeing on broad lines
with the Bantu fetish, has many interesting points, as even my
small knowledge of it showed me, and it is a subject that
would repay further investigation ; and as by fetish I always
mean the governing but underlying ideas of a man's life, we
will commence with the child.   Nothing, as far as I have been
able to make out, happens to him, for fetish reasons, when he
first appears on the scene.   He receives at birth, as is usual, a
name which is changed for another on his initiation into the
secret society, this secret society having also, as usual, a
secret language.   About the age of three or five years the boy
is decorated, under the auspices of the witch doctor, with
certain scars on the face.   These scars run from the root of
the nose across the cheeks, and are sometimes carried up in a
curve on to the forehead.   Tattooing, in the true sense of the
word, they do not use, but they paint themselves, as the mainlanders do, with a red paint made by burning some herb and
mixing the ash with clay or oil, and they occasionally—

whether for ju-ju reasons or for mere decoration I do not know—paint a band of yellow clay round the chest; but of the Bubi secret society I know little, nor have I been able to find any one who knows much more. . Hutchinson,[1] in his exceedingly amusing description of a wedding he was once present at among these people, would lead one to think the period of seclusion of the women's society was twelve months.

The chief god or spirit, O. Wassa, resides in the crater of the highest peak, and by his name the peak is known to the native. Another very important spirit, to whom goats and sheep are offered, is Lobe, resident in a crater lake on the northern slope of the Cordilleras, and the grass you sometimes see a Bubi wearing is said to come from this lake and be a ju-ju of Lobe's. Dr Baumann says that the lake at Riabba from which the spirit Uapa rises is more holy, and that he is small, and resides in a chasm in a rock whose declivity can only be passed by means of bush ropes, and in the wet season he is not get-at-able at all. He will, if given suitable offerings, reveal the future to Bubis, but Bubis only. His priest is the King of all the Bubis, upon whom it is never permitted to a white man, or a Porto, to gaze. Baumann also gives the residence of another important spirit as being the grotto at Banni. This is a sea-cave, only accessible at low water in calm weather. I have heard many legends of this cave, but have never had an opportunity of seeing it, or any one who has seen it first hand.

The charms used by these people are similar in form to those of the mainland Bantu, but the methods of treating paths and gateways are somewhat peculiar. The gateways to the towns are sometimes covered by freshly cut banana leaves, and during the religious feast in November, the paths to the villages are barred across with a hedge of grass which no stranger must pass through.

The government is a peculiar one for West Africa. Every village has its chief, but the whole tribe obey one great chief or king who lives in the crater-ravine at Riabba. This individual is called Moka, but whether he is now the same man referred to by Roguszinsky, Mr. Holland, and the Rev. Hugh

---

[1] *Ten Years' Wanderings among the Ethiopians.* T. J. Hutchinson.

Brown, who attempted to interview him in the seventies, I do not feel sure, for the Bubis are just the sort of people to keep a big king going with a variety of individuals. Even the indefatigable Dr. Baumann failed to see Moka, though he evidently found out a great deal about the methods of his administration and formed a very high opinion of his ability, for he says that to this one chief the people owe their present unity and orderliness ; that before his time the whole island was in a state of internecine war : murder was frequent, and property unsafe. Now their social condition, according to the Doctor's account, is a model to Europe, let alone Africa. Civil wars have been abolished, disputes between villages being referred to arbitration, and murder is swiftly and surely punished. If the criminal has bolted into the forest and cannot be found, his village is made responsible, and has to pay a fine in goats, sheep and tobacco to the value of £16. Theft is extremely rare and offences against the moral code also, the Bubis having an extremely high standard in this matter, even the little children having each a separate sleeping hut. In old days adultery was punished by cutting off the offender's hand. I have myself seen women in Fernando Po who have had a hand cut off at the wrist, but I believe those were slave women who had suffered for theft. Slaves the Bubis do have, but their condition is the mild, poor relation or retainer form of slavery you find in Calabar, and differs from the Dualla form, for the slaves live in the same villages as their masters, while among the Duallas, as among most Bantu slave-holding tribes, the slaves are excluded from the master's village and have separate villages of their own. For marriage ceremonies I refer you to Mr. Hutchinson. Burial customs are exceedingly quaint in the southern and eastern districts, where the bodies are buried in the forest with their heads just sticking out of the ground. In other districts the body is also buried in the forest, but is completely covered and an erection of stones put up to mark the place.

Little is known of all West African fetish, still less of that of these strange people. Dr. Oscar Baumann brought to bear on them his careful unemotional German methods of observation, thereby giving us more valuable information about them

and their island than we otherwise should possess. Mr.
Hutchinson resided many years on Fernando Po, in the
capacity of H. B. M.'s Consul, with his hands full of the affairs
of the Oil Rivers and in touch with the Portos of Clarence,
but he nevertheless made very interesting observations on the
natives and their customs. The Polish exile and his courageous
wife who ascended Clarence Peak, Mr. Rogoszinsky, and
another Polish exile, Mr. Janikowski, about complete our series
of authorities on the island. Dr. Baumann thinks they got
their information from Porto sources—sources the learned
Doctor evidently regards as more full of imagination than
solid fact, but, as you know, all African travellers are occasionally in the habit of pooh-poohing each other, and I own
that I myself have been chiefly in touch with Portos, and that
my knowledge of the Bubi language runs to the conventional
greeting form :— " Ipori ? " " Porto." " Ke Soko ? " " Hatsi
soko ":—"Who are you?"—" Porto." "What's the news?"
" No news."

Although these Portos are less interesting to the ethnologist than the philanthropist, they being by-products of his
efforts, I must not leave Fernando Po without mentioning
them, for on them the trade of the island depends. They are
the middlemen between the Bubi and the white trader. The
former regards them with little, if any, more trust than he
regards the white men, and his view of the position of the
Spanish Governor is that he is chief over the Portos. That
he has any headship over Bubis or over the Bubi land—
Itschulla as he calls Fernando Po—he does not imagine
possible. Baumann says he was once told by a Bubi : " White
men are fish, not men. They are able to stay a little while on
land, but at last they mount their ships again and vanish over
the horizon into the ocean. How can a fish possess land ? "
If the coffee and cacao thrive on Fernando Po to the same
extent that they have already thriven on San Thomé there is
but little doubt that the Bubis will become extinct ; for work
on plantations, either for other people, or themselves, they will
not, and then the Portos will become the most important class,
for they will go in for plantations. Their little factories are
studded all round the shores of the coast in suitable coves and

bays, and here in fairly neat houses they live, collecting palm-oil from the Bubis, and making themselves little cacao plantations, and bringing these products into Clarence every now and then to the white trader's factory.   Then, after spending some time and most of their money in the giddy whirl of that capital, they return to their homes and recover.   There is a class of them permanently resident in Clarence, the city men of Fernando Po, and these are very like the Sierra Leonians of Free Town, but preferable.   Their origin is practically the same as that of the Free Towners.   They are the descendants of liberated slaves set free during the time of our occupation of the island as a naval depot for suppressing the slave trade, and of Sierra Leonians and Accras who have arrived and settled since then.   They have some of the same " Black gennellum, Sar " style about them, but not developed to the same ridiculous extent as in the Sierra Leonians, for they have not been under our institutions. The " Fanny Po " ladies are celebrated for their beauty all along the West Coast, and very justly.   They are not how-ever, as they themselves think, the most beautiful women in this part of the world.   Not at least to my way of thinking. I prefer an Elmina, or an Igalwa, or a M'pongwe, or—but I had better stop and own that my affections have got very scattered among the black ladies on the West Coast, and I no sooner remember one lovely creature whose soft eyes, perfect form and winning, pretty ways have captivated me than I think of another.   The Fanny Po ladies have often a certain amount of Spanish blood in them, which gives a decidedly greater delicacy to their features :—delicate little nostrils, mouths not too heavily lipped, a certain gloss on the hair, and a light in the eye.   But it does not improve their colour, and I am assured that it has an awful effect on their tempers, so I think I will remain, for the present, the faithful admirer of my sable Ingrimma, the Igalwa, with the little red blossoms stuck in her night-black hair, and a sweet soft look and word for every one, but particularly for her ugly husband Isaac the " Jack Wash."

CHAPTER IV

LAGOS BAR

Which the general reader may omit as the voyager gives herein no details of Old Calabar or of other things of general interest, but discourses diffusely on the local geography and the story of the man who wasted coal.

I WILL not detain you with any account of the Oil Rivers here. They are too big a subject to compress for one thing; for another I do not feel that I yet know enough to have the right to speak regarding them, unless I were going to do so along accepted, well-trodden lines, and what I have seen and personally know of the region does not make me feel at all inclined to do this. So I will wait until I have had further opportunities of observing them.

The natives I have worked at, but as their fetish is of exceeding interest, I have relegated it to a separate chapter, owing to its unfitness to be allowed to stray about in the rest of the text, in order to make things generally tidier. The state of confusion the mind of a collector like myself gets into on the West Coast is something simply awful, and my notes for a day will contain facts relating to the kraw-kraw, price of onions, size and number of fish caught, cooking recipes, genealogies, oaths (native form of), law cases, and market prices, &c., &c. And the undertaking of tidying these things up is no small one. As for one's personal memory it becomes a rag-bag into which you dip frantically when some one asks you a question, and you almost always fail to secure your particular fact rag for some minutes.

After returning from the short visit to Fernando Po made in their company, owing to the great kind-

ness of Sir Claude and Lady MacDonald I remained
in Calabar River from January until May, collecting
fish mainly through the kindness of Dr Whitindale,
and insects through the kindness of Mr. Cooper, then in
charge of the botanical station. Most of my time was spent
puddling about the river and the forest round Duke Town
and Creek Town, but I made a point on this visit to Calabar
of going up river to see Miss Slessor at Okÿon, and she
allowed me to stay with her, giving me invaluable help in the
matter of fetish and some of the pleasantest days in my life.
This very wonderful lady has been eighteen years in Calabar ;
for the last six or seven living entirely alone, as far as white
folks go, in a clearing in the forest near to one of the principal
villages of the Okÿon district, and ruling as a veritable white
chief over the entire Okÿon district. Her great abilities,
both physical and intellectual, have given her among the
savage tribe an unique position, and won her, from white and
black who know her, a profound esteem. Her knowledge of
the native, his language, his ways of thought, his diseases,
his difficulties, and all that is his, is extraordinary, and the
amount of good she has done, no man can fully estimate.
Okÿon, when she went there alone—living in the native
houses while she built, with the assistance of the natives, her
present house—was a district regarded with fear by the
Duke and Creek Town natives, and practically unknown to
Europeans. It was given, as most of the surrounding districts still are, to killing at funerals, ordeal by poison, and
perpetual internecine wars. Many of these evil customs she
has stamped out, and Okÿon rarely gives trouble to its
nominal rulers, the Consuls in Old Calabar, and trade passes
freely through it down to the sea-ports.

This instance of what one white can do would give
many important lessons in West Coast administration and
development. Only the sort of man Miss Slessor represents
is rare. There are but few who have the same power of resisting the malarial climate, and of acquiring the language, and
an insight into the negro mind, so perhaps after all it is no
great wonder that Miss Slessor stands alone, as she certainly
does.

After returning down river, I just waited until the *Batanga*, my old friend, came into the river again, and then started for my beloved South West Coast.   The various divisions of the West Coast of Africa are very perplexing to a new comer. Starting from Sierra Leone coming south you first pass the Grain Coast, which is also called the Pepper or Kru Coast, or the Liberian Coast.   Next comes the Ivory Coast, also known as the Half Jack Coast, or the Bristol Coast.   Then comes the Gold Coast ; then the old Slave Coast, now called the Popos ; then Lagos, and then the Rivers, and below the Rivers the South West Coast.   In addition to these names you will hear the Timber Ports, and the Win'ard and Leeward Ports referred to, and it perplexes one when one finds a port, say Axim, referred to by one competent authority, *i.e.* a sea-captain, as a Win'ard port, by the next as a Timber, by the next as a Gold Coast port.   It is just as well to get the matter up if you intend frequenting the Bights of Biafra and Benin. I will just give you, as a hint to facilitate your researches, the information that the Bight of Benin commences at Cape St. Paul and ends at Cape Formosa ; and the Bight of Biafra commences at Cape Formosa and ends at Cape Lopez. The Windward Coast is that portion between Cape Apollonia and the Secum River, just west of Accra.   At this river the Leeward Coast begins, and terminates at the Volta.

When I was on the coast in 1893, Cameroons River was regarded in nautical circles as a River.   Now, alas for me ! it is not, and getting from Calabar to Cameroons is a thing you ought to get a medal for, for the line of vessels that run from Liverpool to Calabar goes no further than the latter place.   In former days they used to call in at Calabar, then go across to Fernando Po and into Cameroons, calling steadily at ports right down to Sant. Paul de Loanda, which was a highly convenient and beautiful arrangement, but I presume did not pay ; so the South West Coast boats, that is to say boats calling below Calabar, now call at Lagos, and thus ignore the Rivers, going straight on into Cameroons River. So you see, if you have providentially kept your head clear during this disquisition, I had to go on a homeward bound boat up as far as Lagos Bar and then catch a South Wester

outward bound, and I assure you changing at Lagos Bar
throws changing at Clapham Junction into the shade. Now
in order to make this latter point clear to that unfortunate
victim the general reader, he, or she, must be dragged through
a disquisition on Lagos and its bar.

Lagos is a marvellous manifestation of the perversity of
man coupled with the perversity of nature, being at one and
the same time one of the most important exporting
ports on the West African seaboard, and one of the
most difficult to get at. The town of Lagos is situated
on an island in the Lagos River, a river which is much
given to going into lagoons and mud, and which has its
bar about two miles out. The entire breadth of the channel
through this bar is half a mile, at least on paper. On each side
of this channel are the worst set of breakers in West Africa, and
its resident population consists of sharks, whose annual toll of
human life is said by some authorities to be fourteen, by others
forty, but like everything else connected with Lagos Bar, it is
uncertain, but bad. This entrance channel, however, at the
best of times has not more than thirteen feet of water on
it, and so although the British African and Royal African
lines of steamers are noble pedestrians, thinking nothing of
walking a mile or so when occasion requires, and as capable
of going over a grass-plot with the dew on it as any ocean
vessels ever built, I am bound to own they do require a
certain amount of water to get on with. They can sit high
and dry on a sand or mud-bank—they prefer mud I may remark—with any vessel. I have often been on them when
engaged in this pastime, but it does undoubtedly cause delay,
and this being the case they do not go alongside at Lagos,
but lie outside the bar. Now such is the pestilential nature of
Lagos Bar that even the carefully built branch boats, the
noble *Dodo* and *Qwarra*, to say nothing of the *Forcados* and
others, although drawing only ten feet, are liable to stick. For
the channel, instead of sticking to its governmentally reported
thirteen feet, is prone to be nine feet, and exceeding prone also
to change its position ; and moreover, even supposing the branch
boat to get across all right, the heavy swell outside with its
great rollers lounging along, intent on breaking on the bar,

looking like coiling snakes under a blanket, make the vessels
lying broadside on to them play pendulum to an extent that
precludes the discharging or taking on of heavy cargo ; and
heavy cargo has to come on and off for Lagos to the value of
£1,566,243 a year. So as the West African trading vessels
are enterprising and determined, particularly where palm
oil is concerned, they arrange the matter by going and
lying up Forcados River. This river, which is 120 miles
below Lagos, is a mouth of the Niger, and has a bar you
can cross (if you don't mind a little walking), drawing seventeen feet nine inches. This being the case they run just
inside Forcados River and then wait for the branch boat
from Lagos to come and bring them their heavy cargo.
When they have got this on board, they proceed up coast
and call off Lagos Bar, and another unfortunate branch boat
brings off mails and passengers to them.

Well, the *Batanga* after leaving Calabar and calling at Bonny
had duly waited for the branch boat in Forcados and ultimately
got her and her cargo, with its attendant uproar ; and an account
of the latest iniquities of Lagos Bar which had one of its bad
fits on just then and was capturing and wrecking branch boats
galore ; and we had the usual scene with Mrs. S. Mrs. S., I may
remark, is a comely and large black lady, an old acquaintance
of mine, hailing from Opobo and frequently going up and
down to Lagos, in connection with trading affairs of her own,
and another lady with whom Mrs. S. is in a sort of partnership.
This trade usually consists of extensive operations in chickens.
She goes up to Lagos and buys chickens, brings them on
board in crates, and takes them to Opobo and there sells them.
It is not for me as a fellow woman to say what Mrs. S. makes
on the transaction, nor does it interest the general public, but
what does interest the general public (at least that portion of
it that goes down to the sea in ships and for its sins wanders
into Forcados River) is Mrs. S.'s return trip to Lagos with
those empty crates and the determination in her heart not to
pay freight for them. Wise and experienced chief officers
never see Mrs. S.'s crates, but young and truculent ones do,
and determine, in their hearts, she shall pay for them, advertising this resolve of theirs openly all the way from Opobo,

which is foolish. When it comes to sending heavy goods overside into the branch boat at Forcados, the wise chief officer lets those crates go, but the truculent one says,

" Here, Mrs. S., *now* you have got to pay for these crates."

" Lor' mussy me, sar," says Mrs. S., " what you talk about ? "

" These here chicken crates of yours, Mrs. S."

" Lor' mussy me," says Mrs. S., " those crates no 'long to me, sar."

" Then," says the truculent one, " heave 'em over side ! We don't want that stuff lumbering up our deck."

Mrs. S. then expostulates and explains they are the property of a lone lorn lady in Lagos to whom Mrs. S. is taking them from the highest motives ; motives " such a nice gentleman " as the first officer must understand, and which it will be a pleasure to him to share in, and she cites instances of other chief officers who according to her have felt, as it were, a ray of sunlight come into their lives when they saw those chicken crates and felt it was in their power to share in the noble work of return- ing them to Lagos freight free. The truculent one then loses his head and some of his temper and avows himself a heart- less villain, totally indifferent to the sex, and says all sorts of things, but my faith in the ultimate victory of Mrs. S. never wavers. My money is on her all the time, and she has never disappointed me, and when I am quite rich some day, I will give Mrs. S. purses of gold in the eastern manner for the many delicious scenes she has played before me with those crates in dreary Forcados.

These affairs being duly disposed of, the *Batanga* left Forcados and duly proceeded up coast to call off Lagos for mails and passengers ; my fate being to go on to the branch boat which brought these out, and which I then expected would take me in to Lagos, to await the arrival of the south-west outward bound boat.

I had been treated, as passengers landing at Lagos are properly and customarily treated, to a course of instruction on the dangers of going on and off branch boats on the bar, with special mention of the case of a gentleman who came down the Coast for pleasure and lost a leg to a shark while so en- gaged, and of the amount of fever of a bad type just then

raging in Lagos ; and then when we saw the branch boat that
was coming out to us get stuck on the bar in the middle of
what a German would call a Wirrwarr of breakers, I own it
took all the fascination of my memories of the South West
Coast to prevent my giving up the journey, and going home to
England comfortably on the *Batanga*, as my best friends
strongly advised my doing.

However presently the branch boat stamped her way over
the bar, and came panting up, and anchored near us, and from
her on to the *Batanga* came a Lagos Government official in a
saturated state.   He said he had just come out to see how a
branch boat could get across the bar at low water—a noble
and enterprising thing which places him in line with the Elder
Pliny.   He entertained us with a calm, utterly dispassionate
account of how the water had washed right over them, gone
down the funnel and all that sort of thing—evidently a horribly
commonplace experience here ; and he said the *Eko* (that was
our branch boat's name) was not going back into Lagos until
she had put the down coast mail and over a hundred deck-
passengers who were going to the Congo, on to the South West
Coast boat, which was hourly expected in the roads, as she had
been telegraphed from Accra.   He casually observed he hoped
she would not be late in the afternoon as he had to go up
country in the morning on the Government steamer.   Well,
things seeming safe and pleasant, I went off to the branch boat,
being most carefully lowered over the side in a chair by the
winch.

" Take care of yourself," said the *Batanga*.

" I will," said I, which shows the futility and vanity of such
resolves, for had not other people taken care of me, goodness
only knows what would have become of me.   Arrived alongside of the *Eko*, I proceeded up her rope-ladder on deck, and
that deck I shall not soon forget.   The Government official
had understated the case ; things were in a spring-cleaning
confusion :   the waves had not made a clean sweep of
her but an uncommonly dirty one, and it would have been
better if she had stuck among the breakers another half hour
and given the sea-nymphs time to tidy up.   They had made
especial hay of the gallant captain's cabin, flinging out on to

the deck his socks and hats and boots just anyhow, and over all and everything was a coating of wet coal-dust. On the little lower deck were the unfortunate native passengers. They were silent, which with native passengers means sick, and every rag they possessed was wringing wet. Rats ran freely about everywhere, and from out of the black patch of silence on the main deck rose no sound save Mrs. S.'s *Chei! Chei! Chei!* of disgust and disapproval of her surroundings. The kindly German captain (for the *Eko* belonged to a great German trading firm in Lagos, and not to the steamboat companies) did all he could to make me comfortable, and the Government official pointed out to me objects of interest on the distant shore : the lighthouse, the Government House, the Wilberforce Hall, and so on, but particularly the little Government steamer which, he observed, was getting up steam to be ready to take him up river early in the morning. He seemed to think they were beginning rather too early, as the Government are vigilant about the sin of wasting coal. As the afternoon wore away, our interest in the coming of the *Benguella* grew until it surpassed all other interests, and the *Benguella* became the one thing we really cared about in life, and yet she came not. The little *Eko* rolled to and fro, to and fro, all the loose gear going slipperty, slop, crash ; slipperty, slop, crash : coal-dust, smuts, and a broiling sun poured down on us quietly, and the only thing or motion that gave us any variety was every three or four minutes the *Eko* making a vicious jerk at her anchor. About six o'clock a steamer was seen coming up into the roads. The experienced captain said she was not the *Benguella*, and she was not, but the *Janette Woermann*, and as soon as she got settled, her captain came on board the *Eko*, of course to ask what prospect there was of cargo on shore. He appeared as a gigantic, lithe, powerful Dane clad in a uniform of great splendour and exceeding tightness, terminating in a pair of Blucher boots and every inch of his six feet four spick and span, but that was only the visible form—his external seeming. What that man really was, was our two guardian cherubs rolled into one, for no sooner did he lay eye on us—the depressed and distracted official and the dilapidated lady—than he claimed us as his own, and in a few more

minutes we were playing bob cherry again with Lagos Bar
sharks, going down into his boat by the *Eko's* rope-ladder.

Were I but Khalif of Bagdad, I would have that captain's
name—which is Heldt—written in letters of gold on ivory
tablets with a full and particular account of all he did for us.
No sooner did he successfully get us on board his comfortable vessel, than he gave me his own cabin on the upper deck
and stowed himself in some sort of outhouse alongside it, which I
observed, when going out on deck during the night to see if that
Benguella had come in to the roads, was far too short for him.
He gave us dinner with great promptitude—an excellent
dinner commencing with what I thought was a plateful of hot
jam, but which anyhow was nice.   Indeed so reconciled did I
become to my environment that my interest in the coming of
the *Benguella* hourly waned, and had it not been for my having
caught a sense of worry about "the way coals were being
wasted" on the Government boat inside the bar, I should have
forgotten the South-Wester.   Not so my companion. You
cannot distract a man from the higher duties and responsi-
bilities of life so easily.   His mind was a prey to the most
dismal thoughts and conjectures.   He regretted having come
out on the *Eko*, although his motive to see how she would get
across the bar at low water was a noble one and arose from
the nature of his particular appointment, and not only did he
regret that, but remembered, with remorse, all the other things
he had done which he should not have done.   Captain Heldt
did his best to cheer him and distract him from the
contemplation of these things and the way coal was being
wasted on his account inside the bar.   The captain offered
him suits of his own clothes to change his sopped ones for ;
but no, he said he was lost enough already without getting
into clothes of that size.   Lager beer, cigars, and stories were
then tried on him, but with little effect. He took a certain
amount of interest in the captain's account of how he had
had his back severely injured and had had to navigate his
vessel among the shoals of Saint Ann while lying in great
agony for weeks owing to an accident in the Grain Coast surf,
and also in the various accounts of the many ribs the captain
had had broken in various ways on the high seas, but any

legend of a more cheerful character than these he evidently felt was unfitted to our situation, and flippant, considering the way those coals were being wasted. Still the *Benguella* came not, though we sat up very late looking for her, and at last we turned in.

The next morning we were up early. There was no *Benguella*. The *Eko* was still rolling about near us waiting for her, and the *Eko's* passengers having had, as I heard, in vivid account some months after from Mrs. S. with many *chei!* *cheis!* a wretched, ratful, foodless night, the *Eko* naturally not laying herself out for water pic-nic parties. We fared well on the *Janette*, our guardian angel providing us with an excellent breakfast. My fellow countryman's anxiety had now passed into a dark despair. He no longer looked for the South-Wester. It was past that ; but he borrowed Captain Heldt's best telescope and watched the Government steamer, which lay smoking away like a Turkish man-of-war, waiting for him. Captain Heldt tried to cheer him with more stories, lager beer, and cigars, and at last produced an auto-harp, an instrument upon which he was himself proficient and capable of playing not only the march from " Ajax," but " Der Wacht am Rhein" and " Annie Laurie." This temporarily took my fellow countryman's mind off coals, and he set about to acquire the management of the auto-harp and rapidly did so, but then he only picked out with infinite feeling and pathos " Home, Sweet Home," so it was taken from him. Then we had long accounts of the region round the Swakop river, from which the *Janette* had just come, and at last, about two o'clock, my fellow countryman sadly said : " Here she comes ! " and there she did come, and in a short time the graceful old *Benguella* was duly anchored in the roads and I was taken on board by my two friends.

We none of us felt very enthusiastic, I fear. I had never been on her before, so regarded her as an utter stranger. My fellow countryman felt it was a hanging matter by now for him on shore, because of those coals, and so did not feel in such a hurry to get there. And to Captain Heldt she was a rival. But often those things which you expect least of ultimately give you the most pleasure, as the moralist would say, and moreover when you are on the Coast you never know whom you may meet ; and as I, after a good deal of trouble in the *Janette's* boat to get my companions to go on deck before me up the rope ladder, elaborately climbed that thrilling nautical institution myself and had got my head over the top of the bulwark, I saw a yard off me, dead ahead, still superintending the hatch—my first tutor in Kru English. It was in '93 that he had last seen me, a very new comer, going ashore at San Paul de Loanda from the *Lagos*, on which vessel he was then officer, and vowing I meant to go home by the next boat ; now seeing me coming on board, in a way I am sure would have done credit to a Half Jack captain, he naturally asked for an explanation, which, being quite busy with the rope-ladder palaver, I did not then and there give him.

In a short time I had said farewell, with many thanks to my two friends who had taken such care of me on Lagos Bar, and my fellow countryman returned in the *Eko*, which, having got her mails and passengers safe and sound on to the *Benguella*, was at last going in to Lagos again, and I am sure it will be a relief to you to know that none of those expected troubles on shore befell the official, but he lived to earn the gratitude and esteem of Lagos and its Government for his noble and determined services in working and surveying that awful bar. When, a few months after our amusing experiences on it, it went on worse than ever, and vessel after vessel was wrecked, he rescued their passengers and crews at the great risk of his own life ; for going alongside a vessel that is breaking up in the breakers, and in an open boat with a native crew, and getting off panic-stricken Africans and their belongings, surrounded by such a sea, with its crowd of expectant sharks, in the West African climate, is good work for a good man, and my fellow-countryman did it and did it well.

CHAPTER V

VOYAGE DOWN COAST

Wherein the voyager before leaving the Rivers discourses on dangers, to which is added some account of Mangrove swamps and the creatures that abide therein, including the devil of an uncle.

MY voyage down coast in the *Benguella* was a very pleasant one and full of instruction, for Mr. Fothergill, who was her purser, had in former years resided in Congo Français as a merchant, and to Congo Français I was bound with an empty hold as regards local knowledge of the district. He was one of that class of men, of which you most frequently find representatives among the merchants, who do not possess the power so many men along here do possess (a power that always amazes me), of living for a considerable time in a district without taking any interest in it, keeping their whole attention concentrated on the point of how long it will be before their time comes to get out of it. Mr. Fothergill evidently had much knowledge and experience of the Fernan Vaz district and its natives. He had, I should say, overdone his experiences with the natives, as far as personal comfort and pleasure at the time went, having been nearly killed and considerably chivied by them. Now I do not wish a man, however much I may deplore his total lack of local knowledge, to go so far as this. Mr. Fothergill gave his accounts of these incidents calmly, and in an undecorated way that gave them a power and convincingness verging on being unpleasant, although useful, to a person who was going into the district where they had occurred, for one felt there was no mortal reason why one should not person-

ally get involved in similar affairs. And I must here acknowledge the great subsequent service Mr. Fothergill's wonderfully
accurate descriptions of the peculiar characteristics of the
Ogowé forests were to me when I subsequently came to deal
with these forests on my own account, as every district of forest
has peculiar characteristics of its own which you require to
know. I should like here to speak of West Coast
dangers because I fear you may think that I am careless of,
or do not believe in them, neither of which is the case.
The more you know of the West Coast of Africa, the more
you realise its dangers. For example, on your first voyage
out you hardly believe the stories of fever told by the old
Coasters. That is because you do not then understand the type
of man who is telling them, a man who goes to his death with
a joke in his teeth. But a short experience of your own,
particularly if you happen on a place having one of its
periodic epidemics, soon demonstrates that the underlying
horror of the thing is there, a rotting corpse which the old
Coaster has dusted over with jokes to cover it so that it hardly
shows at a distance, but which, when you come yourself to
live alongside, you soon become cognisant of. Many men,
when they have got ashore and settled, realise this, and let the
horror get a grip on them ; a state briefly and locally described as funk, and a state that usually ends fatally ; and you
can hardly blame them. Why, I know of a case myself. A
young man who had never been outside an English country
town before in his life, from family reverses had to take
a situation as book-keeper down in the Bights. The factory
he was going to was in an isolated out-of-the-way place and
not in a settlement, and when the ship called off it, he was
put ashore in one of the ship's boats with his belongings, and
a case or so of goods. There were only the firm's beach-boys
down at the surf, and as the steamer was in a hurry the officer
from the ship did not go up to the factory with him, but said
good-bye and left him alone with a set of naked savages as
he thought, but really of good kindly Kru boys on the beach.
He could not understand what they said, nor they what he
said, and so he walked up to the house and on to the
verandah and tried to find the Agent he had come out to

serve under. He looked into the open-ended dining-room and shyly round the verandah, and then sat down and waited for some one to turn up. Sundry natives turned up, and said a good deal, but no one white or comprehensible, so in desperation he made another and a bolder tour completely round the verandah and noticed a most peculiar noise in one of the rooms and an infinity of flies going into the venetian shuttered window. Plucking up courage he went in and found what was left of the white Agent, a considerable quantity of rats, and most of the flies in West Africa. He then presumably had fever, and he was taken off, a fortnight afterwards, by a French boat, to whom the natives signalled, and he is not coming down the Coast again. Some men would have died right out from a shock like this.

But most of the new-comers do not get a shock of this order. They either die themselves or get more gradually accustomed to this sort of thing, when they come to regard death and fever as soldiers, who on a battle-field sit down, and laugh and talk round a camp fire after a day's hard battle, in which they have seen their friends and companions falling round them ; all the time knowing that to-morrow the battle comes again and that to-morrow night they themselves may never see. It is not hard-hearted callousness, it is only their way. Michael Scott put this well in *Tom Cringle's Log*, in his account of the yellow fever during the war in the West Indies. Fever, though the chief danger, particularly to people who go out to settlements, is not the only one ; but as the other dangers, except perhaps domestic poisoning, are incidental to pottering about in the forests, or on the rivers, among the unsophisticated tribes, I will not dwell on them. They can all be avoided by any one with common sense, by keeping well out of the districts in which they occur ; and so I warn the general reader that if he goes out to West Africa, it is not because I said the place was safe, or its dangers overrated. The cemeteries of the West Coast are full of the victims of those people who have said that Coast fever is "Cork fever," and a man's own fault, which it is not ; and that natives will never attack you unless you attack them : which they will—on occasions.

My main aim in going to Congo Français was to get up above the tide line of the Ogowé River and there collect fishes ; for my object on this voyage was to collect fish from a river north of the Congo. I had hoped this river would have been the Niger, for Sir George Goldie had placed at my disposal great facilities for carrying on work there in comfort ; but for certain private reasons I was disinclined to go from the Royal Niger Protectorate into the Royal Niger Company's territory ; and the Calabar, where Sir Claude MacDonald did everything he possibly could to assist me, I did not find a good river for me to collect fishes in. These two rivers failing me, from no fault of either of their own presiding genii, my only hope of doing anything now lay on the South West Coast river, the Ogowé, and everything there depended on Mr. Hudson's attitude towards scientific research in the domain of ichthyology. Fortunately for me that gentleman elected to take a favourable view of this affair, and in every way in his power assisted me during my entire stay in Congo Français. But before I enter into a detailed description of this wonderful bit of West Africa, I must give you a brief notice of the manners, habits and customs of West Coast rivers in general, to make the thing more intellegible.

There is an uniformity in the habits of West Coast rivers, from the Volta to the Coanza, which is, when you get used to it, very taking. Excepting the Congo, the really great river comes out to sea with as much mystery as possible ; lounging lazily along among its mangrove swamps in a what's-it-matter when-one-comes-out and where's-the-hurry style, through quantities of channels inter-communicating with each other. Each channel, at first sight as like the other as peas in a pod, is bordered on either side by green-black walls of mangroves, which Captain Lugard graphically described as seeming " as if they had lost all count of the vegetable proprieties, and were standing on stilts with their branches tucked up out of the wet, leaving their gaunt roots exposed in mid-air." High-tide or low-tide, there is little difference in the water ; the river, be it broad or narrow, deep or shallow, looks like a pathway of polished metal ; for it is as heavy weighted with stinking mud as water e'er can be, ebb or flow, year out and year in.   But the difference in the banks, though an unending alternation between two appearances, is weird.

At high-water you do not see the mangroves displaying their ankles in the way that shocked Captain Lugard.   They look most respectable, their foliage rising densely in a wall irregularly striped here and there by the white line of an aërial root, coming straight down into the water from some upper branch as straight as a plummet, in the strange, knowing way an aërial root of a mangrove does, keeping the hard straight line until it gets some two feet above water-level, and then spreading out into blunt fingers with which to dip into the water and grasp the mud.   Banks indeed at high water can hardly be said to exist, the water stretching away into the mangrove swamps for miles and miles, and you can then go, in a suitable small canoe, away among these swamps as far as you please.

This is a fascinating pursuit.   For people who like that sort of thing it is just the sort of thing they like, as the art critic of a provincial town wisely observed anent an impressionist picture recently acquired for the municipal gallery.   But it is a pleasure to be indulged in with caution ; for one thing, you are certain to come across crocodiles.   Now a crocodile drifting down in deep water, or lying asleep with its jaws open on a sand-bank in the sun, is a picturesque adornment to the landscape when you are on the deck of a steamer, and you can write home about it and frighten your relations on your behalf ; but when you are away among the swamps in a small dug-out canoe, and that crocodile and his relations are awake—a thing he makes a point of being at flood tide because of fish coming along—and when he has got his foot upon his native heath— that is to say, his tail within holding reach of his native mud— he is highly interesting, and you may not be able to write home about him—and you get frightened on your own behalf.   For crocodiles can, and often do, in such places, grab at people in small canoes.   I have known of several natives losing their lives in this way ; some native villages are approachable from the main river by a short cut, as it were, through the mangrove swamps, and the inhabitants of such villages will now and then go across this way with small canoes instead of by the constant channel to the village, which is almost always winding. In addition to this unpleasantness you are liable—until you realise the danger from experience, or have native advice on the point—to get tide-trapped away in the swamps, the water falling round you when you are away in some deep pool or lagoon, and you find you cannot get back to the main river. For you cannot get out and drag your canoe across the stretches of mud that separate you from it, because the mud is of too unstable a nature and too deep, and sinking into it means staying in it, at any rate until some geologist of the remote future may come across you, in a fossilised state, when that mangrove swamp shall have become dry land. Of course if you really want a truly safe investment in Fame, and really care about Posterity, and Posterity's Science, you will jump over into the black batter-like, stinking slime, cheered by the thought of the terrific sensation you will produce 20,000 years hence, and the care you will be taken of then by your fellow-creatures, in a museum. But if you are a mere ordinary person of a retiring nature, like me, you stop in your lagoon until the tide rises again ; most of your attention is directed to dealing with an "at home" to crocodiles and mangrove flies, and with the fearful stench of the slime round you. What little time you have over you will employ in wondering why you came to West Africa, and why, after having reached this point of absurdity, you need have gone and painted the lily and adorned the rose, by being such a colossal ass as to come fooling about in mangrove swamps. Twice this chatty little incident, as Lady MacDonald would call it, has happened to me, but never again if I can help it. On one occasion, the last, a mighty Silurian, as *The Daily Telegraph* would call him, chose to get his front paws over the stern of my canoe, and endeavoured to improve our acquaintance. I had to retire to the bows, to keep the balance right,[1] and fetch him a clip on the snout with a paddle, when he withdrew, and I paddled into the very middle of the lagoon, hoping the water there was too deep for him or any of his friends to repeat the performance. Presumably it was, for no

[1] It is no use saying because I was frightened, for this miserably understates the case.

one did it again. I should think that crocodile was eight feet long ; but don't go and say I measured him, or that this is my outside measurement for crocodiles. I have measured them when they have been killed by other people, fifteen, eighteen, and twenty-one feet odd. This was only a pushing young creature who had not learnt manners.

Still, even if your own peculiar tastes and avocations do not take you in small dug-out canoes into the heart of the swamps, you can observe the difference in the local scenery made by the flowing of the tide when you are on a vessel stuck on a sand-bank, in the Rio del Rey for example. Moreover, as you will have little else to attend to, save mosquitoes and mangrove flies, when in such a situation, you may as well pursue the study. At the ebb gradually the foliage of the lower branches of the mangroves grows wet and muddy, until there is a great black band about three feet deep above the surface of the water in all directions ; gradually a network of gray-white roots rises up, and below this again, gradually, a slope of smooth and lead-brown slime. The effect is not in the least as if the water had fallen, but as if the mangroves had, with one accord, risen up out of it, and into it again they seem silently to sink when the flood comes. But by this more safe, if still unpleasant, method of observing mangrove-swamps, you miss seeing in full the make of them, for away in their fastnesses the mangroves raise their branches far above the reach of tide line, and the great gray roots of the older trees are always sticking up in mid-air. But, fringing the rivers, there is always a hedge of younger mangroves whose lower branches get immersed.

At corners here and there from the river face you can see the land being made from the waters. A mud-bank forms off it, a mangrove seed lights on it, and the thing's done. Well! not done, perhaps, but begun ; for if the bank is high enough to get exposed at low water, this pioneer man-grove grows. He has a wretched existence though. You have only got to look at his dwarfed attenuated form to see this. He gets joined by a few more bold spirits and they struggle on together, their network of roots stopping abundance of mud, and by good chance now and then a consignment of miscellaneous *débris* of palm leaves, or a floating tree-trunk, but they always die before they attain any considerable height. Still even in death they collect. Their bare white sticks remaining like a net gripped in the mud, so that these pioneer mangrove heroes may be said to have laid down their lives to make that mud-bank fit for colonisation, for the time gradually comes when other mangroves can and do colonise on it, and flourish, extending their territory steadily ; and the mud-bank joins up with, and becomes a part of, Africa.

Right away on the inland fringe of the swamp—you may go some hundreds of miles before you get there—you can see the rest of the process. The mangroves there have risen up, and dried the mud to an extent that is more than good for themselves, have over civilised that mud in fact, and so the brackish waters of the tide—which, although their enemy when too deep or too strong in salt, is essential to their existence—cannot get to their roots. They have done this gradually, as a mangrove does all things, but they have done it, and down on to that mud come a whole set of palms from the old mainland, who in their early colonisation days go through similarly trying experiences. First the screw-pines come and live among them ; then the wine-palm and various creepers, and then the oil-palm ; and the *débris* of these plants being greater and making better soil than dead mangroves, they work quicker and the mangrove is doomed. Soon the salt waters are shut right out, the mangrove dies, and that bit of Africa is made. It is very interesting to get into these regions ; you see along the river-bank a rich, thick, lovely wall of soft-wooded plants, and behind this you find great stretches of death ;—miles and miles sometimes of gaunt white mangrove skeletons standing on gray stuff that is not yet earth and is no longer slime, and through the crust of which you can sink into rotting putrefaction. Yet, long after you are dead, buried, and forgotten, this will become a forest of soft-wooded plants and palms ; and finally of hard-wooded trees. Districts of this description you will find in great sweeps of Kama country for example, and in the rich low regions up to the base of the Sierra del Cristal and the Rumby range.

You often hear the utter lifelessness of mangrove-swamps

commented on; why I do not know, for they are fairly heavily stocked with fauna, though the species are comparatively few. There are the crocodiles, more of them than any one wants; there are quantities of flies, particularly the big silent mangrove-fly which lays an egg in you under the skin; the egg becomes a maggot and stays there until it feels fit to enter into external life. Then there are "slimy things that crawl with legs upon a slimy sea," and any quantity of hopping mud-fish, and crabs, and a certain mollusc, and in the water various kinds of cat-fish. Birdless they are save for the flocks of gray parrots that pass over them at evening, hoarsely squarking; and save for this squarking of the parrots the swamps are silent all the day, at least during the dry season; in the wet season there is no silence night or day in West Africa, but that roar of the descending deluge of rain that is more monotonous and more gloomy than any silence can be. In the morning you do not hear the long, low, mellow whistle of the plantain-eaters calling up the dawn, nor in the evening the clock-bird nor the Handel-Festival-sized choruses of frogs, or the crickets, that carry on their vesper controversy of "she did"—"she didn't" so fiercely on hard land.

But the mangrove-swamp follows the general rule for West Africa, and night in it is noisier than the day. After dark it is full of noises; grunts from I know not what, splashes from jumping fish, the peculiar whirr of rushing crabs, and quaint creaking and groaning sounds from the trees; and —above all in eeriness—the strange whine and sighing cough of crocodiles. I shall never forget one moonlight night I spent in a mangrove-swamp. I was not lost, but we had gone away into the swamp from the main river, so that the natives of a village with an evil reputation should not come across us when they were out fishing. We got well in, on to a long pool or lagoon; and dozed off and woke, and saw the same scene around us twenty times in the night, which thereby grew into an æon, until I dreamily felt that I had somehow got into a world that was all like this, and always had been, and was always going to be so. Now and again the strong musky smell came that meant a crocodile close by, and one had to rouse up and see if all the crews' legs were on board, for Africans are reckless, and regardless of their legs during sleep. On one examination I found the leg of one of my most precious men ostentatiously sticking out over the side of the canoe. I woke him with a paddle, and said a few words regarding the inadvisability of wearing his leg like this in our situation ; and he agreed with me, saying he had lost a valued uncle, who had been taken out of a canoe in this same swamp by a crocodile. His uncle's ghost had become, he said, a sort of devil which had been a trial to the family ever since ; and he thought it must have pulled his leg out in the way I com- plained of, in order to get him to join him by means of another crocodile. I thanked him for the information and said it quite explained the affair, and I should do my best to pre- vent another member of the family from entering the state of devildom by aiming blows in the direction of any leg or arm I saw that uncle devil pulling out to place within reach of the crocodiles.

Great regions of mangrove-swamps are a characteristic feature of the West African Coast. The first of these lies north of Sierra Leone ; then they occur, but of smaller dimensions—just fringes of river-outfalls—until you get to Lagos, when you strike the greatest of them all :—the swamps of the Niger outfalls (about twenty-three rivers in all) and of the Sombreiro, New Calabar, Bonny, San Antonio, Opobo (false and true), Kwoibo, Old Calabar (with the Cross Akwayafe Qwa Rivers) and Rio del Rey Rivers. The whole of this great stretch of coast is a mangrove-swamp, each river silently rolling down its great mass of mud-laden waters and constituting each in itself a very pretty problem to the navigator by its network of intercommunicating creeks, and the sand and mud bar which it forms off its entrance by dropping its heaviest mud ; its lighter mud is carried out beyond its bar and makes the nasty-smelling brown soup of the South Atlantic Ocean, with froth floating in lines and patches on it, for miles to seaward.

In this great region of swamps every mile appears like every other mile until you get well used to it, and are able to distinguish the little local peculiarities at the entrance of the rivers and in the winding of the creeks, a thing difficult even for the most experienced navigator to do during those thick wool-like mists called smokes, which hang about the whole Bight from November till May (the dry season), sometimes lasting all day, sometimes clearing off three hours after sunrise.

The upper or north-westerly part of the swamp is round the mouths of the Niger, and it successfully concealed this fact from geographers down to 1830, when the series of heroic journeys made by Mungo Park, Clapperton, and the two Landers finally solved the problem—a problem that was as great and which cost more men's lives than even the discovery of the sources of the Nile.

That this should have been so may seem very strange to us who now have been told the answer to the riddle ; for the upper waters of this great river were known of before Christ and spoken of by Herodotus, Pliny and Ptolemy, and its mouths navigated continuously along by the seaboard by trading vessels since the fifteenth century, but they were not recognised as belonging to the Niger. Some geographers held that the Senegal or the Gambia was its outfall ; others that it was the Zaire (Congo) ; others that it did not come out on the West Coast at all, but got mixed up with the Nile in the middle of the continent, and so on. Yet when you come to know the swamps this is not so strange. You find on going up what looks like a big river—say Forcados, two and a half miles wide at the entrance and a real bit of the Niger. Before you are up it far great, broad, business-like-looking river entrances open on either side, showing wide rivers, mangrove-walled, but two-thirds of them are utter frauds which will ground you within half an hour of your entering them. Some few of them do communicate with other main channels to the great upper river, and others are main channels themselves ; but most of them intercommunicate with each other and lead nowhere in particular, and you can't even get there because of their shallowness. It is small wonder that the earlier navigators did not get far up them in sailing ships, and that the problem had to be solved by men descending the main stream of the Niger before it commences

to what we in Devonshire should call "squander itself about"
in all these channels.   And in addition it must be remembered
that the natives with whom these trading vessels dealt, first
for slaves, afterwards for palm-oil, were not, and are not now,
members of the Lo family of savages.   Far from it: they do
not go in for "gentle smiles," but for murdering any unprotected boat's crew they happen to come across, not only for a
love of sport but to keep white traders from penetrating
to the trade-producing interior, and spoiling prices.   And the
region is practically foodless.   But I need not here go into
further particulars regarding the discovery of the connection
between the Niger and its delta.   It is just the usual bad ju-ju of
all big African rivers.   If you first find the mouth, as in the
case of the Nile, you have awful times finding the source.   If
you find the upper waters, you have awful times in discovering
the mouth.   If you find a bit of its middle, like the Congo,
you have awful times in both directions, but fortunately the
Congo does play fair and does not go and split itself up and
dive into a mass of mangrove-swamps like the Niger ; so that
bit of river work at least was easier.

The rivers of the great mangrove-swamp from the Sombreiro
to the Rio del Rey are now known pretty surely not to be
branches of the Niger, but the upper regions of this part of
the Bight are much neglected by English explorers.   I believe
the great swamp region of the Bight of Biafra is the greatest
in the world, and that in its immensity and gloom it has a
grandeur equal to that of the Himalayas.   I am not saying a
beauty ; I own I see a great beauty in it sometimes, but it is
evidently not of a popular type, for I can never persuade my
companions down in the Rivers to recognise it ; still it produces
an emotion in the stoutest-hearted among them ; yea, even
in those who have sailed the world round ; who have cruised
for years in the Southern seas, know their West Indies by
heart, have run regularly for years to Rio de Janeiro, and have
times and again been to where "thy towers, they say, gleam
fair, Bombay, across the deep blue sea."

Take any such a man, educated or not, and place him on
Bonny or Forcados River in the wet season on a Sunday—
Bonny for choice.   Forcados is good.   You'll keep Forcados

scenery "indelibly limned on the tablets of your mind when a yesterday has faded from its page," after you have spent even a week waiting for the Lagos branch-boat on its inky waters. But Bonny! Well, come inside the bar and anchor off the factories: seaward there is the foam of the bar gleaming and wicked—white against a leaden sky and what there is left of Breaker Island. In every other direction you will see the apparently endless walls of mangrove, unvarying in colour, unvarying in form, unvarying in height, save from perspective. Beneath and between you and them lie the rotting mud waters of Bonny River, and away up and down river, miles of rotting mud waters fringed with walls of rotting mud mangrove-swamp. The only break in them—one can hardly call it a relief to the scenery—are the gaunt black ribs of the old hulks, once used as trading stations, which lie exposed at low water near the shore, protruding like the skeletons of great unclean beasts who have died because Bonny water was too strong even for them.

Raised on piles from the mud shore you will see the white-painted factories and their great store-houses for oil; each factory likely enough with its flag at half-mast, which does not enliven the scenery either, for you know it is because somebody is "dead again." Throughout and over all is the torrential downpour of the wet-season rain, coming down night and day with its dull roar. I have known it rain six mortal weeks in Bonny River, just for all the world as if it were done by machinery, and the interval that came then was only a few wet days, whereafter it settled itself down to work again in the good West Coast waterspout pour for more weeks. I fancy junior clerks of the weather-department must be entrusted with the Bight of Biafra's weather, on account of its extreme simplicity; their duty is just to turn on so many months' wet, and then a tornado season—one tornado administered every forty-eight hours; then stop all water supply and turn on sun; then a tornado season as before, and back again to the water tap. But I cannot say I think the weather does them any credit. Tornados frequently come twice a day, and they frequently leave the water tap running a month more than they ought to. The senior clerks should

attend to the matter, but presumably their time is taken up
with complicated climates like England's.

While your eyes are drinking in the characteristics of
Bonny scenery you notice a peculiar smell—an intensification
of that smell you noticed when nearing Bonny, in the evening, out at sea. That's the breath of the malarial mud, laden
with fever, and the chances are you will be down to-morrow.
If it is near evening time now, you can watch it becoming
incarnate, creeping and crawling and gliding out from the
side creeks and between the mangrove-roots, laying itself
upon the river, stretching and rolling in a kind of grim play,
and finally crawling up the side of the ship to come on board
and leave its cloak of moisture that grows green mildew in a
few hours over all. Noise you will not be much troubled
with ; there is only that rain, a sound I have known make
men who are sick with fever well-nigh mad, and now and
again the depressing cry of the curlews which abound here.
This combination is such that after six or eight hours of it
you will be thankful to hear your shipmates start to work the
winch. I take it you are hard up when you relish a winch.
And you will say—let your previous experience of the world
be what it may—Good Heavens, what a place !

Five times have I been now in Bonny River and I like it.
You always do get to like it if you live long enough to allow
the strange fascination of the place to get a hold on you ; but
when I first entered it, on a ship commanded by Captain
Murray in '93, in the wet season, *i.e.* in August, in spite of
the confidence I had by this time acquired in his skill and
knowledge of the West Coast, a sense of horror seized on me
as I gazed upon the scene, and I said to the old coaster who
then had charge of my education, " Good Heavens ! what an
awful accident. We've gone and picked up the Styx." He
was evidently hurt and said, " Bonny was a nice place when
you got used to it," and went on to discourse on the last
epidemic here, when nine men out of the resident eleven died
in about ten days from yellow fever. I went ashore that
evening to have tea with Captain Boler, and was told many
more details about this particular epidemic, to say nothing of
other epidemics. In one which the captain experienced, at the

fourth funeral, two youngsters (junior clerks of the deceased) from drink brought on by fright, fell into the grave before the coffin, which got lowered on to them, and all three had to be hauled out again. " Barely necessary though, was it ?" said another member of the party, " for those two had to have a grave of their own before next sundown." And the general consensus of opinion was that one of these periodic epidemics was " just about due now." Next to the scenery of " a River," commend me for cheerfulness to the local conversation of its mangrove-swamp region ; and every truly important West African river has its mangrove-swamp belt, which extends inland as far as the tide waters make it brackish, and which has a depth and extent from the banks depending on the configuration of the country. Above this belt comes uniformly a region of high forest, having towards the river frontage clay cliffs, sometimes high, as in the case of the Old Calabar at Adiabo, more frequently dwarf cliffs, as in the Forcados up at Warree, and in the Ogowé,—for a long stretch through Kama country. After the clay cliffs region you come to a region of rapids, caused by the river cutting its way through a mountain range ; such ranges are the Pallaballa, causing the Livingstone rapids of the Congo ; the Sierra del Cristal, those of the Ogowé, and many lesser rivers ; the Rumby and Omon ranges, those of the Old Calabar and Cross Rivers.

Naturally in different parts these separate regions vary in size. The mangrove-swamp may be only a fringe at the mouth of the river, or it may cover hundreds of square miles. The clay cliffs may extend for only a mile or so along the bank, or they may, as on the Ogowé, extend for 130. And so it is also with the rapids : in some rivers, for instance the Cameroons, there are only a few miles of them, in others there are many miles ; in the Ogowé there are as many as 500 ; and these rapids may be close to the river mouth, as in most of the Gold Coast rivers, save the Ancobra and the Volta ; or they may be far in the interior, as in the Cross River, where they commence at about 200 miles ; and on the Ogowé, where they commence at about 208 miles from the sea coast ; this depends on the nearness or remoteness from the

coast line of the mountain ranges which run down the west
side of the continent ; ranges (apparently of very different
geological formations), which have no end of different names,
but about which little is known in detail.[1]

And now we will leave generalisations on West African
rivers and go into particulars regarding one little known in
England, and called by its owners, the French, the greatest
strictly equatorial river in the world—the Ogowé.

[1] The Sierra del Cristal and the Pallaballa range are, by some
geographers, held to be identical ; but I have reason to doubt this, for
the specimens of rock brought home by me have been identified by the
Geological Survey, those of the Pallaballa range as mica schist and
quartz ; those of the Sierra del Cristal as " probably schistose grit, but not
definitely determinable by inspection," and " quartz rock." The quantity
of mica in the sands of the Ogowé, I think, come into it from its affluents
from the Congo region, because you do not get these mica sands in
rivers which are entirely from the Sierra del Cristal, such as the Muni.
The Remby and Omon ranges are probably identical with the Sierra del
Cristal, for in them as in the Sierra you do not get the glistening dove-
coloured rock with a sparse vegetation growing on it, as you do in the
Pallaballa region.

CHAPTER VI

LIBREVILLE AND GLASS

In which the voyager pauses to explain divers things and then gives some account of the country round Libreville and Glass.

I MUST pause here to explain my reasons for giving extracts from my diary, being informed on excellent authority that publishing a diary is a form of literary crime. Such being the case I have to urge in extenuation of my committing it that—Firstly, I have not done it before, for so far I have given a sketchy *résumé* of many diaries kept by me while visiting the regions I have attempted to describe. Secondly, no one expects literature in a book of travel. Thirdly, there are things to be said in favour of the diary form, particularly when it is kept in a little known and wild region, for the reader gets therein notice of things that, although un-important in themselves, yet go to make up the conditions of life under which men and things exist. The worst of it is these things are not often presented in their due and proper proportion in diaries. Many pages in my journals that I will spare you display this crime to perfection. For example: " Awful turn up with crocodile about ten—Paraffin good for over-oiled boots—Evil spirits crawl on ground, hence high lintel—Odeaka cheese is made thus :—" Then comes half a yard on Odeaka cheese making.

When a person is out travelling, intent mainly on geography, it is necessary, if he publishes his journals, that he should pub-lish them in sequence. But I am not a geographer. I have to learn the geography of a region I go into in great detail, so as to get about ; but my means of learning it are not the scientific ones—Taking observations, Surveying, Fixing points, &c., &c. These things I know not how to do. I do not " take lunars ", and I always sympathise with a young friend of mine, who, on hearing that an official had got dreadfully ill from taking them, said, " What do those government men do it for ? It kills them all off. I don't hold with knocking yourself to pieces with a lot of doctor's stuff." I certainly have a dim idea that lunars are not a sort of pill ; but I quite agree that they were unwholesome things for a man to take in West Africa. This being my point of view regarding geography, I have relegated it to a separate chapter and have dealt similarly with trade and Fetish.

I have omitted all my bush journal. It is a journal of researches in Fetish and of life in the forest and in native villages, and I think I have a better chance of making this information understood by collecting it together ; for the African forest is not a place you can, within reasonable limits, give an idea of by chronicling your own experience in it day by day. As a psychological study the carefully kept journal of a white man, from the first day he went away from his fellow whites and lived in the Great Forest Belt of Africa, among natives, who had not been in touch with white culture, would be an exceedingly interesting thing, provided it covered a considerable space of time ; but to the general reader it would be hopelessly wearisome, and as for myself, I am not bent on discoursing on my psychological state, but on the state of things in general in West Africa.

On first entering the great grim twilight regions of the forest you hardly see anything but the vast column-like grey tree stems in their countless thousands around you, and the sparsely vegetated ground beneath. But day by day, as you get trained to your surroundings, you see more and more, and a whole world grows up gradually out of the gloom before your eyes. Snakes, beetles, bats and beasts, people the region that at first seemed lifeless.

It is the same with the better lit regions, where vegetation is many-formed and luxuriant. As you get used to it, what seemed at first to be an inextricable tangle ceases to be so. The separate sorts of plants stand out before your eyes with ever

increasing clearness, until you can pick out the one particular
one you may want; and daily you find it easier to make your
way through what looked at first an impenetrable wall, for
you have learnt that it is in the end easier to worm your way
in among networks of creepers, than to shirk these, and go for
the softer walls of climbing grasses and curtains of lycopodium;
and not only is it easier, but safer, for in the grass and lycopodium there are nearly certain to be snakes galore, and the
chances are you may force yourself into the privacy of a
gigantic python's sleeping place.

There is the same difference also between night and day in
the forest. You may have got fairly used to it by day, and
then some catastrophe keeps you out in it all night, and again
you see another world. To my taste there is nothing so fascinating as spending a night out in an African forest, or plantation; but I beg you to note I do not advise any one to follow
the practice. Nor indeed do I recommend African forest
life to any one. Unless you are interested in it and fall
under its charm, it is the most awful life in death imaginable. It is like being shut up in a library whose books
you cannot read, all the while tormented, terrified, and
bored. And if you do fall under its spell, it takes all the
colour out of other kinds of living. Still, it is good for a
man to have an experience of it, whether he likes it or not,
for it teaches you how very dependent you have been, during
your previous life, on the familiarity of those conditions you
have been brought up among, and on your fellow citizens;
moreover it takes the conceit out of you pretty thoroughly
during the days you spend stupidly stumbling about among
your new surroundings.

When this first period passes there comes a sense of growing
power. The proudest day in my life was the day on which an
old Fan hunter said to me—" Ah! you see." Now he did not
say this, I may remark, as a tribute to the hard work I had been
doing in order to see, but regarded it as the consequence of
a chief having given me a little ivory half-moon, whose special
mission was " to make man see Bush," and when you have
attained to that power in full, a state I do not pretend to have
yet attained to, you can say, " Put me where you like in an

African forest, and as far as the forest goes, starve me or kill me if you can."

As it is with the forest, so it is with the minds of the natives. Unless you live alone among the natives, you never get to know them ; if you do this you gradually get a light into the true state of their mind-forest. At first you see nothing but a confused stupidity and crime; but when you get to see—well! as in the other forest,—you see things worth seeing. But it is beyond me to describe the process, so we will pass on to Congo Français.

My reasons for going to this wildest and most dangerous part of the West African regions were perfectly simple and reasonable. I had not found many fish in the Oil Rivers, and, as I have said, my one chance of getting a collection of fishes from a river north of the Congo lay in the attitude Mr. C. G. Hudson might see fit to assume towards ichthyology. Mr. Hudson I had met in 1893 at Kabinda, when he rescued me from dire dilemmas, and proved himself so reliable, that I had no hesitation in depending on his advice. Since those Kabinda days he had become a sort of commercial Bishop, i.e., an Agent-General for Messrs. Hatton and Cookson in Congo Français, and in this capacity had the power to let me get up the Ogowé river, the greatest river between the Niger and the Congo. This river is mainly known in England from the works of Mr. Du Chaillu, who, however, had the misfortune on both his expeditions to miss actually discovering it. Still, he knew it was there, and said so ; and from his reports other explorers went out to look for it and duly found it ; but of them hereafter. It has been in the possession of France nearly forty years now, and the French authorities keep quite as much order as one can expect along its navigable water way, considering that the density of the forest around it harbours and protects a set of notoriously savage tribes chief among which are the Fans. These Fans are a great tribe that have, in the memory of living men, made their appearance in the regions known to white men, in a state of migration seawards, and are a bright, active, energetic sort of African, who by their pugnacious and predatory conduct do much to make one cease to regret and deplore the sloth and lethargy of the rest of the West Coast tribes ; but of Fans I will speak by and by ; and merely preface my diary by stating that Congo Français has a coast line of about 900 miles, extending from the Campo River to a point a few miles north of Landana, with the exception of the small Corisco region claimed by Spain. The Hinterland is not yet delimitated, except as regards the Middle Congo. The French possession runs from Brazzaville on Stanley Pool up to the confluence of the M'Ubanji with the Congo, then following the western bank of the M'Ubanji. Away to the N.N.E. it is not yet delimitated, and although the French have displayed great courage and enterprise, there are still great stretches of country in Congo Français that have never been visited by a white man ; but the same may be said to as great an extent of the West Coast possessions of England and Germany.

The whole of the territory that is at present roughly de-limitated, may have an area of 220,000 square miles, with a population variously estimated at from two to five millions.

The two main outlets of its trade are Gaboon and Fernan Vaz. Gaboon is the finest harbour on the western side of the continent, and was thought for many years to be what it looks like, namely, the mouth of a great river. Of late years, how-ever, it has been found to be merely one of those great tidal estuaries like Bonny—that go thirty or forty miles inland and then end in a series of small rivers. While under the impression that Gaboon was one of the great water ways of Africa, France made it a head station for her West African Squadron, and the point of development from which to start on exploring the surrounding country. Her attention, it is said, was first attracted to the importance of Gaboon by the reports brought home by the expedition under Prince de Joinville in the *Belle Poule*—who, in 1840, brought the body of Napoleon from St. Helena for interment in Paris—and after de Joinville the northern termination of the Gaboon estuary is officially known, although it is locally called Cape Santa Clara, which is possibly the name given it by the Portuguese navigator, Lopez Gonsalves, who, in 1469, made his great voyage of discovery on this coast, and whose name Cape Lopez —at the mouth of one of the Ogowé streams—still bears.

Fernan Vaz and Cape Lopez are nowadays more important
outlets for trade than Gaboon. To the former comes the
trade of the Rembo river, and a certain amount of the Ogowé
main trade, since the discovery of the Ogololé creek—a sort
of natural canal about twelve miles long and of a fairly
uniform breadth of fifty-five feet. Its course is twisted to
and fro through the dense forest, and during the rains it is
possible to take a small stern wheel steam-boat up and down
it. Cape Lopez is the outlet of the Yombas arm of the lower
Ogowé, which is also navigable by a small steam-boat. The
Chargeur Reunis Company, subsidised by the Government,
supply this vessel, the *Eclaireur*, to run from Cape Lopez to
Njole, the highest navigable point for vessels on the Ogowé.
Messrs. Hatton and Cookson used to have another small
steamer, which went straight to and fro from Gaboon to Njole,
but alas! she is no more. Nowadays Gaboon is merely a
depot, and were it not for her magnificent harbour and the
fact that the government is already established there in firm
solid buildings, Gaboon would be abandoned, for not only has
the trade coming out at Cape Lopez and Fernan Vaz increased, but the trade coming down the Gaboon itself
decreased. This is possibly on account of French enterprise having made the route for trade by the Ogowé main
stream the safer and easier.

There is now another rival to Gaboon in Congo Français,
Loango. Loango owes its importance to the clear-sightedness
and daring of M. de Brazza who, when he reached Brazzaville,
as it is now rightly called, on Stanley Pool, saw that there
was a possibility of a practicable route *via* the Niari Valley
from the Middle Congo regions to the sea. For M. de Brazza
to see the possibility of the practicability of a thing means
that he makes it so, and Loango will gradually become the
outlet for a very large portion of the Congo trade, when the
railway along the Niari Valley is completed. It has also been
suggested that the head station of the government should be
moved from Gaboon to Loango, but against this being done
is the initial expense and the inferiority of the Loango
anchorage. Still, things tend to gravitate towards Loango,
as it is the more important position from a local political

point.   And now, feeling a strong inclination to discourse
of M. de Brazza instead of getting on with my own work, I
descend to diary.

May 20th, 1895.—Landed at Gaboon from the *Benguella*
amidst showers of good advice and wishes from Captain
Eversfield and Mr. Fothergill, to which an unknown but
amiable French official, who came aboard at Batta, adds a
lovely Goliath beetle.

HATTON AND COOKSON'S FACTORY AT GLASS.

The captain winds up with the advice to run the gig on to
the beach, and not attempt the steps of Hatton and Cookson's
wharf, for he asserts   they are only fit for a hen." However,
having had for the present enough of running ashore, I go for
the steps, and they are a little sketchy, but quite practicable.

Mr. Fildes, in the absence of the Agent-General, Mr.
Hudson, receives me most kindly, and in the afternoon I and
Mr. Huyghens, the new clerk out for the firm, are sent off to the
Custom House under the guardian care of a French gentle-
man, who is an agent of Hatton and Cookson's, and who

speaks English perfectly, while retaining his French embellishments and decorations to conversation.

The Post, *i.e.* Custom House, is situated a hundred yards or so from the factory, like it, facing the strand ; and we make our way thither over and among the usual *débris* of a south-west coast beach, logs of waterworn trees, great hard seeds, old tins, and the canoes, which are drawn up out of the reach of the ever-mischievous, thieving sea.

The Custom House is far more remarkable for quaintness than beauty ; it is two stories high, the ground floor being the local lock-up. The officer in charge lives on the topmost floor and has a long skeleton wooden staircase whereby to communicate with the lower world. This staircase is a veritable " hen-roost " one. It is evidently made to kill people, but why ? Individuals desirous of defrauding customs would not be likely to haunt this Custom House staircase, and good people, like me, who want to pay dues, should be encouraged and not killed.

The officer is having his siesta; but when aroused is courteous and kindly, but he incarcerates my revolver, giving me a feeling of iniquity for having had the thing. I am informed if I pay 15s. for a licence I may have it—if I fire French ammunition out of it. This seems a heavy sum, so I ask M. Pichault, our mentor, what I may be allowed to shoot if I pay this ? Will it make me free, as it were, of all the local shooting ? May I daily shoot governors, heads of departments, and *sous officiers ?* M. Pichault says " Decidedly not " ;—I may shoot " hippo, or elephants, or crocodiles." Now I have never tried shooting big game in Africa with a revolver, and as I don't intend to, I leave the thing in pawn. My collecting-cases and spirit, the things which I expected to reduce me to a financial wreck by custom dues, are passed entirely free, because they are for science. *Vive la France !*

21st.—Puddle about seashore. Dr. Nassau comes down from Baraka to see if Messrs. Hatton and Cookson have not appropriated a lady intended for the mission station. One was coming from Batanga by the *Benguella,* he knew, and he is told one has been seen on Hatton and Cookson's quay. Mr. Fildes assures him that the lady they have has been invoiced to the firm, and I am summoned to bear out the

statement which gives me the opportunity I have long desired
of meeting Dr. Nassau, the great pioneer explorer of these
regions and one of the greatest authorities on native subjects
in all their bearings.

Although he has been out here, engaged in mission work,
since 1851, he is an exceedingly active man, and has a
strangely gracious, refined, courteous manner.

22nd.—Uninterrupted sea-shore investigations.

23rd.—M. Pichault conducts Mr. Huyghens and me into
the town of Libreville to be registered.

The road from Glass to Libreville is, at moments, very
lovely, and a fine piece of work for the country and the climate.
Round Glass the land is swampy, a thing that probably induced the English to settle here when they came to Gaboon,
for the English love, above all things, settling in, or as near
as possible to, a good reeking, stinking swamp. We pass
first along a made piece of road with the swamp on the left
hand, and on the other, a sandy bush-grown piece of land with
native houses on it, beyond which lies the sea-shore, and whenever the swamp chooses to go down to the edge of the shore
there is an iron viaduct thrown across it. The making of this
road cost the lives of seventy out of one hundred of the
Tonkinese convicts engaged in its construction. After this
swampy piece the road runs through sandy land, virtually
the shore, with low hills on the one hand and the beach on
the other.

A line of cocoanut palms has been planted along either
side of the road for most of the way, looking beautiful but
behaving badly, for there is a telephone wire running along it
from Libreville to Glass, and these gossiping palms—the most
inveterate chatterer in the vegetable kingdom is a cocoanut
palm—talk to each other with their hard leaves on
the wire, just as they did at Fernando Po, so that
mere human beings can hardly get a word in edgeways. This irritates the human atom, and of course it uses bad
words to the wire, and I fancy these are seventy-five per cent.
of all the words that get through the palm leaves' patter.

Two and a half miles' walk brings us to the office of the
Directeur de l'Administration de l'Intérieur, and we hang about

a fine stone-built verandah.   We wait so long that the feeling
grows on us that elaborate preparations for incarcerating us
for life must be going on, but just as Mr. H. and I have
made up our minds to make a dash for it and escape, we are
ushered into a cool, whitewashed office, and find a French
official, clean, tidy, dark-haired, and melancholy, seated before
his writing-table.   Courteously bidding us be seated, he
asks our names, ages, and avocations, enters them in a book
for future reference, and then writes out a permit for each of
us to reside in the colony, as long as we behave ourselves, and
conform to the laws thereof.   These documents are sent
up stairs to be signed by the acting Governor, and while we
are waiting for their return, he converses with M. Pichault on
death, fever, &c.   Presently a black man is shown in; he is
clad in a blue serge coat, from underneath which float over a
pair of blue canvas trousers the tails of a flannel shirt, and on
his feet are a pair of ammunition boots that fairly hobble him.
His name, the interpreter says, is Joseph.   "Who is your
father?" says the official—clerk interprets into trade English.
"Fader?" says Joseph.   "Yes, fader," says the interpreter.
"My fader?" says Joseph.   "Yes," says the interpreter; "who's
your fader?"   "Who my fader?" says Joseph.   "Take him
away and let him think about it," says the officer with a sad,
sardonic smile.   Joseph is alarmed and volunteers name of
mother; this is no good; this sort of information any fool can
give; Government is collecting information of a more recondite
and interesting character.   Joseph is removed by Senegal
soldiers, boots and all.   As he's going to Boma, in the Congo
Free State, it can only be for ethnological purposes that the
French Government are taking this trouble to get up his
genealogy.

Our stamped papers having arrived now we feel happier
and free, and then M. Pichault alarms us by saying, "Now
for the Police"; and off we trail, subdued, to the Palais de
Justice, where we are promptly ushered into a room containing
a vivacious, gesticulatory old gentleman, kindly civil beyond
words, and a powerful, calm young man, with a reassuring
"He's-all-right; it's-only-his-way" manner regarding his chief.
The chief is clad in a white shirt and white pantaloons cut

à la Turque, but unfortunately these garments have a band that consists of a run-in string, and that string is out of repair. He writes furiously—blotting paper mislaid—frantic flurry round—pantaloons won't stand it—grab just saves them—something wanted the other side of the room—headlong flight towards it—" now's our chance," think the pantaloons, and make off—recaptured.

Formalities being concluded regarding us, the chief makes a dash out from behind his writing-table, claps his heels together, and bows with a jerk that causes the pantaloons to faint in coils, like the White Knight in " Alice in Wonderland," and my last view was of a combat with them, I hope a successful one, and that their owner, who was leaving for home the next day, is now enjoying a well-earned, honourable repose after his long years of service to his country in Congo Français.

24th.—Pouring wet day.

25th.—Called on the Mother Superior, and collected shells from the bay beyond Libreville. In the afternoon called on the missionary lady, who has now arrived with her young son, per German boat from Batanga, and talked on fetish ; Dr. Nassau telling a very pathetic and beautiful story of an old chief at Eloby praying to the spirit of the new moon, which he regarded as a representative of the higher elemental power, to prevent the evil lower spirits from entering his town.

Sunday, 26th.—Mr. Fildes evidently regards it as his duty to devote his Sunday mornings to ladies " invoiced to the firm," and takes me in the gig to go up the little river to the east, ostentatiously only the drainage of the surrounding swamp. The tide just allows us to go over the miniature sand-bar, and then we row up the river, which is about forty feet across, and runs through a perfect gem of a mangrove-swamp, and the stench is quite the right thing—real Odeur de Niger Delta.

As we go higher up, the river channel winds to and fro between walls and slopes of ink-black slime, more sparsely covered with mangrove bushes than near the entrance. This stinking, stoneless slime is honey-combed with crab holes, and the owners of these—green, blue, red, and black—are walking about on the tips of their toes sideways, with that comic pomp peculiar to the crab family. I expected

only to have to sit in the boat and say " Horrible " at intervals,
but no such thing; my companion, selecting a peculiarly
awful-looking spot, says he "thinks that will do," steers the
boat up to it, and jumps out with a squidge into the black
slime. For one awful moment I thought it was suicide, and
that before I could even get the address of his relations to
break the news to them there would be nothing but a Panama
hat lying on the slime before me. But he only sinks in a matter
of a foot or so, and then starts off, to my horror, calling the
boys after him, to hunt crabs for me. Now I have mentioned no
desire for crabs, and was merely looking at them, as I always do
when out with other white folk, noting where they were
so as to come back alone next day and get them; for I don't
want any one's blood, black or white, on my head. As soon
as I recovered speech, I besought him to come back into the
boat and leave them: but no, " tears, prayers, entreaties, all in
vain," as Koko says; he would not, and dashed about in the
stinking mud, regardless, with his four Kruboys far more
cautiously paddling after him.

The affrighted crabs were in a great taking. It seems to be
crab etiquette that, even when a powerfully built, lithe, six
foot high young man is coming at you hard all with a paddle,
you must not go rushing into anybody's house save your
own, whereby it fell out many crabs were captured; but the
thing did not end there. I had never suspected we should
catch anything but our deaths of fever, and so had brought
with me no collecting-box, and before I could remonstrate Mr.
Fildes' handkerchief was full of crabs, and of course mine too. It
was a fine sunny morning on the Equator, and therefore it was
hot, and we had nothing to wipe our perspiring brows with.

All the crabs being caught or scared home on this mud
bank, we proceed higher up river, and after some more crab
hunts we got to a place where I noticed you did not sink very far
in if you kept moving; so I got ashore, and we went towards a
break in the mangroves, where some high trees were growing,
where we fell in with some exceedingly lovely mayflies and had
a great hunt. They have legs two to three inches long, white
at the joints and black between; a very small body with
purple wings belongs to the legs, but you do not suspect this

until you have caught the legs, as they hover and swing to
and fro over some mass of decaying wood stuff. At first I
thought they were spiders hanging from some invisible thread,
so strangely did they move in circumscribed spaces : but
we swept our hands over them and found no thread, and
then we went for the legs in sheer desperation,. and found a
tiny fly body belonging to them and not a tiny spider body.

We then made our way on to the slightly higher land fringing
the swamp. There was at the river end of the swamp a belt
of palms, and beyond this a belt of red-woods, acacias, and
other trees, and passing through these, we were out on an open
grass-covered country, with low, rolling hills, looking strangely
English, with clumps of trees here and there, and running
between the hills, in all directions, densely-wooded valleys—a
pleasant, homely-looking country.

We wandered through a considerable lot of grass, wherein
I silently observed there were millions of ticks, and we made
for a group of hut-homesteads and chatted with the inhabitants, until Mr. Fildes' conscience smote him with the fact that
he had not given out cook's stores for the mid-day meal.
Then we made a short cut to the boat, which involved us in a
lot of mud-hopping, and so home to 12 o'clock breakfast.

At breakfast I find Mr. Fildes regards it as his duty to do
more scientific work, for he asks me to go to Woermann's
farm, and I, not knowing where it is, say yes ; inwardly
trusting that the place may not be far away, and situated in a
reasonably dry country, for I have lost all sense of reliance in
Mr. Fildes' instinct of self-preservation—an instinct usually
strong enough to keep a West Coaster from walking a mile.
Along the windward coast, and in the Rivers, I have always
been accustomed to be regarded as insane for my walking
ways, but this gentleman is worth six of me any day, and
worth sixty for Sundays, it's clear.

At 3 o'clock off we go, turning down the "Boulevard"
towards Libreville, and then up a road to the right opposite
Woermann's beach, and follow it through miles of grass over
low hills. Here and there are huts new to me, and quite
unlike the mud ones of the West Coast, or the grass ones of the
Congo and Angola districts. They are far inferior to the

swish huts of the Effiks, or the Moorish-looking mud ones
you see round Cape Coast Castle, &c., and notably inferior to
the exceedingly neat Dualla huts of Cameroons ; but they are
better than any other type of African house I have seen.

They are made of split bamboo with roofs of mats like the
Effik roofs, but again inferior. I notice sometimes the
sections of the walls are made on the ground and then erected.
The builder drives in a row of strong wooden poles, and then
ties the sections on to them very neatly with "tie-tie." The
door and window-frames and shutters are made of plank
painted a bright cobalt blue as a rule, but now and then red
—a red I believe that had no business there, as it looks like
some white gentleman's red oxide he has had out for painting
the boats with.

Sometimes, however, instead of the sections being made on
the ground of closely set split bamboos, the poles of unsplit
bamboo are driven in, and the split bamboos are lashed on to
them, alternately inside and outside, and between these are fixed
palm-leaf mats. I suspect this style of architecture of being
cheaper. Although there are a good many houses of both
these types being erected on the hills round Glass and Libreville,
I cannot say building operations are carried on with much
vigour, for there are plenty of skeletons up, with just one or
two sections tied in place, and then left as if the builder had
gone on strike or got sick of the job somehow.

The stretch of broiling hot grass is trying, but interesting ;
some of it is intensely fine and a beautiful yellow-green, which
I am told is gathered and dried and made into pillows.
Some again is long lank stuff, carrying a maroon-coloured
ear, which when ripe turns gold colour, and in either state is
very lovely when one comes across stretches of it down a
hillside.

On either side of us show wooded valleys like those we saw
this morning ; and away to the east the line of mangrove
swamp fringing the little river we rowed up. Away to the
west are the groves of mango trees round Libreville ; mango
trees are only pretty when you are close to them, prettiest
of all when you are walking through an avenue of them, and
you can see their richness of colour ; the deep myrtle-green

leaves, with the young shoots a dull crimson, and the soft gray-brown stem, and the luscious-looking but turpentiny-tasting fruit, a glory of gold and crimson, like an immense nectarine.

We gradually get into a more beautiful type of country, and down into a forest. The high trees are the usual high forest series with a preponderance of acacias. It is a forest of varied forms, but flowerless now in the dry season. There are quantities of ferns ; hart's-tongues and the sort that grows on the oil-palms, and elks-horn growing out of its great brown shields on the trees above, and bracken, and pretty trailing lycopodium climbing over things, but mostly over the cardamoms which abound in the under-bush, and here and there great banks of the most lovely ferns I have ever seen save the tree-fern, an am-bitious climber, called, I believe, by the botanists *Nephrodium circutarium*, and walls of that strange climbing grass, and all sorts of other lovely things by thousands in all directions.

Butterflies and dragon-flies were scarce here compared to Okijon, but of other flies there were more than plenty.

The roadway is exceedingly good ; certainly in the grass country you are rather liable to what Captain Eversfield graphically describes as "stub your toe" against lava-like rock, for the grass has overgrown the road, leaving only a single-file path open. In the forest you come across isolated masses of stratified rock, sometimes eight and ten feet high, most prettily overgrown with moss and fern.

We pass through several villages which Mr. Fildes tells me are Fan villages, and are highly interesting after all one has already heard of this tribe of evil repute. Their houses are quite different to the M'pongwe ones we have left behind, and are built of sheets of bark, tied on to sticks.

Frequently in the street one sees the characteristic standing drum painted white in patterns with black or red-brown, and a piece of raw hide stretched across the top, and one or two talking-drums besides.

We cross several pretty streams in the forest carefully bridged with plank. This Woermann's road, I hear, is between six and seven miles long, and its breadth uniformly nine feet, and it must have cost a lot of money to make. It was made with the intention of being used for waggons drawn by oxen, which were to bring down all the produce of the coffee plantation, and the timber that might be cut down in the clearing for it, to Gaboon for shipment. A large house was erected and a quantity of coffee planted, and then the enterprise was abandoned by Messrs. Woermann, and the whole affair, coffee, road, and all is rapidly sinking back into the bush.

There is a considerable-sized Fan village just at the entrance to the farm in which is a big silk-cotton tree. It struck me as strange, after coming from Calabar where these trees are frequently smothered round the roots with fetish objects, to see nothing on this one save a framed and glazed image of the Virgin and Child. Just beyond the Fan town there is a little river.

When we get so far it is too late to proceed further, and nothing but this consideration, backed by the memory of one night when he was compelled to walk to Glass from the farm, prevents Mr. Fildes, I believe, from crossing to Corisco Bay.

So round we turn, and return in the same order we came in, Mr. Fildes lashing along first, I behind him, going like a clock, which was my one chance. When at last we reached the " Boulevard " he wanted to reverse this order, but remembering the awful state that the back of my blouse got in at Fernando Po from a black boot-lace I was reduced to employ as a stay-lace, I refuse to go in front, without explaining why.

27th.—Went up among the grass to see if there was anything to be got; ticks were, and there were any quantity of ants and flocks of very small birds, little finch-like people, with a soft, dull, gray-brown plumage, relieved by a shading of dark green on the back, and little crimson bills ; they have a pretty twittering note, and are little bigger than butterflies ; butterflies themselves are rare now. I see the small boys catch these birds with flake rubber as with birdlime. Down in the wooded hollows there are numbers of other birds, plantain-eaters, and the bird with the long, soft, rich, thrushlike note, and the ubiquitous Wu-tu-tu, the clock bird, so called from its regular habit of giving the cry, from which its native name comes, every two hours during the night, commencing at 4 P.M. and going off duty at 6 A.M.

On my return home, I find Mr. Hudson is back from the Ogowé on the *Mové*, unaltered since '93, I am glad to say. He tells me good Dom Joachim de Sousa Coutinho e Chichorro is dead, and his wife Donna Anna, and her sister Donna Maria de Sousa Coutinho, my valued friends, have returned from Kabinda to Lisbon.

28th.—Go to west side of Libreville shell-hunting ; after passing through the town, and in front of the mango-tree embowered mission station of the Espiritu Santo, the road runs along close to the sea, through a beautiful avenue of cocoa-palms. Then there is a bridge, and a little beyond this the road ends, and so I take to the sandy sea-shore for a mile or so.

The forest fringes the sand, rising in a wall of high trees, not mangroves ; and here and there a stinking stream comes out from under them, and here and there are masses of shingle-formed conglomerate and stratified green-gray rock.

Beyond Libreville there are several little clearings in the forest with a native town tucked into them, the inhabitants of which seem a happy and contented generation mainly devoted to fishing, and very civil. On my walk back I notice the people getting water from the stinking streams ; small wonder the mortality is high in Libreville : this is usually attributed to the inhabitants " going it," but they might " go it " more than they do, without killing themselves if they left off drinking this essence of stinking slime.

29th.—Went to see Mrs. Gault and Dr. Nassau, who says the natives have a legend of a volcano about sixty miles from here.

30th.—Mrs. Gault asks me to go with her to a Bible meeting, held by a native woman. I assent, I go ; Mrs. Sarah, the Biblewoman, is a very handsome, portly lady who speaks English very well. There are besides her, Mrs. Gault and myself, eight or nine native women, and two men. Hymns are sung in M'pongwe, one with a rousing chorus of " Gory

we, gory we, pro pa reary gory we." This M'pongwe does
not sound so musical as the Effik.   Sarah gives an extempore
prayer however, which is very beautiful in sound, and she in-
tones it most tastefully.   But I confess my mind is distracted
by a malignant-looking pig which hovers round us as we
kneel upon the sand.   I well remember Captain ——— being
chivied by a pig in the confines of Die Grosse Colonie, and
then there is the chance of ants and so on up one's
ankles.   Mrs. Gault gives an address which Sarah translates
into M'pongwe, and then come more hymns, and the meeting
closes, and the ladies settle down and have a quiet pipe and a
chat.   We then saunter off and visit native Christians' houses.
Many houses here are built in clumps round a square, but
this form of arrangement seems only a survival, for I find
there is no necessary relationship among the people living in
the square as there is in Calabar: and so home.

31st.—Start out at 2.30 and walk through the grass
country behind Baraka, and suddenly fall down into a strange
place.

On sitting up after the shock consequent on an unpremedi-
tated descent of some thirteen feet or so, I find myself in
a wild place; before me are two cave-like cavities, with
a rough wood seat in each; behind me another similar cavity
or chamber; the space I am in is about three feet wide; to
the left this is terminated by an earth wall; to the right it
goes, as a path, down a cutting or trench which ends in dry
grass.

No sign of human habitation.   Are these sacrifice places, I
wonder, or are they places where those Fans one hears so
much about, come and secretly eat human flesh? Clearly they
are not vestiges of an older civilisation.   In fact, what in the
world are they?   I investigate and find they are nothing in
the world more than markers' pits for a rifle range.

Disgust, followed by alarm, seizes me; those French authorities may take it into their heads to think I am making plans
of their military works! Visions of incarceration flash before my
eyes, and I fly into more grass and ticks, going westwards
until I pick up a path, and following this, find myself in a little
village.   In the centre of the street, see the strange arrow-

head-shaped board mounted on a rough easel and alongside it a bundle of stakes, the whole affair clearly connected with making palm oil, and identical with the contrivance I saw in the far-away Fan village on Sunday morning.

Investigate, find the boiled palm nuts are put into a pine-apple fibre bag, which is hung on the board, then stakes are wedged in between the uprights of the easel, so as to squeeze the bag, one stake after another being put in to increase the pressure. The oil runs out, and off the point of the arrow-shaped board into a receptacle placed to receive it.

The next object of interest is a piece of paper stuck on a stick at the further end of the villages. The inscription is of interest though evidently recent. Find it is " No thoroughfare." There is a bamboo gateway at this end, and so I go through it and find myself to my surprise on the Woermann farm road, and down this I go, butterfly hunting. Presently I observe an old gentleman with a bundle of bamboos watching me intently. Not knowing the natives of this country yet, I feel anxious, and he, in a few minutes without taking his eyes off me, crouches in the grass. I remember my great tutor Captain Boler of Bonny's maxim : " Be afraid of an African if you can't help it, but never show it anyhow," so I walk on intending to pass him with a propitiatory M'bolo.[1] As I get abreast of him he hisses out " Look him ; " he's evidently got something in the grass ; Heaven send it's not a snake, but I " look him,"—a lizard ! The good soul understood collecting, and meant well from the first. I give him tobacco and a selection of amiable observations, and he beams and we go on down the road together, discussing the proper time to burn grass, and the differences in the practical value, for building purposes, of the two kinds of bamboo. Then coming to a path that runs evidently in the direction of the Plateau at Libreville, and thinking it's time I was tacking homewards, I say " good bye " to my companion, and turn down the path. " You sabe 'em road ? " says he in a very questioning voice : I say " yes " airily, and keep on down it.

The path goes on through grass, and then makes for a hollow—wish it didn't, for hollows are horrid at times, and

[1] The M'pongwe greeting ; meaning, " May you live long."

evidently this road has got something against it somewhere, and is not popular, for the grass falls across it like unkempt hair. Road becomes damp and goes into a belt of trees, in the middle of which runs a broad stream with a log laid across it. Congratulating myself on absence of companions, ignominiously crawl across on to the road, which then and there turns round and goes back to the stream again higher up—evidently a joke, "thought-you-were-going-to-get-home-dry-did-you" sort of thing. Wade the stream, rejoin the road on the hither side. Then the precious thing makes a deliberate bolt for the interior of Africa, instead of keeping on going to Libreville. I lose confidence in it. The Wu-tu-tu says it's four o'clock. It's dark at 6.15 down here, and I am miles from home, so I begin to wish I had got an intelligent companion to guide me, as I walk on through the now shoulder-high grass. Suddenly another road branches off to the left. "Saved!" Down it I go, and then it ends in a manioc patch, with no path out the other end, and surrounded by impenetrable bush. Crestfallen, I retrace my steps and continue along my old tormentor, which now attempts to reassure me by doubling round to the left and setting off again for Libreville. I am not deceived, I have had my trust in it too seriously tampered with —Yes, it's up to mischief again, and it turns itself into a stream. Nothing for it but wading, so wade ; but what will be its next manifestation, I wonder? for I begin to doubt whether it is a road at all, and suspect it of being only a local devil, one of the sort that sometimes appears as a road, sometimes as a tree or a stream, &c. I wonder what they will do if they find I don't get in to-night?—wish me—at Liverpool, at least. After a quarter of an hour's knee-deep wading, I suddenly meet a native lady who was at the Bible meeting. She has a grand knowledge of English, and she stands with her skirt tucked up round her, evidently in no hurry, and determined to definitely find out who I am. Recognising this, I attempt to take charge of the conversation, and divert its course. "Nice road this," I say, "but it's a little damp." "Washey, ma," she says, "but ——" "Is this road here to go anywhere," I interposed, "or is it only a kind of joke?" "It no go nowhere 'ticular, ma," she says ; "but ——" "In a civilised community like this of Gaboon," I say, "it's scandalous that roads should be allowed to wander about in this loose way." "That's so for true," she assents; "but, ma, ——" "You must excuse me," I answer, "I am in a great hurry to get in, hope to meet you again. Where do you live? I'll call." She gives me her address, but does not move, and the grass walls either side of the stream road are high and dense. "My husband," she says, "was in H, and C.'s; he die now." "Dear me, that's very sad; you must have been very sorry," I answer, sympathetically, thinking I have turned the conversation. "We all were; he had ten wives. "But, ma, ——" I am damp and desperate. and so pushing into the grass at the side, circumnavigate her portly form successfully, and saying a cheery "good-bye," bolt, and down wind after me comes the uninterrupted question at last; but I do not return to discuss the matter, and soon getting on to drier ground, and seeing a path that goes towards the boulevard, down I go, as quickly as my feet can carry me, and then before I know where I am I find myself in a network of little irrigating canals, running between neatly kept beds of tomatoes, salad, &c., whereon there are working busily a lot of Anamese convicts. The convicts are deported from the French Cochin China possessions and employed by the Public Works Department in various ways. Those who conduct themselves well, and survive, have grants of garden ground given them, which they cultivate in this tidy, carefully minute way, so entirely different from the slummacky African methods of doing things. The produce they sell to the residents in the town, and live very prosperously in this way: but the climate of Western Africa is almost, if not quite, as deadly to the Chinese races as to the white—a fact that has been amply demonstrated not only here; but in Congo Belge, where the railway company carried on a series of experiments with imported labour—a series of experiments that entailed an awful waste of human life—for none of the imported people stood the climate any better than the whites, and you know what that means. This labour question out here, a question that increases daily with the development of plantation enter-

prise, I do not think will ever be solved by importing foreign
labour.   Nor is it advisable that it should be, for our European
Government puts a stop to the action of those causes which
used to keep the native population down, intertribal wars,
sacrifices, &c., &c.; and to the deportation of surplus population
in the form of slaves, and so unless means of support are devised
for "the indigenous ones," as Mrs. Gault calls them, Africa
will have us to thank for some smart attacks of famine, for
the natives, left to their own devices, will never cultivate the
soil sufficiently to support a large population, and moreover a vast percentage of the West African soil is very poor,
sour stuff, that will grow nothing but equally valueless
vegetation.   From this discourse you will argue I did get
home at last.

June 2nd.—*Nubia* in, but she will not call at Batanga, so Mrs.
Gault is stranded until some other steamer calls.   *Nubia* has
lost all her heavy anchors down south, where she reports the
Calemma extra bad this year.

3rd.—Went alone for a long walk to the bend of the mangrove-swamp river to the east.   It stank severely, but was
most interesting, giving one the conditions of life in a mangrove-swamp in what you might call a pocket edition.   Leaving this, I made my way north-west along native paths across
stretches of grass growing on rolling hills and down through
wooded valleys, each of which had a little stream in it, or a patch
of swamp, with enormous arums and other water plants growing, and along through Fan villages, each with just one straight
street, having a club-house at the alternate ends.   I met in
the forest a hunter, carrying home a deer he had shot ; in
addition to his musket, he carried a couple of long tufted
spears, archaic in type.   He was very chatty, and I gave him
tobacco, and we talked sport, and on parting I gave him some
more tobacco, because he kindly gave me a charm to enable
me to see things in the forest.   He was gratified, and said,
" You ver nice," " Good-bye," " Good-day," " So long," " Good-
night," which was very nice of him, as these phrases were
evidently all the amiable greetings in English that he knew.
The " So long " you often hear the natives in Gaboon say : it
always sounds exceedingly quaint.   They have of course

picked it up from the American missionaries, who have been here upwards of thirty years.

4th.—Mr. Hudson announces that the *Mové* will leave at 5.30 on the morning after next.   Later in the day he expects to get her off by 5.30 to-morrow—towards evening he thinks to-morrow at 8.30 is more likely still. Mrs. Gault called with her boy Harry ; she says, " John Holt has got a lovely waist at only two dollars."   I don't want a waist—I am too thin any-how—so I don't investigate the matter. We go up to Dr. Nassau and talk ju-ju.   He agrees with me that dead black men go white when soaked in water.

CHAPTER VII

THE OGOWÉ

Wherein the voyager gives extracts from the Log of the Movè and of the Eclaireur, and an account of the voyager's first meeting with "those fearful Fans," also an awful warning to all young persons who neglect the study of the French language.

June 5th, 1895.—OFF on *Movè* at 9.30. Passengers, Mr. Hudson, Mr. Woods, Mr. Huyghens, Père Steinitz, and I. There are black deck-passengers galore ; I do not know their honourable names, but they are evidently very much married men, for there is quite a gorgeously coloured little crowd of ladies to see them off. They salute me as I pass down the pier, and start inquiries. I say hastily to them : "Farewell, I'm off up river," for I notice Mr. Fildes bearing down on me, and I don't want him to drop in on the subject of society interest. I expect it is settled now, or pretty nearly. There is a considerable amount of mild uproar among the black contingent, and the *Movè* firmly clears off before half the good advice and good wishes for the black husbands are aboard. She is a fine little vessel ; far finer than I expected. The accommodation I am getting is excellent. A long, narrow cabin, with one bunk in it and pretty nearly everything one can wish for, and a copying press thrown in. Food is excellent, society charming, captain and engineer quite acquisitions. The saloon is square and roomy for the size of the vessel, and most things, from rowlocks to teapots, are kept under the seats in good nautical style. We call at the guard-ship to pass our papers, and then steam ahead out of the Gaboon estuary to the south, round Pongara Point, keeping close into the land. About forty feet from shore there is a good free channel for vessels with a light draught which if you do not take, you have to make a big sweep seaward to avoid a reef. Between four and five miles below Pongara, we pass Point Gombi, which is fitted with a lighthouse, a lively and conspicuous structure by day as well as night. It is perched on a knoll, close to the extremity of the long arm of low, sandy ground, and is painted black and white, in horizontal bands, which, in conjunction with its general figure, give it a pagoda-like appearance.

Alongside it are a white-painted, red-roofed house for the light-house keeper, and a store for its oil. The light is either a flashing or a revolving or a stationary one, when it is alight. One must be accurate about these things, and my knowledge regarding it is from information received, and amounts to the above. I cannot throw in any personal experience, because I have never passed it at night-time, and seen from Glass it seems just steady. Most lighthouses on this Coast give up fancy tricks, like flashing or revolving, pretty soon after they are established. Seventy-five per cent. of them are not alight half the time at all. "It's the climate." Gombi, however, you may depend on for being alight at night, and I have no hesitation in saying you can see it, when it is visible, seventeen miles out to sea, and that the knoll on which the lighthouse stands is a grass-covered sand cliff, about forty or fifty feet above sea-level. As we pass round Gombi point, the weather becomes distinctly rough, particularly at lunch-time. The *Mové* minds it less than her passengers, and stamps steadily along past the wooded shore, behind which shows a distant range of blue hills. Silence falls upon the black passengers, who assume recumbent positions on the deck, and suffer. All the things from under the saloon seats come out and dance together, and play puss-in-the-corner, after the fashion of loose gear when there is any sea on.

As the night comes down, the scene becomes more and more picturesque. The moonlit sea, shimmering and breaking on the darkened shore, the black forest and the hills silhouetted against the star-powdered purple sky, and, at my feet, the engine-room stoke-hole, lit with the rose-coloured glow from its furnace, showing by the great wood fire the two nearly naked Krumen stokers, shining like polished bronze in their perspiration, as they throw in on to the fire the billets of red wood that look like freshly-cut chunks of flesh. The white engineer hovers round the mouth of the pit, shouting down directions and ever and anon plunging down the little iron ladder to carry them out himself. At intervals he stands on the rail with his head craned round the edge of the sun deck to listen to the captain, who is up on the little deck above, for there is no telegraph to the engines, and our gallant commander's voice is not strong. While the white engineer is roosting on the rail, the black engineer comes partially up the ladder and gazes hard at me ; so I give him a wad of tobacco, and he plainly regards me as inspired, for of course that was what he wanted. Remember that whenever you see a man, black or white, filled with a nameless longing, it is tobacco he requires. Grim despair accompanied by a gusty temper indicates something wrong with his pipe, in which case offer him a straightened-out hairpin. The black engineer having got his tobacco, goes below to the stoke-hole again and smokes a short clay as black and as strong as himself. The captain affects an immense churchwarden. How he gets through life, waving it about as he does, without smashing it every two minutes, I cannot make out.

At last we anchor for the night just inside Nazareth Bay, for Nazareth Bay wants daylight to deal with, being rich in low islands and sand shoals. We crossed the Equator this afternoon.

June 6th.—Off at daybreak into Nazareth Bay. Anxiety displayed by navigators, sounding taken on both sides of the bows with long bamboo poles painted in stripes, and we go "slow ahead" and "hard astern" successfully, until we get round a good-sized island, and there we stick until four o'clock, high water, when we come off all right, and steam triumphantly but cautiously into the Ogowé. The shores of Nazareth Bay are fringed with mangroves, but once in the river the scenery soon changes, and the waters are walled on either side with a forest rich in bamboo, oil and wine palms. These forest cliffs seem to rise right up out of the mirror-like brown water. Many of the highest trees are covered with clusters of brown-pink young shoots that look like flowers, and others are decorated by my old enemy the climbing palm, now bearing clusters of bright crimson berries. Climbing plants of other kinds are wreathing everything, some blossoming with mauve, some with yellow, some with white flowers, and every now and then a soft sweet heavy breath of fragrance comes out to us as we pass by. There is a native village on the north bank, embowered along its plantations with some very tall cocoa-palms rising high above them.

The river winds so that it seems to close in behind us, opening out in front fresh vistas of superb forest beauty, with the great brown river stretching away unbroken ahead like a broad road of burnished bronze. Astern, it has a streak of frosted silver let into it by the *Mové's* screw. Just about six o'clock, we run up to the *Fallabar*, the *Mové's* predecessor in working the Ogowé, now a hulk, used as a depot by Hatton and Cookson. She is anchored at the entrance of a creek that runs through to the Fernan Vaz ; some say it is six hours' run, others that it is eight hours for a canoe ; all agree that there are plenty of mosquitoes.

The *Fallabar* looks grimly picturesque, and about the last spot in which a person of a nervous disposition would care to spend the night. One half of her deck is dedicated to fuel logs, on the other half are plank stores for the goods, and a room for the black sub-trader in charge of them. I know that there must be scorpions which come out of those logs and stroll into the living room, and goodness only knows what one might not fancy would come up the creek or rise out of the floating grass, or the limitless-looking forest. I am told she was a fine steamer in her day, but those who had charge of her did not make allowances for the very rapid rotting action of the Ogowé water, so her hull rusted through before her engines were a quarter worn out; and there was nothing to be done with her then, but put a lot of concrete in, and make her a depot, in which state of life she is very useful, for during the height of the dry season, the *Mové* cannot get through the creek to supply the firm's Fernan Vaz factories.

Subsequently I heard much of the *Fallabar*, which seems to have been a celebrated, or rather notorious, vessel. Every one declared her engines to have been of immense power, but this I believe to have been a mere local superstition ; because in the same breath, the man who referred to them, as if it would have been quite unnecessary for new engines to have

been made for H.M.S. *Victorious* if those *Fallabar* engines could
have been sent to Chatham dockyard, would mention that
" you could not get any pace up on her ; " and all who knew
her sadly owned " she wouldn't steer," so naturally she spent
the greater part of her time on the Ogowé on a sand bank, or
in the bush. All West African steamers have a mania for
bush, and the delusion that they are required to climb trees.
The *Fallabar* had the complaint severely, because of her
defective steering powers, and the temptation the magnificent
forest, and the rapid currents, and the sharp turns of the creek
district, offered her ; she failed, of course—they all fail—
but it is not for want of practice. I have seen many West
Coast vessels up trees, but never more than fifteen feet
or so.

The trade of this lower part of the Ogowé, from the mouth
to Lembarene, a matter of 130 miles, is almost *nil*. Above
Lembarene, you are in touch with the rubber and ivory
trade.

This *Fallabar* creek is noted for mosquitoes, and the black
passengers made great and showy preparations in the evening
time to receive their onslaught, by tying up their strong
chintz mosquito bars to the stanchions and the cook-house.
Their arrangements being constantly interrupted by the
white engineer making alarums and excursions amongst them ;
because when too many of them get on one side the *Mové*
takes a list and burns her boilers. Conversation and atmosphere are full of mosquitoes. The decision of widely
experienced sufferers amongst us is, that next to the lower
Ogowé, New Orleans is the worst place for them in this
world.

The day closed with a magnificent dramatic beauty.
Dead ahead of us, up through a bank of dun-coloured
mist rose the moon, a great orb of crimson, spreading
down the oil-like, still river, a streak of blood-red reflection. Right astern, the sun sank down into the mist, a
vaster orb of crimson, and when he had gone out of view, sent
up flushes of amethyst, gold, carmine and serpent-green,
before he left the moon in undisputed possession of the black
purple sky.

Forest and river were absolutely silent, but there was a pleasant chatter and laughter from the black crew and passengers away forward, that made the *Mové* seem an island of life in a land of death. I retired into my cabin, so as to get under the mosquito curtains to write ; and one by one I heard my companions come into the saloon adjacent, and say to the watchman : " You sabe six o'clock ? When them long arm catch them place, and them short arm catch them place, you call me in the morning time." Exit from saloon—silence— then : " You sabe five o'clock ? When them long arm catch them place, and them short arm catch them place, you call me in the morning time." Exit—silence—then " You sabe half-past five o'clock ? When them long arm— " Oh, if I were a watchman ! Anyhow, that five o'clocker will have the whole ship's company roused in the morning time.

June 7th.—Every one called in the morning time by the reflex row from the rousing of the five o'clocker. Glorious morning. The scene the reversal of that of last night. The forest to the east shows a deep blue-purple, mounted on a background that changes as you watch it from daffodil and amethyst to rose-pink, as the sun comes up through the night mists. The moon sinks down among them, her pale face flushing crimson as she goes ; and the yellow-gold sunshine comes, glorifying the forest and gilding the great sweep of tufted papyrus growing alongside the bank ; and the mist vanishes, little white flecks of it lingering among the water reeds and lying in the dark shadows of the forest stems. The air is full of the long, soft, rich notes of the plaintive warblers, and the uproar consequent upon the *Mové* taking on fuel wood, which comes alongside in canoe loads from the *Fallabar*.

Père Steinitz and Mr. Woods are busy preparing their respective canoes for their run to Fernan Vaz through the creek. Their canoes are very fine ones, with a remarkably clean run aft. The Père's is quite the travelling canoe, with a little stage of bamboo aft, covered with a hood of palm thatch, under which you can make yourself quite comfortable, and keep yourself and your possessions dry, unless something desperate comes on in the way of rain.

By 10.25 we have got all our wood aboard, and run off up

river full speed. The river seems broader above the *Fallabar*, but this is mainly on account of its being temporarily unencumbered with islands. A good deal of the bank we have passed by since leaving Nazareth Bay on the south side has been island shore, with a channel between the islands and the true south bank.

The day soon grew dull, and looked threatening, after the delusive manner of the dry season. The climbing plants are finer here than I have ever before seen them. They form great veils and curtains between and over the trees, often hanging so straight and flat, in stretches of twenty to forty feet or so wide, and thirty to sixty or seventy feet high, that it seems incredible that no human hand has trained or clipped them into their perfect forms. Sometimes these curtains are decorated with large bell-shaped, bright-coloured flowers, sometimes with delicate sprays of white blossoms. This forest is beyond all my expectations of tropical luxuriance and beauty, and it is a thing of another world to the forest of the Upper Calabar, which, beautiful as it is, is a sad dowdy to this. There you certainly get a great sense of grimness and vastness; here you have an equal grimness and vastness with the addition of superb colour. This forest is a Cleopatra to which Calabar is but a Quaker. Not only does this forest depend on flowers for its illumination, for there are many kinds of trees having their young shoots, crimson, brown-pink, and creamy yellow: added to this there is also the relieving aspect of the prevailing fashion among West African trees, of wearing the trunk white with here and there upon it splashes of pale pink lichen, and vermilion-red fungus, which alone is sufficient to prevent the great mass of vegetation from being a monotony in green.

All day long we steam past ever-varying scenes of loveliness whose component parts are ever the same, yet the effect ever different. Doubtless it is wrong to call it a symphony, yet I know no other word to describe the scenery of the Ogowé. It is as full of life and beauty and passion as any symphony Beethoven ever wrote: the parts changing, interweaving, and returning. There are *leit motifs* here in it, too. See the papyrus ahead; and you know when you get abreast of it you will find the great forest sweeping away in a bay-like curve behind it against the dull gray sky, the splendid columns of its cotton and red woods looking like a façade of some limitless inchoate temple. Then again there is that stretch of sword-grass, looking as if it grew firmly on to the bottom, so steady does it stand ; but as the *Mové* goes by, her wash sets it undulating in waves across its broad acres of extent, showing it is only riding at anchor ; and you know after a grass patch you will soon see a red dwarf clay cliff, with a village perched on its top, and the inhabitants thereof in their blue and red cloths standing by to shout and wave to the *Mové*, or legging it like lamp-lighters from the back streets and the plantation to the river frontage, to be in time to do so, and through all these changing phases there is always the strain of the vast wild forest, and the swift, deep, silent river.

At almost every village that we pass—and they are frequent after the *Fallabar*—there is an ostentatious display of firewood deposited either on the bank, or on piles driven into the mud in front of it, mutely saying in their uncivilised way, " Try our noted chunks : best value for money "—(that is to say, tobacco, &c.), to the *Mové* or any other little steamer that may happen to come along hungry for fuel.

Mr. Hudson is immersed in accounts all day. I stare at the forest, Mr. Huyghens at the engines. The captain is on top of the sun deck most of his time : but he and every one, save Mr. Hudson and Mr. Huyghens, about every twenty minutes go down into the afterhold. If Mr. Hudson were not on board, I'd go down too, just to see what in the world they have got down there. The Krumen on their return have pails of dirty water, which Mr. Hudson, kindly fearing it will give me the idea that the *Mové* is leaking badly, explains that it comes out of something connected with the propeller conditioned by the state of the packing. The captain, with his arms full of tinned provisions. The engineer empty-handed but looking content. Rosa, Mr. Hudson's devoted servant, with the boots and boot-cleaning stuff. I wish to goodness I could go down ; maybe I should find hairpins and ammonia there, both of which I am bitterly in need of, particularly the ammonia, after those mosquitoes.

We stayed a few minutes this afternoon at Ashchyouka, where
there came off to us in a canoe an enterprising young Frenchman who has planted and tended a coffee plantation in this
out-of-the-way region, and which is now, I am glad to hear,
just coming into bearing. After leaving Ashchyouka, high land
showed to the N E., and at 5.15, without evident cause to the
uninitiated, the *Mové* took to whistling like a liner. A few
minutes later a factory shows up on the hilly north bank,
which is Woermann's ; then just beyond and behind
it we see the Government Post ; then Hatton and Cookson's
factory, all in a line. Opposite Hatton and Cookson's
there was a pretty little stern-wheel steamer nestling against
the steep clay bank of Lembarene Island when we come
in sight, but she instantly swept out from it in a perfect
curve, which lay behind her marked in frosted silver on the
water as she dropt down river. I hear now she was the
Éclaireur, the stern-wheeler which runs up and down the
Ogowé in connection with the Chargeurs Réunis Company,
subsidised by the Government, and when the *Mové* whistled,
she was just completing taking on 3,000 billets of wood for
fuel. She comes up from the Cape (Lopez) stoking half wood
and half coal as far as Njole and back to Lembarene ; from
Lembarene to the sea downwards she does on wood. In a
few minutes we have taken her berth close to the bank, and
tied up to a tree. The white engineer yells to the black engineer " Tom-Tom : Haul out some of them fire and open them
drains one time," and the stokers, with hooks, pull out the
glowing logs on to the iron deck in front of the furnace door,
and throw water over them, and the *Mové* sends a cloud of oil-
laden steam against the bank, coming perilously near scalding
some of her black admirers assembled there. I dare say she
felt vicious because they had been admiring the *Éclaireur*.

After a few minutes, I am escorted on to the broad verandah
of Hatton and Cookson's factory, and I sit down under a
lamp, prepared to contemplate, until dinner time, the wild
beauty of the scene. This idea does not get carried out ; in
the twinkling of an eye I am stung all round the neck, and
recognise there are lots too many mosquitoes and sandflies in
the scenery to permit of contemplation of any kind. Never

have I seen sandflies and mosquitoes in such appalling quantities. With a wild ping of joy the latter made for me, and I retired promptly into a dark corner of the verandah, swearing horribly, but internally, and fought them. Mr. Hudson, Agent-general, and Mr. Cockshut, Agent for the Ogowé, walk up and down the beach in front, doubtless talking cargo, apparently unconscious of mosquitoes ; but by and by, while we are having dinner, they get their share. I behave exquisitely, and am quite lost in admiration of my own conduct, and busily deciding in my own mind whether I shall wear one of those plain ring haloes, or a solid plate one, à la Cimabue, when Mr. Hudson says in a voice full of reproach to Mr. Cockshut, " You have got mosquitoes here, Mr. Cockshut." Poor Mr. Cockshut doesn't deny it ; he has got four on his forehead and his hands are sprinkled with them, but he says : " There are none at Njole," which we all feel is an absurdly lame excuse, for Njole is some ninety miles above Lembarene, where we now are. Mr. Hudson says this to him, tersely, and feeling he has utterly crushed Mr. Cockshut, turns on me, and utterly failing to recognise me as a suffering saint, says point blank and savagely, " You don't seem to feel these things, Miss Kingsley." Not feel them, indeed ! Why, I could cry over them. Well ! that's all the thanks one gets for trying not to be a nuisance in this world.

After dinner I go back on to the *Movê* for the night, for it is too late to go round to Kangwe and ask Mme. Jacot, of the Mission Evangelique, if she will take me in. The air is stiff with mosquitoes, and saying a few suitable words to them, I dash under the mosquito bar and sleep, lulled by their shrill yells of baffled rage.

June 8th.—In the morning, up at five. Great activity on beach. *Movê* synchronously taking on wood fuel and discharging cargo. A very active young French pastor from the Kangwe mission station is round after the mission's cargo. Mr. Hudson kindly makes inquiries as to whether I may go round to Kangwe and stay with Mme. Jacot. He says : " Oh, yes," but as I find he is not M. Jacot, I do not feel justified in accepting this statement without its having personal confirmation from Mme. Jacot, and so, leaving my luggage with the

Mové, I get them to allow me to go round with him and his cargo to Kangwe, about three-quarters of an hour's paddle round the upper part of Lembarene Island, and down the broad channel on the other side of it. Kangwe is beautifully situated on a hill, as its name denotes, on the mainland and north bank of the river. Mme. Jacot most kindly says I may come, though I know I shall be a fearful nuisance, for there is no room for me save M. Jacot's beautifully neat, clean, tidy study. I go back in the canoe and fetch my luggage from the *Move*, and say good-bye to Mr. Hudson, who gave me an immense amount of valuable advice about things, which was subsequently of great use to me, and a lot of equally good warnings which, if I had attended to, would have enabled me to avoid many, if not all, my misadventures in Congo Français.

I camped out that night in M. Jacot's study, wondering how he would like it when he came home and found me there ; for he was now away on one of his usual evangelising tours. Providentially Mme. Jacot let me have the room that the girls belonging to the mission school usually slept in, to my great relief, before M. Jacot came home.

I will not weary you with my diary during my first stay at Kangwe. It is a catalogue of the collection of fish, &c., that I made, and a record of the continuous, never-failing kindness and help that I received from M. and Mme. Jacot, and of my attempts to learn from them the peculiarities of the region, the natives, and their language and customs, which they both know so well and manage so admirably. I daily saw there what it is possible to do, even in the wildest and most remote regions of West Africa, and recognised that there is still one heroic form of human being whose praise has never adequately been sung, namely, the missionary's wife. With all the drawbacks and difficulties of the enervating climate, and the lack of trained domestic help, and with the addition of two small children of her own, Edmond the sententious, aged five, and Roger the great, aged eighteen months, and busy teething with phenomenal rapidity and vigour, and a tribe of school children of the Fan and Igalwa tribes, Mme. Jacot had that mission house as clean and tidy, and well ordered, as if it were in Paris.

One of the main comforts I had at Kangwe was the perfect
English spoken by both M. and Mme. Jacot; what that
amounted to I alone know, for I cannot speak a word of
French, neither could I give you dates until I left Kangwe on
the *Eclaireur*, for it is one of my disastrous habits well known
to my friends on the Coast that whenever I am happy, comfortable and content, I lose all knowledge of the date, the time of
day, and my hairpins. "It's the climate." But I kept my
fetish notes, except during two days when my right elbow
was out of repair in consequence of my first visit to a Fan [1]
fireside. It happened this way. Down on the river bank,
some one-and-a-half miles below Kangwe, lies Fula, a large
Fan village. Through Fula that ill-starred day I passed
with all the *éclat* of Wombwell's menagerie. Having been
escorted by half the population for a half mile or so beyond
the town, and being then nervous about Fans, from information received, I decided to return to Kangwe by another road,
if I could find it. I had not gone far on my quest before I
saw another village, and having had enough village work for
one day, I made my way quietly up into the forest on the steep
hillside overhanging the said village. There was no sort of
path up there, and going through a clump of shenja, I slipped,
slid, and finally fell plump through the roof of an unprotected
hut. What the unfortunate inhabitants were doing, I don't
know, but I am pretty sure they were not expecting me to
drop in, and a scene of great confusion occurred. My knowledge of Fan dialect then consisted of Kor-kor, so I said
that in as fascinating a tone as I could, and explained
the rest with three pocket handkerchiefs, a head of tobacco,
and a knife which providentially I had stowed in what
my nautical friends would call my afterhold—my pockets.
I also said I'd pay for the damage, and although this
important communication had to be made in trade English,
they seemed to understand, for when I pointed to the roof
and imitated writing out a book for it, the master of the house

---

[1] The proper way to spell this tribe's name is Faung, but as they are
called by the first writer on them, Du Chaillu, Fans, I keep that name.
They are also referred to as the M'pangwe, the Pahouines, the Fam-Fam,
the Osheba, and the Ba-fann. The latter is a plural form.

said " Um," and then laid hold of an old lady and pointed to her
and then to the roof, meaning clearly I had equally damaged
both, and that she was equally valuable.   I squared the family
all right, and I returned to Kangwe *viâ* Fula, without delay
and without the skin on my elbow.   Wishing to get higher
up the Ogowé, I took the opportunity of the river boat of
the Chargeurs Réunis going up to the Njole on one of her
trips, and joined her.

VIEW OF ONE BRANCH OF THE OGOWÉ FROM KANGWE.

June 22nd.—*Éclaireur,* charming little stern wheel steamer,
exquisitely kept.   She has an upper and a lower deck.   The
lower deck for business, the upper deck for white passengers
only.   On the upper deck there is a fine long deck house,
running almost her whole length.   In this are the officers' cabins,
the saloon and the passengers' cabins (two), both large and
beautifully fitted up.   Captain Verdier exceedingly pleasant
and constantly saying " N'est ce pas ? "   A quiet and singularly
clean engineer completes the white staff.   The passengers
consist of Mr. Cockshut, going up river to see after the

sub-factories; a French official bound for Franceville, which it will take him thirty-six days, go as quick as he can, in a canoe after Njole; a tremendously lively person who has had black water fever four times, while away in the bush with nothing to live on but manioc, a diet it would be far easier to die on under the circumstances. He is excellent company; though I do not know a word he says, he is perpetually giving lively and dramatic descriptions of things which I cannot but recognise. M. S——, with his pince-nez, the Doctor, and, above all, the rapids of the Ogowé, rolling his hands round and round each other and dashing them forward with a descriptive ejaculation of "Whish, flash, bum, bum, bump," and then comes what evidently represents a terrific fight for life against terrific odds. Wish to goodness I knew French, for wishing to see these rapids, I cannot help feeling anxious and worried at not fully understanding this dramatic entertainment regarding them. There is another passenger said to be the engineer's brother, a quiet, gentlemanly man. Captain argues violently with every one; with Mr. Cockshut on the subject of the wicked waste of money in keeping the *Mové* and not shipping all goods by the *Éclaireur*, "n'est-ce pas?" and with the French official on goodness knows what, but I fancy it will be pistols for two and coffee for one in the morning time. When the captain feels himself being worsted in argument, he shouts for support to the engineer and his brother. "N'est-ce pas?" he says, turning furiously to them. "Oui, oui, certainement," they say dutifully and calmly, and then he, refreshed by their support, dashes back to his controversial fray. He even tries to get up a row with me on the subject of the English merchants at Calabar, whom he asserts have sworn a kind of blood oath to ship by none but British African Company's steamers. I cannot stand this, for I know my esteemed and honoured friends the Calabar traders would ship by the *Flying Dutchman* or the devil himself if either of them would take the stuff at 15s. the ton. We have, however, to leave off this row for want of language, to our mutual regret, for it would have been a love of a fight.

Soon after leaving Lembarene Island, we pass the

mouth of the chief southern affluent of the Ogowé,
the Ngunie ; it flows in unostentatiously from the E.S.E.,
a broad, quiet river here with low banks and two
islands (Walker's islands) showing just off its entrance.
Higher up, it flows through a mountainous country, and at
Samba, its furthest navigable point, there is a wonderfully
beautiful waterfall, the whole river coming down over a low cliff,
surrounded by an amphitheatre of mountains. It takes the
Éclaireur two days steaming from the mouth of the Ngunie to
Samba, when she can get up ; but now, in the height of the
long dry season neither she nor the *Mové* can go because of the
sand banks ; so Samba is cut off until next October. Hatton
and Cookson have factories up at Samba, for it is an outlet
for the trade of Achango land in rubber and ivory, a trade
worked by the Akele tribe, a powerful, savage and difficult
lot to deal with, and just in the same condition, as far as I
can learn, as they were when Du Chaillu made his wonderful
journeys among them. While I was at Lembarene, waiting
for the *Éclaireur*, a notorious chief descended on a Ngunie
sub-factory, and looted it. The wife of the black trading agent
made a gallant resistance, her husband was away on a trading
expedition, but the chief had her seized and beaten, and
thrown into the river. An appeal was made to the Doctor, then
Administrator of the Ogowé, a powerful and helpful official,
and he soon came up with the little cannonier, taking Mr.
Cockshut with him to vindicate the honour of the French
flag, under which all factories here are. They, having got to
the scene of action, sent a message to the chief to come down
and talk the palaver. The chief being a natural-born idiot,
came with two of his head men and some retainers. Only he
and the head men were allowed into the room, and three or
four Senegalese soldiers held the door, while the three white men,
the Doctor, the captain of the cannonier and Mr. Cockshut took
a black man apiece, and after a fine fight, threw them and
bound them. The injured lady was then admitted, and given
a Kasanguru with which she returned thanks personally to the
chief with all her might, accompanying her operations with
verbal commentary on the way he had behaved to her, as any
lady would. The chief and his two head men were then

taken up to Njole, where they are at present engaged in the healthy and invigorating pursuit of navvying a stiff clay bank in the interest of the government.

The Samba natives are in no hurry for that job to be completed. They are quite tired of that chief themselves, and would have had to poison him off on their own account had not the Doctor intervened. In fact, every one is satisfied except the chief and the two head men, who have not acquired a taste for manual labour yet.

The banks of the Ogowé just above Lembarene Island are low ; with the forest only broken by village clearings and seeming to press in on those, ready to absorb them should the inhabitants cease their war against it. The blue mountains of Achango land show away to the E.S.E. in a range. Behind us, gradually sinking in the distance, is the high land on Lembarene Island.

Soon we run up alongside a big street of a village with four high houses rising a story above the rest, which are strictly ground floor ; it has also five or six little low open thatched huts along the street in front.[1] These may be fetish huts, or, as the captain of the *Sparrow* would say, " again they mayn't." For I have seen similar huts in the villages round Libreville, which were store places for roof mats, of which the natives carefully keep a store dry and ready for emergencies in the way of tornadoes, or to sell. We stop abreast of this village. Inhabitants in scores rush out and form an excited row along the vertical bank edge, several of the more excited individuals falling over it into the water.

Yells from our passengers on the lower deck. Yells from inhabitants on shore. Yells of *vite, vite* from the Captain. Dogs bark, horns bray, some exhilarated individual thumps the village drum, canoes fly out from the bank towards us. Fearful scrimmage heard going on all the time on the deck below. As soon as the canoes are alongside, our passengers from the lower deck, with their bundles and their dogs, pour

---

[1] The villages of the Fans and Bakele are built in the form of a street. When in the forest there are two lines of huts, the one facing the other, and each end closed by a guard house. When facing a river there is one line of huts facing the river frontage.

over the side into them. Canoes rock wildly and wobble off
rapidly towards the bank, frightening the passengers because
they have got their best clothes on, and fear that the
Éclaireur will start and upset them altogether with her
wash.

On reaching the bank, the new arrivals disappear into brown
clouds of wives and relations, and the dogs into fighting
clusters of resident dogs. Happy, happy day! For those men
who have gone ashore have been away on hire to the government and factories for a year, and are safe home in the bosoms
of their families again, and not only they themselves, but all the
goods they have got in pay. The remaining passengers below
still yell to their departed friends; I know not what they say,
but I expect it's the Fan equivalent for " Mind you write.
Take care of yourself. Yes, I'll come and see you soon," &c.,
&c. While all this is going on, the *Éclaireur* quietly slides
down river, with the current, broadside on as if she smelt her
stable at Lembarene. This I find is her constant habit whenever the captain, the engineer, and the man at the wheel are
all busy in a row along the rail, shouting overside, which
occurs whenever we have passengers to land. Her iniquity
being detected when the last canoe load has left for the shore,
she is spun round and sent up river again at full speed. Just
as this is being done, the inhabitants of the country salute the
captain with a complimentary salvo of guns. I am quietly
leaning against the side of his cabin door at the time, when
bang comes his answering salute from out of it, within three-
and-a-half inches of my right ear. Sensation of stun for
minutes. Captain apologetic; he " did not know I was there."
I am apologetic too; I did know he was there, " but I did
not know he was going to fire off his gun?" " He is forgiven."
" N'est-ce pas?" " Oui, oui, certainement," say I, quoting the
engineer. Peace restored.

We go on up stream; now and again stopping at little villages
to land passengers or at little sub-factories to discharge cargo,
until evening closes in, when we anchor and tie up at
O'Saomokita, where there is a sub-factory of Messrs. Woermann's, in charge of which is a white man, the only white man
between Lembarene and Njole. He comes on board and looks

only a boy, but is really aged twenty.   He is a Frenchman, and
was at Hatton and Cookson's first, then he joined Woermann's,
who have put him in charge of this place.   The isolation for
a white man must be terrible; sometimes two months will go
by without his seeing another white face but that in his look-
ing-glass, and when he does see another, it is only by a fleeting
visit such as we now pay him, and to make the most of this, he
stays on board to dinner.   While waiting for dinner that
night, as I am sitting at the saloon table, I see an apparition
on the settee opposite.   Is it fever coming on?   Or does it
arise from having got some brain cells permanently shaken
out of their place by that gun shock this afternoon?   I don't
mention it to my fellow passengers, who I notice do not seem
to see it, for fear of exciting their derision, but watch it
furtively during dinner.   It does not move nor multiply itself,
nor has it any phosphorescent halo.   Good signs, all these, but
still it cannot be a black silk chimney-pot hat.   After all, it
was, and it belongs to the captain.   How or why or when he
got it, I do not know—neither do I exactly know what he and
the passengers do with it, now I have gone to my cabin, which
is next to the saloon.   That the French official is the leading
spirit in proceedings I am quite sure, for I know his voice
wherein he is now singing tunes I have heard at the Jacots' as
hymn tunes. I am convinced of this, however, that they are not
hymn tunes now, because you don't dance a species of High-
land fling, which from the vibrations communicated to me I
know is being danced, to hymns; neither do you greet them
with shouts of laughter.   I wish—no, of course I don't, for it
comes neither under the head of fetish, nor fishes, and
moreover in the intervals, filled with violent conversation, I
hear the French official, I am perfectly sure, trying to convince
the others that I am an English officer in disguise on the spy;
which makes me feel embarrassed, and anything but flattered.
Wish to goodness I knew French, or how to flirt with that
French official so as to dispel the illusion.

June 23rd.—Start off steaming up river early in the
morning time.   Land ahead showing mountainous.   Rather
suddenly the banks grow higher.   Here and there in the
forest are patches which look like regular hand-made plant-

ations, which they are not, but only patches of engombie-gombie
trees, showing that at this place was once a native town.
Whenever land is clear along here, this tree springs up all over
the ground. It grows very rapidly, and has great leaves something like a sycamore leaf, only much larger. These leaves
growing in a cluster at the top of the straight stem give an
umbrella-like appearance to the affair; so the natives call them
and an umbrella by the same name, but whether they think
the umbrella is like the tree or the tree is like the umbrella, I
can't make out. I am always getting myself mixed over
this kind of thing in my attempts "to contemplate
phenomena from a scientific standpoint," as Cambridge
ordered me to do. I'll give the habit up. "You can't do
that sort of thing out here—It's the climate," and I will
content myself with stating the fact, that when a native
comes into a store and wants an umbrella, he asks for an
engombie-gombie.

The uniformity of the height of the individual trees in one
of these patches is striking, and it arises from their all starting
fair. I cannot make out other things about them to my
satisfaction, for you very rarely see one of them in the wild
bush, and then it does not bear a fruit that the natives collect
and use, and then chuck away the stones round their domicile.
Anyhow, there they are, all one height, and all one colour, and
apparently allowing no other vegetation to make any headway
among them. But I found when I carefully investigated
engombie-gombie patches that there were a few of the great,
slower-growing forest trees coming up amongst them, and in
time when these attain a sufficient height, their shade kills off
the engombie-gombie, and the patch goes back into the great
forest from which it came. The frequency of these patches
arises from the nomadic habits of the chief tribe in these
regions, the Fans. They rarely occupy one site for a
village for any considerable time on account—firstly, of their
wasteful method of collecting rubber by cutting down the vine,
which soon stamps it out of a district; and, secondly, from
their quarrelsome ways. So when a village of Fans has
cleared all the rubber out of its district, or has made the said
district too hot to hold it by rows with other villages, or has

got itself very properly shelled out and burnt for some attack on traders or the French flag in any form, its inhabitants clear off into another district, and build another village; for bark and palm thatch are cheap, and house removing just nothing; when you are an unsophisticated cannibal Fan you don't require a pantechnicon van to stow away your one or two mushroom-shaped stools, knives, and cooking-pots, and a calabash or so. If you are rich, maybe you will have a box with clothes in as well, but as a general rule all your clothes are on your back. So your wives just pick up the stools and the knives and the cooking-pots, and the box, and the children toddle off with the calabashes. You have, of course, the gun to carry, for sleeping or waking a Fan never parts with his gun, and so there you are "finish," as M. Pichault would say, and before your new bark house is up, there grows the engombie-gombie, where your house once stood. Now and again, for lack of immediate neighbouring villages to quarrel with, one end of a village will quarrel with the other end. The weaker end then goes off and builds itself another village, keeping an eye lifting for any member of the stronger end who may come conveniently into its neighbourhood to be killed and eaten. Meanwhile, the engombie-gombie grows over the houses of the empty end, pretending it's a plantation belonging to the remaining half. I once heard a new-comer hold forth eloquently as to how those Fans were maligned. "They say," said he, with a fine wave of his arm towards such a patch, "that these people do not till the soil—that they are not industrious—that the few plantations they do make are ill-kept —that they are only a set of wandering hunters and cannibals. Look there at those magnificent plantations!" I did look, but I did not alter my opinion of the Fans, for I know my old friend engombie-gombie when I see him.

This morning the French official seems sad and melancholy. I fancy he has got a Monday head (Kipling), but he revives as the day goes on. As we go on, the banks become hills and the broad river, which has been showing sheets of sandbanks in all directions, now narrows and shows only neat little beaches of white sand in shallow places along the bank. The current is terrific. The *Éclaireur* breathes hard, and has all she can do to fight her way up against it. Masses of black weathered rock in great boulders show along the exposed parts of both banks, left dry by the falling waters. Each bank is steep, and quantities of great trees, naked and bare, are hanging down from them, held by their roots and bush-rope entanglement from being swept away with the rushing current, and they make a great white fringe to the banks. The hills become higher and higher, and more and more abrupt, and the river runs between them in a gloomy ravine, winding to and fro ; we catch sight of a patch of white sand ahead, which I mistake for a white painted house, but immediately after doubling round a bend we see the houses of the Talagouga Mission Station. The *Éclaireur* forthwith has an hysteric fit on her whistle, so as to frighten M. Forget and get him to dash off in his canoe to her at once. Apparently he knows her, and does not hurry, but comes on board quietly. I find there will be no place for me to stay at at Njole, so I decide to go on in the *Éclaireur* and use her as an hotel while there, and then return and stay with Mme. Forget if she will have me. I consult M. Forget on this point. He says, " Oh, yes," but seems to have lost something of great value recently, and not to be quite clear where. Only manner, I suppose. When M. Forget has got his mails he goes, and the *Éclaireur* goes on ; indeed, she has never really stopped, for the water is too deep to anchor in here, and the terrific current would promptly whisk the steamer down out of Talagouga gorge were she to leave off fighting it. We run on up past Talagouga Island, where the river broadens out again a little, but not much, and reach Njole by nightfall, and tie up to a tree by Dumas factory beach. Usual uproar, but as Mr. Cockshut says, no mosquitoes. The mosquito belt ends abruptly at O' Soamokita.

June 24th.—Mr. Cockshut, who went ashore last night, kindly comes on board and asks me if I will go ashore to his sub-factory. Say yes, and go, but when ashore decide not to embarrass Hatton and Cookson's domestic economy by going into the factory. Besides, I see before me to the left a real road, the first road I have seen for months. I tell Mr. Cockshut I will go for a walk ; he seems relieved, and I start off down the road alone. Lovely road, bright yellow clay, as hard as paving stone. On each side it is most neatly hedged with pine-apples ; behind these, carefully tended, acres of coffee bushes planted in long rows. Certainly coffee is one of the most lovely of crops. Its grandly shaped leaves are like those of our medlar tree, only darker and richer green, the berries set close to the stem, those that are ripe, a

CAFFEA LIBERICA—LIBERIAN COFFEE.

rich crimson ; these trees, I think, are about three years old, and just coming into bearing ; for they are covered with full-sized berries, and there has been a flush of bloom on them this morning, and the delicious fragrance of their stephanotis-shaped and scented flowers lingers in the air. The country spreads before me a lovely valley encompassed by purple-blue mountains. Mount Talagouga looks splendid in a soft, infinitely deep blue, although it is quite close, just the other side of the river. The road goes on into the valley, as pleasantly as ever and more so. How pleasant it would be now, if our government along the Coast had the enterprise and public spirit of the French, and made such roads just on the remote chance of stray travellers dropping in on a steamer once in ten years or so and wanting a walk. Observe extremely neatly Igalwa built huts, people sitting on the bright clean ground outside them, making mats and baskets. " Mboloani," say I. " Ai Mbolo," say they, and knock off work to stare. Observe large wired-in enclosures on left-hand side of road—investigate—find they are tenanted by animals—goats, sheep, chickens, &c. Clearly this is a *jardin d'acclimatation*. No wonder the colony does not pay, if it goes in for this sort of thing, 206 miles inland, with simply no public to pay gate-money. While contemplating these things, hear awful hiss. Serpents ! No, geese. Awful fight. Grand things, good, old-fashioned, long skirts are for Africa ! Get through geese and advance in good order, but somewhat rapidly down road, turn sharply round corner of native houses. Turkey cock—terrific turn up. Flight on my part forwards down road, which is still going strong, now in a northerly direction, apparently indefinitely. Hope to goodness there will be a turning that I can go down and get back by, without returning through this ferocious farmyard. Intent on picking up such an outlet, I go thirty yards or so down the road. Hear shouts coming from a clump of bananas on my left. Know they are directed at me, but it does not do to attend to shouts always. Expect it is only some native with an awful knowledge of English, anxious to get up my family history—therefore accelerate pace. More shouts, and louder, of " Madame Gacon ! Madame Gacon ! " and out of the banana clump comes a big, plump, pleasant-looking gentleman, clad in a singlet and a divided skirt. White people must be attended to, so advance carefully towards him through a plantation of young coffee, apologising humbly for intruding on his domain. He smiles and bows beautifully, but—horror ! —he knows no English, I no French. Situation *très inexplicable et très interessante*, as I subsequently heard him remark ; and the worst of it is he is evidently bursting to know who I am, and what I am doing in the middle of his coffee plantation, for his it clearly is, as appears from his obsequious body-guard of blacks, highly interested in me also. We gaze at each other, and smile some more, but stiffly, and he stands bareheaded in the sun in an awful way. It's murder I'm committing, hard all! He, as is fitting for his superior sex, displays intelligence first and says, " Interpreter," waving his hand to the south. I say " Yes," in my best Fan, an enthusiastic, intelligent grunt which any one must understand. He leads the way back towards those geese—perhaps, by the by, that is why he wears those divided skirts—and we enter a beautifully neatly built bamboo house, and sit down opposite to each other at a table and wait for the interpreter who is being fetched. The house is low on the ground and of native construction, but most beautifully kept, and arranged with an air of artistic feeling quite as unexpected as the rest of my surroundings. I notice upon the walls sets of pictures of terrific incidents in Algerian campaigns, and a copy of that superb head of M. de Brazza in Arab headgear. Soon the black minions who have been sent to find one of the plantation hands who is supposed to know French and English, return with the " interpreter." That young man is a fraud. He does not know English—not even coast English —and all he has got under his precious wool is an abysmal ignorance darkened by terror ; and so, after one or two futile attempts and some frantic scratching at both those regions which an African seems to regard as the seats of intellectual inspiration, he bolts out of the door. *Situation terrible !* My host and I smile wildly at each other, and both wonder in our respective languages what, in the words of Mr. Squeers as mentioned in the classics—we " shall do in this 'ere most awful go." We are both going mad with the strain of the situation, when in walks the engineer's brother from the *Éclaireur.* He seems intensely surprised to find me sitting in his friend the planter's parlour after my grim and retiring conduct on the *Éclaireur* on my voyage up. But the planter tells him all, sousing him in torrents of words, full of the violence of an outbreak of pent-up emotion. I do not understand what he says, but I catch " *très inexplicable* " and things like that. The calm brother of the engineer sits down at the table, and I am sure tells the planter something like this : " Calm yourself, my friend, we picked up this curiosity at Lembarene. It seems quite harmless." And then the planter calmed, and mopped a perspiring brow, and so did I, and we smiled more freely, feeling the mental atmosphere had become less tense and cooler. We both simply beamed on our deliverer, and the planter gave him lots of things to drink. I had nothing about me except a head of tobacco in my pocket, which I did not feel was a suitable offering. Now the engineer's brother, although he would not own to it, knew English, so I told him how the beauty of the road had lured me on, and how I was interested in coffee-planting, and how much I admired the magnificence of this plantation, and all the enterprise and energy it represented.

" *Oui, oui, certainement,*" said he, and translated. My friend the planter seemed charmed ; it was the first sign of anything approaching reason he had seen in me. He wanted me to have *eau sucrée* more kindly than ever, and when I rose, intending to bow myself off and go, geese or no geese, back to the *Éclaireur,* he would not let me go. I must see the plantation, *toute la plantation.* So presently all three of us go out and thoroughly do the plantation, the most well-ordered, well-cultivated plantation I have ever seen, and a very noble monument to the knowledge and industry of the planter. For two hot hours these two perfect gentlemen showed me over it. I also behaved well, for petticoats, great as they are, do not prevent insects and catawumpuses of sorts walking up one's ankles and feeding on one as one stands on the long grass which has been most wisely cut and laid round the young trees for mulching. This plantation is of great extent on the hill-sides and in the valley bottom, portions of it are just coming into bearing. The whole is kept as perfectly as a garden, amazing as the work of one white man with only a staff of unskilled native labourers—at present only eighty of them. The coffee planted is of three kinds, the Elephant berry, the Arabian, and the San Thomé. During our inspection, we only had one serious misunderstanding, which arose from my seeing for the first time in my life tree-ferns growing in the Ogowé. There were three of them evidently carefully taken care of, among some coffee plants. It was highly exciting, and I tried to find out about them. It seemed, even in this centre of enterprise, unlikely that they had been brought just "for dandy" from the Australasian region, and I had never yet come across them in my wanderings save on Fernando Po. Unfortunately, my friends thought I wanted them to keep, and shouted for men to bring things and dig them up; so I had a brisk little engagement with the men, driving them from their prey with the point of my umbrella, ejaculating Kor Kor, like an agitated crow. When at last they understood that my interest in the ferns was scientific, not piratical, they called the men off and explained that the ferns had been found among the bush, when it was being cleared for the plantation.

Ultimately, with many bows and most sincere thanks from me, we parted, providentially beyond the geese, and I returned down the road to Njole, where I find Mr. Cockshut waiting outside his factory. He insists on taking me to the Post to see the Administrator, and from there he says I can go on to the *Éclaireur* from the Post beach, as she will be up there from Dumas'. Off we go up the road which skirts the river bank, a dwarf clay cliff, overgrown with vegetation, save where it is cleared for beaches. The road is short, but exceedingly pretty; on the other side from the river is a steep bank on which is growing a plantation of cacao. Lying out in the centre of the river you see Njole Island, a low, sandy one, timbered not only with bush, but with orange and other fruit trees; for formerly the Post and factories used to be situated on the island—now only their trees remain for various reasons, one being that in the wet season it is a good deal under water. Everything is now situated on the mainland north bank, in a straggling but picturesque line; first comes Woermann's factory, then Hatton and Cookson's, and John Holt's, close together with a beach in common, in a sweetly amicable style for factories, who as a rule firmly stockade themselves off from their next door neighbours. Then Dumas' beach, a little native village, the cacao patch and the Post at the up river end of things European, an end of things European, I am told, for a matter of 500 miles. Immediately beyond the

Post is a little river falling into the Ogowé, and on its further bank a small village belonging to a chief, who, hearing of the glories of the Government, came down like the Queen of Sheba—in intention, I mean, not personal appearance—to see it, and so charmed has he been that here he stays to gaze on it.

Although Mr. Cockshut hunted the Administrator of the Ogowé out of his bath, that gentleman is exceedingly amiable and charming, all the more so to me for speaking good English.   Personally, he is big, handsome, exuberant, and energetic.   He shows me round with a gracious enthusiasm, all manner of things—big gorilla teeth and heads, native spears and brass-nail-ornamented guns ; and explains, while we are in his study, that the little model canoe full of Kola nuts is the supply of Kola to enable him to sit up all night and work.   Then he takes us outside to see the new hospital which he, in his capacity as Administrator, during the absence of the professional Administrator on leave in France, has granted to himself in his capacity as Doctor ; and he shows us the captive chief and headman from Samba busily quarrying a clay cliff behind it so as to enlarge the governmental plateau, and the ex-ministers of the ex-King of Dahomey, who are deported to Njole, and apparently comfortable and employed in various non-menial occupations.   Then we go down the little avenue of cacao trees in full bearing, and away to the left to where there is now an encampment of Adoomas, who have come down as a convoy from Franceville, and are going back with another under the command of our vivacious fellow passenger, who, I grieve to see, will have a rough time of it in the way of accommodation in those narrow, shallow canoes which are lying with their noses tied to the bank, and no other white man to talk to.   What a blessing he will be conversationally to Franceville when he gets in.   The Adooma encampment is very picturesque, for they have got their bright-coloured chintz mosquito-bars erected as tents.

Dr. Pélessier then insists on banging down monkey bread-fruit with a stick, to show me their inside.   Of course they burst over his beautiful white clothes.   I said they would, but men will be men.   Then we go and stand under the two lovely odeaka trees that make a triumphal-arch-like gateway to the Post's beach from the river, and the doctor discourses in a most interesting way on all sorts of subjects. We go on waiting for the *Éclaireur*, who, although it is past four o'clock, is still down at Dumas' beach. I feel nearly frantic at detaining the Doctor, but neither he nor Mr. Cockshut seem in the least hurry. But at last I can stand it no longer. The vision of the Administrator of the Ogowé, worn out, but chewing Kola nut to keep himself awake all night while he finishes his papers to go down on the *Éclaireur* to-morrow morning, is too painful ; so I say I will walk back to Dumas' and go on the *Éclaireur* there, and try to liberate the Administrator from his present engagements, so that he may go back and work. No good! He will come down to Dumas' with Mr. Cockshut and me. Off we go, and just exactly as we are getting on to Dumas' beach, off starts the *Éclaireur* with a shriek for the Post beach. So I say good-bye to Mr. Cockshut, and go back to the Post with Dr. Pélessier, and he sees me on board, and to my immense relief he stays on board a good hour and a half, talking to other people, so it is not on my head if he is up all night.

June 25th.—*Éclaireur* has to wait for the Administrator until ten, because he has not done his mails. At ten he comes on board like an amiable tornado, for he himself is going to Cape Lopez. I am grieved to see them carrying on board, too, a French official very ill with fever. He is the engineer of the cannonier, and they are taking him down to Cape Lopez, where they hope to get a ship to take him up to Gaboon, and to the hospital on the *Minervé*. I heard subsequently that the poor fellow died about forty hours after leaving Njole at Achyouka in Kama country.

We get away at last, and run rapidly down river, helped by the terrific current. The *Éclaireur* has to call at Talagouga for planks from M. Gacon's sawmill. As soon as we are past the tail of Talagouga Island, the *Éclaireur* ties her whistle string to a stanchion, and goes off into a series of screaming fits, as only she can. What she wants is to get M. Forget or M. Gacon, or better still both, out in their canoes with the wood waiting for her, because " she cannot anchor in the depth,"

" nor can she turn round," and " backing plays the mischief with any ship's engines," and " she can't hold her own against the current," and—then Captain Verdier says things I won't repeat, and throws his weight passionately on the whistle string, for we are in sight of the narrow gorge of Talagouga, with the Mission Station apparently slumbering in the sun. This puts the *Éclaireur* in an awful temper. She goes down towards it as near as she dare, and then frisks round again, and runs up river a little way and drops down again, in violent hysterics the whole time. Soon M. Gacon comes along among the trees on the bank, and laughs at her. A rope is thrown to him, and the panting *Éclaireur* tied up to a tree close in to the bank, for the water is deep enough here to moor a liner in, only there are a good many rocks. In a few minutes M. Forget and several canoe loads of beautiful red-brown mahogany planks are on board, and things being finished, I say good-bye to the captain, and go off with M. Forget in a canoe, to the shore.

CHAPTER VIII

TALAGOUGA

Concerning the district of Talagouga, with observations and admonitions
on the capture of serpents.

MME. FORGET received me most kindly and hospitably, she,
with her husband and her infant daughter, and M. and Mme.
Gacon represent the Mission Evangélique and the white race
at Talagouga. Mme. Gacon is the lady the planter took
me for; and when I saw her, with her sweet young face and
masses of pale gold-coloured hair, I felt highly flattered.
Either that planter must be very short-sighted or the colour
of my hair must have misled him, not that mine is pale gold,
but hay-coloured. I don't know how he did it. Mme. Forget
is a perfectly lovely French girl, with a pale transparent skin
and the most perfect great dark eyes, with indescribable
charm, grace of manner, and vivacity in conversation. It
grieves me to think of her, wasted on this savage wilderness
surrounded by its deadly fever air. Oranie Forget, otherwise
the baby, although I am not a general admirer of babies of
her age—a mere matter of months—is also charming; I am
not saying this because she flattered me by taking to me—
all babies and children do that—but she has great style, and
I have no doubt she will grow up to be a beauty too, but she
would have made a dead certainty of it, if she had taken after
her mother.

The mission station at Talagouga is hitched on to the rocky
hillside, which rises so abruptly from the river that there is
hardly room for the narrow footpath which runs along the
river frontage of it. And when you are on the Forgets'
verandah it seems as if you could easily roll right off it into the
dark, deep, hurrying Ogowé. I suggest this to Mme. Forget as

an awful future for Oranie, but she has thought of it and wired
the verandah up.   You go up a steep flight of steps into the
house, which is raised on poles some fifteen feet above the
ground in front, and you walk through it against the hillside,
made up mostly of enormous boulders of quartz, for Talagouga
mountains are the western termination of the side of the Sierra
del Cristal range. When you get through the house you come to
more stairs, cut out now in the hillside rock and leading to the

STATION OF THE MISSION ÉVANGÉLIQUE, TALAGOUGA.

kitchen to the right, and to the store buildings ; to the left they
continue up to the church, which is still higher up the hill-face.
That church is the prettiest I have seen in Africa.   I do not
say I should like to sit in it, because there seems to me no
proper precautions taken to exclude snakes, lizards, or insects,
and there would be great difficulty in concentrating one's
mind on the higher life in the presence of these fearfully
prevalent lower forms. Talagouga church commences as a

strong wooden framework on which is hung the bell, and then
to the right of this structure, is another which is a roof supported by bare poles. At its lower end there is a little daïs on
which stands a table and a chair, the yellow clay floor slopes
abruptly up hill and the pews consist of round, none too thick,
poles, neatly mounted on stumps, some ten inches from the
ground. I should have thought those pews were quite perfection for an African congregation ; but they tell me I am wrong
and that even Elders go off sound asleep on them, quite comfortably, I suppose like bats ; I don't mean upside down, you
understand, but merely by an allied form of muscular action,
the legs clinching on to the pole-pew during sleep. Beyond the
church, the hillside is cut by a ravine, and out of the dense
forest that grows in it runs a beautiful, clear stream. It has
been dammed back above, for it is harnessed to M. Gacon's
saw-mill. The building of this dam, the erection of the two
big water-wheels, the saw, and the shed that covers it, indeed
all the work connected with the affair, has been done by
M. Gacon with his own hands, and not only has he dammed
back the water, and put up his saw-mill, but he still works
hard at it daily, cutting hundreds of fine red-wood planks
for the service of the mission, shipping them by the *Éclaireur*,
in flighty little canoes in this risky bit of river, and keeping a
big store of them under his house—a bamboo structure, once
Talagouga church—and all this with no other assistance but
unskilled native labour. What this means you might understand a little if I were to write details from June to January,
and then you were to come out here and take a turn at some
such job yourself, to finish off your education. Across the
other side of the ravine and high up, is perched the house
which Dr. Nassau built, when he first established mission
work on the Upper Ogowé. The house is now in ruins ;
but in front of it, as an illustration of the transitory nature
of European life in West Africa, is the grave of Mrs. Nassau,
among the great white blocks of quartz rock, its plain stone
looking the one firm, permanent, human-made-thing about the
place ; below it, down the hill, are some houses inhabited by the
native employés on the station : and passing these, still going
down towards the river, you come to a wooden bridge spanning

the mill-stream, and crossing this, you find yourself back on the
path which goes in front of M. Gacon's house; passing
this you come to the house inhabited by the girls in the
mission school, presided over by the comely Imgrimina, wife
of Isaac, the Jack-Wash, and a few steps more bring you to
the foot of the Forgets' verandah staircase. The path runs
on a little beyond this to the east, on a slightly broader, level
bit of ground, behind which rises the hillside, and it ends
abruptly at another ravine with another, but smaller, stream ;
beyond this the hills come down right into the river, and on
the small, flat piece of ground there are a few more native
houses, belonging to the Bible-readers, and so on ; up on the
hillside above them hangs a garden, apparently kept in position
by quantities of stout wooden pegs driven into the ground ;
these really are to keep the artificially levelled beds of
mould, and the things in them, from being washed down
into the river by the torrential wet season's rains. All sorts of
things are supposed by the gardener to grow in those beds,
but Mme. Forget declares there is nothing but a sort of salad.
It is a very nice salad; I believe it to be dandelion, and there is
plenty of it, and Mme. Forget might be more resigned about it ;
on the other hand, I agree with her, and quite fail to see why the
gardener's salary should be continually raised, as he desires,
nor exactly what bearing his abdominal afflictions have on the
non-productiveness of the tomato plants, nor why, again, he
should be paid more because of them, for curious abdominal
symptoms are very common among the whole of the West
African tribes. My own opinion about that garden is that
there are too many plantains in it, and too much shade.
The whole station is surrounded by dense, dark-coloured,
and forbidding-looking forest ; in front of it runs the
dark rapid river, profoundly deep, but not more than 400
yards wide here ; on the opposite side of it there is another
hillside similarly forested, and unbroken by clearing, save in
one little spot higher up than the mission, where there is
a little native town and a small sub-factory of Hatton and
Cookson's.

Talagouga is grand, but its scenery is undoubtedly grim,
and its name, signifying the gateway of misery, seems applic-

able.[1] It must be a melancholy place to live in, the very air lies heavy and silent. I never saw the trees stirred by a breeze the whole time I was there, even the broad plantain leaves seemed to stand sleeping day out and day in, motionless. This is because the mountains shelter it back and front ; and on either side, promontories, running out from both banks, make a narrow winding gorge for the river channel. The only sign of motion you get is in the Ogowé ; if you look at it you see, in spite of its dark quiet face, that it is sweeping past at a terrific pace. One great gray rock sticks up through it just below the mission beach, and from that lies ever a silver streak from the hindrance it gives the current. Every now and again you will notice a canoe full of wild, naked, or nearly naked savages, silent because they are Fans, and don't sing like Igalwas or M'pongwe when in canoes. They are either paddling very hard and creeping very slowly upwards, against one of the banks, or just keeping her head straight and going rapidly down. Now and again you will hear the laboured beat of the engines of either the *Mové* or *Éclaireur*, before you see the vessel and hear the warning shriek of their whistles ; and you can watch her as she comes up fighting her way to Njole, or see her as she comes down, slipping past like a dream in a few seconds, and that is all. My first afternoon sufficed to allow of my seeing the station. M. Jacot reports it to have thirty-two buildings on it, but he is a slave to truth, and counts all the cook-houses, &c. Houses deserving of the name there are but three—the Gacons', the girls' and the Forgets'.

Mme. Forget took no end of care of me, and I look at my clean, tidy, comfortable room with terror, until I find a built out bath-room wherein I shall be able to make awful messes with fish, &c., without disgracing myself and country ; and joy inexpressible ! " no mosquitoes," yet still curtain.   I told you before I had heard they ended at O Soamokita, but when I see people putting up mosquito-curtains over their beds I always have doubts ; besides, along here you always find people deny having mosquitoes, if they can, without committing violent per-

---

[1] Mr. R. B. N. Walker, I believe, holds this name is Otal a ma gouga ; A gouga = hardship, privation.

jury ; if they cannot deny it, as was the case with Mr. Cockshut at Lembarene, they try and turn the conversation or say other places are worse.   Owing to this blissful absence of irritation I slept profoundly my first night at Talagouga, but roused by awful sounds in the morning—time, 5.30—sit straight up in bed " one time."   Never noticed mission had donkey yesterday, but they have, and it's off in an epileptic fit.   As the sound amplifies and continues a flash of reason succeeds this first impression.   It's morning service in the church, and the natives are just singing hymns.   In after days the sound always produces the same physical shock, but the mental one dies out crushed under the weight of knowledge of the sound's origin.

I spent my second day talking to Mme. Forget, whose English is perfectly good, although she tells me she resisted education most strenuously in this direction from patriotic motives.   I must say I bow down and worship the spirit of patriotic fire in the French, not that I would imply for one moment that I, as an Englishwoman, suffered from it in Congo Français.   They always gave me the greatest help in getting about their territory and every kindness—of course there was no reason why they should not do so, for they have no reason to be anything but proud of the great things they have done here and the admirable way this noble province of theirs is administered.   Congo Français is a very different thing to Congo Belge, a part of the world I shall not wander into again until it becomes Congo Français, and that won't be long.   I now salve my pride as an Englishwoman with the knowledge that were a Frenchwoman to travel in any of our West Coast settlements, she would have as warm and helpful a welcome as I get here, and I will be femininely spiteful, and say she would do more harm in the English settlements than ever I did in the French.   Think of Mme. Jacot, Mme. Forget, or Mme. Gacon going into Calabar, for example, why there wouldn't be a whole heart left in the place in twenty-four hours !

On the second day I spent at Talagouga I also made the acquaintance of Monsieur Pichon, a very stately, homing, Antwerp pigeon ; his French feeling was a hopeless barrier to a mutual friendship arising between us. I admire him sincerely. His personal appearance, his grand manner, the regular way in which he orders his life, going down regularly on to one particular stone at the river's brink to make his toilet ; attending every meal during the day ; and going to roost on one particular door-top, commands admiràtion and respect. But to me he behaved cruelly. He bullied me out of food at meal times, always winding up with a fight, holding on to my finger with his beak like a vice. I know he regards me as a defeated slave and took as mere due service my many rescues of him from behind a mirror, which hung tilted from the wall and behind which he used constantly to fall, dazzled by the vision of his own beauty as he flew up in front of the glass. There is another low-down pigeon domesticated at Talagouga, but he was a nobody, and Monsieur let him know it, in spite of several rebellions on his part. And there were also two very small, very black kittens which were being carefully, but alas unavailingly nursed, for their mother had abandoned them.

M. Forget did not think I should have much chance of getting fish for specimens, because he said, although the Fans catch plenty, they do not care to sell them, as they are the main article of food in this foodless region, still he would try and persuade them to bring them to me, and so success-ful were his efforts that that afternoon several Fans turned up with specimens. For these I gave, as usual when opening a trade in a district, fancy prices, a ruse that proved so successful here that I was soon at my wits' end for bottles and spirit—trade gin I might have got, but there is not sufficient alcohol in trade gin to preserve specimens in. Again M. Forget came to the rescue and let me have a bottle of alcohol out of the dispensary.

I got a fearful fright during my second night at Talagouga. I went to bed quite lulled into a sense of security by the mosquitolessness of the previous night. I was aroused be-tween 2 and 3 o'clock A.M. by acute pain from punctured wounds on the chest and the mosquito curtain completely down and smothering me. My first fear was that I had brought a mosquito or so of the Lembarene strain up to

Talagouga with me, who had just recovered from the journey and were having their evening meal. I fought my way out of the mosquito-curtain and trod on a cold flabby thing which kindly said " Croak "—introducing itself as a harmless frog, and dispelling fear number two, namely that it was a snake. I then had a sporting hunt for matches in the inky dark—upset half the room before I found them, but when this was done, and I got the candle alight, I found a big black cat sitting smiling on my bed, and conjecturing she was the bereaved mother of those afflicted, deserted, kittens, I got her off, and tied up the mosquito-bar to the ceiling again, and then took her in with me under it to finish my night's rest ; for I feared if I left her outside she would cause another tender awakening of memories of those Lembarene mosquitoes. The frog, having got his wind again, flip-flapped about the floor all night, croak, croak-ing to his outdoor relations about the unprovoked outrage that had been committed on him.

I spent the succeeding days in buying fish from the natives, who brought it in quantities, mostly of two sorts, and of course wanted enormous prices for it ; but I confess I rather enjoy the give-and-take fun of bartering against their extor-tion, and my trading with them introduced us to each other so that when we met in the course of the long climbing walks I used to take beetle-hunting in the bush behind the mission station, we knew about each other, and did not get much shocked or frightened.

That forest round Talagouga was one of the most difficult bits of country to get about in I ever came across, for it was dense and there were no bush paths. No Fan village wants to walk to another Fan village for social civilities, and all their trade goes up and down the river in canoes. No doubt some miles inland there are bush paths, but I never struck one, so they must be pretty far away. Neither did I come across any villages in the forest, they seem all to be on the river bank round here.

The views from the summits of the abruptly shaped hills round Talagouga are exceedingly grand, and give one a good idea of the trend of the Sierra del Cristal range in this district ; to the east, the higher portions of the ranges showed, just beyond Njole, a closely set series of strangely shaped summits beautifully purple-blue, running away indefinitely to the N.N.W. and S.E.; and when the day was clear, one could see the mountains of Achangoland away to the S.S.E., from their shape evidently the same formation, but not following the same direction as the range of the Sierra del Cristal. The hills I had personally to deal with were western flanking hills of the Sierra—all masses of hard black rock with veins and blocks of crystalline quartz. Between the interstices of the rocks, was the rich vegetable mould made by hundreds of thousands of years of falling leaves and timber. The undergrowth was very dense and tangled among the great gray-white columns of the high trees; the young shoots of this undergrowth were interesting, not so often rose-coloured as those round Lembarene, but usually in the denser parts a pale creamy-white, or a deep blue. I was fool enough to fancy that a soft, delicate-leaved, white-shoot-bearing plant had, on its own account, a most fragrant scent, but I soon found the scent came from the civet cats, which abound here, and seem to affect this shrub particularly. It is very quaint the intense aversion the Africans have to this scent, and the grimaces and spitting that goes on when they come across it; their aversion is shared by the elephants. I once saw an elephant put his trunk against one of these scented bushes, have it up in a second, and fly off into the forest with an Oh lor! burn-some-brown-paper! pocket-handkerchief-please expression all over him. The natives, knowing this, use civet in hunting elephants, as I will some day describe. The high trees were of various kinds—acacias, red-wood, African oak, a little ebony, and odeaka, and many other kinds I know not even the native names of to this day. One which I know well by sight gives, when cut, a vividly yellow wood of great beauty. Now and again on exposed parts of the hillside, one comes across great falls of timber which have been thrown down by tornadoes either flat on to the ground—in which case under and among them are snakes and scorpions, and getting over them is slippery work; or thrown sideways and hanging against their fellows, all covered with gorgeous drapery of climbing, flowering plants—in which case they present to the human atom a wall made up of strong tendrils and climbing grasses, through which the said atom has to cut its way with a matchette and push into the crack so made, getting, the while covered with red driver-ants, and such like, and having sensational meetings with blue-green snakes, dirty green snakes with triangular horned heads, black cobras, and boa constrictors. I never came back to the station without having been frightened half out of my wits, and with one or two of my smaller terrifiers in cleft sticks to bottle. When you get into the way, catching a snake in a cleft stick is perfectly simple. Only mind you have the proper kind of stick, split far enough up, and keep your attention on the snake's head, that's his business end, and the tail which is whisking and winding round your wrist does not matter : there was one snake, by the way, of which it was impossible to tell, in the forest, which was his head. The natives swear he has one at each end ; so you had better " Lef 'em," even though you know the British Museum would love to have him, for he is very venomous, and one of the few cases of death from snake-bite I have seen, was from this species.

Several times, when further in the forest, I came across a trail of flattened undergrowth, for fifty or sixty yards, with a horrid musky smell that demonstrated it had been the path of a boa constrictor, and nothing more.

It gave me more trouble and terror to get to the top of those Talagouga hillsides than it gave me to go twenty miles in the forests of Old Calabar, and that is saying a good deal, but when you got to the summit there was the glorious view of the rest of the mountains, stretching away, interrupted only by Mount Talagouga to the S.E. by E. and the great, grim, dark forest, under the lowering gray sky, common during the dry season on the Equator. No glimpse or hint did one have of the Ogowé up here, so deep down in its ravine does it flow. A person coming to the hill tops close to Talagouga from the N. or N.N.W. and turning back in his track from here might be utterly unconscious that one of the great rivers of the world was flowing, full and strong, within some 800 feet of him. There is a strange sense of secretiveness about all these West African forests ; but I never saw it so marked as in these that shroud the Sierra del Cristal. I very rarely met any natives in this part; those that I did were hunters, big, lithe men with all their toilet attention concentrated on their hair. On two occasions I ran some risk from having been stalked in mistake for game by these hunters. " Hoots toots, mon, a verra pretty thing it would hae been for an Englishwoman to hae been shot in mistake for a gorilla by a cannibal Fan of all folks," was a Scotch friend's commentary. I escaped, how-ever, because these men get as close as they can to their prey before firing; and when they found out their mistake they were not such cockney sportsmen as to kill me because I was something queer, and we stood and stared at each other, said a few words in our respective languages, and parted. One thing that struck me very much in these forests was the absence of signs of fetish worship which are so much in evidence in Calabar, where you constantly come across trees worshipped as the residences of spirits, and little huts put up over offerings to bush souls.

Thanks to the kindness of M. Forget, I had an opportunity of visiting Talagouga Island—a grant of which has been made by the French Government to the Mission Évangélique, who, owing to the inconveniences of being hitched precariously on a hillside, intend shortly removing from their present situation, and settling on the island.

Talagouga Island is situated in the middle of the river, about halfway between the present mission beach and Njole. It is a mile long and averages about a quarter of a mile wide; the up-river end of it is a rocky low hill, and it tapers down river from this, ending in a pretty little white sandbank. At the upper end there is a reef of black rocks against which the Ogowé strikes, its brown face turning white with agitation at being interrupted, when it is in such a tearing hurry to get to the South Atlantic. When going up river to it in a canoe, creeping up along by the bank, I had more chance of seeing details than when on the *Éclaireur* with her amusing distractions. The first object of interest was Talagouga rock; seen at close quarters, it rises a gray, rough, weathered head, much water-worn, some twenty feet above the dry season level of the water. Goodness knows how far it is down to its bed on the river bottom. Up to a few years ago it was regarded as the mark between the regions of Gaboon and Congo Français, but this division is now done away with, and there is no Gaboon, but the whole province is Congo Français. So Talagouga rock gets no official position, and is left to the veneration it is held in, as the dwelling-place of an Ombuiri. On the edge on the top of the bank, adjacent to Talagouga rock, is a small swamp, and by the side of it stands another gigantic monolith which, judging the height of Talagouga rock above water to be twenty feet, must be between fifty and sixty feet high. It does not get any veneration at all ; but if that great Stonehenge-like thing were in the Rivers, it would be a great ju-ju, and be covered round its base with bits of white calico, and have bottles of gin set in front of it, and calabashes of hard-boiled eggs and goodness knows what. That rock is thrown away on these Bantu ; that comes of being magnificent at the wrong time and place. Opposite to Talagouga rock, on the other bank, is perched on top of a dwarf clay cliff the village of Talagouga (Fan) with Hatton and Cookson's sub-factory in it, presided over by a Sierra Leonian. On the north bank, a little higher up, M. Forget pointed out to me a place in the forest where, a year or two ago, the strange dwarf people had a village ; there are none of them there now, as they wander to and fro in the forest, never remaining many months in one spot. They are diffused, in small communities, all over the forest of Congo Francais ; but their chief haunt seems to be among the Bakele tribe in Achangoland. We crossed the river and then landed, clambering up a steep bank on to the lower end of the island. M. Forget stated that a path ran up to the upper end, which had been cut when the island was surveyed before being registered to the mission. I did not think much of it as a path, nor did M. Forget, I fancy, after ten minutes' experience of it, for it had considerably grown up : and although this island is not quite so densely timbered as the mainland, nor made in such acute angles, still it has these attributes to a considerable extent, as it is a real island of a rocky nature, and not a glorified sandbank that has grabbed its earth and vegetation from shipwrecked pieces of the main bank and dead trees, like those islands round and below Lembarene. However, scratched but safe we got to the upper end; and M. Forget went off to see after the orange, lime, banana, and plantain trees that had been planted on the upper end of the island where the mission houses are to be built. I wandered about seeing things, among others an encampment of Fans who are cutting down the timber to make room for the building, which is not yet commenced; and some wonderful tiny bays in the bank, along the southern side, where the current is less strong, or rather, I suppose, deflected against the mainland bank by the rock reef. These bays are filled in the dry season by banks of white sand in which sparkle fragments of mica, and when you walk on them they give out a musical, soft hum in a strange way. "Unfortunately," M. Forget says, so far no spring water has been found on the island. I say unfortunately in notes of quotation as I do not agree with him that the absence of spring water is a misfortune, but regard it as a blessing in disguise, for, to my way of thinking, the Ogowé water, exposed to the air, with its swift current, is safer stuff to drink than *decoc terræ Africano*—spring water, I mean.

While we are waiting for the return of the canoe which has gone to the mainland to deposit an Evangelist in a village, M. Forget has a palaver with the Fans, who are very slowly shaving the trees from the top of the hill. They agreed to do this thing for the wood, but it has since occurred to them that they would like to be paid wages as well. They are sweet unsophisticated children of nature, these West African tribes; little thoughts like these are constantly arising in their minds, and on all hands—missionary, governmental and trading—I am told these Fans are exceedingly treacherous and you can never trust them to hold to a bargain. I will say this is not the case with other African tribes I have come across. In the Rivers, for example, when a jam is made, it's made, and they will stick to it all, save the time clause, more honourably than twenty per cent. of white men would. Our canoe returns before "palaver done set"; and we go off home, the blue mists rising among the trees and reflecting in the Ogowé a deeper and more intense blue, adding

another element to a wonderfully lovely scene that is well
accompanied by the elaborate songs of the canoe crew and
the sound of their paddles. We are down again at Talagouga
beach in a far shorter time than it took us to come up.

All the balance of the time I was at Talagouga I spent in
trying to find means to get up into the rapids above Njole,
for my heart got more and more set on them now that I saw
the strange forms of the Talagouga fishes, and the differences
between them and the fishes at Lembarene. For some time
no one whom I could get hold of regarded it as a feasible
scheme, but, at last, M. Gacon thought it might be managed ;
I said I would give a reward of 100 francs to any one who
would lend me a canoe and a crew, and I would pay the
working expenses, food, wages, &c. M. Gacon had a good
canoe and could spare me two English-speaking Igalwas, one
of whom had been part of the way with MM. Allégret and
Teisserès, when they made their journey up to Franceville
and then across to Brazzaville and down the Congo two years
ago. He also thought we could get six Fans to complete the
crew. I was delighted, packed my small portmanteau with a
few things, got some trade goods, wound up my watch,
ascertained the date of the day of the month, and borrowed
three hairpins from Mme. Forget, then down came disappointment. On my return from the bush that evening, Mme. Forget
said M. Gacon said " it was impossible," the Fans round
Talagouga wouldn't go at any price above Njole, because
they were certain they would be killed and eaten by the
up-river Fans. Internally consigning the entire tribe to
regions where they will get a rise in temperature, even on this
climate, I went with Mme. Forget to M. Gacon, and we
talked it over ; finally, M. Gacon thought he could let me
have two more Igalwas from Hatton and Cookson's beach
across the river. Sending across there we found this could
be done, so I now felt I was in for it, and screwed my courage
to the sticking point —no easy matter after all the information
I had got into my mind regarding the rapids of the River
Ogowé.

CHAPTER IX

THE RAPIDS OF THE OGOWÉ

The Log of an Adooma canoe during a voyage undertaken to the rapids of the River Ogowé, with some account of the divers disasters that befell thereon.

I ESTABLISH myself on my portmanteau comfortably in the canoe, my back is against the trade box, and behind that is the usual mound of pillows, sleeping mats, and mosquito-bars of the Igalwa crew ; the whole surmounted by the French flag flying from an indifferent stick.

M. and Mme. Forget provide me with everything I can possibly require, and say, that the blood of half my crew is half alcohol ; on the whole it is patent they don't expect to see me again, and I forgive them, because they don't seem cheerful over it ; but still it is not reassuring—nothing is about this affair, and it's going to rain. It does, as we go up the river to Njole, where there is another risk of the affair collapsing, by the French authorities declining to allow me to proceed. On we paddled, M'bo the head man standing in the bows of the canoe in front of me, to steer, then I, then the baggage, then the able-bodied seamen, including the cook also standing and paddling ; and at the other extremity of the canoe—it grieves me to speak of it in this unseamanlike way, but in these canoes both ends are alike, and chance alone ordains which is bow and which is stern—stands Pierre, the first officer, also steering ; the paddles used are all of the long-handled, leaf-shaped Igalwa type. We get up just past Talagouga Island and then tie up against the bank of M. Gazenget's plantation, and make a piratical raid on its bush for poles. A gang of his mèn come down to us, but only to chat. One of them, I notice, has had something happen severely to one side of his face. I ask M'bo what's the matter, and he answers, with a derisive laugh, " He be fool man, he go for tief plantain and done got shot." M'bo does not make it clear where the sin in this affair is exactly located ; I expect it is in being " fool man." Having got our supply of long stout poles we push off and paddle on again. Before we reach Njole I recognise my crew have got the grumbles, and at once inquire into the reason. M'bo sadly informs me that " they no got chop," having been provided only with plantain, and no meat or fish to eat with it. I promise to get them plenty at Njole, and contentment settles on the crew, and they sing. After about three hours we reach Njole, and I proceed to interview the authorities. Dr. Pélessier is away down river, and the two gentlemen in charge don't understand English ; but Pierre translates, and the letter which M. Forget has kindly written for me explains things, and so the palaver ends satisfactorily, after a long talk. First, the official says he does not like to take the responsibility of allowing me to endanger myself in those rapids. I explain I will not hold any one responsible but myself, and I urge that a lady has been up before, a Mme. Quinee. He says " Yes, that is true, but Madame had with her a husband and many men, whereas I am alone and have only eight Igalwas and not Adoomas, the proper crew for the rapids, and they are away up river now with the convoy." " True, oh King ! " I answer, " but Madame Quinee went right up to Lestourville, whereas I only want to go sufficiently high up the rapids to get typical fish. And these Igalwas are great men at canoe work, and can go in a canoe anywhere that any mortal man can go "—this to cheer up my Igalwa interpreter—" and as for the husband, neither the Royal Geographical Society's list, in their ' Hints to Travellers,' nor Messrs. Silver, in their elaborate lists of articles necessary for a traveller in tropical climates, make mention of husbands." If they did, by the by, they would say he was to be green, but they don't say a word about one. However, the official ultimately says Yes, I may go, and parts with me as with one bent on self-destruction. This affair being settled I start off, like an old hen with a brood of chickens to provide for, to get chop for my men, and go first to Hatton and Cookson's factory. I find its white Agent is down river after stores, and John Holt's Agent says he has got no beef nor fish, and is precious short of provisions for himself ; so I go back to Dumas', where I find a most amiable French gentleman, who says he will let me have as much fish or beef as I want, and to this supply he adds some delightful bread biscuits. M'bo and the crew beam with satisfaction ; mine is clouded by finding, when they have carried off the booty to the canoe, that the Frenchman will not let me pay for it. Therefore taking the opportunity of his back being turned for a few minutes, I buy and pay for, across the store counter, some trade things, knives, cloth, &c. Then I say good-bye to the Agent. " Adieu, Mademoiselle," says he in a for-ever tone of voice. Indeed I am sure I have caught from these kind people a very pretty and becoming mournful manner, and there's not another white station for 500 miles where I can show it off. Away we go, still damp from the rain we have come through, but drying nicely with the day, and cheerful about the chop.

The Ogowé is broad at Njole and its banks not mountainous, as at Talagouga ; but as we go on it soon narrows, the current runs more rapidly than ever, and we are soon again surrounded by the mountain range. Great masses of black rock show among the trees on the hillsides, and under the fringe of fallen trees that hang from the steep banks. Two hours after leaving Njole we are facing our first rapid. Great gray-black masses of smoothed rock rise up out of the whirling water in all directions. These rocks have a peculiar appearance which puzzle me at the time, but in subsequently getting used to it I accepted it quietly and admired. When the sun shines on them they have a soft light blue haze round them, like a halo. The effect produced by this, with the forested hillsides and the little beaches of glistening white sand was one of the most perfect things I have ever seen.

We kept along close to the right-hand bank, dodging out of the way of the swiftest current as much as possible. Ever and again we were unable to force our way round projecting parts of the bank, so we then got up just as far as we could to the

point in question, yelling and shouting at the tops of our voices.
M'bo said "Jump for bank, sar," and I "up and jumped," followed
by half the crew.   Such banks ! sheets, and walls, and rubbish
heaps of rock, mixed up with trees fallen and standing.   One
appalling corner I shall not forget, for I had to jump at a rock
wall, and hang on to it in a manner more befitting an insect
than an insect-hunter, and then scramble up it into a close-set
forest, heavily burdened with boulders of all sizes.   I wonder
whether the rocks or the trees were there first ? there is evidence
both ways, for in one place you will see a rock on the top of
a tree, the tree creeping out from underneath it, and in another
place you will see a tree on the top of a rock, clasping it with
a network of roots and getting its nourishment, goodness
knows how, for these are by no means tender, digestible sand-
stones, but uncommon hard gneiss and quartz which has no idea
of breaking up into friable small stuff, and which only takes
on a high polish when it is vigorously sanded and canvassed
by the Ogowé.   While I was engaged in climbing across these
promontories, the crew would be busy shouting and hauling
the canoe round the point by means of the strong chain provided for such emergencies fixed on to the bow.   When this was
done, in we got again and paddled away until we met our next
affliction.

M'bo had advised that we should spend our first night at the
same village that M. Allégret did : but when we reached it,
a large village on the north bank, we seemed to have a lot of
daylight still in hand, and thought it would be better to stay
at one a little higher up, so as to make a shorter day's work
for to-morrow, when we wanted to reach Kondo Kondo ; so
we went against the bank just to ask about the situation and
character of the up-river villages.   The row of low, bark huts
was long, and extended its main frontage close to the edge of
the river bank.   The inhabitants had been watching us as we
came, and when they saw we intended calling that afternoon,
they charged down to the river edge hopeful of excitement.
They had a great deal to say, and so had we.   After compliments, as they say, in excerpts of diplomatic communications,
three of their men took charge of the conversation on their
side, and M'bo did ours.   To M'bo's questions they gave a

dramatic entertainment as answer, after the manner of these brisk, excitable Fans. One chief, however, soon settled down to definite details, prefacing his remarks with the silence-commanding " Azuna ! Azuna ! " and his companions grunted approbation of his observations. He took a piece of plantain leaf and tore it up into five different-sized bits. These he laid along the edge of our canoe at different intervals of space, while he told M'bo things, mainly scandalous, about the characters of the villages these bits of leaf represented, save of course about bit A, which represented his own. The interval between the bits was proportional to the interval between the villages, and the size of the bits was proportional to the size of the village. Village number four was the only one he should recommend our going to. When all was said, I gave our kindly informants some heads of tobacco and many thanks. Then M'bo sang them a hymn, with the assistance of Pierre, half a line behind him in a different key, but every bit as flat. The Fans seemed impressed, but any crowd would be by the hymn-singing of my crew, unless they were inmates of deaf and dumb asylums. Then we took our farewell, and thanked the village elaborately for its kind invitation to spend the night there on our way home, shoved off and paddled away in great style just to show those Fans what Igalwas could do.

We hadn't gone 200 yards before we met a current coming round the end of a rock reef that was too strong for us to hold our own in, let alone progress. On to the bank I was ordered and went ; it was a low slip of rugged confused boulders and fragments of rocks, carelessly arranged, and evidently under water in the wet season. I scrambled along, the men yelled and shouted and hauled the canoe, and the inhabitants of the village, seeing we were becoming amusing again, came, legging it like lamp-lighters, after us, young and old, male and female, to say nothing of the dogs. Some good souls helped the men haul, while I did my best to amuse the others by diving headlong from a large rock on to which I had elaborately climbed, into a thick clump of willow-leaved shrubs. They applauded my performance vociferously, and then assisted my efforts to extricate my-

self, and during the rest of my scramble they kept close to
me, with keen competition for the front row, in hopes that I
would do something like it again.   But I refused the *encore*,
because, bashful as I am, I could not but feel that my last
performance was carried out with all the superb reckless
abandon of a Sarah Bernhardt, and a display of art of this
order should satisfy any African village for a year at least.
At last I got across the rocks on to a lovely little beach of
white sand, and stood there talking, surrounded by my
audience, until the canoe got over its difficulties and arrived
almost as scratched as I ; and then we again said farewell
and paddled away, to the great grief of the natives, for they
don't get a circus up above Njole every week, poor dears.

Now there is no doubt that that chief's plantain - leaf
chart was an ingenious idea and a credit to him.   There is
also no doubt that the Fan mile is a bit Irish, a matter of
nine or so of those of ordinary mortals, but I am bound to
say I don't think, even allowing for this, that he put those
pieces far enough apart.   On we paddled a long way before
we picked up village number one, mentioned in that chart.   On
again, still longer, till we came to village number two.   Village
number three hove in sight high up on a mountain side soon
after, but it was getting dark and the water worse, and the hillsides growing higher and higher into nobly shaped mountains,
forming, with their forest-graced steep sides, a ravine that,
in the gathering gloom, looked like an alley-way made of iron,
for the foaming Ogowé.   Village number four we anxiously
looked for ; village number four we never saw; for round us came
the dark, seeming to come out on to the river from the forests
and the side ravines, where for some hours we had seen it
sleeping, like a sailor with his clothes on in bad weather.
On we paddled, looking for signs of village fires, and seeing
them not.   The *Erd-geist* knew we wanted something, and
seeing how we personally lacked it, thought it was beauty ;
and being in a kindly mood, gave it us, sending the lovely
lingering flushes of his afterglow across the sky, which, dying,
left it that divine deep purple velvet which no one has dared to
paint.   Out in it came the great stars blazing high above us,
and the dark round us was be-gemmed with fire-flies : but

we were not as satisfied with these things as we should have
been ; what we wanted were fires to cook by and dry ourselves by, and all that sort of thing.   The *Erd-geist* did
not understand, and so left us when the afterglow had died
away, with only enough starlight to see the flying foam of
the rapids ahead and around us, and not enough to see the
great trees that had fallen from the bank into the water.
These, when the rapids were not too noisy, we could listen
for, because the black current rushes through their branches
with an impatient "lish, swish" ; but when there was a rapid
roaring close alongside we ran into those trees, and got ourselves mauled, and had ticklish times getting on our course
again.   Now and again we ran up against great rocks sticking
up in the black water—grim, isolated fellows, who seemed to
be standing silently watching their fellow rocks noisily fighting in the arena of the white water.   Still on we poled and
paddled.   About 8 P.M. we came to a corner, a bad one ; but
we were unable to leap on to the bank and haul round, not
being able to see either the details or the exact position of the
said bank, and we felt, I think naturally, disinclined to spring
in the direction of such bits of country as we had had experience of during the afternoon, with nothing but the aid
we might have got from a compass hastily viewed by the
transitory light of a lucifer match, and even this would not
have informed us how many tens of feet of tree fringe lay between us and the land, so we did not attempt it.   One must
be careful at times, or nasty accidents may follow.   We fought
our way round that corner, yelling defiance at the water, and
dealt with succeeding corners on the *vi et armis* plan, breaking,
ever and anon, a pole.   About 9.30 we got into a savage rapid.
We fought it inch by inch.   The canoe jammed herself on
some barely sunken rocks in it.   We shoved her off over them.
She tilted over and chucked us out.   The rocks round being
just awash, we survived and got her straight again, and got
into her and drove her unmercifully ; she struck again and
bucked like a broncho, and we fell in heaps upon each other,
but stayed inside that time—the men by the aid of their
intelligent feet, I by clinching my hands into the bush rope
lacing which ran round the rim of the canoe and the meaning of

which I did not understand when I left Talagouga. We sorted ourselves out hastily and sent her at it again. Smash went a sorely tried pole and a paddle. Round and round we spun in an exultant whirlpool, which, in a light-hearted, maliciously joking way, hurled us tail first out of it into the current. Now the grand point in these canoes of having both ends alike declared itself; for at this juncture all we had to do was to revolve on our own axis and commence life anew with what had been the bow for the stern. Of course we were defeated, we could not go up any further without the aid of our lost poles and paddles, so we had to go down for shelter somewhere, anywhere, and down at a terrific pace in the white water we went. While hitched among the rocks the arrangement of our crew had been altered, Pierre joining M'bo in the bows; this piece of precaution was frustrated by our getting turned round; so our position was what you might call precarious, until we got into another whirlpool, when we persuaded nature to start us right end on. This was only a matter of minutes, whirlpools being plentiful, and then M'bo and Pierre, provided with our surviving poles, stood in the bows to fend us off rocks, as we shot towards them; while we midship paddles sat, helping to steer, and when occasion arose, which occasion did with lightning rapidity, to whack the whirlpools with the flat of our paddles, to break their force. Cook crouched in the stern concentrating his mind on steering only. A most excellent arrangement in theory and the safest practical one no doubt, but it did not work out what you might call brilliantly well; though each department did its best. We dashed full tilt towards high rocks, things twenty to fifty feet above water. Midship backed and flapped like fury; M'bo and Pierre received the shock on their poles; sometimes we glanced successfully aside and flew on; sometimes we didn't. The shock being too much for M'bo and Pierre they were driven back on me, who got flattened on to the cargo of bundles which, being now firmly tied in, couldn't spread the confusion further aft; but the shock of the canoe's nose against the rock did so in style, and the rest of the crew fell forward on to the bundles, me, and themselves. So shaken up together were we several times that night, that it's a wonder to me, considering the hurry, that we sorted ourselves out correctly with our own particular legs and arms. And although we in the middle of the canoe did some very spirited flapping, our whirlpool-breaking was no more successful than M'bo and Pierre's fending off, and many a wild waltz we danced that night with the waters of the River Ogowé.

Unpleasant as going through the rapids was, when circumstances took us into the black current we fared no better. For good all-round inconvenience, give me going full tilt in the dark into the branches of a fallen tree at the pace we were going then—and crash, swish, crackle and there you are, hung up, with a bough pressing against your chest, and your hair being torn out and your clothes ribboned by others, while the wicked river is trying to drag away the canoe from under you. I expect we should have been an amusing spectacle for hard-hearted onlookers ; but onlookers there were none, neither could we form a co-operative society for consuming our own ridiculousness as we did when we had light to see it by. After a good hour and more of these experiences, we went hard on to a large black reef of rocks So firm was the canoe wedged that we in our rather worn-out state couldn't move her so we wisely decided to "lef 'em" and see what could be done towards getting food and a fire for the remainder of the night. Our eyes, now trained to the darkness, observed pretty close to us a big lump of land, looming up out of the river. This we subsequently found out was Kembe Island. The rocks and foam on either side stretched away into the darkness, and high above us against the star-lit sky stood out clearly the summits of the mountains of the Sierra del Cristal.

The most interesting question to us now was whether this rock reef communicated sufficiently with the island for us to get to it. Abandoning conjecture ; tying very firmly our canoe up to the rocks, a thing that seemed, considering she was jammed hard and immovable, a little unnecessary—but you can never be sufficiently careful in this matter with any kind of boat—off we started among the rock boulders. I would climb up on to a rock table, fall off it on the other side

on to rocks again, with more or less water on them—then
get a patch of singing sand under my feet, then with varying
suddenness get into more water, deep or shallow, broad or
narrow pools among the rocks ; out of that over more rocks,
&c., &c., &c. : my companions, from their noises, evidently
were going in for the same kind of thing, but we were quite
cheerful, because the probability of reaching the land seemed
increasing.   Most of us arrived into deep channels of water
which here and there cut in between this rock reef and the bank
M'bo was the first to find the way into certainty ; he was, and
I hope still is, a perfect wonder at this sort of work.   I
kept close to M'bo, and when we got to the shore, the rest of
the wanderers being collected, we said " chances are there's a
village round here " ; and started to find it.   After a gay time
in a rock-encumbered forest, growing in a tangled, matted way
on a rough hillside, at an angle of 45 degrees, M'bo sighted
the gleam of fires through the tree stems away to the left, and
we bore down on it, listening to its drum.   Viewed through
the bars of the tree stems the scene was very picturesque.
The village was just a collection of palm mat-built huts
very low and squalid.   In its tiny street, an affair of some
sixty feet long and twenty wide, were a succession of small
fires.   The villagers themselves, however, were the striking
features in the picture.   They were painted vermilion all over
their nearly naked bodies, and were dancing enthusiastically
to the good old rump-a-tump-tump-tump tune, played energetically by an old gentleman on a long, high-standing, white-
and-black painted drum.   They said that as they had been
dancing when we arrived they had failed to hear us.   M'bo
secured a—well, I don't exactly know what to call it—for my
use.   It was, I fancy, the remains of the village club-house.
It had a certain amount of palm-thatch roof and some of its
left-hand side left, the rest of the structure was bare old poles
with filaments of palm mat hanging from them here and
there ; and really if it hadn't been for the roof one wouldn't
have known whether one was inside or outside it.   The floor
was trodden earth and in the middle of it a heap of white ash
and the usual two bush lights, laid down with their burning
ends propped up off the ground with stones, and emitting, as is

their wont, a rather mawkish, but not altogether unpleasant smell, and volumes of smoke which finds its way
out through the thatch, leaving on the inside of it a rich
oily varnish of a bright warm brown colour. They give
a very good light, provided some one keeps an eye on
them and knocks the ash off the end as it burns gray ; the
bush lights' idea of being snuffed. Against one of the openwork sides hung a drum covered with raw hide, and a long
hollow bit of tree trunk, which served as a cupboard for a few
small articles. I gathered in all these details as I sat on one
of the hard wood benches, waiting for my dinner, which Isaac
was preparing outside in the street. The atmosphere of the
hut, in spite of its remarkable advantages in the way of venti-
lation, was oppressive, for the smell of the bush lights, my wet
clothes, and the natives who crowded into the hut to look at
me, made anything but a pleasant combination. The people
were evidently exceedingly poor ; clothes they had very little
of. The two head men had on old French military coats in
rags ; but they were quite satisfied with their appearance, and
evidently felt through them in touch with European culture,
for they lectured to the others on the habits and customs of
the white man with great self-confidence and superiority. The
majority of the village had a slight acquaintance already with
this interesting animal, being, I found, Adoomas. They had
made a settlement on Kembe Island some two years or so
ago. Then the Fans came and attacked them, and killed and
ate several. The Adoomas left and fled to the French
authority at Njole and remained under its guarding
shadow until the French came up and chastised the
Fans and burnt their village ; and the Adoomas—
when things had quieted down again and the Fans had
gone off to build themselves a new village for their burnt
one—came back to Kembe Island and their plantain patch.
They had only done this a few months before my
arrival and had not had time to rebuild, hence the dilapidated
state of the village. They are, I am told, a Congo region
tribe, whose country lies south-west of Franceville, and, as
I have already said, are the tribe used by the French
authorities to take convoys up and down the Ogowé to France-

ville, more to keep this route open than for transport purposes ;
the rapids rendering it impracticable to take heavy stores this
way, and making it a thirty-six days' journey from Njole with
good luck.   The practical route is *viâ* Loango and Brazzaville.
The Adoomas told us the convoy which had gone up with the
vivacious government official had had trouble with the rapids
and had spent five days on Kondo Kondo, dragging up
the canoes empty by means of ropes and chains, carrying the
cargo that was in them along on land until they had passed the
worst rapid and then repacking.   They added the information
that the rapids were at their worst just now, and entertained us
with reminiscences of a poor young French official who had
been drowned in them last year—indeed they were just
as cheering as my white friends.   As soon as my dinner
arrived they politely cleared out, and I heard the devout M'bo
holding a service for them, with hymns, in the street, and this
being over they returned to their drum and dance, keeping
things up distinctly late, for it was 11.10 P.M., when we first
entered the village.

While the men were getting their food I mounted
guard over our little possessions, and when they turned
up to make things tidy in my hut, I walked off down to
the shore by a path, which we had elaborately avoided when
coming to the village, a very vertically inclined, slippery little
path, but still the one whereby the natives went up and down
to their canoes, which were kept tied up amongst the rocks.
The moon was rising, illumining the sky, but not yet sending
down her light on the foaming, flying Ogowé in its deep ravine.
The scene was divinely lovely ; on every side out of the
formless gloom rose the peaks of the Sierra del Cristal.
Tomanjawki, on the further side of the river surrounded by
his companion peaks, looked his grandest, silhouetted hard
against the sky.   In the higher valleys where the dim light
shone faintly, one could see wreaths and clouds of silver-gray
mist lying, basking lazily or rolling to and fro.   Olangi
seemed to stretch right across the river, blocking with his
great blunt mass all passage ; while away to the N.E. a cone-
shaped peak showed conspicuous, which I afterwards knew as
Kangwe.   In the darkness round me flitted thousands of fire-

flies and out beyond this pool of utter night flew by unceasingly the white foam of the rapids; sound there was none save their thunder. The majesty and beauty of the scene fascinated me, and I stood leaning with my back against a rock pinnacle watching it. Do not imagine it gave rise, in what I am pleased to call my mind, to those complicated, poetical reflections natural beauty seems to bring out in other people's minds. It never works that way with me; I just lose all sense of human individuality, all memory of human life, with its grief and worry and doubt, and become part of the atmosphere. If I have a heaven, that will be mine, and I verily believe that if I were left alone long enough with such a scene as this or on the deck of an African liner in the Bights, watching her funnel and masts swinging to and fro in the great long leisurely roll against the sky, I should be found soulless and dead; but I never have a chance of that. This night my absent Kras, as my Fanti friends would call them, were sent hurrying home badly scared to their attributive body by a fearful shriek tearing through the voice of the Ogowé up into the silence of the hills. I woke with a shudder and found myself sore and stiff, but made hastily in the direction of the shriek, fancying some of our hosts had been spearing one of the crew—a vain and foolish fancy I apologise for. What had happened was that my men, thinking it wiser to keep an eye on our canoe, had come down and built a fire close to her and put up their mosquito-bars as tents. One of the men, tired out by his day's work, had sat down on one of the three logs, whose ends, pointed to a common centre where the fire is, constitute the universal stove of this region. He was taking a last pipe before turning in, but sleep had taken him, and the wretch of a fire had sneaked along in the log under him and burnt him suddenly. The shriek was his way of mentioning the fact. Having got up these facts I left the victim seated in a remedial cool pool of water and climbed back to the village, whose inhabitants, tired at last, were going to sleep. M'bo, I found, had hung up my mosquito-bar over one of the hard wood benches, and going cautiously under it I lit a night-light and read myself asleep with my damp dilapidated old Horace.

Woke at 4 A.M. lying on the ground among the plantain stems, having by a reckless movement fallen out of the house. Thanks be there are no mosquitoes. I don't know how I escaped the rats which swarm here, running about among the huts and the inhabitants in the evening, with a tameness shocking to see. I turned in again until six o'clock, when we started getting things ready to go up river again, carefully providing ourselves with a new stock of poles, and subsidising a native to come with us and help us to fight the rapids.

The greatest breadth of the river channel we now saw, in the daylight, to be the S.S.W. branch ; this was the one we had been swept into, and was almost completely barred by rock. The other one to the N.N.W. was more open, and the river rushed through it, a terrific, swirling mass of water. Had we got caught in this, we should have got past Kembe Island, and gone to glory. Whenever the shelter of the spits of land or of the reefs was sufficient to allow the water to lay down its sand, strange shaped sandbanks showed, as regular in form as if they had been smoothed by human hands. They rise above the water in a slope, the low end or tail against the current ; the down-stream end terminating in an abrupt miniature cliff, sometimes six and seven feet above the water ; that they are the same shape when they have not got their heads above water you will find by sticking on them in a canoe, which I did several times, with a sort of automatic devotion to scientific research peculiar to me. Your best way of getting off is to push on in the direction of the current, carefully preparing for the shock of suddenly coming off the cliff end.

We left the landing place rocks of Kembe Island about 8, and no sooner had we got afloat, than, in the twinkling of an eye; we were swept, broadside on, right across the river to the north bank, and then engaged in a heavy fight with a severe rapid. After passing this, the river is fairly un-interrupted by rock for a while, and is silent and swift. When you are ascending such a piece the effect is strange ; you see the water flying by the side of your canoe, as you vigorously drive your paddle into it with short rapid strokes, and you forthwith fancy you are travelling at the rate of a North-Western express ; but you just raise your eyes, my friend, and

look at that bank, which is standing very nearly still, and you
will realise that you and your canoe are standing very nearly
still too ; and that all your exertions are only enabling you to
creep on at the pace of a crushed snail, and that it's the water
that is going the pace.   It's a most quaint and unpleasant dis-
illusionment.

Above the stretch of swift silent water we come to the
Sengelade Islands, and the river here changes its course
from N.N.W., S.S.E. to north and south.   A bad rapid,
called by our ally from Kembe Island "Unfanga," being
surmounted, we seem to be in a mountain-walled lake, and
keeping along the left bank of this, we get on famously for
twenty whole restful minutes, which lulls us all into a false
sense of security, and my crew sing M'pongwe songs, descriptive of how they go to their homes to see their wives, and
families, and friends, giving chaffing descriptions of their
friends' characteristics and of their failings, which cause bursts of
laughter from those among us who recognise the allusions,
and how they go to their boxes, and take out their clothes,
and put them on—a long bragging inventory of these things is
given by each man as a solo, and then the chorus, taken heartily
up by his companions, signifies their admiration and astonishment at his wealth and importance—and then they sing how,
being dissatisfied with that last dollar's worth of goods they
got from "Holty's," they have decided to take their next
trade to Hatton and Cookson, or *vice versa ;* and then comes the
chorus, applauding the wisdom of such a decision, and extol-
ling the excellence of Hatton and Cookson's goods or Holty's.
These M'pongwe and Igalwa boat songs are all very pretty,
and have very elaborate tunes in a minor key.   I do not believe
there are any old words to them ; I have tried hard to find out
about them, but I believe the tunes, which are of a limited number and quite distinct from each other, are very old.   The words
are put in by the singer on the spur of the moment, and only
restricted in this sense, that there would always be the domestic
catalogue—whatever its component details might be—sung to
the one fixed tune, the trade information sung to another,
and so on.   A good singer, in these parts, means the man who
can make up the best song—the most impressive, or the most

amusing; I have elsewhere mentioned pretty much the same state of things among the Ga's and Krumen and Bubi, and in all cases the tunes are only voice tunes, not for instrumental performance.   The instrumental music consists of that marvellously developed series of drum tunes—the attempt to understand which has taken up much of my time, and led me into queer company—and the many tunes played on the 'mrimba and the orchid-root-stringed harp: they are, I believe, entirely distinct from the song tunes.   And these peaceful tunes my

SOUTH BANK OF THE OGOWÉ RIVER NEAR SENGELADE ISLANDS.

men were now singing were, in their florid elaboration very different from the one they fought the rapids to, of—So Sir—So Sur—So Sir—So Sur—Ush!   So Sir, &c.

On we go singing elaborately, thinking no evil of nature, when a current, a quiet devil of a thing, comes round from behind a point of the bank and catches the nose of our canoe; wringing it well, it sends us scuttling right across the river in spite of our ferocious swoops at the water, upsetting us among a lot of rocks with the water boiling over them; this lot of rocks being however of the table-top kind, and not those precious, close-set pinnacles rising up sheer out of profound depths, between which you are so likely to get your canoe wedged in and split. We, up to our knees in water that nearly tears our legs off, push and shove the canoe free, and re-embarking return singing "So Sir" across the river, to have it out with that current. We do; and at its head find a rapid, and notice on the mountain-side a village clearing, the first sign of human habitation we have seen to-day.

Above this rapid we get a treat of still water, the main current of the Ogowé flying along by the south bank. On our side there are sandbanks with their graceful sloping backs and sudden ends, and there is a very strange and beautiful effect produced by the flakes and balls of foam thrown off the rushing main current into the quiet water. These whirl among the eddies and rush backwards and forwards as though they were still mad with wild haste, until, finding no current to take them down, they drift away into the land-locked bays, where they come to a standstill as if they were bewildered and lost and were trying to remember where they were going to and whence they had come; the foam of which they are composed is yellowish-white, with a spongy sort of solidity about it. In a little bay we pass we see eight native women, Fans clearly, by their bright brown faces, and their loads of brass bracelets and armlets; likely enough they had anklets too, but we could not see them, as the good ladies were pottering about waist-deep in the foam-flecked water, intent on breaking up a stockaded fish-trap. We pause and chat, and watch them collecting the fish in baskets, and I acquire some specimens; and then, shouting farewells when we are well away, in the proper civil way, resume our course.

The middle of the Ogowé here is simply forested with high rocks, looking, as they stand with their grim forms above the foam, like a regiment of strange strong creatures breasting it, with their straight faces up river, and their more flowing curves down, as though they had on black mantles which were swept backwards. Across on the other bank rose the black-forested spurs of Tomanjawki. Our channel was

free until we had to fight round the upper end of our bay
into a long rush of strong current with bad whirlpools curving
its face ; then the river widens out and quiets down and then
suddenly contracts—a rocky forested promontory running
out from each bank. There is a little village on the north
bank's promontory, and, at the end of each, huge monoliths rise
from the water, making what looks like a gateway
which had once been barred and through which the Ogowé
had burst.

BOKO BOKO RAPIDS, OGOWÉ RIVER.

For the first time on this trip I felt discouraged ; it seemed
so impossible that we, with our small canoe and scanty crew,
could force our way up through that gateway, when the whole
Ogowé was rushing down through it.   But we clung to the
bank and rocks with hands, poles, and paddle, and did it ;
really the worst part was not in the gateway but just before
it, for here there is a great whirlpool, its centre hollowed some
two or three feet below its rim.   It is caused, my Kembe
islander says, by a great cave opening beneath the water.
Above the gate the river broadens out again and we see

the arched opening to a large cave in the south bank;
the mountain-side is one mass of rock covered with the
unbroken forest; and the entrance to this cave is just on the
upper wall of the south bank's promontory; so, being sheltered
from the current here, we rest and examine it leisurely. The
river runs into it, and you can easily pass in at this season,
but in the height of the wet season, when the river level would
be some twenty feet or more above its present one, I doubt if
you could. They told me this place is called Boko Boko,
and that the cave is a very long one, extending on a level
some way into the hill, and then ascending and coming out
near a mass of white rock that showed as a speck high up on
the mountain.

If you paddle into it you go "far far," and then "no more
water live," and you get out and go up the tunnel, which is sometimes broad, sometimes narrow, sometimes high, sometimes so
low that you have to crawl, and so get out at the other end.

One French gentleman has gone through this performance,
and I am told found "plenty plenty" bats, and hedgehogs,
and snakes. They could not tell me his name, which I much
regretted. As we had no store of bush lights we went no
further than the portals; indeed, strictly between ourselves, if
I had had every bush light in Congo Français I personally
should not have relished going further. I am terrified of
caves; it sends a creaming down my back to think of them.

We went across the river to see another cave entrance on the
other bank, where there is a narrow stretch of low rock-covered
land at the foot of the mountains, probably under water in the
wet season. The mouth of this other cave is low, between tumbled blocks of rock. It looked so suspiciously like a short cut to
the lower regions, that I had less exploring enthusiasm about
it than even about its opposite neighbour; although they
told me no man had gone down "them thing." Probably
that much-to-be-honoured Frenchman who explored the other
cave, allowed like myself, that if one did want to go from the
Equator to Hades, there were pleasanter ways to go than this.
My Kembe Island man said that just hereabouts were five cave
openings, the two that we had seen and another one we had
not, on land, and two under the water, one of the sub-fluvial

ones being responsible for the whirlpool we met outside the
gateway of Boko Boko.

The scenery above Boko Boko was exceedingly lovely, the
river shut in between its rim of mountains. As you pass up
it opens out in front of you and closes in behind, the closely-
set confused mass of mountains altering in form as you view
them from different angles, save one, Kangwe—a blunt cone,
evidently the record of some great volcanic outburst ; and
the sandbanks show again wherever the current deflects and
leaves slack water, their bright glistening colour giving a
relief to the scene.

For a long period we paddle by the south bank, and pass a
vertical cleft-like valley, the upper end of which seems blocked
by a finely shaped mountain, almost as conical as Kangwe.
The name of this mountain is Njoko, and the name of the
clear small river, that apparently monopolises the valley floor,
is the Ovata. Our peace was not of long duration, and we
were soon again in the midst of a bristling forest of rock ; still
the current running was not dangerously strong, for the
river-bed comes up in a ridge, too high for much water to
come over at this season of the year ; but in the wet season
this must be one of the worst places. This ridge of rock runs
two-thirds across the Ogowé, leaving a narrow deep channel
by the north bank. When we had got our canoe over the
ridge, mostly by standing in the water and lifting her, we
found the water deep and fairly quiet.

On the north bank we passed by the entrance of the Okana
River. Its mouth is narrow, but, the natives told me, always
deep, even in the height of the dry season. It is a very considerable river, running inland to the N.N.E. Little is known
about it, save that it is narrowed into a ravine course
above which it expands again ; the banks of it are thickly
populated by Fans, who send down a considerable trade, and
have an evil reputation. In the main stream of the Ogowé
below the Okana's entrance, is a long rocky island called
Shandi. When we were getting over our ridge and paddling
about the Okana's entrance my ears recognised a new sound.
The rush and roar of the Ogowé we knew well enough, and
could locate which particular obstacle to his headlong course

was making him say things ; it was either those immovable rocks, which threw him back in foam, whirling wildly, or it was that fringe of gaunt skeleton trees hanging from the bank playing a " pull devil, pull baker " contest that made him hiss with vexation. But this was an elemental roar. I said to M'bo : " That's a thunderstorm away among the mountains." " No, sir," says he, " that's the Alemba."

We paddled on towards it, hugging the right-hand bank again to avoid the mid-river rocks. For a brief space the mountain wall ceased, and a lovely scene opened before us ; we seemed to be looking into the heart of the chain of the Sierra del Cristal, the abruptly shaped mountains encircling a narrow plain or valley before us, each one of them steep in slope, every one of them forest-clad ; one, whose name I know not unless it be what is sometimes put down as Mt. Okana on the French maps, had a conical shape which contrasted beautifully with the more irregular curves of its companions. The colour down this gap was superb, and very Japanese in the evening glow. The more distant peaks were soft gray-blues and purple, those nearer, indigo and black. We soon passed this lovely scene and entered the walled-in channel, creeping up what seemed an interminable hill of black water, then through some whirlpools and a rocky channel to the sand and rock shore of our desired island Kondo Kondo, along whose northern side tore in thunder the Alemba. We made our canoe fast in a little cove among the rocks, and landed, pretty stiff and tired and considerably damp. This island, when we were on it, must have been about half a mile or so long, but during the long wet season a good deal of it is covered, and only the higher parts—great heaps of stone, among which grows a long branched willow-like shrub—are above or nearly above water. The Adooma from Kembe Island especially drew my attention to this shrub, telling me his people who worked the rapids always regarded it with an affectionate veneration ; for he said it was the only thing that helped a man when his canoe got thrown over in the dreaded Alemba, for its long tough branches swimming in, or close to, the water are veritable life lines, and his best chance ; a chance which must have failed some poor fellow, whose knife and leopard-skin belt we found wedged in among the rocks on Kondo Kondo. The main part of the island is sand, with slabs and tables of polished rock sticking up through it ; and in between the rocks grew in thousands most beautiful lilies, their white flowers having a very strong scent of vanilla and their bright light-green leaves looking very lovely on the glistening pale sand among the black-gray rock. How they stand the long submersion they must undergo I do not know ; the natives tell me they begin to spring up as soon as ever the water falls and leaves the island exposed ; that they very soon grow up and flower, and keep on flowering until the Ogowé comes down again and rides roughshod over Kondo Kondo for months. While the men were making their fire I went across the island to see the great Alemba rapid, of which I had heard so much, that lay between it and the north bank. Nobler pens than mine must sing its glory and its grandeur. Its face was like nothing I have seen before. Its voice was like nothing I have heard. Those other rapids are not to be compared to it ; they are wild, headstrong, and malignant enough, but the Alemba is not as they. It does not struggle, and writhe, and brawl among the rocks, but comes in a majestic springing dance, a stretch of waltzing foam, triumphant.

The beauty of the night on Kondo Kondo was superb ; the sun went down and the afterglow flashed across the sky in crimson, purple, and gold, leaving it a deep violet-purple, with the great stars hanging in it like moons, until the moon herself arose, lighting the sky long before she sent her beams down on us in this valley. As she rose, the mountains hiding her face grew harder and harder in outline, and deeper and deeper black, while those opposite were just enough illumined to let one see the wefts and floating veils of blue-white mist upon them, and when at last, and for a short time only, she shone full down on the savage foam of the Alemba, she turned it into a soft silver mist. Around, on all sides flickered the fire-flies, who had come to see if our fire was not a big relation of their own, and they were the sole representatives, with ourselves, of animal life. When the moon had gone, the sky, still lit by the stars, seeming indeed to be in itself lambent, was very lovely, but it shared none of its light with us, and we sat round our fire surrounded by an utter darkness. Cold, clammy drifts of almost tangible mist encircled us ; ever and again came cold faint puffs of wandering wind, weird and grim beyond description.

The individual names of the mountains round Kondo Kondo and above I cannot give you, though I was told them. For in my last shipwreck before reaching Kondo Kondo, I had lost my pencil ; and my note-book, even if I had had a pencil, was unfit to get native names down on, being a pulpy mass, because I had kept it in my pocket after leaving the Okana river so as to be ready for submergencies. And I also had several fish and a good deal of water in my pocket too, so that I am thankful I have a note left.

I will not weary you further with details of our ascent of the Ogowé rapids, for I have done so already sufficiently to make you understand the sort of work going up them entails, and I have no doubt that, could I have given you a more vivid picture of them, you would join me in admiration of the fiery pluck of those few Frenchmen who traverse them on duty bound. I personally deeply regret it was not my good fortune to meet again the French official I had had the pleasure of meeting on the *Éclaireur*. He would have been truly great in his description of his voyage to Franceville. I wonder how he would have " done " his unpacking of canoes and his experiences on Kondo Kondo, where, by the by, we came across many of the ashes of his expedition's attributive fires. Well ! he must have been a pleasure to Franceville, and I hope also to the good fathers at Lestourville, for those places must be just slightly sombre for Parisians.

Going down big rapids is always, everywhere, more dangerous than coming up, because when you are coming up and a whirlpool or eddy does jam you on rocks, the current helps you off—certainly only with a view to dashing your brains out and smashing your canoe on another set of rocks it's got ready below ; but for the time being it helps, and when off, you take charge and convert its plan into an incompleted fragment ; whereas in going down the current is against your backing off. M'bo had a series of prophetic visions as to what would happen to us on our way down, founded on reminiscence and tradition.

I tried to comfort him by pointing out that, were any one of his prophecies fulfilled, it would spare our friends and relations all funeral expenses; and, unless they went and wasted their money on a memorial window, that ought to be a comfort to our well-regulated minds. M'bo did not see this, but was too good a Christian to be troubled by the disagreeable conviction that was in the minds of other members of my crew, namely, that our souls, unliberated by funeral rites from this world, would have to hover for ever over the Ogowé near the scene of our catastrophe.

SOUTH BANK OF THE OGOWÉ ABOVE BOKO BOKO.

I own this idea was an unpleasant one—fancy having to pass the day in those caves with the bats, and then come out and wander all night in the cold mists! However, like a good many likely-looking prophecies, those of M'bo did not quite come off, and a miss is as good as a mile. Twice we had a near call, by being shot in between two pinnacle rocks, within half an inch of being fatally close to each other for us; but after some alarming scrunching sounds, and creaks from the canoe, we were shot ignominiously out down river. Several times we got on to partially submerged table rocks, and were

unceremoniously bundled off them by the Ogowé, irritated at
the hindrance we were occasioning ; but we never met the rocks
of M'bo's prophetic soul—that lurking, submerged needle, or
knife-edge of a pinnacle rock which was to rip our canoe from
stem to stern, neat and clean into two pieces.

A comic incident happened to us one evening.   The canoe
jammed among a clump of rocks, and out we went anyhow into
the water.   Fortunately, there were lots of rocks about ; unfortunately, we each chose different ones to perch on ; mine was
exceedingly inconvenient, being a smooth pillar affair, to which
it was all I and the French flag, which always accompanied
me in upsets, could do to hold on.   There was considerable
delay in making up our party again, for the murkiness of
the night only allowed each of us to see the foam which
flew round our own particular rock, and the noise of the
rapids made it difficult for us to interchange information
regarding our own individual position and plan of action.
However, owing to that weak-minded canoe swinging round
broadside on to the rocks, she did not bolt down the river.
When Pierre got to her she was trying to climb sideways over
them, " like a crab," he said.   We seven of us got into her—
number eight we could not find and were just beginning to
think the Ogowé had claimed another victim when we heard
the strains of that fine hymn " Notre port est au Ciel,"—which is
a great favourite hereabouts owing to its noble tune,—coming
to us above the rapids' clamour in an agonised howl.   We went
joyfully and picked the singer off his rock, and then dashed
downwards to further dilemmas and disasters.   The course we
had to take coming down was different to that we took coming
up.   Coming up we kept as closely as might be to the most
advisable bank, and dodged behind every rock we could,
to profit by the shelter it afforded us from the current.
Coming down, fallen-tree-fringed banks and rocks were converted from friends to foes ; so we kept with all our power
in the very centre of the swiftest part of the current in order to
avoid them.   The grandest part of the whole time was coming
down, below the Alemba, where the whole great Ogowé
takes a tiger-like spring for about half a mile, I should
think, before it strikes a rock reef below.   As you come out

from among the rocks in the upper rapid it gives you—or I
should perhaps confine myself to saying, it gave me—a peculiar internal sensation to see that stretch of black water,
shining like a burnished sheet of metal, sloping down before
one, at such an angle. All you have got to do is to keep your
canoe-head straight—quite straight, you understand—for any
failure so to do will land you the other side of the tomb, instead of in a cheerful no-end-of-a-row with the lower rapid's
rocks. This lower rapid is one of the worst in the dry season ;
maybe it is so in the wet too, for the river's channel here turns
an elbow-sharp curve which infuriates the Ogowé in a most
dangerous manner.

I hope to see the Ogowé next time in the wet season—
there must be several more of these great sheets of water then
over what are rocky rapids now. Just think what coming
down over that ridge above Boko Boko will be like ! I do
not fancy however it would ever be possible to get up the river
when it is at its height, with so small a crew as we were when
we went and played our knock-about farce, before King Death,
in his amphitheatre in the Sierra del Cristal.

CHAPTER X

LEMBARENE

In which is given some account of the episode of the Hippopotame, and of the voyager's attempts at controlling an Ogowé canoe ; and also of the Igalwa tribe.

On my return to Talagouga, I find both my good friends sick with fever—M. Forget very ill indeed. Providentially the *Éclaireur* came up river, with the Doctor Administrator on board, and he came ashore and prescribed, and in a few days M. Forget was better. I say good-bye to Talagouga with much regret, and go on board the *Éclaireur*, when she returns from Njole, with all my bottles and belongings. On board I find no other passenger ; the captain's English has widened out considerably ; and he is as pleasant, cheery, and spoiling for a fight as ever ; but he has a preoccupied manner, and a most peculiar set of new habits, which I find are shared by the engineer. Both of them make rapid dashes to the rail, and nervously scan the river for a minute and then return to some occupation, only to dash from it to the rail again. During breakfast their conduct is nerve-shaking. Hastily taking a few mouthfuls, the captain drops his knife and fork and simply hurls his seamanlike form through the nearest door out on to the deck. In another minute he is back again, and with just a shake of his head to the engineer, continues his meal. The engineer shortly afterwards flies from his seat, and being far thinner than the captain, goes through his nearest door with even greater rapidity ; returns, and shakes his head at the captain, and continues his meal. Excitement of this kind is infectious, and I also wonder whether I ought not to show a sympathetic friendliness by flying from my seat and hurling myself on to the deck through my nearest door, too.

But although there are plenty of doors, as four enter the
saloon from the deck, I do not see my way to doing this performance aimlessly, and what in this world they are both after I
cannot think. So I confine myself to woman's true sphere, and
assist in a humble way by catching the wine and Vichy water
bottles, glasses, and plates of food, which at every performance
are jeopardised by the members of the nobler sex starting
off with a considerable quantity of the ample table-cloth
wrapped round their legs. At last I can stand it no longer,
so ask the captain point-blank what is the matter. " Nothing," says he, bounding out of his chair and flying out of his
doorway ; but on his return he tells me he has got a bet on
of two bottles of champagne with Woermann's agent for
Njole, as to who shall reach Lembarene first, and the German
agent has started off some time before the *Éclaireur* in his
little steam launch.

During the afternoon we run smoothly along ; the free
pulsations of the engines telling what a very different thing
coming down the Ogowé is to going up against its terrific current.
Every now and again we stop to pick up cargo, or discharge
over-carried cargo, and the captain's mind becomes lulled by
getting no news of the Woermann's launch having passed
down. He communicates this to the engineer ; it is impossible
she could have passed the *Éclaireur* since they started, therefore she must be somewhere behind at a subfactory, " *N'est-ce
pas ?* " " *Oui, oui, certainement,*" says the engineer. The
engineer is, by these considerations, also lulled, and
feels he may do something else but scan the river
à la sister Ann. What that something is puzzles me ;
it evidently requires secrecy, and he shrinks from detec-
tion. First he looks down one side of the deck, no one there ;
then he looks down the other, no one there ; good so far. I
then see he has put his head through one of the saloon port-
holes ; no one there ; he hesitates a few seconds until I begin
to wonder whether his head will suddenly appear through my
port ; but he regards this as an unnecessary precaution, and I
hear him enter his cabin which abuts on mine and there is
silence for some minutes. Writing home to his mother, think
I, as I go on putting a new braid round the bottom of a worn

skirt. Almost immediately after follows the sound of a little click from the next cabin, and then apparently one of the denizens of the infernal regions has got its tail smashed in a door and the heavy hot afternoon air is reft by an inchoate howl of agony. I drop my needlework and take to the deck ; but it is after all only that shy retiring young man practising secretly on his clarionet.

The captain is drowsily looking down the river. But repose is not long allowed to that active spirit ; he sees something in the water—what? " *Hippopotame*," he ejaculates. Now both he and the engineer frequently do this thing, and then fly off to their guns—bang, bang, finish ; but this time he does not dash for his gun, nor does the engineer, who flies out of his cabin at the sound of the war shout " *Hippopotame*." In vain I look across the broad river with its stretches of yellow sandbanks, where the " *hippopotame* " should be, but I can see nothing but four black stumps sticking up in the water away to the right. Meanwhile the captain and the engineer are flying about getting off a crew of blacks into the canoe we are towing alongside. This being done the captain explains to me that on the voyage up " the engineer had fired at, and hit a hippopotamus, and without doubt this was its body floating." We are now close enough even for me to recognise the four stumps as the deceased's legs, and soon the canoe is alongside them and makes fast to one, and then starts to paddle back, hippo and all, to the *Éclaireur*. But no such thing ; let them paddle and shout as hard as they like, the hippo's weight simply anchors them. The *Éclaireur* by now has dropped down the river past them, and has to sweep round and run back. Recognising promptly what the trouble is, the energetic captain grabs up a broom, ties a light cord belonging to the leadline to it, and holding the broom by the end of its handle, swings it round his head and hurls it at the canoe. The arm of a merciful Providence being interposed, the broom-tomahawk does not hit the canoe, wherein, if it had, it must infallibly have killed some one, but falls short, and goes tearing off with the current, well out of reach of the canoe. The captain seeing this gross dereliction of duty by a Chargeur Réunis broom, hauls it in hand over hand and talks to it. Then he ties the other end of its

line to the mooring rope, and by a better aimed shot sends the
broom into the water, about ten yards above the canoe, and it
drifts towards it.   Breathless excitement! surely they will get
it now.   Alas, no!   Just when it is within reach of the canoe, a
fearful shudder runs through the broom.   It throws up its head
and sinks beneath the tide.   A sensation of stun comes over all
of us.   The crew of the canoe, ready and eager to grasp the
approaching aid, gaze blankly at the circling ripples round
where it sank.   In a second the captain knows what has
happened.   That heavy hawser which has been paid out after
it has dragged it down, so he hauls it on board again.

The *Éclaireur* goes now close enough to the hippo-anchored
canoe for a rope to be flung to the man in her bows ; he catches
it and freezes on gallantly.   Saved!   No!   Oh horror!   The
lower deck hums with fear that after all it will not taste that
toothsome hippo chop, for the man who has caught the rope
is as nearly as possible jerked flying out of the canoe when
the strain of the *Éclaireur* contending with the hippo's
inertia flies along it, but his companion behind him grips him
by the legs and is in his turn grabbed, and the crew holding
on to each other with their hands, and on to their craft with
their feet, save the man holding on to the rope and the whole
situation ; and slowly bobbing towards us comes the hippopotamus, who is shortly hauled on board by the winners in
triumph.

My esteemed friends, the captain and the engineer, who of
course have been below during this hauling, now rush on to the
upper deck, each coatless, and carrying an enormous butcher's
knife.   They dash into the saloon, where a terrific sharpening of
these instruments takes place on the steel belonging to the
saloon carving-knife, and down stairs again.   By looking down
the ladder, I can see the pink, pig-like hippo, whose colour
has been soaked out by the water, lying on the lower deck
and the captain and engineer slitting down the skin intent
on gralloching operations.   Providentially, my prophetic soul
induces me to leave the top of the ladder and go forward—
"run to win'ard," as Captain Murray would say—for within
two minutes the captain and engineer are up the ladder as if
they had been blown up by the boilers bursting, and go as

one man for the brandy bottle ; and they wanted it if ever
man did ; for remember that hippo had been dead and in the
warm river-water for more than a week.

The captain had had enough of it, he said, but the engineer
stuck to the job with a courage I profoundly admire, and he
saw it through and then retired to his cabin ; sand-and-can-
vassed himself first, and then soaked and saturated himself in
Florida water. The flesh gladdened the hearts of the crew
and lower-deck passengers and also of the inhabitants of
Lembarene, who got dashes of it on our arrival there. Hippo
flesh is not to be despised by black man or white ; I have
enjoyed it far more than the stringy beef or vapid goat's
flesh one gets down here.

I stayed on board the *Éclaireur* all night ; for it was dark
when we reached Lembarene, too dark to go round to Kangwe ;
and next morning, after taking a farewell of her—I
hope not a final one, for she is a most luxurious little vessel
for the Coast, as the feeding on board is excellent and the
society varied and charming—I went round to Kangwe. M.
and Mme. Jacot received me back most kindly, and they
both looked all the better for my having been away. M.
Haug and a young missionary from Baraka, who had come up
to Lembarene for a change after fever, were busy starting
to go up to Talagouga in a canoe, which I was very glad of,
because M. Haug, at any rate, would be of immense help
to Mme. and M. Forget, while they were in such bad health ;
only during his absence M. Jacot had enough work for any
five men.

I remained some time in the Lembarene district and saw and
learnt many things ; I owe most of what I learnt to M.
and Mme. Jacot who knew a great deal about both the
natives and the district, and I owe much of what I saw to
having acquired the art of managing by myself a native
canoe. This " recklessness " of mine I am sure did not merit the
severe criticism it has been subjected to, for my performances
gave immense amusement to others (I can hear Lembarene's
shrieks of laughter now) and to myself they gave great
pleasure.

My first attempt was made at Talagouga one very hot

afternoon.   M. and Mme. Forget were, I thought, safe
having their siestas, Oranie was with Mme. Gacon.   I
knew where Mme. Gacon was for certain ; she was with
M. Gacon ; and I knew he was up in the sawmill shed,
out of sight of the river, because of the soft thump, thump,
thump of the big water-wheel.   There was therefore no one to
keep me out of mischief, and I was too frightened to go into
the forest that afternoon, because on the previous afternoon I
had been stalked as a wild beast by a cannibal savage, and I am
nervous.   Besides, and above all, it is quite impossible to see
other people, even if they are only black, naked savages, gliding
about in canoes, without wishing to go and glide about yourself.
So I went down to where the canoes were tied by their noses to
the steep bank, and finding a paddle, a broken one, I unloosed
the smallest canoe.   Unfortunately this was fifteen feet or so
long, but I did not know the disadvantage of having, as it
were, a long-tailed canoe then—I did shortly afterwards.

The promontories running out into the river on each side of
the mission beach give a little stretch of slack water between
the bank and the mill-race-like current of the Ogowé, and I
wisely decided to keep in the slack water, until I had found
out how to steer—most important thing steering.   I got into
the bow of the canoe, and shoved off from the bank all right ;
then I knelt down—learn how to paddle standing up by and
by—good so far.   I rapidly learnt how to steer from the
bow, but I could not get up any pace.   Intent on acquiring
pace, I got to the edge of the slack water ; and then displaying more wisdom, I turned round to avoid it, proud as a
peacock, you understand, at having found out how to turn
round.   At this moment, the current of the greatest equatorial
river in the world, grabbed my canoe by its tail.   We spun
round and round for a few seconds, like a teetotum, I
steering the whole time for all I was worth, and then the
current dragged the canoe ignominiously down river, tail foremost.

Fortunately a big tree was at that time temporarily hanging
against the rock in the river, just below the sawmill beach.
Into that tree the canoe shot with a crash, and I hung on, and
shipping my paddle, pulled the canoe into the slack water

again, by the aid of the branches of the tree, which I was in
mortal terror would come off the rock, and insist on accompanying me and the canoe, viâ Kama country, to the Atlantic
Ocean ; but it held, and when I had got safe against the side of
the pinnacle-rock I wiped a perspiring brow, and searched in
my mind for a piece of information regarding navigation that
would be applicable to the management of long-tailed Adooma
canoes. I could not think of one for some minutes. Captain
Murray has imparted to me at one time and another an
enormous mass of hints as to the management of vessels,
but those vessels were all presupposed to have steam power.
But he having been the first man to take an ocean-going
steamer up to Matadi on the Congo, through the terrific
currents that whirl and fly in Hell's Cauldron, knew
about currents, and I remembered he had said regarding taking vessels through them, " Keep all the headway you can on
her." Good ! that hint inverted will fit this situation like a
glove, and I'll keep all the tailway I can off her. Feeling now
as safe as only a human being can feel who is backed up by a
sound principle, I was cautiously crawling to the tail-end of
the canoe, intent on kneeling in it to look after it, when
I heard a dreadful outcry on the bank. Looking there I
saw Mme. Forget, Mme. Gacon, M. Gacon, and their attributive crowd of mission children all in a state of frenzy. They
said lots of things in chorus. " What ? " said I. They said
some more and added gesticulations. Seeing I was wasting
their time as I could not hear, I drove the canoe from
the rock and made my way, mostly by steering, to
the bank close by ; and then tying the canoe firmly
up I walked over the mill stream and divers other
things towards my anxious friends. " You'll be drowned,"
they said. " Gracious goodness ! " said I, " I thought that half
an hour ago, but it's all right now ; I can steer." After much
conversation I lulled their fears regarding me, and having
received strict orders to keep in the stern of the canoe, because
that is the proper place when you are managing a canoe
single-handed, I returned to my studies. I had not however
lulled my friends' interest regarding me, and they stayed on
the bank watching.

I found first, that my education in steering from the bow was of no avail, second, that it was all right if you reversed it. For instance, when you are in the bow, and make an inward stroke with the paddle on the right-hand side, the bow goes to the right; whereas, if you make an inward stroke on the right-hand side, when you are sitting in the stern, the bow then goes to the left. Understand? Having grasped this law, I crept along up river; and, by Allah! before I had gone twenty yards, if that wretch, the current of the greatest, &c., did not grab hold of the nose of my canoe, and we teetotummed round again as merrily as ever. My audience screamed. I knew what they were saying, "You'll be drowned! Come back! Come back!" but I heard them and I heeded not. If you attend to advice in a crisis you're lost; besides, I couldn't "Come back" just then. However, I got into the slack water again, by some very showy, high-class steering. Still steering, fine as it is, is not all you require and hanker after. You want pace as well, and pace, except when in the clutches of the current, I had not so far attained. Perchance, thought I, the pace region in a canoe may be in its centre; so I got along on my knees into the centre to experiment. Bitter failure; the canoe took to sidling down river broadside on, like Mr. Winkle's horse. Shouts of laughter from the bank. Both bow and stern education utterly inapplicable to centre; and so, seeing I was utterly thrown away there, I crept into the bows, and in a few more minutes I steered my canoe, perfectly, in among its fellows by the bank and secured it there. Mme. Forget ran down to meet me and assured me she had not laughed so much since she had been in Africa, although she was frightened at the time lest I should get capsized and drowned. I believe it, for she is a sweet and gracious lady; and I quite see, as she demonstrated, that the sight of me, teetotumming about, steering in an elaborate and showy way all the time, was irresistibly comic. And she gave a most amusing account of how, when she started looking for me to give me tea, a charming habit of hers, she could not see me in among my bottles, and so asked the little black boy where I was. "There," said he, pointing to the tree hanging against the rock out in the river ; and she, seeing me hitched with a canoe against the rock, and knowing the danger and depth of the river, got alarmed.

Well, when I got down to Lembarene I naturally went on with my canoeing studies, in pursuit of the attainment of pace. Success crowned my efforts, and I can honestly and truly say that there are only two things I am proud of—one is that Doctor Günther has approved of my fishes, and the other is that I can paddle an Ogowé canoe. Pace, style, steering and all, "All same for one" as if I were an Ogowé African. A strange, incongruous pair of things : but I often wonder what are the things other people are really most proud of ; it would be a quaint and repaying subject for investigation.

Mme. Jacot gave me every help in canoeing, for she is a remarkably clear-headed woman, and recognised that, as I was always getting soaked, anyhow, I ran no extra danger in getting soaked in a canoe ; and then, it being the dry season, there was an immense stretch of water opposite Andande beach, which was quite shallow. So she saw no need of my getting drowned.

The sandbanks were showing their yellow heads in all directions when I came down from Talagouga, and just opposite Andande there was sticking up out of the water a great, graceful, palm frond. It had been stuck into the head of the pet sandbank, and every day was visited by the boys and girls in canoes to see how much longer they would have to wait for the sandbank's appearance. A few days after my return it showed, and in two days more there it was, acres and acres of it, looking like a great, golden carpet spread on the surface of the centre of the clear water—clear here, down this side of Lembarene Island, because the river runs fairly quietly, and has time to deposit its mud. Dark brown the Ogowé flies past the other side of the island, the main current being deflected that way by a bend, just below the entrance of the Nguni.

There was great rejoicing. Canoe-load after canoe-load of boys and girls went to the sandbank, some doing a little fishing round its rim, others bringing the washing there, all skylarking and singing. Few prettier sights have I ever seen than those

on that sandbank—the merry brown forms dancing or lying
stretched on it : the gaudy-coloured patchwork quilts and
chintz mosquito-bars that have been washed, spread out
drying, looking from Kangwe on the hill above, like beds
of bright flowers. By night when it was moonlight
there would be bands of dancers on it with bush-light torches,
gyrating, intermingling and separating till you could think
you were looking at a dance of stars.

They commenced affairs very early on that sandbank, and
they kept them up very late ; and all the time there came from
it a soft murmur of laughter and song. Ah me ! if the aim of
life were happiness and pleasure, Africa should send us missionaries instead of our sending them to her—but, fortunately
for the work of the world, happiness is not. One thing I remember which struck me very much regarding the sandbank,
and this was that Mme. Jacot found such pleasure in taking her
work on to the verandah, where she could see it. I knew
she did not care for the songs and the dancing. One day she
said to me, " It is such a relief." " A relief ? " I said. " Yes,
do you not see that until it shows there is nothing but forest,
forest, forest, and that still stretch of river. That bank is the
only piece of clear ground I see in the year, and that only
lasts a few weeks until the wet season comes, and then it goes,
and there is nothing but forest, forest, forest, for another year.
It is two years now since I came to this place ; it may be I know
not how many more before we go home again." I grieve to
say, for my poor friend's sake, that her life at Kangwe was nearly
at its end. Soon after my return to England I heard of the
death of her husband from malignant fever. M. Jacot was
a fine, powerful, energetic man, in the prime of life. He
was a tectotaler and a vegetarian ; and although constantly
travelling to and fro in his district on his evangelising
work, he had no foolish recklessness in him. No one would
have thought that he would have been the first to go of
us who used to sit round his hospitable table. His delicate
wife, his two young children or I would have seemed far
more likely. His loss will be a lasting one to the people he
risked his life to (what he regarded) save. The natives held
him in the greatest affection and respect, and his influence

over them was considerable, far more profound than that of any other missionary I have ever seen. His loss is also great to those students of Africa who are working on the culture or on the languages ; his knowledge of both was extensive, particularly of the little known languages of the Ogowé district. He was, when I left, busily employed in compiling a dictionary of the Fan tongue, and had many other works on language in contemplation. His work in this sphere would have had a high value, for he was a man with a university education and well grounded in Latin and Greek, and thoroughly acquainted with both English and French literature, for although born a Frenchman, he had been brought up in America. He was also a cultivated musician, and he and Mme. Jacot in the evenings would sing old French songs, Swiss songs, English songs, in their rich full voices ; and then if you stole softly out on to the verandah, you would often find it crowded with a silent, black audience, listening intently.

The amount of work M. and Mme. Jacot used to get through was, to me, amazing, and I think the Ogowé Protestant mission sadly short-handed—its missionaries not being content to follow the usual Protestant plan out in West Africa, namely, quietly sitting down and keeping house, with just a few native children indoors to do the housework, and close by a school and a little church where a service is held on Sundays. The representatives of the Mission Évangélique, go to and fro throughout the district round each station on evangelising work, among some of the most dangerous and uncivilised tribes in Africa, frequently spending a fortnight at a time away from their homes, on the waterways of a wild and dangerous country. In addition to going themselves, they send trained natives as evangelists and Bible readers, and keep a keen eye on the trained native, which means a considerable amount of worry and strain too. The work on the stations is heavy in Ogowé districts, because when you have got a clearing made and all the buildings up, you have by no means finished with the affair, for you have to fight the Ogowé forest back, as a Dutchman fights the sea. But the main cause of work is the store, which in this exhausting climate is more than enough work for one man alone.

Payments on the Ogowé are made in goods ; the natives do
not use any coinage-equivalent, save in the strange case of the
Fans, which does not touch general trade and which I will
speak of later. They have not even the brass bars and cheetems
that are in used in Calabar, or cowries as in Lagos. In order
to expedite and simplify this goods traffic, a written or printed
piece of paper is employed—practically a cheque, which is
called a " bon " or " book," and these " bons " are cashed—*i.e.*
gooded, at the store. They are for three amounts. Five
fura = a dollar.   One fura = a franc.   Desu = fifty centimes =
half a fura. The value given for these " bons " is the
same from government, trade, and mission. Although the
Mission Évangélique does not trade—*i.e.* buy produce and
sell it at a profit, its representatives have a great deal of
business to attend to through the store, which is practically a
bank. All the native evangelists, black teachers, Bible-
readers and labourers on the stations are paid off in these bons ;
and when any representative of the mission is away on a journey, food bought for themselves and their canoe crews is
paid for in bons, which are brought in by the natives at their
convenience, and changed for goods at the store. Therefore
for several hours every weekday the missionary has to devote
himself to store work, and store work out here is by no means
playing at shop. It is very hard, tiring, exasperating work
when you have to deal with it in full, as a trader, when it is
necessary for you to purchase produce at a price that will give
you a reasonable margin of profit over storing, customs' duties,
shipping expenses, &c., &c. But it is quite enough to try the
patience of any saint when you are only keeping store to pay
on bons, *à la* missionary ; for each class of article used in trade
—and there are some hundreds of them—has a definite and
acknowledged value, but where the trouble comes in is that
different articles have the same value ; for example, six fish-
hooks and one pocket-handkerchief have the same value, or
you can make up that value in lucifer matches, pomatum, a
mirror, a hair comb, tobacco, or scent in bottles..

Now, if you are a trader, certain of these articles cost you
more than others, although they have an identical value to
the native, and so it is to your advantage to pay what we

should call, in Cameroons, " a Kru, cheap copper," and you have
a lot of worry to effect this. To the missionary this does not
so much matter. It makes absolutely no difference to the
native, mind you ; so he is by no means done by the trader.
Take powder for an example. There is no profit on powder
for the trader in Congo Français, but the native always wants
it because he can get a tremendous profit on it from his black
brethren in the bush ; hence it pays the trader to give him
his bon out in Boma check, &c., better than in gunpowder.
This is a fruitful spring of argument and persuasion. However, whether the native is passing in a bundle of rubber
or a tooth of ivory, or merely cashing a bon for a week's
bush catering, he is in Congo Français incapable of deciding
what he will have when it comes to the point. He comes into
the shop with a bon in his hand, and we will say, for example,
the idea in his head that he wants fish-hooks—"jupes," he
calls them—but, confronted with the visible temptation of
pomatum, he hesitates, and scratches his head violently.
Surrounding him there are ten or twenty other natives with
their minds in a similar wavering state, but yet anxious to be
served forthwith. In consequence of the stimulating scratch,
he remembers that one of his wives said he was to bring some
lucifer matches, another wanted cloth for herself, and another
knew of some rubber she could buy very cheap, in tobacco, of a
Fan woman who had stolen it. This rubber he knows he can
take to the trader's store and sell for pocket-handkerchiefs of
a superior pattern, or gunpowder, or rum, which he cannot get
at the mission store. He finally gets something and takes it
home, and likely enough brings it back, in a day or so,
somewhat damaged, desirous of changing it for some other
article or articles. Remember also that these Bantu, like
the Negroes, think externally, in a loud voice ; like Mr. Kipling's 'oont, " he smells most awful vile," and, if he be a
Fan, he accompanies his observations with violent dramatic
gestures, and let the customer's tribe or sex be what it may,
the customer is sadly, sadly liable to pick up any portable
object within reach, under the shadow of his companions'
uproar, and stow it away in his armpits, between his legs, or,
if his cloth be large enough, in that. Picture to yourself the

perplexities of a Christian minister, engaged in such an occupation as storekeeping under these circumstances, with, likely enough, a touch of fever on him and jiggers in his feet; and when the store is closed the goods in it requiring constant vigilance to keep them free from mildew and white ants.

Then in addition to the store work, a fruitful source of work and worry are the schools, for both boys and girls. It is regarded as futile to attempt to get any real hold over the children unless they are removed from the influence of the country fashions that surround them in their village homes ; therefore the schools are boarding ; hence the entire care of the children, including feeding and clothing, falls on the missionary.

The French government has made things harder by decreeing that the children should be taught French. It does not require that evangelistic work should be carried on in French, but that if foreign languages are taught, that language shall be French first. The general feeling of the missionaries is against this, because of the great difficulty in teaching the native this delicate and highly complex language. English, the Africans pick up sooner than any foreign language. I do not like to think that my esteemed friend Donna Maria de Sousa Coutinho is right in saying " because it is so much more like their own savage tongue," but regard this facility in acquiring it to the universal use of it in the form of trade English in the villages round them. Indeed, I believe that if the missionary was. left alone he would not teach any European language, but confine himself to using the native languages in his phonetically written-down form; because the Africans learn to read this very quickly, and the missionary can confine their reading to those books he thinks suitable for perusal by his flock—namely, the Bible, hymn-book, and Bunyan's *Holy War*.

The native does not see things in this light, and half the time comes to the schools only to learn, what he calls " sense," *i.e.*, white man's ways and language, which will enable him to trade with greater advantage. Still, I think the French government is right, from what I have seen in our own possessions of the disadvantage, expense, and inconvenience of the

bulk of the governed not knowing the language of their
governors, both parties having therefore frequently to depend
on native interpreters ; and native interpreters are "deceitful
above all things and desperately wicked" occasionally, and the
just administration of the country under these conditions is
almost impossible.

You may say, Why should not the government official learn
the native language like the missionary? and I think government officials who are settled like missionaries on the Coast
should do so, but if you enforced this rule in Congo Français,
where the government officials fly to and fro, Mezzofantis
only need apply for appointments. Take the Gaboon district,
to use the handy, but now obsolete division of the colony.
This district, being the seaboard one, is where most of the
dealings with the natives occur. In my small way I have met
there with representatives of tribes speaking Shekani, Balungi,
M'benga, M'billo, M'pongwe, Bakele, Ncomi, Igalwa, Adooma,
Ajumba, and Fan, and there are plenty more. Neither are any
of these tribes neatly confined to distinct districts, so that you
might teach your unfortunate official one language, and then tie
him down in one place, where he could use it. Certain districts
have a preponderance of certain tribes, but that is all. The
Fans are everywhere in the northern districts of the Ogowé :
but among them, in the districts below Lembarene, you will
find Igalwa and Ajumba villages, side by side, with likely
enough just across the stream a Bàkele one. Above
Talagouga, until you get to Boué, you could get along with
Fan alone ; but there is no government rule that requires
languages up there because, barring keeping the Ogowé open
to the French flag, it is not interfered with ; and then when
you get up to Franceville above Boué, there is quite another
group of languages, Okota, Batoke, Adooma, &c., &c., and
the Middle Congo languages. To require a knowledge of all
these languages would be absurd, and necessitate the multipli-
cation of officials to an enormous extent.

But to return to the Mission Évangélique schools. This
mission does not undertake technical instruction. All the
training the boys get is religious and scholastic. The girls
fare somewhat better, for they get in addition instruction from

the mission ladies in sewing, washing, and ironing, and for the rest of it they have an uncommonly pleasant and easy time, which they most bitterly regret as past when they go to their husbands, for husbands they each of them have.

It is strange that no technical instruction is given by any government out here. All of the governments support mission schools by grants : but the natives turned out by the schools are at the best only fit for clerks, and the rest of the world seems to have got a glut of clerks already, and Africa does not want clerks yet, it wants planters—I do not say only plantation hands, for I am sure from what I have seen in Cameroons of the self-taught native planters there, that intelligent Africans could do an immense amount to develop the resources of the country. The Roman Catholic mission at Landana carries on a great work in giving agricultural instruction in improved methods : but most of the other technical mission stations confine their attention to teaching carpentering, bricklaying, smith's work, tailoring, book-binding and printing, trades which, save the two first named, Africa is not yet in urgent need to be taught.

The teaching even of sewing, washing, and ironing is a little previous. Good Mme. Jacot will weary herself for months to teach a Fan girl how to make herself a dress, and the girl will learn eagerly, and so keenly enjoy the dress when it is made that it breaks one's heart when one knows that this same girl, when her husband takes her to his village soon, in spite of the two dresses the mission gave her, will be reduced to a bit of filthy rag, which will serve her for dress, sheet, towel and dish cloth ; for even were her husband willing to get her more cloth to exercise her dressmaking accomplishments on, he dare not. Men are men, and women are women all the world over ; and what would his other wives, and his mother and sisters say? Then the washing and ironing are quite parlour accomplishments when your husband does not wear a shirt, and household linen is non existent as is the case among the Fans and many other African tribes. There are other things that the women might be taught with greater advantage to them and those round them.

It is strange that all the cooks employed by the Europeans

should be men, yet all the cooking among the natives themselves is done by women, and done abominably badly in all the
Bantu tribes I have ever come across ; and the Bantu are in
this particular, and indeed in most particulars, far inferior to
the true Negro ; though I must say this is not the orthodox
view.   The Negroes cook uniformly very well, and at moments
are inspired in the direction of palm-oil chop and fish cooking.
Not so the Bantu, whose methods cry aloud for improvement,
they having just the very easiest and laziest way possible of
dealing with food.   The food supply consists of plantain,
yam, koko, sweet potatoes, maize, pumpkin, pineapple, and
ochres, fish both wet and smoked, and flesh of many kinds—
including human in certain districts—snails, snakes, and crayfish, and big maggot-like pupæ of the rhinoceros beetle and the
Rhyncophorus palmatorum.   For sweetmeats the sugar-cane
abounds, but it is only used chewed *au naturel.*   For seasoning there is that bark that tastes like an onion, an onion distinctly *passé,* but powerful and permanent, particularly if it
has been used in one of the native-made, rough earthen pots.
These pots have a very cave-man look about them ; they are
unglazed, unlidded bowls.   They stand the fire wonderfully
well, and you have got to stand, as well as you can, the taste
of the aforesaid bark that clings to them, and that of the smoke
which gets into them during cooking operations over an open
wood fire, as well as the soot-like colour they impart to even
your own white rice.   Out of all this varied material the
natives of the Congo Français forests produce, dirtily,
carelessly and wastefully, a dull, indigestible diet.   Yam,
sweet potatoes, ochres, and maize are not so much cultivated
or used as among the Negroes, and the daily food is practically
plantain—picked while green and the rind pulled off, and the
tasteless woolly interior baked or boiled and the widely distributed manioc treated in the usual way.   The sweet or non-
poisonous manioc I have rarely seen cultivated, because it
gives a much smaller yield, and is much longer coming to
perfection.   The poisonous kind is that in general use ; its
great dahlia-like roots are soaked in water to remove the
poisonous principle, and then dried and grated up, or more
commonly beaten up into a kind of dough in a wooden trough

that looks like a model canoe, with wooden clubs, which I have seen the curiosity hunter happily taking home as war clubs to alarm his family with. The thump, thump, thump of this manioc beating is one of the most familiar sounds in a bush village. The meal, when beaten up, is used for thickening broths, and rolled up into bolsters about a foot long and two inches in diameter, and then wrapped in plantain leaves, and tied round with tie-tie and boiled, or more properly speaking steamed, for a lot of the rolls are arranged in a brass skillet—a kettle Mr. Hudson persists in calling it ; but, much as I respect his statements, I cannot blindly accept this one, for any woman knows a kettle must have a spout, and these utensils are spoutless and round, with a handle across the top, just for all the world like the skillet I make jam in in England —skillet, I repeat. A small quantity of water is poured over the rolls of plantain, a plantain leaf is tucked in over the top tightly, so as to prevent the steam from escaping, and the whole affair is poised on the three cooking-stones over a wood fire, and left there until the contents are done, or more properly speaking, until the lady in charge of it has delusions on the point, and the bottom rolls are a trifle burnt or the whole insufficiently cooked.

This manioc meal is the staple food, the bread equivalent, all along the coast. As you pass along you are perpetually meeting with a new named food, fou-fou on the Leeward, kank on the Windward, m'vada in Corisco, agooma in the Ogowé ; but acquaintance with it demonstrates that it is all the same—manioc. If I ever meet a tribe that refers to buttered muffins I shall know what to expect and so not get excited.

It is a good food when it is properly prepared ; but when a village has soaked its soil-laden manioc tubers in one and the same pool of water for years, the water in that pool becomes a trifle strong, and both it and the manioc get a smell which once smelt is never to be forgotten ; it is something like that resulting from bad paste with a dash of vinegar, but fit to pass all these things, and has qualities of its own that have no civilised equivalent.

I believe that this way of preparing the staple article of

diet is largely responsible for that dire and frequent disease
"cut him belly," and several other quaint disorders, possibly
even for the sleep disease. The natives themselves say that
a diet too exclusively maniocan produces dimness of vision,
ending in blindness if the food is not varied; the poisonous
principle cannot be anything like soaked out in the surcharged
water, and the meal when it is made up and cooked has just
the same sour, acrid taste you would expect it to have from
the smell.

The fish is boiled, or wrapped in leaves and baked. The
dried fish, very properly known as stink-fish, is much preferred ;
this is either eaten as it is, or put into stews as seasoning, as
also are the snails. The meat is eaten either fresh or smoked,
boiled or baked. By baked I always mean just buried in the
ground and a fire lighted on top, or wrapped in leaves and
buried in hot embers.

The smoked meat is badly prepared, just hung up in the
smoke of the fires, which hardens it, blackening the outside
quickly ; but when the lumps are taken out of the smoke, in a
short time cracks occur in them, and the interior part proceeds to go bad, and needless to say maggoty. If it is kept
in the smoke, as it often is to keep it out of the way of dogs
and driver ants, it acquires the toothsome taste and texture
of a piece of old tarpaulin. . I have gone into this bush cooking here in detail, so that you may understand why
on the Coast, when a man comes in and says he has been
down on native chop, we say " Good gracious ! " and give out
the best tins on the spot.

I may be judging the coast tribes too harshly if I include
them with the bush tribes in my culinary indictment, so I
confine my accusations to the Fans and up-river tribes, with
whose culinary methods I have been more in contact, for when
on the coast I have been either in European houses, or in those
of educated natives who have partially, at any rate, adopted
European ways of cooking, and I must say that among the
M'pongwe and Igalwas I came across a bright ray of intelligence—nay, I will say genius, in the matter of Odeaka cheese.
It is not cheese, but, as the schoolboy said anent the author
of the *Iliad*, somebody else of the same name ; but it is good,

and I will sing its praises when I talk of the M'pongwe, and now ask the surviving reader who has waded through this dissertation on cookery if something should not be done to improve the degraded condition of the Bantu cooking culture? Not for his physical delectation only, but because his present methods are bad for his morals, and drive the man to drink, let alone assisting in riveting him in the practice of polygamy, which the missionary party say is an exceedingly bad practice for him to follow. The inter-relationship of these two subjects may not seem on the face of it very clear, but inter-relationships of customs very rarely are; I well remember M. Jacot coming home one day at Kangwe from an evangelising visit to some adjacent Fan towns, and saying he had had given to him that afternoon a new reason for polygamy, which was that it enabled a man to get enough to eat. This sounds sinister from a notoriously cannibal tribe; but the explanation is that the Fans are an exceedingly hungry tribe, and require a great deal of providing for. It is their custom to eat about ten times a day when in village, and the men spend most of their time in the palaver-houses at each end of the street, the women bringing them bowls of food of one kind or another all day long. When the men are away in the forest rubber or elephant-hunting, and have to cook their own food, they cannot get quite so much; but when I have come across them on these expeditions, they halted pretty regularly every two hours and had a substantial snack, and the gorge they all go in for after a successful elephant hunt is a thing to see —once.

There are other reasons which lead to the prevalence of this custom, beside the cooking. One is that it is totally impossible for one woman to do the whole work of a house—look after the children, prepare and cook the food, prepare the rubber, carry the same to the markets, fetch the daily supply of water from the stream, cultivate the plantation, &c., &c. Perhaps I should say it is impossible for the dilatory African woman, for I once had an Irish charwoman, who drank, who would have done the whole week's work of an African village in an afternoon, and then been quite fresh enough to knock some of the nonsense out of her husband's head with that of

the broom, and throw a kettle of boiling water or a paraffin
lamp at him, if she suspected him of flirting with other ladies.
That woman, who deserves fame in the annals of her country,
was named Harragan. She has attained immortality some
years since, by falling down stairs one Saturday night from
excitement arising from "the Image's" (Mr. Harragan) conduct; but we have no Mrs. Harragan in Africa. The African
lady does not care a travelling whitesmith's execration if her
husband does flirt, so long as he does not go and give to other
women the cloth, &c., that she should have. The more wives
the less work, says the African lady; and I have known men
who would rather have had one wife and spent the rest of the
money on themselves, in a civilised way, driven into polygamy
by the women; and of course this state of affairs is most
common in non-slave-holding tribes like the Fan. But then
there is that custom which, as far as I know, is common to all
African tribes, and I suspect to Asiatic, which is well known
to ethnologists, and which once caused a missionary to say to
me: "A blow must be struck at polygamy, and that blow
must be dealt with a feeding-bottle." He was a practical
man, so there are a gross or two of Alexandra feeding-bottles
at a place on the Coast; but they don't go off, and the
missionary has returned to America.

Now polygamy is, like most other subjects, a difficult thing
to form an opinion on, if, before forming that opinion, you go
and make a study of the facts and bearings of the case. It is
therefore advisable to follow the usual method employed by
the majority of people. Just take a prejudice of your own,
and fix it up with the so-called opinions of people who go in
for that sort of prejudice too. This method is absolutely
essential to the forming of an opinion on the subject of polygamy among African tribes, that will be acceptable in
enlightened circles. Polygamy is the institution which above
all others governs the daily life of the native; and it is therefore the one which the missionaries who enter into this daily life,
and not merely into the mercantile and legal, as do the trader
and the government official, are constantly confronted with
and hindered by. All the missionaries have set their faces
against it and deny Church membership to those men who

practise it ; whereby it falls out that many men are excluded
from the fold who would make quite as good Christians as
those within it.   They hesitate about turning off from their
homes women who have lived and worked for them for years,
and not only for them, but often for their fathers before them.
One case in the Rivers I know of is almost tragic if you
put yourself in his place.   An old chief, who had three wives,
profoundly and vividly believed that exclusion from the Holy
Communion meant an eternal damnation.   The missionary
had instructed him in the details of this damnation thoroughly,
and the chief did not like the prospect at all ; but on the other
hand he did not like to turn off the three wives he had lived
with for years.   He found the matter was not even to be
compromised, by turning off two and going to church to be
married with accompanying hymns and orange-blossoms with
number three, for the ladies held together ; not one of them
would marry him and let the other two go, so the poor old
chief worried himself to a shammock and anybody else he
could get to listen to him.   His white trader friends told him
not to be such an infernal ass.   Some of his black fellow
chiefs said the missionary was quite right, and the best thing
for him to do would be to hand over to them the three old
wives, and go and marry a young girl from the mission school.
Personally they were not yet afflicted with scruples on the
subject of polygamy, and of course (being " missionary man "
now) he would not think of taking anything for his wives, so
they would do their best, as friends, to help him out of the
difficulty.   Others of his black fellow chiefs, less advanced in
culture, just said : " What sort of fool palaver you make ; "
and spat profusely.   The poor old man smelt hell fire, and
cried " Yo, yo, yo," and beat his hands upon the ground.   It
was a moral mess of the first water all round.   Still do not
imagine the mission-field is full of yo yo-ing old chiefs ; for
although the African is undecided, he is also very ingenious,
particularly in dodging inconvenient moral principles.

Many a keen old chief turns on his pastor and asks driving
questions regarding the patriarchs, until I have heard a sorely
tried pastor question the wisdom of introducing the Old
Testament to the heathen.   Many a young man hesitates

about joining the Church that will require his entering into the married state with only one woman, whom he knows he may not whack, and who, he knows, will also know this and carry on in all directions, and go and report all his little failings up at the mission, and get him into hot water with the missionary whose good opinion he values highly. And he is artful enough to know he enjoys this good opinion more as an interesting possible convert, than he would as a Church member requiring " discipline."

The worst classes of cases wherein polygamy troubles the missionary are those of boys trained in the mission school and married to school-trained girls. For a time they live according to Church ordinance ; and then they keep it to the eye, and break it to the heart ; and during this period of transition, during which the missionary fights a hard and losing fight for these souls against their inherited sensualism and sloth, they sink into a state that to my mind, seems worse than they would have been in had they never seen a missionary. But I will not go into the disintegrating effects of mission training here, because my opinions on them have no reference to the work done by the Mission Évangélique whose influence upon the natives has been, and is, all for good ; and the amount of work they have done, considering the small financial resources behind them, is to a person who has seen other missions most remarkable, and is not open to the criticism lavished on missions in general.

Mission work was first opened upon the Ogowé by Dr. Nassau, the great pioneer and explorer of these regions. He was acting for the American Presbyterian Society ; but when the French Government demanded education in French in the schools, the stations on the Ogowé, Lembarene (Kangwe), and Talagouga were handed over to the Mission Évangélique of Paris, and have been carried on by its representatives with great devotion and energy. I am unsympathetic, for reasons of my own, with Christian missions, so my admiration for this one does not arise from the usual ground of admiration for missions, namely, that however they may be carried on, they are engaged in a great and holy work ; but I regard the Mission Évangélique, judging from the results I have seen, as the perfection of what one may call a purely spiritual mission.

Lembarene is strictly speaking a district which includes Adânlinan lângâ and the Island, but the name is locally used to denote the great island in the Ogowé, whose native name is Nenge Ezangy ; but for the sake of the general reader I will keep to the everyday term of Lembarene Island.

Lembarene Island is the largest of the islands on the Ogowé. It is some fifteen miles long, east and west, and a mile to a mile and a half wide. It is hilly and rocky, uniformly clad with forest, and several little permanent streams run from it on both sides into the Ogowé. It is situated 130 miles from the sea, at the point, just below the entrance of the N'guni, where the Ogowé commences to divide up into that network of channels by which, like all great West African rivers save the Congo, it chooses to enter the ocean. The island, as we mainlanders at Kangwe used to call it, was a great haunt of mine, particularly after I came down from Talagouga and saw fit to regard myself as competent to control a canoe. I do not mean that I was cut off from it before ; for M. Jacot and M. Haug were always willing to send me across in a big canoe, with the mission boys to paddle, and the boys were always ready to come because it meant " dash," and the dissipation of going to what was the local equivalent of Paris ; but there was always plenty of work for them on the station, and so I did not like taking them away. Therefore when I could get there alone I went more frequently.

From Andande, the beach of Kangwe, the breadth of the arm of the Ogowé to the nearest village on the island, was about that of the Thames at Blackwall. One half of the way was slack water, the other half was broadside on to a stiff current. Now my pet canoe at Andande was about six feet long, pointed at both ends, flat bottomed, so that it floated on the top of the water ; its freeboard was, when nothing was in it, some three inches, and the poor thing had seen trouble in its time, for it had a hole you could put your hand in at one end ; so in order to navigate it successfully, you had to squat in the other, which immersed that to the water level but safely elevated the damaged end in the air. Of course you had to stop in your end firmly, because if you went forward the hole went down into the water, and the water went into the hole, and forthwith you foundered with all hands—*i.e.*, you and the paddle and the calabash baler. This craft also had a strong weather helm, owing to a warp in the tree of which it had been made. I learnt all these things one afternoon, paddling round the sandbank ; and the next afternoon, feeling confident in the merits of my vessel, I started for the island, and I actually got there, and associated with the natives, but feeling my arms were permanently worn out by paddling against the current, I availed myself of the offer of a gentleman to paddle me back in his canoe. He introduced himself as Samuel, and volunteered the statement that he was "a very good man." We duly settled ourselves in the canoe, he occupying the bow, I sitting in the middle, and a Mrs. Samuel sitting in the stern. Mrs. Samuel was a powerful, pretty lady, and a conscientious and continuous paddler. Mr. S. was none of these things, but an ex-Bible reader, with an amazing knowledge of English, which he spoke in a quaint, falsetto, far-away sort of voice, and that man's besetting sin was curiosity. "You be Christian, ma?" said he. I asked him if he had ever met a white man who was not ? "Yes, ma," says Samuel. I said "You must have been associating with people whom you ought not to know." Samuel fortunately not having a repartee for this, paddled on with his long paddle for a few seconds. "Where be your husband, ma?" was the next conversational bomb he hurled at me. "I no got one," I answer. "No got," says Samuel, paralysed with astonishment ; and as Mrs. S., who did not know English, gave one of her vigorous drives with her paddle at this moment, Samuel as near as possible got jerked head first into the Ogowé, and we took on board about two bucketfuls of water. He recovered himself, however and returned to his charge. "No got one, ma?" "No," say I furiously. "Do you get much rubber round here?" "I no be trade man," says Samuel, refusing to fall into my trap for changing conversation. "Why you no got one?" The remainder of the conversation is unreportable, but he landed me at Andande all right, and got his dollar.

The next voyage I made, which was on the next day, I decided to go by myself to the factory, which is on the other side of the island, and did so. I got some goods to buy fish with, and heard from Mr. Cockshut that the poor boy-agent at Osoamokita, had committed suicide. It was a grievous thing. He was, as I have said, a bright, intelligent young Frenchman ; but living in the isolation, surrounded by savage, tiresome tribes, the strain of his responsibility had been too much for him. He had had a good deal of fever, and the very kindly head agent for Woermann's had sent Dr. Pélessier to see if he had not better be invalided home ; but he told the Doctor he was much better, and as he had no one at home to go to he begged him not to send him, and the Doctor, to his subsequent regret, gave in. No one knows, who has not been to visit Africa, how terrible is the life of a white man in one of these out-of-the-way factories, with no white society, and with nothing to look at, day out and day in, but the one set of objects—the forest, the river, and the beach, which in a place like Osoamokita you cannot leave for months at a time, and of which you soon know every plank and stone. I felt utterly wretched as I started home again to come up to the end of the island, and go round it and down to Andande ; and paddled on for some little time, before I noticed that I was making absolutely no progress. I redoubled my exertions, and crept slowly up to some rocks projecting above the water ; but pass them I could not, as the main current of the Ogowé flew in hollow swirls round them against my canoe. Several passing canoefuls of natives gave me good advice in Igalwa ; but facts were facts, and the Ogowé was too strong for me. After about twenty minutes an old Fan gentleman came down river in a canoe and gave me good advice in Fan, and I got him to take me in tow—that is to say, he got into my canoe and I held on to his and we went back down river. I then saw his intention was to take me across to that disreputable village, half Fan, half Bakele, which is situated on the main bank of the river opposite the island ; this I disapproved of, because I had heard that some Senegal soldiers who had gone over there, had been stripped of every rag they had on, and maltreated ; besides, it was growing very late, and I wanted to get home to dinner. I communicated my feelings to my pilot, who did not seem to understand at first, so I feared I should have to knock them into him with the paddle ; but at last he understood I wanted to be landed on the island and duly landed me, when he seemed much surprised at the reward I gave him in pocket-handker-chiefs. Then I got a powerful young Igalwa dandy to paddle me home.

I did not go to the island next day, but down below Fula, watching the fish playing in the clear water, and the lizards and birds on the rocky high banks ; but on my next journey round to the factories I got into another and a worse disaster. I went off there early one morning ; and thinking the only trouble lay in getting back up the Ogowé, and having devel-oped a theory that this might be minimised by keeping very close to the island bank, I never gave a thought to dangers attributive to going down river ; so, having by now acquired pace, my canoe shot out beyond the end rocks of the island into the main stream. It took me a second to realise what had happened, and another to find out I could not get the canoe out of the current without upsetting it, and that I could not force her back up the current, so there was nothing for it but to keep her head straight now she had bolted. A group of native ladies, who had followed my pro-ceedings with much interest, shouted observations which I believe to have been " Come back, come back ; you'll be drowned." " Good-bye, Susannah, don't you weep for me," I courteously retorted, and flew past them and the factory beaches and things in general, keenly watching for my chance to run my canoe up a siding, as it were, off the current main line. I got it at last—a projecting spit of land from the island with rocks projecting out of the water in front of it bothered the current, and after a wild turn round or so, and a near call from my terrified canoe trying to climb up a rock, I got into slack water and took a pause in life's pleasures for a few minutes. Knowing I must be near the end of the island, I went on pretty close to the bank, finally got round into the Kangwe branch of the Ogowé by a connecting creek, and

after an hour's steady paddling I fell in with three big canoes
going up river; they took me home as far as Fula, whence a
short paddle landed me at Andande only slightly late for
supper, convinced that it was almost as safe and far more
amusing to be born lucky than wise.

Now I have described my circumnavigation of the island, I
will proceed to describe its inhabitants. The up-river end of
Lembarene Island is the most inhabited. A path round
the upper part of the island passes through a succession of
Igalwa villages and by the Roman Catholic missionary station.
The slave villages belonging to these Igalwas are away down
the north face of the island, opposite the Fan town of Fula,
which I have mentioned. It strikes me as remarkable that
the Igalwa, like the Dualla of Cameroons, have their slaves in
separate villages; but this is the case, though I do not know
the reason of it. These Igalwa slaves cultivate the plantations,
and bring up the vegetables and fruit to their owners' villages,
and do the housework daily.

The interior of the island is composed of high, rocky, heavily
forested hills, with here and there a stream, and here and
there a swamp; the higher land is towards the up-river end;
down river there is a lower strip of land with hillocks. This
is, I fancy, formed by deposits of sand, &c., catching in among
the rocks, and connecting what was at one time several isolated
islands. There are no big game or gorillas on the island, but
it has a peculiar and awful house ant, much smaller than the
driver ant, but with a venomous, bad bite; its only good point
is that its chief food is the white ants, which are therefore
kept in abeyance on Lembarene Island, although flourishing
destructively on the mainland banks of the river in this
locality. I was never tired of going and watching those
Igalwa villagers, nor were, I think, the Igalwa villagers ever
tired of observing me. Although the physical conditions of
life were practically identical with those of the mainland, the
way in which the Igalwas dealt with them, i.e., the culture, was
distinct from the culture of the mainland Fans.

The Igalwas are a tribe very nearly akin, if not ethnically
identical with, the M'pongwe, and the culture of these two
tribes is on a level with the highest native African culture.

African culture, I may remark, varies just the same as
European in this, that there is as much difference in the
manners of life between, say, an Igalwa and a Bubi of Fernando
Po, as there is between a Londoner and a Laplander.

The Igalwa builds his house like that of the M'pongwe,
of bamboo, and he surrounds himself with European-
made articles. The neat houses, fitted with windows, with
wooden shutters to close at night, and with a deal door—a
carpenter-made door—are in sharp contrast with the ragged
ant-hill looking performances of the Akkas, or the bark huts
of the Fan, with no windows, and just an extra broad bit of
bark to slip across the hole that serves as a door. On going
into an Igalwa house you will see a four-legged table, often
covered with a bright-coloured tablecloth, on which stands a
water bottle, with two clean glasses, and round about you
will see chairs—Windsor chairs. These houses have usually
three, sometimes more rooms, and a separate closed-in little
kitchen, built apart, wherein you may observe European-made
saucepans, in addition to the ubiquitous skillet. Outside, all
along the clean sandy streets, the inhabitants are seated.
The Igalwa is truly great at sitting, the men pursuing a policy
of masterly inactivity, broken occasionally by leisurely netting
a fishing net, the end of the netting hitched up on to the roof
thatch, and not held by a stirrup. The ladies are employed in
the manufacture of articles pertaining to a higher culture—I
allude, as Mr. Micawber would say, to bed-quilts and pillow
cases—the most gorgeous bed-quilts and pillow-cases—made
of patchwork, and now and again you will see a mosquito-bar
in course of construction, of course not made of net or muslin
because of the awesome strength and ferocity of the Lembarene strain of mosquitoes, but of stout, fair-flowered and
besprigged chintzes ; and you will observe these things are
often being sewn with a sewing machine. Here and there
you will see a misguided woman making a Hubbard. Forgive me, but I must break out on the subject of Hubbards ;
I will promise to keep clear of bad language let the effort
cost me what it may. A Hubbard is a female garment
patronised by the whole set of missions from Sierra Leone
to Congo Belge, so please understand I am not criticising

the Mission Évangélique in this affair. I think these things are one of the factors producing the well-known torpidity of the mission-trained girl ; and they should be suppressed in her interest, apart from their appearance, which is enough to constitute a hanging matter. Their formation is this—a yoke round the neck and shoulders fastens at the back with three buttons—two usually lost ; from this yoke protrude dwarf sleeves, and round its lower rim, on a level with the armpits, is sewn on a flounce, set in with full gathers, which falls to the heels of the wearer. Sometimes this flounce is sewn on with a chain-stitch machine, whereby I once saw a dreadful accident on the Leeward Coast. In church a limb of a child, seeking for amusement during the long extemporary prayer of its pastor, came across a thread of white sticking out from the back of the yoke of the Hubbard of the woman in front of her, and pulled it out by the yard. Of course, when the unconscious victim rose up, the whole of what might be called the practical part of her attire subsided on to the floor. This is only an occasional danger ; but the constant habit of the garment is to fall forward and reap the dirt whenever the wearer stoops forward to do anything, going into the fire, and the cooking, and things in general, and impeding all rapid movement. These garments are usually made at working parties in Europe ; and what idea the pious ladies in England, Germany, Scotland, and France can have of the African figure I cannot think, but evidently part of their opinion is that it is very like a tub. I was once helping to unpack a mission box. "What have they sent out these frills for palm-oil puncheons for ? " I inquired of my esteemed friend, the lady missionary. " Don't be more foolish than you can help," she answered. " Don't you see the sleeves ? They are Hubbards." I was crushed ; but even she acknowledged that it was trying of the home folk to make them like that, all the more so because their delusion on the African figure was not confined to the making of Hubbards, but extended to the making of shirts and chemises. There is nothing like measurements in ethnology, so I measured and found one that with a depth of thirty inches had a breadth of beam of forty-two inches ; one with a depth of thirty-six

inches had a breadth of sixty inches. It is not in nature
for people to be made to fit these things. So I suggested
that a few stuffed negroes should be sent home for distribution
in working-party centres, and then the ladies could try the
things on. My friend's answer was far from being personally
complimentary, so I will not give it, but return hurriedly to
the Igalwa ladies in the Lembarene village, sitting on the
sunny sandy street on their low, wood country stools. The

IGALWA WOMEN.

chairs I have mentioned before are "for dandy" not for
use.

Those among them who may not be busy sewing, are busy
doing each other's hair. Hair-dressing is quite an art among
the Igalwa and M'pongwe women, and their hair is very
beautiful; very crinkly, but fine. It is plaited up, close to
the head, partings between the plaits making elaborate
parterres. Into the beds of plaited hair are stuck long pins
of river ivory (hippo), decorated with black tracery and

openwork, and made by their good men. A lady will stick
as many of these into her hair as she can get, but the prevailing mode is to have one stuck in behind each ear, showing
their broad, long heads above like two horns ; they are exceedingly becoming to these black but comely ladies, verily
I think, the comeliest ladies I have ever seen on the Coast.
Very black they are, blacker than many of their neighbours,
always blacker than the Fans, and although their skin lacks
that velvety pile of the true negro, it is not too shiny, but it is
fine and usually unblemished, and their figures are charmingly
rounded, their hands and feet small, almost as small as a high-
class Calabar woman's, and their eyes large, lustrous, soft and
brown, and their teeth as white as the sea surf and undisfigured
by filing.

The native dress for men and women alike is the cloth or
paun. The men wear it by rolling the upper line round
the waist, and in addition they frequently wear a singlet
or a flannel shirt worn *more Africano*, flowing free. Rich
men will mount a European coat and hat, and men connected with the mission or trading stations occasionally wear
trousers. The personal appearance of the men does not
amount to much when all's done, so we will return to the
ladies. They wrap the upper hem of these cloths round under
the armpits, a graceful form of drapery, but one which requires
continual readjustment. The cloth is about four yards long
and two deep, and there is always round the hem a border,
or false hem, of turkey red twill, or some other coloured
cotton cloth to the main body of the paun. In addition
to the cloth there is worn, when possible, a European shawl,
either one of those thick cotton cloth ones printed with
Chinese-looking patterns in dull red on a dark ground, this
sort is wrapped round the upper part of the body : or what
is more highly esteemed is a bright, light-coloured, fancy wool
shawl, pink or pale blue preferred, which being carefully
folded into a roll is placed over one shoulder, and is entirely
for dandy. I am thankful to say they do not go in for hats ;
when they wear anything on their heads it is a handkerchief
folded shawlwise ; the base of the triangle is bound round
the forehead just above the eyebrows, the ends carried round

over the ears and tied behind over the apex of the triangle
of the handkerchief, the three ends being then arranged fan-
wise at the back. Add to this costume a sober-coloured silk
parasol, not one of your green or red young tent-like, brutally
masculine, knobby-sticked umbrellas, but a fair, lady-like
parasol, which, being carefully rolled up, is carried handle
foremost right in the middle of the head, also for dandy. Then
a few strings of turquoise-blue beads, or imitation gold ones,
worn round the shapely throat; and I will back my Igalwa or
M'pongwe belle against any of those South Sea Island young
ladies we nowadays hear so much about, thanks to Mr. Steven-
son, yea, even though these may be wreathed with fragrant
flowers, and the African lady very rarely goes in for flowers.
The only time I have seen the African ladies wearing them for
ornament has been among these Igalwas, who now and again
stud their night-black hair with pretty little round vividly red
blossoms in a most fetching way. I wonder the Africans do
not wear flowers more frequently, for they are devoted to
scent, both men and women.

The usual statements that the African women age—go off,
I believe, is the technical term—very early is, I am sure,
wrong in many cases. Look at those Sierra Leone mammies,
slightly spherical, I own, but undeniably charming; and the
Calabar women, although belonging to a very ugly tribe, are
very little the worse for twenty years one way or the other;
and these women along Congo Français way, Well! I know
one who is all forty-five, and yet at present is regarded by a
French official, a judge one might think, as *une belle femme*.

The Igalwas are a proud race, one of the noble tribes, like
the M'pongwe and the Ajumba. The women do not intermarry with lower-class tribes, and in their own tribe they
are much restricted, owing to all relations on the mother's
side being forbidden to intermarry. This well-known form of
accounting relationships only through the mother (*Mutter-
recht*) is in a more perfected and elaborated form among the
Igalwa than among any other tribe I am personally acquainted
with; brothers and cousins on the mother's side being in one
class of relationship, and called by one name, Ndako.

The father's responsibility, as regards authority over his own children is very slight. The really responsible male relative is the mother's elder brother. From him must leave to marry be obtained for either girl, or boy ; to him and the mother must the present be taken which is exacted on the marriage of a girl ; and should the mother die, on him and not on the father, lies the responsibility of rearing the children ; they go to his house, and he treats and regards them as nearer and dearer to himself than his own children, and at his death, after his own brothers by the same mother, they become his heirs.

Marriage among the Igalwa and M'pongwe is not direct marriage by purchase, but a certain fixed price present is made to the mother and uncle of the girl. Other propitiatory presents are made, but do not count legally, and have not necessarily to be returned in case of post-nuptial differences arising leading to a divorce—a very frequent catastrophe in the social circle ; for the Igalwa ladies are spirited, and devoted to personal adornment, and they are naggers at their husbands. Many times when walking on Lembarene Island, have I seen a lady stand in the street and let her husband, who had taken shelter inside the house, know what she thought of him, in a way that reminded me of some London slum scenes. When the husband loses his temper, as he surely does sooner or later, being a man, he whacks his wife—or wives, if they have been at him in a body. This crisis usually takes place at night ; and when staying on board the *Mové*, or the *Éclaireur*, moored alongside the landing place at Lembarene Island, I have heard yells and squalls of a most dismal character. He may whack with impunity so long as he does not draw blood ; if he does, be it never so little, his wife is off to her relations, the present he has given for her is returned, the marriage is annulled, and she can re-marry as soon as she is able.

Her relations are only too glad to get her, because, although the present has to be returned, yet the propitiatory offerings remain theirs, and they know more propitiatory offerings as well as another present will accrue with the next set of suitors. This of course is only the case with the younger women ; the older women for one thing do not nag so much, and moreover they have usually children willing and able to support them.

If they have not, their state is, like that of all old childless women in Africa, a very desolate one.

Infant marriage is now in vogue among the Igalwa, and to my surprise I find it is of quite recent introduction and adoption. Their own account of this retrograde movement in culture is that in the last generation—some of the old people indeed claim to have known him—there was an exceedingly ugly and deformed man who could not get a wife, the women being then, as the men are now, great admirers of physical beauty. So this man, being very cunning, hit on the idea of becoming betrothed to one before she could exercise her own choice in the matter; and knowing a family in which an interesting event was likely to occur, he made heavy presents in the proper quarters and bespoke the coming infant if it should be a girl. A girl it was, and thus, say the Igalwa, arose the custom; and nowadays, although they do not engage their wives so early as did the founder of the custom, they adopt infant marriage as an institution.

I inquired carefully, in the interests of ethnology, as to what methods of courting were in vogue previously. They said people married each other because they loved each other. I think other ethnologists will follow this inquiry up, for we may here find a real golden age, which in other races of humanity lies away in the mists of the ages behind the kitchen middens and the Cambrian rocks. My own opinion in this matter is that the earlier courting methods of the Igalwa involved a certain amount of effort on the man's part, a thing abhorrent to an Igalwa. It necessitated his dressing himself up, and likely enough fighting that impudent scoundrel who was engaged in courting her too ; and above all serenading her at night on the native harp, with its strings made from the tendrils of a certain orchid, or on the marimba, amongst crowds of mosquitoes. Any institution that involved being out at night amongst crowds of those Lembarene mosquitoes would have to disappear, let that institution be what it might.

The Igalwa are one of the dying-out coast tribes. As well as on Lembarene Island, their villages are scattered along the banks of the Lower Ogowé, and on the shores and islands of Elivã Z'onlange. On the island they are, so far, undisturbed by the Fan invasion, and laze their lives away like lotus-eaters. Their slaves work their large plantations, and bring up to them magnificent yams, ready prepared agooma, sweet-potatoes, papaw, &c., not forgetting that delicacy Odeaka cheese; this is not an exclusive inspiration of theirs, for the M'pongwe and the Benga use it as well. It is made from the kernel of the wild mango, a singularly beautiful tree of great size and stately spread of foliage. I can compare it only in appearance and habit of growth to our Irish, or ever-green, oak, but it is an idealisation of that fine tree. Its leaves are a softer, brighter, deeper green, and in due season (August) it is covered—not ostentatiously like the real mango, with great spikes of bloom, looking each like a gigantic head of mignonette—but with small yellow-green flowers tucked away under the leaves, filling the air with a soft sweet perfume, and then falling on to the bare shaded ground beneath to make a deep-piled carpet. I do not know whether it is a mango tree at all, for I am no botanist: but anyhow the fruit is rather like that of the mango in external appearance, and in internal still more so, for it has a disproportionately large stone. These stones are cracked, and the kernel taken out. The kernels are spread a short time in the shade to dry; then they are beaten up into a pulp with a wooden pestle, and the pulp put into a basket lined carefully with plantain leaves and placed in the sun, which melts it up into a stiff mass. The basket is then removed from the sun and stood aside to cool. When cool, the cheese can be turned out in shape, and can be kept a long time if it is wrapped round with leaves and a cloth, and hung up inside the house. Its appearance is that of almond rock, and it is cut easily with a knife; but at any period of its existence, if it is left in the sun it melts again rapidly into an oily mass.

The natives use it as a seasoning in their cookery, stuffing fish and plantains with it and so on, using it also in the pre-paration of a sort of sea-pie they make with meat and fish. To make this, a thing well worth doing, particularly with hippo or other coarse meat, reduce the wood fire to embers, and make plantain leaves into a sort of bag, or cup; small pieces of the meat should then be packed in layers with red pepper and odeaka in between. The tops of the leaves are then tied together with fine tie-tie, and the bundle, without any saucepan of any kind, stood on the glowing embers, the cook taking care there is no flame. The meat is done, and a superb gravy formed, before the containing plantain leaves are burnt through—plantain leaves will stand an amazing lot in the way of fire. This dish is really excellent, even when made with boa constrictor, hippo, or crocodile. It makes the former most palatable ; but of course it does not remove the musky taste from crocodile ; nothing I know of will.

The Igalwa have been under missionary influence since 1874, when Dr. Nassau founded the mission station at Kangwe. To this influence they owe their very frequent ability to read and write, and maybe also their somewhat refined culture. Nevertheless, this influence has not permeated their social institutions much yet.

The great and important difference between the M'pongwe,[1] Igalwa, and Ajumba fetish, and the fetish of those tribes round them, consists in their conception of a certain spirit called Mbuiri. They have, as is constant among the Bantu races of South-West Africa, a great god—the creator, a god who has made all things, and who now no longer takes any interest in the things he has created. Their name for this god is Anyambie, which when pronounced sounds to my ears like anlynlah—the l's being very weak,—the derivation of this name, however, is from Anyima a spirit, and Mbia, good. This god, unlike other forms of the creating god in fetish, has a viceroy or minister who is a god he has created, and to whom he leaves the government of affairs. This god is Mbuiri or Ombwiri, and this Ombwiri is of very high interest to the student of comparative fetish. He has never been, nor can he ever become, a man, i.e. be born as a man, but he can transfuse with his own personality that of human beings, and also the souls of all those things we white men regard as inanimate, such as rocks, trees, &c., in a similar manner.

The M'pongwe know that his residence is in the sea, and some of them have seen him as an old white man, not flesh-

[1] The M'pongwe speaking tribes are the M'pongwe, Orungu, Nkâmi, Ajumba, Inlenga and the Igalwa.

colour white, but chalk white. There is another important
point here, but it wants a volume to itself, so I must pass
it. Mbuiri's appearance in a corporeal form denotes ill luck,
not death to the seer, but misfortune of a severe and
diffused character. The ruin of a trading enterprise, the
destruction of a village or a family, are put down to Mbuiri's
action. Yet he is not regarded as a malevolent god, a devil,
but as an avenger, or punisher of sin ; and the M'pongwe
look on him as the Being to whom they primarily owe the
good things and fortunes of this life, and as the Being who
alone has power to govern the host of truly malevolent spirits
that exist in nature.

The different instruments with which he works in the
shaping of human destiny bear his name when in his employ.
When acting by means of water, he is Mbuiri Aningo ;
when in the weather, Mbuiri Ngali ; when in the forests,
Mbuiri Ibaka ; when in the form of a dwarf, Mbuiri Akkoa,
and so on.

The great difference between Mbuiri and the lesser spirits
is this :—the lesser spirits cannot incarnate themselves except
through extraneous things ; Mbuiri can, he can become visible
without anything beyond his own will to do so. The other
spirits must be in something to become visible. This is an
extremely delicate piece of fetish which it took me weeks to
work out. I think I may say another thing about Mbuiri,
though I say it carefully, and that is, that among the
M'pongwe and the tribe who are the parent tribe of the
M'pongwe—the now rapidly dying out Ajumba, and their
allied tribe the Igalwa—Mbuiri is a distinct entity, while
among the neighbouring tribes he is a class, *i.e.* there are
hundreds of Mbuiri or Ombwiri, one for every remarkable
place or thing, such as rock, tree, or forest thicket, and for
every dangerous place in a river. Had I not observed a
similar state of affairs regarding Sasabonsum, a totally
different kind of spirit on the Windward coast, I should have
had even greater trouble than I had, in finding a key to what
seemed at first a mass of conflicting details regarding this
important spirit Mbuiri.

There is one other very important point in M'pongwe fetish ;

and that is that the souls of men exist before birth as well as after death. This is indeed, as far as I have been able to find out, a doctrine universally held by the West African tribes, but among the M'pongwe there is this modification in it, which agrees strangely well with the idea I found regarding reincarnated diseases, existent among the Okÿon tribes (pure negroes). The malevolent minor spirits are capable of being born with, what we will call, a man's soul, as well as going in with the man's soul during sleep. For example, an Olâgâ may be born with a man and that man will thereby be born mad; he may at any period of his life, given certain conditions, become possessed by an evil spirit, Onlogho Abambo, Iniembe, Nkandada, and become mad, or ill; but if he is born mad, or sickly, one of the evil spirits such as an Olâgâ or an Ibambo, the soul of a man that has not been buried properly, has been born with him.

The rest of the M'pongwe fetish is on broad lines common to other tribes, so I relegate it to the general collection of notes on fetish. M'pongwe jurisprudence is founded on the same ideas as those on which West African jurisprudence at large is founded, but it is so elaborated that it would be desecration to sketch it. It requires a massive monograph.

CHAPTER XI

ON THE WAY FROM KANGWE TO LAKE NCOVI

In which the voyager goes for bush again and wanders into a new lake and a new river.

July 22nd, 1895.—Left Kangwe. The four Ajumba[1] did not turn up early in the morning as had been arranged, but arrived about eight, in pouring rain, so decided to wait until two o'clock, which will give us time to reach their town of Arevooma before nightfall, and may perhaps give us a chance of arriving there dry. At two we start. Good Mme. Jacot comes down to Andande beach to see us off, accompanied by Edmond; M. Jacot, I am sorry to say, has a bad touch of fever, but insists that he will be all right to-morrow; and as he is a person whom one automatically believes in, and also is a disciple of Kühne, one can do nothing; so I go, though feeling anxious for Mme. Jacot. I myself have an awful headache, complicated by the conviction that I am in for a heavy bout of fever : but as an Aduma canoe is one of the most comfortable things in Africa, or out of it, this is no cause for delay. We go down river on the Kangwe side of Lembarene Island, make a pause in front of the Igalwa slave town, which is on the Island and nearly opposite the Fan town of Fula on the mainland bank, our motive being to get stores of yam and plantain—and magnificent specimens of both we get—and then, when our

[1] These four Ajumba had been engaged, through the instrumentality of M. Jacot, to accompany me to the Rembwé River. The Ajumba are one of the noble tribes and are the parent stem of the M'pongwe; their district is the western side of Lake Ayzingo.

canoe is laden with them to an extent that would get us into
trouble under the Act if it ran here, off we go again. Every
canoe we meet shouts us a greeting, and asks where we are
going, and we say "Rembwé"—and they say "What!
Rembwé!"—and we say "Yes, Rembwé," and paddle on. I
lay among the luggage for about an hour, not taking much
interest in the Rembwé or anything else, save my own headache; but this soon lifted, and I was able to take notice, just
before we reached the Ajumba's town, called Arevooma.
The sandbanks stretch across the river here nearly awash, so
all our cargo of yams has to be thrown overboard on to the
sand, from which they can be collected by being waded out
to. The canoe, thus lightened, is able to go on a little
further, but we are soon hard and fast again, and the crew
have to jump out and shove her off about once every five
minutes, and then to look lively about jumping back into
her again, as she shoots over the cliffs of the sandbanks.

When we reach Arevooma, I find it is a very prettily situated
town, on the left-hand bank of the river—clean and well kept,
and composed of houses built on the Igalwa and M'pongwe
plan with walls of split Bamboo and a palm thatch roof. I
own I did not much care for these Ajumbas on starting, but
they are evidently going to be kind and pleasant companions.
One of them is a gentlemanly-looking man, who wears a gray
shirt; another looks like a genial Irishman who has
accidentally got black, very black; he is distinguished by
wearing a singlet; another is a thin, elderly man, notably
silent; and the remaining one is a strapping, big fellow, as
black as a wolf's mouth, of gigantic muscular development,
and wearing quantities of fetish charms hung about him.
The two first mentioned are Christians; the other two pagans,
and I will refer to them by their characteristic points, for their
honourable names are awfully alike when you do hear them,
and, as is usual with Africans, rarely used in conversation.

Gray Shirt places his house at my disposal, and both he
and his exceedingly pretty wife do their utmost to make me
comfortable. The house lies at the west end of the town. It
is one room inside, but has, I believe, a separate cooking shed.
In the verandah in front is placed a table, an ivory bundle chair

and a gourd of water, and I am also treated to a calico table-cloth, and most thoughtfully screened off from the public gaze with more calico so that I can have my tea in privacy. After this meal, to my surprise Ndaka turns up. Certainly he is one of the very ugliest men—black or white—I have ever seen, and I fancy one of the best. He is now on a holiday from Kangwe, seeing to the settlement of his dead brother's affairs. The dead brother was a great man in Arevooma and a pagan, but Ndaka, the Christian Bible-reader, seems to get on perfectly with the family and is holding to-night a meeting outside his brother's house and comes with a lantern to fetch me to attend it. Of course I have to go, headache or no headache

Most of the town was there, mainly as spectators. Ndaka and my two Christian boatmen manage the service between them, and what with the hymns and the mosquitoes the experience is slightly awful. We sit in a line in front of the house, which is brilliantly lit up—our own lantern on the ground before us acting as a rival entertainment to the house lamps inside for some of the best insect society in Africa, who after the manner of the insect world, insist on regarding us as responsible for their own idiocy in getting singed, and sting us in revenge, while we slap hard, as we howl hymns in the fearful Igalwa and M'pongwe way. Next to an English picnic, the most uncomfortable thing I know is an open-air service in this part of Africa. Service being over, Ndaka takes me over the house to show its splendours. The great brilliancy of its illumination arises from its being lit by two hanging lamps supplied by Messrs Woermann at five dollars apiece and burning Devoe's patent paraffin oil in them. This is not an advertisement, because no other firm sells this type of lamp round here, neither can you get, all along the Coast, any other sort of paraffin oil. The most remarkable point about the house is the floor which is made of split, plaited bamboo, the like of which I have never before seen. It gives under your feet in an alarming way, being raised some three or four feet above the ground, and I am haunted by the fear that I shall go through it and give pain to myself, and great trouble to others before I could be got out. It is a beautiful piece of workmanship, and Arevooma has every reason to be proud of it. Having admired these things, I go, dead tired and still headachy, down the road with my host who carries the lantern, through an atmosphere that has 45 per cent. of solid matter in the shape of mosquitoes ; then wishing him good-night, I shut myself in, and illuminate, humbly, with a candle.   The furniture of the house consists mainly of boxes, containing the wealth of Gray Shirt, in clothes, mirrors, &c.   One corner of the room is taken up by great calabashes full of some sort of liquor, and there is an ivory bundle chair, a hanging mirror, several rusty guns, and a considerable collection of china basins and jugs.   Evidently Gray Shirt is rich.   The most interesting article to me, however, just now is the bed hung over with a clean, substantial, chintz mosquito bar, and spread with clean calico and adorned with patchwork-covered pillows. So I take off my boots and put on my slippers ; for it never does in this country to leave off boots altogether at any time, and risk getting bitten by mosquitoes on the feet, when you are on the march ; because the rub of your boot on the bite always produces a sore, and a sore when it comes in the Gorilla country, comes to stay.

No sooner have I carefully swished all the mosquitoes from under the bar and turned in, than a cat scratches and mews at the door—turn out and let her in.   She is evidently a pet, so I take her on to the bed with me.   She is a very nice cat— sandy and fat—and if I held the opinion of Pythagoras concerning wild fowl, I should have no hesitation in saying she had in her the soul of Dame Juliana Berners, such a whole-souled devotion to sport does she display, dashing out through the flaps of the mosquito bar after rats which, amid squeals from the rats and curses from her, she kills amongst the china collection.   Then she comes to me, triumphant, expecting congratulations, and accompanied by mosquitoes, and purrs and kneads upon my chest until she hears another rat.

Tuesday, July 23rd.—Am aroused by violent knocking at the door in the early gray dawn—so violent that two large centipedes and a scorpion drop on to the bed.   They have evidently been tucked away among the folds of the bar all night.   Well " when ignorance is bliss 'tis folly to be wise," particularly along here. I get up without delay, and find myself quite well. The cat has thrown a basin of water neatly over into my bag during her nocturnal hunts; and when my tea comes I am informed a man "done die" in the night, which explains the firing of guns I heard. I inquire what he has died of, and am told "He just truck luck, and then he die." His widows are having their faces painted white by sympathetic lady friends, and are attired in their oldest, dirtiest clothes, and but very few of them; still, they seem to be taking things in a resigned spirit. These Ajumba seem pleasant folk. They play with their pretty brown children in a taking way. Last night I noticed some men and women playing a game new to me, which consisted in throwing a hoop at each other. The point was to get the hoop to fall over your adversary's head. It is a cheerful game. Quantities of the common house-fly about—and, during the early part of the morning, it rains in a gentle kind of way; but soon after we are afloat in our canoe it turns into a soft white mist.

We paddle still westwards down the broad quiet waters of the O'Rembo Vongo. I notice great quantities of birds about here—great hornbills, vividly coloured kingfishers, and for the first time the great vulture I have often heard of, and the skin of which I will take home before I mention even its approximate spread of wing.[1] There are also noble

---

[1] Since my return home I have read that rather rare and very charming book, *Ten Years' Wanderings among the Ethiopians*, by T. J. Hutchinson, a gentleman who was for a long time H.B.M. Consul in Calabar. He also has heard of this bird, which was described as "measuring five fathoms, *i e.*, thirty feet,—from the tip of one wing to the tip of the other. Its beak is a fathom, or six feet long. No man dares to go near it, and no gun fit to kill it. Its favourite food is obtained by killing the elephant, whose eyes it devours." Mr. Hutchinson goes on to say that "inquiring the colour of the bird's plumage the answer I received—namely, that its feathers were green," made me shut my note-book, with a "mental reservation" as to the ignorance of Baron Cuvier (p. 242). I am not going bail for these measurements being correct to an inch or so, and must state that the bird is not green but brown and gray, and the noise it makes when settling in the forest trees over one's head is very great, but for further particulars, you must wait until I or some other West Coaster brings home a specimen, and then—— !

white cranes, and flocks of small black and white birds, new to me, with heavy razor-shaped bills, reminding one of the Devonian puffin. The hornbill is perhaps the most striking in appearance. It is the size of a small, or say a good-sized hen-turkey. Gray Shirt says the flocks, which are of eight or ten, always have the same quantity of cocks and hens, and that they live together "white man fashion," *i.e.*, each couple keeping together. They certainly do a great deal of courting, the cock filling out his wattles on his neck like a turkey, and spreading out his tail with great pomp and ceremony, but very awkwardly. To see hornbills on a bare sandbank is a solemn sight, but when they are dodging about in the hippo grass they sink ceremony, and roll and waddle, looking—my man said —for snakes and the little sand-fish, which are close in under the bank ; and their killing way of dropping their jaws—I should say opening their bills—when they are alarmed is comic. I think this has something to do with their hearing, for I often saw two or three of them in a line on a long branch, standing, stretched up to their full height, their great eyes opened wide, and all with their great beaks open, evidently listening for something. Their cry is most peculiar and can only be mistaken for a native horn ; and although there seems little variety in it to my ear, there must be more to theirs, for they will carry on long confabulations with each other across a river, and, I believe, sit up half the night and talk scandal.

There were plenty of plantain-eaters here, but, although their screech was as appalling as I have heard in Angola, they were not regarded, by the Ajumba at any rate, as being birds of evil omen, as they are in Angola. Still, by no means all the birds here only screech and squark. Several of them have very lovely notes. There is one who always gives a series of infinitely beautiful, soft, rich-toned whistles just before the first light of the dawn shows in the sky, and one at least who has a prolonged and very lovely song. This bird, I was told in Gaboon, is called *Telephonus erythropterus*. I expect an ornithologist would enjoy himself here, but I cannot —and will not—collect birds. I hate to have them killed any how, and particularly in the barbarous way in which these natives kill them.

The broad stretch of water looks like a long lake. In all directions sandbanks are showing their broad yellow backs, and there will be more showing soon, for it is not yet the height of the dry. We are perpetually grounding on those which by next month will be above water. These canoes are built, I believe, more with a view to taking sandbanks comfortably than anything else ; but they are by no means yet sufficiently specialised for getting off them. Their flat bottoms enable them to glide on to the banks, and sit there, without either upsetting or cutting into the sand, as a canoe with a keel would ; but the trouble comes in when you are getting off the steep edge of the bank, and the usual form it takes is upsetting. So far my Ajumba friends have only tried to meet this difficulty by tying the cargo in.

I try to get up the geography of this region conscientiously. Fortunately I find Gray Shirt, Singlet, and Pagan can speak trade English ; for my interpreter's knowledge of that language seems confined to "Praps," "'Tis better so," and "Lordy, Lordy, helpee me"—a valueless vocabulary. None of them, however, seem to recognise a single blessed name on the chart, which is saying nothing against the chart and its makers, who probably got their names up from M'pongwes and Igalwas instead of Ajumba, as I am trying to. Geographical research in this region is fraught with difficulty, I find, owing to different tribes calling one and the same place by different names ; and I am sure the Royal Geographical Society ought to insert among their "Hints" that every traveller in this region should carefully learn every separate native word, or set of words, signifying "I don't know,"—four villages and two rivers I have come across out here solemnly set down with various forms of this statement, for their native name. Really I think the old Portuguese way of naming places after Saints, &c., was wiser in the long run, and it was certainly pleasanter to the ears. My Ajumba, however, know about my Ngambi and the Vinue all right and Elivã z'Ayzingo, so I must try and get cross bearings from these.

We have an addition to our crew this morning—a man who wants to go and get work at John Holt's sub-factory away on the Rembwé. He has been waiting a long while at Arevooma, unable to get across, I am told, "because the road is now stopped between Ayzingo and the Rembwé by "those fearful Fans." "How are we going to get through that way?" says I, with natural feminine alarm. "We are not, sir," says Gray Shirt. This is what Lady MacDonald would term a chatty little incident ; and my hair begins to rise as I remember what I have been told about those Fans and the indications I have already seen of its being true when on the Upper Ogowé. Now here we are going to try to get through the heart of their country, far from a French station, and without the French flag. Why did I not obey Mr. Hudson's orders not to go wandering about in a reckless way ! Anyhow I am in for it, and Fortune favours the brave. The only question is : Do I individually come under this class ? I go into details. It seems Pagan thinks he can depend on the friendship of two Fans he once met and did business with, and who now live on an island in Lake Ncovi—Ncovi is not down on my map and I have never heard of it before—anyhow thither we are bound now.

Each man has brought with him his best gun, loaded to the muzzle, and tied on to the baggage against which I am leaning—the muzzles sticking out each side of my head : the flint locks covered with cases, or sheaths, made of the black-haired skins of gorillas, leopard skin, and a beautiful bright bay skin, which I do not know, which they say is bush cow— but they call half a dozen things bush cow. These guns are not the "gas-pipes" I have seen up north ; but decent rifles which have had the rifling filed out and the locks replaced by flint locks and converted into muzzle loaders, and many of them have beautiful barrels. I find the Ajumba name for the beautiful shrub that has long bunches of red yellow and cream-coloured young leaves at the end of its branches is " obāa." I also learn that in their language ebony and a monkey have one name. The forest on either bank is very lovely. Some enormously high columns of green are formed by a sort of climbing plant having taken possession of lightning-struck trees, and in one place it really looks exactly as if some one had spread a great green coverlet over the forest, so as to keep it dry. No high land showing in any direction. Pagan tells

me the extinguisher-shaped juju filled with medicine and made
of iron is against drowning—the red juju is "for keep foot in
path." Beautiful effect of a gleam of sunshine lighting up a
red sandbank till it glows like the Nibelungen gold. Indeed
the effects are Turneresque to-day owing to the mist, and the
sun playing in and out among it.

The sandbanks now have their cliffs to the N.N.W. and
N.W. At 9.30, the broad river in front of us is apparently
closed by sandbanks which run out from the banks thus :—

                yellow ⎫
S. bank bright-red ⎬ N. bank.   Current running strong along
                yellow ⎭

south bank. This bank bears testimony of this also being the
case in the wet season, for a fringe of torn-down trees hangs
from it into the river. Pass Seke, a town on north bank,
interchanging the usual observations regarding our destination.
The river seems absolutely barred with sand again ; but as we
paddle down it, the obstructions resolve themselves into spits
of sand from the north bank and the largest island in mid-
stream, which also has a long tail, or train, of sandbank down
river. Here we meet a picturesque series of canoes, fruit and
trade laden, being poled up stream, one man with his pole
over one side, the other with his pole over the other, making
a St. Andrew's cross as you meet them end on.

Most luxurious, charming, and pleasant trip this. The
men are standing up swinging in rhythmic motion their long;
rich red wood paddles in perfect time to their elaborate melancholy, minor key boat song. Nearly lost with all hands.
Sandbank palaver—only when we were going over the end
of it, slipped sideways over its edge. River deep, bottom
sand and mud. This information may be interesting to the
geologist, but I hope I shall not be converted by circumstances
into a human sounding apparatus again to-day. Next time
she strikes I shall get out and shove behind.

We are now skirting the real north bank, and not the bank
of an island or islands as we have been for some time heretofore. Lovely stream falls into this river over cascades.
The water is now rough in a small way and the width of the
river great, but it soon is crowded again with wooded islands.

There are patches and wreaths of a lovely, vermilion-flowering bush rope decorating the forest, and now and again clumps of a plant that shows a yellow and crimson spike of bloom, very strikingly beautiful. We pass a long tunnel in the bush, quite dark as you look down it—evidently the path to some native town. The south bank is covered, where the falling waters have exposed it, with hippo grass. Terrible lot of mangrove flies about, although we are more than one hundred miles above the mangrove belt. River broad again—tending W.S.W., with a broad flattened island with attributive sand-banks in the middle. The fair way is along the south bank of the river. Gray Shirt tells me this river is called the O'Rembo Vongo, or small River, so as to distinguish it from the main stream of the Ogowé which goes down past the south side of Lembarene Island, as well I know after that canoe affair of mine. Ayzingo now bears due north—and native mahogany is called " Okooma." Pass village called Welli on north bank. It looks like some gipsy caravans stuck on poles. I expect that village has known what it means to be swamped by the rising river; it looks as if it had, very hastily in the middle of some night, taken to stilts, which I am sure, from their present rickety condition, will not last through the next wet season, and then some unfortunate spirit will get the blame of the collapse. I also learn that it is the natal spot of my friend Kabinda, the carpenter at Andande. Now if some of these good people I know would only go and distinguish themselves, I might write a sort of county family history of these parts ; but they don't, and I fancy won't. For example, the entrance—or should I say the exit ?—of a broadish little river is just away on the south bank. If you go up this river—it runs S.E.—you get to a good-sized lake ; in this lake there is an island called Adole ; then out of the other side of the lake there is another river which falls into the Ogowé main stream—but that is not the point of the story, which is that on that island of Adole, Ngouta, the interpreter, first saw the light. Why he ever did—there or anywhere—Heaven only knows! I know I shall never want to write his biography.

On the western bank end of that river going to Adole, there

is an Igalwa town, notable for a large quantity of fine white
ducks and a clump of Indian bamboo. My informants say,
" No white man ever live for this place," so I suppose the
ducks and bamboo have been imported by some black trader
whose natal spot this is. The name of this village is
Wanderegwoma. Stuck on sandbank—I flew out and shoved
behind, leaving Ngouta to do the balancing performances in
the stern. This O'Rembo Vongo divides up just below here, I
am told, when we have re-embarked, into three streams. One
goes into the main Ogowé opposite Ayshouka in Nkami
country—Nkami country commences at Ayshouka and goes
to the sea—one into the Ngumbi, and one into the Nunghi—
all in the Ouroungou country. Ayzingo now lies N.E.
according to Gray Shirt's arm. On our river there is here
another broad low island with its gold-coloured banks shining
out, seemingly barring the entire channel, but there is really a
canoe channel along by both banks.

We turn at this point into a river on the north bank that
runs north and south—the current is running very swift to
the north. We run down into it, and then, it being more than
time enough for chop, we push the canoe on to a sandbank in
our new river, which I am told is the Karkola. I, after having
had my tea, wander off. I find behind our high sandbank,
which like all the other sandbanks above water now, is getting
grown over with hippo grass—a fine light green grass, the
beloved food of both hippo and manatee—a forest, and entering this I notice a succession of strange mounds or heaps,
made up of branches, twigs, and leaves, and dead flowers.
Many of these heaps are recent, while others have fallen into
decay. Investigation shows they are burial places. Among
the *débris* of an old one there are human bones, and out from
one of the new ones comes a stench and a hurrying, exceedingly busy line of ants, demonstrating what is going on.
I own I thought these mounds were some kind of bird's or
animal's nest. They look entirely unhuman in this desolate
reach of forest. Leaving these, I go down to the water edge
of the sand, and find in it a quantity of pools of varying
breadth and expanse, but each surrounded by a rim of dark
red-brown deposit, which you can lift off the sand in a skin.

On the top of the water is a film of exquisite iridescent colours like those on a soap bubble, only darker and brighter. In the river alongside the sand, there are thousands of those beautiful little fish with a black line each side of their tails. They are perfectly tame, and I feed them with crumbs in my hand. After making every effort to terrify the unknown object containing the food—gallant bulls, quite two inches long, sidling up and snapping at my fingers—they come and feed right in the palm, so that I could have caught them by the handful had I wished. There are also a lot of those weird, semi-transparent, yellow, spotted little sand-fish with cup-shaped pectoral fins, which I see they use to enable them to make their astoundingly long leaps. These fish are of a more nervous and distrustful disposition, and hover round my hand but will not come into it. Indeed I do not believe the other cheeky little fellows would allow them to. They have grand butting matches among themselves, which wind up with a most comic tail fight, each combatant spinning round and going in for a spanking match with his adversary with his pretty little red-edged tail—the red rim round it and round his gill covers going claret-coloured with fury. I did not make out how you counted points in these fights—no one seemed a scale the worse.

The men, having had their rest and their pipes, shout for me, and off we go again. The Karkola [1] soon widens to about 100 feet ; it is evidently very deep here ; the right bank (the east) is forested, the left, low and shrubbed, one patch looking as if it were being cleared for a plantation, but no village showing. A big rock shows up on the right bank, which is a change from the clay and sand, and soon the whole character of the landscape changes. We come to a sharp turn in the river, from north and south to east and west—the current very swift. The river channel dodges round against a big bank of sword grass, and then widens out to the breadth of the Thames at Putney. I am told that a river runs out of it here to the west to Ouroungou country, and so I imagine

---

[1] As this river is not mentioned on maps, and as I was the first white traveller on it, I give my own phonetic spelling ; but I expect it would be spelt by modern geographers " Kâkola."

this Karkola falls ultimately into the Nazareth.   We skirt the
eastern banks, which are covered with low grass with a scanty
lot of trees along the top.   High land shows in the distance
to the S.S.W. and S.W., and then we suddenly turn up into a
broad river or straith, shaping our course N.N.E.   On the
opposite bank, on a high dwarf cliff, is a Fan town.   " All
Fan now," says Singlet in anything but a gratified tone of
voice.

It is a strange, wild, lonely bit of the world we are now in,
apparently a lake or broad—full of sandbanks, some bare and
some in the course of developing into permanent islands by
the growth on them of that floating coarse grass, any joint of
which being torn off either by the current, a passing canoe, or
hippos, floats down and grows wherever it settles.   Like most
things that float in these parts, it usually settles on a sandbank,
and then grows in much the same way as our couch grass
grows on land in England, so as to form a network, which
catches for its adopted sandbank all sorts of floating *débris ;*
so the sandbank comes up in the world.   The waters of the
wet season when they rise drown off the grass ; but when they
fall, up it comes again from the root, and so gradually the
sandbank becomes an island and persuades real trees and
shrubs to come and grow on it, and its future is then
secured.

We skirt alongside a great young island of this class ; the
sword grass some ten or fifteen feet high.   It has not got any
trees on it yet, but by next season or so it doubtless will have.
The grass is stubbled down into paths by hippos, and just as
I have realised who are the road-makers, they appear in
person.   One immense fellow, hearing us, stands up and
shows himself about six feet from us in the grass, gazes
calmly, and then yawns a yawn a yard wide and grunts his
news to his companions, some of whom—there is evidently a
large herd—get up and stroll towards us with all the flowing
grace of Pantechnicon vans in motion.   We put our helm
paddles hard a starboard and leave that bank.   These hippos
always look to me as if they were the first or last creations in
the animal world.   At present I am undecided whether
Nature tried " her 'prentice hand " on them in her earliest

youth, or whether, having got thoroughly tired of making the delicately beautiful antelopes, corallines, butterflies, and orchids, she just said : " Goodness ! I am quite worn out with this finicking work.   Here, just put these other viscera into big bags—I can't bother any more."

Our hasty trip across to the bank of the island on the other side being accomplished, we, in search of seclusion and in the hope that out of sight would mean out of mind to hippos, shot down a narrow channel between semi-island sandbanks, and those sandbanks, if you please, are covered with specimens— as fine a set of specimens as you could wish for—of the West African crocodile.   These interesting animals are also having their siestas, lying sprawling in all directions on the sand, with their mouths wide open.   One immense old lady has a family of lively young crocodiles running over her, evidently playing like a lot of kittens.   The heavy musky smell they give off is most repulsive, but we do not rise up and make a row about this, because we feel hopelessly in the wrong in intruding into these family scenes uninvited, and so apologetic-ally pole ourselves along rapidly, not even singing.   The pace the canoe goes down that channel would be a wonder to Henley Regatta.   When out of ear-shot I ask Pagan whether there are many gorillas, elephants, or bush-cows round here.   " Plenty too much," says he ; and it occurs to me that the corn-fields are growing golden green away in England ; and soon there rises up in my mental vision a picture that fascinated my youth in the *Fliegende Blätter*, represent-ing " Friedrich Gerstaeker auf der Reise."   That gallant man is depicted tramping on a serpent, new to M. Boulenger, while he attempts to club, with the butt end of his gun, a most lively savage who, accompanied by a bison, is attacking him in front.   A terrific and obviously enthusiastic crocodile is grabbing the tail of the explorer's coat, and the explorer says " Hurrah ! das gibt wieder einen prächtigen Artikel für *Die Allgemeine Zeitung.*"   I do not know where in the world Gerstaeker was at the time, but I should fancy hereabouts. My vigorous and lively conscience also reminds me that the last words a most distinguished and valued scientific friend had said to me before I left home was, " Always take measurements,

Miss Kingsley, and always take them from the adult male." I
know I have neglected opportunities of carrying this commission out on both those banks, but I do not feel like going back.
Besides, the men would not like it, and I have mislaid my
yard measure.

The extent of water, dotted with sandbanks and islands in
all directions, here is great, and seems to be fringed uniformly
by low swampy land, beyond which, to the north, rounded
lumps of hills show blue. On one of the islands is a little
white house which I am told was once occupied by a black
trader for John Holt. It looks a desolate place for any man
to live in, and the way the crocodiles and hippo must have
come up on the garden ground in the evening time could not
have enhanced its charms to the average cautious man. My
men say, "No man live for that place now." The factory, I
believe, has been, for some trade reason, abandoned. Behind
it is a great clump of dark-coloured trees. The rest of the
island is now covered with hippo grass looking like a
beautifully kept lawn. We lie up for a short rest at another
island, also a weird spot in its way, for it is covered with a
grove of only one kind of tree, which has a twisted, con-
torted, gray-white trunk and dull, lifeless-looking, green, hard
foliage.

I learn that these good people, to make topographical
confusion worse confounded, call a river by one name when you
are going up it, and by another when you are coming down ;
just as if you called the Thames the London when you were
going up, and the Greenwich when you were coming down. The
banks all round this lake or broad, seem all light-coloured sand
and clay. We pass out of it into a channel. Current flowing
north. As we are entering the channel between banks of
grass-overgrown sand, a superb white crane is seen standing
on the sand edge to the left. Gray Shirt attempts to get a
shot at it, but it—alarmed at our unusual appearance—
raises itself up with one of those graceful preliminary
curtseys, and after one or two preliminary flaps spreads
its broad wings and sweeps away, with its long legs trailing
behind it like a thing on a Japanese screen. Gray Shirt does
not fire, but puts down his gun on the baggage again with its

muzzle nestling against my left ear.   A minute afterwards we strike a bank, and bang goes off the gun, deafening me, singeing my hair and the side of my face slightly.   Fortunately the two men in front are at the moment in the recumbent position attributive to the shock of the canoe jarring against the cliff edge of a bank, or they would have had a miscellaneous collection of bits of broken iron pots and lumps of lead frisking among their vitals.   It is a little difficult to make out how much credit Providence really deserves in this affair, but a good deal.   Of course if It had taken the trouble to keep us off the bank, or to remind Gray Shirt to uncock his weapon, the thing would not have happened at all, but preliminary precaution is not Providence's peculiarity.   Still, when the thing happened It certainly rose to it.   I might have had the back of my head blown out, and the men might have been killed.   I only hope this won't confirm Pagan permanently into superstition ; for only a few minutes before, he had been showing me a big charm to keep him from being hurt by a gun.   If he thinks about it, he will see there is nothing in the charm, because the other man who equally escaped was a charmless Christian.

The river into which we ran zig-zags about, and then takes a course S.S.E.   It is studded with islands slightly higher than those we have passed, and thinly clad with forest.   The place seems alive with birds ; flocks of pelican and crane rise up before us out of the grass, and every now and then a crocodile slides off the bank into the water.   Wonderfully like old logs they look, particularly when you see one letting himself roll and float down on the current.   In spite of these interests I began to wonder where in this lonely land we were to sleep to-night.   In front of us were miles of distant mountains, but in no direction the slightest sign of human habitation.   Soon we passed out of our channel into a lovely, strangely melancholy, lonely-looking lake—Lake Ncovi, my friends tell me.   It is exceedingly beautiful.   The rich golden sunlight of the late afternoon soon followed by the short-lived, glorious flushes of colour of the sunset and the after-glow, play over the scene as we paddle across the lake to the N.N.E.—our canoe leaving a long trail of frosted silver behind her as she glides over the mirror-like

water, and each stroke of the paddle sending down air with it
to come up again in luminous silver bubbles—not as before
in swirls of sand and mud. The lake shore is, in all directions,
wreathed with nobly forested hills, indigo and purple in the
dying daylight. On the N.N.E. and N.E. these come
directly down into the lake ; on N.W., N., S.W., and S.E.
there is a band of well-forested ground, behind which they
rise. In the north and north-eastern part of the lake several
exceedingly beautiful wooded islands show, with gray rocky
beaches and dwarf cliffs.

Sign of human habitation at first there was none ; and
in spite of its beauty, there was something which I was
almost going to say was repulsive. The men evidently
felt the same as I did. Had any one told me that the
air that lay on the lake was poison, or that in among its
forests lay some path to regions of utter death, I should have
said—" It looks like that " ; but no one said anything, and we
only looked round uneasily, until the comfortable-souled
Singlet made the unfortunate observation that he " smelt
blood." [1] We all called him an utter fool to relieve our minds,
and made our way towards the second island. When we got
near enough to it to see details, a large village showed among
the trees on its summit, and a steep dwarf cliff, overgrown
with trees and creeping plants came down to a small beach
covered with large water-washed gray stones. There was
evidently some kind of a row going on in that village, that
took a lot of shouting too. We made straight for the
beach, and drove our canoe among its outlying rocks, and
then each of my men stowed his paddle quickly, slung on his
ammunition bag, and picked up his ready loaded gun,
sliding the skin sheath off the lock. Pagan got out on to the
stones alongside the canoe just as the inhabitants became
aware of our arrival, and, abandoning what I hope was a mass
meeting to remonstrate with the local authorities on the
insanitary state of the town, came—a brown mass of naked
humanity—down the steep cliff path to attend to us, whom
they evidently regarded as an imperial interest. Things did

---

[1] A common African sensation among natives when alarmed, somewhat akin to our feeling some one walk over our graves.

not look restful, nor these Fans personally pleasant. Every man among them—no women showed—was armed with a gun, and they loosened their shovel-shaped knives in their sheaths as they came, evidently regarding a fight quite as imminent as we did. They drew up about twenty paces from us in silence. Pagan and Gray Shirt, who had joined him, held out their unembarrassed hands, and shouted out the name of the Fan man they had said they were friendly with : " Kiva-Kiva." The Fans stood still and talked angrily among themselves for some minutes, and then, Silence said to me, " It would be bad palaver if Kiva no live for this place," in a tone that conveyed to me the idea he thought this unpleasant contingency almost a certainty. The Passenger exhibited unmistakable symptoms of wishing he had come by another boat. I got up from my seat in the bottom of the canoe and leisurely strolled ashore, saying to the line of angry faces " M'boloani " in an unconcerned way, although I well knew it was etiquette for them to salute first. They grunted, but did not commit themselves further. A minute after they parted to allow a fine-looking, middle-aged man, naked save for a twist of dirty cloth round his loins and a bunch of leopard and wild cat tails hung from his shoulder by a strip of leopard skin, to come forward. Pagan went for him with a rush, as if he were going to clasp him to his ample bosom, but holding his hands just off from touching the Fan's shoulder in the usual way, while he said in Fan, " Don't you know me, my beloved Kiva ? Surely you have not forgotten your old friend ? " Kiva grunted feelingly, and raised up his hands and held them just off touching Pagan, and we breathed again. Then Gray Shirt made a rush at the crowd and went through great demonstrations of affection with another gentleman whom he recognised as being a Fan friend of his own, and whom he had not expected to meet here. I looked round to see if there was not any Fan from the Upper Ogowé whom I knew to go for, but could not see one that I could on the strength of a previous acquaintance, and on their individual merits I did not feel inclined to do even this fashionable imitation embrace. Indeed I must say that never—even in a picture book—have I seen such a set of wild wicked-looking savages as those we

faced this night, and with whom It was touch-and-go for twenty
of the longest minutes I have ever lived, whether we fought
—for our lives, I was going to say, but it would not have
been even for that, but merely for the price of them.

Peace having been proclaimed, conversation became general.
Gray Shirt brought his friend up and introduced him to me,
and we shook hands and smiled at each other in the conventional way. Pagan's friend, who was next introduced, was
more alarming, for he held his hands for half a minute just
above my elbows without quite touching me, but he meant
well; and then we all disappeared into a brown mass of
humanity and a fog of noise. You would have thought, from
the violence and vehemence of the shouting and gesticulation,
that we were going to be forthwith torn to shreds; but not a
single hand really touched me, and as I, Pagan, and Gray
Shirt went up to the town in the midst of the throng, the
crowd opened in front and closed in behind, evidently half
frightened at my appearance. The row when we reached the
town redoubled in volume from the fact that the ladies, the
children, and the dogs joined in. Every child in the place as
soon as it saw my white face let a howl out of it as if it had
seen his Satanic Majesty, horns, hoofs, tail and all, and fled
into the nearest hut, headlong, and I fear, from the continuance
of the screams, had fits. The town was exceedingly filthy —
the remains of the crocodile they had been eating the week
before last, and piles of fish offal, and remains of an elephant,
hippo or manatee—I really can't say which, decomposition
was too far advanced—united to form a most impressive
stench. The bark huts are, as usual in a Fan town, in
unbroken rows; but there are three or four streets here, not
one only, as in most cases. The palaver house is in the innermost street, and there we went, and noticed that the village
view was not in the direction in which we had come, but across
towards the other side of the lake. I told the Ajumba to
explain we wanted hospitality for the night, and wished to hire
three carriers for to-morrow to go with us to the Rembwé.

For an hour and three-quarters by my watch I stood in
the suffocating, smoky, hot atmosphere listening to, but only
faintly understanding, the war of words and gesture that raged

round us. At last the fact that we were to be received being settled, Gray Shirt's friend led us out of the guard house— the crowd flinching back as I came through it—to his own house on the right-hand side of the street of huts. It was a very different dwelling to Gray Shirt's residence at Arevooma. I was as high as its roof ridge and had to stoop low to get through the door-hole. Inside, the hut was fourteen or fifteen feet square, unlit by any window. The door-hole could be closed by pushing a broad piece of bark across it under two horizontally fixed bits of stick. The floor was sand like the street outside, but dirtier. On it in one place was a fire, whose smoke found its way out through the roof. In one corner of the room was a rough bench of wood, which from the few filthy cloths on it and a wood pillow I saw was the bed. There was no other furniture in the hut save some boxes, which I presume held my host's earthly possessions. From the bamboo roof hung a long stick with hooks on it, the hooks made by cutting off branching twigs. This was evidently the hanging wardrobe, and on it hung some few fetish charms, and a beautiful ornament of wild cat and leopard tails, tied on to a square piece of leopard skin, in the centre of which was a little mirror, and round the mirror were sewn dozens of common shirt buttons. In among the tails hung three little brass bells and a brass rattle ; these bells and rattles are not only " for dandy," but serve to scare away snakes when the ornament is worn in the forest. A fine strip of silky-haired, young gorilla skin made the band to sling the ornament from the shoulder when worn. Gorillas seem well enough known round here. One old lady in the crowd out- side, I saw, had a necklace made of sixteen gorilla canine teeth slung on a pine-apple fibre string. Gray Shirt explained to me that this is the best house in the village, and my host the most renowned elephant hunter in the district.

We then returned to the canoe, whose occupants had been getting uneasy about the way affairs were going " on top," on account of the uproar they heard and the time we had been away. We got into the canoe and took her round the little promontory at the end of the island to the other beach, which is the main beach. By arriving at the beach when

we did, we took our Fan friends in the rear, and they did not
see us coming in the gloaming.   This was all for the best
it seems, as they said they should have fired on us before they
had had time to see we were rank outsiders, on the apprehension that we were coming from one of the Fan towns we
had passed, and with whom they were on bad terms regarding
a lady who bolted there from her lawful lord, taking with her
—cautious soul!—a quantity of rubber.   The only white man
who had been here before in the memory of man, was a French
officer who paid Kiva six dollars to take him somewhere, I was
told—but I could not find out when, or what happened to that
Frenchman.[1] It was a long time ago, Kiva said, but these
folks have no definite way of expressing duration of time nor,
do I believe, any great mental idea of it; although their
ideas are, as usual with West Africans, far ahead of their
language.

All the goods were brought up to my hut, and while Ngouta
gets my tea we started talking the carrier palaver again.   The
Fans received my offer, starting at two dollars ahead of what
M. Jacot said would be enough, with utter scorn, and every
dramatic gesture of dissent ; one man, pretending to catch
Gray Shirt's words in his hands, flings them to the ground
and stamps them under his feet.   I affected an easy take-it-or-
leave-it-manner, and looked on.   A woman came out of the
crowd to me, and held out a mass of slimy gray abomination
on a bit of plantain leaf—smashed snail.   I accepted it and gave
her fish hooks.   She was delighted and her companions excited,
so she put them into her mouth for safe keeping.   I hurriedly
explained in my best Fan that I do not require any more snail ;
so another lady tried the effect of a pine-apple.   There might be
no end to this, so I retired into trade and asked what she would
sell it for.   She did not want to sell it—she wanted to give it
me ; so I gave her fish hooks.   Silence and Singlet interposed,

---

[1] Since my return I think the French gentleman may have been M. F.
Tenaille d'Estais, who is down on the latest map French as having visited
a lake in this region in 1882, which is set down as Laç Ebouko. He seems
to have come from and returned to Lake Ayzingo—on map Lac Azingo—
but on the other hand " Ebouko " was not known on the lake, Ajumba
and Fans alike calling it Ncovi.

saying the price for pine-apples is one leaf of tobacco, but I explained I was not buying. Ngouta turned up with my tea, so I went inside, and had it on the bed. The door-hole was entirely filled with a mosaic of faces, but no one attempted to come in. All the time the carrier palaver went on without cessation, and I went out and offered to take Gray Shirt's and Pagan's place, knowing they must want their chop, but they refused relief, and also said I must not raise the price ; I was offering too big a price now, and if I once rise the Fan will only think I will keep on rising, and so make the palaver longer to talk. " How long does a palaver usually take to talk round here ?" I ask. " The last one I talked," says Pagan, " took three weeks, and that was only a small price palaver." " Well," say I, " my price is for a start to-morrow—after then I have no price—after that I go away." Another hour however sees the jam made, and to my surprise I find the three richest men in this town of M'fetta have personally taken up the contract—Kiva my host, Fika a fine young fellow, and Wiki, another noted elephant hunter. These three Fans, the four Ajumba and the Igalwa, Ngouta, I think will be enough. Moreover I fancy it safer not to have an overpowering per-centage of Fans in the party, as I know we shall have considerable stretches of uninhabited forest to traverse ; and the Ajumba say that the Fans will kill people, *i.e.*, the black traders who venture into their country, and cut them up into neat pieces, eat what they want at the time, and smoke the rest of the bodies for future use. Now I do not want to arrive at the Rembwé in a smoked condition, even should my frag-ments be neat, and I am going in a different direction to what I said I was when leaving Kangwe, and there are so many ways of accounting for death about here—leopard, canoe capsize, elephants, &c.—that even if I were traced—well, nothing could be done then, anyhow—so will only take three Fans. One must diminish dead certainties to the level of sporting chances along here, or one can never get on.

No one, either Ajumba or Fan, knew the exact course we were to take. The Ajumba had never been this way before— the way for black traders across being *via* Lake Ayzingo, the way Mr. Goode of the American Mission once went, and the

Fans said they only knew the way to a big Fan town called
Efoua, where no white man or black trader had yet been.
There is a path from there to the Rembwé they knew, because
the Efoua people take their trade all to the Rembwé.   They
would, they said, come with me all the way if I would guarantee
them safety if they " found war " on the road.   This I agreed to
do, and arranged to pay off at Hatton and Cookson's sub-factory
on the Rembwé, and they have " Look my mouth and it be
sweet, so palaver done set."   Every load then, by the light of
the bush lights held by the women, we arranged.   I had to
unpack my bottles of fishes so as to equalise the weight
of the loads.   Every load is then made into a sort of cocoon
with bush rope.

I was left in peace at about 11.30 P.M., and clearing off the
clothes from the bench threw myself down and tried to get
some sleep, for we were to start, the Fans said, before dawn.
Sleep impossible—mosquitoes ! lice !!—so at 12.40 I got up
and slid aside my bark door.   I found Pagan asleep under his
mosquito bar outside, across the doorway, but managed to get
past him without rousing him from his dreams of palaver
which he was still talking aloud, and reconnoitred the town. The
inhabitants seemed to have talked themselves quite out and
were sleeping heavily. I went down then to our canoe and found
it safe, high up among the Fan canoes on the stones, and then I
slid a small Fan canoe off, and taking a paddle from a
cluster stuck in the sand, paddled out on to the dark lake.

It was a wonderfully lovely quiet night with no light save that
from the stars.   One immense planet shone pre-eminent in
the purple sky, throwing a golden path down on to the
still waters.   Quantities of big fish sprung out of the water,
their glistening silver-white scales flashing so that they look
like slashing swords. Some bird was making a long, low boom-
booming sound away on the forest shore.   I paddled leisurely
across the lake to the shore on the right, and seeing crawling
on the ground some large glow-worms, drove the canoe on to
the bank among some hippo grass, and got out to get them.

While engaged on this hunt I felt the earth quiver under
my feet, and heard a soft big soughing sound, and looking
round saw I had dropped in on a hippo banquet.   I made

out five of the immense brutes round me, so I softly returned
to the canoe and shoved off, stealing along the bank, paddling
under water, until I deemed it safe to run out across the lake
for my island. I reached the other end of it to that on which
the village is situated ; and finding a miniature rocky bay
with a soft patch of sand and no hippo grass, the incidents
of the Fan hut suggested the advisability of a bath. Moreover,
there was no china collection in that hut, and it would be a
long time before I got another chance, so I go ashore again,
and, carefully investigating the neighbourhood to make
certain there was no human habitation near, I then indulged
in a wash in peace. Drying one's self on one's cummerbund is
not pure joy, but it can be done when you put your mind to it.
While I was finishing my toilet I saw a strange thing happen.
Down through the forest on the lake bank opposite came a
violet ball the size of a small orange. When it reached the sand
beach it hovered along it to and fro close to the ground. In
a few minutes another ball of similarly coloured light came
towards it from behind one of the islets, and the two waver to
and fro over the beach, sometimes circling round each other.
I made off towards them in the canoe, thinking—as I still
do—they were some brand new kind of luminous insect.
When I got on to their beach one of them went off into the
bushes and the other away over the water. I followed in the
canoe, for the water here is very deep, and, when I almost
thought I had got it, it went down into the water and I could
see it glowing as it sunk until it vanished in the depths. I made
my way back hastily, fearing my absence with the canoe might
give rise, if discovered, to trouble, and by 3.30 I was back in
the hut safe, but not so comfortable as I had been on the lake.
A little before five my men are stirring and I get my tea. I
do not state my escapade to them, but ask what those
lights were. "Akom," said the Fan, and pointing to the
shore of the lake where I had been during the night they
said, "they came there, it was an 'Aku'"—or devil bush.
More than ever did I regret not having secured one of those sort
of two phenomena. What a joy a real devil, appropriately put
up in raw alcohol, would have been to my scientific friends !

Wednesday, July 24th.—We get away about 5.30, the Fans

coming in a separate canoe. We call at the next island to M'fetta to buy some more aguma. The inhabitants are very interested in my appearance, running along the stony beach as we paddle away, and standing at the end of it until we are out of sight among the many islands at the N.E. end of Lake Ncovi. The scenery is savage; there are no terrific cliffs nor towering mountains to make it what one usually calls wild or romantic, but there is a distinction about it which is all its own. This N.E. end has beautiful sand beaches on the southern side, in front of the forested bank, lying in smooth ribbons along the level shore, and in scollops round the promontories where the hills come down into the lake. The forest on these hills, or mountains—for they are part of the Sierra del Cristal—is very dark in colour, and the undergrowth seems scant. We presently come to a narrow but deep channel into the lake coming from the eastward, which we go up, winding our course with it into a valley between the hills. After going up it a little way we find it completely fenced across with stout stakes, a space being left open in the middle, broader than the spaces between the other stakes; and over this is poised a spear with a bush rope attached, and weighted at the top of the haft with a great lump of rock. The whole affair is kept in position by a bush rope so arranged just under the level of the water that anything passing through the opening would bring the spear down. This was a trap for hippo or manatee, and similar in structure to those one sees set in the hippo grass near villages and plantations, which serve the double purpose of defending the vegetable supply, and adding to the meat supply of the inhabitants. We squeeze through between the stakes so as not to let the trap off, and find our little river leads us into another lake, much smaller than Ncovi. It is studded with islands of fantastic shapes, all wooded with high trees of an equal level, and with little or no undergrowth among them, so their pale gray stems look like clusters of columns supporting a dark green ceiling. The forest comes down steep hill sides to the water edge in all directions; and a dark gloomy-looking herb grows up out of black slime and water, in a bank or ribbon in front of it. There is another channel out of this lake, still to the N.E. The Fans say they think it goes into the big lake far far away, *i.e.*, Lake Ayzingo. From the look of the land, I think this river connecting Ayzingo and Lake Ncovi wanders down this valley between the mountain spurs of the Sierra del Cristal, expanding into one gloomy lake after another. We run our canoe into a bank of the dank dark-coloured water herb to the right, and disembark into a fitting introduction to the sort of country we shall have to deal with before we see the Rembwé—namely, up to our knees in black slime.

CHAPTER XII

FROM NCOVI TO ESOON

Concerning the way in which the voyager goes from the island of M'fetta· to no one knows exactly where, in doubtful and bad company, and of what this led to, and giving also some accounts of the Great Forest and of those people that live therein.

I WILL not bore you with my diary in detail regarding our land journey, because the water-washed little volume attri- butive to this period is mainly full of reports of law cases, for reasons hereinafter to be stated ; and at night, when passing through this bit of country, I was usually too tired to do any- thing more than make an entry such as : " 5 S., 4 R. A., N.E Ebony. T. 1—50, &c., &c."—entries that require amplification to explain their significance, and I will proceed to explain.

Our first day's march was a very long one. Path in the ordinary acceptance of the term there was none. Hour after hour, mile after mile, we passed on, in the under-gloom of the great forest. The pace made by the Fans, who are in- finitely the most rapid Africans I have ever come across, severely tired the Ajumba, who are canoe men, and who had been as fresh as paint, after their exceedingly long day's paddling from Arevooma to M'fetta. Ngouta, the Igalwa interpreter, felt pumped, and said as much, very early in the day. I regretted very much having brought him ; for, from a mixture of nervous exhaustion arising from our M'fetta ex- periences, and a touch of chill, he had almost entirely lost his voice, and I feared would fall sick. The Fans were evi- dently quite at home in the forest, and strode on over fallen trees and rocks with an easy, graceful stride. What saved us weaklings was the Fans' appetites ; every two hours they sat down, and had a snack of a pound or so of meat and aguma apiece, followed by a pipe of tobacco. We used to come up with them at these halts. Ngouta and the Ajumba used to sit down ; and rest with them, and I also, for a few minutes, for a rest and chat, and then I would go on alone, thus getting a good start. I got a good start, in the other meaning of the word, on the afternoon of the first day when descending into a ravine.

I saw in the bottom, wading and rolling in the mud, a herd of five elephants. I am certain that owing to some misapprehension among the Fates I was given a series of magnificent sporting chances, intended as a special treat for some favourite Nimrod of those three ladies, and I know exactly how I ought to have behaved. I should have felt my favourite rifle fly to my shoulder, and then, carefully sighting for the finest specimen, have fired. The noble beast should have stumbled forward, recovered itself, and shedding its life blood behind it have crashed away into the forest. I should then have tracked it, and either with one well-directed shot have given it its quietus, or have got charged by it, the elephant passing completely over my prostrate body ; either termination is good form, but I never have these things happen, and never will. (In the present case I remembered, hastily, that your one chance when charged by several elephants is to dodge them round trees, working down wind all the time, until they lose smell and sight of you, then to lie quiet for a time, and go home.) It was evident from the utter unconcern of these monsters that I was down wind now, so I had only to attend to dodging, and I promptly dodged round a tree, thinking perhaps a dodge in time saves nine—and I lay down. Seeing they still displayed no emotion on my account, and fascinated by the novelty of the scene, I crept forward from one tree to another, until I was close enough to have hit the nearest one with a stone, and spats of mud, which they sent flying with their stamping and wallowing came flap, flap among the bushes covering me.

One big fellow had a nice pair of 40 lb. or so tusks on him, singularly straight, and another had one big curved tusk and one broken one. If I were an elephant I think I would wear the tusks straight ; they must be more effective weapons thus, but there seems no fixed fashion among elephants here in this matter. Some of them lay right down like pigs in the deeper part of the swamp, some drew up trunkfuls of water and syringed themselves and each other, and every one of them indulged in a good rub against a tree. Presently when they had had enough of it they all strolled off up wind, a way elephants have ;[1] but why I do not know, because they know the difference, always carrying their trunk differently when they are going up wind to what they do when they are going down — arrested mental development,[2] I suppose. They strolled through the bush in Indian file, now and then breaking off a branch, but leaving singularly little dead water for their tonnage and breadth of beam. One laid his trunk affectionately on the back of the one in front of him, which I believe to be the elephant equivalent to walking arm-in-arm. When they had gone I rose up, turned round to find the men, and trod on Kiva's back then and there, full and fair, and fell sideways down the steep hillside until I fetched up among some roots.

It seems Kiva had come on, after his meal, before the others, and seeing the elephants, and being a born hunter, had crawled like me down to look at them. He had not expected to find me there, he said. I do not believe he gave a thought of any sort to me in the presence of these fascinating creatures, and so he got himself trodden on. I suggested to him we should pile the baggage, and go and have an elephant hunt. He shook his head reluctantly, saying " Kor, kor," like a depressed rook, and explained we were not strong enough ; there were only three Fans—the Ajumba, and Ngouta did not count— and moreover that we had not brought sufficient ammunition owing to the baggage having to be carried, and the ammunition that we had must be saved for other game than elephant, for we might meet war before we met the Rembwé River.

We had by now joined the rest of the party, and were all soon squattering about on our own account in the elephant bath. It was shocking bad going—like a ploughed field

---

[1] Foolish, because natives always attack them in the rear.

[2] The usual explanation for anything you do not understand in a native of Africa's conduct.

exaggerated by a terrific nightmare. It pretty nearly pulled all the legs off me, and to this hour I cannot tell you if it is best to put your foot into a footmark—a young pond, I mean —about the size of the bottom of a Madeira work arm-chair, or whether you should poise yourself on the rim of the same, and stride forward to its other bank boldly and hopefully. The footmarks and the places where the elephants had been rolling were by now filled with water, and the mud underneath was in places hard and slippery. In spite of my determination to preserve an awesome and unmoved calm while among these dangerous savages, I had to give way and laugh explosively; to see the portly, powerful Pagan suddenly convert himself into a quadruped, while Gray Shirt poised himself on one heel and waved his other leg in the air to advertise to the assembled nations that he was about to sit down, was irresistible. No one made such palaver about taking a seat as Gray Shirt; I did it repeatedly without any fuss to speak of. That lordly elephant-hunter, the Great Wiki, would, I fancy, have strode over safely and with dignity, but the man who was in front of him spun round on his own axis and flung his arms round the Fan, and they went to earth together; the heavy load on Wiki's back drove them into the mud like a pile-driver. However we got through in time, and after I had got up the other side of the ravine I saw the Fan let the Ajumba go on, and were busy searching themselves for something.

I followed the Ajumba, and before I joined them felt a fearful pricking irritation. Investigation of the affected part showed a tick of terrific size with its head embedded in the flesh; pursuing this interesting subject, I found three more, and had awfully hard work to get them off and painful too for they give one not only a feeling of irritation at their holding-on place, but a streak of rheumatic-feeling pain up from it. On completing operations I went on and came upon the Ajumba in a state more approved of by Praxiteles than by the general public nowadays. They had found out about elephant ticks, so I went on and got an excellent start for the next stage.

By this time, shortly after noon on the first day, we had struck into a mountainous and rocky country, and also struck a track—a track you had to keep your eye on or you lost it in a minute, but still a guide as to direction.

The forest trees here were mainly ebony and great hard wood trees,[1] with no palms save my old enemy the climbing palm, *calamus*, as usual, going on its long excursions, up one tree and down another, bursting into a plume of fronds, and in the middle of each plume one long spike sticking straight up, which was an unopened frond, whenever it got a gleam of sunshine ; running along the ground over anything it meets, rock or fallen timber, all alike, its long, dark-coloured, rope-like stem simply furred with thorns. Immense must be the length of some of these climbing palms. One tree I noticed that day that had hanging from its summit, a good one hundred and fifty feet above us, a long straight rope-like palm stem. Interested, I went to it, and tried to track it to root, and found it was only a loop that came down from another tree. I had no time to trace it further ; for they go up a tree and travel along the surrounding tree-tops, take an occasional dip, and then up again.

The character of the whole forest was very interesting. Sometimes for hours we passed among thousands upon thousands of gray-white columns of uniform height (about 100—150 feet) ; at the top of these the boughs branched out and interlaced among each other, forming a canopy or ceiling, which dimmed the light even of the equatorial sun to such an extent that no undergrowth could thrive in the gloom. The statement of the struggle for existence was published here in plain figures, but it was not, as in our climate, a struggle against climate mainly, but an internecine war from over population. Now and again we passed among vast stems of buttressed trees, sometimes enormous in girth ; and from their far-away summits hung great bush-ropes, some as straight as plumb lines, others coiled round, and intertwined among each other, until one could fancy one was looking on some mighty battle between armies of gigantic serpents, that had been arrested at its height by some magic spell. All these bush-ropes were as bare of foliage as a ship's wire rigging, but a good many had thorns. I was very curious as

[1] *Diospyros* and *Copaifua mopane*.

to how they got up straight, and investigation showed me that many of them were carried up with a growing tree. The only true climbers were the *calamus* and the rubber vine (*Landolphia*), both of which employ hook tackle.

Some stretches of this forest were made up of thin, spindly stemmed trees of great height, and among these stretches I always noticed the ruins of some forest giant, whose death by lightning or by his superior height having given the demoniac tornado wind an extra grip on him, had allowed sunlight to penetrate the lower regions of the forest ; and then evidently the seedlings and saplings, who had for years been living a half-starved life for light, shot up. They seemed to know that their one chance lay in getting with the greatest rapidity to the level of the top of the forest. No time to grow fat in the stem. No time to send out side branches, or any of those vanities. Up, up to the light level, and he among them who reached it first won in this game of life or death ; for when he gets there he spreads out his crown of upper branches, and shuts off the life-giving sunshine from his competitors, who pale off and die, or remain dragging on an attenuated existence waiting for another chance, and waiting sometimes for centuries. There must be tens of thousands of seeds which perish before they get their chance ; but the way the seeds of the hard wood African trees are packed, as it were, in cases specially made durable, is very wonderful. Indeed the ways of Providence here are wonderful in their strange dual intention to preserve and to destroy ; but on the whole, as Peer Gynt truly observes, " *Ein guter Wirth—nein das ist er nicht.*"

We saw this influence of light on a large scale as soon as we reached the open hills and mountains of the Sierra del Cristal, and had to pass over those fearful avalanche-like timber falls on their steep sides. The worst of these lay between Efoua and Egaja, where we struck a part of the range that was exposed to the south-east. These falls had evidently arisen from the tornados, which from time to time have hurled down the gigantic trees whose hold on the superficial soil over the sheets of hard bed rock was insufficient, in spite of all the anchors they had out in the shape of roots and buttresses, and all the rigging in the shape of bush ropes.

Down they had come, crushing and dragging down with them those near them or bound to them by the great tough climbers.

Getting over these falls was perilous, not to say scratchy work. One or another member of our party always went through; and precious uncomfortable going it was I found, when I tried it in one above Egaja; ten or twelve feet of crashing creaking timber, and then flump on to a lot of rotten, wet *débris*, with more snakes and centipedes among it than you had any immediate use for, even though you were a collector; but there you had to stay, while Wiki, who was a most critical connoisseur, selected from the surrounding forest a bush-rope that he regarded as the correct remedy for the case, and then up you were hauled, through the sticks you had turned the wrong way on your down journey.

The Duke had a bad fall, going twenty feet or so before he found the rubbish heap; while Fika, who went through with a heavy load on his back, took us, on one occasion, half an hour to recover; and when we had just got him to the top, and able to cling on to the upper sticks, Wiki, who had been superintending operations, slipped backwards, and went through on his own account. The bush-rope we had been hauling on was too worn with the load to use again, and we just hauled Wiki out with the first one we could drag down and cut; and Wiki, when he came up, said we were reckless, and knew nothing of bush ropes, which shows how ungrateful an African can be. It makes the perspiration run down my nose whenever I think of it. The sun was out that day; we were neatly situated on the Equator, and the air was semi-solid, with the stinking exhalations from the swamps with which the mountain chain is fringed and intersected; and we were hot enough without these things, because of the violent exertion of getting these twelve to thirteen-stone gentlemen up among us again, and the fine varied exercise of getting over the fall on our own account.

When we got into the cool forest beyond it was delightful; particularly if it happened to be one of those lovely stretches of forest, gloomy down below, but giving hints that far away above us was a world of bloom and scent and beauty which we saw as much of as earth-worms in a flower-bed. Here and there the ground was strewn with great cast blossoms, thick, wax-like, glorious cups of orange and crimson and pure white, each one of which was in itself a handful, and which told us that some of the trees around us were showing a glory of colour to heaven alone. Sprinkled among them were bunches of pure stephanotis-like flowers, which said that the gaunt bush-ropes were rubber vines that had burst into flower when they had seen the sun. These flowers we came across in nearly every type of forest all the way, for rubber abounds here.

I will weary you no longer now with the different kinds of forest and only tell you I have let you off several. The natives have separate names for seven different kinds, and these might, I think, be easily run up to nine.

A certain sort of friendship soon arose between the Fans and me. We each recognised that we belonged to that same section of the human race with whom it is better to drink than to fight. We knew we would each have killed the other, if sufficient inducement were offered, and so we took a certain amount of care that the inducement should not arise. Gray Shirt and Pagan also, their trade friends, the Fans treated with an independent sort of courtesy; but Silence, Singlet, the Passenger, and above all Ngouta, they openly did not care a row of pins for, and I have small doubt that had it not been for us other three they would have killed and eaten these very amiable gentlemen with as much compunction as an English sportsman would kill as many rabbits. They on their part hated the Fan, and never lost an opportunity of telling me " these Fan be bad man too much." I must not forget to mention the other member of our party, a Fan gentleman with the manners of a duke and the habits of a dustbin. He came with us, quite uninvited by me, and never asked for any pay; I think he only wanted to see the fun, and drop in for a fight if there was one going on, and to pick up the pieces generally. He was evidently a man of some importance, from the way the others treated him; and moreover he had a splendid gun, with a gorilla skin sheath for its lock, and ornamented all over its stock with brass nails. His costume consisted of a small piece of dirty rag round his loins; and whenever we were going through dense undergrowth, or wading a swamp, he wore that filament tucked up scandalously short. Whenever we were sitting down in the forest having one of our nondescript meals, he always sat next to me and appropriated the tin. Then he would fill his pipe, and turning to me with the easy grace of aristocracy, would say what may be translated as " My dear Princess, could you favour me with a lucifer ? "

I used to say, " My dear Duke, charmed, I'm sure," and give him one ready lit.

I dared not trust him with the box whole, having a personal conviction that he would have kept it. I asked him what he would do suppose I was not there with a box of lucifers ; and he produced a bush-cow's horn with a neat wood lid tied on with tie tie, and from out of it he produced a flint and steel and demonstrated. Unfortunately all his grace's minor possessions, owing to the scantiness of his attire, were in one and the same pine-apple-fibre bag which he wore slung across his shoulder ; and these possessions, though not great, were as dangerous to the body as a million sterling is said to be to the soul, for they consisted largely of gunpowder and snuff, and their separate receptacles leaked and their contents commingled, so that demonstration on fire-making methods among the Fan ended in an awful bang and blow-up in a small way, and the Professor and his pupil sneezed like fury for ten minutes, and a cruel world laughed till it nearly died, for twenty. Still that bag with all its failings was a wonder for its containing power.

The first day in the forest we came across a snake [1]—a beauty with a new red-brown and yellow-patterned velvety skin, about three feet six inches long and as thick as a man's thigh. Ngouta met it, hanging from a bough, and shot backwards like a lobster, Ngouta having among his many weaknesses a rooted horror of snakes. This snake the Ogowé natives all hold in great aversion. For the bite of other sorts of snakes they profess to have remedies, but for this they have none. If, however, a native is stung by one he usually conceals the fact that it was this particular kind, and tries to get any chance the native doctor's medicine may give. The Duke stepped

[1] *Vipera nasicornis ;* M'pongwe, *Ompenle.*

forward and with one blow flattened its head against the tree
with his gun butt, and then folded the snake up and got as
much of it as possible into the bag, while the rest hung dangling
out.   Ngouta, not being able to keep ahead of the Duke, his
Grace's pace being stiff, went to the extreme rear of the party,
so that other people might be killed first if the snake returned
to life, as he surmised it would.   He fell into other dangers
from this caution, but I cannot chronicle Ngouta's afflictions
in full without running this book into an old-fashioned folio
size.   We had the snake for supper, that is to say the Fan
and I ; the others would not touch it, although a good snake,
properly cooked, is one of the best meats one gets out here,
far and away better than the African fowl.

The Fans also did their best to educate me in every way :
they told me their names for things, while I told them mine,
throwing in besides as "a dash for top" a few colloquial
phrases such as : " Dear me, now," " Who'd have thought it,"
" Stuff, my dear sir," and so on ; and when I left them they
had run each together as it were into one word, and a nice
savage sound they had with them too, especially " dearmenow,"
so I must warn any philologist who visits the Fans, to beware
of regarding any word beyond two syllables in length as
being of native origin.   I found several European words
already slightly altered in use among them, such as " Amuck "
—a mug, " Alas "—a glass, a tumbler.   I do not know whether
their " Ami "—a person addressed, or spoken of—is French or
not.   It may come from " Anwĕ "—M'pongwe for " Ye,"
" You."   They use it as a rule in addressing a person after the
phrase they always open up conversation with, " Azuna "—
Listen, or I am speaking.

They also showed me many things : how to light a fire
from the pith of a certain tree, which was useful to me in after
life, but they rather overdid this branch of instruction one way
and another ; for example, Wiki had, as above indicated, a
mania for bush-ropes and a marvellous eye and knowledge of
them ; he would pick out from among the thousands surrounding us now one of such peculiar suppleness that you
could wind it round anything, like a strip of cloth, and as
strong withal as a hawser ; or again another which has

a certain stiffness, combined with a slight elastic spring, excellent for hauling, with the ease and accuracy of a lady who picks out the particular twisted strand of embroidery silk from a multi-coloured tangled ball. He would go into the bush after them while other people were resting, and particularly after the sort which, when split is bright yellow, and very supple and excellent to tie round loads.

On one occasion, between Egaja and Esoon, he came back from one of these quests and wanted me to come and see something, very quietly ; I went, and we crept down into a rocky ravine, on the other side of which lay one of the outermost Egaja plantations. When we got to the edge of the cleared ground, we lay down, and wormed our way, with elaborate caution, among a patch of Koko ; Wiki first, I following in his trail.

After about fifty yards of this, Wiki sank flat, and I saw before me some thirty yards off, busily employed in pulling down plantains, and other depredations, five gorillas : one old male, one young male, and three females. One of these had clinging to her a young fellow, with beautiful wavy black hair with just a kink in it. The big male was crouching on his haunches, with his long arms hanging down on either side, with the backs of his hands on the ground, the palms upwards. The elder lady was tearing to pieces and eating a pine-apple, while the others were at the plantains destroying more than they ate.

They kept up a sort of a whinnying, chattering noise, quite different from the sound I have heard gorillas give when enraged, or from the one you can hear them giving when they are what the natives call " dancing " at night. I noticed that their reach of arm was immense, and that when they went from one tree to another, they squattered across the open ground in a most inelegant style, dragging their long arms with the knuckles downwards. I should think the big male and female were over six feet each. The others would be from four to five. I put out my hand and laid it on Wiki's gun to prevent him from firing, and he, thinking I was going to fire, gripped my wrist.

I watched the gorillas with great interest for a few seconds, until I heard Wiki make a peculiar small sound, and looking at him saw his face was working in an awful way as he clutched his throat with his hand violently.

Heavens! think I, this gentleman's going to have a fit; it's lost we are entirely this time. He rolled his head to and fro, and then buried his face into a heap of dried rubbish at the foot of a plantain stem, clasped his hands over it, and gave an explosive sneeze. The gorillas let go all, raised themselves up for a second, gave a quaint sound between a bark and a howl, and then the ladies and the young gentleman started home. The old male rose to his full height (it struck me at the time this was a matter of ten feet at least, but for scientific purposes allowance must be made for a lady's emotions) and looked straight towards us, or rather towards where that sound came from. Wiki went off into a paroxysm of falsetto sneezes the like of which I have never heard; nor evidently had the gorilla, who doubtless thinking, as one of his black co-relatives would have thought, that the phenomenon favoured Duppy, went off after his family with a celerity that was amazing the moment he touched the forest, and disappeared as they had, swinging himself along through it from bough to bough, in a way that convinced me that, given the necessity of getting about in tropical forests, man has made a mistake in getting his arms shortened. I have seen many wild animals in their native wilds, but never have I seen anything to equal gorillas going through bush; it is a graceful, powerful, superbly perfect hand-trapeze performance.[1]

After this sporting adventure, we returned, as I usually return from a sporting adventure, without measurements or the body.

Our first day's march, though the longest, was the easiest, though, providentially I did not know this at the time. From my Woermann road walks I judge it was well twenty-five miles. It was easiest however, from its lying for the greater part of

[1] I have no hesitation in saying that the gorilla is the most horrible wild animal I have seen. I have seen at close quarters specimens of the most important big game of Central Africa, and, with the exception of snakes, I have run away from all of them; but although elephants, leopards, and pythons give you a feeling of alarm, they do not give that feeling of horrible disgust that an old gorilla gives on account of its hideousness of appearance.

the way through the gloomy type of forest. All day long we never saw the sky once.

The earlier part of the day we were steadily going up hill, here and there making a small descent, and then up again, until we came on to what was apparently a long ridge, for on either side of us we could look down into deep, dark, ravine-like valleys. Twice or thrice we descended into these to cross them, finding at their bottom a small or large swamp with a river running through its midst. Those rivers all went to Lake Ayzingo.

We had to hurry because Kiva, who was the only one among us who had been to Efoua, said that unless we did we should not reach Efoua that night. I said, " Why not stay for bush?" not having contracted any love for a night in a Fan town by the experience of M'fetta; moreover the Fans were not sure that after all the whole party of us might not spend the evening at Efoua, when we did get there, simmering in its cooking-pots.

Ngouta, I may remark, had no doubt on the subject at all, and regretted having left Mrs. N. keenly, and the Andande store sincerely. But these Fans are a fine sporting tribe, and allowed they would risk it; besides, they were almost certain they had friends at Efoua ; and, in addition, they showed me trees scratched in a way that was magnification of the condition of my own cat's pet table leg at home, demonstrating leopards in the vicinity. I kept going, as it was my only chance, because I found I stiffened if I sat down, and they always carefully told me the direction to go in when they sat down ; with their superior pace they soon caught me up, and then passed me, leaving me and Ngouta and sometimes Singlet and Pagan behind, we, in our turn, overtaking them, with this difference that they were sitting down when we did so.

About five o'clock I was off ahead and noticed a path which I had been told I should meet with, and, when met with, I must follow. The path was slightly indistinct, but by keeping my eye on it I could see it. Presently I came to a place where it went out, but appeared again on the other side of a clump of underbush fairly distinctly. I made a short cut for it and the next news was I was in a heap, on a lot of spikes, some fifteen feet or so below ground level, at the bottom of a bag-shaped game pit.

It is at these times you realise the blessing of a good thick skirt. Had I paid heed to the advice of many people in England, who ought to have known better, and did not do it themselves, and adopted masculine garments, I should have been spiked to the bone, and done for. Whereas, save for a good many bruises, here I was with the fulness of my skirt tucked under me, sitting on nine ebony spikes some twelve inches long, in comparative comfort, howling lustily to be hauled out. The Duke came along first, and looked down at me. I said, "Get a bush-rope, and haul me out." He grunted and sat down on a log. The Passenger came next, and he looked down. "You kill?" says he. "Not much," say I; "get a bush-rope and haul me out." "No fit," says he, and sat down on the log. Presently, however, Kiva and Wiki came up, and Wiki went and selected the one and only bush-rope suitable to haul an English lady, of my exact complexion, age, and size, out of that one particular pit. They seemed rare round there from the time he took; and I was just casting about in my mind as to what method would be best to employ in getting up the smooth, yellow, sandy-clay, incurved walls, when he arrived with it, and I was out in a twinkling, and very much ashamed of myself, until Silence, who was then leading, disappeared through the path before us with a despairing yell. Each man then pulled the skin cover off his gun lock, carefully looked to see if things there were all right and ready loosened his knife in its snake-skin sheath; and then we set about hauling poor Silence out, binding him up where necessary with cool green leaves; for he, not having a skirt, had got a good deal frayed at the edges on those spikes. Then we closed up, for the Fans said these pits were symptomatic of the immediate neighbourhood of Efoua. We sounded our ground, as we went into a thick plantain patch, through which we could see a great clearing in the forest, and the low huts of a big town. We charged into it, going right through the guard-house gateway, at one end, in single file, as its narrowness obliged us, and into the street-shaped town, and formed ourselves into as imposing a looking party as possible

in the centre of the street. The Efouerians regarded us with
much amazement, and the women and children cleared off into
the huts, and took stock of us through the door-holes. There
were but few men in the town, the majority, we subsequently
learnt, being away after elephants. But there were quite sufficient left to make a crowd in a ring round us. Fortunately
Wiki and Kiva's friends were present, and we were soon
in another word—fog, but not so bad a one as that at M'fetta ;
indeed Efoua struck me, from the first, favourably ; it was, for
one thing, much cleaner than most Fan towns I have been in.

As a result of the confabulation, one of the chiefs had his
house cleared out for me. It consisted of two apartments
almost bare of everything save a pile of boxes, and a small
fire on the floor, some little bags hanging from the roof poles,
and a general supply of insects. The inner room contained
nothing save a hard plank, raised on four short pegs from the
earth floor.

I shook hands with and thanked the chief, and directed
that all the loads should be placed inside the huts. I must
admit my good friend was a villainous-looking savage, but he
behaved most hospitably and kindly. From what I had
heard of the Fan, I deemed it advisable not to make any
present to him at once, but to base my claim on him on the
right of an amicable stranger to hospitality. When I had
seen all the baggage stowed I went outside and sat at the
doorway on a rather rickety mushroom-shaped stool in the
cool evening air, waiting for my tea which I wanted bitterly.
Pagan came up as usual for tobacco to buy chop with ; and
after giving it to him, I and the two chiefs, with Gray Shirt
acting as interpreter, had a long chat. Of course the first
question was, Why was I there ?

I told them I was on my way to the factory of H. and C.
on the Rembwé. They said they had heard of " Ugumu," *i.e.*,
Messrs Hatton and Cookson, but they did not trade direct
with them, passing their trade into towns nearer to the
Rembwé, which were swindling bad towns, they said ; and
they got the idea stuck in their heads that I was a trader, a
sort of bagman for the firm, and Gray Shirt could not get this
idea out, so off one of their majesties went and returned with

twenty-five balls of rubber, which I bought to promote good feeling, subsequently dashing them to Wiki, who passed them in at Ndorko when we got there.   I also bought some elephant-hair necklaces from one of the chiefs' wives, by exchanging my red silk tie with her for them, and one or two other things. I saw fish-hooks would not be of much value because Efoua was not near a big water of any sort ; so I held fish-hooks and traded handkerchiefs and knives.

One old chief was exceedingly keen to do business, and I bought a meat spoon, a plantain spoon, and a gravy spoon off him ; and then he brought me a lot of rubbish I did not want, and I said so, and announced I had finished trade for that night.   However the old gentleman was not to be put off, and after an unsuccessful attempt to sell me his cooking-pots, which were roughly made out of clay, he made energetic signs to me that if I would wait he had got something that he would dispose of which Gray Shirt said was " good too much." Off he went across the street, and disappeared into his hut, where he evidently had a thorough hunt for the precious article.   One box after another was brought out to the light of a bush torch held by one of his wives, and there was a great confabulation between him and his family of the " I'm sure you had it last," " You must have moved it," " Never touched the thing," sort.   At last it was found, and he brought it across the street to me most carefully.   It was a bundle of bark cloth tied round something most carefully with tie tie.   This being removed, disclosed a layer of rag, which was unwound from round a central article.   Whatever can this be ? thinks I ; some rare and valuable object doubtless, let's hope connected with Fetish worship, and I anxiously watched its unpacking ; in the end, however, it disclosed, to my disgust and rage, an old shilling razor.   The way the old chief held it out, and the amount of dollars he asked for it, was enough to make any one believe that I was in such urgent need of the thing, that I was at his mercy regarding price.   I waved it off with a haughty scorn, and then feeling smitten by the expression of agonised bewilderment on his face, I dashed him a belt that delighted him, and went inside and had tea to soothe my outraged feelings.

The chiefs made furious raids on the mob of spectators who pressed round the door, and stood with their eyes glued to every crack in the bark of which the hut was made. The next door neighbours on either side might have amassed a comfortable competence for their old age, by letting out seats for the circus. Every hole in the side walls had a human eye in it, and I heard new holes being bored in all directions ; so I deeply fear the chief, my host, must have found his palace sadly draughty. I felt perfectly safe and content, however, although Ngouta suggested the charming idea that " P'r'aps them M'fetta Fan done sell we." The only grave question I had to face was whether I should take off my boots or not ; they were wet through, from wading swamps, &c., and my feet were very sore ; but on the other hand, if I took those boots off, I felt confident that I should not be able to get them on again next morning, so I decided to lef 'em.

As soon as all my men had come in, and established themselves in the inner room for the night, I curled up among the boxes, with my head on the tobacco sack, and dozed.

After about half an hour I heard a row in the street, and looking out,—for I recognised his grace's voice taking a solo part followed by choruses,—I found him in legal difficulties about a murder case. An *alibi* was proved for the time being ; that is to say the prosecution could not bring up witnesses because of the elephant hunt ; and I went in for another doze, and the town at last grew quiet. Waking up again I noticed the smell in the hut was violent, from being shut up I suppose, and it had an unmistakably organic origin. Knocking the ash end off the smouldering bush-light that lay burning on the floor, I investigated, and tracked it to those· bags, so I took down the biggest one, and carefully noted exactly how the tie tie had been put round its mouth ; for these things are important and often mean a lot. I then shook its contents out in my hat, for fear of losing anything of value. They were a human hand, three big toes, four eyes, two ears, and other portions of the human frame. The hand was fresh, the others only so so, and shrivelled.

Replacing them I tied the bag up, and hung it up again. I subsequently learnt that although the Fans will eat their

fellow friendly tribesfolk, yet they like to keep a little something belonging to them as a memento. This touching trait
in their character I learnt from Wiki ; and, though it's to their
credit, under the circumstances, still it's an unpleasant
practice when they hang the remains in the bedroom you
occupy, particularly if the bereavement in your host's family
has been recent. I did not venture to prowl round Efoua ;
but slid the bark door aside and looked out to get a breath of
fresh air.

It was a perfect night, and no mosquitoes. The town, walled
in on every side by the great cliff of high black forest, looked
very wild as it showed in the starlight, its low, savage-built bark
huts, in two hard rows, closed at either end by a guard-house.
In both guard-houses there was a fire burning, and in their
flickering glow showed the forms of sleeping men. Nothing
was moving save the goats, which are always brought into the
special house for them in the middle of the town, to keep
them from the leopards, which roam from dusk to dawn.

Dawn found us stirring, I getting my tea, and the rest of
the party their chop, and binding up anew the loads with
Wiki's fresh supple bush-ropes. Kiva amused me much ;
during our march his costume was exceeding scant, but when
we reached the towns he took from his bag garments, and
attired himself so resplendently that I feared the charm of his
appearance would lead me into one of those dreadful wife
palavers which experience had taught me of old to dread :
and in the morning time he always devoted some time to repacking. I gave a big dash to both chiefs, and they came out
with us, most civilly, to the end of their first plantations ; and
then we took farewell of each other, with many expressions
of hope on both sides that we should meet again, and many
warnings from them about the dissolute and depraved
character of the other towns we should pass through before
we reached the Rembwé.

Our second day's march was infinitely worse than the first,
for it lay along a series of abruptly shaped hills with deep
ravines between them ; each ravine had its swamp and each
swamp its river. This bit of country must be absolutely impassable for any human being, black or white, except during

the dry season. There were representatives of the three chief forms of the West African bog. The large deep swamps were best to deal with, because they make a break in the forest, and the sun can come down on their surface and bake a crust, over which you can go, if you go quickly. From experience in Devonian bogs, I knew pace was our best chance, and I fancy I earned one of my nicknames among the Fans on these. The Fans went across all right with a rapid striding glide, but the other men erred from excess of caution, and while hesitating as to where was the next safe place to plant their feet, the place that they were standing on went in with a glug. Moreover, they would keep together, which was more than the crust would stand. The portly Pagan and the Passenger gave us a fine job in one bog, by sinking in close together. Some of us slashed off boughs of trees and tore off handfuls of hard canna leaves, while others threw them round the sinking victims to form a sort of raft, and then with the aid of bush-rope, of course, they were hauled out.

The worst sort of swamp, and the most frequent hereabouts, is the deep narrow one that has no crust on, because it is too much shaded by the forest. The slopes of the ravines too are usually covered with an undergrowth of shenja, beautiful beyond description, but right bad to go through. I soon learnt to dread seeing the man in front going down hill, or to find myself doing so, for it meant that within the next half hour we should be battling through a patch of shenja. I believe there are few effects that can compare with the beauty of them, with the golden sunlight coming down through the upper forest's branches on to their exquisitely shaped, hard, dark green leaves, making them look as if they were sprinkled with golden sequins. Their long green stalks, which support the leaves and bear little bunches of crimson berries, take every graceful curve imaginable, and the whole affair is free from insects ; and when you have said this, you have said all there is to say in favour of shenja, for those long green stalks of theirs are as tough as twisted wire, and the graceful curves go to the making of a net, which rises round you shoulder high, and the hard green leaves when lying on the ground are fearfully slippery. It is not nice going down through them, particularly when nature is so arranged that the edge of the bank you are descending is a rock-wall ten or twelve feet high with a swamp of unknown depth at its foot ; this arrangement was very frequent on the second and third day's marches, and into these swamps the shenja seemed to want to send you head first and get you suffocated. It is still less pleasant, however, going up the other side of the ravine when you have got through your swamp. You have to fight your way upwards among rough rocks, through this hard tough network of stems ; and it took it out of all of us except the Fans.

These narrow shaded swamps gave us a world of trouble and took up a good deal of time. Sometimes the leader of the party would make three or four attempts before he found a ford, going on until the black, batter-like ooze came up round his neck, and then turning back and trying in another place ; while the rest of the party sat upon the bank until the ford was found, feeling it was unnecessary to throw away human life, and that the more men there were paddling about in that swamp, the more chance there was that a hole in the bottom of it would be found ; and when a hole is found, the discoverer is liable to leave his bones in it. If I happened to be in front, the duty of finding the ford fell on me ; for none of us after leaving Efoua knew the swamps personally. I was too frightened of the Fan, and too nervous and uncertain of the stuff my other men were made of, to dare show the white feather at anything that turned up. The Fan took my conduct as a matter of course, never having travelled with white men before, or learnt the way some of them require carrying over swamps and rivers and so on. I dare say I might have taken things easier, but I was like the immortal Schmelzle, during that omnibus journey he made on his way to Flætz in the thunder-storm—afraid to be afraid. I am very certain I should have fared very differently had I entered a region occupied by a powerful and ferocious tribe like the Fan, from some districts on the West Coast, where the inhabitants are used to find the white man incapable of personal exertion, requiring to be carried in a hammock, or wheeled in a go-cart or a Bath-chair about the streets of their coast towns, depending for the defence of their settlement on a body of black soldiers. This is not so in Congo Français, and I had behind me the prestige of a set of white men to whom for the native to say, "You shall not do such and such a thing;" "You shall not go to such and such a place," would mean that those things would be done. I soon found the name of Hatton and Cookson's agent-general for this district, Mr. Hudson, was one to conjure with among the trading tribes; and the Ajumba, moreover, although their knowledge of white men had been small, yet those they had been accustomed to see were fine specimens. Mr. Fildes, Mr. Cockshut, M. Jacot, Dr. Pélessier, Père Lejeune, M. Gacon, Mr. Whittaker, and that vivacious French official, were not men any man, black or white, would willingly ruffle; and in addition there was the memory among the black traders of "that white man MacTaggart," whom an enterprising trading tribe near Setta Khama had had the hardihood to tackle, shooting him, and then towing him behind a canoe and slashing him all over with their knives the while; yet he survived, and tackled them again in a way that must almost pathetically have astonished those simple savages, after the real good work they had put in to the killing of him. Of course it was hard to live up to these ideals, and I do not pretend to have succeeded, or rather that I should have succeeded had the real strain been put on me.

Particularly sure am I that I should never flourish under the treatment Mr. MacTaggart habitually receives. I had the pleasure of meeting him on my way home the other day and found him quite convalescent from another overdose of steel. He had gone, about six weeks previously with divers other white men, on a perfectly peaceable mission into a town. The treacherous inhabitants, after receiving them kindly and talking the palaver, went for Mr. MacTaggart as the party were returning to their boats, with sharpened cutlasses; took the top off his head, and a large chip out of the back of it, and then, evidently knowing their man, proceeded to remove him in his stunned condition into the bush on a door. They there thought of taking off his head thoroughly, to make a Ju Ju of. The securing of the head of a notably brave man is a great desideratum among West Coast tribes, and they thought by securing Mr. MacTaggart's head they would do this, and also remove him from his then sphere of activity, the prevention of gin smuggling. Their plan seems excellent in theory; but I would not stake any money on its having succeeded, even if they had been able to get him well away on that door, which owing to his companions they were not. It is almost as risky to be notoriously brave among a West African tribe, as it is to be notoriously holy in the East. I know another case in which they desired to collect the head of a gentleman for their Ju Ju house. It showed in this case a lofty devotion on their part, for it would have caused them grave domestic inconvenience to have removed, at one fell swoop, their entire set of tradesmen. Still more did it show an artistic feeling of a high order ; for the head is a very handsome one. Though they command my respect as a fellow collector by the care they took in the attempt to collect it by shooting the specimen in the legs, from other standpoints I am very glad they have failed. This idea of the advantage of having a big man's head is somewhat like the Eastern one that I remember reading of in one of Richard Burton's memoirs. He was once among some very pious Easterns disguised as a dervish and enjoying such an amount of admiration from them that he felt safe and content, until one day a native friend came to him, secretly, and advised him to fly, " because the people of this city are desirous of having the shrine of a very holy man among them—both because of the spiritual advantages it bestows, and the temporal ones arising from pilgrims coming to the town from other places to visit it, and they have decided that you are so very holy, and wise, and learned in the Koran that you will do." Burton left.

But to return to that gorilla-land forest. All the. rivers we crossed on the first, second, and third day I was told went into one or other of the branches of the Ogowé, showing that the long slope of land between the Ogowé and the Rembwé is towards the Ogowé. The stone of which the mountains were composed was that same hard black rock that I had found on the Sierra del Cristal, by the Ogowé rapids ; only hereabouts there was not amongst it those great masses of white quartz,

which are so prominent a feature from Talagouga upwards in
the Ogowé valley; neither were the mountains anything like so
high, but they had the same abruptness of shape.   They look
like very old parts of the same range worn down to stumps
by the disintegrating forces of the torrential rain and sun, and
the dense forest growing on them.   Frost of course they had
not been subject to, but rocks, I noticed, were often being
somewhat similarly split by rootlets having got into some tiny
crevice, and by gradual growth enlarged it to a crack.

Of our troubles among the timber falls on these mountains
I have already spoken; and these were at their worst between
Efoua and Egaja.   I had suffered a good deal from thirst
that day, unboiled water being my ibet and we were all very
nearly tired out with the athletic sports since leaving Efoua.
One thing only we knew about Egaja for sure, and that
was that not one of us had a friend there, and that it was a
town of extra evil repute, so we were not feeling very cheerful
when towards evening time we struck its outermost plantations, their immediate vicinity being announced to us by
Silence treading full and fair on to a sharp ebony spike
driven into the narrow path and hurting himself. Fortunately,
after we passed this first plantation, we came upon a camp of
rubber collectors—four young men ; I got one of them to
carry Silence's load and show us the way into the town,
when on we went into more plantations.

There is nothing more tiresome than finding your path
going into a plantation, because it fades out in the cleared
ground, or starts playing games with a lot of other little
paths that are running about amongst the crops, and no West
African path goes straight into a stream or a plantation, and
straight out the other side, so you have a nice time picking it
up again.

We were spared a good deal of fine varied walking by our
new friend the rubber collector ; for I noticed he led us out by
a path nearly at right angles to the one by which we had
entered.   He then pitched into a pit which was half full of
thorns, and which he observed he did not know was there,
demonstrating that an African guide can speak the truth.
When he had got out, he handed back Silence's load and got

a dash of tobacco for his help ; he left us to devote the rest of his evening by his forest fire to unthorning himself, while we proceeded to wade a swift, deepish river that crossed the path he told us led into Egaja, and then went across another bit of forest and down hill again. " Oh, bless those swamps !" thought I, " here's another," but no—not this time. Across the bottom of the steep ravine, from one side to another, lay an enormous tree as a bridge, about fifteen feet above a river, which rushed beneath it, over a boulder-encumbered bed. I took in the situation at a glance, and then and there I would have changed that bridge for any swamp I have ever seen, yea, even for a certain bush-rope bridge in which I once wound myself up like a buzzing fly in a spider's web. I was fearfully tired, and my legs shivered under me after the falls and emotions of the previous part of the day, and my boots were slippery with water soaking.

The Fans went into the river, and half swam, half waded across. All the Ajumba, save Pagan, followed, and Ngouta got across with their assistance. Pagan thought he would try the bridge, and I thought I would watch how the thing worked. He got about three yards along it and then slipped, but caught the tree with his hands as he fell, and hauled himself back to my side again ; then he went down the bank and through the water. This was not calculated to improve one's nerve ; I knew by now I had got to go by the bridge, for I saw I was not strong enough in my tired state to fight the water. If only the wretched thing had had its bark on it would have been better, but it was bare, bald, and round, and a slip meant death on the rocks below. I rushed it, and reached the other side in safety, whereby poor Pagan got chaffed about his failure by the others, who said they had gone through the water just to wash their feet.

The other side, when we got there, did not seem much worth reaching, being a swampy fringe at the bottom of a steep hillside, and after a few yards the path turned into a stream or backwater of the river. It was hedged with thickly pleached bushes, and covered with liquid water on the top of semi-liquid mud. Now and again for a change you had a foot of water on top of fearfully slippery harder mud, and then

we light-heartedly took headers into the bush, sideways, or
sat down ; and when it was not proceeding on the evil tenor of
its way, like this, it had holes in it ; in fact, I fancy the bottom of
the holes was the true level, for it came near being as full of
holes as a fishing-net, and it was very quaint to see the man in
front, who had been paddling along knee-deep before, now plop
down with the water round his shoulders ; and getting out of
these slippery pockets, which were sometimes a tight fit, was
difficult.

However that is the path you have got to go by, if you're
not wise enough to stop at home ; the little bay of shrub overgrown swamp fringing the river on one side and on the other
running up to the mountain side.

At last we came to a sandy bank, and on that bank stood
Egaja, the town with an evil name even among the Fan,
but where we had got to stay, fair or foul. We went
into it through its palaver house, and soon had the usual
row.

I had detected signs of trouble among my men during the
whole day ; the Ajumba were tired, and dissatisfied with the
Fans ; the Fans were in high feather, openly insolent to
Ngouta, and anxious for me to stay in this delightful locality,
and go hunting with them and divers other choice spirits, whom
they assured me we could easily get to join us at Efoua.
Ngouta kept away from them, and I was worried about him
on account of his cold and loss of voice. I kept peace as well
as I could, explaining to the Fans I had not enough money
with me now, because I had not, when starting, expected such
magnificent opportunities to be placed at my disposal ; and
promising to come back next year—a promise I hope to keep—
and then we would go and have a grand time of it. This state
of a party was a dangerous one in which to enter a strange Fan
town, where our security lay in our being united. When the
first burst of Egaja conversation began to boil down into
something reasonable, I found that a villainous-looking
scoundrel, smeared with soot and draped in a fragment
of genuine antique cloth, was a head chief in mourning.
He placed a house at my disposal, quite a mansion, for it had
no less than four apartments. The first one was almost

entirely occupied by a bedstead frame that was being made up inside on account of the small size of the door.

This had to be removed before we could get in with the baggage at all. While this removal was being effected with as much damage to the house and the article as if it were a quarter-day affair in England, the other chief arrived. He had been sent for, being away down the river fishing when we arrived. I saw at once he was a very superior man to any of the chiefs I had yet met with. It was not his attire, remarkable though that was for the district, for it consisted of a gentleman's black frock-coat such as is given in the ivory bundle, a bright blue felt sombrero hat, an ample cloth of Boma check ; but his face and general bearing was distinctive, and very powerful and intelligent ; and I knew that Egaja, for good or bad, owed its name to this man, and not to the mere sensual, brutal-looking one. He was exceedingly courteous, ordering his people to bring me a stool and one for himself, and then a fly-whisk to battle with the evening cloud of sand-flies. I got Pagan to come and act as interpreter while the rest were stowing the baggage, &c. After compliments, " Tell the chief," I said, " that I hear this town of his is thief town."

" Better not, sir," says Pagan.

" Go on," said I, " or I'll tell him myself."

So Pagan did. It was a sad blow to the chief.

" Thief town, this highly respectable town of Egaja ! a town whose moral conduct in all matters (Shedule) was an example to all towns, called a thief town ! Oh, what a wicked world ! "

I said it was ; but I would reserve my opinion as to whether Egaja was a part of the wicked world or a star-like exception, until I had experienced it myself. We then discoursed on many matters, and I got a great deal of interesting fetish information out of the chief, which was valuable to me, because the whole of this district had not been in contact with white culture ; and altogether I and the chief became great friends.

Just when I was going in to have my much-desired tea, he brought me his mother—an old lady, evidently very bright and able, but, poor woman, with the most disgusting hand and

arm I have ever seen.   I am ashamed to say I came very near
being sympathetically sick in the African manner on the
spot.   I felt I could not attend to it, and have my tea afterwards, so I directed one of the canoe-shaped little tubs, used
for beating up the manioc in, to be brought and filled with hot
water, and then putting into it a heavy dose of Condy's fluid,
I made her sit down and lay the whole arm in it, and went
and had my tea.   As soon as I had done I went outside, and
getting some of the many surrounding ladies to hold bush-
lights, I examined the case.   The whole hand was a mass of
yellow pus, streaked with sanies, large ulcers were burrowing
into the fore-arm, while in the arm-pit was a big abscess.   I
opened the abscess at once, and then the old lady frightened
me nearly out of my wits by gently subsiding, I thought dying,
but I soon found out merely going to sleep.   I then washed
the abscess well out, and having got a lot of baked plantains, I
made a big poultice of them, mixed with boiling water and
more Condy in the tub, and laid her arm right in this ; and
propping her up all round and covering her over with cloths I
requisitioned from her son, I left her to have her nap while I
went into the history of the case, which was that some forty-
eight hours ago she had been wading along the bank, catching
crawfish, and had been stung by "a fish like a snake" ; so I
presume the ulcers were an old-standing palaver.   The hand
had been a good deal torn by the creature, and the pain and
swelling had been so great she had not had a minute's sleep
since.   As soon as the poultice got chilled I took her arm out
and cleaned it again, and wound it round with dressing, and
had her ladyship carried bodily, still asleep, into her hut, and
after rousing her up, giving her a dose of that fine preparation,
pil. crotonis cum hydrargi, saw her tucked up on her own plank
bedstead for the night, sound asleep again.   The chief was
very anxious to have some pills too ; so I gave him some, with
firm injunctions only to take one at the first time.   I knew
that that one would teach him not to take more than one for
ever after, better than I could do if I talked from June to
January.   Then all the afflicted of Egaja turned up, and
wanted medical advice.   There was evidently a good stiff
epidemic of the yaws about ; lots of cases of dum with the

various symptoms ; ulcers of course galore ; a man with a bit
of a broken spear head in an abscess in the thigh ; one which
I believe a professional enthusiast would call a "lovely case" of
filaria, the entire white of one eye being full of the active little
worms and a ridge of surplus population migrating across the
bridge of the nose into the other eye, under the skin, looking
like the bridge of a pair of spectacles. It was past eleven before
I had anything like done, and my men had long been sound
asleep, but the chief had conscientiously sat up and seen the
thing through. He then went and fetched some rolls of bark
cloth to put on my plank, and I gave him a handsome cloth I
happened to have with me, a couple of knives, and some heads
of tobacco and wished him good-night ; blockading my bark
door, and picking my way over my sleeping Ajumba into an
inner apartment which I also blockaded, hoping I had done
with Egaja for some hours. No such thing. At 1.45 the whole
town was roused by the frantic yells of a woman. I judged
there was one of my beauties of Fans mixed up in it, and there
was, and after paying damages, got back again by 2.30 A.M.,
and off to sleep again instantly. At four sharp, whole town of
Egaja plunged into emotion, and worse shindy. I suggested
to the Ajumba they should go out ; but no, they didn't care
a row of pins if one of our Fans did get killed, so I went,
recognising Kiva's voice in high expostulation. Kiva, it
seems, a long time ago had a transaction *in re* a tooth of ivory
with a man who, unfortunately, happened to be in this town
to-night, and Kiva owed the said man a coat.[1]

Kiva, it seems, has been spending the whole evening
demonstrating to his creditor that, had he only known they
were to meet, he would have brought the coat with him—a
particularly beautiful coat—and the reason he has not paid it
before is that he has mislaid the creditor's address. The
creditor says he has called repeatedly at Kiva's village, that
notorious M'fetta, and Kiva has never been at home ; and
moreover that Kiva's wife (one of them) stole a yellow dog
of great value from his (the creditor's) canoe. Kiva says,
women will be women, and he had gone off to sleep thinking

---

[1] An European coat or its equivalent value is one of the constant
quantities in an ivory bundle.

the affair had blown over and the bill renewed for the time
being. The creditor had not gone to sleep ; but sat up thinking the affair over and remembered many cases, all cited in
full, of how Kiva had failed to meet his debts ; also Kiva's
brother on the mother's side and uncle ditto ; and so has
decided to foreclose forthwith on the debtor's estate, and as
the estate is represented by and consists of Kiva's person, to
take and seize upon it and eat it.

It is always highly interesting to observe the germ of any
of our own institutions existing in the culture of a lower race
Nevertheless it is trying to be hauled out of one's sleep
in the middle of the night, and plunged into this study
Evidently this was a trace of an early form of the Bankruptcy Court ; the court which clears a man of his debt, being
here represented by the knife and the cooking pot ; the whitewashing, as I believe it is termed with us, also shows, only it
is not the debtor who is whitewashed, but the creditors doing
themselves over with white clay to celebrate the removal of
their enemy from his sphere of meretricious activity. This
inversion may arise from the fact that whitewashing a creditor
who was about to be cooked would be unwise, as the stuff
would boil off the bits and spoil the gravy. There is always
some fragment of sound sense underlying African institutions.
Kiva was, when I got out, tied up, talking nineteen to the
dozen ; and so was every one else ; and a lady was working
up white clay in a pot.

I dare say I ought to have rushed at him and cut his bonds,
and killed people in a general way with a revolver, and then
flown with my band to the bush ; only my band evidently
had no flying in them, being tucked up in the hut pretending
to be asleep, and uninterested in the affair ; and although I
could have abandoned the band without a pang just then, I
could not so light-heartedly fly alone with Kiva to the bush
and leave my fishes ; so I shouted Azuna to the Bankruptcy
Court, and got a Fan who spoke trade English to come and
interpret for me ; and from him I learnt the above stated
outline of the proceedings up to the time. Regarding the
original iniquity of Kiva, my other Fans held the opinion that
the old Scotch lady had regarding certain passages in the

history of the early Jews—that it was a long time ago, and habelings it was no true.

Fortunately for the reader it is impossible for me to give in full detail the proceedings of the Court. I do not think if the whole of Mr. Pitman's school of shorthand had been there to take them down the thing could possibly have been done in word-writing. If the late Richard Wagner, however, had been present he could have scored the performance for a full orchestra ; and with all its weird grunts and roars, and pistol-like finger clicks, and its elongated words and thigh slaps, it would have been a masterpiece.

I got my friend the chief on my side ; but he explained he had no jurisdiction, as neither of the men belonged to his town ; and I explained to him, that as the proceedings were taking place in his town he had a right of jurisdiction *ipso facto*. The Fan could not translate this phrase, so we gave it the chief raw, and he seemed to relish it, and he and I then cut into the affair together, I looking at him with admiration and approval when he was saying his say, and after his " Azuna " had produced a patch of silence he could move his tongue in, and he similarly regarding me during my speech for the defence. We neither, I expect, understood each other, and we had trouble with our client, who would keep pleading " Not guilty," which was absurd. Anyhow we produced our effect, my success arising from my concluding my speech with the announcement that I would give the creditor a book on Hatton and Cookson for the coat, and I would deduct it from Kiva's pay.

But, said the Court : " We look your mouth and it be sweet mouth, but with Hatton and Cookson we can have no trade." This was a blow to me. Hatton and Cookson was my big Ju Ju, and it was to their sub-factory on the Rembwé that I was bound. On inquiry I elicited another cheerful little fact, which was they could not deal with Hatton and Cookson, because there was " blood war on the path that way." The Court said they would take a book on Holty, but with Holty, *i.e.* Mr. John Holt, I had no deposit of money, and I did not feel justified in issuing cheques on him, knowing also he could not feel amiable towards wandering scientists, after what he had

recently gone through with one. Not that I doubt for one
minute but that his representatives would have honoured my
book ; for the generosity and helpfulness of West African
traders is unbounded and long-suffering. But I did not like to
encroach on it, all the more so from a feeling that I might
never get through to refund the money. So at last I paid the
equivalent value of the coat out of my own trade-stuff; and
the affair was regarded by all parties as satisfactorily closed
by the time the gray dawn was coming up over the forest
wall. I went in again and slept in snatches until I got my
tea about seven, and then turned out to hurry my band out of
Egaja. This I did not succeed in doing until past ten. One
row succeeded another with my men ; but I was determined to
get them out of that town as quickly as possible, for I had
heard so much from perfectly reliable and experienced people
regarding the treacherousness of the Fan. I feared too that
more cases still would be brought up against Kiva, from the
résumé of his criminal career I had had last night, and I knew it
was very doubtful whether my other three Fans were any better
than he. There was his grace's little murder affair only
languishing for want of evidence owing to the witnesses for
the prosecution being out elephant-hunting not very far away ;
and Wiki was pleading an *alibi*, and a twin brother, in a bad
wife palaver in this town. I really hope for the sake of
Fan morals at large, that I did engage the three worst villains
in M'fetta, and that M'fetta is the worst town in all Fan land,
inconvenient as this arrangement was to me personally.
Anyhow, I felt sure my Pappenheimers would take a lot of beating for good solid crime, among any tribe anywhere. Moreover, the Ajumba wanted meat, and the Fans, they said,
offered them human. I saw no human meat at Egaja, but
the Ajumba seem to think the Fans eat nothing else, which is
a silly prejudice of theirs, because the Fans do. I think in
this case the Ajumba thought a lot of smoked flesh offered
was human. It may have been ; it was in neat pieces ; and
again, as the Captain of the late ss. *Sparrow* would say, " it
mayn't." But the Ajumba have a horror of cannibalism, and
I honestly believe never practise it, even for fetish affairs,
which is a rare thing in a West African tribe where sacrificial

and ceremonial cannibalism is nearly universal. Anyhow the Ajumba loudly declared the Fans were "bad men too much," which was impolitic under existing circumstances, and inexcusable, because it by no means arose from a courageous defiance of them ; but the West African ! Well ! "he's a devil and an ostrich and an orphan child in one."

The chief was very anxious for me to stay and rest, but as his mother was doing wonderfully well, and the other women seemed quite to understand my directions regarding her, I did not feel inclined to risk it. The old lady's farewell of me was peculiar : she took my hand in her two, turned it palm upwards, and spat on it. I do not know whether this is a constant form of greeting among the Fan ; I fancy not. Dr. Nassau, who explained it to me when I saw him again down at Baraka, said the spitting was merely an accidental by-product of the performance, which consisted in blowing a blessing ; and as I happened on this custom twice afterwards, I feel sure from observation he is right.

The two chiefs saw us courteously out of the town as far as where the river crosses the out-going path again, and the blue-hatted one gave me some charms "to keep my foot in path," and the mourning chief lent us his son to see us through the lines of fortification of the plantation. I gave them an equal dash, and in answer to their question as to whether I had found Egaja a thief-town, I said that to call Egaja a thief-town was rank perjury, for I had not lost a thing while in it ; and we parted with mutual expression of esteem and hopes for another meeting at an early date.

The defences of the fine series of plantations of Egaja on this side were most intricate, to judge from the zigzag course our guide led us through them. He explained they had to be because of the character of the towns towards the Rembwé. After listening to this young man, I really began to doubt that the Cities of the Plain had really been destroyed, and wondered whether some future revision committee will not put transported for destroyed. This young man certainly hit off the character of Sodom and Gomorrah to the life, in describing the towns towards the Rembwé, though he had never heard Sodom and Gomorrah named. He assured me I should see

the difference between them and Egaja the Good, and I
thanked him and gave him his dash when we parted ; but told
him as a friend, I feared some alteration must take place, and
some time elapse before he saw a regular rush of pilgrim
worshippers of virtue coming into even Egaja the Good,
though it stood just as good a chance and better than most
towns I had seen in Africa.

We went on into the gloom of the Great Forest again ;
that forest that seemed to me without end, wherein, in a
lazy, hazy-minded sort of way, I expected to wander through
by day and drop in at night to a noisy savage town for the
rest of my days.

We climbed up one hill, skirted its summit, went through
our athletic sports over sundry timber falls, and struck down
into the ravine as usual. But at the bottom of that ravine,
which was exceeding steep, ran a little river free from swamp.
As I was wading it I noticed it had a peculiarity that distinguished it from all the other rivers we had come through ;
and then and there I sat down on a boulder in its midst and
hauled out my compass. Yes, by Allah! it's going north-
west and bound as we are for Rembwé River. I went out the
other side of that river with a lighter heart than I went in, and
shouted the news to the boys, and they yelled and sang as we
went on our way.

All along this bit of country we had seen quantities of
rubber vines, and between Egaja and Esoon we came across
quantities of rubber being collected. Evidently there was
a big camp of rubber hunters out in the district very busy.
Wiki and Kiva did their best to teach me the trade. Along
each side of the path we frequently saw a ring of stout bush
rope, raised from the earth on pegs about a foot to eighteen
inches. On the ground in the middle stood a calabash, into
which the ends of the pieces of rubber vine were placed, the
other ends being supported by the bush rope ring. Round
the outside of some of these rings was a slow fire, which just
singes the tops of the bits of rubber vine as they project over
the collar or ring, and causes the milky juice to run out of
the lower end into the calabash, giving out as it does so a
strong ammoniacal smell. When the fire was alight there

would be a group of rubber collectors sitting round it watching the cooking operations, removing those pieces that had run dry and placing others, from a pile at their side, in position. On either side of the path we continually passed pieces of rubber vine cut into lengths of some two feet or so, and on the top one or two leaves plaited together, or a piece of bush rope tied into a knot, which indicated whose property the pile was.

The method of collection employed by the Fan is exceed-

FANS WITH IVORY AND RUBBER.

ingly wasteful, because this fool of a vegetable *Landolphia florida (Ovariensis)* does not know how to send up suckers from its root, but insists on starting elaborately from seeds only. I do not, however, see any reasonable hope of getting them to adopt more economical methods. The attempt made by the English houses, when the rubber trade was opened up in 1883 on the Gold Coast, to get the more tractable natives there to collect by incisions only, has failed ; for in the early days a man could get a load of rubber almost at his own door on the Gold Coast, and now he has to go fifteen days' journey

inland for it. When a Fan town has exhausted the rubber in
its vicinity, it migrates, bag and baggage, to a new part of the
forest. The young unmarried men are the usual rubber
hunters. Parties of them go out into the forest, wandering
about in it and camping under shelters of boughs by night,
for a month and more at a time, during the dry seasons,
until they have got a sufficient quantity together ; then they
return to their town, and it is manipulated by the women, and
finally sold, either to the white trader, in districts where he is
within reach, or to the M'pongwe trader who travels round
buying it and the collected ivory and ebony, like a Norfolk
higgler. In districts like these I was in, remote from the
M'pongwe trader, the Fans carry the rubber to the town nearest
to them that is in contact with the black trader, and sell it to
the inhabitants, who in their turn resell it to their next town,
until it reaches him.

This passing down of the rubber and ivory gives rise between
the various towns to a series of commercial complications
which rank with woman palaver for the production of rows ; it
being the sweet habit of these Fans to require a life for a life,
and to regard one life as good as another. Also rubber trade
and wife palavers sweetly intertwine, for a man on the kill *in
re* a wife palaver knows his best chance of getting the life
from the village he has a grudge against lies in catching one
of that village's men when he may be out alone rubber hunting.
So he does this thing, and then the men from the victim's
village, go and lay for a rubber hunter, from the killer's village ;
and then of course the men from the killer's village go and lay
for rubber hunters from victim number one's village, and thus
the blood feud rolls ˋdown the vaulted chambers of the ages,
so that you, dropping in on affairs, cannot see one end or the
other of it, and frequently the people concerned have quite
forgotten what the killing was started for. Not that this discourages them in the least. Really if Dr. Nassau is right, and
these Fans are descendants of Adam and Eve, I expect the
Cain and Abel killing palaver is still kept going among
them.

Wiki, being great on bush rope, gave me much information
regarding rubber, showing me the various other vines besides

the true rubber vine, whose juice, mingled with the true sap by
the collector when in the forest, adds to the weight ; a matter
of importance, because rubber is bought by weight. The
other adulteration gets done by the ladies in the villages
when the collected sap is handed over to them to prepare
for the markets.

This preparation consists of boiling it in water slightly, and
adding a little salt, which causes the gummy part to separate
and go to the bottom of the pot, where it looks like a thick
cream. The water is carefully poured off this deposit,
which is then taken out and moulded, usually in the hands ;
but I have seen it run into moulds made of small calabashes
with a stick or piece of iròn passing through, so that when
the rubber is set this can be withdrawn. A hole being thus
left the balls can be threaded on to a stick, usually five on
one stick, for convenience of transport. It is during the
moulding process that most of the adulteration gets in.
Down by the side of many of the streams there is a white
chalky-looking clay which is brought up into the villages,
powdered up, and then hung up over the fire in a basket to
attain a uniform smuttiness ; it is then worked into the
rubber when it is being made up into balls. Then a good
chunk of Koko, *Arum esculentum* (Koko is better than yam,
I may remark, because it is heavier), also smoked approxi-
mately the right colour, is often placed in the centre of the
rubber ball. In fact, anything is put there, that is hopefully
regarded as likely to deceive the white trader.

I once overheard a long discussion between two ladies : " I
always clay my rubber up well," says number one. " I think,"
says number two, " a bit of yam is better, with just a coat of
rubber outside, then he hop good too much when Mr.——
frows him for floor." They did not convince each other as to
the superiority of their individual methods, but became very
friendly over the foolishness of a mutual friend, who both
clayed and yammed her rubber to such an extent that when
Mr.—— " frowed him for floor he done squat." Mr.—— then
cut him open and " frowed " both the pieces at her head—a
performance that raised Mr.—— in their esteem, as it demonstrated commercial intelligence, a thing universally admired

down here. So great is the adulteration, that most of the traders have to cut each ball open. Even the Kinsembo rubber, which is put up in clusters of bits shaped like little thimbles formed by rolling pinches of rubber between the thumb and finger, and which one would think difficult to put anything inside of, has to be cut, because "the simple children of nature" who collect it and bring it to that "swindling white trader" struck upon the ingenious notion that little pieces of wood shaped like the thimbles and coated by a dip in rubber were excellent additions to a cluster.

The pure rubber, when it is made, looks like putty, and has the same dusky-white colour; but, owing to the balls being kept in the huts in baskets in the smoke, and in wicker-work cages in the muddy pools to soak up as much waste as possible before going into the hands of the traders, they get almost inky in colour.

CHAPTER XIII

FROM ESOON TO AGONJO

In which the Voyager sets forth the beauties of the way from Esoon to N'dorko, and gives some account of the local Swamps.

OUR next halting place was Esoon, which received us with the usual row, but kindly enough ; and endeared itself to me by knowing the Rembwé, and not just waving the arm in the air, in any direction, and saying " Far, far plenty bad people live for that side," as the other towns had done. Of course they stuck to the bad people part of the legend ; but I was getting quite callous as to the moral character of new acquaintances, feeling sure that for good solid murderous rascality several of my old Fan acquaintances, and even my own party, would take a lot of beating ; and yet, one and all, they had behaved well to me. I am glad to see from my diaries that I knew this at the time ; for I see in my Cameroon journal an entry " Wish to Allah the Fans were in this country ; have been inquiring in vain for a cannibal tribe to associate with, but there is not one round here " ; but that's another story. Esoon gave me to understand that of all the Sodoms and Gomorrahs that town of Egaja was an easy first, and it would hardly believe we had come that way. Still Egaja had dealt with us well. However I took less interest—except, of course, as a friend, in some details regarding the criminal career of Chief Blue-hat of Egaja—in the opinion of Esoon regarding the country we had survived, than in the information it had to impart regarding the country we had got to survive on our way to the Big River, which now no longer meant the Ogowé, but the Rembwé. I meant to reach one of Hatton and Cookson's sub-factories there, but—strictly between ourselves—I knew no more at what town that factory was than a Kindergarten

Board School child does. I did not mention this fact ; and a
casual observer might have thought that I had spent my youth
in that factory, when I directed my inquiries to the finding out
the very shortest route to it. Esoon shook its head. " Yes, it
was close, but it was impossible to reach Uguma's factory."
" Why ? " " There was blood war on the path." I said it was
no war of mine. But Esoon said, such was the appalling
depravity of the next town on the road, that its inhabitants
lay in wait at day with loaded guns and shot on sight any
one coming up the Esoon road, and that at night they tied
strings with bells on across the road and shot on hearing them.
No one had been killed since the first party of Esoonians
were fired on at long range, because no one had gone that
way ; but the next door town had been heard by people who
had been out in the bush at night, blazing down the road when
the bells were tinkled by wild animals. Clearly that road was
not yet really healthy.

The Duke, who as I have said before, was a fine courageous
fellow, ready to engage in any undertaking, suggested I should
go up the road—alone by myself—first—a mile ahead of the
party—and the next town, perhaps, might not shoot at sight,
if they happened to notice I was something queer ; and I
might explain things, and then the rest of the party would
follow. " There's nothing like dash and courage, my dear
Duke," I said, " even if one display it by deputy, so this plan
does you great credit ; but as my knowledge of this charming
language of yours is but small, I fear I might create a wrong
impression in that town, and it might think I had kindly
brought them a present of eight edible heathens—you and the
remainder of my followers, you understand." My men saw
this was a real danger, and this was the only way I saw of
excusing myself. It is at such a moment as this that the
Giant's robe gets, so to speak, between your legs and threatens
to trip you up. Going up a forbidden road, and exposing
yourself as a pot shot to ambushed natives would be jam and
fritters to Mr. MacTaggart, for example ; but I am not up to
that form yet. So I determined to leave that road severely
alone, and circumnavigate the next town by a road that leaves
Esoon going W.N.W., which struck the Rembwé by N'dorko,

I was told, and then follow up the bank of the river until I picked up the sub-factory. Subsequent experience did not make one feel inclined to take out a patent for this plan, but at the time in Esoon it looked nice enough.

Some few of the more highly cultured inhabitants here could speak trade English a little, and had been to the Rembwé, and were quite intelligent about the whole affair. They had seen white men. A village they formerly occupied nearer the Rembwé had been burnt by them, on account of a something that had occurred to a Catholic priest who visited it. They were, of course, none of them personally mixed up in this sad affair, so could give no details of what had befallen the priest. They knew also "the *Mové*," which was a great bond of union between us. "Was I a wife of them *Mové* white man," they inquired—"or them other white man?" I civilly said them *Mové* men were my tribe, and they ought to have known it by the look of me. They discussed my points of re-semblance to "the *Mové* white man," and I am ashamed to say I could not forbear from smiling, as I distinctly recognised my friends from the very racy description of their personal appear-ance and tricks of manner given by a lively Esoonian belle who had certainly met them. So content and happy did I become under these soothing influences, that I actually took off my boots, a thing I had quite got out of the habit of doing, and had them dried. I wanted to have them rubbed with palm oil, but I found, to my surprise, that there was no palm oil to be had, the tree being absent, or scarce in this region, so I had to content myself with having them rubbed with a piece of animal fat instead. I chaperoned my men, while among the ladies of Esoon—a forward set of minxes—with the vigilance of a dragon ; and decreed, like the Mikado of Japan, "that who-soever leered or winked, unless connubially linked, should forthwith be beheaded," have their pay chopped, I mean ; and as they were beginning to smell their pay, they were careful, and we got through Esoon without one of my men going into jail ; no mean performance when you remember that every man had a past—to put it mildly. Fika remained behind here, the others promising to bring back his pay bundle with them on their return journey home. I think Fika heard rumours in Esoon of some gentlemen he had met before and was not keen to meet again, being just then at N'dorko, so I parted with him and Esoon, with suitable dashes, in peace.

Esoon is not situated like the other towns, with a swamp and the forest close round it; but it is built on the side of a fairly cleared ravine among its plantain groves. When you are on the southern side of the ravine, you can see Esoon looking as if it were hung on the hillside before you. You then go through a plantation down into the little river, and up into the town—one long, broad, clean-kept street. Leaving Esoon you go on up the hill through another plantation to the summit. Immediately after leaving the town we struck westwards; and when we got to the top of the next hill we had a view that showed us we were dealing with another type of country. The hills to the westward are lower, and the valleys between them broader and less heavily forested, or rather I should say forested with smaller sorts of timber. All our paths took us during the early part of the day up and down hills, through swamps and little rivers, all flowing Rembwéwards. About the middle of the afternoon, when we had got up to the top of a high hill, after having had a terrible time on a timber fall of the first magnitude, into which four of us had fallen, I of course for one, I saw a sight that made my heart stand still. Stretching away to the west and north, winding in and out among the feet of the now isolated mound-like mountains, was that never to be mistaken black-green forest swamp of mangrove; doubtless the fringe of the River Rembwé, which evidently comes much further inland than the mangrove belt on the Ogowé. This is reasonable and as it should be, though it surprised me at the time; for the great arm of the sea which is called the Gaboon is really a fjord, just like Bonny and Opobo rivers, with several rivers falling into it at its head, and this fjord brings the sea water further inland. In addition to this the two rivers, the 'Como (Nkâmâ) and Rembwé that fall into this Gaboon, with several smaller rivers, both bring down an inferior quantity of fresh water, and that at nothing like the tearing, tide-beating back pace of the Ogowé. As my brother would say, " It's perfectly simple if you think

about it ; " but thinking is not my strong point.   Anyhow I
was glad to see the mangrove-belt ; all the gladder because I
did not then know how far it was inland from the sea, and
also because I was fool enough to think that a long line I
could see, running E. and W. to the north of where I stood,
was the line of the Rembwé river ; which it was not, as we
soon found out.   Cheered by this pleasing prospect, we
marched on forgetful of our scratches, down the side of the
hill, and down the foot slope of it, until we struck the edge
of the swamp.   We skirted this for some mile or so, going
N.E.   Then we struck into the swamp, to reach what we had
regarded as the Rembwé river.   " Nature was at its ghastliest,"
as *Chambers's Magazine* said, and hurt the feelings of the
locality by saying, of the Oil Rivers scenery.   We found ourselves at the edge of that open line we had seen from the
mountain.   Not standing, because you don't so much as try
to stand on mangrove roots unless you are a born fool, and
then you don't stand long, but clinging, like so many monkeys,
to the net of aërial roots which surrounded us, looking blankly
at a lake of ink-black slime.   It was half a mile across,
and some miles long.   We could not see either the west or
east termination of it, for it lay like a rotten serpent twisted
between the mangroves.   It never entered into our heads to try
to cross it, for when a swamp is too deep for mangroves to grow
in it, " No bottom lib for them dam ting," as a Kruboy once
said to me, anent a small specimen of this sort of ornament
to a landscape.   But we just looked round to see which direction we had better take.   Then I observed that the roots,
aërial and otherwise, were coated in mud, and had no leaves
on them, for a foot above our heads.   Next I noticed that
the surface of the mud before us had a sort of quiver running
through it, and here and there it exhibited swellings on its
surface, which rose in one place and fell in another.   No need
for an old coaster like me to look at that sort of thing twice
to know what it meant, and feeling it was a situation more
suited to Mr. Stanley than myself, I attempted to emulate his
methods and addressed my men.   " Boys," said I, " this
beastly hole is tidal, and the tide is coming in.   As it took
us two hours to get to this sainted swamp, it's time we started

out, one time, and the nearest way. It's to be hoped the
practice we have acquired in mangrove roots in coming, will
enable us to get up sufficient pace to get out on to dry land
before we are all drowned." The boys took the hint. Fortunately one of the Ajumbas had been down in Ogowé, it was
Gray Shirt, who "sabed them tide palaver." The rest of them,
and the Fans, did not know what tide meant, but Gray Shirt
hustled them along and I followed, deeply regretting that my
ancestors had parted prematurely with prehensile tails for
four limbs, particularly when two of them are done up in
boots and are not sufficient to enable one to get through a mangrove swamp network of slimy roots rising out of the water,
and swinging lines of aërial ones coming down to the water
à la mangrove, with anything approaching safety. Added to
these joys were any quantity of mangrove flies, a broiling hot
sun, and an atmosphere three quarters solid stench from the pu-
trifying ooze all round us. For an hour and a half thought I,
Why did I come to Africa, or why, having come, did I not
know when I was well off and stay in Glass? Before these
problems were settled in my mind we were close to the true
land again, with the water under us licking lazily among the
roots and over our feet.

We did not make any fuss about it, but we meant to stick
to dry land for some time, and so now took to the side of a
hill that seemed like a great bubble coming out of the swamp,
and bore steadily E. until we found a path. This path,
according to the nature of paths in this country, promptly
took us into another swamp, but of a different kind to our
last—a knee-deep affair, full of beautiful palms and strange
water plants, the names whereof I know not. There was
just one part where that abomination, *pandanus*, had to be
got through, but, as swamps go, it was not at all bad.
I ought to mention that there were leeches in it, lest I
may be thought too enthusiastic over its charms. But the
great point was that the mountains we got to on the other
side of it, were a good solid ridge, running, it is true, E. and W.,
while we wanted to go N.; still on we went waiting for developments, and watching the great line of mangrove-swamp
spreading along below us to the left hand, seeing many of

the lines in its dark face, which betokened more of those
awesome slime lagoons that we had seen enough of at close
quarters.

About four o'clock we struck some more plantations, and
passing through these, came to a path running north-east,
down which we went. I must say the forest scenery here was
superbly lovely. Along this mountain side cliff to the mangrove-swamp the sun could reach the soil, owing to the
steepness and abruptness and the changes of curves of the
ground ; while the soft steamy air which came up off the swamp
swathed everything, and although unpleasantly strong in smell
to us, was yet evidently highly agreeable to the vegetation.
Lovely wine palms and rafia palms, looking as if they had been
grown under glass, so deliciously green and profuse was their
feather-like foliage, intermingled with giant red woods, and lovely
dark glossy green lianes, blooming in wreaths and festoons of
white and mauve flowers, which gave a glorious wealth of
beauty and colour to the scene. Even the monotony of the
mangrove-belt alongside gave an additional charm to it, like
the frame round a picture.

As we passed on, the ridge turned N. and the mangrove
line narrowed between the hills. Our path now ran east and
more in the middle of the forest, and the cool shade was charming after the heat we had had earlier in the day. We crossed
a lovely little stream coming down the hillside in a cascade ;
and then our path plunged into a beautiful valley. We had
glimpses through the trees of an amphitheatre of blue mist-
veiled mountains coming down in a crescent before us, and
on all sides, save due west where the mangrove-swamp came
in. Never shall I forget the exceeding beauty of that valley,
the foliage of the trees round us, the delicate wreaths and
festoons of climbing plants, the graceful delicate plumes of
the palm trees, interlacing among each other, and showing
through all a background of soft, pale, purple-blue mountains
and forest, not really far away, as the practised eye knew,
but only made to look so by the mist, which has this trick
of giving suggestion of immense space without destroying the
beauty of detail. Those African misty forests have the same
marvellous distinctive quality that Turner gives one in his

greatest pictures. I am no artist, so I do not know exactly
what it is, but I see it is there. I luxuriated in the exquisite beauty of that valley, little thinking or knowing what
there was in it besides beauty, as Allah "in mercy hid the
book of fate." On we went among the ferns and flowers.
until we met a swamp, a different kind of swamp to those we
had heretofore met, save the little one last mentioned. This
one was much larger, and a gem of beauty ; but we had to
cross it. It was completely furnished with characteristic flora.
Fortunately when we got to its edge we saw a woman
crossing before us, but unfortunately she did not take a
fancy to our appearance, and instead of staying and having a
chat about the state of the roads, and the shortest way to
N'dorko, she bolted away across the swamp. I noticed
she carefully took a course, not the shortest, although that
course immersed her to her arm-pits. In we went after
her, and when things were getting unpleasantly deep, and
feeling highly uncertain under foot, we found there was a
great log of a tree under the water which, as we had
seen the lady's care at this point, we deemed it advisable to
walk on. All of us save one, need I say that one was myself,
effected this with safety. As for me, when I was at the
beginning of the submerged bridge, and busily laying about in
my mind for a definite opinion as to whether it was better
to walk on a slippy tree trunk bridge you could see, or on
one you could not, I was hurled off by that inexorable fate that
demands of me a personal acquaintance with fluvial and
paludial ground deposits ; whereupon I took a header, and am
thereby able to inform the world, that there is between
fifteen and twenty feet of water each side of that log. I conscientiously went in on one side, and came up on the other.
The log, I conjecture, is dum or ebony, and it is some fifty
feet long ; anyhow it is some sort of wood that won't float. I
really cannot be expected, by the most exigent of scientific
friends, to go botanising under water without a proper outfit.
Gray Shirt says it is a bridge across an under-swamp river.
Having survived this and reached the opposite bank, we
shortly fell in with a party of men and women, who were
taking, they said, a parcel of rubber to Holty's. They told us

N'dorko was quite close, and that the plantations we saw
before us were its outermost ones, but spoke of a swamp, a
bad swamp. We knew it, we said, in the foolishness of our
hearts thinking they meant the one we had just forded, and
leaving them resting, passed on our way ; half-a-mile further
on we were wiser and sadder, for then we stood on the rim of
one of the biggest swamps I have ever seen south of the Rivers.
It stretched away in all directions, a great sheet of filthy water,
out of which sprang gorgeous marsh plants, in islands, great
banks of screw pine, and coppices of wine palm, with their
lovely fronds reflected back by the still, mirror-like water, so
that the reflection was as vivid as the reality, and above all
remarkable was a plant,[1] new and strange to me, whose pale-
green stem came up out of the water and then spread out in
a flattened surface, thin, and in a peculiarly graceful curve.
This flattened surface had growing out from it leaves, the
size, shape and colour of lily of the valley leaves ; until I saw
this thing I had held the wine palm to be the queen of grace
in the vegetable kingdom, but this new beauty quite surpassed her.

Our path went straight into this swamp over the black
rocks forming its rim, in an imperative, no alternative, " Come-
along-this-way" style. Singlet, who was leading, carrying a good
load of bottled fish and a gorilla specimen, went at it like a
man, and disappeared before the eyes of us close following
him, then and there down through the water. He came up,
thanks be, but his load is down there now, worse luck. Then
I said we must get the rubber carriers who were coming this
way to show us the ford ; and so we sat down on the bank a
tired, disconsolate, dilapidated-looking row, until they arrived.
When they came up they did not plunge in forthwith ; but
leisurely set about making a most nerve-shaking set of preparations, taking off their clothes, and forming them into
bundles, which, to my horror, they put on the tops of their
heads. The women carried the rubber on their backs still, but
rubber is none the worse for being under water. The men
went in first, each holding his gun high above his head. They
skirted the bank before they struck out into the swamp, and

[1] Specimen placed in Herbarium at Kew.

were followed by the women and by our party, and soon we were all up to our chins.

We were two hours and a quarter passing that swamp. I was one hour and three-quarters ; but I made good weather of it, closely following the rubber-carriers, and only going in right over head and all twice. Other members of my band were less fortunate. One finding himself getting out of his depth, got hold of a palm frond and pulled himself into deeper water still, and had to roost among the palms until a special expedition of the tallest men went and gathered him like a flower. Another got himself much mixed up and scratched because he thought to make a short cut through screw pines. He did not know the screw pine's little ways,[1] and he had to have a special relief expedition. One and all, we got horribly infested with leeches, having a frill of them round our necks like astrachan collars, and our hands covered with them, when we came out. The depth of the swamp is very uniform, at its ford we went in up to our necks, and climbed up on to the rocks on the hither side out of water equally deep.

Knowing you do not like my going into details on such matters, I will confine my statement regarding our leeches, to the fact that it was for the best that we had some trade salt with us. It was most comic to see us salting each other ; but in spite of the salt's efficacious action I was quite faint from loss of blood, and we all presented a ghastly sight as we made our way on into N'dorko. Of course the bleeding did not stop at once, and it attracted flies and—but I am going into details, so I forbear.

We had to pass across the first bit of open country I had seen for a long time—a real patch of grass on the top of a low ridge, which is fringed with swamp on all sides save the one we made our way to, the eastern. Shortly after passing through another plantation, we saw brown huts, and

[1] *Pandanus candelabrum*—a marsh tree from 20 to 30 feet high growing in dense thickets, the stout aërial roots coming down into the water and forming with the true stems a network even more dense than that of mangroves. Their leaves, which grow in clusters, are sword-shaped, and from 4 to 6 feet in length with sharp spiney margins, and the whole affair is exceedingly tough and scratchy.

in a few minutes were standing in the middle of a ramshackle village, at the end of which, through a high stockade, with its gateway smeared with blood which hung in gouts, we saw our much longed for Rembwe River. I made for it, taking small notice of the hubbub our arrival occasioned, and passed through the gateway to its bank ; then, setting its guarding bell ringing violently, I stood on the steep, black, mud slime bank, surrounded by a noisy crowd. It is a big river, but nothing to the Ogowé, either in breadth or beauty ; what beauty it has is of the Niger delta type— black mud-laden water, with a mangrove swamp fringe to it in all directions. I soon turned back into the village and asked for Ugumu's factory. " This is it," said an exceedingly dirty, good-looking, civil-spoken man in perfect English, though as pure blooded an African as ever walked. " This is it, sir," and he pointed to one of the huts on the right-hand side, indis- tinguishable in squalor from the rest. " Where's the Agent ? " said I. " I'm the Agent," he answered. You could have knocked me down with a feather. " Where's John Holt's factory?" said I. " You have passed it ; it is up on the hill." · This showed Messrs. Holt's local factory to be no bigger than Ugumu's. At this point a big, scraggy, very black man with an irregularly formed face the size of a tea-tray and looking generally as if he had come out of a pantomime on the *Arabian Nights*, dashed through the crowd, shouting, " I'm for Holty, I'm for Holty." " This is my trade, you go 'way," says Agent number one. Fearing my two Agents would fight and damage each other, so that neither would be any good for me, I firmly said, " Have you got any rum ? " Agent number one looked crestfallen, Holty's triumphant. " Rum, fur sure," says he ; so I gave him a five-franc piece, which he regarded with great pleasure, and putting it in his mouth, he legged it like a lamplighter away to his store on the hill. " Have you any tobacco ? " said I to Agent number one. He brightened, " Plenty tobacco, plenty cloth," said he ; so I told him to give me out twenty heads. I gave my men two heads apiece. I told them rum was coming, and ordered them to take the loads on to Hatton and Cookson's Agent's hut and then to go and buy chop and make themselves comfortable. They highly

approved of this plan, and grunted assent ecstatically ; and just
as the loads were stowed Holty's anatomy hove in sight with
a bottle of rum under each arm, and one in each hand ; while
behind him came an acolyte, a fat, small boy, panting and
puffing and doing his level best to keep up with his long-
legged flying master.   I gave my men some and put the
rest in with my goods, and explained that I belonged to
Hatton and Cookson's (it's the proper thing to belong to somebody), and that therefore I must take up my quarters at their
Store ; but Holty's energetic agent hung about me like a vulture
in hopes of getting more five franc-piece pickings.   I sent
Ngouta off to get me some tea, and had the hut cleared of an
excited audience, and shut myself in with Hatton and Cookson's agent, and asked him seriously and anxiously if there
was not a big factory of the firm's on the river, because it was
self-evident he had not got anything like enough stuff to pay
off my men with, and my agreement was to pay off on the
Rembwé, hence my horror at the smallness of the firm's
N'dorko store.   "Besides," I said, " Mr. Glass (I knew the
head Rembwé agent of Hatton and Cookson was a Mr. Glass),
you have only got cloth and tobacco, and I have promised
the Fans to pay off in whatever they choose, and I know for
sure they want powder."   "I am not Mr. Glass," said my
friend ; " he is up at Agonjo, I only do small trade for him here."
Joy ! ! ! ! but where's Agonjo?   To make a long story short
I found Agonjo was an hour's paddle up the Rembwé and the
place we ought to have come out at.   There was a botheration
again about sending up a message, because of a war palaver ;
but I got a pencil note, with my letter of introduction from
Mr. Cockshut to Sanga Glass, at last delivered to that gentleman ; and down he came, in a state of considerable astonishment, not unmixed with alarm, for no white man of any kind
had been across from the Ogowé for years, and none had ever
come out at N'dorko.   Mr. Glass I found an exceedingly neat,
well-educated M'pongwe gentleman in irreproachable English
garments, and with irreproachable, but slightly *floreate*, English
language.   We started talking trade, with my band in the
middle of the street ; making a patch of uproar in the moonlit
surrounding silence.   As soon as we thought we had got one

gentleman's mind settled as to what goods he would take his pay in, and were proceeding to investigate another gentleman's little fancies ; gentleman number one's mind came all to pieces again, and he wanted " to room his bundle," *i.e.* change articles in it for other articles of an equivalent value, if it must be, but of a higher, if possible.   Oh ye shopkeepers in England who grumble at your lady customers, just you come out here and try to serve, and satisfy a set of Fans ! Mr. Glass was evidently an expert at the affair, but it was past 11 p.m. before we got the orders written out, and getting my baggage into some canoes, that Mr. Glass had brought down from Agonjo, for N'dorko only had a few very wretched ones, I started off up river with him and all the Ajumba, and Kiva, the Fan, who had been promised a safe conduct.   He came to see the bundles for his fellow Fans were made up satisfactorily.

The canoes being small there was quite a procession of them.   Mr. Glass and I shared one, which was paddled by two small boys ; how we ever got up the Rembwé that night I do not know, for although neither of us were fat, the canoe was a one man canoe, and the water lapped over the edge in an alarming way.   Had any of us sneezed, or had it been daylight when two or three mangrove flies would have joined the party, we must have foundered ; but all went well ; and on arriving at Agonjo Mr. Glass most kindly opened his store, and by the light of lamps and lanterns, we picked out the goods from his varied and ample supply, and handed them over to the Ajumba and Kiva, and all, save three of the Ajumba, were satisfied.   The three, Gray Shirt, Silence, and Pagan quietly explained to me that they found the Rembwé price so little better than the Lembarene price that they would rather get their pay off Mr. Cockshut, than risk taking it back through the Fan country, so I gave them books on him.   I gave all my remaining trade goods, and the rest of the rum to the Fans as a dash, and they were more than satisfied.   I must say they never clamoured for dash for top.   The Passenger we had brought through with us, who had really made himself very helpful, was quite surprised at getting a bundle of goods from me.   My only anxiety was as to whether Fika would get his share all right ; but I expect he did, for the Ajumbas are very honest men ; and they were going back with my Fan friends. I found out, by the by, the reason of Fika's shyness in coming through to the Rembwé ; it was a big wife palaver.

I had a touching farewell with the Fans ; and so in peace, good feeling, and prosperity I parted company for the second time with "the terrible M'pongwe," whom I hope to meet with again, for with all their many faults and failings, they are real men. I am faint-hearted enough to hope, that our next journey together, may not be over a country that seems to me to have been laid down as an obstacle race track for Mr. G. F. Watts's Titans, and to have fallen into shocking bad repair.

CHAPTER XIV

BUSH TRADE AND FAN CUSTOMS

Wherein the Voyager, having fallen among the black traders, discourses on these men and their manner of life; and the difficulties and dangers attending the barter they carry on with the bush savages; and on some of the reasons that makes this barter so beloved and followed by both the black trader and the savage. To which is added an account of the manner of life of the Fan tribe; the strange form of coinage used by these people; their manner of hunting the elephant, working in iron; and such like things.

I SPENT a few, lazy, pleasant days at Agonjo, Mr. Glass doing all he could to make me comfortable, though he had a nasty touch of fever on him just then. His efforts were ably seconded by his good lady, an exceedingly comely Gaboon woman, with pretty manners, and an excellent gift in cookery. The third member of the staff was the store-keeper, a clever fellow : I fancy a Loango from his clean-cut features and spare make, but his tribe I know not for a surety. What I do know is that he can sing " Partant pour la Syrie " with intense power and a penetrating pathos in the depths of the night. But I do not chronicle this as a discovery of my own ; it was common knowledge to every sentient being within a radius of half a mile of the factory.

Mosquitoes here we met again : some one ought to go into the local distribution of mosquitoes in Congo Français instead of just saying hard things about them. I leave the work for a nobler soul than mine, and to assist him, note the fact that they are simply awful throughout all Kama country and Ouroungou. Up at Lembarene, which is above Kama country, they are worse, and remain so until you get to Osamokita ; there they cease from troubling—although there is still a stretch of flat country and a supply of stagnant water in the shape of small lakes ; I say this regretfully, but science is truth. I once had a nice little theory, that worked well in the Niger Delta, that you never had mosquitoes if you had a 4-knot current water supply ; unless you bred the said mosquitoes for yourself, in tanks or barrels ; because, said the theory, the larva got washed away down. But although the Ogowé has a 4-knot current twice over at Osamokita, and there are no mosquitoes ; still there are those lakes in the forest at the back of it; so any one who can patch that theory up, and make it go again, is welcome to it. Again regarding mosquito distribution, there's a pretty solid fog of them from Kangwe to Arevooma, from Arevooma on to Lake Ncovi, and at Lake Ncovi they—but it's no use my writing down my opinion about mosquitoes in Lake Ncovi because no one will print it. When we left Ncovi, and got well into the forest, we missed them, and were no more troubled with them, until we got here to Agonjo, where there is not a 4-knot current ; but I will not revert to that, and merely remark a peculiarity I have observed in mosquitoes since I have been so much in touch with them in Congo Français, and that is that they evidently feed on oil ; several—many hundreds that I have crushed have left quite a pool of oil—I presume palm oil, but it may be animal fat. I should remark before leaving this subject that there are two schools in this district which quarrel much over the merits of their separate methods of destroying mosquitoes—the Flappists and the Crushers. I am a Crusher, holding it better to allow the vermin to get a hold, and his entire mind set on blood, and then to descend on him quietly, but firmly, with a finger ; as for those heretics the Flappists they always hurt themselves, and frequently fail to bag their game, by their more showy methods.

I really thought that I was again getting a chance to secure a valuable specimen of *spectra domestica*—or the common domestic ghost—the first night in Agonjo. I held it to be the ghost of a carpenter, for it made a continuous sawing noise in the bamboo wall by the side of my bed, but again I was disappointed : it was only the usual rat. This enterprising rodent indeed was a fellow collector, and had stolen the bladder off one of my bottles, and was determined to get it up into the roof whether the wall bamboos would let him or no. I helped him up with it, he holding on to his end while I poked the other up with a stick, and we got the thing done between us, and I hope he is happy.

One of these black trader factories is an exceedingly interesting place to stay at, for in these factories you are right down on the bed rock of the trade. On the Coast, for the greater part, the white traders are dealing with black traders, middlemen, who have procured their trade stuff from the bush natives, who collect and prepare it. Here, in the black trader factory, you see the first stage of the export part of the trade : namely the barter of the collected trade stuff between the collector and the middleman. I will not go into details regarding it. What I saw merely confirmed my opinion from my other experience, and this opinion had been further strengthened by what I had been seeing, during the previous months, while living among bush men collecting trade stuff ; and that is that the native is not cheated ; no, not even by a fellow African trader ; and I will merely here pause to sing a pæan to a very unpopular class—the black middleman as he exists on the South West Coast. It is impossible to realise the gloom of the lives of these men in bush factories, unless you have lived in one. It is no use saying "they know nothing better and so don't feel it," for they do know several things better, being very sociable men, fully appreciative of the joys of a Coast town, and their aim, object and end in life is, in almost every case, to get together a fortune that will enable them to live in one, give a dance twice a week, card parties most nights, and dress themselves up so that their fellow Coast townsmen may hate them and their townswomen love them. From their own accounts of the dreadful state of trade ; and the awful and unparalleled series of losses they have had, from the upsetting of canoes, the raids and robberies made on them and their goods by " those awful bush savages " ; you would, if you were of a trustful disposition, regard the black trader with an admiring awe as the man who has at last solved the great commercial problem of how to keep a shop and live by the loss. Nay, not only live, but build for himself an equivalent to a palatial residence, and keep up, not only it, but half a dozen wives, with a fine taste for dress every one of them. I am not of a trustful disposition and I accept those "losses" with a heavy discount, and know most of the rest of them have come out of my friend the white trader's pockets. Still I can never feel the righteous indignation that I ought to feel, when I see the black trader "down in a seaport town with his Nancy," &c., as Sir W. H. S. Gilbert classically says, because I remember those bush factories.

Mr. Glass, however, was not a trader who made a fortune by losing those of other people ; for he had been many years in the employ of the firm. He had risen certainly to the high post and position of charge of the Rembwé, but he was not down giddy-flying at Gaboon. His accounts of his experiences when he had been many years ago away up the still little known Nguni River, in a factory in touch with the lively Bakele, then in a factory among Fans and Igalwa on the Ogowé, and now among Fans and Skekiani on the Rembwé, were fascinating, and told vividly of the joys of first starting a factory in a wild district. The way in which your customers, for the first month or so, enjoyed themselves by trying to frighten you, the trader, out of your wits and goods, and into giving them fancy prices for things you were trading in, and for things no earthly use to you, or any one else ! The trader's existence during this period is marked by every unpleasantness save dulness ; from that he is spared by the presence of a mob of noisy, dangerous, thieving savages all over his place all day ; invading his cook-house, to put some nastiness into his food as a trade charm ; helping themselves to portable property at large ; and making themselves at home to the extent of sitting on his dining-table. At night those customers proceed to sleep all over the premises, with a view to being on hand to start shopping in the morning. Woe betide the trader if he gives in to this, and tolerates the invasion, for there is no chance of that house ever being his own again ; and in addition to the local flies, &c., on the table-cloth, he will always have several big black gentlemen to share his meals. If he raises prices, to tide over some extra row, he is a lost man; for the Africans can understand prices going up, but never prices coming down; and time being no object, they will hold back their trade. Then the district is ruined, and the trader along with it, for he cannot raise the price he gets for the things he buys.

What that trader has got to do, is to be a " Devil man." They always kindly said they recognised me as one, which is a great compliment. He must betray no weakness, but a character which I should describe as a compound of the best parts of those of Cardinal Richelieu, Brutus, Julius Cæsar, Prince Metternich, and Mettzofante, the latter to carry on the native language part of the business ; and he must cast those customers out, not only from his house ; but from his yard ; and adhere to the " No admittance except on business " principle. This causes a good deal of unpleasantness, and the trader's nights are now cheered by lively war-dances outside his stockade ; the accompanying songs advertising that the customers are coming over the stockade to raid the store, and cut up the trader "into bits like a fish." Sometimes they do come—and then—finish ; but usually they don't ; and gradually settle down, and respect the trader greatly as " a Devil man " ; and do business on sound lines during the day. Over the stockade at night, by ones and twos, stealing, they will come to the end of the chapter.

At Agonjo Mr. Glass, his wife, and the " Partant pour la Syrie " vocalist used to have to take it in turns to keep watch, because it was the habit of these local " children of nature " to sell a log or so of ebony during the day, and come and re-gain possession of it at night. They would then take it down to the next factory, and sell it there—similarly regaining it, and bringing it back, and re-selling it, and so on, *da capo*. Thereby it falls out that one man might live for quite a time on a few billets, with no exertion, or hard work, stealing being a beloved pastime—a kind of a sort of a game in which you only lose if you are found out.

Moonlight nights are fairly restful for the bush trader, but when it is inky black, or pouring with rain, he has got to be very much out and about, and particularly vigilant has he got to be on tornado nights—a most uncomfortable sort of weather to attend to business in, I assure you.

The factory at Agonjo was typical; the house is a fine specimen of the Igalwa style of architecture; mounted on poles above the ground ; the space under the house being used as. a store for rubber in barrels, and ebony in billets ; thereby enabling the trader to hover over these precious possessions, sleeping and waking, like a sitting hen over her eggs.

Near to the house are the sleeping places for the beach hands, and the cook-house. In front, in a position commanded by the eye from the verandah, and well withdrawn from the stockade, are great piles of billets of red bar wood. The whole of the clean, sandy yard containing these things, and divers others, is surrounded by a stout stockade, its main face to the river frontage, the water at high tide lapping its base, and at low tide exposing in front of it a shore of black slime. Although I cite this factory as a typical factory of a black trader, it is a specimen of the highest class, for, being in connection with Messrs. Hatton and Cookson it is well kept up and stocked. Firms differ much in this particular. Messrs. Hatton and Cookson, like Messrs. Miller Brothers in the Bights, take every care that lies in their power of the people who serve them, down to the Kruboys working on their beaches, giving ample and good rations and providing good houses. But this is not so with all firms on the Coast. I have seen factories belonging to the Swedish houses beside which this factory at Agonjo is a palace, although those factories are white man factories, and the unfortunate white men in them are expected by these firms to live on native chop—an expectation the Agents by no means realise, for they usually die. Black hands, however, do not suffer much at the hands of such firms, for the Swedish Agents are a quiet, gentlemanly set of men, in the best sense of that much misused term, and they do not employ on their beaches such a staff of black helpers as the English houses, so the two or three Kruboys on a starvation beach can fairly well fend for themselves, for there is always an adjacent village, and in that village there are always chickens, and on the shore crabs, and in the river fish, and for the rest of his diet the Kruboy flirts with the local ladies.

Although, as I have laid down, the bush factory at its best

is a place, as Mr. Tracey Tupman would say, more fitted for
a wounded heart than for one still able to feast on social joys,
it is a luxurious situation for a black trader compared to
the other form of trading he deals with—that of travelling
among the native villages in the bush. This has one hundred
times the danger, and a thousand times the discomfort, and is
a thoroughly unhealthy pursuit. The journeys these bush
traders make are often remarkable, and they deserve great
credit for the courage and enterprise they display. Certainly
they run less risk of death from fever than a white man
would ; but, on the other hand, their colour gives them no
protection ; and their chance of getting murdered is distinctly
greater ; and also the white governmental powers cannot
revenge their death, in the way they would the death of a
white man, for these murders usually take place away in some
forest region, in a district no white man has ever penetrated;
and when the account of it reaches the main trading station,
or the sea coast town, to whom the man belongs—for many of
them are not attached to any factory, but trading on their own
accounts—it is usually in the form of the statement that So-
and-so died of a disease. The relatives of the deceased never
believe this, but the Government naturally feel disinclined to
start off on a highly expensive expedition ; which is next to
certain in the bargain to cost a white man who goes with it
his life ; on a month or so's march, through trackless swamp
and bush ; on the off chance of finding out at the end of
their quest that So and so did really die of a disease ; or that
the village where he died is utterly deserted ; the natives on
hearing of their approach having gone for a pic-nic in the
surrounding forest.

You will naturally ask how it is that so many of these men
do survive " to lead a life of sin " as a missionary described
to me their Coast town life to be. This question struck me as
requiring explanation. The result of my investigations, and
the answers I have received from the men themselves, show
that there is a reason why the natives do not succumb every
time to the temptation to kill the trader, and take his goods,
and this is twofold : firstly, all trade in West Africa follows
definite routes, even in the wildest parts of it; and so a village

far away in the forest, but on the trade route, knows, that as
a general rule twice a year, a trader will appear to purchase
its rubber and ivory. If he does not appear somewhere
about the expected time, that village gets uneasy. The
ladies are impatient for their new clothes; the gentlemen half
wild for want of tobacco ; and things coming to a crisis, they
make inquiries for the trader down the road, one village to
another, and then, if it is found that a village has killed the
trader, and stolen all his goods, there is naturally a big
palaver, and things are made extremely hot, even for
equatorial Africa, for that village by the tobaccoless husbands
of the clothesless wives. Herein lies the trader's chief safety,
the village not being an atom afraid, or disinclined to kill him,
but afraid of their neighbouring villages, and disinclined to
be killed by them. But the trader is not yet safe. There is
still a hole in his armour, and this is only to be stopped up in
one way, namely, by wives ; for you see although the village
cannot safely kill him, and take all his goods, they can still
safely let him die of a disease, and take part of them, passing
on sufficient stuff to the other villages to keep them
quiet. Now the most prevalent disease in the African bush
comes out of the cooking pot, and so to make what goes into
the cooking pot—which is the important point, for earthen
pots do not in themselves breed poison—safe and wholesome,
you have got to have some one who is devoted to your health to
attend to the cooking affairs, and who can do this like a wife ?
So you have a wife—one in each village up the whole of your
route. I know myself one gentleman whose wives stretch
over 300 miles of country, with a good wife base in a Coast
town as well. This system of judiciously conducted alliances,
gives the black trader a security nothing else can, because
naturally he marries into influential families at each village,
and all his wife's relations on the mother's side regard him as
one of themselves, and look after him and his interests.
That security can lie in women, especially so many women,
the so-called civilised man may ironically doubt, but the
security is there, and there only, and on a sound basis, for remember the position of a travelling trader's wife in a village
is a position that gives the lady prestige, the discreet husband

showing little favours to her family and friends, if she asks
for them when he is with her ; and then she has not got the
bother of having a man always about the house, and liable to
get all sorts of silly notions into his head if she speaks to
another gentleman, and then go and impart these notions
to her with a cutlass, or a kassengo, as the more domestic
husband, I am assured by black ladies, is prone to.

You may now, I fear, be falling into the other adjacent
error—from the wonder why any black trader survives, namely,
into the wonder why any black trader gets killed, with all
these safeguards, and wives.   But there is yet another danger,
which no quantity of wives, nor local jealousies avail to guard
him through.   This danger arises from the nomadic habits of
the bush tribes, notably the Fan.   For when a village has made
up its mind to change its district, either from having made the
district too hot to hold it, with quarrels with neighbouring
villages ; or because it has exhausted the trade stuff, *i.e.* rubber
and ivory in reach of its present situation ; or because some
other village has raided it, and taken away all the stuff it was
saving to sell to the black trader ; it resolves to give itself a
final treat in the old home, and make a commercial *coup* at
one fell swoop.   Thus when the black trader turns up with his
boxes of goods, it kills him, has some for supper, smokes the
rest, and takes it and the goods, and departs to found new
homes in another district.

The bush trade I have above sketched is the bush trade
with the Fans.   In those districts on the southern banks of
the Ogowé the main features of the trade, and the trader's life
are the same, but the details are more intricate, for the Igalwa
trader from Lembarene, Fernan Vaz, or Njole, deals with
another set of trading tribes, not first hand with the collectors.
The Fan villages on the trade routes may, however, be regarded
as trade depots, for to them filters the trade stuff of the more
remote villages, so the difference is really merely technical,
and in all villages alike the same sort of thing occurs.

The Igalwa or M'pongwe trader arrives with the goods he
has received from the white trader, and there are great rejoicing and much uproar as his chests and bundles and demijohns
are brought up from the canoe.   And presently, after a great

deal of talk, the goods are opened.   The chiefs of the village
have their pick, and divide this among the principal men of
the village, who pay for it in part with their store of collected
rubber or ivory, and take the rest on trust, promising to collect
enough rubber to pay the balance on the next visit of the
trader.   Thereby the trader has a quantity of debts outstanding in each village, liable to be bad debts, and herein lies his
chief loss.   Each chief takes a certain understood value in
goods as a commission for himself—*nyeno*—giving the trader,
as a consideration for this, an understood bond to assist him in
getting in the trust granted to his village.   This *nyeno* he
utilises in buying trade stuff from villages not on the trade
route.   Among the Fans the men who have got the goods
stand by with these to trade for rubber with the general public
and bachelors of the village, in a way I will presently explain.
In tribes like Ajumbas, Adooma, &c., the men having the
goods travel off, as traders, among their various bush tribes,
similarly paying their *nyeno*, and so by the time the goods
reach the final producing men, only a small portion of them
is left, but their price has necessarily risen.   Still it is quite absurd for a casual white traveller, who may have dropped in on
the terminus of a trade route, to cry out regarding the small
value the collector (who is often erroneously described as the
producer, giving a false " won-by-the-sweat-of-his-brow " halo
to him) gets for his stuff, compared to the price it fetches in
Europe.   For before it even reaches the factory of the Coast
Settlement, that stuff has got to keep a whole series of traders.
It appears at first bad that this should be the case, but the
case it is along the west coast of the continent save in the
districts commanded by the Royal Niger company, who, with
courage and enterprise, have pushed far inland, and got in touch
with the great interior trade routes—a performance which has
raised in the breasts of the Coast trader tribes who have been
supplanted, a keen animosity, which like most animosity in
Africa, is not regardful of truth.   The tribes that have had the
trade of the Bight of Biafra passing through their hands have
been accustomed, according to the German Government who
are also pressing inland, to make seventy-five per cent. profit
on it, and they resent being deprived of this.   A good deal is to

be said in favour of their views ; among other things that the greater part of the seaboard districts of West Africa, I may say every part from Sierra Leone to Cameroon, is structurally incapable of being self-supporting under existing conditions. Below Cameroon, on my beloved South-west coast, which is infinitely richer than the Bight of Benin, rich producing districts come down to the sea in most places until you reach the Congo; but here again the middleman is of great use to the interior tribes, and if they do have to pay him seventy-five per cent, serve them right. They should not go making wife palaver, and blood palaver all over the place to such an extent that the inhabitants of no village, unless they go *en masse*, dare take a ten mile walk, save at the risk of their lives, in any direction, so palaver no live.

We will now enter into the reason that induces the bush man to collect stuff to sell among the Fans, which is the expensiveness of the ladies in the tribe. A bush Fan is bound to marry into his tribe, because over a great part of the territory occupied by them there is no other tribe handy to marry into ; and a Fan residing in villages in touch with other tribes, has but little chance of getting a cheaper lady. For there is, in the Congo Français and the country adjacent to the north of it (Batanga), a regular style of aristocracy which may be summarised firstly thus : All the other tribes look down on the Fans, and the Fans look down on all the other tribes. This aristocracy has sub-divisions, the M'pongwe of Gaboon are the upper circle tribe ; next come the Benga of Corisco ; then the Bapoka ; then the Banaka. This system of aristocracy is kept up by the ladies. Thus a M'pongwe lady would not think of marrying into one of the lower tribes, so she is restricted, with many inner restrictions, to her own tribe. A Benga lady would marry a M'pongwe, or a Benga, but not a Banaka, or Bapoka ; and so on with the others ; but not one of them would marry a Fan. As for the men, well of course they would marry any lady of any tribe, if she had a pretty face, or a good trading connection, if they were allowed to : that's just man's way. To the south-east the Fans are in touch with the Achille, Bakele, Dakele, practically one and the same tribe and a tribe

that has much in common with the Fan, but who differ from
them in getting on in a very friendly way with the little dwarf
people, the Matimbas, or Watwa, or Akkoa: people the Fans
cannot abide. With these Achille the Fan can intermarry,
but there is not much advantage in so doing, as the price is
equally high, but still marry he must.

A young Fan man has to fend for himself, and has a
scratchy kind of life of it, aided only by his mother until—if
he be an enterprising youth—he is able to steal a runaway

AN AKKOA DWARF OF CONGO FRANÇAIS.

wife from a neighbouring village, or if he is a quiet and steady
young man, until he has amassed sufficient money to buy a
wife. This he does by collecting ivory and rubber and selling
it to the men who have been allotted goods by the chief of
the village, from the consignment brought up by the black
trader. He supports himself meanwhile by, if the situation of
his village permits, fishing and selling the fish, and hunting
and killing game in the forest. He keeps steadily at it in his
way, reserving his roysterings until he is settled in life. A
truly careful young man does not go and buy a baby girl

cheap, as soon as he has got a little money together; but works and saves on until he has got enough to buy a good, tough widow lady, who, although personally unattractive, is deeply versed in the lore of trade, and who knows exactly how much rubbish you can incorporate in a ball of india rubber, without the white trader, or the black bush factory trader, instantly detecting it. The bush travelling trader has, in certain of the more savage districts, to take rubber without making an examination of it; that would hurt the sensitive feelings of his Fan friends. But then in these districts he carefully keeps the price low to allow for this. When the Fan young man has married his wife, in a legitimate way on the cash system, he takes her round to his relations, and shows her off; and they make little presents to help the pair set up housekeeping. But the young man cannot yet settle down, for his wife will not allow him to. She is not going to slave herself to death doing all the work of the house, &c., and so he goes on collecting, and she preparing, trade stuff, and he grows rich enough to buy other wives—some of them young children, others widows, no longer necessarily old. But it is not until he is well on in life that he gets sufficient wives, six or seven. For it takes a good time to get enough rubber to buy a lady, and he does not get a grip on the ivory trade until he has got a certain position in the village, and plantations of his own which the elephants can be discovered raiding, in which case a percentage of the ivory taken from the herd is allotted to him. Now and again he may come across a dead elephant, but that is of the nature of a windfall; and on rubber and ebony he has to depend during his early days. These he changes with the rich men of his village for a very peculiar and interesting form of coinage—bikĕi—little iron imitation axe-heads which are tied up in bundles called ntet, ten going to one bundle, for with bikĕi must the price of a wife be paid. You cannot do so with rubber or ivory, or goods. These bikĕi pass, however, as common currency among the Fans, for other articles of trade as well, but I do not think they will pass bikĕi out of the tribe. Possibly no one else will take this form of change. Thousands of these bikĕi, done up into ntets, go to the price of a wife. I was much interested in this coinage-equivalent, and found out all I could regarding it, but there is plenty more to be found out, and I hope the next voyager among the Fans will keep his eye on it. You do not find bikëi close down to Libreville, among the Fans who are there in a semi-civilised state, or more properly speaking in a state of disintegrating culture. You must go for bush. I thought I saw in bikči a certain resemblance in underlying idea with the early Greek coins I have seen at Cambridge, made like the fore-parts of cattle ; and I have little doubt that the articles of barter among the Fans before the introduction of the rubber, ebony, and ivory trades, which in their districts are comparatively recent, were iron implements. For the Fans are good workers in iron ; and it would be in consonance with well-known instances among other savage races in the matter of stone implements, that these things, important of old, should survive, and be employed in the matter of such an old and important affair as marriage. They thus become ju-ju ; and indeed all West African legitimate marriage, although appearing to the casual observer a mere matter of barter, is never solely such, but always has ju-ju in it.

We may as well here follow out the whole of the domestic life of the Fan, now we have got him married. His difficulty does not only consist in getting enough bikëi together but in getting a lady he can marry. No amount of bikëi can justify a man in marrying his first cousin, or his aunt ; and as relationship among the Fans is recognised with both his father and his mother, not as among the Igalwa with the latter's blood relations only, there are an awful quantity of aunts and cousins about from whom he is debarred. But when he has surmounted his many difficulties, and dodged his relations, and married, he is seemingly a better husband than the man of a more cultured tribe. He will turn a hand to anything, that does not necessitate his putting down his gun outside his village gateway. He will help chop firewood, or goat's chop, or he will carry the baby with pleasure, while his good lady does these things ; and in bush villages, he always escorts her so as to be on hand in case of leopards, or other local unpleasantnesses. When inside the village he will lay down his gun, within handy reach, and build the house, tease out fibre to make game nets with, and plait baskets, or make pottery with the ladies, cheerily chatting the while.

Fan pottery, although rough and sunbaked, is artistic in form and ornamented, for the Fan ornaments all his work ; the articles made in it consist of cooking pots, palm-wine bottles, water bottles and pipes, but not all water bottles, nor all pipes are made of pottery. I wish they were, particularly the former, for they are occasionally made of beautifully plaited fibre coated with a layer of a certain gum with a vile taste, which it imparts to the water in the vessel. They say it does not do this if the vessel is soaked for two days in water, but it does, and I should think contaminates the stream it was soaked in into the bargain. The pipes are sometimes made of iron very neatly. I should imagine they smoked hot, but of this I have no knowledge. One of my Ajumba friends got himself one of these pipes when we were in Efoua, and that pipe was, on and off, a curse to the party. Its owner soon learnt not to hold it by the bowl, but by the wooden stem, when smoking it ; the other lessons it had to teach he learnt more slowly. He tucked it, when he had done smoking, into the fold in his cloth, until he had had three serious conflagrations raging round his middle. And to the end of the chapter, after having his last pipe at night with it, he would lay it on the ground, before it was cool. He learnt to lay it out of reach of his own cloth, but his fellow Ajumbas and he himself persisted in always throwing a leg on to it shortly after, and there was another row.

The Fan basket-work is strongly made, but very inferior to the Fjort basket-work. Their nets are, however, the finest I have ever seen. These are made mainly for catching small game, such as the beautiful little gazelles (*Ncheri*) with dark gray skins on the upper part of the body, white underneath, and satin-like in sleekness all over. Their form is very dainty, the little legs being no thicker than a man's finger, the neck long and the head ornamented with little pointed horns and broad round ears. The nets are tied on to trees in two long lines, which converge to an acute angle, the bottom part of the net lying on the ground. Then a party of men and women accompanied by their trained dogs, which have bells hung round

their necks, beat the surrounding bushes, and the frightened
small game rush into the nets, and become entangled. The
fibre from which these nets are made has a long staple, and is
exceedingly strong. I once saw a small bush cow caught in
a set of them and unable to break through, and once a leopard ;
he, however, took his section of the net away with him, and a
good deal of vegetation and sticks to boot. In addition to
nets, this fibre is made into bags, for carrying things
in while in the bush, and into the water bottles already mentioned.

The iron-work of the Fans deserves especial notice for its
excellence. The anvil is a big piece of iron which is
embedded firmly in the ground. Its upper surface is flat, and
pointed at both ends. The hammers are solid cones of iron,
the upper part of the cones prolonged so as to give a good
grip, and the blows are given directly downwards, like the
blows of a pestle. The bellows are of the usual African
type, cut out of one piece of solid but soft wood ; at the upper
end of these bellows there are two chambers hollowed out in
the wood and then covered with the skin of some animal, from
which the hair has been removed. This is bound firmly round
the rim of each chamber with tie-tie, and the bag of it at the top
is gathered up, and bound to a small piece of stick, to give a
convenient hand hold. The straight cylinder, terminating in
the nozzle, has two channels burnt in it which communicate with each of the chambers respectively, and half-way up
the cylinder, there are burnt from the outside into the air
passages, three series of holes, one series on the upper surface,
and a series at each side. This ingenious arrangement gives
a constant current of air up from the nozzle when the bellows
are worked by a man sitting behind them, and rapidly and
alternately pulling up the skin cover over one chamber, while
depressing the other. In order to make the affair firm it is
lashed to pieces of stick stuck in the ground in a suitable way
so as to keep the bellows at an angle with the nozzle directed
towards the fire. As wooden bellows like this if stuck into
the fire would soon be aflame, the nozzle is put into a cylinder
made of clay. This cylinder is made sufficiently large at the
end, into which the nozzle of the bellows goes, for the air to

have full play round the latter. On my first meeting with
this performance, I must needs think that the clay affair did
not fit the bellows, and asked if they had no bigger bellows.
When finally the Fan blacksmith found out what error I was
suffering from, he jammed his bellows into the clay cylinder
and there was no end of a smother; for of course when fixed
tight, instead of getting the perpetual current of fresh air, it
alternately sucked up and blew out the smoke and hot air
from the fire itself. I apologised.

ANGOLA BLACKSMITHS.

The Fan bellows only differ from those of the other iron-
working West Coast tribes in having the channels from the two
chambers in one piece of wood all the way; in the other bellows
I have seen the two channels unite just above the nozzle. And
also the Fan decorates the bellows with spearhead forms, the
points whereof are directed towards the fire; he seems to think
this helps. His forge is the same as the other forges, a round
cavity scooped in the ground; his fuel also is charcoal. His
other smith's tool consists of a pointed piece of iron, with which

he works out the patterns he puts at the handle-end of his swords, &c.

I must now speak briefly on the most important article with which the Fan deals, namely ivory. His methods of collecting this are several, and many a wild story the handles of your table knives could tell you, if their ivory has passed through Fan hands. For ivory is everywhere an evil thing before which the quest for gold sinks into a parlour game ; and when its charms seize such a tribe as the Fans, " conclusions pass their careers." A very common way of collecting a tooth is to kill the person who owns one. Therefore in order to prevent this catastrophe happening to you yourself, when you have one, it is held advisable, unless you are a powerful person in your own village, to bury or sink the said tooth and say nothing about it until the trader comes into your district or you get a chance of smuggling it quietly down to him. Some of these private ivories are kept for years and years before they reach the trader's hands. And quite a third of the ivory you see coming on board a vessel to go to Europe is dark from this keeping : some teeth a lovely brown like a well-coloured meerschaum, others quite black, and gnawed by that strange little creature much heard of, and abused, yet little known in ivory ports—the ivory rat. This squirrel-like creature was first brought to Europe by Paul du Chaillu, and as far as I know no further specimen has been secured. I got two, but I am ashamed to say I lost them. Du Chaillu called it *Sciurus eborivorus*. Its main point, as may be imagined, is its teeth. The incisors in the upper jaw are long, and closely set together ; those in the lower are still longer, and as they seem always to go in under the upper teeth, I wonder how the creature gets its mouth shut. The feet are hairless, and somewhat like those of a squirrel. The tail is long, and marked with transverse bars, and it is not carried over the back. Over the eyes, and on either side of the mouth, are very long stiff bristles. The mischief these little creatures play with buried ivory is immense, because, for some inscrutable reason, they seem to prefer the flavour of the points of the teeth, the most valuable part.

Ivory, however, that is obtained by murder is private ivory. The public ivory trade among the Fans is carried on in a way

more in accordance with European ideas of a legitimate trade.
The greater part of this ivory is obtained from dead elephants.
There are in this region certain places where the elephants are
said to go to die.   A locality in one district pointed out to
me as such a place, was a great swamp in the forest.   A
swamp that evidently was deep in the middle, for from out its
dark waters no swamp plant, or tree grew, and evidently its
shores sloped suddenly, for the band of swamp plants round
its edge was narrow.   It is just possible that during the rainy
season when most of the surrounding country would be under
water, elephants might stray into this natural trap and get
drowned, and on the drying up of the waters be discovered, and
the fact being known, be regularly sought for by the natives
cognisant of this.   I inquired carefully whether these places
where the elephants came to die always had water in them, but
they said no, and in one district spoke of a valley or round-
shaped depression in among the mountains.   But natives were
naturally disinclined to take a stranger to these ivory mines,
and a white person who has caught—as any one who has been
in touch must catch—ivory fever, is naturally equally disinclined to give localities.

A certain percentage of ivory collected by the Fans is
from live elephants, but I am bound to admit that their method
of hunting elephants is disgracefully unsportsmanlike.   A herd
of elephants is discovered by rubber hunters or by depredations
on plantations, and the whole village, men, women, children,
babies and dogs turn out into the forest and stalk the monsters
into a suitable ravine, taking care not to scare them.   When
they have gradually edged the elephants on into a suitable
place, they fell trees and wreathe them very roughly together with bush rope, all round an immense enclosure, still
taking care not to scare the elephants into a rush.   This fence
is quite inadequate to stop any elephant in itself, but it is made
effective by being smeared with certain things, the smell
whereof the elephants detest so much that when they wander
up to it, they turn back disgusted.   I need hardly remark that
this preparation is made by the witch doctors and its con-
stituents a secret of theirs, and I was only able to find out
some of them.   Then poisoned plantains are placed within

the enclosure, and the elephants eat these and grow drowsier and drowsier; if the water supply within the enclosure is a pool it is poisoned, but if it is a running stream this cannot be done. During this time the crowd of men and women spend their days round the enclosure, ready to turn back any elephant who may attempt to break out, going to and fro to the village for their food. Their nights they spend in little bough shelters by the enclosure, watching more vigilantly than by day, as the elephants are more active at night, it being their usual feeding time. During the whole time the witch doctor is hard at work making incantations and charms, with a view to finding out the proper time to attack the elephants. In my opinion, his decision fundamentally depends on his knowledge of the state of poisoning the animals are in, but his version is that he gets his information from the forest spirits. When, however, he has settled the day, the best hunters steal into the enclosure and take up safe positions in trees, and the outer crowd set light to the ready-built fires, and make the greatest uproar possible, and fire upon the staggering, terrified elephants as they attempt to break out. The hunters in the trees fire down on them as they rush past, the fatal point at the back of the skull being well exposed to them.

When the animals are nearly exhausted, those men who do not possess guns dash into the enclosure, and the men who do, reload and join them, and the work is then completed. One elephant hunt I chanced upon at the final stage had taken two months' preparation, and although the plan sounds safe enough, there is really a good deal of danger left in it with all the drugging and ju-ju. There were eight elephants killed that day, but three burst through everything, sending energetic spectators flying, and squashing two men and a baby as flat as botanical specimens.

The subsequent proceedings were impressive. The whole of the people gorged themselves on the meat for days, and great chunks of it were smoked over the fires in all directions. A certain portion of the flesh of the hind leg was taken by the witch doctor for ju-ju, and was supposed to be put away by him, with certain suitable incantations in the recesses of

the forest ; his idea being apparently either to give rise to
more elephants, or to induce the forest spirits to bring more
elephants into the district. Meanwhile the carcases were going
bad, rapidly bad, and the smell for a mile round was strong
enough to have taken the paint off a door. Moreover there
were flies, most of the flies in West Africa, I imagine, and—
but I will say no more. I thought before this experience
that I had touched bottom in smells when once I spent the
outside of a week in a village, on the sand bank in front of
which a portly hippopotamus, who had been shot up river, got
stranded, and proceeded energetically to melt into its elemental gases ; but that was a passing whiff to this.

Dr. Nassau tells me that the manner in which the ivory
gained by one of these hunts is divided is as follows :—" The
witch doctor, the chiefs, and the family on whose ground the
enclosure is built, and especially the household whose women
first discovered the animals, decide in council as to the division of the tusks and the share of the flesh to be given to the
crowd of outsiders. The next day the tusks are removed and
each family represented in the assemblage cuts up and distri-
butes the flesh." In the hunt I saw finished, the elephants had
not been discovered, as in the case Dr. Nassau above speaks
of, in a plantation by women, but by a party of rubber hunters
in the forest some four or five miles from any village, and the
ivory that would have been allotted to the plantation holder
in the former case, went in this case to the young rubber
hunters.

Of the method of catching game in traps I have already
spoken. Such are the pursuits, sports and pastimes of my
friends the Fans. I have been considerably chaffed both by
whites and blacks about my partiality for this tribe, but as I
like Africans in my way—not *à la* Sierra Leone—and
these Africans have more of the qualities I like than any
other tribe I have met, it is but natural that I should prefer
them. They are brave and so you can respect them, which
is an essential element in a friendly feeling. They are on
the whole a fine race, particularly those in the mountain districts of the Sierra del Cristal, where one continually sees
magnificent specimens of human beings, both male and

female. Their colour is light bronze, many of the men have beards, and albinoes are rare among them. The average height in the mountain districts is five feet six to five feet eight, the difference in stature between men and women not being great. Their countenances are very bright and expressive, and if once you have been among them, you can never mistake a Fan. But it is in their mental characteristics that their difference from the lethargic, dying-out coast tribes is most marked. The Fan is full of fire, temper, intelligence and go ; very teachable, rather difficult to manage, quick to take offence, and utterly indifferent to human life. I ought to say that other people, who should know him better than I, say he is a treacherous, thievish, murderous cannibal. I never found him treacherous ; but then I never trusted him, remembering one of the aphorisms of my great teacher Captain Boler of Bonny, " It's not safe to go among bush tribes, but if you are such a fool as to go, you needn't go and be a bigger fool still, you've done enough." And Captain Boler's other great aphorism was : " Never be afraid of a black man." " What if I can't help it ? " said I. " Don't show it," said he. To these precepts I humbly add another : " Never lose your head." My most favourite form of literature, I may remark, is accounts of mountaineering exploits, though I have never seen a glacier or a permanent snow mountain in my life. I do not care a row of pins how badly they may be written, and what form of bumble-puppy grammar and composition is employed, as long as the writer will walk along the edge of a precipice with a sheer fall of thousands of feet on one side and a sheer wall on the other ; or better still crawl up an *arête* with a precipice on either. Nothing on earth would persuade me to do either of these things myself, but they remind me of bits of country I have been through where you walk along a narrow line of security with gulfs of murder looming on each side, and where in exactly the same way you are as safe as if you were in your easy chair at home, as long as you get sufficient holding ground : not on rock in the bush village inhabited by murderous cannibals, but on ideas in those men's and women's minds ; and these ideas, which I think I may say you will always find, give you safety.

It is not advisable to play with them, or to attempt to eradicate them, because you regard them as superstitious; and never, never shoot too soon. I have never had to shoot, and hope never to have to; because in such a situation, one white alone with no troops to back him means a clean finish. But this would not discourage me if I had to start, only it makes me more inclined to walk round the obstacle, than to become a mere blood splotch against it, if this can be done without losing your self-respect, which is the mainspring of your power in West Africa.

As for flourishing about a revolver and threatening to fire, I hold it utter idiocy. I have never tried it, however, so I speak from prejudice which arises from the feeling that there is something cowardly in it. Always have your revolver ready loaded in good order, and have your hand on it when things are getting warm, and in addition have an exceedingly good bowie knife, not a hinge knife, because with a hinge knife you have got to get it open—hard work in a country where all things go rusty in the joints—and hinge knives are liable to close on your own fingers. The best form of knife is the bowie, with a shallow half moon cut out of the back at the point end, and this depression sharpened to a cutting edge. A knife is essential, because after wading neck deep in a swamp your revolver is neither use nor ornament until you have had time to clean it. But the chances are you may go across Africa, or live years in it, and require neither. It is just the case of the gentleman who asked if one required a revolver in Carolina? and was answered, "You may be here one year, and you may be here two and never want it; but when you do want it you'll want it very bad."

The cannibalism of the Fans, although a prevalent habit, is no danger, I think, to white people, except as regards the bother it gives one in preventing one's black companions from getting eaten. The Fan is not a cannibal from sacrificial motives like the negro. He does it in his common sense way. Man's flesh, he says, is good to eat, very good, and he wishes you would try it. Oh dear no, he never eats it himself, but the next door town does. He is always very much abused for

eating his relations, but he really does not do this. He will
eat his next door neighbour's relations and sell his own

IN A FAN VILLAGE.

deceased to his next door neighbour in return ; but he does
not buy slaves and fatten them up for his table as some of

the Middle Congo tribes I know of do.   He has no slaves, no prisoners of war, no cemeteries, so you must draw your own conclusions.   No, my friend, I will not tell you any cannibal stories.   I have heard how good M. du Chaillu fared after telling you some beauties, and now you come away from the Fan village and down the Rembwé river.

CHAPTER XV

DOWN THE REMBWÉ

Setting forth how the Voyager descends the Rembwé River, with divers excursions and alarms, in the company of a black trader, and returns safely to the Coast. To which is added some account of the geography of this region, the Gaboon and its chief affluents.

GETTING away from Agonjo seemed as if it would be nearly as difficult as getting to it, but as the quarters were comfortable and the society fairly good, I was not anxious. I own the local scenery was a little too much of the Niger Delta type for perfect beauty, just the long lines of mangrove, and the muddy river lounging almost imperceptibly to sea, and nothing else in sight. Mr. Glass, however, did not take things so philosophically. I was on his commercial conscience, for I had come in from the bush and there was money in me. Therefore I was a trade product—a new trade stuff that ought to be worked up and developed ; and he found himself unable to do this, for although he had secured the first parcel, as it were, and got it successfully stored, yet he could not ship it, and he felt this was a reproach to him.

Many were his lamentations that the firm had not provided him with a large sailing canoe and a suitable crew to deal with this new line of trade. I did my best to comfort him, pointing out that the most enterprising firm could not be expected to provide expensive things like these, on the extremely remote chance of ladies arriving per bush at Agonjo—in fact not until the trade in them was well developed. But he refused to see it in this light and harped upon the subject, wrapped up, poor man, in a great coat and a muffler, because his ague was on him. In not accepting my view I think he was in error, undoubted authority on bush trade though he is ; for I feel fairly certain that even if Messrs. Hatton and Cookson, or any other firm, were to run a weekly line of Palace steamboats with brass bands, and red-velvet saloons up and down the Rembwé river, there would not be sufficient white passenger traffic to pay for coal. Certainly not by my route, one that had never been taken even by a black trader before. But I am not thinking of taking out a patent for it ; for one thing, I am sure it would never become sufficiently popular to pay the patentee's preliminary expenses, and for another, the relatives of people who might attempt to use it at any but the short time in the year it is usable, would come down on me for damages.

I next tried to convince Mr. Glass that any canoe would do for me to go down in. " No," he said, " any canoe will not do ; " and he explained that when you got down the Rembwé to 'Como Point you were in a rough, nasty bit of water, the Gaboon, which has a fine confused set of currents from the tidal wash and the streams of the Rembwé and 'Como rivers, in which it would be improbable that a river canoe could live any time worth mentioning. Progress below 'Como Point by means of mere paddling he considered impossible. There was nothing for it but a big sailing canoe, and there was no big sailing canoe to be had. I think Mr. Glass got a ray of comfort out of the fact that Messrs. John Holt's sub-agent was, equally with himself, unable to ship me.

At this point in the affair there entered a highly dramatic figure. He came on to the scene suddenly and with much uproar, in a way that would have made his fortune in a trans-pontine drama. I shall always regret I have not got that man's portrait, for I cannot do him justice with ink. He dashed up on to the verandah, smote the frail form of Mr. Glass between the shoulders, and flung his own massive one into a chair. His name was Obanjo, but he liked it pronounced Captain Johnson, and his profession was a bush and river trader on his own account. Every movement of the man was theatrical, and he used to look covertly at you every now and then to see if he had produced his impression, which was evidently intended to be that of a reckless, rollicking skipper. There was a Hallo-my-Hearty atmosphere coming off him from the top of his hat to the soles of his feet, like the scent off a flower ; but it did not require a genius in judging men to see that behind, and under this was a very different sort of man, and if I should ever want to engage in a wild and awful career up a West African river I shall start on it by engaging Captain Johnson. He struck me as being one of those men, of whom I know five, whom I could rely on, that if one of them and I went into the utter bush together, one of us at least would come out alive and have made something substantial by the venture; which is a great deal more than I could say, for example, of Ngouta, who was still with me, as he desired to see the glories of Gaboon and buy a hanging lamp. I will not commence that hanging lamp palaver here, however, but remark that Ngouta persisted in regarding himself as still surrounded by danger at Agonjo.

Captain Johnson's attire calls for especial comment and admiration. However disconnected the two sides of his character might be, his clothes bore the impress of both of his natures to perfection. He wore, when first we met, a huge sombrero hat, a spotless singlet, and a suit of clean, well-got-up dungaree, and an uncommonly picturesque, powerful figure he cut in them, with his finely moulded, well-knit form and good-looking face, full of expression always, but always with the keen small eyes in it watching the effect his genial smiles and hearty laugh produced. The eyes were the eyes of Obanjo, the rest of the face the property of Captain Johnson. I do not mean to say that they were the eyes of a bad bold man, but you had not to look twice at them to see they belonged to a man courageous in the African manner, full of energy and resource, keenly intelligent and self-reliant, and all that sort of thing.

I left him and the refined Mr. Glass together to talk over the palaver of shipping me, and they talked it at great length. Finally the price I was to pay Obanjo was settled and we proceeded to less important details. It seemed Obanjo, when up the river this time, had set about constructing a new and large trading canoe at one of his homes, in which he was just

thinking of taking his goods down to Gaboon. The only
drawback was this noble vessel was not finished ; but
that did not discourage any of us, except Mr. Glass, who
seemed to think the firm would debit me to his account if
I got lost. However, next morning Obanjo with his vessel
turned up, and saying farewell to my kind host, Mr. Sanga
Glass, I departed.

She had the makings of a fine vessel in her ; though roughly
hewn out of an immense hard-wood tree : her lines were good,
and her type was that of the big sea-canoes of the Bight of
Panavia. Very far forward was a pole mast, roughly made,
but European in intention, and carrying a long gaff. Shrouds
and stays it had not, and my impression was that it would
be carried away if we dropped in for half a tornado, until I
saw our sail and recognised that it would go to darning cotton
instantly if it fell in with even a breeze. It was a bed quilt that
had evidently been in the family some years, and although it
had been in places carefully patched with pieces of previous
sets of the captain's dungarees, in other places, where it had not,
it gave " free passage to the airs of Heaven " ; which I may
remark does not make for speed in the boat mounting such
canvas. Partly to this sail, partly to the amount of trading
affairs we attended to, do I owe the credit of having made
a record trip down the Rembwé, the slowest white man time
on record.

Fixed across the stern of the canoe there was the usual
staging made of bamboos, flush with the gunwale. Now
this sort of staging is an exceedingly good idea when it is
fully finished. You can stuff no end of things under it ;
and over it there is erected a hood of palm-thatch, giving
a very comfortable cabin five or six feet long and about
three feet high in the centre, and you can curl yourself up in
it and, if you please, have a mat hung across the opening.
But we had not got so far as that yet on our vessel, only just
got the staging fixed in fact ; and I assure you a bamboo staging is but a precarious perch when in this stage of formation.
I made myself a reclining couch on it in the Roman manner
with my various belongings, and was exceeding comfortable
until we got nearly out of the Rembwé into the Gaboon.

Then came grand times. Our noble craft had by this time got a good list on her from our collected cargo—ill stowed. This made my home, the bamboo staging, about as reposeful a place as the slope of a writing desk would be if well polished; and the rough and choppy sea gave our vessel the most peculiar set of motions imaginable. She rolled, which made it precarious for things on the bamboo staging, but still a legitimate motion, natural and foreseeable. In addition to this, she had a cataclysmic kick in her, that I think the heathenish thing meant to be a pitch—which no mortal being could foresee or provide against, and which projected portable property into the waters of the Gaboon over the stern and on to the conglomerate collection in the bottom of the canoe itself, making Obanjo repeat, with ferocity and feeling, words he had heard years ago, when he was boatswain on a steamboat trading on the Coast. It was fortunate, you will please understand, for my future, that I have usually been on vessels of the British African or the Royal African lines when voyaging about this West African sea-board, as the owners of these vessels prohibit the use of bad language on board, or goodness only knows what words I might not have remembered and used in the Gaboon estuary.

We left Agonjo with as much bustle and shouting and general air of brisk seamanship as Obanjo could impart to the affair, and the hopeful mind might have expected to reach somewhere important by nightfall. I did not expect that; neither, on the other hand, did I expect that after we had gone a mile and only four, as the early ballad would say, that we should pull up and anchor against a small village for the night; but this we did, the captain going ashore to see for cargo, and to get some more crew.

There were grand times ashore that night, and the captain returned on board about 2 A.M. with some rubber and pissava and two new hands whose appearance fitted them to join our vessel; for a more villainous-looking set than our crew I never laid eye on. One enormously powerful fellow looked the incarnation of the horrid negro of buccaneer stories, and I admired Obanjo for the way he kept them in hand. We had now also acquired a small dug-out canoe as tender, and a large fishing-net.

About 4 A.M. in the moonlight we started to drop down river on the tail of the land breeze, and as I observed Obanjo wanted to sleep I offered to steer. After putting me through an examination in practical seamanship, and passing me, he gladly accepted my offer, handed over the tiller which stuck out across my bamboo staging, and went and curled himself up, falling sound asleep among the crew in less time than it takes to write. On the other nights we spent on this voyage I had no need to offer to steer ; he handed over charge to me as a matter of course, and as I prefer night to day in Africa, I enjoyed it. Indeed, much as I have enjoyed life in Africa, I do not think I ever enjoyed it to the full as I did on those nights dropping down the Rembwé. The great, black, winding river with a pathway in its midst of frosted silver where the moonlight struck it : on each side the ink-black mangrove walls, and above them the band of star and moonlit heavens that the walls of mangrove allowed one to see. Forward rose the form of our sail, idealised from bed-sheetdom to glory ; and the little red glow of our cooking fire gave a single note of warm colour to the cold light of the moon. Three or four times during the second night, while I was steering along by the south bank, I found the mangrove wall thinner, and standing up, looked through the network of their roots and stems on to what seemed like plains, acres upon acres in extent, of polished silver—more specimens of those awful slime lagoons, one of which, before we reached Ndorko, had so very nearly collected me. I watched them, as we leisurely stole past, with a sort of fascination. On the second night, towards the dawn, I had the great joy of seeing Mount Okoneto, away to the S.W., first showing moonlit, and then taking the colours of the dawn before they reached us down below. Ah me ! give me a West African river and a canoe for sheer good pleasure. Drawbacks, you say ? Well, yes, but where are there not drawbacks ? The only drawbacks on those Rembwé nights were the series of horrid frights I got by steering on to tree shadows and thinking they were mud banks, or trees

themselves, so black and solid did they seem. I never roused
the watch fortunately, but got her off the shadow gallantly
single-handed every time, and called myself a fool instead of
getting called one. My nautical friends carp at me for getting on shadows, but I beg them to consider before they judge
me, whether they have ever steered at night down a river quite
unknown to them an unhandy canoe, with a bed-sheet sail,
by the light of the moon. And what with my having a theory
of my own regarding the proper way to take a vessel round
a corner, and what with having to keep the wind in the bed-
sheet where the bed-sheet would hold it, it's a wonder to me
I did not cast that vessel away, or go and damage Africa.

By daylight the Rembwé scenery was certainly not so
lovely, and might be slept through without a pang. It had
monotony, without having enough of it to amount to
grandeur. Every now and again we came to villages, each of
which was situated on a heap of clay and sandy soil, presumably the end of a spit of land running out into the
mangrove swamp fringing the river. Every village we saw
we went alongside and had a chat with, and tried to look up
cargo in the proper way. One village in particular did we
have a lively time at. Obanjo had a wife and home there,
likewise a large herd of goats, some of which he was desirous
of taking down with us to sell at Gaboon. It was a pleasant-
looking village, with a clean yellow beach which most of the
houses faced. But it had ramifications in the interior. I
being very lazy, did not go ashore, but watched the pantomime from the bamboo staging. The whole flock of goats
enter at right end of stage, and tear violently across the
scene, disappearing at left. Two minutes elapse. Obanjo
and his gallant crew enter at right hand of stage, leg it
like lamplighters across front, and disappear at left. Fearful pow-wow behind the scenes. Five minutes elapse. Enter
goats at right as before, followed by Obanjo and company as
before, and so on *da capo*. It was more like a fight I once
saw between the armies of Macbeth and Macduff than anything I have seen before or since ; only our Rembwé play was
better put on, more supers, and noise, and all that sort of
thing, you know. It was a spirited performance I assure you

and I and the inhabitants of the village, not personally
interested in goat-catching, assumed the *rôle* of audience and
cheered it to the echo. While engaged in shouting "Encore"
to the third round, I received a considerable shock by hearing
a well-modulated evidently educated voice saying in most
perfect English :

"Most diverting spectacle, madam, is it not ?"

Now you do not expect to hear things called "diverting
spectacles" on the Rembwé ; so I turned round and saw standing on the bank against which our canoe was moored, what
appeared to me to be an English gentleman who had from
some misfortune gone black all over and lost his trousers and
been compelled to replace them with a highly ornamental
table-cloth. The rest of his wardrobe was in exquisite condition, with the usual white jean coat, white shirt and collar,
very neat tie, and felt hat affected by white gentlemen out
here. Taking a large and powerful cigar from his lips with one
hand, he raised his hat gracefully with the other and said :

"Pray excuse me, madam."

I said, "Oh, please go on smoking."

"May I ?" he said, offering me a cigar-case.

"Oh, no thank you," I replied.

"Many ladies do now," he said, and asked me whether I
"preferred Liverpool, London, or Paris."

I said, "Paris ; but there were nice things in both the other
cities."

"Indeed that is so," he said ; "they have got many very
decent works of art in the St. George's Hall."

I agreed, but said I thought the National Gallery preferable
because there you got such fine representative series of works
of the early Italian schools. I felt I had got to rise to this
man whoever he was, somehow, and having regained my nerve,
I was coming up hand over hand to the level of his culture
when Obanjo and the crew arrived, carrying goats. Obanjo
dropped his goat summarily into the hold, and took off his hat
with his very best bow to my new acquaintance, who acknowledged the salute with a delicious air of condescension.

"Introduce me," said the gentleman.

"I cannot," said Obanjo.

" I regret, madam," said the gentleman, " I have not
brought my card-case with me. One little expects in
such a remote region to require one ; my name is Prince
Makaga." [1]

I said I was similarly card-caseless for reasons identical with
his own, but gave him my name and address, and Obanjo,
having got all aboard, including a member of the crew, fetched
by the leg, shoved off, and with many bows we and the
black gentleman parted. As soon as we were out of earshot
from shore " Who is he, Obanjo ? " said I. Obanjo laughed,
and said he was a M'pongwe gentleman who had at one time
been agent for one of the big European firms at Gaboon, and
had been several times to Europe. Thinking that he could
make more money on his own account, he had left the firm
and started trading all round this district. At first he made a
great deal of money, but a lot of his trust had recently gone
bad, and he was doubtless up here now looking after some
such matter. Obanjo evidently thought him too much of a
lavender-kid-glove gentleman to deal with bush trade, and
held it was the usual way ; a man got spoilt by going to
Europe. I quite agree with him on general lines, but Prince
Makaga had a fine polish on him without the obvious conceit
usually found in men who have been home.

We had another cheerful little incident that afternoon
While we were going along softly, softly as was our wont, in
the broiling heat, I wishing I had an umbrella—for sitting on
that bamboo stage with no sort of protection from the sun
was hot work after the forest shade I had had previously—
two small boys in two small canoes shot out from the bank
and paddled hard to us and jumped on board. After a few

[1] " Makaga, an honourable name, which only one man, and he the
bravest and best hunter in the tribe, may bear. The office of the Makaga
is to lead all desperate affairs—for instance, if any one has murdered one
of his fellow-villagers, and the murderer's town refuses to give him up
(which is almost always the case, they thinking it is a shame to surrender
any one who has taken refuge with them), then it is the business of the
Makaga to take the best men of his village, and lead them to the
assault of that which protects the murderer, and destroy it with its
nhabitants."—*Du Chaillu's Explorations and Adventures in Equatorial
Africa*, 1861, p. 393.

minutes' conversation with Obanjo one of them carefully sank
his canoe; the other just turned his adrift and they joined
our crew. I saw they were Fans, as indeed nearly all the
crew were, but I did not think much of the affair. Our
tender, the small canoe, had been sent out as usual with the
big black man and another A. B. to fish; it being one of our
industries to fish hard all the time with that big net. The
fish caught, sometimes a bushel or two at a time, almost all
grey mullet, were then brought alongside, split open, and
cleaned. We then had all round as many of them for supper
as we wanted, the rest we hung on strings over our fire, more
or less insufficiently smoking them to prevent decomposition,
it being Obanjo's intention to sell them when he made his next
trip up the 'Como; for the latter being less rich in fish than
the Rembwé they would command a good price there. We
always had our eye on things like this, being, I proudly
remark, none of your gilded floating hotel of a ferry-boat like
those Cunard or White Star liners are, but just a good trader
that was not ashamed to pay, and not afraid of work.

Well, just after we had leisurely entered a new reach of
the river, round the corner after us, propelled at a phenomenal pace, came our fishing canoe, which we had left
behind to haul in the net and then rejoin us. The occupants, particularly the big black A. B., were shouting something
in terror stricken accents. "What?" says Obanjo springing
to his feet. "The Fan! the Fan!" shouted the canoe men
as they shot towards us like agitated chickens making for
their hen. In another moment they were alongside and
tumbling over our gunwale into the bottom of the vessel still
crying "The Fan! The Fan! The Fan!" Obanjo then by
means of energetic questioning externally applied, and accompanied by florid language that cast a rose pink glow, smelling of
sulphur, round us, elicited the information that about 40,000
Fans, armed with knives and guns, were coming down the
Rembwé with intent to kill and slay us, and might be expected
to arrive within the next half wink. On hearing this, the whole
of our gallant crew took up masterly recumbent positions in
the bottom of our vessel and turned gray round the lips.
But Obanjo rose to the situation like ten lions. "Take the

rudder," he shouted to me, "take her into the middle of the stream and keep the sail full." It occurred to me that perhaps a position underneath the bamboo staging might be more healthy than one on the top of it, exposed to every microbe of a bit of old iron and what not and a half that according to native testimony would shortly be frisking through the atmosphere from those Fan guns ; and moreover I had not forgotten having been previously shot in a somewhat similar situation, though in better company. However I did not say anything ; neither, between ourselves, did I somehow believe in those Fans. So regardless of danger, I grasped the helm, and sent our gallant craft flying before the breeze down the bosom of the great wild river (that's the proper way to put it, but in the interests of science it may be translated into crawling towards the middle). Meanwhile Obanjo performed prodigies of valour all over the place. He triced up the mainsail, stirred up his faint-hearted crew, and got out the sweeps, *i.e.* one old oar and four paddles, and with this assistance we solemnly trudged away from danger at a pace that nothing slower than a Thames dumb barge, going against stream, could possibly overhaul. Still we did not feel safe, and I suggested to Ngouta he should rise up and help ; but he declined, stating he was a married man. Obanjo cheering the paddlers with inspiriting words sprang with the agility of a leopard on to the bamboo staging aft, standing there with his gun ready loaded and cocked to face the coming foe, looking like a statue put up to himself at the public expense. The worst of this was, however, that while Obanjo's face was to the coming foe, his back was to the crew, and they forthwith commenced to re-subside into the bottom of the boat, paddles and all. I, as second in command, on seeing this, said a few blood-stirring words to them, and Obanjo sent a few more of great power at them over his shoulder, and so we kept the paddles going.

Presently from round the corner shot a Fan canoe. It contained a lady in the bows, weeping and wringing her hands, while another lady sympathetically howling, paddled it. Obanjo in lurid language requested to be informed why they were following us. The lady in the bows said, "My son ! my son ! " and in a second more three other canoes shot round the corner full of men with guns. Now this looked like business, so Obanjo and I looked round to urge our crew to greater exertions and saw, to our disgust, that the gallant band had successfully subsided into the bottom of the boat while we had been eying the foe. Obanjo gave me a recipe for getting the sweeps out again. I did not follow it, but got the job done, for Obanjo could not take his eye and gun off the leading canoe and the canoes having crept up to within some twenty yards of us, poured out their simple tale of woe.

It seemed that one of those miscreant boys was a runaway from a Fan village. He had been desirous, with the usual enterprise of young Fans, of seeing the great world that he knew lay down at the mouth of the river, *i.e.* Libreville Gaboon. He had pleaded with his parents for leave to go down and engage in work there, but the said parents holding the tenderness of his youth unfitted to combat with Coast Town life and temptation, refused this request, and so the young rascal had run away without leave and with a canoe, and was surmised to have joined the well-known Obanjo. Obanjo owned he had (more armed canoes were coming round the corner), and said if the mother would come and fetch her boy she could have him. He for his part would not have dreamed of taking him if he had known his relations disapproved. Every one seemed much relieved, except the *causa belli*. The Fans did not ask about two boys and providentially we gave the lady the right one. He went reluctantly. I feel pretty nearly sure he foresaw more kassengo than fatted calf for him on his return home. When the Fan canoes were well back round the corner again, we had a fine hunt for the other boy, and finally unearthed him from under the bamboo staging. When we got him out he told the same tale. He also was a runaway who wanted to see the world, and taking the opportunity of the majority of the people of his village being away hunting, he had slipped off one night in a canoe, and dropped down river to the village of the boy who had just been reclaimed. The two boys had fraternised, and come on the rest of their way together, lying waiting, hidden up a creek, for Obanjo, who they knew was coming down river ; and having successfully got picked up by him, they thought they were safe. But after this affair boy number two judged there was no more safety yet, and that his family would be down after him very shortly; for he said he was a more valuable and important boy than his late companion, but his family were an uncommon savage set. We felt not the least anxiety to make their acquaintance, so clapped heels on our gallant craft and kept the paddles going, and as no more Fans were in sight our crew kept at work bravely. While Obanjo, now in a boisterous state of mind, and flushed with victory, said things to them about the way they had collapsed when those two women in a canoe came round that corner, that must have blistered their feelings, but they never winced. They laughed at the joke against themselves merrily. The other boy's family we never saw and so took him safely to Gaboon, where Obanjo got him a good place.

Really how much danger there was proportionate to the large amount of fear on our boat I cannot tell you. It never struck me there was any, but on the other hand the crew and Obanjo evidently thought it was a bad place ; and my white face would have been no protection, for the Fans would not have suspected a white of being on such a canoe and might have fired on us if they had been unduly irritated and not treated by Obanjo with that fine compound of bully and blarney that he is such a master of.

Whatever may have been the true nature of the affair, however, it had one good effect, it got us out of the Rembwé into the Gaboon, and although at the time this seemed a doubtful blessing, it made for progress. I had by this time mastered the main points of incapability in our craft. *A.* we could not go against the wind. *B.* we could not go against the tide. While we were in the Rembwé there was a state we will designate as *C*—the tide coming one way, the wind another. With this state we could progress, backwards if the wind came up against us too strong, but seawards if it did not, and the tide was running down. If the tide was running up, and the wind was coming down, then we went seaward, softly, softly alongside the mangrove bank, where the rip of the tide stream is least. When, however, we got down off 'Como Point, we met there a state I will designate as *D*—a fine confused set of marine and fluvial phenomena.   For away to the north the 'Como and Boqué and two other lesser, but considerable streams, were, with the Rembwé, pouring down their waters in swirling, intermingling, interclashing currents ; and up against them, to make confusion worse confounded, came the tide, and the tide up the Gaboon is a swift strong thing, and irregular, and has a rise of eight feet at the springs, two-and-a-half at the neaps.   The wind was lulled too, it being evening time.   In this country it is customary for the wind to blow from the land from 8 P.M. until 8 A.M., from the south-west to the east. Then comes a lull, either an utter dead hot brooding calm, or light baffling winds and draughts that breathe a few panting hot breaths into your sails and die.   Then comes the sea breeze up from the south-south-west or north-west, some days early in the forenoon, some days not till two or three o'clock.   This breeze blows till sundown, and then comes another and a hotter calm.

Fortunately for us we arrived off the head of the Gaboon estuary in this calm, for had we had wind to deal with we should have come to an end.   There were one or two wandering puffs, about the first one of which sickened our counterpane of its ambitious career as a marine sail, so it came away from its gaff and spread itself over the crew, as much as to say, " Here, I've had enough of this sailing.   I'll be a counterpane again." We did a great deal of fine varied, spirited navigation, details of which, however, I will not dwell upon because it was successful. We made one or two circles, taking on water the while and then returned into the south bank backwards.   At that bank we wisely stayed for the night, our meeting with the Gaboon so far having resulted in wrecking our sail, making Ngouta sea-sick and me exasperate ; for from our noble vessel having during the course of it demonstrated for the first time her cataclysmic kicking power, I had had a time of it with my belongings on the bamboo stage.   A basket constructed for catching human souls in, given me as a farewell gift by a valued friend, a witch doctor, and in which I kept the few things in life I really cared for, *i.e.*, my brush, comb, tooth brush, and pocket handkerchiefs, went over the stern ; while I

was recovering this with my fishing line (such was the excellent
nature of the thing, I am glad to say it floated) a black bag
with my blouses and such essentials went away to leeward,
Obanjo recovered that, but meanwhile my little portmanteau
containing my papers and trade tobacco slid off to leeward ;
and as it also contained geological specimens of the Sierra del
Cristal, a massive range of mountains, it must have hopelessly
sunk had it not been for the big black, who grabbed it. All
my bedding, six Equetta cloths, given me by Mr. Hamilton in
Opobo River before I came South, did get away successfully,
but were picked up by means of the fishing line, wet but safe.
After this I did not attempt any more Roman reclining couch
luxuries, but stowed all my loose gear under the bamboo
staging, and spent the night on the top of the stage, dozing
precariously with my head on my knees.

When the morning broke, looking seaward I saw the welcome forms of König and Perroquet Islands away in the
distance, looking, as is their wont, like two lumps of cloud that
have dropped on to the broad Gaboon, and I felt that I was
at last getting near something worth reaching, *i.e.* Glass,
which though still out of sight, I knew lay away to the west
of those islands on the northern shore of the estuary. And if
any one had given me the choice of being in Glass within
twenty-four hours from the mouth of the Rembwé, or in Paris
or London in a week, I would have chosen Glass without
a moment's hesitation. Much as I dislike West Coast towns
as a general rule, there are exceptions, and of all exceptions,
the one I like most is undoubtedly Glass Gaboon; and its
charms loomed large on that dank chilly morning after
a night spent on a bamboo staging in an unfinished native
canoe.

I may as well attempt to give you here a brief sketch of the
local geography of the head of the Gaboon estuary, for I seem
the immediate English successor, in the way of travellers, to
Mr. Winwood Reade, who was here in '63. He came up the
estuary, and up into the 'Como, which he ascended as far as
the rapids—rapids caused as usual in this country by the rocks
of the Sierra del Cristal. Above these rapids, I hear from
native sources, the 'Como is formed by a succession of smaller

streams having their origin in the mountain range. The 'Como falls into the Gaboon on its northern bank, at its eastern end, and is probably the largest of its tributaries. A little distance up, the 'Como, or more properly written, the Nkâmâ, is joined on its south bank by the Boqué or Bakwe. Their joint stream, called the Olomb'ompolo, falls into the Gaboon. On the broad peninsula of land that separates the mouth of the 'Como from that of the Rembwé are two other rivers of less magnitude. The mouth of the Rembwé, about one and a half miles wide, is on the southern bank of the eastern end of the Gaboon. This southern bank is one low stretch of sandy land between thirty-five and forty miles long, having on it numerous native M'pongwe villages, but no white settlement whatsoever. It ends at Pongara Point, the western seaward termination of the estuary, which is above nine miles off from the northern shore's western termination—Cape Santa Clara.

The Rembwé, like the 'Como, is said to rise in the Sierra del Cristal. It is navigable to a place called Isango which is above Agonjo ; just above Agonjo it receives an affluent on its southern bank and runs through mountain country, where its course is blocked by rapids for anything but small canoes. Obanjo did not seem to think this mattered, as there was not much trade up there, and therefore no particular reason why any one should want to go higher up. Moreover he said the natives were an exceedingly bad lot ; but Obanjo usually thinks badly of the bush natives in these regions. Anyhow they are Fans—and Fans are Fans. He was anxious for me, however, to start on a trading voyage with him up another river, a notorious river, in the neighbouring Spanish territory. The idea was I should buy goods at Glass and we should go together and he would buy ivory with them in the interior. I anxiously inquired where my profits were to come in. Obanjo who had all the time suspected me of having trade motives, artfully said, " What for you come across from Ogowé ? You say, see this country. Ah ! I say you come with me. I show you plenty country, plenty men, elephants, leopards, gorillas. Oh ! plenty thing. Then you say where's my trade ? " I disclaimed trade motives in a lordly way. Then says he,

" You come with me up there." I said I'd see about it later on,
for the present I had seen enough men, elephants, gorillas and
leopards, and I preferred to go into wild districts under the
French flag to any flag.   I am still thinking about taking that
voyage, but I'll not march through Coventry with the crew we
had down the Rembwé—that's flat, as Sir John Falstaff says.
Picture to yourselves, my friends, the charming situation of
being up a river surrounded by rapacious savages with a lot
of valuable goods in a canoe and with only a crew to defend
them possessed of such fighting mettle as our crew had
demonstrated themselves to be.   Obanjo might be all right,
would be I dare say ; but suppose he got shot and you had
eighteen stone odd of him thrown on your hands in addition
to your other little worries.   There is little doubt such an
excursion would be rich in incident and highly interesting,
but I am sure it would be, from a commercial point of view, a
failure.

Trade however, even when carried on in a safer, saner way
than our above scheme provides, is falling off on the Rembwé
and 'Como.   The white firms no longer find it pays to put
white agents up at the factories on the Rembwé at Agonjo
and Isango, and on the 'Como at N'enge N'enge, although they
still keep the factories going under black agents.   N'enge
N'enge, a large island just inside the 'Como mouth by the confluence with the Boqué, has still a white representative
missionary of the American Presbyterian Mission—the mission that first commenced working in this Gaboon, Ogowé,
and Batanga region ; and the station at N'enge N'enge is still
in connection with the headquarters of this mission at Baraka,
not having been handed over with the Ogowé stations to the
Mission Évangélique of Paris.   But apart from this mission
station and the evangelising tours made by the energetic
Roman Catholic priests, the upper Gaboon region is not
much troubled by white enterprise.   Now and again that very
hard-working little vessel, the gunboat stationed at Libreville,
goes up river to see whether the natives are behaving properly,
or to point out their errors to them.

The reason for the falling off of the trade in this particular
district is, I suspect, not—as is suggested —the impoverishment

of the country from export trade articles being exhausted, but arises from the Fan invasion having upset things, and also from the trade being diverted to the Ogowé; owing to the enterprising way the French have opened up that river since say the sixties. Before the sixties, the Ogowé was practically only a legend in the native tongue. Now the enterprise of France has made it a practical trade outlet for a great part of some of the richest country in West Africa; and the upper Rembwé trade has been drained in that direction. A very similar case to that of Bonny, whose trade has of late years pitifully fallen away, being drained towards Opobo by the greater ability and power of the Opobo chiefs.

Trade has a fascination for me, and going transversely across the nine-mile-broad rough Gaboon estuary in an unfinished canoe with an inefficient counterpane sail has none; but I return duty bound to this unpleasant subject. We started very early in the morning. We reached the other side entangled in the trailing garments of the night. I was thankful during that broiling hot day of one thing, and that was that if Sister Ann was looking out across the river, as was Sister Ann's invariable way of spending spare moments, Sister Ann would never think I was in a canoe that made such audaciously bad tacks, missed stays, got into irons, and in general behaved in a way that ought to have lost her captain his certificate. Just as the night came down, however, we reached the northern shore of the Grand Gaboon at Dongila, just off the mouth of the 'Como, still some eleven miles east of König Island, and further still from Glass, but on the same side of the river, which seemed good work. The foreshore here is very rocky, so we could not go close alongside but anchored out among the rocks. At this place there is a considerable village and a station of the Roman Catholic Mission. When we arrived a nun was down on the shore with her school children, who were busy catching shell-fish and generally merry-making. Obanjo went ashore in the tender, and the holy sister kindly asked me, by him, to come ashore and spend the night; but I was dead tired and felt quite unfit for polite society after the long broiling hot day and getting soaked by water that had washed on board. Moreover I learnt

she could not speak English, and I shrank in my condition
from attempting to evolve the French language out of my
inner consciousness ; feeling quite certain I should get much
misunderstood by the gentle, clean, tidy lady, and she might
put me down as an ordinary specimen of Englishwoman, and
so I should bring disgrace on my nation. If I had been able
to dress up, ashore I would have gone, but as it was I wrote
her a note explaining things and thanking her.

We lay off Dongila all night, because of the tide. I lay off
everything, Dongila, canoe and all a little after midnight.
Obanjo and almost all the crew stayed on shore that night,
and I rolled myself up in an Equetta cloth and went sound
and happily asleep on the bamboo staging, leaving the canoe
pitching slightly. About midnight some change in the tide,
or original sin in the canoe, caused her to softly swing round
a bit, and the next news was that I was in the water. I had
long expected this to happen, so was not surprised, but highly
disgusted, and climbed on board, needless to say, streaming.
So, in the darkness of the night I got my portmanteau from
the hold and thoroughly tidied‧ up. The next morning we
were off early, coasting along to Glass, and safely arriving
there, I attempted to look as unconcerned as possible, and
vaguely hoped Mr. Hudson would be down in Libreville ; for I
was nervous about meeting him, knowing that since he had
carefully deposited me in safe hands with Mme. Jacot, with
many injunctions to be careful, that there were many incidents in my career that would not meet with his approval.
Vain hope ! he was on the pier. He did not approve. He
had heard of most of my goings on.

The agent for the German house at Lembarene had come
to Libreville a few days before in the legitimate way, i.e. down
the Ogowé in a little steamer, and on to a mail boat at Fernan
Vaz, and thence to Libreville, and had brought the news that I
was reported to have left Kangwe, going in the direction of
the Rembwé. Knowing I ought to reach Agonjo, Mr. Hudson
had most kindly sent a surf-boat with a good crew up the
Rembwé to fetch me down. We never saw this surf-boat as
we came down. I expect we were dodging round some
corner or another after trade, or lying away in a swamp creek

for the night. But this in no way detracts from my great obligation to Mr. Hudson for sending up for me, but adds another item to the great debt of gratitude I owe him ; for had it not been for him I should never have seen the interior of this beautiful region of the Ogowé. I tried to explain to him how much I had enjoyed myself and how I realised I owed it all to him ; but he persisted in his opinion that my intentions and ambitions were suicidal, and took me down the Woermann Road, the ensuing Sunday, as it were on a string.

CHAPTER XVI

CONGO FRANÇAIS

*In which a pæan in honour of the great Ogowé explorers is sung by the
Voyager, to which is added a great deal of very congested information
on the geography in general of Congo Français.[1]*

BEFORE leaving the Ogowé region I must attempt to give
you a general *résumé* of its geography ; for my own journals
kept, while in it, contain this information in so scattered a
state, that no one save an expert in this bit of Africa would
understand the full bearing of them ; and it would have to be
an enthusiastic expert who would take the trouble of piecing
the information together.

My reason for going into these geographical details at
all, is that I think I may say no region in Africa, certainly
no region of equal importance, is so little known in England.
The history of the exploration of the upper regions of the
Ogowé may be written in the life of one man, that of the
greatest of all West African explorers, M. de Brazza ; and it
is impossible for any one to fail to regard him with the
greatest veneration, when one knows from personal acquaintance the make of country and the dangerousness of the
native population with which he has had to deal and with
which he still deals, restlessly but wisely pushing always
onwards to expand the territories of the country of his

---

[1] I have used the names of places as they have been published by the
various travellers referred to ; but, owing to the kindness of Mr. R. B. N.
Walker, I have since my return had from him a list of these names
spelt in conformation with the native pronunciation, and, thinking that
they may be valuable to subsequent travellers, I will occasionally append
them in footnotes.

adoption, France.   It requires indeed some one who has personally sampled Africa to form a just estimate of the value of certain bits of work from what I may call an artistic standpoint.   The "arm-chair explorer" may be impressed by the greatness of length of the red line route of an explorer ; but the person locally acquainted with the region may know that some of those long red lines are very easily made in Africa—thanks to the exertions of travellers who have gone before, or to what one of my German friends once poetically called the lamblike-calfheadedness of the natives, or to the country itself being of a reasonably traversable nature.   In other regions a small red line means 400 times the work and danger, and requires 4,000 times the pluck, perseverance and tact.   These regions we may call choice spots.

I do not mean to depreciate the value of extensive travel in Africa, far from it.   It has an enormous value and so obvious a one that I need not dwell on it ; but the man who combines the two—who makes his long red line pass through great regions of choice spots—deserves especial admiration; and when in addition to traversing them, he attains power over their natives, and retains it, welding the districts into a whole, making the flag of his country respected and feared therein, he is a very great man indeed ; and such a man is de Brazza. Such a man Mr. Stanley might have been had it not been for matters I will not enter into here, for it would involve us in a discussion on the Congo Free State.

M. de Brazza's first journey into the interior [1] of Congo Français was made in 1875–78 when, accompanied by MM. Ballay and Marche he reached the upper waters of the Ogowé and then pushed east and northwards, discovering two new rivers, the Alima and the Licona, both of which he surmised were tributaries of the Congo.   He at once saw the importance of these rivers to the French possessions ; for, by them, access would be obtained to the Congo, above the great barrier of navigation on that river, the Livingstone rapids. He convinced the authorities at home of this and was commanded by the African Association (French Committee) and

[1] See *Proceedings of Geographical Society of Paris* for June 23rd, 1882, quoted in *Proceedings of Royal Geographical Societv*, August, 1882.

by the Government to make a second journey in order to trace the Alima to the Congo ; to establish civilising stations, one on the Ogowé and one on the Congo; and to cultivate the friendship of the native tribes throughout the region.

The Chambers voted a grant towards the expenses, and he left France for Africa on the 27th of December, 1879—M. Ballay, his companion on the first journey, remaining behind to complete the preparations for the exploration, more especially the fitting out of a steamer that was to be used in the navigation of the Ogowé and the Alima. When the said steamer should be ready in sections, M. Ballay was to bring it out and join M. de Brazza. There is always a steamer in sections in every story of a good expedition, and that steamer is invariably a curse that costs men's lives, and M. de Brazza's steamer was no exception to the rule ; but of that hereafter.

Two Europeans went out with de Brazza, M. Noguez and and M. Michaud. On landing on the Coast he organised his expedition at Gaboon, and ascended the Ogowé, the worst part of the journey being from Lembarene [1] to Boué, on account of the Fans all along this region, and the rapids along a great part of it, these having to be navigated through the Sierra de Cristal, owing to the wildness of the banks preventing portage. When these mountains are passed, however, there is an open park-like country where carriers can be employed, and you are no longer at the entire mercy of the flying furious river that makes this bit of the voyage from Njole to Boué a peculiarly choice spot. Beyond the Sierra del Cristal, moreover, de Brazza got in touch with the Okanda and Adooma tribes, people less ferocious and more helpful than the Fans ; and over these two tribes he attained a great influence, arranging with them the regular system of communication with Njole that at present goes on, the Adoomas conveying supplies up and down through the region of the rapids.

---

[1] Lembarene is now an official district under the charge of a Chef de Poste, whose residence is on Lembarene Island, and to the island the name of Lembarene is colloquially limited. The native name for the island is Ezange'-nenge'. In 1866 the name Lembarene was borne by one of the three Inlenga villages just below the confluence with the lake or lagoon Zele'.

He fixed on a point for his first station at the confluence of the Passa with the Ogowé, and founded there the station now know as Franceville in June, 1880. In the middle of the same month he sent down to the coast M. Michaud with 770 men and forty-four canoes to meet M. Ballay, whom he expected would by this time have arrived at Gaboon with the sections of the steamer ; and leaving M. Noguez at Franceville to get on with making it, de Brazza started off in a way characteristic of him, alone, with a small party of

AN UPPER OGOWÉ VILLAGE.

natives for the Congo ; although he fully expected to meet with opposition from the Apfuru tribe, who had on his previous journey barred the way to him down the Alima. He says he " relied on his growing reputation for friendliness, throughout the region, for softening the hostility of the natives." He may have done so ; but if he had not had time to acquire it, de Brazza would have gone on, relying on something else, his luck, most likely—that luck which, as the story on the Ogowé goes, once saved him from immolation at the hands of the Fans by arranging for a pyrotechnic display to take place without human aid, with a quantity of fireworks he had with him.

Two or three days' journey from Franceville going east, the nature of the country changes. To the clayey soil of the Ogowé basin and its richly wooded moist valleys succeeds a sandy, arid, hilly country, with here and there in the neighbourhood of a village a group of palm trees.

This is the aspect of the country which forms the water-

BATEKE PORTERS, OGOWÉ.

shed between the Ogowé and the tributaries of the Upper Congo. On the northern bank of the Congo, and on the southern bank of the Congo, I found this same make of country, more seaward, in the Pallaballa mountains above Matadi.

De Brazza remarks it is a singular fact that narrow sandy tracts of country are everywhere inhabited by one and the same tribe, the Bateke, reputed, probably erroneously he says, to be cannibals.

When he had passed the Leketi, a southern branch of the
Alima, his route lay across the plateau of Achicuya, an
elevated district lying about 2,600 feet above sea level, and
separated from another similar plateau (the Aboma) by the
river Mpama.   (Mpama = Ox.)

The chief of Achicuya received the traveller in a friendly
manner, and a similar reception awaited him on reaching the
Abooma tribe.   These latter people he describes as being the
handsomest and bravest he had met ; and it was from them he
received information regarding the Congo and the powerful
chief Makoko, whose sovereignty the Abooma acknowledge.

Leaving the Abooma district he travelled along the Lefini
(the Lawson of Mr. Stanley), and just as he was finishing the
construction of a raft to descend the Lefini, he received
messengers from King Makoko with friendly greetings and
offers of assistance.   This much facilitated his further proceedings.   He descended the Lefini with the envoy as far as
Ngampo on his raft, and then landed and went overland
for two days across an uninhabited tableland.   He states his
march over the sun-scorched plateau was most wearisome ;
and that two days' march must have been a choice spot,
if, as I conjecture, this tableland was of the same formation
as those truly horrible Pallaballa mountains, that have in their
composition an immense percentage of mica, which glistens
in the sun like diamond dust, and dazzles you, and which,
bare of vegetation, reflect back the burning heat in a scorching way, forming a layer of hot air, and making the whole
desolate, hideous scene vibrate before your eyes as you can
see things vibrating through the hot air over a line of gas jets.
Never shall I forget my short experience in the Pallaballa
range.   Never have I in all West Africa come across a thing
that came up to one's ideals of the infernal region so completely.   And the nights, when you had the whole earth
round you exhaling a heavy, hot breath with the heat it
had been soaking in during the day.   Small wonder M. de
Brazza should have " begun to find fault with his guide,
Makoko's envoy, just before eleven o'clock on the second
night after a forced march."   Fortunately shortly afterwards he
came in sight of the Congo.   " It appeared like an immense

AN ANGOLA FISHERMAN AT HOME.

CAPE COAST.

FERNANDO PO AND AMBAO ISLAND FROM THE N.E.

CALLE DE LA MARINA CLARENCE, FERNANDO PO.

CALLE DE SACRAMENTO, CLARENCE, FERNANDO PO.

A TYPICAL WEST AFRICAN RIVER BANK.

FAN CHIEF AND FAMILY

FANS.

M. DE BRAZZA

CARAVAN FOR STANLEY POOL, PALLABALLA MOUNTAINS, CONGO.

THE FALLS OF THE NGUNIE AT SAMBA.

DEATH DANCE COSTUMES, OLD CALABAR

TRADE BOYS OF A CHIEF AT EQUETTA, OPOBO.

CAMEROONS RIVER, FROM ABOVE AKKWA TOWN.

A MAHOGANY TREE, GOLD COAST.

SHIPPING MAHOGANY, AXIM.

sheet of water, the silver sheen of which contrasted with the sombre hue of the lofty mountains around. Towards the N.W. the waterline extended to the horizon, and the river swept in a noiseless slow current past the foot of the hills beneath."

His first object on reaching the banks of the Great River was to establish peaceful relations with the Apfuru and other tribes of the 'Ubanji nation. The principal tribe of this family are the Alhialumo "sailors of the Congo," who are born, live, and die with their families on board the fine canoes, in which they carry on their trade in ivory and other goods between the Alima and Stanley Pool. This was so on de Brazza's first visit. Now I am informed that trade route is to a considerable extent diverted.

De Brazza addressed himself to Ngampey their chief, who seemed inclined to be friendly. "Choose," said he, "between the cartridge and the flag I send you. One will be the sign of a war without mercy, the other a symbol of a peace as profitable to you as to us." He left the tribes on this side time to think over the answer and went on to King Makoko.

De Brazza here says he felt his rights of priority and those of France now clearly established over the whole region between the Ogowé, the Equator, and the Congo ; and he next wished to extend this over the left bank of the Congo, the N., as far as the confluence of the river Djué to the south of Stanley Pool. In this part of the country the plateaus are more fertile and better cultivated than those in the interior and the population denser and equally pacific. "The Mussulman element," says de Brazza, "being unknown in this region, European civilisation need not expect to encounter the hostility, hatred, and fanaticism which oblige the French, for instance, not to advance except with armed forces from the Senegal to the Niger. There is nothing to be feared there except the natural opposition of the natives to whatever is new."

Makoko received him with all available magnificence, and he remained twenty-five days with the chief and for a longer period in his provinces, and "could not have been better treated."

In the end a treaty was concluded by which the king placed his states under the protection of France, and ceded a tract of country, to be selected by M. de Brazza, on the shores of the Congo. The treaty was ratified on a day appointed, in the presence of all the vassal chiefs of Makoko. On its completion the grand fetish master put a little earth in a box and presented it to M. de Brazza, saying, "Take this earth and carry it to the great chief of the whites. It will remind him that we belong to him." De Brazza then planted the French flag before Makoko's house, saying, "This is the symbol of friendship and protection which I will leave with you. Wherever waves this emblem of peace there is France, and she will cause to be respected the rights of all those whom it covers."

I have no hesitation in saying that as far as Congo Français goes (I have no experience of other French possessions), this high-flown statement is true ; and although de Brazza did a good thing for France that day, Makoko also did well, for he saved himself from the Congo Free State.

Soon after the signing of this treaty with Makoko, de Brazza left him and attended a meeting of the 'Ubanji chiefs at Nganchuno on the Congo. The chiefs came in an unsettled state of mind, and showed at first much opposition to the conclusion of a treaty, expressing their mistrust on account of a previous white traveller who had shot a member of the tribe and escaped down river too swiftly to be followed. However, after a second grand meeting, a treaty of peace was arranged and war was buried. This ceremony consisted in each chief and each man of de Brazza's small party burying some implement of war in a hole, over which a quickly growing tree was afterwards planted. French colours were distributed among the chiefs and the treaty definitely agreed to.

De Brazza then set off to choose the site for the station on the Congo, making five days' journey down the river to the west into Stanley Pool, and finally selecting Ntamo, now known as Brazzaville. He took possession of this site duly under his agreement with Makoko, and hoisted the French flag here on the 1st of October 1880. Its

selection has been subjected to a good deal of criticism,
but it is clear that it is a commanding strategical position,
for save with the goodwill of Brazzaville no one can pass
from the Upper to the Lower Congo *viâ* the river.   The
Livingstone rapids of the Congo, that commence to the westward of it, are indeed permanent bars to steam vessels navigating the Congo, for about 200 miles ; yet they are not bars
to canoe transport because the banks of the Congo, unlike
those of the Ogowé, permit of portage.

It must be confessed that these rapids of the Congo *are* a
difficulty.   The waters collected by the great river in its catchment basin of 1,600,000 square miles come through a narrow
channel 170 miles in length, cut by them in the rocks of the
Pallaballa range, and take the descent of 1,000 feet in fierce
stretches of rushing water, broken by thirty-two distinct cataracts. But to overcome these a railway is in course of construction from Matadi to Stanley Pool ; for the courage and good
seamanship of Captain Murray demonstrated the fact that it
was possible to take an ocean-going steamer up through the
whirlpools of Hell's Cauldron, to Matadi, close to the foot of the
last of the thirty-two cataracts, the Yellala, and 120 miles from
the sea.   But it is certain that the Congo Free State must soon
be split up among the Powers in Africa ; and then the long
stretch of country from Brazzaville to the 'Ubanji confluence
already in the possession of France, thanks to M. de Brazza,
will give France command over the whole district of the Middle
Congo, *i.e.* that district draining its trade into the Congo for
the 1,000 miles that separate the Livingstone Falls from the
Stanley Falls.

Access to the right bank of the Congo at Stanley Pool
is undoubtedly easier ; but those southern regions, not now in
the possession of the Congo Free State, belong to Portugal,
and Portugal would have little chance of obtaining a tract of
country when her rival for it is France.   Portugal has
already been almost completely ousted from the Congo, which
her great explorer Diogo Cão discovered in 1482, but she
still holds the southern bank of the Congo, from the sea to
a point (Nkoi) just below Matadi ; and a very considerable
quantity of the Congo trade filters into her country owing

to her imposts being more reasonable than those of the Free State.

I will not here attempt to go further into the political side of de Brazza's journey and its attendant conquests for France but will pass on to his return journey to the Coast.

ADOOMAS, UPPER OGOWÉ.

He left a Senegal sergeant and a few men at Brazzaville and proceeded to explore a new route from the Stanley Pool to the sea. This was by the valley of the N'Duo, which empties itself into the Niari [1] and leads from Ntamo to the Atlantic in a nearly due westerly direction. He thought this would

[1] In M'pongwe, Nyari = Buffalo.

be the easiest way to the sea ; but it was so entirely unexplored that the very name under which the Niari enters the sea was unknown.   Moreover the route proved so hazardous that he was compelled to continue his journey down the Congo, on his way meeting with Mr. Stanley, who gave him a cordial reception.

From the mouth of the Congo he sailed to Gaboon, reaching Libreville on the 15th of December, 1880.   Here a cruel disappointment awaited him, needless to say connected with that steamer.   Neither de Ballay nor the steamer had arrived, and a very bitter nuisance this must have been, and one that would have caused many a man to throw up the whole undertaking ; for he had sent down those 770 men and 44 canoes, promising them divers wonderful manifestations of white man's power and plenty of work, and there was neither ; and de Brazza owned it was with painful feelings that he found himself so ill supported, and obliged, instead of returning to Europe to rest from his fatigues, having performed himself all he had undertaken to do, to hasten again into the interior in order to carry reinforcements to the men left in charge of the two stations he had founded, distant, the one 500, the other 800 miles.

He started back into the interior with a party strengthened by two French sailors, Guiral and Amiel, and a number of native carpenters, gardeners, &c.   In ascending the Ogowé for the third time his canoe was upset at the Boué Falls and he suffered much from illness brought on by having to work long in the water to save his baggage.   Arriving at Franceville in February, 1881, he found there 100 natives satisfactorily established and engaged in various industries.   The gardens had been well cared for and the settlement was self-supporting. De Brazza however had not lost faith in that steamer even yet, and he set about preparing means of transport for the thing when it should arrive.   There were seventy-five miles of portage intervening between the station Franceville and the confluence of the Obia and Lekiba with the Alima, the point chosen for the commencement of the navigation of the Alima. The clearing of a path for the transport of the sections of the steamer was accomplished by the aid of 400 labourers superintended by Michaud, Guiral, and Amiel.

The organisation of a service of transport was then proceeded with, a business of some difficulty owing to the jealousies of the tribes with regard to the profits of conveyance over different sections of the route. M. de Brazza then thought to surmount this difficulty by establishing a body of carriers of his own, but various obstacles intervened to prevent his accomplishing this forthwith, and in the meantime he had to send supplies to Brazzaville on the Congo. While thus engaged he was fortunately joined on the 27th of September by M. Mizon of the French navy, who had been sent from France in company with de Ballay. He brought de Brazza news that the latter was detained at Gaboon and that the steamer had been discovered to have defects in construction that would prevent her joining the expedition for a long time.

M. de Brazza then resolved to leave Franceville in charge of M. Mizon and go off on an entirely new bit of exploration. He was by now, after those three voyages up and down them, aware that the rapids of the Ogowé are not what you might call a safe and pleasant route to Franceville, particularly for heavy goods ; and he reverted to his old idea, that he had had to abandon testing when leaving Brazzaville in 1880, namely that a safer route to the sea-coast than the Ogowé affords, existed down the Niari valley. He first went to Nhango on the route between the Ogowé and the Congo, near the M'paka country of the latter river. There he learnt that Mr. Stanley had been attempting to persuade the chiefs of the Bateke to withdraw from their engagements with France and endeavouring to win over Malamine, the chief of Ntamo (Brazzaville). But de Brazza did not surmise there was any danger of Mr. Stanley succeeding in either of these diplomatic ventures, so proceeded on his exploration.

He started at the end of January, 1882, passing over mountains by the sources of the Leketi and M'paka, and on the 8th of February he discovered one of the sources of the Ogowé at a point where it formed a mere rivulet of water. A month later he arrived on the banks of his desired Niari, which proved to be a beautiful river 270 feet broad and to enter the ocean under the name of Quilliou (Kouilou or

Killiou) just north of Loango. Not far from its left bank
were found mines of copper and lead.

Along this left bank he continued his march, finding to his
great satisfaction that the river, as far as its confluence with
the Lalli, flowed without rapids or falls along a broad, fertile,

A KONGAS, THE CHIEF GONIONE, AND HIS TWO WIVES.

and densely peopled valley, lying athwart the great parallel
terraces over which, ladderlike, the neighbouring Congo has
cut its bed on its way to the ocean. About sixty miles
further the Niari tends a little towards the north and he
quitted its banks after having crossed its little affluent the

Nkenge. From here he began the ascent of the plateau, where the villagers no longer received him and his party with the friendliness he had encountered along the valley of the Niari. The mistrust with which he had to contend led at last to an hostile encounter at the village of Kimbendge, in which six of his men were wounded, and the expedition was obliged to beat a retreat. They marched without taking food, in a pouring rain all night long, going south, finding themselves in the morning at the summit of a mountain range at the foot of which extended a verdant plain through which flowed the Lundima (Loema). In the plain they passed a group of villages named Mboko, where copper ore is found on the surface ; and then journeying westwards arrived at Kimbunda, a Basundi village situated between Lundima and the Loango. This place is within five days' march of Boma (Emboma) on the Congo on one side and Landana on the Atlantic. The party arrived, exhausted with the fatigues of their long and difficult march, at Landana on the 17th of April, 1882.

M. de Brazza claimed by this expedition a tract of country one-third the area of France as an addition to his previous discoveries, and he insisted on the importance of the position at Ntamo (Brazzaville) which he said was the key to the whole western interior of Equatorial Africa. It was in the hands of France and the route *viâ* the Niari was the best road to it and the best line for a railway, which ought to be undertaken by the French as the most effectual means of opening up the country.

The construction of this railroad has been undertaken, and that it has not been already completed I think, no doubt, arises from the idea that the Congo Free State will shortly fall into the hands of France, and then the route up the Congo, with a railway round the Livingstone rapids, will be the best and shortest way to Brazzaville, and things in general on the Middle Congo. However until that day dawns France has done much to utilise the Niari valley route and regular convoys now use it to the interior. De Brazza has of late years been ceaselessly working at the development and expansion of Congo Français to the north and east, particularly to the establishment of a safe and easy line of transport to the southern shores of Lake Chad. With the insight into African geographical problems so characteristic of him, de Brazza saw the Sanga river was more likely to afford a route to the central Soudan from the Congo than the apparently more important M'ubungi. Camfurel was the first man sent to trace the course of the Sanga, and he and his expedition were annihilated. Furneaux was then sent and succeeded in getting several days' journey above the rapids of the Sanga when he fell in with war, and got one white and seventeen black men of his party killed. Then he returned to de Brazza, who went up the river himself as far as the rapids and established a station there that black traders now frequent. He sent a lieutenant and fifty-five men on, and this good man got right through to Yola on the Niger and then returned to de Brazza safely. On his way I may remark, as proof that he had struck an interior trade-route, he met traders who had passports from Algeria on the Mediterranean, and these he countersigned. Some of these people accompanied him, and when he returned to Brazzaville, horses from the Soudan were photographed alongside a steamer on the Congo.

He reported that as soon as you got out of the Ogowé forests to the north, the country became extremely healthy and none of the expedition suffered from sickness, and that this country abounds with cattle and horses. The lieutenant must have been traversing high land, for a part of the time while between the Ogowé and the Niger ; but that the country is healthy for white men I expect is only because there are no white men there for it to kill and make a death-rate. I do not believe that any part of Africa between the Zambesi and the Sahara is healthy for white men.

There is in course of construction a railroad which is to open up the route from Congo Français to Lake Chad, following the course of the Sanga ; and this when completed will form a line of markets that must be of great importance from the richness of the country they will drain. It should be the trade-route for the whole north central African ivory and other trades ; and there is no doubt de Brazza is manifesting his usual far-sightedness in turning his attention to the expansion of Congo Français to the north-east, and unless Providence in the shape of death, or Sir George Goldie— de Brazza's only rival in administrative ability in West Africa —intervenes, he will succeed in uniting Congo Français with the French Soudan. De Brazza has done so much and done it so well that I, as a woman, may be excused a sentimental hope that he may live to see his edifice of power completed.

After sketching the work of de Brazza the completer, we must turn to the work of Du Chaillu, the inaugurator of geographical knowledge in this region ; but I will only briefly sketch Du Chaillu's work, because his books are accessible to English readers and not given in scattered journals of geographical societies, as are the notices of de Brazza.

Du Chaillu's works should be read carefully by every one interested in the forest region of Africa, for you find in them a series of wonderfully vivid pictures of life, both of man and beast, and of the country itself with its dense, gloriously beautiful, gloomy forests and its wild rivers, as true in all these things as on the day on which Du Chaillu wrote. On his return to England great doubt was cast upon his accounts ; but I have no hesitation in saying that I never came across anything while in his region that discredited Du Chaillu's narrative on the whole. His deductions from the things he saw are a matter apart, for no two West African travellers will ever be found to agree in their deductions ; but his descriptions of the country and the animals are truthful—yes, including those gorillas ; I know places where the gorilla population is every bit as thick as he says and the individuals every bit as big ; and his account of the natives and their ways are recognisable by any one having personal knowledge in the matter. Nor am I alone, I am glad to say ; for one of the greatest authorities on this matter, Dr. Nassau, who was on the Coast when Du Chaillu was, says there is nothing Du Chaillu relates that might not have happened in this country. More can be said of no one of the school of travellers of which Du Chaillu, Dr. Barth, Joseph Thomson, and Livingstone are past masters, and of which I am an humble member. We have not a set of white companions with us to confirm our statements and say, " *Oui, oui, certainement, Monsieur*," as the engineer and his brother used to say on the *Éclaireur* to their captain; but we

have great compensations for this. We have no awful rows
with each other in inconvenient places in Africa, or on our return
home, and we can say to our critics : " Have you been
there ? No ! Then go there or to whatever place you may
happen to believe in ! and till then—shut up." Mr. Winwood
Reade accepted this sort of answer from Du Chaillu and
went down to the regions of the Panavia Bight and Gaboon
with a pre-determination to prove Du Chaillu was wrong ;
and I am bound to say I think he utterly failed. He
did not follow Du Chaillu's course throughout by any means,
doing little more than going in behind Corisco Bay and up the
Gaboon estuary and the 'Como, a very good bit of work, and
charmingly described in his *Savage Africa*, but he was not
in the country rich in gorillas in either place.

Du Chaillu's journeys may be divided into two main groups,
one of which is described in his first book, *Explorations and
Adventures in Equatorial Africa*, 1861. During this journey
he ascended the Muni River as far as the Osheba [1] country, the
'Como and Boqué as far as the Sierra del Cristal, marched
overland from the Gaboon estuary to the rivers of the Delta
of the Ogowé, and did a great deal of work in the whole
of this great dangerous network ; going up and down the
N'Poulounay [2] and the O'Rembo and striking the upper waters
of the Ngunie, going to and fro among the tribes of the
Sierra del Cristal and Achangoland mountains. On his
second journey, made in 1864–65, he was entirely in regions
south of the Ogowé. He went into Fernan Vaz, followed the
O'Rembo for some little distance, and then struck away east
by south, crossing the Ngunie at a point south of the spot he
had reached on it when he discovered this river in 1858.
Thence he went on into the mountains of Achangoland,
where he was attacked and had to beat a very hurried
retreat to the ocean.

Nearly the whole of Du Chaillu's two journeys were

[1] The Osheba are now recognised as Fans.
[2] Mr. R. B. N. Walker says Du Chaillu's N'Poulounay should read
Mplunie, and that it is merely an inferior stream connecting the lower
main Ogowé (Ngony-Oulange) and the Bandu, with the Fernan Vaz,
partly by means of the Ogâlote.

through successions of choice spots. Many of his districts have not been revisited. In a few I was his immediate successor.

By ill-luck M. Du Chaillu on both journeys just missed striking the main stream of the Ogowé, but he knew that it was there, and the information he brought back of the existence of a great river whose delta he recognised he had been exploring, was received in France with a more proper spirit

MOUNT LOPE, OGOWÉ.

than in England or Germany; and in 1862 MM. Serval, Bellay, and Griffon were commanded by the French government to trace the Nazareth, which Du Chaillu regarded as the chief mouth of his great river. This they did almost to the bend of it by Elivä z'onlange (called by Du Chaillu Anengué); but they failed to reach the junction of the Ogowé (called by Du Chaillu the Okanda) with the great river discovered by Du Chaillu, the Ngunie, which junction he had surmised occurred. The confluence of these two rivers, as I have already described, is just above Lembarene, some twenty miles from the point this expedition reached. M. Serval, however, after the return of the expedition to Gaboon, made another attempt, and crossed by land from the Gaboon to the Ogowé, reaching Orongo a little above Osoamokita, definitely proving that the Gaboon estuary was not a mouth of the Ogowé and quite disconnected from it. In 1864 another expedition sent by the French Government succeeded in reaching the confluence of the Ngunie with the Ogowé (the Ngouyai with the Okanda of Du Chaillu). From those days, up to the time of de Brazza, the most important worker on the Ogowé has been Mr. R. B. N. Walker, of whose journey I regret to say no full account has been published, for it was a most remarkable one, undertaken before the Fans on the river bank had been overawed by M. de Brazza. Mr. Walker reached Lope, the furthest point attained until de Brazza's 1889 journey, and in addition to this, made many exploring expeditions in the region.[1] Then come the missionary journeys of Dr. Nassau, who was well-established up at Talagouga [2] with his house and church built when de Brazza came by in 1879. Since the latter opened up the district, the only travellers I know of, passing through the region up the Ogowé rapids, are MM. Alegret and Tesseris, who made a journey right up the Ogowé and out on to the Congo with a view to selecting a site for mission stations, and to these gentlemen I am indebted for many photographs of native types on the Upper Ogowé. Financial reasons have, I believe, militated against the establishment of further stations above Talagouga by the Mission Évangélique, to which these gentlemen belong ; and this station, and a Roman Catholic Mission

[1] Since my return to England, feeling much interested in the travels of Mr. Walker, I have hunted up several papers by him scattered among the transactions of various societies *circa* 1876, and from them fully recognise the great loss to our knowledge of the actual geography and ethnology of this region, that we suffer from Mr. Walker never having collected and published in book form the results of his travels and residence in Congo Français.

[2] The natives sometimes call it Otalamaguga. Aguga means want, privation, hardship.

at a place called Lestourville, close to Franceville, established
in memory of a Governor who died, are now the outposts of
Christianity in these West African regions. The main results
of these travels on the Ogowé may be summarised as having
shown that the Ogowé is one of the great rivers of Africa, the
largest river between the Niger and the Congo, the largest
strictly Equatorial river in the world, its course lying fairly
neatly along the line for over 700 miles. It has a catchment
basin roughly computed—for its basin is not yet thoroughly
explored—of 130,000 square miles, and its discharge of water
into the Atlantic is, according to the season, between 360,000
and 1,750,000 cubic feet per second.

Its main affluents are, in order of merit, the Ngunie entering on its south bank, and the Ivindo, and the Okanda, both of
which enter on its north bank.

The Ogowé is, on the whole, more of the nature of the
Congo than of the Niger, save that unlike the Congo, it has an
immense delta. This delta commences at Lembarene, just
below the point where it receives the waters of the Ngunie
river. The delta region is tremendously interesting both in
flora, fauna, and fetish ; but it is tradeless, and its main population is made up of malaria microbes and mosquitoes, and it
is supremely damp. Indeed the whole of it and the country
from the Gaboon to Cette Kama,[1] save the strange bubble-
shaped mountains like Mount Sangatō, Mount Mandji and
Mount Okoneto, is under water when the Ogowé and its neighbouring rivers come down in the "long wet" ; and the lakes
in the Lembarene district, Elivă Ayzingo and the still larger
Elivă z'onlange, and all the string of lakes along the O'Rembo,
Ungo, and Vinue overflow into the forest. The Sierra del
Cristal cuts the course of the Ogowé just above Njole, forming the region of the rapids. There are 500 miles of these
rapids, rendering navigation impossible in any other craft

[1] Sĕtĕ Kama—the natives call it Masetyi. One or two Europeans profess to believe that it was named by the Spaniards Siete Camas (the
seven beds or graves) from the fact of seven men from some ship
being buried there. It was first opened up as a trading station by Henry
Walker in 1849, who traded from a ship. His brother, R. B. N. Walker
established a factory on shore there in 1857. The natives have to this
day a bad name.

but a canoe, and highly perilous work in that, I assure you, from personal experience ; and when you get above them the river is not much use except for canoes, until you get to Franceville ; beyond Franceville it is only available for canoes in the wet season, but you do not want the Ogowé, being in touch with the great rivers flowing transversely to it into the Congo.

Below the rapids, however, the Ogowé is a grand waterway, as waterways go on the West Coast. You can go up its main stream to Njole for over 200 miles, and up its affluent the Ngunie as far as Samba, where there are lovely falls. Above these falls and a set of rapids the Ngunie would be again available for small steamboats, but there are none there at present.

In addition to the main stream of the Ogowé, you can with the exercise of great care, and with the assistance of good fortune, navigate a small steamboat into Lake Ayzingo and Lake Z'onlange in the wet season, and also enter this main stream of the Ogowé from the ocean by two side creeks running down to Fernan Vaz. The current of the Ogowé is extremely swift, particularly above Lembarene, and the rise of the river in the Talagouga narrows, during the wet season, is from eighteen to twenty feet. This rise commences a month before the wet season gets established here, probably on account of the latter being earlier on the upper waters of the affluents that come in above Njole—the Okanda, and the Ivindo.

The region of the delta to the south is more water-eaten than to the north. The stretch of country to the north, between the delta of the Ogowé and the Gaboon, is rimmed along the seashore, and the estuary shore, by a sort of sand rampart which keeps in the overflow waters of the wet season, and forms the most impossible morass to get about in during this period. The human population of this region is sparse, and what there is resides in villages on the abruptly shaped bubble-like hills that rise isolated here and there. This region is very little explored ; the main stream of the Ogowé, entered either from Nazareth Bay or from Fernan Vaz, being the highway to and from the interior, and the unhealthiness and absence of trade in this great swampy forest belt offer but little inducement to travelling about in it. Along the banks of the main waterways passing through it, the villages are all situated in similar sites, namely perched on the top of a clay bank, or dwarf cliff, behind which the land slopes steeply into what, in the wet season, is a swamp. On all sides rises the colossal, white-trunked, liane-hung forest ; on all sides one may say, making no exception even for the broad river the villages face ; for across it there is the tree-cliff again and in its deep dark waters are mirrored back the forest and the sky—all that the world is made of to the inhabitants of these villages ; they are born, live, and die with no interval save sleep from the sight of that universe of forest, river and sky—and only a little sky—that which they can see over the river. All the change they get the seasons bring ; the gloomy dry season when the wind steals softly up the river in the morning time, and down the river in the evening ; the tornado seasons with their burst of earth-shaking thunder, and their lightnings coming down into the forest in great forked splashes, and their howling, squealing, moaning winds, that rush devastating through it, claiming as many victims among its giants as even the lightnings do.

The course of a grand tornado through a high forest is a thing to see, but anything but pleasant to experi-ence. The heavy brooding suffocating heat when the great storm seems pressing its hot breast down on the very ground—the sensation of depression and wretchedness that creeps over you—and the evident apprehension of all living things of what they know is coming ; an appre-hension which changes into terror when the storm bursts and comes sweeping seawards with all the frenzy of its de-moniac power and the roar of its rain. Behind it lie the bodies of many of the noblest trees, either lightning-seared, still standing, but turned in a moment from luxuriant living things into gaunt skeletons ; or thrown down, with all their bravery of foliage and bush-rope, by the winged force which has wrung them round, and pulled them sheer out by the roots—things 100 to 200 feet high, just as you would pull out a root of groundsel—flinging them crashing among their fellows, wrecks to rot.

Then comes the wet season, not here like the wet season in the Rivers, one grim, torrential waterfall ; but daily heavy sheets of rain diversified with intervals of bright sunshine and accompanied by heavy steamy heat ; with the Ogowé coming down daily muddier and muddier, floating along on its swift current bits of bank with the trees still growing on them, and surrounded ·by tangled masses of grass and drift-wood, forming the well-known floating islands which mariners often meet with miles out to sea off this coast.

Every day the river rises up the banks, flowing over their lowest parts into the low reaches of the forest, and threatening with destruction the clay or mud-cliffs with the villages perched on them ; and often carrying this threat out, and tearing down parts of the clay bank, swamping and sweeping away the frail houses and ruining the plantations of plantains close by.

Between the Kama[1] country and the Ouroungou country the channel of the Ogowé is, fortunately, broad, and there are opportunities for the swollen waters to flow easily away into the low-lying uninhabited parts of the forest. Were it not so those clay cliffs would have worse times of it than they now do, and villages would be more precarious residential sites than is now the case. In the Talagouga gorge, where the current is more fierce—the waters being hemmed in to a narrower channel, and the banks made of the hard rocks of the Sierra del Cristal —the rise of the waters twenty and thirty feet above the dry-season level does not work the destruction that occurs in the clay bank region.

The long wet season commences in September and lasts till the end of January, its greatest intensity being in November and December.[2] In February comes the short dry, then the short wet till May. From May till September is the long dry. The seasons, however, are not to be depended on with that calm reliance you may place in their wetness or dryness on the Gold Coast or in the Rivers. The long dry is fairly worthy of its name, the long wet also.

The peculiarity of the dry season being the coolest season,

---

[1] Sometimes spelt Camma country. The native name is Akama. The tribes living in it are known as the Nkâmi, frequently Ncomi.

[2] Long dry season, Enomo ; long wet, Nlyanja.

and its sky overhung with gray threatening-looking cloud, is
one that extends from just below Cameroons to Angola,
i.e., to the edge of the Kalahari desert, where wet seasons
are not; it strikes the person coming south from the Bights,
where the dry season is the hot season and the wet the cooler,
as most strange and peculiar. One of the many difficulties of
travelling down the West African coast is that you are certain
to get your season wrong somewhere. It is not so bad for me
as it is for some people, because I rather prefer the wet and am
reconciled to the climate. Now a person with a predilection for
dry seasons has an awful life of it, and I must in justice remark
that this predilection is the sane one to possess. I know
an American gentleman, who " 'lowed he'd do West Africa,"
but ultimately " 'lowed West Africa had done him," who got
so bothered by the different times different seasons were going
on in different parts of the Coast that he characterised the
entire West African climate as "a fried eel." Why fried I do
not know. We do not fry in the Coast climate, we stew,—
and I consider the statement harsh. Of course we have got
the worst climate in the world and we are proud of it. Some
day I will write a work in ten volumes that will be an ABC
of the whole affair, and be what my German friends would call
the essential pocket-book for West African travellers, and it
will let them know what to expect, when, where, and how ; but
meantime I may note that both wet and dry seasons have
their points. If you want to go far up a river, without
having ample opportunities of studying the various ways in
which your craft can get wrecked on sandbanks, you must go
in the full wet. Of course this ends in your returning, or
attempting to return in the dry, and as when you have penetrated the interior any distance you usually start on your
return journey full tilt, pursued by rapacious and ferocious
cannibals, the fact that you stick on sandbanks on an
average three times in a mile, gives you considerable worry.
If you wish to penetrate the interior on foot, you must choose
the dry season because of those swamps—a good bottomless
swamp is impassable in the wet. In the dry it bears a crust
over it, which, with suitable precautions, can be crossed, while
the shallow swamps can be waded. And all the rivers are

navigable in canoes in the dry, if too shallow for steamers, and canoes are the most comfortable things to travel in in the whole world. The predilection in favour of small steam launches is to me a mystery. What joy any sane person can have in one, who is not in a hurry, I do not know. I have had some experience in them, and some of those ex-periences have been the worst I have gone through. I remember one occasion when I tried to get a little launch through a creek which was, al-though deep, full of water grass. Well! I will be careful, but it was enough to make my distin-guished Liverpool friends use bad language. You see you could not get the screw to work because of the grass. Attempts at using the screw merely made the poor thing into a chaff cutter, and it was not made for that, so choked. You could not get up a sail, because there was no wind sufficiently strong to get through the grass, which towered in a dense mass some ten feet above your funnel. You

A GIANTESS OF THE UPPER OGOWÉ.

could not row or paddle, because of the said grass, and you could not get out and walk or tow because the water was too deep. I should like to have the situation put as a problem at a nautical examination. The only solution I found to it was to get two brawny blacks with matchets in the bows to cut a way for her, and the rest of the crew to pull her forward by catching hold of the grass ahead.

If any one can suggest a better I shall be only too delighted, for it was laborious work, and these choice spots are anything but uncommon in West African rivers. Then I remember another steam lanch—the *Dragon Fly*. She had been built for coal, but there was no coal, so she had to burn wood. Wood, as my nautical friends would say, blows a ship out, and to store enough wood to go twenty miles you had to have wood billets everywhere ; all over the deck, and on top of the sun-deck, &c., to such an extent that there was no room for you, and the gunwale was nearly awash. Then you always got on a sandbank, several sandbanks, so the wood got burnt right up before you got anywhere you wanted to, and you had to return by the current and the help of poles. If I had been bound to go on in her, we must have spent the greater part of our lives wood-chopping in wet forests ; but I am of too nervous a disposition to penetrate the interior on the *Dragon Fly* with her dilapidated boiler.

Then there was a patent launch that progressed theoretically by the explosion of small quantities of gunpowder ; but the trade powder we had did not suit her somehow, so she pursued a policy of masterly inactivity, making awesome noises in her works, and the quickest trip she ever did was to the bottom. And she certainly did make that on trade powder. I own I am prejudiced against launches. The heat of the West Coast climate is quite enough for me without having a large hot water bottle, in the shape of a boiler, to sit by. And a canoe is a craft you can take almost anywhere, and is therefore better for general work, unless you have a good deep channel large enough for you to have a steamer of a respectable size.

In addition to grass creeks and sandbanks, the obstacles to the navigation of side streams, on the Ogowé and its neighbouring rivers are swamps of papyrus, exceedingly lovely, but difficult to get through, and great floating masses of river lettuce (*Pistia stratiotes*). It is very like a nicely grown cabbage lettuce, and it is very charming when you look down a creek full of it, for the beautiful tender green makes a perfect picture against the dark forest that rises from the banks of the creek. If you are in a canoe, it gives you little apprehension to know you have got to go through it, but if you are in a small steam launch, every atom of pleasure in its beauty goes, the moment you lay eye on the thing. You dash into it as hard as you can go, with a sort of geyser of lettuces flying up from the screw; but not for long, for this interesting vegetable grows after the manner of couch-grass.

I used to watch its method of getting on in life. Take a typical instance: a bed of river-lettuces growing in a creek become bold, and grow out into the current, which tears the

UPPER OGOWÉ NATIVES.

outsider pioneer lettuce off from the mat. Down river that young thing goes, looking as innocent as a turtle-dove. If you pick it up as it comes by your canoe and look underneath, you see it has just got a stump. Roots? Oh dear no! What does a sweet green rose like that want roots for? It only wants to float about on the river and be happy; so you put the precious humbug back, and it drifts away with a smile and gets up some suitable quiet inlet and then sends out roots galore longitudinally, and at every joint on them buds up another lettuce; and if you go up its creek eighteen months or so after, with a little launch, it goes and winds those roots round your propeller. The fierce current of the wet season, when the main river scours into the creeks, and the creeks start fierce currents of their own with their increased waters, play great havoc with these lettuce beds, and plots of them get cut off from the main bodies. These plots float off down river, and as soon as they get into a bit of slack water or hitch on a rising sandbank, they collect all other floating things that come their way and start as islands. The grass soon chokes off its companion the lettuce, and makes the island habitable for other plants ; and so you have a floating island. These floating islands have a weird fascination, and I never saw so many of them in any river as in the Ogowé. To see a bit of seeming solid land, solemnly going past you down the river, as if it were out on business ; or if it is in tidal ways and you on a fixed point, to see it coming up to you, hanging about, and then retiring, is unsettling to one's general ideas of the propriety of nature. One of the largest of these floating islands I saw, was in the Karkola River. It had got caught in an eddy made by another stream entering this river, and it kept swimming round and round slowly and quietly.

I have not here given an account of half the difficulties of navigating a tropical river in the forest-region, because they are so numerous, and so many of them not to be guarded against. Those logs which from their specific gravity float down just under water and strike you unexpectedly ; and even those logs that float on the surface, are nasty things to meet on an ink-black night. I well remember the miscellaneous joys we happened on once when dropping down the Ogowé in the dark in a small canoe. Half the way it was a steeplechase for the canoe over floating logs. Sometimes she refused her fences point-blank and butted them ; sometimes she would climb up them and fall over on the other side ; and even my experienced native companion owned that it was difficult to tell, during the subsequent aquatic sports which her crew indulged in, which was the bottom of the canoe and which was the unsophisticated log. Sometimes she would clear her log-fence at a bound in a showy way, but then when she came down the other side, she went too deep and filled herself and foundered, and so the only thing was to pole the logs off. Some of those logs, by the by, had queer ways with them. One, on being poked on the end as it floated towards, us opened its front section and bit the pole with such a grip that the man using it let go all one time. Yes, I dare say it was a crocodile —still African vegetation is a queer thing.

You would naturally think that, in spite of sandbanks with cliff-edges down stream, of sections of the continent floating round, and of logs liable to bite and not liable to bite, you had at least one thing left to rely on—the bank. But that bank may be all right, and again, as the captain of the late ss. *Sparrow* would say, it mayn't. A friend of mine, for example, who got stuck in a launch up a river-creek on a sandbank, got a hawser out, and winding it round some mangroves on the bank, proceeded " to have her off in no time " with the steam winch. She did not budge an inch, but the African continent did: the whole bit of bank came away, and down on the boat came the trees with a swish, burying everything and everybody in branches and foliage. As he said, we were " like the babes in the wood after robins had been along, on a big scale "; and he also stated, as we climbed up on top of our arboreal superstructure, that " Africa was a rotten continent."

CHAPTER XVII

THE LOG OF THE *LAFAYETTE*

During a voyage undertaken to the island of Corisco, to which is added some account of the present condition of the island and its inhabitants, and also of that of Cape Esterias and things in general, as is customary with the author.

As soon as I returned to Glass I naturally went to discourse with Doctor Nassau on Fetish. We discoursed, I may mention, at length and to my advantage. In one of these talks the doctor mentioned that there were lakes in the centre of the Island of Corisco, and that in those lakes were quantities of fish, which fish were always and only fished by the resident ladies, at duly appointed seasons. Needless to say, I felt it a solemn duty to go and investigate personally; and equally needless to say, Doctor Nassau gave me every assistance, which took the form of lending me a small vessel called the *Lafayette*. She had been long in his possession, but of late years little used, still she was a fine seaworthy boat, so with a crew headed by the Doctor's factotum, Eveke, who was a native of the said island, together with a few friends of his, we set sail.

Left Libreville at 8 A.M. so as to get full advantage of wind and tide. Doctor Nassau kindly comes along the wharf to see us clear away. We then make for the guard-ship, to pass our papers, and do this in an unyachtsmanlike way, lowering our gaff too soon, hence have ignominiously to row alongside. The off-shore breeze blows strong this morning and the tide is running out like a mill-race, so the *Lafayette* flies seaward

gallantly, Libreville looks very bright and pleasing—with its
red roofs and white walls amongst the surrounding wealth of
dark green mango trees ; but we soon leave it behind, passing
along in front of the low, rolling hills, all densely clad with
forests, out to Cape Clara, or Cape Joinville as some maps will
have it—the end of the northern shore of the Gaboon
estuary. When we get to the Cape we find a pretty fair sea
running, and Eveke, whose seamanship I am beginning to
view with suspicion, lets her gybe, and I get knocked into
the bottom of the boat by the boom, and stay there. There
is nothing like entering into the spirit of a thing like this if
you mean to enjoy it, and after all that's the wisest thing to
do out here, for there's nothing between enjoying it and dying
of it. The sun is broiling hot ; everything one has got to sit
on or catch hold of is as hot as a burning brick, and there is
no cabin, nor even locker, on our craft ; so I prop myself up
against my collecting-box and lazily take stock of the things
round me, and write.

My crew are a miscellaneous lot of M'pongwe, black but
not comely. One gentleman, however, evidently thinks he is,
as he has a beautiful pair of carefully tended whiskers, rare
adjuncts to the African. He also has a pair of kerseymere
trousers, far too tight for him ; but a man with whiskers "all
same for one with white man" must dress the part, and
trousers are scarce in this country. Our cargo consists of two
bags of salt, several bags and boxes of sand for ballast, several
bottles of water for drinking, a bundle of bedding—a loan from
the Doctor, and a deck chair—a loan from Mr. Hudson. Owing
to the *Lafayette* having no deck, the latter is "not required
on the voyage," and is folded up. I observe with anxiety that
the cargo is not stowed in a manner that would meet with the
approval of Captain Murray, and decide to get dunnage and
do it in style the first port we call at. Can't possibly shift
cargo in this sea. The crew drink the water in such quantities
that there will be an ocean tragedy if we get becalmed. We
run along close in shore from Cape Clara to Cape Esterias—a
fine, sandy, rock-strewn shore, backed by a noble bush—for
eight miles. The land falls away then, for Esterias is the
southernmost point of Corisco Bay. Close to Cape Esterias

I see the familiar bark-built village that betokens Fans, and on sighting this we change our course and lay one apparently for the Brazilian ports.

The *Lafayette* flies along before a heavy sea, and from my position at the bottom of her I can see nothing but her big white mainsail and her mast with its shrouds and stays standing out clear, rocking to and fro, against the hard blue sky; and just the white crests of the waves as they go dancing by. I have nothing to hear save the pleasantest sounds in the world—the rustle of the sail and the swish of the waves as they play alongside the vessel. Now and then there is added to these the lazy, laughing talk of the black men; and now and then an extra lively wave throws its crest in among us. Soon all the crew drop softly off to sleep, Eveke joining them, so I rouse up and take the main sheet and the tiller and keep her so. I feel as if I were being baked to a cinder, but there's no help for it, and some of it is very pleasant. About four o'clock I see two lumps of land on the sky-line. I wake Eveke up and he seems surprised at my not knowing what they are. " That's Corisco and Banã, sir," says he. I explain to Eveke, as I hand over the navigation to him, that every one has not been born on Corisco, and the fact of his having had this advantage is the reason of his being pilot now ; and I reseat myself in the bottom of the boat and carefully look over the side, mindful of that boom palaver. We head for the bigger and most western bit of land, soon seeing the details of its undulating, black-green forests. When we get within a mile, Eveke asks me to wake up the man in front of me, and I stir him firmly, but gently, with a chart ; for I know what waking black men leads to sometimes ; and when he rouses I order him to wake up the others, and in a few minutes they are all more or less awake, even the man on the look-out. They wash their mouths out with sea-water, and then re-commence their laughing, talking and water-drinking again.

We run into a small, sandy-shored, wooded bay where, as I find is Eveke's habit, we lower our gaff prematurely and drift, in the proper way, leisurely towards the above, stern foremost. At last the *Lafayette*, finding everything is left to her, says : " Look here, you fellows, if you don't help

I won't play," and stops and commences to swing broadside on. So the oars—or sweeps I should call them, for we have evidently returned to fourteenth century seamanship—are got out and in a few minutes we are bumping violently on the strand. We let go the anchor, make all snug and go ashore. When ashore, of course with the exception of myself and the pilot, the crew indulge in a dance to stretch their cramped limbs. As no inhabitants turn up, Eveke runs up into the little village that fronts us and hunts a few out, who come and stare at us in a woolly stupid way, very different from my friends, the vivacious Fans. Eveke has tremendous greetings with them—particularly with the young ladies. He hastily informs me that he is related to them. I hope he is. He says most of the people are away at the farms—which is not an affliction to me, for Eveke wastes enough time on those we have got, and they seem to me a churlish lot for Africans. The only question they ask us is : Have we any tobacco ? Corisco is nearly out of tobacco, owing to the weather having been too rough of late for them to get across either to Eloby, or Cocco Beach, where the factories are, for more. They are gratified by our affirmative answer, and sit down, in a line, on a large log, and beam at us in a subdued way, while we get the things we want off the *Lafayette* and finish securing her for the night. This being done, Eveke and I go off to his father's house—his father, the Rev. Mr. Ibea, being the sole representative of the American Presbyterian mission now on Corisco Island.

I have heard much of the strange variety of scenery to be found on this island : how it has, in a miniature way, rivers, lakes, forests, prairies, swamps and mountains ; and our walk demonstrates to me the baldness of the truth of the statement. The tide being now nearly in, we cannot keep along the beach all the way, which is a mercy—for the said beach is, where it is dry, of the softest, whitest sand imaginable ; where it is wet, of the softest, pink-dove-coloured sand, and it is piled with fresh, rotting, and rotten seaweed into which, at every step, you sink over your ankles in an exhausting way, and on the surface of which you observe centipedes crawling, and, needless to say, sandflies galore. When we come to a point of any one of the many little bays or indentations in the coast-line where the sea is breaking, we clamber up the bank and turn inland, still ankle deep in sand, and go through this museum of physical geography.   First a specimen of grass land, then along a lane of thickly pleached bush, then down into a wood with a little (at present) nearly dried up swamp in its recesses ; then up out on to an open heath which has recently been burnt and is covered with dead bracken and scorched oil palms ; then through a village into grass again, and back to the beach to plough our way through seaweed across another bay ; then round some remarkable rocks, up into a wood, then grass, and more bush and more beach, and up among a cluster of coco-palms, more grass ; and then a long stretch of path with one side of it a thick hedge which is encroaching in a way that calls for energetic lopping, for the bush leans so across the path that you also have to lean at an angle of nearly 45° towards the other side.   I begin to despair, my boots being full of sand, and to fear we shall never get through the specimens before nightfall.   There is such an air of elaborate completeness about this museum, and we have not even com- menced the glacier or river departments.   However, at length we see what seems to be the entrance to an English park, and coming up to this find a beautiful avenue of mango trees.

Corisco evidently feels the dry season severely.   The dry sandy soil is thickly strewn with dead leaves.   At the end of the avenue there is a pretty wooden house, painted white, with its doors and window-frames painted a bold bright blue. Around it are a cluster of outbuildings like it, each mounted on poles, the little church, the store, and the house for the children in the mission school.   A troop of children rush out and greet Eveke effusively.   One of them, I am informed, is his brother, and he commences to bubble out conversation in Benga.   I send Eveke off to find his mother, thinking he will like to get his greetings with her over unobserved, and after a few minutes she comes forward to greet me,—a pretty, bright- looking lady whom it is hard to believe old enough to be Eveke's mother ; and not only Eveke's but the mother of a lot of strapping young women who come forward with her, and the grandmother of other strapping young women mixed up among them. I must really try and find out which is which. Until I do so perhaps it will be diplomatic to regard them all as her daughters. Mrs. Ibea insists, in the kindliest way possible, on my taking possession of her own room. Mr. Ibea is away, she says, on an evangelising visit to the mainland at Cape St. John (the northern extremity of Corisco Bay), intending to call at Eloby Island ; so he may not be here for some days, and she promptly gives me tea and alligator pears, both exceedingly welcome.

The views from the windows of my clean and comfortable room are very beautiful. The house stands on a high promontory called Alondo Point, the turning point of the south and west sides of the island, and almost overhangs the sea. A reef of rock runs out at the foot of the cliff for about a mile, on which the sea breaks constantly. The great rollers of the South Atlantic, meeting here their first check since they left Cape Horn and the Americas, fly up in sheets of foam with a never-ending thunder. I go to bed early, thankfully observing that the gay mosquito curtain is entirely " for dandy "— decorative and not defensive.

The obtaining of specimens of fish from the lakes in the centre of the island being my main object in visiting Corisco, I set to work by starting immediately after breakfast to the bay that we came to last night, and which I will call Nassau Bay in future. I go along the same variegated path I came by yesterday. Eveke has slept at the village in the Bay among his relatives so as to keep an eye, he says, on the *Lafayette*. When I find him, he says that only women can catch the lake fish, and that they always catch them in certain baskets, and as these have to be made they cannot be ready to-day. Having heard Corisco is famous for shells, and having seen nothing on any of the many beaches on the southern side of the island more conchologically charming than half a dozen dilapidated whelks, I ask where the main deposits of shells are. Eveke says there is any quantity of them on the other little islands, Laval to the south, and Baña to the S.E. in Corisco Bay. To his horror I say I will go to those islands now, and we get our scattered crew together and

the *Lafayette* under way, and run across first to some sandbanks, whose heads are exposed at low water—beautiful
stretches of dove-coloured sand, but apparently not even a
whelk as far as shells go. Up through the sand are sticking
thousands of little white tubes, apparently empty ; but after a
few minutes,—having parted· from the riot of the crew and
quietness reigning—I find, when the sand is wetted by the
foam, some lovely little sea anemones looking out of the tops
of the tubes. After a time I rejoin the crew and find they
have dug out a few olive and harp shells, but nothing remarkable ; and I hurt Eveke's feelings by saying I consider Corisco,
as a collecting ground for shells, a fraud. He assures me
solemnly that in the wet season, which has calmer seas than
the dry, when the sun comes out and shines upon the
exposed sandbanks, they are covered with thousands of shells,
but from his description I think they are mostly olives. We
go across from the sandbank to Laval, a little rock island
with a patch of bush on its summit, and from its edges
—the size does not run to shores—I get some sponges. Then
on to Baña, a larger island, which has a population of rats
only, from whence it is sometimes called Rat Island—but I
get no more shells. Before I get back to Corisco, Eveke
solemnly assures me that the women with their fishing baskets
will be ready to-morrow early.

Get up and hurry off early to Nassau Bay. Women not
ready. Wait for two hours sitting on the steps of a native's
house, which is built in the European style, and situated across
the top of the village. There are two other houses like this one,
I notice, between here and Alondo, each ostentatiously placed
across the street. At last Eveke comes and says, " The
women make trouble. They no get the baskets ready to-day ;
they have them ready to-morrow for sure, but not to-day."
Internally blessing Eveke and the ladies, I go to see how the
world is made along the southern shores of the island—along the
dove-coloured sand, hedged on my right hand by the spray wall
of the surf, and on the left by low-growing bushes, flowering
profusely with long sprays of intensely sweet-scented, white
mimosa-like flower. Behind these rises the high bush of one
of the miniature forests. Every now and then I pass a path

to some native village, which, though hidden behind the trees, has its existence betrayed by the canoes, three or four of them drawn high up out of the reach of the surf under a group of coco-palms, which, as a general rule, stand as a gateway to these paths. About a mile along, perhaps a little more, the point runs out which makes the eastern end of Nassau Bay, the largest bay on this southern side of the island, and the only reasonably safe anchorage on all Corisco's shores. This point is composed of similar rock to that which juts out and forms the western end of this bay.[1] The rocks are exceedingly strange and picturesque. The surf play has hollowed them out underneath, until the upper part overhangs like a snow cornice ; and in several places masses of rock jut out beyond the others, weathered into strange forms, looking wonderfully like the heads of great lizard and serpent monsters stretched out, gazing towards the mainland of Africa. Some of these points of rock have trees growing along the neck of them, looking like a bristling mane. The under part of the rock is eaten back into a concavity, and in this again are eaten out groups of caves, a network of them intercommunicating in places, and pillars of rock rising in them from floor to ceiling. In the floor are perfectly lovely, clear pools of sea-water ; the rock in which they are hollowed out is a soft gray-green, and some zoophyte of an exquisite bright mauve or pink-violet colour grows in a broad band round the upper edge ; and in the water, lambent with the light reflected from the roof, float in a tangled skein the seaweeds—the softest, sweetest commingling of golden-browns, greens, and reds imaginable. These little caves are gems of beauty, and nothing but becoming suddenly aware that the tide is rapidly coming in, makes me tear myself away and return across the bay, past where the *Lafayette* lies anchored, towards Alondo. After a mile over this trying track of rotten seaweed, on going round a little point, I find a lot of wild, uncivil children, who yell and dance round me half-terrified, but wholly malignant. They spit at me and shout, " Frenchy no good," " Frenchy no good," in English, such as it is, and equally broken Spanish. At first I think, Well ! France is no business of mine ; but I

---

[1] Specimen identified by the Geological Survey as calcareous grit.

instantly receive a severe rap on my moral knuckles from my conscience, which tells me that as I chose to place myself under the protection of the French flag above Njole, and a great protection it undoubtedly was, I must, in my turn, protect it from insult when it flies on the *Lafayette* in foreign waters. Moreover, the blood of the Vikings that is in me gets up on its own account at such treatment, and I make up my mind to suitably correct those children forthwith, particularly a male albino about fourteen years old, who is clad in the remains of an antique salt sack, which he wears unaltered, inverted over him. Unfortunately, holes have been roughly cut in the bottom and sides of it to let out his unnecessary head and arms; but at this identical moment I catch sight of a sweet-looking nun doing needle-work as she sits on the rocks. I go up to her and pass compliments, but do not complain to her about her flock, because she must be perfectly aware how they are going on, and secondly I am sure she is too meek to deal with them, even if she disapproves. Moreover, my knowledge of Spanish consists almost entirely of expressions of thanks and greetings—expressions which you are most in need of when dealing with Spaniards, as a general rule. So, finding she knows no English, I bow myself off and go my way round the rocky point that forms the end of another shallow bay, looking ostentatiously tired and feeble. Round that rocky point after me come the yelling pack led by the albino, and there things happen to those children that cause them to prefer the nun's company to mine. I make my way on, and to my dismay find the sea flying and churning up in a roaring rock cauldron at the extremity of the next point, so that I cannot get past. There is no path up inland that I can reach without passing the place where I have left the nun sitting. I feel naturally shy about doing this because of the male albino having gone off leaving his sack with me, and I do not know the Spanish idiom for " Please, ma'am, it came off in my hand;" though doubtless this idiom exists, for there are parlour-maids and wine-glasses in Spain, and I am sure they employ this phrase every time when, in washing a wine-glass, they have gripped one end like a vice and wrung the other off. And not the albino alone has got out of repair this

side of the rock, for neither that promising young lady who
spat in my face, nor the one who threw sand in my eyes are
what they were this morning.   There is nothing for it then
but the dwarf cliff; so I climb it and get into the bush and
try and strike a path.   I get into a plantain plantation,
which means there is a village close at hand, and on the
further side I come into a three-hut one, and find a
most amiable old lady sunning herself in the centre of
it.   Unfortunately she does not know any English, but I shed
a box of lucifer matches on her, wishing to show that I
mean well, and knowing that one of the great charms of a
white man to a black is this habit of shedding things.   It is
their custom to hang round one in their native wilds in the
hope something will be shed, either intentionally or uninten-
tionally.   Not, I fancy, for the bald sake of the article itself,
but from a sort of sporting interest in what the next thing
shed will be.   I know it is my chief charm to them, and
they hang round wondering whether it will be matches,
leaf tobacco, pocket-handkerchiefs, or fish-hooks ; and when
the phenomena flag they bring me various articles for sale
to try to get me into working order again.   My present
old lady is glad of her matches and they brighten up her
intelligence, and she begins to understand I want something.
After experimenting on me with a bunch of plantains and
a paw-paw unsuccessfully, she goes and fetches a buxom young
woman who soon comprehends I want Mrs. Ibea's house, and
instantly she and the old lady escort me down a grass path
and through some galleries of specimens of physical geography.
We are soon joined by two pretty young girls, and wind our
way back to the shore again on the further side of the point
that had driven me inland.   The elders then take themselves
off after a mutual interchange of compliments and thanks ;
the young women come on with me.   Mighty pretty pictures
they make with their soft dusky skins, lithe, rounded figures,
pretty brown eyes, and surf-white teeth showing between their
laughing lips as they dance before me ; and I cannot help
thinking what a comfort they would be to a shipwrecked
mariner and how he would enjoy it all.

On we go, climbing round every rocky point until we

find the tide too far in for any more beach at all, and strike into an inland path. These Corisco paths require understanding to get on with. They all seem to start merely with the intention of taking you round a headland because the tide happens to be in ; but, like all African paths, once they are started Allah or Sheitan only knows where they will go, and their presiding spirits might quote Kipling and sing, " God knows where we shall go, dear lass, and the deuce knows what we shall see," to the wayfarer who follows them. One thing and one thing only you can safely prognosticate of the African path ; and that is that it will not follow the shortest line between any two given points. A Corisco one turns up off the beach, springs inland saying to you, "Want to go round that corner, do you ? Oh ! well ; just come and see some of our noted scenery while you are here," and takes you through a miniature forest, small swamp, and a prairie. " It's a pity," says the path, " not to call at So-and-so's village now we are so near it," and off you have to go through a patch of grass and a plantation to the village. " We must hurry up and get back to that beach again. Blessed if I hadn't nearly forgotten what I came out for ! " it continues ; and back on to the beach it plunges, landing you about fifty yards from the place where you left it on account of the little headland.

At last we reach Alondo, and I give my guides buttons, reels of cotton, pocket-handkerchiefs, fish-hooks, and matches, and we part friends ; they to show their treasures in their village, and to give rise to the hope that I may get lost on Corisco again, soon and often, I to tea and talk with Mrs. Ibea. I tell her Eveke had said in the forenoon, when I last saw him, that he was coming home in the evening ; but he does not turn up and his mother says she "expects he is courting his mother-in-law." Regarding this as probably a highly interesting piece of native custom, in the interests of Science, I prop open my sleepy eyelids and listen. After all it isn't—but only a piece of strange native morality. His lady-love, it seems, is house-keeper to a man on the mainland who is always talking of leaving the district but doesn't do so, so the marriage gets perpetually postponed. I hope that man won't try the patient

affection of the engaged pair too long, for I should fancy it
might lead to some internal disorder.

I heard a quantity of details of Corisco family affairs—
one very sad one, of how a young man who was a native
trader for one of the German houses up the Cameroons
River, came to his death a short time ago. The firm had
decided to break factory at the place where he was stationed,
a thing the natives of this country cannot bear ; for having a
factory that has once been established among them removed,
brings them into derision and contempt among their neighbours. " You're a pretty town," say the scornful. " You can't
keep a factory. Yah ! " Moreover, a factory in a town is an
amusement and a convenience, let alone being lucrative to the
native. Well, this unfortunate young Benga man was left
behind by the white men to see the last of the goods cleared
out and brought down river; and while he was faithfully looking
to these things, the local natives attacked him and killed him
and " cut him up like a fish into small pieces and threw them
into the water," says Mrs. Ibea. These native sub-traders
have very risky lives of it, travelling undefended, with goods,
amongst the savage tribes on this South-West Coast. They
frequently get killed and robbed, and the only thing that
keeps them from not being so treated still more frequently is
that the commercial instinct of the bush tribes warns them
that it would completely stamp out trade. In Corisco Bay
the river Muni, a name given it by the Portuguese early
navigators from the native word for " take care," is notoriously
unsafe—all the more so because there is no settled European
authority over it, France and Spain being at loggerheads about
the ownership of the piece of coast from Cape Esterias to
Batta. This had doubtless a good deal to do with those
children's conduct this afternoon ; for Corisco Island and Eloby
Islands are Spanish possessions, and are under a Vice-
Governor to the Governor of Fernando Po. I remember
when I was out before, being led to believe that the Vice-
Governorship of Eloby was a sort of pensioning-off place for
Spanish officials who had gone mad, or that it was held by
London County Councillors in disguise. One of the Vice-
Governors was truly great at domestic legislation, and nothing

but the habit of forgetting in a day or so the orders he had issued made the place habitable at all.   At one time there was an ordinance that all lights on the island should be out at 10 P.M., and as your African is a sad dog for late hours, this bored him terribly.   Shortly after, there was another that all goats should be kept tied up.   This fairly ran the native off his legs trying to catch them.   The goats, I believe, liked it, regarding it as a kind of a game, though they made an awful ba-aaing which kept the lightless Africans awake.   I do not know what the present Governor is like.   Maybe he would have seen fit to regard me as a filibuster coming in flying the French flag, intent on annexing Corisco to Gaboon, and might have sent me off to prison at Fernando Po, as happened to Mr. Ibea once for some religious palaver he got into with the two Catholic priests who are on the island.

These priests, and I believe three nuns, are the only white live people on the island now.   Dead white people are there in the two cemeteries in a sad quantity ; for in the early fifties, when the American Presbyterian Mission opened work on this Coast, their opinion was that the fever risk for the white ministers would be less on this island, separated as it is by some twenty miles of sea from the mainland, and that they could establish a station on it and live in comparative safety, while they educated natives to go and do the work on the mainland.   But Corisco Island behaved like every other West Coast " sanatorium," and demonstrated that it was no healthier than its neighbouring country ; and several ministers having died and most of the remainder suffering severely from fever, they decided to move on to the continent, where they could carry on their work directly and could not be much worse off than they were on the island.

Dr. Nassau, of whom I have already spoken, and Mrs. Hog-den, whose husband lies buried on Corisco, are the surviving members of the early days of the American Presbyterian Mission ; and on the Mission moving to the continent, the Doctor, *more suo*, made some wonderful journeys hundreds of miles into the interior, where no white man had been before, and where in many places no white man has been since.   I am quite aware that Dr. Nassau was the first white man to send home

gorillas' brains ; still I deeply regret he has not done more for
science and geography.   Had he but had Livingstone's conscientious devotion to taking notes and publishing them,
we should know far more than we do at present about the
hinterland from Cameroons to the Ogowé, and should have, for
ethnological purposes, an immense mass of thoroughly reliable
information about the manners and religions of the tribes
therein, and Dr. Nassau's fame would be among the greatest
of the few great African explorers—not that he would care a
row of pins for that.   I beg to state I am not grumbling at
him, however, as I know he would say I was, because of his
disparaging remarks on my pronunciation of M'pongwe
names, but entirely from the justifiable irritation a student of
fetish feels at knowing there is but one copy of this collection
of materials, and that that copy is in the form of a human
being and will disappear with him before it is half learnt by
us, who cannot do the things he has done.

Get up very early, make a hasty breakfast, and walk to
Nassau Bay, full of pleasant anticipations of a day's good fishing in those lakes.   When I arrive at the village find I need
not have hurried, so sit down for my usual wait.

At last Eveke, who has been making demonstrations of
great activity in getting the ladies under way, succeeds in
so doing—or, I fancy, more properly speaking, those ladies
who are ready, and disposed to start on their own account,
do so.   Several men accompany the party and we leave the
village by a path that goes round to the right of the plank-
built house, plunges forthwith into a little ravine, goes across
a dried swamp, up a hill and out on to an open prairie, all in
about twenty minutes.   The prairie has recently been burnt,
and is a stretch of blackened green with the ruins of a few
singed, or burnt up, trees rising from it.

These burnt lands are interesting, though they make one in
a horrid mess.   I now understand the *rationale* of the statement the natives have often made to me ; namely, that if you
fire the grass too soon, or when there is no wind, you kill it for
good.   If you wait until it is " dry too much " it is all right
and you don't kill it.   This is because the grass grows in a
lot of bulb-like bottom tufts ; when the outer and upper parts

are quite dry it catches fire and, fanned by the wind, the fire licks this up and sweeps on with great rapidity, leaving the moist heart of the tuft comparatively uninjured ; and this sends out fresh green leaves when the wet season's tornado rain comes down on it. Whereas if you burn it too soon, and without wind, the outer stuff, being insufficiently dry to burn with this rapidity, smoulders, and the heat of it lasting longer, kills the inside.

Some of the low-growing, bamboo-like palms act in the same way; but should there happen to be a lot of dry grass, or their own dry cast-off leaves round them, close up to the stem, their vital part just above the root gets injured, and they die or make very bad convalescences. I do not know whether it is so in Corisco, but at other places where I have been there is always a fire-doctor, who by means of ju-ju, backed as ju-ju often is by sound common sense and local knowledge, decides which is the proper day to set the grass on fire.

We go across this prairie into a little wood mainly made up of beautiful wild fig-trees, with their muscles showing through the skin like our own beech-trees' muscles do, only the wild fig stem is whitish-grey and most picturesquely twisted and branching. Then out of this on to another prairie, larger and unburnt. During the whole of our walk from the village we have been yelling in prolonged, intoned howls for ladies, whose presence is necessary to the legitimate carrying on of our fishing—lady representatives of each village being expected to attend and see the fish are properly divided. I cannot find there is any fetish at the bottom of this custom, and think its being restricted to the women is originally founded on the male African's aversion to work ; and in the representation of the villages, on the Africans' distrust of each other.

Notably, and grievously, we howl for En-gou-ta-a-a and Engouta comes not ; so we throw ourselves down on the deliciously soft, fine, golden brown grass, in the sun, and wait for the tardy, absent ones, smoking, and laughing, and sleeping, and when any of the avocations palls on any of us we rise up and howl " Engouta." After about two mortal hours of this, and when my companions have for some time settled down, quite reconciled, to sleep peacefully, I hear a crackle-crackle-like fusillade of miniature guns.   Looking towards the place whence the sound comes I notice a cloud of bright blue smoke surmounting a rapidly advancing wall of crimson fire.   I get up and mention this fact briefly to my drowsy companions, adding in the case of the more profound sleepers an enlightening kick, and make an exemplary bee-line to the bush in front of us.   The others follow my example with a rapidity I should not have expected in their tribe, but, in spite of some very creditable and spirited sprint performances, three members of the party get scorched and spent the balance of the afternoon sitting in mud-holes, comforting themselves with the balmy black slime.

The fire swept across our bit of the prairie in the line of the breeze, and died out when it came to the green wood in a very short time ; and shortly afterwards the absent ones, including Engouta, turn up.   These ladies explained "some fool man been done burn " a patch on the other side to plant manioc. The whole island is busy planting now before the rains come on.   Some days ago he thought the fire was out, and safe, but it wasn't, and the stiff breeze fanned it up.   " People should be careful with fire," I say sententiously and they all agree with me, the scorched ones enthusiastically.

A little clamber down into the wood we are in brings us to the lakes.   There is a little chain of them—they are just basins in the rock strata of varying sizes, and each has a thick lining of black mud.   The water is at its lowest now, as it is the end of the dry season, and the water they contain is, I think, the accumulation of rain water from wet seasons.

As far as I can see there are no streams running into or out of them.   In the wet season probably there may be both. One of them the ladies refuse to fish in, saying it was too deep ; possibly being a deep crack in the rock like the one you see as you pass the enclosed grounds of the Catholic Mission at Evangelanda ; and I think they are prevented from evaporating, as that one does in the dry season, by being surrounded with the dense bush of this tangled little wood, which occupies the hollow of the interior of the island in which they are situated.

Even with this I believe they would dry, were the dry season the hot season, as it is on the Gold Coast. Most of these lakes have an encircling rim of rock, from which, if you are a fisher, you jump down into unmitigated black slime to your knees ; you then waddle, and squatter, and grunt, and sky-lark generally, to the shallow remnant of water. If it is one of the larger lakes, you and your companions drive in two rows of stakes, cutting each other at right angles, more or less, in the centre of the lake.

This being done, the women, with the specially made baskets—affairs shaped like bed-pillows with one side open—form a line with their backs towards the banks, their faces to the water, in the enclosure ; the other women go into the water by the stakes, and splash with hands and feet and sticks as hard as they can, needless to say shouting hard the while. The terrified fish fly from them into the baskets, and are scooped up by the peck. In little basins of water the stakes are not required, but the rest of the proceedings are the same, some women standing with their backs to the bank, holding their baskets' mouths just under water, and scooping up the fish flying from the beaters in the middle.

From twelve to fourteen bushels is the usual result of the day's fishing, and the fish are divided between the representatives and distributed among the villages. A tremendous fish dinner ensues in the evening, and what fish are left are smoked and kept as relishes and dainties until next fishing time comes round.

I was told on the island that this fishing takes place every year in August, that is after the farm planting and just before the tornado rains come on. On the mainland the tradition is that it takes place here every two years, in August. I dare say this was the case in old days ; although, by the way, I heard that this regular institution of fishing with its representatives, &c., was of comparatively recent introduction, and arose from the fear that the fish, by irregular and constant fishing, would be exterminated. Corisco would not accept this view at all, and insisted that the fashion had come down from the old times, meaning it had an unlimited antiquity. But with all this formality, after all I had gone through, and all my

walks and waitings, those wretched fish were nothing and
nobody else but an African mud-fish, a brute I cordially hate,
for whenever I ask native fishermen for fish, they bring me
him, if I start catching fish for myself, nine times in ten it's
him I catch.   It was a bitter disappointment, for I had looked
forward to getting some strange fish, or strongly modified
form, in the middle of this little sea island, in fresh-water, some
twenty miles from the mainland shore.   But there! it's Africa all
over; presenting one with familiar objects when one least requires
them, like that razor in the heart of Gorilla-land; and un-
familiar, such as elephants and buffaloes when you are out for
a quiet stroll armed with a butterfly net, to say nothing of
snakes in one's bed and scorpions in one's boots and sponge.
One's view of life gets quite distorted; I don't believe I should
be in the least surprised to see a herd of hippo stroll on to the
line out of one of the railway tunnels of Notting Hill Gate
station.   West Africa is undoubtedly bad for one's mind.

I did not go completely round all the lakes, having to watch
the fishing, and at last, finding there was only this one kind of
fish to be had, and that it was getting late, I set off on my
weary, long walk back to Alondo, where I found on arriving that
Mrs. Ibea had got tea waiting for me, and that Mr. Ibea was back
from his evangelising mission to Cape St. John and Eloby.
He is a splendidly built, square-shouldered man, a pure Benga,
of the finest type, full of energy and enthusiasm.   I found
some difficulty in accepting his statement regarding the age
of Mrs. Ibea and himself, and I still think he stuck a good
ten years on.

His views on native social questions I had less difficulty in
accepting, more particularly those which coincide with my
own.   We talked about the Fan—the backbone of native,
and a good big factor in white conversation, all along here.

In this part of the world the descent of this great tribe is
ousting the older inhabitants of the land.   Mr. Ibea says that
one of the first white members of the American Presbyterian
Mission that came to this Coast some thirty years ago, made
a journey into the interior behind Batanga.   At the further
end of this journey he heard of the coming Fan, even then
in a state of migration westwards; and, from what he heard,

on his return to Corisco he prophesied that before another ten years were past they would have the Fan to deal with on the sea-coast districts. Natives and Europeans both laughed at him ; but before the ten years were past the Fans were over the border line of the M'pongwe and Igalwa, but the prophet was not alive to see the realisation of his prophecy. At this present time, the Fans are, in a few places, down by the sea-shore itself, busy learning how to manage a canoe on the open and deep sea—not yet so proficient in the art as the M'pongwe or Benga, who are great masters, but getting on well with their studies, for they are an indefatigable race, and plucky, which is the main element in any race's success. It is very evident to an observer that the Fans on the Ogowé are comparatively recent, and that when they came they brought with them no experience in dealing with a great rapid river ; but they tackle it in a game way, and are getting on. In addition to the causes of decay that the presence of the Fan among the Coast tribes brings into play, there are many others helping the extinction of the latter. It always seems to me a wonder we have so many traces of early man as we have, when one sees here in Africa how one tribe sweeps out another tribe that goes like the foam of a broken wave into the *Ewigkeit* before it, leaving nothing, after the lapse of a century, to show it ever existed.

Here the Dualla and the M'pongwe, both tribes now becoming on their own account extinct, have their traditions of having come down to the sea-board from nearly the same region from whence the Fan are now swarming. The inhabitants of Fernando Po, the so-called Bubi, probably the oldest race now on the sea-board, remember the coming of the M'pongwe too, for they say these M'pongwe drove them out of the districts round Gaboon. How long ago this happened it is impossible to say, owing to the absence of monuments, and the weak-mindedness of the African regarding time ; but I am sure, from many conversations, that you may place a limit of 500 years as the extreme one for the very oldest Negro or Bantu historical tradition. Indeed I doubt much whether any Bantu tradition would run to that ; I say historical, because the religious tradition may be of intense antiquity, being handed down from generation to generation unaltered for immense periods of time. The child would be told, for example, that a dangerous spirit lived in the rapids of a river, or lurked in the forest, which it would be advisable for him to keep an eye on, for his own safety. But who would trouble to tell him that a chief of such and such a name once lived there where the Engombie-Gombie trees have been shadowed down again by the great forest? The chief is dead. The village is dead, " palaver done set," so the historical tradition fades out like smoke.

Even the invasion of another tribe, like the Fans, for example, does not affect the religious tradition much. For it is not on the whole a war invasion : they come down in villagefuls among the older tribes, and hear the local spirit-gossip, and take it to their ample bosom, of belief, and pass the traditions on to their children. Meanwhile, the tribe that told them these things has moved West, away from them, because they have got the best bush places cleared and covered with their planta-tions, and they catch all the fish, and they get all the trade, and they eat respectable people occasionally, and steal from them continually, and they kick up such a noise, and have such perpetual rows among each other, and respectable villages belonging to the older tribe; that the older tribe has the opinion forced upon it, that no decent people can live near those filthy, fearful Fans, and so move nearer in to Lembarene or Libre-ville.

In addition to this cause of a tribe leaving its old districts, there are others which move tribes completely off earthly dis-tricts of any kind altogether : among these are the smallpox, and the sleep disease. The former is most common in Congo Français, where it receives the graphically descriptive name of " the spotted death " among the natives, the latter appears in its worst form in Kacongo and Angola, where whole villages are, at intervals, depopulated by it. The visitations of these maladies, indeed of all maladies in West Africa, take the form of epidemics, and seem periodic. I have collected much material, but not sufficient yet to make deductions from, as to the duration of the periods between the outbreaks. The natives all along the Coast from Calabar to the South will tell you : " It is when the crabs come up the river," which means when the crayfish come down the rivers; but that is just their artless, unobservant way of putting things. This swarming of the crayfish occurs about every five years, and for days the river-water is crowded with them, so that you can bale them out by basketfuls. This the native does, accompanying his operations with songs and tom-toms, and he then eats any quantity of them ; another quantity he smokes and preserves, in what he pleases to regard as a dried state, for sauce making ; and the greatest quantity of all he chucks in heaps to fester round his dwelling.

There are plenty more causes of the extinction of tribes besides these—so many in fact, that one gets to wonder that there are any Coast tribes of 100 years old or so left.

Mr. Ibea himself says that there are not now more than 2,000 of his own tribe left, and that those that are now representing it are far inferior, physically, to those he remembers as having seen as old men, when he was a boy.

These Benga were once an exceedingly powerful and proud tribe. Now they have little save their pride left. In old days they were very busy making war on their neighbours, elephant hunting, shipping themselves as crew to whaling vessels, and other people as slaves to slaving vessels, and so on. Great hands at the slave trade were these Benga, and slave-owners are they still ; but gone is their glory, and in a few years more the Benga will themselves have gone to join the shades of the tribes that were before them in this land, leaving behind them no sign, not even a flint arrow-head, to show that they ever existed ; for their wooden utensils and their iron weapons will rot like rag in the hot moist earth ; and then " finish."

Mr. Ibea and I got quite low about this. He agreed it was partially the Benga's own fault ; they had of late years taken to bad habits, he said ; amongst these to infant marriage. This struck me as strange, for as I have already mentioned, the also dying-out Igalwas have only recently adopted this custom. He says that forty years ago it was quite unknown among the Benga, and that in former days both men and women were frequently over fifteen and twenty before they married. Now the old men buy girl children, both as wives for themselves and for their infant sons. Then Mr. Ibea blamed the rum ; although he owned they had plenty of rum in the old prosperous whaling and slaving days. Indeed he said he thought the main reason of their extinction was the indolence that had come over the tribe, now these incentives to activity were gone ; for inactivity in Africa is death. He said, of course as a Christian minister, he knew it was for the best that the old warlike, bloodthirsty Benga spirit was broken, but—but well, I think he felt as I feel myself when I come across quantities of my fellow countrymen talking of the wickedness of war, and the necessity of checking our growing population, and so on ; only I feel it more than Mr. Ibea, for I am not a Christian minister and am more of a savage than he is.

Nothing strikes one so much, in studying the degeneration of these native tribes, as the direct effect that civilisation and reformation has in hastening it. The worst enemy to the existence of the African tribe, is the one who comes to it and says :—Now you must civilise, and come to school, and leave off all those awful goings-on of yours, and settle down quietly. The tribe does so ; the African is teachable and tractable ; and then the ladies and some of the young men are happy and content with the excitement of European clothes and frequent Church services ; but the older men and some of the bolder young men soon get bored with these things and the, to them, irksome restraints, and they go in for too much rum, or mope themselves to death, or return to their native customs. The African treats his religion much as other men do : when he gets slightly educated, a little scientific one might say, he removes from his religion all the disagreeable parts. He promptly eliminates its equivalent Hell, represented in Fetishism by immediate and not future retribution. Then goes his rigid Sabbath-keeping, and food-restriction equivalent, and he has nothing left but the agreeable portions : dances, polygamy, and so on; and it's a very bad thing for him. I only state these things so as to urge upon people at home the importance of combining technical instruction in their mission teaching ; which by instilling into the African mind ideas of discipline, and providing him with manual occupation, will save him from these relapses which are now the reproach of missionary effort, and the curse and degradation of the African. I do not feel sure that one must accept Mr. Ibea's opinion, and class infant marriage among the causes of tribe extinction, because this custom is in vogue among many tribes that are still swarming, and among these Fans it is in vogue as regards the women. This, I think, is the earliest stage of the custom.

The island of Corisco is three miles in length, north and south, and averages one and three-quarters in breadth. Its north-west point is in lat. 0°, 58′ north and long. 9°, 20′ east. I have acquired a good deal of information from local traditions, charts, and personal experience, the latter being of course largely of the situation of rocks and banks when personally navigating ; so I will set the general results of my studies down.

Corisco Island is situated in the middle of Corisco Bay and is most seaward of the islands in the bay. It is surrounded by a hollow bank, irregular in outline, extending in some places two-and-a-half miles off shore ; and in addition to this extensive shoal are several detached rocky patches off the N.E. shore of the island. Off the N.E. point lie Corisco Banks, the outer patch with three-and-a-half fathoms of water three miles off shore. On the outer large patch you may get twelve feet of water, but I found bottom at two feet. On the inner and larger it averages three feet ; among both these patches there are boat channels ; and Mr. Ibea's accounts of his experiences among them during the many voyages he has made to and from the mainland, with the stiff current that runs round Cape St. John, are thrilling, but not such as would induce any one to make Corisco a yachting centre.

Laval Island, which I have mentioned above, is about 200 yards long but makes the most of itself with rocks and trees, and stands high above the water. It is one mile south of Corisco Island. It has a line of bank, on which the sea breaks, north and north-east. The " West Coast Pilot "says there is only a canoe passage between it and Corisco Island. This is not the case, for you can take a small schooner between them, though I do not advise it because of the rock reef running out from Alondo Point. The edge of the encircling bank of Corisco Island goes round outside Laval one and a half miles to the west,

and two miles to the southward.   About a mile S.E. of Laval
there is a reef which, when I was on Corisco, was a perpetual
line of foam.

Laval Bank lies S.W. ¾ S. three-and-a-half miles from
Laval Island.   It is rock and sand.   There is good fishing
near it, but the sea breaks over the head of it furiously.   It
stretches two miles north and south and is one and a half
broad, the Pilot says.   I passed through it on my return voyage
to Gaboon and think it is in many places two miles wide, but
this being the rough season in these seas it showed itself off
in full.

Baña Island is a quarter of a mile long, and is lower than
Laval.   It is five miles S. of the S.E. end of Corisco Island,
that is, Alondo.   Its surrounding plinth of rock shows in
places at low water and one large rock, which is never covered,
shows about a mile out to sea, W. by S.

But Baña Island is nothing to Baña Bank, which supports
Obanjo's—I beg his pardon, Captain Johnson's—statement
that " half dem dar 'fernal Corisco Bay Islands lib under water."

This bank is nine miles long, in an east by north and west
by south direction, averaging three and a half miles in breadth.
On it the depths are very shallow and variable.   The
eastern part of the bank is called the Crown Sand and a patch
dries, for I was shell-hunting on it.   About two miles S.E. by
E. ¾ E. of Baña, that is to say shorewards to the mainland,
there is another patch of the Crown Sand which dries, which
is called the East Sand ; on this I got some sponges and
Gorgonia.   After trying to give a conscientious account of
Baña Bank, I notice my friend the " West Coast Pilot " collapses
and pathetically beseeches you, if you will, or must, go into
Corisco Bay, to be very careful.   I think these patches of
the Crown Sand that dry must be near to the end of
the bank ; for Captain Porter, who knows this bit of coast
well, tells me there is a passage for vessels out of Corisco
Bay by Oranda Point, towards Cape Esterias, provided
they do not draw more than two fathoms and know the way;
but this passage is not used now.

Eleven miles east from the north-east end of Corisco Island,
further into the bay, lie the two Eloby Islands. They are on the

top of an extensive shoal, running in most directions for miles, but particularly eastwards and southwards. Mail steamers that come in to call at Messrs. Holt's factory on little Eloby, and off the mouth of the Muni River where Hatton and Cookson have a factory, come into Corisco Bay, from the north, round to the east of the Eloby islands, and leave by the same channel, which averages six fathoms; and go south, if they want to, well outside to the west of all Corisco Bay's banks. I do not know why little Eloby Island should be the inhabited one. Big Eloby is a fine, likely-looking island. I was told by a Benga on Cape Esterias that it was once inhabited, but there was a war and the inhabitants were killed and carried off as slaves, and it has not since been re-colonised.

The northern part of the bay I have had no personal experience in navigating, but, according to the "Pilot" it has its drawbacks, and according to people who have to work it, these drawbacks are by no means down in all their beauty in the charts. It was in this bay that the *Benguella* struck on a something. I cannot be more definite because some of my friends who ought to know say it was a wreck—the old wreck of the *David MacLean*; others, who ought to know, say it was rocks; anyhow she tore, then and there, a big wound in herself, and nothing but the fine seamanship of Captain Eversfield ever got her up into Cameroons River and successfully beached her and repaired her there. During her convalescence she was the haven of refuge for the unfortunate white folk of Cameroon while the mutiny of the Dahomeyan soldiers went on ashore in 1894.

There is another wreck not down in the chart, just off Alondo, the south-east point of Corisco Island; it is that of the schooner *Elfie*, belonging to the American Presbyterian Mission.

This Corisco Bay, when you look at it on the map, seems an ideally formed harbour, and I once heard it strongly recommended as a suitable site for a coaling station; but a glance at its chart will show you it is only a subtly rock-set trap for vessels, imperfect as the chart is. Its width is thirty-five miles south by west and three-quarters west. This line touches the eastern end of Corisco Island, and eastwards of it the bay is fourteen miles deep.

Two rivers fall into Corisco Bay, the Muni and the Moondah. The latter runs up behind Libreville. There is a creek, the entrance to which is on the right-hand bank near the mouth of the Moondah as you enter ; this runs behind Cape Esterias, in a south-east direction, and nearly communicates with the Gaboon estuary ; so nearly that it is possible to utilise it as a short cut to Corisco Bay from Libreville, it being possible to drag a boat over the intervening strip of land.

The Muni is a longer and more important river than the Moondah ; its outfall is north of it, opposite little Eloby Island, on the mainland shore. On a chart it looks like the usual African river turned upside down, its upper course being split up into several streams instead of its lower. Both these rivers, like many others in this region, rise in the range of the Sierra del Cristal, an enormous belt of mountainous country the eastern limitations of which are at present unexplored.

A few great rivers cut through this range from sources beyond the Sierra, such as the Ogowé and the joint streams of the Mbam and Sanaga which come into the Atlantic under the names of the O'Bengo and the Boungo. The ranges round the Ogowé are the best known parts of the Sierra del Cristal; for the Ogowé places at the traveller's disposal a path, such as I have partially described, through 500 miles of it ; and the Ogowé's chief affluent, the Nguni, cuts through it again from Samba south-eastwards ; and the Okanda's course lies, as far as that river has been ascended, in the very heart of it, going away north-east. It is a range of old volcanic origin, running in series of ridges parallel to each other, and following the long line of the continent. Its general trend is north-west and south-east. It comes down almost to the sea beach behind Batanga, and the beautiful little Loway River falls from a small cliff some twenty or thirty feet high belonging to, it on to the sea shore itself.

It is this range which gives the coast from Cameroon to Landana the marked superiority in beauty it possesses over the rest of the West Coast ; excepting, of course, the splendours of Ambas Bay, which is a thing apart and out of all keeping with the Coast. These western ridges of the Sierra make a beautiful purple blue background to the splendid band of forest that runs behind the bright yellow sands of the sea shore, which are again bordered to seaward by the white wall of surf. The mountains forming it are distinct in outline and fantastic in form, notably the one behind Batanga, which seen from seaward takes the exact form of a kneeling elephant. Its height is 1707 feet and I am told there is another one of almost identical shape in the same parallel of latitude on the East African Coast. It was first ascended by Sir Richard Burton, since then Mr. Newberry of Batanga has been up it. He tells me the view from the summit to the east is into a mountainous country as far as eye can see. Several of the other peaks of this range that have been measured, and are visible from the sea, are higher than the Elephant. The Mitre, inland from Cape St. John, is 3940 feet ; the highest of a stretch of hills called the Seven Hills, but belonging to one range, is 2786 feet. Mount Alouette is 3415 feet but none are so striking in form as Mount Elephant.

Behind Corisco Bay the range takes a trend inland, in a direction nearly at right angles to the shore, going inland to the south-east by south ; but the details of its peaks are not known, this district being little explored. The range seems to turn more eastward still behind Cape Esterias, and runs towards, and unites with, that part of the Sierra del Cristal that cuts the course of the Ogowé some 170 miles from the sea at Talagouga ; only a few isolated bubble-shaped hills, like Mount Sangataõ, being in the Ogowé delta region. The position of this range when I struck its western flank, coming across from the Ogowé to the Rembwé, was some 140 to 150 miles inland, the main chain of this part lying to the eastward of where I was. The Rembwé cuts through a portion of it just above Agonjo, but the Rembwé itself rises in the range. The 'Como, which it joins with at 'Como Point to form the Gaboon estuary, is said to rise inlands behind this range, and is formed like the Muni by several streams uniting. Obanjo told me, when I was at Ajongo, that the range was going from there in a north by east direction, but of the upper part of the 'Como little or nothing is personally known by white men.

The inhabitants of the shores and hinterland of Corisco Bay are a wild set of savages of several tribes. The Benga were once the ruling race among them, but they have diminished rapidly of late years.   The country is very rich in rubber and ebony, which is bought by the Benga native traders, and M'pongwe, and sold to the white traders at Eloby and Cocoa Beach.

Those traders who know the inland tribes describe them as savage and treacherous.   The Fans are coming down through this part of the country to the beach all the way along from Batanga to the Gaboon estuary.   I cannot hold out much hope that they will enlighten or ameliorate the manners and customs of the older inhabitants as regards trade, but they can teach them a thing or two worth knowing in the way of activity and courtesy.   That they will suffer the same extinction that the previous migrants to the Coast have suffered, there is no reason to doubt, for they will be under similar conditions ; and Mr. Ibea and myself agree again, that there is something inimical to human life, black or white, in the immediate Coast region of West and South-West Africa, as far down as Congo : and the interior tribes also join us in our opinion.   Many times have I, and others, been told by interior tribes that there is a certain air which comes from the sea that kills men—that is just their way of putting it.   I call it Paludisme Malariæ, which is just my way of putting it, and of course I fancy that it comes from the rotting, reeking swamp land and lagoons, and not from the sea. Anyhow, white men and black feel it, and suffer and die.

CHAPTER XVIII

FROM CORISCO TO GABOON

The log of the *Lafayette* on her return voyage from Corisco to Gaboon, giving some account of Cape Esterias and the inhabitants thereof; to which is added a full and particular account of a strange sailing manœuvre, first carried out by this voyager, and not included in any published treatise on the art of seamanship in the known world.

August 8th, 1895.—Weather still very rough, the two mile spit of rock running seawards from Alondo Point is a white stretch of flying foam, and the roar and thunder of it shakes the rocky cliff on which the house stands. Mr. Ibea thinks, however, that we should make Cape Esterias by nightfall, presumably because we are all sober ; for he tells me an enlivening tale of how he "started from Corisco, on just such a day as this," in a boat commanded and owned by a native, who was drunk at starting and became more so. In addition to himself and this disreputable person, there were some women, and a crew of four or five men. "Shortly," says Mr. Ibea, "we were upset, and I had to swim about and put them all back into the boat again. I had not got them in half-an-hour before he got the boat over again, and I again had to fetch them out of the water." Mr. Ibea is a magnificent swimmer, and a fine dashing sailor, and I wish he were coming with me instead of Eveke, and would leave Eveke to look after pastoral matters ; but this I know is not possible, and it may be worse to-morrow, so I'm off, and shall spend my time keeping the *Lafayette* from being upset, for I cannot swim round like ten Newfoundland story-book dogs, or one Mr. Ibea, gathering people from the South Atlantic waves and replacing them on board her, or any vessel. So I take a grateful farewell of Mrs. Ibea and the

family at large. Mr. Ibea and his younger son, who is bubbling
out conversation in Benga, as he has ever been doing since I
came to the island, come with me a little way, and then
we part.

I notice that the sea is rough, and the lagoons behind the
beaches stink worse even than usual : no wonder the mission
found it as unhealthy here as on the mainland! The fine sand
blows in the wind, stinging my face—in fact it is bad weather,
but I have had enough of walking to and fro along this sandy
beach, while Eveke courts his mother-in-law elect, and, in
order to get more time to do so, tries to frighten me about
the weather.

Arrived at Nassau Bay and have the usual job of hunting
out Eveke and the crew from the village, and the usual delays.
We wait for the turn of the tide on Eveke's advice. It would,
I am sure, have been better to have gone out before the
slack, so as to have had the full tide for Esterias, but I
let him have his way and wait patiently in the wooden,
European-fashion built house which I learn belongs to Eveke's
uncle. It does not give one the idea of being much lived in.

It is fairly clean, the walls inside are painted white, with
the door and window-frames a bright cobalt blue. Cobalt
blue, by the bye, seems a great feature on this island. I
wonder whether a cargo of it was ever washed ashore from a
wreck, or whether it is a special line of goods for " paying off "
in ? One rarely sees any other coloured paint. There is one
other little village I have been passing through daily since I
have been here, that has each house door painted with it and
white paint in stripes, diagonal bands, straight bands, plain and
chess-board patterns, till it's as good as names and numbers to
that village. It would be far and away better for postmen and
diners-out than a plan in vogue in a far away London suburb I
know of, wherein the christening of the villas seems to have
been done by a gardener, giving the more ordinary individual
gay times—for the houses are named after trees, and which
particular shrub your friend lives at often slips down a hole
in your memory, when you find yourself confronted by the
front gates of " the Bays," " Lilacs," " Elms," " Oaks," " Labur-
nums," &c. This house of Eveke's uncle wants no name or

number to distinguish it from the neighbouring bamboo huts,
—you couldn't miss it in a London fog, for were you once to
get into the village street, you would be bound to run up
against it, as it stands right across the top.

It is considerately furnished inside. In the room in which I
await the tide turn there are two chests of drawers, a real dining
table, nine chairs, another table, three looking-glasses and a
big wooden bedstead of the native type—a wooden bench without sides, but with a head- and foot-board ; one usually sees
this sort of bedstead basking in the sun in the street. There
are four I see now at it in the broad village street below me,
to the end of compelling the surplus parasitic population to
leave. On the one in this room lies a heap of muddled dirty
clothes, giving it an air of being the one thing in the house that
is used. The rest seems all "for dandy." On the table,
scattered anyhow together, are glass scent-bottles, a hanging-
lamp, framed oleographs of English farmyard scenes ; and
amongst them an old album full of faded photographs,
evidently once the valued treasure of some white man who is
dead now ; for were he living he would never have parted with
it, after pasting in against the pictures those little English wild
roses and bits of heather and bluebells.

At last Eveke rushes up with one of those spasmodic attacks
of activity which he simulates, and which never impose on any
one but himself, and we all go aboard. Yesterday I met a
lady on the shore who asked me if I would take her to
Gaboon. I said, as any skipper would, "delighted, my
dear"; and here she is sitting on the top of the cargo with her
head just exactly in the proper position to get it bashed in, or
knocked off by the boom ; and her five bundles, one tin box, a
peck of limes and a husband. In fact, things are in such a
muddle on board that before we weigh anchor, I decide to stow
cargo, as befits the pupil of Captain Murray. No black man
can stow cargo. I say so viciously, from my canoe experiences. The *Lafayette's* "hold" is in a condition that would
bleach the hair of any "British African" officer on the
Coast, even if he only caught sight of it through a telescope.
For it partakes strongly of the arrangement of a rubbish heap ;
the lady passenger's belongings, mine, the crew's, the deck

chair, the bundle of bedding, the boxes of sand for ballast, all together anyhow; and for dunnage, parcels of the men's aguma and neat little packets of salt, done up in plantain leaves tied round with tie-tie; and an untidily made up bundle of yam, pieces whereof have got out of the plantain leaf and evaded the tie-tie, and are now wandering about, mixed up with most things. I think, at first, that Mr. Hudson's clean, tidy, deck-chair is underneath everything; I can just see a corner of it sticking out beneath a box of sand, like Mr. Pecksniff's feelings, or the Princes in the Tower, only it is anything but pillows that are smothering it. On making a spirited rescue of the chair, I find, however, that Dr. Nassau's bedding is the thing that really is in the bilge water. During these operations, I jump forward, on to what I imagine is a lot of the crew's clothes, and "Oh! that's my husband," cries the lady passenger, "you fit to hurt him proper"; he upsets me on to the cargo, and groans a good deal and talks about compensation; but I say "he had come at shipper's own risk," and I have "no liability," so he settles down again. When I have finished stowing cargo we set out to sea—Eveke at the helm. I find I am expected to sit surrounded by a rim of alligator pears and bananas, as though I were some kind of joint garnished for table, instead of a West Coast skipper. The *Lafayette* having neither cabin nor locker is extremely difficult to keep tidy. There is, unavoidably, an "all the coals adrift on deck, half the rails below" look about her, do what one will. I stow the pears in under the end strut, where there is a hole with an ornamental woodwork flourish round it, but no door; so those charming fruit will persist in coming larking out again as soon as ever I have got them in. "Oh, it's a dog's life, is the sea, for a man," as my sailor friends say. Eveke meanwhile takes us out of Nassau Bay through Baña Bank and then goes to sleep and I take charge. My lady passenger is quite the lady passenger, frightened of the sea, and dissatisfied with the accommodation. I have stowed her with every care in the bottom of the boat, on the bedding athwart-ships, and she is grateful for the attention; but says "the vessel is not big enough," and goes on eating excruciatingly sour limes in a

way that sets my teeth on edge. Half her sufferings arise
from her disastrous habit of falling asleep ; and then her head
goes flump off the seat she is leaning it against, and crack
against the ribs of the boat's side ; I put my leather photograph case in her usual striking place, but she dodges it in her
descent seven times in ten.

The sea is running high, and all the afternoon we beat up
and tack, and the *Lafayette* has a larky way, giving herself
the airs of a duck washing itself, putting her head down and
shaking the water out over her stern ; a good deal of water
comes on board one way and another, over one side on one
tack, over the other side on the other tack, over the bows
always. The man with the whiskers is a smart seaman, and
the only one worth his salt, and he attends to the jib ; the
others sleep and eat and talk and attend to the jiggers in
their feet, which they have picked up on Corisco, where they
swarm.

The weather is a bit thick, so we do not sight the continent
until four o'clock, and it is borne in on me that there's no Cape
Esterias for us to-night. Eveke pilots us close in towards the
shore, and we run among the long line of rollers, attributive to
the great rock reefs that fringe it, and which run out to sea in an
irregular cone shape, stretching true north and north-north-east
from the blunt headland that has for its north-west extremity
Akanda point and for its southern, Cape Clara. Cape Esterias
runs out further seaward than Akanda, and is the real south-
east point of Corisco Bay; but from Akanda to Cape Clara (or
Joinville) may be taken as the limits of the headland that
separates Corisco Bay from the Gaboon Estuary : and the
Moondah River mouth is here. "The sun's rim sinks, the stars
rush out, at one stride comes the dark" and finds us still
lolloping about in the breaking swell. Half an hour after
sundown the wind drops, with that suddenness that the
breeze, be it light or heavy, always drops alongshore down
here ; and although we could do little when we had it, as it was
nearly in our teeth, we can of course do nothing without it,
so we run the *Lafayette* on to a tongue of sand between rock
reefs, that were breathing heavily, just North of Akanda point.

Well do I remember now the time I spent sitting on a

deck chair on the deck of the 2,000 ton *Rochelle* in 1893, with
all anxiety as to locality and navigation on the mind of Captain
Harrison, while I lazily wondered what it was like ashore here.
The stretch of land looked there so desolate and wild : a long
line of surf, a long line of dove-coloured sand, a long line of
green shrub-brushes, backed by a low, dark forest.   We soon
lost sight of it on the *Rochelle*, as she swung out west to give
its dangers a wide berth.   Little did I think then that I should
ever be in circumstances so pre-eminently fitted for acquiring
detailed knowledge of the entire phenomena, surf, rocks, sand,
beach and all, as I am at present in.   We lower our gaff
and anchor as hard as we can, and then, leaving two men
in the boat and the lady passenger ; the rest of us jump over
the side into the surf, and wade ashore to stretch our limbs
and pick up firewood.   We do not stay long, because we are
afraid of the *Lafayette* dragging her anchors.   Don't mention
it, pray, in "British African" circles ; but as we back her
stern-foremost on to the sand, we want a hand-line for
soundings to find a suitable sand tongue to settle on.   I give
Whiskers my fishing-line ; its lead sinker does very well, only
you see we haven't time to take off the line of fish hooks, and,
so when he, in proper style, swings the lead to take a cast, those
hooks just hitch in the cargo.   I cut them adrift with a jack
knife with commendable promptitude, Eveke meanwhile
handles the sail and I, when danger becomes imminent, energetically take soundings over the stern with my umbrella.   It
is magnificent, but not navigation, still it works well.

We wade back to the *Lafayette*, clamber on board, and
start to get our supper in the dark, for by now the last
light has died out of the sky, and artificial light we have none.
Unfortunately I have packed my eatables in my collecting box,
so attempt to eat a very interesting dead-wood fungus in
lieu of biscuit.   Giving this up, I decide to confine my
attention to my one surviving tin, the opening of which costs
me skin and blood.   I am not surprised, but grieved, to find
that after all it contains only vegetables for putting into
soups, because I have had experience with this species of tinned
product before.   This particular tin is one of the consignment so kindly sent by Mr. Hudson to my rescue on the

Ogowé, and I did not feel justified in returning it to store
when I got back to Gaboon, because its little golden label had,
as is usual with those French forms of labels, come off, and after
all, I being an optimistic ass, hoped there might be something
in the tin good to eat.   Well there isn't, and what is worse, I
have nothing to drink, for the *Lafayette* is too agitated to
allow us to make a fire to boil water for tea.   There is plenty
of water in bottles for the men, but unboiled water is my
ibet.   There are always little somethings that are not quite
pleasant in African travel.

The lady passenger groans a good deal and eats those
excruciating limes and the biscuits, of which I had given her
a good store in the afternoon, in the hopes of distracting her
from a series of observations she was then making on the
height of Atlantic waves.   She soon goes off to sleep as
I hear by the sound of the crack of her head against the ribs
of the boat.   In my dual capacity of skipper and stewardess, I
search her head out from amongst a bunch of bananas, an iron
pot and the photograph case, and, eliminating the other factors,
arrange it nicely on the banana bunch and wrap her up completely in my thick rug and shawl, because she only has on
one thin cloth, and the seas that have come on board have
soaked that through long ago.

The men, after their supper on the provisions I had rescued
from a state of dunnage, light their pipe—I say pipe advisedly,
for they had one, a thing about the size of a young model-
dwelling washing copper.   It takes a whole leaf of tobacco
rolled round and placed into it horizontally, with three lucifer
matches broken up and placed in the hole in the middle, and
of course a bit of plantain leaf folded and put on top to
prevent its roaring away too rapidly.   They hand it on
from one to the other, while they make their arrangements for
the night.   These arrangements consist in placing the main
sail across the boom like a tent, they then creep in under this
and go to sleep on the cargo.   They want to erect a tent for
me with the jib, because they say it is very bad to sleep
in the light of the moon which is rising ; but I do not feel
like sleeping, so I refuse.   I have no hesitation in saying
that they pass an uneasy night.   For one reason, in under

their tent with them is a large ram Mr. Ibea is sending
to Gaboon, and that sheep has scimitar-shaped sharp
horns and restless habits, and I can see he does things that
hurt and rouse the sleepers to groaning-point perpetually.
I sit up by the rudder watching the black heaving ocean, too
rough for the weak moon to brighten save when it flies aloft
in angry white foam and surf over the shoals and rocks ; and
the dimly moonlit sky with the clouds flying in the ever
blowing upper wind from the equator ; and the motionless
black line of the forest with the soft white mist rolling low
and creeping and crawling out between its stems from the
lagoons behind the sand-ridged beach. The mist comes stretching out from under the bushes over the sand towards the sea,
now raising itself up into peaks, now crouching down upon
the sand, and sending out long white arms or feelers towards
the surf and then drawing them back as if it were some spirit-
possessed thing, poisonous and malignant, that wanted to
reach us, and yet is timorous and frightened of the surf's
thunder-roar and spray. It gets over its alarm after about an
hour, however, and comes curling out in a white wall and
during the rest of the calm before the dawn-wind comes,
wraps itself round us, dankly-smelling like some foul corpse.

I don't think this sort of mist is healthy, but it is often
supremely lovely and always fascinates me. I have seen it
play the weirdest wildest tricks many a time, in many a place
in West Africa. I have, when benighted, walked hurriedly
through it for miles in the forest while it has mischievously
hidden the path at my feet from the helpful illumination
of the moon, swishing and swirling round my moving
skirts. I have seen it come out of the forests and gather
on the creek before and round me when out o' nights in
canoes, gradually as we glided towards the breeze-swept
river, forming itself into a great ball which has rolled before
us, alongside, or behind us, showing dimly now in the shadow,
ghostly white now in the moonshine, and bursting into
thousands of flakes if the river breeze when it met it was too
strong for it ; if it were not, just melting away into the sheet of
mist that lay sleeping on the broad river itself. Now and again
you will see it in the forest stretch up a gradually lengthening

arm, and wind it lazily round and round some grand column
of a tree-stem, to the height of ten or twenty feet from the
ground, spread out its top like a plume and then fall back
again to the mist-river from which it came. It has weird ways,
this mist of the West Coast.   I have often, when no one has
been near to form opinions of my frivolity, played with
it, scooping it up in my hands and letting it fall again, or
swished it about with a branch, when it lay at a decent level
of three or four feet from the ground.   When it comes higher
and utterly befogs you, you don't feel much inclination to
play with it.   The worst of it is, you never quite know how
high it is coming.   I have seen it rise out of Bimbia flats and
cover the Great Cameroon as though it said, " Ah you are
Grand Mungo, but I am grander—I am Death."

I drop off to sleep now and then, only to be aroused
either by the *Lafayette* having dragged her anchor and got
off skylarking with a lot of rough rocks so that she must
be rescued and re-anchored, or by ejaculations from under
the sail because of that ram.   The tent amidships would
afford a series of fine studies for any one who wanted to
illustrate anything *à la* Doré; it looks like a great grave-cloth
spread over a tumbled heap of corpses, which vaguely show
their outlines through its heavy white folds.   When my crew
do a good writhe they are particularly fine.   My attention
gets riveted on them because one of them has an abominable
quavering, hysterical, falsetto snore, which, as I want to go
to sleep myself, rouses in my mind a desire to slay the per-
former, for that snore cuts through the sound of the surf
on to my nerves like a knife.   Three times during the night
I arose, and grasping the stump of a plantain bunch and
walking along the thwarts, hovered, like a revengeful fiend,
over the shrouded sleepers, hesitating for a few minutes to
locate the seat of the disorder, for I used all suitable care
and precaution to avoid hitting the innocent, but this is
difficult, for the snore seems to come from underneath the
upper layer, whose heads show through the sail like plums
through a pie-crust, so I am regretfully compelled to take
swipes at the excrescence nearest the source of the nuisance.
This remedy is only a temporary one, but during the lull it

produces I fall asleep, after the third application firmly, and do not wake up until the scratching of the crew to extricate itself from under the sail arouses me, and I then find my head under the seat and my unlucky body bent wherever nature had omitted to provide a joint. I have to get up and undo the sail, for I had tied the ends of it securely together to bottle up some of the noise last time the snore aroused me.

August 10th.—The morning breaks gray, cheerless and chilly, the sea looks angry and wicked. For half-an-hour, while the crew are getting things straight, I comb my tangled hair and meditate on the problem "Why did I come to Africa?" This done we heave up anchor and shove off at about 5.30 A.M. and from that time till 1.45 go along near in-shore on the land breeze, among the rollers. I do not cite this as the proper course to lay, but give it as an example of the impossibility of getting a black crew to run out of smell of land ; they always like to hug the shore, as not only my own experiences but those of sympathetic friends with whom I have interchanged experiences demonstrate. Let the shore be what it may they cling to it. Poor Mr. S., going from Gaboon to Eloby, got run well up the Moondah River on one occasion, owing to this persistent habit, and other adventurers have fared no better.

The shore along from Akanda to Cape Clara is one to which any white seaman would give a lot of room. Immediately south of our anchorage it begins to rise into dwarf vertical cliffs overhung by bush and trailing plants between which the cliff-face shows strange-looking slabs of white clay and rock. The sea plays furiously against them at high tide, and at low leaves a very narrow beach heavily strewn with immense rock boulders. By 1.30 we find we cannot get round Cape Esterias, so run in under the shallow lea of its northern side. There is here a narrow sand-beach, with plenty of rock on it, and a semi-vertical and supremely slippery path leading up to an ostentatiously European plank-built house. We fix up the *Lafayette* safely and all go ashore.

The inhabitants of this country have been watching us beating in, and taking a kindly interest in the performance, and so as soon as everything is all right they sing out in a

chorus *Mboloani*. They did not do so before because it is not
etiquette to distract people when they are engaged in the
crucial occupation of landing a boat or canoe. I am taken
possession of by a very comely-looking brown young lady,
gracefully attired in my favourite coloured cloth, bright pink
with a cardinal twill hem round it, and we go up the hill
together. I note that she wears a tight rope of large green
and white beads round her beautiful throat ; she tells me
her name is Agnes and that she is a subtrader for Messrs.
Holt's factory at Eloby, and I find, thanks be ! she talks fluent
trade English, and further that on account of its European
planks the ostentatious house is regarded by these kindly
people as *ipso facto* my fit and proper dwelling for the time
I may think good to stay at Cape Esterias. Its enterprising
builder and owner apologises for its unfinished state ; indeed,
when at close quarters with it, I see it has merely got its
walls up and its roof on. It is perched some four feet above
the ground, on poles, and the owner has not yet decided what
flight of stairs he will erect to the verandah. He has purchased an old ready-made flight, and has himself constructed
a bamboo ladder, its cross pieces tied on to the uprights, I
need hardly say, with tie-tie. This being done he has got
both ladders lying on the ground beside each other, while he
thinks the matter well out as to their respective advantages.
Of course the additional fluster of my unexpected arrival
renders him more than ever incapable of coming to a decision
on their rival merits. I relieve his mind by ignoring them
and swing up on to the verandah and enter the house.
The furniture consists of shavings, tools, the skeleton of a
native bedstead, and a bag of something which evidently
serves as a bed. The owner proudly displays the charms of
the establishment ; he intends, he remarks, to paint the inside
of the walls white, with the door and window frames a bright
blue. . . . I recognise the good old cobalt in a pot. I applaud
the idea, not that it is new on this Coast, but it is better than
all white, or dunduckety mud-colour paint, the only other
colour schemes in vogue for domestic decoration, and worlds
an' away ahead of varnish, which acts as a " catch 'em alive oh "
for all manner of insects, and your clothes when you hang

them against it. I note there will be a heavy percentage of
blue here, because in the fifteen feet square living room there
are three doors and two windows—each one of which, from a
determination to be quite the white man, is fitted with a lock
and a bolt. The next room, there are only two, is particularly
strong in windows, being provided with three. Out of the
two to the north there is a lovely view of wooded valleys and
low hills seen across that charming bright foreground of a
banana plantation. The window to the east commands the
line of back arrangements of one side of the little village, a
view full of interest to the ethnologist, only just at present I
am too wet and tired for the soulful contemplation of science,
or of scenic beauty, so I close all three windows up with their
wooden shutters,—glass, of course, there is none—and having
got my portmanteau, and a pudding basin of European
origin—with a lively combination of blue, maroon, and gas
greens all over it—full of water and, joy! a towel from Agnes,
I proceed to wash and dress in the dark. I hear, meanwhile,
great uproar in the next room ; the entire settlement seems to
be doing things and talking about it! On re-entering the
other apartment I find one kindly native has lent me a
four-legged table, and another an ivory bundle chair, and
the population of Cape Esterias has been enterprisingly employed in hauling and hoisting the furniture on to the stairless
verandah and into the house, or standing by and giving advice
as to how this was to be done. Agnes also adds a slip of
new calico for a table cloth, and I am exceedingly grateful,
but, Allah ! how stiff and bruised and tired ! So after having
some food and a cup of sugarless and milkless coffee, I excuse
myself and go and lie down on the most luxurious bed, that
bag of old salt sack stuff, filled with sweating sea-weed, just
a bit over-populated, perhaps, with fleas, but very enjoyable,
on the plank floor.

It is 5 o'clock when I awake, and I am still thirsty ; not
liking to bother Agnes for more coffee and being mortal
frightened of raw water, I ask her for a " paw-paw." She gets
me some unripe ones, explaining " that those nasty boys done
gone chop all them ripe one "—such is the universal nature of
boys ! I regretfully decline the hard fruit, and as they attract

quantities of ants I say, "Agnes, just throw them away." "What you mean?" says my charmer. "Put 'em outside," say I. She gazes blankly, "Chuck 'em," says I, descending still further in my language. A gleam of comprehension comes to Agnes. "You mean I hev them?" says she. "That's it, heave them," I answer, and she forthwith "hev 'em" out of one of our many windows. I feel it is my duty to go and pay my respects to the Mission; Agnes quite agrees, and off we go among the scattered bamboo-built houses, one of which in a skeleton state she tells me she is building for herself.

The Roman Catholic Mission, the only representative of white men here, is on the southern face of Cape Esterias. Its buildings consist of a small residence and a large church. The church has a concrete floor and wooden benches, the white walls relieved by a frieze of framed prints of a religious character, a pretty altar with its array of bright brass candlesticks, and above it the tinted and gilt figure of the Virgin and Child. Every part of the place is sweet and clean, giving evidence of the loving care with which it is tended. As I pass the residence, the missionary, seeing me, sends one of his black retainers to fetch me in, and leads me on to the verandah, where I am most cordially received by the Père in charge, who has practical views on hospitality, and is anxious for me to have wine and many things else he can ill afford to spare from his own store. I thankfully confine my depredations to some sugar and a loaf of excellent bread, but he insists on handing to Agnes for me a tin of beef and a lot of oranges. As I cannot speak French, nor he English, I do my best to convey my sense of his kindness and bow myself off.

Agnes, who is very proud of the Mission, tells me there is only one Père and one Frère stationed here, but she says "they are very good—good too much." They educate the children, teaching them to read French, &c., and should a child display any aptitude it is forwarded round to Gaboon to acquire a further training in the technical schools there in connection with the headquarters of the Mission. She herself, I gather, was educated primarily by the Mission, but she has continued her studies on her own account, for not only does

she speak French grammatically, as the natives are taught to,
and read and write it, but also English—Coast English no
doubt, but comforting to the wanderer who falls in with her,
while she claims an equal knowledge of Spanish ; no mean
range of accomplishments for a lady. I return to my abode
and have a square meal and sugar in my coffee, thanks to the
missionary, and so to bed, as Mr. Pepys would say. I am
sure, by the way, Mr. Pepys would like Agnes, she is quite
his style of beauty, plump and pleasant ; I don't expect he
would care for my seaweed bed though, unless he had been
broken into it by African travel, for Mr. Pepys had great
ideas of being comfortable in a conventional way.

August 11th.—Agnes rouses me from my thalassic couch and
suggests Mass at 5.30 A.M.   It seems a very proper suggestion,
so I carry it out.   I find the rest of the inhabitants already on
their knees in the church, singing their Salve Maria responses
in that musical, metallic twang the Latin seems to bring out
so strangely in the African voice, usually so full and throaty.
I endeavour to follow properly, and when my whole attention
is absorbed in so doing, a terrific tug at my skirts alarms me,
I look carefully round and see Agnes on her knees behind me.
" What's the matter ? " I ask. She whispers something. " Salve
Maria," I say, joining the congregational chorus hastily, and
add in a whisper " I no fit to hear you, speak them thing
softly, softly,"—she then emits a hissing whisper, full of earnest
meaning but incomprehensible as to detail ; " Salve Maria "
comes again and I, feeling frightened that I am doing something awfully wrong somehow, answer anxiously " What ? "
and then right out loud and clear, Agnes says, " I be his Jack
wash." " Salve Maria," say I, with the congregation.   Then
we have an explanation outside, and it seems she does his
reverence's washing, and feeling, justly enough, proud of the
white lace petticoats which he was displaying before the altar
she was compelled to communicate the fact to me and claim
her share in their beauty.   Vanity, thy name is Woman !

I take leave of Agnes with gifts, and of my host, the owner
of the house, giving him a present. He is more than satisfied,
but explains this must be regarded as a gift and not as pay
for the hire of his house—it not being the fashion of his

country to take this from a traveller. While waiting about for the *Lafayette* to get ready for sea, *i.e.*, for the water bottles to be refilled, I learn the cause of the weird howls and screams I have heard during the night. A poor maniac who has run from Gaboon to Cape Esterias haunts the rocky narrow beach at night and flies from any one who approaches him to give him food, or offer him shelter. He soon returns and hangs about near the houses again and runs at night along the beach screaming and moaning as he jumps about among the rocks. When I get on to the beach he is sitting playing on a rock, not far off, tearing up a plantain leaf into shreds. I take up some packages of aguma and biscuits, and softly and cautiously make my way towards him, but he just lets me get within a few yards and then is off with a howl, at a pace which, if it holds, must by now have landed him on the shores of Victoria Nyanza. In addition to this fortuitous lunatic, there is at Cape Esterias a local one, quite the biggest black man I have ever seen ; he must be little short of seven feet high, and his muscular development is such that he looks very heavily built for his height. They tell me he is a slave who was brought in his youth, like most Benga slaves, from one of the Fernan Vaz tribes, and is quite harmless and hard-working, but quite mad, "some witch has stolen one of his souls." I have seen it stated that insanity is almost unknown among the Africans ; I can truly say I have never stayed any time in a district among them without coming across several cases of it. In the Rivers, indeed among all the true negro tribes, it is customary to kill lunatics off. On the South-West Coast insanity usually takes the form of malignant melancholy and they kill themselves off. Amongst the Kacongo and Bas-congo tribes, this suicide is at times almost an epidemic, and it is there customary when a man shows symptoms of its coming on by hanging himself, without rhyme or reason, about the place or by trying to knock his brains out against a post, for a family conclave to be held. The utter folly of his proceedings are then pointed out to him by his relations, as only relations can point it out, and should he after this still persist in attempting to kill himself, spoiling things, and disturbing people, the job is taken off his hands and his relations

club him on the head, and throw the body in the river, so
"palaver done set." These Benga and M'pongwe people seem
just to let lunatics alone, though to their credit be it said they
had tried to feed this poor fellow from Gaboon, because, they
said, they feared he would starve. When lunatics are dangerous
they secure them to trees by a chain. There was one, I am
told, chained near Glass a long time, but one night he broke
loose and was never heard of again.

I should say my lady passenger left here. I fancy she had
had enough of the *Lafayette*. She said she " would walk the
rest of the way," which may be translated into she'd write to
Mr. A. L. Jones. We get out through the breakers and hoist
our mainsail and beat along among the rollers, rolling ourselves
like mad as the heavy waves sweep broadside on under us.
Just off the Cape itself we have to run almost out of smell of
land, to get round a rock reef; I am bound to confess the
consequences of this spirited display of seamanship are not
encouraging. A terrific marine phenomenon exhibits itself
suddenly off our weather bow, at a distance of fifteen to
twenty feet. My first opinion is that it is the blow-up of
a submarine volcano, not because I am a specialist in marine
volcanic methods, having never seen one out of a picture-book,
but this is very like the picture-book, waves and foam and
flying water. In another second it explains itself completely, for out of the centre of it springs aloft the immense
fluke of a great whale, as high as our mainmast. It swings
round with a flourish and then comes flop down on to and into
the broken sea, sending sheets of water over us and into the
boat. We bale hard all, and stand by for another performance, but, to my intense relief, we see the whale blow a few
minutes later a good distance off, and then have another
flourish—a most charming spectacle on the horizon. My crew
then say, as they take the baling easier, it is a common
affair in Corisco Bay just about now, for it is the courting
time for whales. I don't come again into Corisco Bay in
canoes or small craft while any of that wretched foolishness is
going on. They also tell me that the other day four people
coming from Cape Esterias to Gaboon in a canoe were
drowned, all hands, and they think they must have fallen in

with this whale ; certainly if a small canoe had been as close as we were it would have had a bad time of it, for with us the mainsail protected us from a lot of water coming on board. Goodness knows, however, we had enough, and did some brilliant baling.

Rounding the reef we run inshore again, and beat up to Cape Clara, the shore showing the same type of dwarf cliff and forest on top. Here and there a village shows, some of them Fans who have arrived in the easterly end of their migration and are, according to my crew, making by no means good preparations for their eternal one.

On going round Cape Clara, to my joy we see the Grand Estuary of Gaboon running inland before us, and the wind being favourable, we run up it in grand style, looking, I am sure, quite the well-handled racer. But "short is human glory, vain the vanity of man," our true nature shows up again soon in the way we approach the stately *Minerve*, the guardship, to pass our papers. I hand over to Eveke, making ·it a rule, since I placed my bowsprit into a conservatory and took the paint off one side of a small-pox hospital, not to keep charge when approaching valuable objects. Eveke promptly lowers the gaff, dropping the mainsail completely over me, and hastily getting out our oars, we avoid a collision and hook on to her ladder. A frantic conversation is already going on between my crew and the authorities before I extricate myself. It is a difficult thing to get anything like gracefully and amiably from under a wet mainsail, but my prophetic soul tells me we are in disgrace, so I do my best and beam upon an officer, who is at the bottom of the ladder, asking leading questions about the health of Corisco, and demanding the official bill of the same. Eveke is much alarmed, for I tell him we shall get quarantined, and he ought to have seen about this, and at last by means of the feeble French of one of our crew, we demonstrate to the officer that bills of health simply can't be got on Corisco, there being no Spanish official on the forsaken island to issue them. The official is unconvinced and goes up the ladder to see other officers about it. The interval of suspense I employ in blowing up Eveke, and he in attempting to

exculpate himself and inculpate Dr. Nassau for not having
told him one was necessary.   However, in a few minutes down
the ladder comes the doctor, saying that a merciful view has
been taken of the case, only we must not do it again.   I
solemnly assure him I will not ; nor will I, for it's not my
present intention to revisit an island that has only mud-fish
in its lakes and courting whales in its encircling seas.   While
we have been busy over this affair, the lively *Lafayette* has
been availing herself, as usual when my eye is off her, of the
opportunity to get into mischief and bring down disgrace and
derision upon her captain and crew ; this time by jamming her
topmast, with a nice, clean, new French flag on it, up the tap of
a cistern—a most unseamanlike proceeding, and one which the
instruction I have received from Captain Murray and Professor Roy—instruction, I am aware, I do small credit to
—gives me no hints as to the proper way of dealing with,
so we have to be ignominiously extricated by the *Minerve's*
crew, who roar at us, as we shove off, drifting, waddling and
wobbling away, until we get our mainsail up again.

As the manœuvre of placing your main-top up a tap is not
mentioned, even in my friend *The Sailor's Sea Book* I had
better explain how the thing is done.   The *Minerve* is an old
line-of-battle ship, moored off Libreville to serve as a guard
ship, a depot, and a hospital.   She is by nature high out of
water, on her gun deck is the hospital, on the main deck the
officers' quarters and the exercise ground for the sailors and
marines, and above this again is another structure with
cisterns on, their taps projecting overside—why I do not know,
unless they screw hose on them, for I have never been aboard
her or had her geography explained ; above all is a roof of
palm-leaf mats, in good old Coast style.   The whole fabric,
as Clark Russell would say, towers high into the air, just high
enough about the cisterns for the lively *Lafayette* to get her
precious spar up the nozzle of one of those taps, and of course
it was a joke she could not resist trying on.   I wish it clearly
to be understood that I am not saying a syllable against the
staid, stately *Minerve*.   The only indiscretion she was ever
guilty of was once leaving her moorings and going off with a
heavy tornado, to the horror of Glass and Libreville, drifting

away, hospital and all, to what seemed destruction. She was rescued, but what the feelings of those on board were, save that they had a lurid glow of glory in them and a determination that they would die in a manner creditable to La France, I know not. The feelings of those ashore I am faintly able to realise, and they must have been painful in the extreme, for the *Minerve* is beloved ; many a man, nay, almost every man, knows that he owes his life to the skill and care he received on board her when he had "that attack." No man is, I think, regarded as being initiated into the inner life of Congo Français until he has been carried on board her in a dying condition from the fearful Coast fever, and duly pulled round. It would be an immense advantage to the other settlements along here had they such an institution. She is infinitely better than the so-called "Sanatorium" on higher ground. The idea of the efficacy of such stations is one of the most dangerous illusions rife on the West Coast—I even learn now that this Government is thinking of doing away with the floating hospital and building one ashore which will not have anything like so good a record to show as the wards of the *Minerve* now have.

After our incident with the authorities we pull ourselves together, and arrive at Hatton and Cookson's Wharf with a delusive dash, and glad I am to get there and return to all the comforts, society, and safety associated with it.

CHAPTER XIX

FETISH

In which the Voyager attempts cautiously to approach the subject of
Fetish, and gives a classification of spirits, and some account of the
Ibet and Orundas.

HAVING given some account of my personal experiences
among an African tribe in its original state, *i.e.*, in a state un-
influenced by European ideas and culture, I will make an
attempt to give a rough sketch of the African form of
thought and the difficulties of studying it, because the study
of this thing is my chief motive for going to West Africa.
Since 1893 I have been collecting information in its native
state regarding Fetish, and I use the usual terms fetish and
ju-ju because they have among us a certain fixed value—a
conventional value, but a useful one. Neither "fetish" nor
"ju-ju" are native words. Fetish comes from the word
the old Portuguese explorers used to designate the objects
they thought the natives worshipped, and in which they
were wise enough to recognise a certain similarity to their
own little images and relics of Saints, " *Feitiço*." Ju-ju, on the
other hand, is French, and comes from the word for a toy or
doll,[1] so it is not so applicable as the Portuguese name, for
the native image is not a doll or toy, and has far more affinity to
the image of a saint, inasmuch as it is not venerated for
itself, or treasured because of its prettiness, but only because
it is the residence, or the occasional haunt, of a spirit.

[1] It is held by some authorities to come from gru-gru, a Mandingo word
for charm, but I respectfully question whether gru-gru has not come from
ju-ju, the native approximation to the French joujou.

Stalking the wild West African idea is one of the most
charming pursuits in the world. Quite apart from the intellectual, it has a high sporting interest ; for its pursuit is
as beset with difficulty and danger as grizzly bear hunting,
yet the climate in which you carry on this pursuit—vile as
it is—is warm, which to me is almost an essential of existence.
Personally I prefer it to elephant hunting ; and I shall never
forget the pleasure with which, in the forest among the Fans,
I netted one reason for the advantage of possessing a white
man's eye-ball, and, as I wrote it down in my water-worn
notebook, saw it joined up with the reason why it is advisable
to cut off big men's heads in the Niger Delta. Above all,
I beg you to understand that I make no pretension to a
thorough knowledge of Fetish ideas ; I am only on the
threshold. " Ich weiss nicht all doch viel ist mir bekannt," as
Faust said—and, like him after he had said it, I have got a lot
to learn.

I do not intend here to weary you with more than a small
portion of even my present knowledge, for I have great
collections of facts that I keep only to compare with those
of other hunters of the wild idea, and which in their present
state are valueless to the cabinet ethnologist. Some of these
may be rank lies, some of them mere individual mind-freaks,
others have underlying them some idea I am not at present
in touch with.

The difficulty of gaining a true conception of the savage's
real idea is great and varied.

In places on the Coast where there is, or has been, much
missionary influence the trouble is greatest, for in the first case
the natives carefully conceal things they fear will bring them
into derision and contempt, although they still keep them in
their innermost hearts ; and in the second case, you have a set
of traditions which are Christian in origin, though frequently
altered almost beyond recognition by being kept for years in
the atmosphere of the African mind. For example, there is
this beautiful story now extant among the Cabindas. God made
at first all men black—He always does in the African story—
and then He went across a great river and called men to follow
Him, and the wisest and the bravest and the best plunged into

the great river and crossed it ; and the water washed them white, so they are the ancestors of the white men. But the others were afraid too much, and said, " No, we are comfortable here ; we have our dances, and our tom-toms, and plenty to eat—we won't risk it, we'll stay here" ; and they remained in the old place, and from them come the black men. But to this day the white men come to the bank, on the other side of the river, and call to the black men, saying, " Come, it is better over here." I fear there is little doubt that this story is a modified version of some parable preached to the Cabindas at the time the Jesuit Fathers had such influence among them, before they were driven out of the lower Congo regions more than a hundred years ago, for political reasons, by the Portuguese. The Cabindas have quite forgotten its origin—" it is old story "—and they keep it on, in much the same way as a neighbouring tribe keeps on the ringing of the old bells, morning and evening, that were once bells in a Jesuit monastery long since forgotten. " Our Fathers did it " ; so palaver done set.

In the bush—where the people have been little, or not at all, in contact with European ideas—in some ways the investigation is easier ; yet another set of difficulties confronts you. The difficulty that seems to occur most easily to people is the difficulty of the language. My brother the other day derided me, as is his wont, saying, " What a great advantage it was, that peculiar power African travellers all seemed to have of conversing on the most obscure metaphysical questions with the natives ; whereas when *he* was in Singapore, things were otherwise—if you said carefully, ' Pergi ka Mercantile Bank,' the chances were your rick-shaw runner took you to the waterworks." But the truth is that the West African languages are not difficult to pick up ; nevertheless, there are an awful quantity of them and they are at the best most imperfect mediums of communication. No one who has been on the Coast can fail to recognise how inferior the native language is to the native mind behind it—and the prolixity and repetition he has therefore to employ to make his thoughts understood.

The great comfort is the wide diffusion of that peculiar

language, " trade English " ; it is not only used as a means
of intercommunication between whites and blacks, but between natives using two distinct languages.   On the south-west
Coast you find individuals in villages far from the sea, or a
trading station, who know it, and this is because they have
picked it up and employ it in their dealings with the coast
tribes and travelling traders.   It is by no means an easy
language to pick up—it is not a farrago of bad words and
broken phrases, but is a definite structure, has a great
peculiarity in its verb forms, and employs no genders.   There
is no grammar of it out yet ; and one of the best ways of
learning it is to listen to a seasoned second mate regulating
the unloading or loading, of cargo, over the hatch of the hold.
No, my Coast friends, I have *not* forgotten—but though you
did not mean it helpfully, this was one of the best hints you
ever gave me.

Another good way is the careful study of examples which
display the highest style and the most correct diction ; so I
append the letter given by Mr. Hutchinson as being about
the best bit of trade English I know.

" To Daddy nah Tampin Office,—

Ha Daddy, do, yah, nah beg you tell dem people for me ;
make dem Sally-own pussin know.   Do yah.   Berrah well.

Ah lib nah Pademba Road—one bwoy lib dah oberside
lakah dem two Docter lib overside you Tampin office.   Berrah
well.

Dah bwoy head big too much—he say nah Militie Ban—he
got one long long ting so so brass, someting lib dah go flip
flap, dem call am key.   Berrah well.   Had ! Dah bwoy kin
blow !—she ah !—na marin, oh !—nah sun time, oh ! nah evenin,
oh !—nah middle night, oh !—all same—no make pussin sleep.
Not ebry bit dat, more lib da !   One Boney bwoy lib oberside
nah he like blow bugle.   When dem two woh-woh bwoy blow
dem ting de nize too much too much.

When white man blow dat ting and pussin sleep he kin tap
wah make dem bwoy carn do so ?   Dem bwoy kin blow ebry
day eben Sunday dem kin blow.   When ah yerry dem blow
Sunday ah wish dah bugle kin go down na dem troat or
dem kin blow them head-bone inside.

Do nah beg you yah tell all dem people 'bout dah ting wah dem two bwoy dah blow. Till am Amtrang Boboh hab febah bad. Till am titty carn sleep nah night. Dah nize go kill me two pickin, oh!

Plabba done. Good by Daddy.

Crashey Jane."

Now for the elementary student we will consider this letter. The complaint in Crashey Jane's letter is about two boys who are torturing her morning, noon, and night, Sunday and week day, by blowing some " long long brass ting " as well as a bugle, and the way she dwells on their staying power must bring a sympathetic pang for that black sister into the heart of many a householder in London who lives next to a ladies' school, or a family of musical tastes. "One touch of nature," &c. " Daddy " is not a term of low familiarity but one of esteem and respect, and the " Tampin Office " is a respectful appellation for the Office of the " New Era " in which this letter was once published. " Bwoy head big too much," means that the young man is swelled with conceit because he is connected with " Militie ban." " Woh woh " you will find, among all the natives in the Bights, to mean extremely bad. I think it is native, having some connection with the root Wo—meaning power, &c. ; but Mr. Hutchinson may be right, and it may mean " a capacity to bring double woe."

" Amtrang Boboh " is not the name of some uncivilised savage, as the uninitiated may think ; far from it. It is Bob Armstrong—upside down, and slightly altered, and refers to the Hon. Robert Armstrong, stipendiary magistrate of Sierra Leone, &c.

" Berrah well " is a phrase used whenever the native thinks he has succeeded in putting his statement well. He sort of turns round and looks at it, says " Berrah well," in admiration of his own art, and then proceeds.

" Pickin " are children.

" Boney bwoy " is not a local living skeleton, but a native from Bonny River.

" Sally own " is Sierra Leone.

" Blow them head-bone inside " means, blow the top off their heads.

I have a collection of trade English letters and documents, for it is a language that I regard as exceedingly charming, and it really requires study, as you will see by reading Crashey Jane's epistle without the aid of a dictionary. It is, moreover, a language that will take you unexpectedly far in Africa, and if you do not understand it, land you in some pretty situations. One important point that you must remember is that the African is logically right in his answer to such a question as " You have not cleaned this lamp ? "—he says, " Yes, sah "—which means, " yes, I have not cleaned the lamp." It does not mean a denial to your accusation ; he always uses this form, and it is liable to confuse you at first, as are many other of the phrases, such as " I look him, I no see him " ; this means " I have been searching for the thing but have not found it " ; if he really meant he had looked upon the object but had been unable to get to it, he would say : " I look him, I no catch him," &c.

There is another class of letters written by Africans who have had school teaching to a high degree, and these are very fine literature—quite as fine as that of the Indian Baboo and with more ability and go in them. They are usually written in really exquisite handwriting, and abound in grandiloquence. I will not quote any here, save a phrase written in a letter I heard read out before the Court of the Chiefs at Bonny by young George Peppel—anent a quarrel then going on between him and his brother. " The subject," George eloquently stated, " has now become so delicately distended as to require the united wisdom of the wisest heads in Bonny for its solution." I like " delicately distended," much. I know so many subjects in England that are in this condition from the quantity of gas that has been put into them.

The difficulty of the language is, however, far less than the whole set of difficulties with your own mind. Unless you can make it pliant enough to follow the African idea step by step, however much care you may take, you will not bag your game. I heard an account the other day—I have forgotten where— of a representative of her Majesty in Africa who went out for a day's antelope shooting. There were plenty of antelope about, and he stalked them with great care ; but always, just before he got within shot of the game, they saw something and bolted. Knowing he and the boy behind him had been making no sound and could not have been seen, he stalked on, but always with the same result ; until happening to look round, he saw the boy behind him was supporting the dignity of the Empire at large, and this representative of it in particular, by steadfastly holding aloft the consular flag. Well, if you go hunting the African idea with the flag of your own religion or opinions floating ostentatiously over you, you will similarly get a very poor bag.

A few hints as to your mental outfit when starting on this port may be useful. Before starting for West Africa, burn all your notions about sun-myths and worship of the elemental forces. My own opinion is you had better also burn the notion, although it is fashionable, that human beings got their first notion of the origin of the soul from dreams.

I went out with my mind full of the deductions of every book on Ethnology, German or English, that I had read during fifteen years—and being a good Cambridge person, I was particularly confident that from Mr. Frazer's book, *The Golden Bough*, I had got a semi-universal key to the underlying idea of native custom and belief. But I soon found this was very far from being the case. His idea is a true key to a certain quantity of facts, but in West Africa only to a limited quantity.

I do not say, do not read Ethnology—by all means do so; and above all things read, until you know it by heart, *Primitive Culture*, by Dr. E. B. Tylor, regarding which book I may say that I have never found a fact that flew in the face of the carefully made, broad-minded deductions of this greatest of Ethnologists. In, addition you must know your Westermarck on *Human Marriage*, and your Waitz *Anthropologie*, and your Topinard—not that you need expect to go measuring people's skulls and chests as this last named authority expects you to do, for no self-respecting person black or white likes that sort of thing from the hands of an utter stranger, and if you attempt it you'll get yourself disliked in West Africa. Add to this the knowledge of all A. B. Ellis's works ; Burton's *Anatomy of Melancholy ;* Pliny's *Natural History ;* and

as much of Aristotle as possible. If you have a good knowledge of the Greek and Latin classics, I think it would be an
immense advantage; an advantage I do not possess, for my
classical knowledge is scrappy, and in place of it I have a
knowledge of Red Indian dogma : a dogma by the way that
seems to me much nearer the African in type than Asiatic
forms of dogma.

Armed with these instruments of observation, with a little
industry and care you should in the mill of your mind be able
to make the varied tangled rag-bag of facts that you will
soon become possessed of into a paper. And then I advise
you to lay the results of your collection before some great
thinker and he will write upon it the opinion that his greater
and clearer vision makes him more fit to form.

You may say, Why not bring these home their things in the
raw state? And bring them home in a raw state you must, for
purposes of reference ; but in this state they are of little use
to a person unacquainted with the conditions which
surround them in their native homes. Also very few
African stories bear on one subject alone, and they hardly
ever stick to a point. Take this Fernando Po legend. Windwood Reade (*Savage Africa*, p. 62) gives it, and he says he
heard it twice. I have heard it, in variants, four times—once
on Fernando Po, once in Calabar and twice in Gaboon. So
it is evidently an old story :—

" The first man called all people to one place. His name
was Raychow. 'Hear this, my people' said he, 'I am going
to give a name to every place, I am King in this River.' One
day he came with his people to the Hole of Wonga Wonga,
which is a deep pit in the ground from which fire comes at
night. Men spoke to them from the Hole, but they could not
see them. Raychow said to his son, 'Go down into the
Hole'—and his son went. The son of the King of the Hole
came to him and defied him to a contest of throwing the
spear. If he lost he should be killed, if he won he should go
back in safety. He won—then the son of the King of the
Hole said, 'It is strange you should have won, for I am a
spirit. Ask whatever you wish,' and the King's son asked
for a remedy for every disease he could remember ; and the

spirit gave him the medicines, and when he had done so, he said, ' There is one sickness you have forgotten—it is the Kraw-kraw, and of that you shall die.'

" ' A tribe named Ndiva was then strong but now none remain (Windwood Reade says four remain). They gave Raychow's son a canoe and forty men, to take him back to his father's town, and when he saw his father he did not speak. His father said, ' My son, if you are hungry eat.' He did not answer, and his father said, ' Do you wish me to kill a goat?' He did not answer ; his father said, ' Do you wish me to give you new wives?' He did not answer. Then his father said, ' Do you want me to build you a fetish hut?' Then he answered, 'Yes,' and the hut was built, and the medicines he had brought back from the Hole were put into it.

" ' Now,' said the son of King Raychow, ' I go to make the Moondah enter the Orongo' (Gaboon); so he went and dug a canal and when this was finished all his men were dead. Then he said, ' I will go and kill river-horse in the Benito.' He killed four, and as he was killing the fifth, the people descended from the mountains against him. So he made fetish on his great war-spear and sang

> My spear, go kill these people,
> Or these people will kill me ;

and the spear went and killed the people, except a few who got into canoes and flew to Fernando Po. Then said their King, ' My people shall never wear cloth till we have con-quered the M'pongwe,' and to this day the Fernando Poians go naked and hate with a special hatred the M'pongwe.' "

Now this is a noble story—there is a lot of fine confused feeding in it, as the Scotchman said of boiled sheep's head.

You learn from it—A. The name of the first man, and also that he was filled with a desire for topographical nomenclature.

B. You hear of the Hole Wonga Wonga, and this is most interesting because to this day, apart from the story, you are told by the natives of a hole that emits fire, and Dr. Nassau says it is always said to be north of Gaboon ; but so far no white man has any knowledge of an active volcano there, although the district is of volcanic origin. The crater of Fernando Po may be referred to in the legend because of the king's son being sent home in a canoe ; but I do not think it is, because the Hole is known not to be Fernando Po, and it has got, according to local tradition, a river running from it or close to it.

C. The kraw-kraw is a frightfully prevalent disease ; no one has a remedy for it, presumably owing to Raychow's son's forgetfulness.

D. The silence of the son to the questions is remarkable, because you always find people who have been among spirits lose their power of asking for what they want, for a time, and can only answer to the right question.

E. The sudden way in which Raychow's son gets fired with the desire to turn civil engineer just when he has got a magnificent opening in life as a doctor is merely the usual flightiness of young men, who do not see where their true advantages lie—and the conduct of the men in dying, after digging a canal is normal, and modern experiences support it, for men who dig canals down in West Africa die plentifully, be they black, white, or yellow ; so you can't help believing in those men, although it is strange a black man should have been so enterprising as to go in for canal digging at all. There is no other case of it extant to my knowledge, and a remarkable fact is, that the Moondah does so nearly connect, by one creek, with the Gaboon estuary that you can drag a boat across the little intervening bit of land.

F. Is a sporting story that turns up a little unexpectedly, certainly ; but the Benito is within easy distance north of the Moondah, so the geography is all right.

G. The inhabitants of Fernando Po have still an especial hatred for the M'pongwe, and both they and the M'pongwe have this account of the one tribe driving the other off the mainland. Then the Bubis [1]—as the inhabitants on Fernando Po are called, from a confusion arising in the minds of the sailors calling at Fernando Po, between their stupidity and their word Bâbi = stranger, which they use as a word of greet-

[1] The proper way to spell this name is booby, *i.e.*, silly, but as Bubi is the accepted spelling, I bow to authority.

ing—these Bubis are undoubtedly a very early African race. Their culture, though presenting some remarkable points, is on the whole exceedingly low. They never wear clothes unless compelled to, and their language depends so much on gesture that they cannot talk in it to each other in the dark.

I give this as a sample of African stories. It is far more connected and keeps to the point in a far more business-like way than most of them. They are of great interest when you know the locality and the tribe they come from; but I am sure if you were to bring home a heap of stories like this, and empty them over any distinguished ethnologist's head, without ticketing them with the culture of the tribe they belonged to, the conditions it lives under, and so forth, you would stun him with the seeming inter-contradiction of some, and utter pointlessness of the rest, and he would give up ethnology and hurriedly devote his remaining years to the attempt to collect a million postage stamps, so as to do some-thing definite before he died. Remember, you must always have your original material—carefully noted down at the time of occurrence—with you, so that you may say in answer to his Why? Because of this, and this, and this.

However good may be the outfit for your work that you take with you, you will have, at first, great difficulty in realising that it is possible for the people you are among really to believe things in the way they do. And you cannot associate with them long before you must recognise that these Africans have often a remarkable mental acuteness and a large share of common sense; that there is nothing really " child-like " in their form of mind at all. Observe them further and you will find they are not a flighty-minded, mystical set of people in the least. They are not dreamers, or poets, and you will observe, and I hope observe closely—for to my mind this is the most important difference between their make of mind and our own—that they are notably deficient in all mechanical arts : they have never made, unless under white direction and instruction, a single fourteenth-rate piece of cloth, pottery, a tool or machine, house, road, bridge, picture or statue; that a written language of their own construction they none of them possess. A careful study of the things a man, black or

white, fails to do, whether for good or evil, usually gives you a
truer knowledge of the man than the things he succeeds in
doing. When you fully realise this acuteness on one hand
and this mechanical incapacity on the other which exist in
the people you are studying, you can go ahead. Only, I
beseech you, go ahead carefully. When you have found the
easy key that opens the reason underlying a series of facts, as
for example, these : a Benga spits on your hand as a greeting ;
you see a man who has been marching regardless through the
broiling sun all the forenoon, with a heavy load, on entering
a village and having put down his load, elaborately steal round
in the shelter of the houses, instead of crossing the street ; you
come across a tribe that cuts its dead up into small pieces and
scatters them broadcast, and another tribe that thinks a white
man's eye-ball is a most desirable thing to be possessed of—
do not, when you have found this key, drop your collecting
work, and go home with a shriek of " I know all about Fetish,"
because you don't, for the key to the above facts will not open
the reason why it is regarded advisable to kill a person who
is making Ikung ; or why you should avoid at night a cotton
tree that has red earth at its roots ; or why combings of hair and
paring of nails should be taken care of ; or why a speck of
blood that may fall from your flesh should be cut out of wood—
if it has fallen on that—and destroyed, and if it has fallen on
the ground stamped and rubbed into the soil with great care.
This set requires another key entirely.

I must warn you also that your own mind requires protection
when you send it stalking the savage idea through the tangled
forests, the dark caves, the swamps and the fogs of the
Ethiopian intellect. The best protection lies in recognising
the untrustworthiness of human evidence regarding the unseen,
and also the seen, when it is viewed by a person who has in
his mind an explanation of the phenomenon before it occurs.
For example, take a person who, believing in ghosts, sees a
white figure in a churchyard, bolts home, has fits, and on revival
states he has seen a ghost, and gives details. He has seen a
ghost and therefore he is telling the truth. Another person
who does not believe in ghosts sees the thing, flies at it and
finds its component parts are boy and bed-sheet.

Do not applaud this individual, for he is quite conceited enough to make him comfortable ; yet when he says the phenomenon was a boy and a bed-sheet, he is also telling the truth, and not much more of the truth than observer number one, for, after all, inside the boy there is a real ghost that made him go and do the thing. I know many people have doubts as to the existence of souls in small boys of this class, holding that they contain only devils ; but devils can become ghosts, according to a mass of testimony. Great as the protection to the mind is, to keep it, as Hans Breitmann says, " still skebdical," I warn you that, with all precaution, the study of African metaphysics is bad for the brain, when you go and carry it on among all the weird, often unaccount-able surroundings, and depressing scenery of the Land of the Shadow of Death—a land that stretches from Goree to Loanda.

The fascination of the African point of view is as sure to linger in your mind as the malaria in your body. Never then will you be able to attain to the gay, happy cock-sureness regarding the Deity and the Universe of those people who stay at home, and whom the *Saturday* so aptly called " the suburban agnostics." You will always feel inclined to ask this class of people, " Yes ; well, what is Force ? What is Motion ; and above all, tell me what is Matter that you talk so glibly of ? and if so why ? " And the suburban agnostic looks down on you, and says pityingly, " Read Schopenhauer and Clifford," as if he were ordering you pills ; which revolts you, and you retort " Read Kant and Darwin," and the con-versation disappears into a fog of words.

The truth is, the study of natural phenomena knocks the bottom out of any man's conceit if it is done honestly and not by selecting only those facts that fit in with his pre-con-ceived or ingrafted notions. And, to my mind, the wisest way is to get into the state of mind of an old marine engineer who oils and sees that every screw and bolt of his engines is clean and well watched, and who loves them as living things, caressing and scolding them himself, defending them, with stormy language, against the aspersions of the silly, uninformed outside world, which persists in regarding them as mere machines, a thing his superior intelligence and experience knows they are not. Even animistic-minded I got awfully sat upon the other day in Cameroon by a superior but kindred spirit, in the form of a First Engineer. I had thoughtlessly repeated some scandalous gossip against the character of a naphtha launch in the river. "Stuff!" said he furiously; "she's all right, and she'd go from June to January if those blithering fools would let her alone." Of course I apologised.

The religious ideas of the Negroes, *i.e.*, the West Africans in the district from the Gambia to the Cameroon region, say roughly to the Rio del Rey (for the Bakwiri appear to have more of the Bantu form of idea than the negro, although physically they seem nearer the latter), differ very considerably from the religious ideas of the Bantu South-West Coast tribes. The Bantu is vague on religious subjects; he gives one accustomed to the negro the impression that he once had the same set of ideas, but has forgotten half of them, and those that he possesses have not got that hold on him that the corresponding or super-imposed Christian ideas have over the true Negro; although he is quite as keen on the subject of witchcraft, and his witchcraft differs far less from the witchcraft of the Negro than his religious ideas do.

Witchcraft is a wonderful thing in its way. In Africa I constantly come upon ideas and methods of procedure in it that are identical with those of Irish, Devonian, and Semitic witchcraft, but this subject is too large to enter upon here.

The god, in the sense we use the word, is in essence the same in all of the Bantu tribes I have met with on the Coast: a non-interfering and therefore a negligeable quantity. He varies his name: Anzambi, Anyambi, Nyambi, Nzambi, Anzam, Nyam, Ukuku, Suku, and Nzam, but a better investigation shows that Nzam of the Fans is practically identical with Suku south of the Congo in the Bihe country, and so on.

They regard their god as the creator of man, plants, animals, and the earth, and they hold that having made them, he takes no further interest in the affair. But not so the crowd of spirits with which the universe is peopled, they take only too much interest and the Bantu wishes they would not and is perpetually saying so in his prayers, a large percentage whereof amounts to "Go away, we don't want you." "Come not into this house, this village, or its plantations." He knows from experience that the spirits pay little heed to these objurgations, and as they are the people who must be attended to, he develops a cult whereby they may be managed, used, and understood. This cult is what we call witchcraft.

As I am not here writing a complete work on Fetish I will leave Nzam on one side, and turn to the inferior spirits. These are almost all malevolent; sometimes they can be coaxed into having creditable feelings, like generosity and gratitude, but you can never trust them. No, not even if you are yourself a well-established medicine man. Indeed they are particularly dangerous to medicine men, just as lions are to lion tamers, and many a professional gentleman, in the full bloom of his practice, gets eaten up by his own particular familiar which he has to keep in his own inside whenever he has not sent it off into other people's.

I am indebted to the Reverend Doctor Nassau for a great quantity of valuable information regarding Bantu religious ideas—information which no one is so competent to give as he, for no one else knows the West Coast Bantu tribes with the same thoroughness and sympathy. He has lived among them since 1851, and is perfectly conversant with their languages and culture, and he brings to bear upon the study of them a singularly clear, powerful, and highly-educated intelligence.

I shall therefore carefully ticket the information I have derived from him, so that it may not be mixed with my own. I may be wrong in my deductions, but Dr. Nassau's are above suspicion.

He says the origin of these spirits is vague—some of them come into existence by the authority of Anzam (by which you will understand, please, the same god I have quoted above as having many names), others are self-existent—many are distinctly the souls of departed human beings, "which in the future which is all around them" retain their human wants and feelings, and the Doctor assures me he has heard dying people with their last breath threatening to return as spirits to revenge themselves upon their living enemies. He could not tell me if there was any duration set upon the existence as spirits of these human souls, but two Congo Français natives, of different tribes, Benga and Igalwa, told me that when a family had quite died out, after a time its spirits died too. Some, but by no means all, of these spirits of human origin, as is the case among the negro Effiks, undergo reincarnation. The Doctor told me he once knew a man whose plantations were devastated by an elephant. He advised that the beast should be shot, but the man said he dare not because the spirit of his dead father had passed into the elephant.

Their number is infinite and their powers as varied as human imagination can make them ; classifying them is therefore a difficult work, but Doctor Nassau thinks this may be done fairly completely into :—

1. Human disembodied spirits—*Manu*.

2. Vague beings, well described by our word ghosts : *Abambo*.

3. Beings something like dryads, who resent intrusion into their territory, on to their rock, past their promontory, or tree. When passing the residence of one of these beings, the traveller must go by silently, or with some cabalistic invocation, with bowed or bared head, and deposit some symbol of an offering or tribute even if it be only a pebble. You occasionally come across great trees that have fallen across a path that have quite little heaps of pebbles, small shells, &c., upon them deposited by previous passers-by. This class is called *Ombwiri*.

4. Beings who are the agents in causing sickness, and either aid or hinder human plans—*Mionde*.

5. There seems to be, the Doctor says, another class of spirits somewhat akin to the ancient Lares and Penates, who especially belong to the household, and descend by inheritance with the family. In their honour are secretly kept a bundle of finger, or other bones, nail-clippings, eyes, brains, &c., accumulated from deceased members of successive generations.

Dr. Nassau says "secretly," and he refers to this custom being existent in non-cannibal tribes. I saw bundles of this character among the cannibal Fans, and among the non-cannibal Adooma, openly hanging up in the thatch of the sleeping apartment.

6. He also says there may be a sixth class, which may, however only be a function of any of the other classes—namely, those that enter into any animal body, generally a leopard. Sometimes the spirits of living human beings do this, and the animal is then guided by human intelligence, and will exercise its strength for the purposes of its temporary human possessor. In other cases it is a non-human soul that enters into the animal, as in the case of Ukuku.

Spirits are not easily classified by their functions because those of different class may be employed in identical undertakings. Thus one witch doctor may have, I find, particular influence over one class of spirit and another over another class ; yet they will both engage to do identical work. But in spite of this I do not see how you can classify spirits otherwise than by their functions ; you cannot weigh and measure them, and it is only a few that show themselves in corporeal form.

There are characteristics that all the authorities seem agreed on, and one is that individual spirits in the same class vary in power : some are strong of their sort, some weak.

They are all to a certain extent limited in the nature of their power ; there is no one spirit that can do all things ; their efficiency only runs in certain lines of action and all of them are capable of being influenced, and made subservient to human wishes, by proper incantations. This latter characteristic is of course to human advantage, but it has its disadvantages, for you can never really trust a spirit, even if you have paid a considerable sum to a most distinguished medicine man to get a powerful one put up in a ju-ju, or monde,[1] as it is called in several tribes.

The method of making these charms is much the same among Bantu and Negroes. I have elsewhere described the

[1] This article has different names in different tribes ; thus it is called a bian among the Fan, a tarwiz, gree-gree, &c., on other parts of the Coast.

Gold Coast method, so here confine myself to the Bantu. This similarity of procedure naturally arises from the same underlying idea existing in the two races.

You call in the medicine man, the "oganga," as he is commonly called in Congo Français tribes. After a variety of ceremonies and processes, the spirit is induced to localise itself in some object subject to the will of the possessor. The things most frequently used are antelopes' horns, the large snail-shells, and large nut-shells, according to Doctor

MAKING A CHARM IN THE UPPER OGOWÉ REGION.

Nassau. Among the Fan I found the most frequent charm-case was in the shape of a little sausage, made very neatly of pineapple fibre, the contents being the residence of the spirit or power, and the outside coloured red to flatter and please him—for spirits always like red.

The substance put inside charms is all manner of nasti-ness, usually on the sea coast having a high percentage of fowl dung.

The nature of the substance depends on the spirit it is

intended to be attractive to—attractive enough to induce it to leave its present abode and come and reside in the charm.

In addition to this attractive substance I find there are other materials inserted which have relation towards the work the spirit will be wanted to do for its owner.   For example, charms made either to influence a person to be well disposed towards the owner, or the still larger class made with intent to work evil on other human beings against whom the owner has a grudge, must have in them some portion of the person to be dealt with—his hair, blood, nail-parings, &c.—or, failing that, his or her most intimate belonging, something that has got his smell in—a piece of his old waist-cloth for example.

This ability to obtain power over people by means of their blood, hair, nails, &c., is universally diffused ; you will find it down in Devon, and away in far Cathay, and the Chinese, I am told, have in some parts of their empire little ovens to burn their nail- and hair-clippings in.   The fear of these latter belongings falling into the hands of evilly-disposed persons is ever present to the West Africans.   The Igalwa and other tribes will allow no one but a trusted friend to do their hair, and bits of nails and hair are carefully burnt or thrown away into a river ; and blood, even that from a small cut or a fit of nose-bleeding, is most carefully covered up and stamped out if it has fallen on the earth.   Dr. Nassau says, " If it falls on the side of a canoe, or a tree, the place is carefully cut out and the chip destroyed.   Blood from a wound on a woman is held in high horror.   This has probably something to do with the drawing of blood constituting grounds of divorce among the Igalwa.   A Fan told me that a man in the village, who was so weak from some cause or other that he could hardly crawl about, had fallen into this state by seeing the blood of a woman who had been killed by a falling tree.   The underlying idea regarding blood is of course the old one that the blood is the life.

The life in Africa means a spirit, hence the liberated blood is the liberated spirit, and liberated spirits are always whipping into people who do not want them.   In the case of the young Fan, the opinion held was that the weak spirit of the woman had got into him.   I could not help being reminded of the saying one often hears from a person in England who has seen some tragedy,—" I cannot get the horror of it out of my eyes." This "horror" would mean to an African a spirit coming from the thing itself.

Charms are made for every occupation and desire in life— loving, hating, buying, selling, fishing, planting, travelling, hunting, &c., and although they are usually in the form of things filled with a mixture in which the spirit nestles, yet there are other kinds ; for example, a great love charm is made of the water the lover has washed in, and this, mingled with the drink of the loved one, is held to soften the hardest heart. Of a similar nature is the friendship-compelling charm I know of on the Ivory Coast, which I have been told is used also in the Batanga regions. This is obtained on the death of a person you know really cared for you —like your father or mother, for example—by cutting off the head and suspending it over a heap of chalk, as the white earth that you find in river beds is called here, then letting it drip as long as it will and using this saturated chalk to mix in among the food of any one you wish should think kindly of you and trust you. This charm, a Bassa man said to me, " was good too much for the white trader," and made him give you " good price too much " for palm oil, &c., and that statement revived my sympathy for a friend who once said to me that when he used first to come to the Coast he had "pretty well had the inside raked up out of him " from the sickness caused by the charms that his local cook administered to him in the interest of the cook's friends. That man keeps an Accra cook now, and I trust lives a life of healthy, icy, unemotional calm.

Some kinds of charms, such as those to prevent your getting drowned, shot, seen by elephants, &c., are worn on a bracelet or necklace. A new-born child starts with a health-knot tied round the wrist, neck, or loins, and throughout the rest of its life its collection of charms goes on increasing. This collection does not, however, attain inconvenient dimensions, owing to the failure of some of the charms to work.

That is the worst of charms and prayers. The thing you wish of them may, and frequently does, happen in a strikingly direct way, but other times it does not. In Africa this is held to arise

from the bad character of the spirits; their gross ingratitude and fickleness. You may have taken every care of a
spirit for years, given it food and other offerings that you
wanted for yourself, wrapped it up in your cloth on chilly
nights and gone cold, put it in the only dry spot in the canoe,
and so on, and yet after all this, the wretched thing will be
capable of being got at by your rival or enemy and lured
away, leaving you only the case it once lived in.

Finding, we will say, that you have been upset and half-
drowned, and your canoe-load of goods lost three times in a
week, that your paddles are always breaking, and the amount
of snags in the river and so on is abnormal, you judge that
your canoe charm has stopped. Then you go to the medicine
man who supplied you with it and complain. He says it was
a perfectly good charm when he sold it you and he never had
any complaints before, but he will investigate the affair ; when
he has done so, he either says the spirit has been lured away
from the home he prepared for it by incantations and
presents from other people, or that he finds the spirit is dead ;
it has been killed by a more powerful spirit of its class, which
is in the pay of some enemy of yours. In all cases the little
thing you kept the spirit in is no use now, and only fit to sell
to a white man as "a big curio!" and the sooner you let
him have sufficient money to procure you a fresh and still
more powerful spirit—necessarily more expensive—the safer
it will be for you, particularly as your misfortunes distinctly
point to some one being desirous of your death. You of
course grumble, but seeing the thing in his light you pay up,
and the medicine man goes busily to work with incantations,
dances, looking into mirrors or basins of still water, and con-
coctions of messes to make you a new protecting charm.

Human eye-balls, particularly of white men, I have already
said are a great charm. Dr. Nassau says he has known graves
rifled for them. This, I fancy, is to secure the "man that
lives in your eyes" for the service of the village, and naturally
the white man, being regarded as a superior being, would
be of high value if enlisted into its service. A similar idea
of the possibility of gaining possession of the spirit of a dead
man obtains among the Negroes, and the heads of important

chiefs in the Calabar districts are usually cut off from the body on burial and kept secretly for fear the head, and thereby the spirit, of the dead chief, should be stolen from the town. If it were stolen it would be not only a great advantage to its new possessor, but a great danger to the chief's old town, because he would know all the peculiar ju-ju relating to it. For each town has a peculiar one, kept exceedingly secret, in addition to the general ju-jus, and this secret one would then be in the hands of the new owners of the spirit. It is for similar reasons that brave General MacCarthy's head was treasured by the Ashantees, and so on.

Charms are not all worn upon the body, some go to the plantations, and are hung there, ensuring an unhappy and swift end for the thief who comes stealing. Some are hung round the bows of the canoe, others over the doorway of the house, to prevent evil spirits from coming in—a sort of tame watch-dog spirits.

The entrances to the long street-shaped villages are frequently closed with a fence of saplings and this sapling fence you will see hung with fetish charms to prevent evil spirits from entering the village and sometimes in addition to charms you will see the fence wreathed with leaves and flowers. I tried to find out whether these leaves were for the residence or amusement of the protecting spirits or whether they were traps for the evil spirits attempting to enter the town. Both reasons were given me, the latter most definitely. Bells are frequently hung on these fences, but I do not fancy ever for fetish reasons. At Ndorko, on the Rembwé, there were many guards against spirit visitors, but the bell, which was carefully hung so that you could not pass through the gateway without ringing it, was a guard against thieves and human enemies only. It was entirely a piece of native manufacture, shaped very like the cow-bells my friends bring home from Switzerland, with the same hoarse note, and I was informed, when at Lembarene, that down in a corner of the Lake of Islands there were a party of Fans who could not get out because they had quarrelled, *more suo*, with a village of fellow Fans who guard the entrance for canoes to the said corner, keeping a bright look out by day, to see the imprisoned ones did not escape, and by night stretching a line hung with bells from stake to stake, so that the least touch of a canoe on it set the bells ringing and the captors on the alert. The opinion was that unless the Government intervened the imprisoned Fans would gradually get killed and eaten by their fellow tribesmen, and then there will be a brief peace in that corner. They seem, I must say, to be a nice set down in that Eliva Z'onange, for they had eaten a returning communicant from the Catholic mission a few weeks before I reached Lembarene; but this is mere chop palaver, for the cannibalism of the Fan is not a sacrificial cannibalism like that of the Niger Delta tribes, so we will leave it on one side and return to the gateways.

Frequently a sapling is tied horizontally near the ground across the entrance. Dr. Nassau could not tell me why, but says it must never be trodden on. When the smallpox, a dire pestilence in these regions, is raging, or when there is war, these gateways are sprinkled with the blood of sacrifices, and for these sacrifices and for the payments of heavy blood fines, &c., goats and sheep are kept. They are rarely eaten for ordinary purposes, and these West Coast Africans have all a perfect horror of the idea of drinking milk, holding this custom to be a filthy habit, and saying so in unmitigated language.

The villagers eat the meat of the sacrifice, that having nothing to do with the sacrifice to the spirits, which is the blood, for the blood is the life.[1]

Beside the few spirits that the Bantu regards himself as having got under control in his charms, he has to worship the uncontrolled army of the air. This he does by sacrifice and incantation.

The sacrifice is the usual killing of something valuable as an offering to the spirits. The value of the offering in these S.W. Coast regions has certainly a regular relationship to the value of the favour required of the spirits. Some favours are worth a dish of plantains, some a fowl, some a goat and some

[1] Care must be taken not to confuse with sacrifices propitiations of spirits; the killing of men and animals as offerings to the souls of deceased persons.

a human being, though human sacrifice is very rare in Congo Français, the killing of people being nine times in ten a witchcraft palaver.

Dr. Nassau, however, says that "the intention of the giver ennobles the gift," the spirit being supposed, in some vague way, to be gratified by the recognition of itself, and even sometimes pleased with the homage of the mere simulacrum of a gift. I believe the only class of spirits that have this convenient idea are the Ombwiri; thus the stones heaped by passers-by on the foot of some great tree, or rock, or the leaf cast from a passing canoe towards a promontory on the river, &c., although intrinsically valueless and useless to the Ombwiri nevertheless gratify him. It is a sort of bow or taking off one's hat to him. Some gifts, the Doctor says, are supposed to be actually utilised by the spirit.

In some part of the long single street of most villages there is built a low hut in which charms are hung, and by which grows a consecrated plant, a lily, a euphorbia, or a fig. In some tribes a rudely carved figure, generally female, is set up as an idol before which offerings are laid. I saw at Egaja two figures about 2 feet 6 inches high, in the house placed at my disposal. They were left in it during my occupation, save that the rolls of cloth (their power) which were round their necks, were removed by the owner chief; of the significance of these rolls I will speak elsewhere.

Incantations may be divided into two classes, supplications analogous to our idea of prayers, and certain cabalistic words and phrases. The supplications are addresses to the higher spirits. Some are made even to Anzam himself, but the spirit of the new moon is that most commonly addressed to keep the lower spirits from molesting.

Dr. Nassau gave me many instances out of the wealth of his knowledge. One night when he was stopping at a village, he saw standing out in the open street a venerable chief who addressed the spirits of the air and begged them, "Come ye not into my town;" he then recounted his good deeds, praising himself as good, just, honest, kind to his neighbours, and so on. I must remark that this man had not been in touch with Europeans, so his ideal of goodness was the native one—which you will find everywhere among the most remote West Coast natives. He urged these things as a reason why no evil should befall him, and closed with an impassioned appeal to the spirits to stay away. At another time, in another village, when a man's son had been wounded and a bleeding artery which the Doctor had closed had broken out again and the hæmorrhage seemed likely to prove fatal, the father rushed out into the street wildly gesticulating towards the sky, saying, "Go away, go away, go away, ye spirits, why do you come to kill my son?" In another case a woman rushed into the street, alternately objurgating and pleading with the spirits, who, she said, were vexing her child which had convulsions. "Observe," said the Doctor in his impressive way, "these were distinctly prayers, appeals for mercy, agonising protests, but there was no praise, no love, no thanks, no confession of sin." I said, considering the underlying idea, I did not see how that could be, thinking of the thing as they did, and the Doctor and I had one of our little disagreements. I shall always feel grateful to him for his great toleration of me, but I am sure this arose from his feeling that I saw there was an underlying idea in the minds of the people he loved well enough to lay down his life for in the hope of benefiting and ennobling them, and that I did not, as many do, set them down as idiotic brutes, glorying in an aimless cruelty that would be a disgrace to a devil.

Regarding the cabalistic words and phrases, things which had long given me great trouble to get any comprehension of, the Doctor gave me great help. He says some of these phrases and words are coined by the person himself, others are archaisms handed down from ancestors and believed to possess an efficacy, though their actual meaning is forgotten. He says they are used at any time as defence from evil, when a person is startled, sneezes, or stumbles. Among these I think I ought to class that peculiar form of friendly farewell or greeting which the Doctor poetically calls a "blown blessing" and the natives Ibata. I thought the three times it was given to me that it was just spitting on the hand. Practically it is so, but the Doctor says the spitting is accidental, a by-product I suppose. The method consists in taking the right hand in both yours, turning it palm upwards, bending your head low over it, and saying with great energy and a violent propulsion of the breath, Ibata.

Idols are comparatively rare in Congo Français, but where they are used the people have the same idea about them as the true negroes have, namely, that they are things which spirits reside in, or haunt, but not in their corporeal nature adorable. The resident spirit in them and in the charms and plants, which are also regarded as residences of spirits, has to be placated with offerings of food and other sacrifices. You will see in the Fetish huts above mentioned dishes of plantain and fish left till they rot. Dr. Nassau says the life or essence of the food only is eaten by the spirit, the form of the vegetable or flesh being left to be removed when its life is gone out. The Calabar negroes told me that the spirits often take the forms of lizards—which abound in this country —and come and eat the food, and they always seem to doubt whether the offered food has reached its proper destination unless some animal has eaten it. But for one thing, as I have said before, the true Negro is more definite in his ideas, and his gods and spirits very practical individuals, whereas the Bantu are vaguer, and moreover there are not so many lizards in Congo Français, so perhaps the native metaphysician is forced to be more spiritual in his ideas about his sacrifice.

In cases of emergency a fowl with its blood is laid at the door of the Fetish hut, or when pestilence is expected, or an attack by enemies, or a great man or woman is very ill, goats and sheep are sacrificed and the blood put in the Fetish hut as well as on the gateways of the village. These sacrifices among the Fan are made with a very peculiar-shaped knife, a fine specimen of which I secured by the kindness of Captain Davies ; it is shaped like the head of a hornbill and is quite unlike the knives in common use among the tribes, which are either long, leaf-shaped blades sharpened along both edges, or broad, trowel-shaped, almost triangular daggers. All Fan knives are fine weapons, superior to the knives of all other Coast tribes I have met with, but the sacrifice knife is distinctly peculiar. Du Chaillu figures one in his book, calling it a tomahawk. Other people besides him speak of it and call it a throwing knife. I believe it is entirely used for sacrificing. I do not believe you could throw it, as its curve and heavy weight at the back bring it round when you attempt to, and it is quite unlike the multi-bladed, real throwing knives of some middle Congo tribes. But it is perfectly adapted for killing animals by a blow behind the head, at the top of the spine, and this is the way I have seen it used, and if I remember right, Du Chaillu does not say that he himself saw it thrown. I have never seen any knife like it except in an illustration to Junker's *Reiser im Afrika* (1891, vol. iii. p. 122), where one very similar is figured among the knives of the Mungabatu.

There are several other implements of this cannibal tribe figured by Junker that have a great resemblance to the Fan things used for similar purposes, and I am much tempted to think that these two tribes are, if not identical, at least very nearly related. The same dwarf people, the pygmies, are in the Mungabatu region, and are fairly frequent in the forest among the Fans, and the north-east and east limitations of the Fans are not yet known.

I found to my great interest the same superstition in Congo Français that I met with first in the Oil Rivers. Its meaning I am unable to fully account for, but I believe it to be a form of sacrifice. In Calabar each individual has a certain forbidden thing or things. These things are either forms of food, or the method of eating. In Calabar this prohibition is called Ibet, and when, in consequence of the influence of white culture, a man gives up his Ibet, he is regarded by good sound ju-juists as leading an irregular and dissipated life, and even the unintentional breaking of the Ibet is regarded as very dangerous. For example, in buying a slave the purchaser always inquires what is the slave's Ibet, because if the slave were given his Ibet to eat, he would get ill ; again, once when staying with my esteemed friend Miss Mary Slessor at Okÿon, there arrived among her crowd of patients a small boy with a very " sick foot." On being asked from what it had arisen, instead of getting the usual answer, " picked up medicine on the road," the boy said he had broken his Ibet. Miss Slessor told me that shortly after a child is born some of the elderly female relatives meet together and find out, by their magic, what the child's Ibet during life is to be. When they have done so, it is made known and he has to keep to it.

Special days are set apart by each individual; on these days he eats only the smallest quantity and plainest quality of food. No one must eat with him, nor any dog, fowl, &c., feed off the crumbs, nor any one watch him while eating. I suspect on this day the Ibet is eaten, but I have not verified this, only getting, from an untrustworthy source, a statement that supported it.

Dr. Nassau told me that among Congo Français tribes certain rites are performed for children during infancy or youth, in which a prohibition is laid upon the child as regards the eating of some particular article of food, or the doing of certain acts. "It is difficult," he said, "to get the exact object of the 'Orunda.' Certainly the prohibited article is not in itself evil, for others but the inhibited individual may eat or do with it as they please. Most of the natives blindly follow the custom of their ancestors without being able to give any *raison d'être*, but again, from those best able to give a reason, you learn the prohibited article is a sacrifice ordained for the child by its parents and the magic doctor as a gift to the governing spirit of its life. The thing prohibited becomes removed from the child's common use, and is made sacred to the spirit. Any use of it by the child or man would therefore be a sin, which would bring down the spirit's wrath in the form of sickness or other evil, which can be atoned for only by expensive ceremonies or gifts to the magic doctor who intercedes for the offender."

Anything may be an Orunda provided only that it is connected with food; I have been able to find no definite ground for the selection of it. The Doctor said, for example, that "once when on a boat journey, and camped in the forest for the noon-day meal, the crew of four had no meat. They needed it. I had a chicken but ate only a portion, and gave the rest to the crew. Three men ate it with their manioc meal, the fourth would not touch it. It was his Orunda." "On another journey," said the Doctor, "instead of all my crew leaving me respectfully alone in the canoe to have my lunch and going ashore to have theirs, one of them stayed behind in the canoe, and I found his Orunda was only to eat over water when on a journey by water." "At another place, a chief at whose village we once anchored in a small steamer when a glass of rum was given him, had a piece of cloth held up before his mouth that the people might not see him drink, which was his Orunda."

I know some ethnologists will think this last case should be classed under another head, but I think the Doctor is right. He is well aware of the existence of the other class of prohibitions regarding chiefs and I have seen plenty of chiefs myself up the Rembwé who have no objection to take their drinks *coram publico*, and I have no doubt this was only an individual Orunda of this particular Rembwé chief.

Great care is requisite in these matters, because a man may do or abstain from doing one and the same thing for divers reasons.

The word Orunda means prohibition, the Doctor says. In Effik I found the word Ibet meant a command—a law—an abstinence.

CHAPTER XX

FETISH—(*Continued*)

In which the Voyager discourses on deaths and witchcraft, and, with no
intentional slur on the medical profession, on medical methods and
burial customs, concluding with sundry observations on twins.

IT is exceedingly interesting to compare the ideas of the
Negroes with those of the Bantu. At present I have
a more definite knowledge of the former, but I have
gained sufficient knowledge of the West Coast Bantu to be
able to commence a regular comparative study of these two
analogous, but by no means identical, sets of ideas.

I fancy you find the earliest forms, both of religion and
witchcraft, among the negroes, and I hope in some future
sojourn on the Bantu border-line to work up the subject
more thoroughly, for it is one of great interest to the student
of mental evolution.

The mental condition of the lower forms of both races
seems very near the other great border-line that separates
man from the anthropoid apes, and I believe that if we had
the material, or rather if we could understand it, we should
find little or no gap existing in mental evolution in this old,
undisturbed continent of Africa.

There is one point in evolution, and one only, on which
I am a little heterodox, and that is the dogma that all human
beings came in the beginning from a single pair, appearing
somewhere in Asia, and that their descendants then migrated
about the earth accustoming themselves, their religion, their
cooking, and their culture to new environments, turning the
while all sorts of colours, and developing peculiarities of no

mortal use, and half the time of no ornament, in the matter of hair.

I know, of course, that the South-West Coast tribes have all migrated from a region in the north-east that seems to be perpetually throwing off tribe after tribe, which all come west, and die out in the swamp-lands of the West Coast ; but at the same time we know, and have known for hundreds of years, quite enough of the regions beyond those from which the South-West Coast tribes—Duallas, M'pongwe, Benga, and Fan —have come during modern times, to be certain that these interesting and striking-looking hosts of human beings have not come trapesing across from Asia. I am not planting an African garden of Eden to rival the Asiatic one. I am only saying I agree with the French ethnologists and fancy there have been several points of origin of the human race.

Let, however, these things be as they may, one thing about Negro and Bantu races is very certain, and that is that their lives are dominated by a profound belief in witchcraft and its effects.

Among both alike the rule is that death is regarded as a direct consequence of the witchcraft of some malevolent human being, acting by means of spirits, over which he has, by some means or another, obtained control.

To all rules there are exceptions. Among the Calabar negroes, who are definite in their opinions, I found two classes of exceptions. The first arises from their belief in a bush-soul. They believe every man has four souls : a, the soul that survives death ; b, the shadow on the path ; c, the dream-soul ; d, the bush-soul.

This bush-soul is always in the form of an animal in the forest—never of a plant. Sometimes when a man sickens it is because his bush-soul is angry at being neglected, and a witch-doctor is called in, who, having diagnosed this as being the cause of the complaint, advises the administration of some kind of offering to the offended one. When you wander about in the forests of the Calabar region, you will frequently see little dwarf huts with these offerings in them. You must not confuse these huts with those of similar construction you are continually seeing in plantations, or near roads, which refer to quite other affairs. These offerings, in the little huts in the forest, are placed where your bush-soul was last seen. Unfortunately, you are compelled to call in a doctor, which is an expense, but you cannot see your own bush-soul, unless you are an Ebumtup, a sort of second-sighter.

Ebumtupism is rare, and if you do happen to possess this gift, it is discovered by the presiding elders during your initiation to the secret society of your tribe. When it is discovered the presiding elders strongly advise that you should enter the medical profession and become a witch doctor, as this profession is a paying one, although the training for it is dreadfully expensive to your parents, for it has to be carried on by the established witch-doctor. Your parents, if you are discovered to be an Ebumtup, usually make sacrifices after the way of parents, black or white, and you proceed with your studies.

But to return to the bush-soul of an ordinary person. If the offering in the hut works well on the bush-soul, the patient recovers, but if it does not he dies. Diseases arising from derangements in the temper of the bush-soul however, even when treated by the most eminent practitioners, are very apt to be intractable, because it never realises that by injuring you it endangers its own existence. For when its human owner dies, the bush-soul can no longer find a good place, and goes mad, rushing to and fro—if it sees a fire it rushes into it ; if it sees a lot of people it rushes among them, until it is killed, and when it is killed it is "finish" for it, as M. Pichault would say, for it is not an immortal soul.

The bush-souls of a family are usually the same for a man and for his sons, for a mother and for her daughters. Sometimes, however, I am told all the children take the mother's, sometimes all take the father's. They may be almost any kind of animal, sometimes they are leopards, sometimes fish, or tortoises, and so on.

There is another peculiarity about the bush-soul, and that is that it is on its account that old people are held in such esteem among the Calabar tribes. For, however bad these old people's personal record may have been, the fact of their longevity demonstrates the possession of powerful and astute bush-souls. On the other hand, a man may be a quiet, respectable citizen, devoted to peace and a whole skin, and yet he may have a sadly flighty disreputable bush-soul which will get itself killed or damaged and cause him death or continual ill-health.

There is another way by which a man dies apart from the action of bush-souls or witchcraft ; he may have had a bad illness from some cause in his previous life and, when reincarnated, part of this disease may get reincarnated with him and then he will ultimately die of it. There is no medicine of any avail against these reincarnated diseases.

The idea of reincarnation is very strong in the Niger Delta tribes. It exists, as far as I have been able to find out, throughout all Africa, but usually only in scattered cases, as it were ; but in the Delta, most— I think I may say all—human souls of the " surviving soul " class are regarded as returning to the earth again, and undergoing a reincarnation shortly after the due burial of the soul.

These two exceptions from the rule of all deaths and sickness being caused by witchcraft are, however, of minor importance, for infinitely the larger proportion of death and sickness is held to arise from witchcraft itself, more particularly among the Bantu.

Witchcraft acts in two ways, namely, witching something out of a man, or witching something into him. The former method is used by both Negro and Bantu, but is decidedly more common among the Negroes, where the witches are continually setting traps to catch the soul that wanders from the body when a man is sleeping ; and when they have caught this soul, they tie it up over the canoe fire and its owner sickens as the soul shrivels.

This is merely a regular line of business, and not an affair of individual hate or revenge. The witch does not care whose dream-soul gets into the trap, and will restore it on payment. Also witch-doctors, men of unblemished professional reputation, will keep asylums for lost souls, *i.e.*, souls who have been out wandering and found on their return to their body that their place has been filled up by a Sisa, a low class soul I will speak of later. These doctors keep souls and administer them to patients who are short of the article.

But there are other witches, either wicked on their own account, or hired by people who are moved by some hatred to individuals, and then the trap is carefully set and baited for the soul of the particular man they wish to injure, and concealed in the bait at the bottom of the pot are knives and sharp hooks which tear and damage the soul, either killing it outright, or mauling it so that it causes its owner sickness on its return to him. I knew the case of a Kruman who for several nights had smelt in his dreams the savoury smell of smoked crawfish seasoned with red peppers. He became anxious, and the headman decided some witch had set a trap baited with this dainty for his dream-soul, with intent to do him grievous bodily harm, and great trouble was taken for the next few nights to prevent this soul of his from straying abroad.

My attention was drawn to the case by snorts, snores, and flumps on the Kruman's part of even more than usual violence, and I went to see what was up with the man, mentally deciding that what he wanted was a dose of my pet pill. I found him under a blanket and his nose and mouth tied over with a handkerchief. It was a sweltering hot night and the man was as wet with sweat as if he had been dragged through a river, so I suggested his muzzle should be removed and then being informed of the state of affairs regarding his soul, I of course did not interfere.

The witching of things into a man is far the most frequent method among the Bantu, hence the prevalence among them of the post-mortem examination,—a practice I never found among the Negroes.

The idea of the majority of deaths arising from witchcraft is, I believe, quite true if you will read witchcraft as poison. In a dull sort of way sometimes the black man understands it so too, as is shown by his very generally regarding the best remedy for witching as being a brisk purgative and emetic, accompanied of course with suitable ceremonies.

The belief in witchcraft is the cause of more African deaths than anything else. It has killed and still kills more men and women than the slave-trade. Its only rival is perhaps the smallpox, the Grand Kraw-Kraw, as the Krumen graphically call it.

At almost every death a suspicion of witchcraft arises. The witch-doctor is called in, and proceeds to find out the guilty person. Then woe to the unpopular men, the weak women, and the slaves ; for on some of them will fall the accusation that means ordeal by poison, or fire, followed, if these point to guilt, as from their nature they usually do, by a terrible death : slow roasting alive—mutilation by degrees before the throat is mercifully cut—tying to stakes at low tide that the high tide may come and drown—and any other death human ingenuity and hate can devise.

The terror in which witchcraft is held is interesting in spite of all its horror. I have seen mild, gentle men and women turned by it, in a moment, to incarnate fiends, ready to rend and destroy those who a second before were nearest and dearest to them. Terrible is the fear that falls like a spell upon a village when a big man, or big woman is just known to be dead. The very men catch their breaths, and grow grey round the lips, and then every one, particularly those belonging to the household of the deceased, goes in for the most demon-strative exhibition of grief. Long, low howls creep up out of the first silence—those blood-curdling, infinitely melancholy, wailing howls—once heard, never to be forgotten.

The men tear off their clothes and wear only the most filthy rags ; women, particularly the widows, take off orna-ments and almost all dress ; their faces are painted white with chalk, their heads are shaven, and they sit crouched on the earth in the house, in the attitude of abasement, the hands resting on the shoulders, palm downwards, not crossed across the breast, unless they are going into the street.

Meanwhile the witch-doctor has been sent for, if he is not already present, and he sets to work in different ways to find out who are the persons guilty of causing the death.

Whether the methods vary with the tribe, or with the in-dividual witch-doctor, I cannot absolutely say, but I think largely with the latter.

Among the Benga I saw a witch-doctor going round a village ringing a small bell which was to stop ringing outside the hut of the guilty. Among the Cabindas (Fjort) I saw, at different times, two witch-doctors trying to find witches, one by means of taking on and off the lid of a small basket while he repeated the names of all the people in the village. When the lid refused to come off at the name of a person, that person was doomed. The other Cabinda doctor first tried throwing nuts upon the ground, also repeating names. That method apparently failed. Then he resorted to another, rubbing the flattened palms of his hands against each other. When the palms refused to meet at a name, and his hands flew about wildly, he had got his man.

The accused person, if he denies the guilt, and does not claim the ordeal, is tortured until he not only acknowledges his guilt but names his accomplices in the murder, for re-member this witchcraft is murder in the African eyes. It is not just producing the parlour tricks of modern spiritualists.

If he claims the ordeal, as he usually does, he usually has to take a poison drink. Among all the Bantu tribes I know this is made from Sass wood (sass = bad ; sass water = rough water ; sass surf = bad surf, &c.), and is a decoction of the freshly pulled bark of a great hard wood forest tree, which has a tall unbranched stem, terminating in a crown of branches bearing small leaves. Among the Calabar tribes the ordeal drink is of two kinds : one made from the Calabar bean, the other, the great ju-ju drink Mbiam, which is used also in taking oaths.

In both the sass-wood and Calabar bean drink the only chance for the accused lies in squaring the witch-doctor, so that in the case of the sass-wood drink it is allowed to settle before administration, and in the bean that you get a very heavy dose, both arrangements tending to produce the immediate emetic effect indicative of innocence. If this effect does not come on quickly you die a miserable death from the effects of the poison interrupted by the means taken to kill you as soon as it is decided from the absence of violent sickness that you are guilty.

The Mbiam is not poisonous, nor is its use confined, as the

use of the bean is, entirely to witch palaver ; but it is the most
respected and dreaded of all oaths, and from its decision there
is but one appeal, the appeal open to all condemned persons,
but rarely made—the appeal to Long ju-ju.   This Long ju-ju
means almost certain death, and before it a severe frightening
that is worse to a negro mind than mere physical torture.

The Mbiam oath formula I was able to secure in the upper
districts of the Calabar.   One form of it runs thus, and it is
recited before swallowing the drink made of filth and blood :—

" If I have been guilty of this crime,

" If I have gone and sought the sick one's hurt,

" If I have sent another to seek the sick one's hurt,

" If I have employed any one to make charms or to cook
bush,

" Or to put anything in the road,

" Or to touch his cloth,

" Or to touch his yams,

" Or to touch his goats,

" Or to touch his fowl,

" Or to touch his children,

" If I have prayed for his hurt,

" If I have thought to hurt him in my heart,

" If I have any intention to hurt him,

" If I ever, at any time, do any of these things (recite in
full),

" Or employ others to do these things (recite in full)

" Then, Mbiam ! *Thou* deal with me."

This form I give was for use when a man was sick, and
things were generally going badly with him, for it is not customary in cases of disease to wait until death occurs before
making an accusation of witchcraft.   In the case of Mbiam
being administered after a death this long and complicated
oath would be worded to meet the case most carefully, the
future intention clauses being omitted.   In all cases, whenever
it is used, the greatest care is taken that the oath be recited
in full, oath-takers being sadly prone to kiss their thumb, as it
were, particularly ladies who are taking Mbiam for accusations
of adultery, in conjunction with the boiling oil ordeal.   Indeed,
so unreliable is this class of offenders, or let us rather say this

class of suspected persons, that some one usually says the oath for them.

From the penalty and inconveniences of these accusations of witchcraft there is but one escape, namely flight to a sanctuary. There are several sanctuaries in Congo Français. The great one in the Calabar district is at Omon. Thither mothers of twins, widows, thieves, and slaves fly, and if they reach it are safe. But an attempt at flight is a confession of guilt ; no one is quite certain the accusation will fall on him, or her, and hopes for the best until it is generally too late. Moreover, flying anywhere beyond a day's march, is difficult work in West Africa. So the killing goes on and it is no uncommon thing for ten or more people to be destroyed for one man's sickness or death ; and thus over immense tracts of country the death-rate exceeds the birth-rate. Indeed some of the smaller tribes have thus been almost wiped out. In the Calabar district I have heard of entire villages taking the bean voluntarily because another village had accused it *en bloc* of witchcraft. It amounts almost to a mania with these people. Miss Slessor has frequently told me how, during a quarrel, one person has accused another of witchcraft, and the accused has bolted off in a towering rage and swallowed the bean.

The witch-doctor is not always the cause of people being subjected to the ordeal or torture. In Calabar and the Okÿon districts all the widows of a dead man are subjected to ordeal.

They have to go the next night after the death, before an assemblage of chiefs and the general surrounding crowd, to a cleared space where there is a fire burning. A fowl is tied to the right hand of each widow, and should that fowl fail to cluck at the sight of the fire the woman is held guilty of having bewitched her dead husband and is dealt with accordingly.

Among the Bantu, although the killing among the wives from the accusation of witchcraft is high, some of them being almost certain to fall victims, yet there is not the wholesale slaughter of women and slaves sent down with the soul of the dead that there is among the Negroes.

Dr. Nassau told me of an interesting case which had come under his notice. Once he met a native heathen Akele chief who showed him a string of shells, horns, and wild cats' tails which he said could turn aside bullets. Although the Doctor is well known as a dead shot, the Akele dared him, in a friendly way, to shoot at him with a rifle, and to try him the Doctor pointed the rifle at him, at the distance of a few paces, but the Akele never quailed, and " of course," said the Doctor, " I did not fire." Two years after, that same man when hunting was charged by a wounded elephant and pierced by its tusks. His attendants drove off the beast, and the fearfully lacerated man survived just long enough to accuse one of his women and some slaves of having bewitched his gun and thus caused his death, and on this accusation four people were killed. The ingenious ethnologist may trace from this the accusations made against guns by European sportsmen and recognise survivals in them.

In doubtful cases of death, *i.e.,* in all cases not arising from actual violence, when blood shows in the killing, the Bantu of the S.W. Coast make post-mortem examinations. Notably common is this practice among the Cameroons and Batanga region tribes. The body is cut open to find in the entrails some sign of the path of the injected witch.

I am informed that it is the lung that is most usually eaten by the spirit. If the deceased is a witch-doctor it is thought, as I have mentioned before, that his familiar spirit has eaten him internally, and he is opened with a view of securing and destroying his witch. In 1893 I saw in a village in Kacongo five unpleasant-looking objects stuck on sticks. They were the livers and lungs, and in fact the plucks, of witch-doctors, and the inhabitants informed me they were the witches that had been found in them on post-mortems and then been secured.

Mrs. Grenfell, of the Upper Congo, told me in the same year, when I had the pleasure of travelling with her from Victoria to Matadi, that a similar practice was in vogue among several of the Upper Congo tribes.

Again in 1893 I came across another instance of the post-mortem practice. A woman had dropped down dead on a factory beach at Corisco Bay. The natives could not make it out at all. They were irritated about her conduct: "She no sick. she no complain, she no nothing, and then she go die one time."

The post-mortem showed a burst aneurism. The native verdict was "She done witch herself," *i.e.*, she was a witch eaten by her own familiar.

The general opinion held by people living near a river is that the spirit of a witch can take the form of a crocodile to do its work in; those who live away from large rivers or in districts like Congo Français, where crocodiles are not very savage, hold that the witch takes on the form of a leopard. Still the crocodile spirit form is believed in in Congo Français, and to a greater extent in Kacongo, because here the crocodiles of the Congo are very ferocious and numerous, taking as heavy a toll in human life as they do in the delta of the Niger and the estuaries of the Sierra Leone and Sherboro' Rivers.

One witch-doctor I know in Kacongo had a strange professional method. When, by means of his hand rubbings, &c., he had got hold of a witch or a bewitched one, he always gave the unfortunate an emetic and always found several lively young crocodiles in the consequence, and the stories of the natives in this region abound in accounts of people who have been carried off by witch crocodiles, and kept in places underground for years. I often wonder whether this idea may not have arisen from the well-known habit of the crocodile of burying its prey on the bank. Sometimes it will take off a limb of its victim at once, but frequently it buries the body whole for a few days before eating it. The body is always buried if it is left to the crocodile.

I have a most profound respect for the whole medical profession, but I am bound to confess that the African representatives of it are a little empirical in their methods of treatment. The African doctor is not always a witch-doctor in the bargain, but he is usually. Lady doctors abound. They are a bit dangerous in pharmacy, but they do not often venture on surgery, so on the whole they are safer, for African surgery is heroic. Dr. Nassau cited the worst case of it I know of.

A man had been accidentally shot in the chest by another man with a gun on the Ogowé. The native doctor who was called in made a perpendicular incision into the man's chest, extending down to the last rib ; he then cut diagonally across, and actually lifted the wall of the chest, and groped about among the vitals for the bullet which he successfully extracted. Patient died. No anæsthetic was employed.

I came across a minor operation. A man had broken the ulna of the left arm. The native doctor got a piece—a very nice piece—of bamboo, drove it in through the muscles and integuments from the wrist to the elbow, then encased the limb in plantain leaves, and bound it round, tightly and neatly, needless to say with tie-tie. The arm and hand when I saw it, some six or seven months after the operation, was quite useless, and was withering away.

Many of their methods, however, are better. The Dualla medicos are truly great on poultices for extracting foreign substances, such as bits of iron cooking-pot—a very frequent form of foreign substance in a man out here, owing to their being generally used as bullets. Almost incredible stories are told by black and white of the efficacy of these poultices ; one case I heard from a reliable source of a man who had been shot with fragments of iron pot in the thigh. The white doctor extracted several pieces and said he had got all out, but the man still went on suffering, and could not walk, so, at his request, a native doctor was called in, and he applied his poultice. In a few minutes he removed it, and on its face were two pieces of jagged iron pot. Probably they had been in the poultice when it was applied, anyhow the patient recovered rapidly.

Baths accompanied by massage are much esteemed. The baths are sometimes of hot water with a few herbs thrown in, sometimes they are made by digging a hole in the earth and putting into it a quantity of herbs, and bruised cardamoms, and peppers. Boiling water is then plentifully poured over these and the patient is placed in the bath and is covered over with the parboiled green stuff ; a coating of clay is then placed over all, leaving just the head sticking out. The patient remains in this bath for a period of a few hours, up to a day and a half, and when taken out is well rubbed and kneaded. This form of bath I saw used by the M'pongwe and Igalwas, and it is undoubtedly good for many diseases, notably for that curse of the Coast, rheumatism, which afflicts black and white alike. Rubbing and kneading and hot baths are, I think, the best native remedies, and the plaster of grains-of-paradise pounded up, and mixed with clay, and applied to the forehead as a remedy for malarial headache, or brow ague, is often very useful, but apart from these, I have never seen, in any of these herbal remedies, any trace of a really valuable drug.

The Calabar natives are notably behindhand in their medical methods, depending more on ju-ju than the Bantus. In a case of rheumatism, for example, instead of ordering the hot bath, the local practitioner will "woka" his patient and extract from the painful part, even when it has not been wounded, pieces of iron pot, millepedes, etc., and, in cases of dysentery, bundles of shred-up palm-leaves. These things, he asserts, have been by witchcraft inserted into the patient. His conduct can hardly be regarded as professional; and moreover as he goes on to diagnose who has witched these things into the patient's anatomy, it is highly dangerous to the patient's friends, relations, and neighbours into the bargain.

The strangest thing, however, that I ever heard of being witched into a man I was told of by a most intelligent Igalwa, a Christian, and a very trustworthy man, and his statement was attested by another man, equally reliable, but not a Christian. They said that a relation of theirs had been witched two years previously. An emetic was administered, and there appeared upon the scene a strange little animal which grew with visible rapidity. An hour after its coming to light it crawled about, got out of its basin, and then flew away. I tried my best to identify the species, but the nearest thing I could get to it was that it was like a small bat. It had bat's wings, but then it had a body and tail like a lizard, which was distracting of it, to a naturalist. This thing, they said, had been given to the man when it was "small small," (*i.e.*, very small) in some drink or food, and if it had been left undisturbed by that emetic, it would have grown up inside the man, killing him by feeding on his vitals. There was no want of information or verbal testimony in the case, but I should have felt more sure about the affair if I could have got that thing in a bottle of pure alcohol. The only other case of this winged lizard I heard of was at Batanga, when a witch-doctor had been opened and a winged, lizard-like thing found in his inside, which, Batanga said, was his power. I was reminded of this case, however, the other day when I was in Cameroon. Two traders that I know had been up river, and had had to remain out all night in an open boat. One of them was pretty ill after the experience, and he is, I hear, since dead.

" No, Miss Kingsley," said the other to me, " it is not fever ; we don't quite know what it is, but we think Mr. ——— must have swallowed a parasite."

With no intentional slur on the medical profession, after this discussion on their methods I will pass on to the question of dying.

Dying in West Africa particularly in the Niger Delta, is made very unpleasant for the native by his friends and relations.

When a person is insensible, violent means are taken to recall the spirit to the body. Pepper is forced up the nose and into the eyes. The mouth is propped open with a stick. The shredded fibres of the outside of the oil-nut are set alight and held under the nose and the whole crowd of friends and relations with whom the stifling hot hut is tightly packed yell the dying man's name at the top of their voices, in a way that makes them hoarse for days, just as if they were calling to a person lost in the bush or to a person struggling and being torn or lured away from them. " Hi, hi, don't you hear ? come back, come back. See here. This is your place," &c.

This custom holds good among both Negroes and Bantus ; but the funeral ceremonies vary immensely, in fact with every tribe, and form a subject the details of which I will reserve for a separate work on Fetish.

Among the Okÿon tribes especial care is taken in the case of a woman dying and leaving a child over six months old. The underlying idea is that the spirit of the mother is sure to come back and fetch the child, and in order to pacify her and prevent the child dying, it is brought in and held just in front of the dead body of the mother and then gradually carried away behind her where she cannot see it, and the person holding the child makes it cry out and says, " See, your child is here, you are going to have it with you all right." Then the child is hastily smuggled out of the hut, while a bunch of plantains is put in with the body of the woman and bound up with the funeral binding clothes.

Very young children they do not attempt to keep, but throw them away in the bush alive, as all children are thrown who have not arrived in this world in the way considered orthodox, or who cut their teeth in an improper way. Twins are killed among all the Niger Delta tribes, and in districts out of English control the mother is killed too, except in Omon, where the sanctuary is.

There twin mothers and their children are exiled to an island in the Cross River. They have to remain on the island and if any man goes across and marries one of them he has to remain on the island too. This twin-killing is a widely diffused custom among the Negro tribes.

I doubt whether the Bantus do it so much, but I distrust those Bantus in the matter of twins. They lulled my mind into an unsuspicious, restful state regarding twins, and then played it low, so I won't go bail for them. It was this way. When I first came out to the Coast, my friends told me everything they could lay tongue on until I frequently smelt their souls scorching, and a brief experience of my friends' conversation warned me that the phrase, " We've some very peculiar customs down here " was the *Leit Motif* of the entrance of twins into the conversation. Regarding this subject as unfit for general discussion, I therefore used to smother those twins by leading the conversation off by the ear immediately I heard the warning note, and exceedingly skilful in this I became.

When, however, I was past the Negro ports Bonny, Calabar, &c., and across the Bantu border line, below Cameroon, I found the subject did not arise, and I became lulled into a sense of false security. All went well for some time, until one day I was walking with an Englishman across a stretch

of country where there were several villages.   At one of these
high festival was evidently being held, a dance of women was
taking place in the main street, the usual wriggle and stamp
affair, to the thump, thump, thump of the native drums.   Before one house, on either side of the doorway, stood a man
and a woman.   The remarkable point about the affair was
that their legs were painted white, and as the view of them
was not interrupted by clothes, the effect was somewhat
startling.   "Dear me, Mr.——," I said, "that's rather quaint."
"We've some very peculiar customs down here regarding
twins," said he, before I, being unprepared, had time to turn
the conversation.

These customs (Akele) amounted to the mother of twins
being kept in her hut for a year after the birth.   Then there
was a great dance and certain ceremonies, during which the
lady and the doctor, not the husband, had their legs painted
white.   When the ceremonials were over the woman returned
to her ordinary avocations.

There is always a sense of there being something uncanny
regarding twins in West Africa, and in those tribes where
they are not killed they are regarded as requiring great care to
prevent them from dying on their own account.   I remember
once among the Tschwi trying to amuse a sickly child with
an image which was near it and which I thought was its doll.
The child regarded me with its great melancholy eyes pityingly, as much as to say, "A pretty fool *you* are making of
yourself," and so I was, for I found out that the image was
not a doll at all but an image of the child's dead twin which
was being kept near it as a habitation for the deceased
twin's soul, so that it might not have to wander about, and,
feeling lonely, call its companion after it.

The terror with which twins are regarded in the Niger
Delta is exceedingly strange and real.   When I had the
honour of being with Miss Slessor at Okÿon, the first twins
in that district were saved with their mother from immolation
owing entirely to Miss Slessor's great influence with the
natives and her own unbounded courage and energy.   The
mother in this case was a slave woman—an Eboe, the most
expensive and valuable of slaves.   She was the property of a

big woman who had always treated her—as indeed most slaves are treated in Calabar—with great kindness and consideration, but when these two children arrived all was changed; immediately she was subjected to torrents of virulent abuse, her things were torn from her, her English china basins, possessions she valued most highly, were smashed, her clothes were torn, and she was driven out as an unclean thing. Had it not been for the fear of incurring Miss Slessor's anger, she would, at this point, have been killed with her children, and the bodies thrown into the bush.

As it was, she was hounded out of the village. The rest of her possessions were jammed into an empty gin-case and cast to her. No one would touch her, as they might not touch to kill. Miss Slessor had heard of the twins' arrival and had started off, barefooted and bareheaded, at that pace she can go down a bush path. By the time she had gone four miles she met the procession, the woman coming to her and all the rest of the village yelling and howling behind her. On the top of her head was the gin-case, into which the children had been stuffed, on the top of them the woman's big brass skillet, and on the top of that her two market calabashes. Needless to say, on arriving Miss Slessor took charge of affairs, relieving the unfortunate, weak, staggering woman from her load and carrying it herself, for no one else would touch it, or anything belonging to those awful twin things, and they started back together to Miss Slessor's house in the forest-clearing, saved by that tact which, coupled with her courage, has given Miss Slessor an influence and a power among the negroes unmatched in its way by that of any other white.

She did not take the twins and their mother down the village path to her own house, for though had she done so the people of Okÿon would not have prevented her, yet so polluted would the path have been, and so dangerous to pass down, that they would have been compelled to cut another, no light task in that bit of forest, I assure you. So Miss Slessor stood waiting in the broiling sun, in the hot season's height, while a path was being cut to enable her just to get through to her own grounds. The natives worked away hard, knowing that it saved the polluting of a long stretch of market road, and when it was finished Miss Slessor went to her own house by it and attended with all kindness, promptness, and skill, to the woman and children.   I arrived in the middle of this affair for my first meeting with Miss Slessor, and things at Okÿon were rather crowded, one way and another, that afternoon.   All the attention one of the children wanted—the boy, for there was a boy and a girl—was burying, for the people who had crammed them into the box had utterly smashed the child's head.   The other child was alive, and is still a member of that household of rescued children all of whom owe their lives to Miss Slessor.   There are among them twins from other districts, and delicate children who must have died had they been left in their villages, and a very wonderful young lady, very plump and very pretty, aged about four.   Her mother died a few days after her birth, so the child was taken and thrown into the bush, by the side of the road that led to the market.   This was done one market-day some distance from the Okÿon town.   This particular market is held every ninth day, and on the succeeding market-day some women from the village by the side of Miss Slessor's house happened to pass along the path and heard the child feebly crying : they came into Miss Slessor's yard in the evening, and sat chatting over the day's shopping, &c., and casually mentioned in the way of conversation that they had heard the child crying, and that it was rather remarkable it should be still alive.   Needless to say, Miss Slessor was off, and had that waif home.   It was truly in an awful state, but just alive.   In a marvellous way it had been left by leopards and snakes, with which this bit of forest abounds, and, more marvellous still, the driver ants had not scented it.   Other ants had considerably eaten into it one way and another ; nose, eyes, &c., were swarming with them and flies ; the cartilage of the nose and part of the upper lip had been absolutely eaten into, but in spite of this she is now one of the prettiest black children I have ever seen, which is saying a good deal, for negro children are very pretty with their round faces, their large mouths not yet coarsened by heavy lips, their beautifully shaped flat little ears, and their immense melancholy deer-like eyes, and above these charms they possess that of being fairly quiet. This child is not an object of terror, like the twin children ; it was just thrown away because no one would be bothered to rear it, but when Miss Slessor had had all the trouble of it the natives had no objection to pet and play with it, calling it " the child of wonder," because of its survival.

With the twin baby it was very different. They would not touch it and only approached it after some days, and then only when it was held by Miss Slessor or me. If either of us wanted to do or get something, and we handed over the bundle to one of the house children to hold, there was a stampede of men and women off the verandah, out of the yard, and over the fence, if need be, that was exceedingly comic, but most convincing as to the reality of the terror and horror in which they held the thing. Even its own mother could not be trusted with the child ; she would have killed it. She never betrayed the slightest desire to have it with her, and after a few days' nursing and feeding up she was anxious to go back to her mistress, who, being an enlightened woman, was willing to have her if she came without the child.

The main horror is undoubtedly of the child, the mother being killed more as a punishment for having been so intimately mixed up in bringing the curse, danger, and horror into the village than for anything else.

The woman went back by the road that had been cut for her coming, and would have to live for the rest of her life an outcast, and for a long time in a state of isolation, in a hut of her own into which no one would enter, neither would any one eat or drink with her, nor partake of the food or water she had cooked or fetched. She would lead the life of a leper, working in the plantation by day, and going into her lonely hut at night, shunned and cursed. I tried to find out whether there was any set period for this quarantine, and all I could arrive at was that if—and a very considerable if—a man were to marry her and she were subsequently to present to society an acceptable infant, she would be to a certain extent socially rehabilitated, but she would always be a woman with a past—a thing the African, to his credit be it said, has no taste for.

The woman's own lamentations were pathetic. She would

sit for hours singing or rather mourning out a kind of dirge over herself: "Yesterday I was a woman, now I am a horror, a thing all people run from. Yesterday they would eat with me, now they spit on me. Yesterday they would talk to me with a sweet mouth, now they greet me only with curses and execrations. They have smashed my basin, they have torn my clothes," and so on, and so on. There was no complaint against the people for doing these things, only a bitter sense of injury against some superhuman power that had sent this withering curse of twins down on her. She knew not why; she sang "I have not done this, I have not done that"—and highly interesting information regarding the moral standpoint a good deal of it was. I have tried to find out the reason of this widely diffused custom which is the cause of such a pitiful waste of life; for in addition to the mother and children being killed it often leads to other people, totally unconcerned in the affair, being killed by the relatives of the sufferer on the suspicion of having caused the calamity by witchcraft, and until one gets hold of the underlying idea, and can destroy that, the custom will be hard to stamp out in a district like the great Niger Delta. But I have never been able to hunt it down, though I am sure it is there, and a very quaint idea it undoubtedly is. The usual answer is, "It was the custom of our fathers," but that always and only means, "We don't intend to tell." Another explanation is that the dislike is grounded on the idea that it is like the lower animals. The teeth-filing I think undoubtedly does arise from this; you often hear a native of tribes that go in for filing or knocking out teeth say contemptuously of those who do not follow the custom, "Those men have teeth all same for one with dog." Although I grant that when you are a Niger Delta native you have to be a little careful for fear of being taken for one of the lower animals, just as seedy young men with us object to carrying paper parcels for fear of being taken for tailors, still this idea does not explain the terror, the abject terror, with which twins are regarded, nor the conviction that their existence and proximity bring down on all diseases, difficulties, and disaster. I overheard once a rational reason given, but again the reason was not strong

enough, and moreover the source of information was intoxicated.

Affiliated to this custom of twin-killing, and having, I suspect, the same underlying idea, is the custom common in Negro
and Bantu tribes of throwing away the body of a woman who
has died in her confinement without the child being born,
burning everything belonging to her, and blotting out her
name and memory. The name of such a woman is never
mentioned after the catastrophe, and the body is thrown far
away into the bush, not near the path, where the bodies of
little children are thrown in order that their souls may choose
a new mother from the women who pass by.

Funeral customs vary considerably between the Negro and
Bantu, and I never yet found among the Bantu those unpleasant
death-charms which are in vogue in the Niger Delta. One of
these is the custom of the nearest relatives sitting round the
body during the time—an awesome long time considering the
climate—that elapses before burial under the house floor, the
assembled relatives sniffing frequently and powerfully at the
body. The young children are brought in and held over it so
that they can sniff too.

I was once in a canoe with four men and women and three
children, and a corpse came towards us on the current. My
companions paddled towards it with enthusiasm and getting
it against the side of the canoe, dipped their calabashes into
the water round the corpse, and drank calabash after calabash,
until they had got their back teeth under water and then they
emptied, in that fine swallow-or-choke and hang-the-spilling
style of theirs, calabashes of water into the children until the
unfortunate infants fairly overflowed.

"Good death-charm," they said to me. " I shouldn't wonder
if it were," said I, " paddle away," for I was frightened lest
these people, who are, barring their manners and customs,
kindly and affectionate, should have the corpse on board and
take it home to their families and make a decoction for home
consumption, and it was an unpleasant corpse—smallpox and
all that sort of thing, you know. I am told this custom occurs
in the Niger estuaries and in the Old Calabar regions. I was
in Bantu regions, but my companions were not pure Bantu.

The Calabar people, when the consular eye is off them, bury
under the house. In the case of a great chief the head is cut
off and buried with great secrecy somewhere else, for reasons
I have already stated. The body is buried a few days after
death, but the really important part of the funeral is the
burying of the spirit, and this is the thing that causes all the
West Africans, Negro and Bantu alike, great worry, trouble,
and expense. For the spirit, no matter what its late owner
may have been, is malevolent—all native-made spirits are.
The family have to get together a considerable amount of
wealth to carry out this burial of the spirit, so between the
body-burying and the spirit-burying a considerable time
usually elapses ; maybe a year, maybe more. The custom
of keeping the affair open until the big funeral can be made
obtains also in Cabinda and Loango, but there, instead of burying the body in the meantime, it is placed upon a platform of
wood, and slow fires kept going underneath to dry it, a mat roof
being usually erected over it to keep off rain. When sufficiently dried, it is wrapped in clothes and put into a coffin,
until the money to finish the affair is ready. The Duallas are
more tied down ; their death-dances must be celebrated, I am
informed, on the third, seventh, and ninth day after death. On
these days the spirit is supposed to be particularly present in
its old home. In all the other cases, I should remark, the
spirit does not leave the home until its devil is made and if
this is delayed too long he naturally becomes fractious.

Among the Congo Français tribes there are many different
kinds of burial—as the cannibalistic of the Fan. I may remark,
however, that they tell me themselves that it is considered
decent to bury a relative, even if you subsequently dig him up
and dispose of the body to the neighbours. Then there is
the earth-burial of the Igalwas and M'pongwe, and the
beating into unrecognisable pulp of the body which, I am
told on good native authority, is the method of several
Upper Ogowé tribes, including the Adoomas. I had no
opportunity of making quiet researches on burial customs
when I was above Njoli, because I was so busy trying to
avoid qualifying for a burial myself ; so I am not quite sure
whether this method is the general one among these little-

known tribes, as I am told by native traders, who have it among them that it is—or whether it is reserved for the bodies of people believed to have been possessed of dangerous souls.

Destroying the body by beating up, or by cutting up, is a widely diffused custom in West Africa in the case of dangerous souls, and is universally followed with those that have contained wanderer-souls, *i.e.*, those souls which keep turning up in the successive infants of a family. A child dies, then another child comes to the same father or mother, and that dies, after giving the usual trouble and expense. A third arrives and if that dies, the worm—the father, I mean—turns, and if he is still desirous of more children, he just breaks one of the legs of the body before throwing it in the bush.

This he thinks will act as a warning to the wanderer-soul and give it to understand that if it will persist in coming into his family, it must settle down there and give up its flighty ways. If a fourth child arrives in the family, " it usually limps," and if it dies, the justly irritated parent cuts its body up carefully into very small pieces, and scatters them, doing away with the soul altogether.

The Kama country people of the lower Ogowé are more superstitious and full of observances than the upper river tribes.

Particularly rich in Fetish are the Ncomi, a Fernan Vaz tribe. I once saw a funeral where they had been called in to do the honours, and M. Jacot told me of an almost precisely similar occurrence that he had met with in one of his many evangelising expeditions from Lembarene. I will give his version because of his very superior knowledge of the language.

He was staying in a Fan town where one of the chiefs had just died. The other chief (there are usually two in a Fan town) decided that his deceased *confrère* should have due honour paid him, and resolved to do the thing handsomely.

The Fans openly own to not understanding thoroughly about death and life and the immortality of the soul, and things of that sort, and so the chief called in the Ncomi, who are specialists in these subjects, to make the funeral customs.

M. Jacot said the chief made a speech to the effect that the Fans did not know about these things, but their neighbours, the Ncomi, were known to be well versed in them and the proper things to do, so he had called them in to pay honour to the dead chief. Then the Ncomi started and carried on their weird, complicated death-dance.

The Fans sat and stood round watching them in a ring for a long time, but to a rational, common-sense, shrewd, unimaginative set of people like the Fans, just standing hour after hour gazing on a dance you do not understand, and which consists of a wriggle and a stamp, a wriggle and a stamp, in a solemn walk, or prance, round and round, to the accompaniment of a monotonous phrase thumped on a tom-tom and a monotonous, melancholy chant, uttered in a minor key interspersed every few minutes with an emphatic howl, produces a feeling of boredom, therefore the Fans softly stole away and went to bed, which disgusted the Ncomi, and there was a row. In the dance I saw the same thing happened, only when the Ncomi saw the audience getting thin they complained and said that they were doing this dance in honour of the Fans' chief, in a neighbourly way, and the very least the Fans could do, as they couldn't dance themselves, was to sit still and admire people who could. The Fan chief in my village quite saw it, and went and had the Fans who had gone home early turned up and made them come and see the performance some more; this they did for a time, and then stole off again, or slept in their seats, and the Ncomi were highly disgusted at those brutes of Fans, whom they regarded, they said in their way, as Philistines of an utterly obtuse and degraded type.

The Ncomi themselves put the body into coffins. A barrel is the usual one, but two gun-cases, the ends knocked out and the gun-cases fitted together, is another frequent form of coffin used by them. These coffins are not buried, but are put into special places in the forest.

Along the bank of the Ogowé you will notice here and there long stretches of uninhabited bush. These are not all mere stretches of swamp forest. If you land on some of these and go in a little way you will find the forest full of mounds—or rather heaps, because they have no mould over them—made of branches of trees and leaves ; underneath each of these heaps there are the remains of a body. One very evil-looking place so used I found when I was on the Karkola river. Dr. Nassau tells me they are the usual burying grounds of the Ajumbas.

He said that once, when on a boat journey up the Ogowé, wanting to camp to get the mid-day meal, he ordered his men to pull ashore to a bank. They did not like to, saying it was a bad place, but its badness not being apparent, the Doctor stuck to the point, and ashore they went. He then found for the first time these mounds, and not knowing what they were, he pulled out some of the sticks and saw under them the remains of a body. He went back to the canoe and had his lunch elsewhere, to the evident pleasure of his companions.

CHAPTER XXI

FETISH—*(continued)*

In which the Voyager discourses on the legal methods of natives of this
country, the ideas governing forms of burial, of their manner of
mourning for their dead, and the condition of the African soul in its
under-world.

GREAT as are the incidental miseries and dangers surrounding death to all the people in the village in which a
death occurs, undoubtedly those who suffer most are the
widows of a chief or free man.

The uniform custom among both Negroes and Bantus is
that those who escape execution on the charge of having
witched the husband to death, shall remain in a state of filth
and abasement, not even removing vermin from themselves,
until after the soul-burial is complete—the soul of the dead
man being regarded as hanging about them and liable to be
injured. Therefore, also to the end of preventing his soul
from getting damaged, they are confined to their huts; this
latter restriction is not rigidly enforced, but it is held theoretically to be the correct thing.

They maintain the attitude of grief and abasement, sitting
on the ground, eating but little food, and that of a coarse
kind. In Calabar their legal rights over property, such as
slaves, are meanwhile considerably in abeyance, and they are
put to great expense during the time the spirit is awaiting
burial. They have to keep watch, two at a time, in the hut,
when the body is buried, keeping lights burning, and they
have to pay out of their separate estate for the entertainment
of all the friends of the deceased who come to pay him

compliment ; and if he has been an important man, a big man, the whole district will come, not in a squadron, but just when it suits them, exactly as if they were calling on a live friend. Thus it often happens that even a big woman is bankrupt by the expense. I will not go into the legal bearings of the case here, for they are intricate, and, to a great extent, only interesting to a student of Negro law.

The Bantu women occupy a far inferior position in regard to the rights of property to that held by the Negro women.

The disposal of wives after the death of the husband among the M'pongwe and Igalwa is a subject full of interest ; but it is, like most of their law, very complicated. The brothers of the deceased are supposed to take them—the younger brother may not marry the elder brother's widows, but the elder brothers may marry those of the younger brother. Should any of the women object to the arrangement, they may " leave the family."

I own that the ground principle of African law practically is " the simple plan that they should take who have the power, and they should keep who can," and this tells particularly against women and children who have not got living, powerful relations of their own. Unless the children of a man are grown up and sufficiently powerful on their own account, they have little chance of sharing in the distribution of his estate ; but in spite of this abuse of power there is among Negroes and Bantus a definite and acknowledged law, to which an appeal can be made by persons of all classes, provided they have the wherewithal to set the machinery of it in motion. The difficulty the children and widows have in sharing in the distribution of the estate of the father and husband arises, I fancy, in the principle of the husband's brothers being the true heir, which has sunk into a fossilised state near the trading stations in the face of the white culture. The reason for this inheritance of goods passing from the man to his brother by the same mother has no doubt for one of its origins the recognition of the fact that the brother by the same mother must be a near relation, whereas, in spite of the strict laws against adultery, the relationship to you of the children born of your wives is not so certain. Nevertheless

this is one of the obvious and easy explanations for things it
is well to exercise great care before accepting, for you must
always remember that the African's mind does not run on
identical lines with the European—what may be self-evident
to you is not so to him, and *vice versa*. I have frequently
heard African metaphysicians complain that white men make
great jumps in their thought-course, and do not follow an
idea step by step. You soon become conscious of the careful
way a Negro follows his idea. Certain customs of his you
can, by the exercise of great patience, trace back in a
perfectly smooth line from their source in some natural
phenomenon. Others, of course, you cannot, the traces of
the intervening steps of the idea having been lost, owing
partly to the veneration in which old customs are held,
which causes them to regard the fact that their fathers had
this fashion as reason enough for their having it, and above
all to the total absence of all but oral tradition. But so great
a faith have I in the lack of inventive power in the African,
that I feel sure all their customs, had we the material that has
slipped down into the great swamp of time, could be traced
back either, as I have said, to some natural phenomenon, or to
the thing being advisable, for reasons of utility.

The uncertainty in the parentage of offspring may seem to
be such a utilitarian underlying principle, but, on the other
hand, it does not sufficiently explain the varied forms of the
law of inheritance, for in some tribes the eldest or most influential son does succeed to his father's wealth ; in other
places you have the peculiar custom of the chief slave in-
heriting. I think, from these things, that the underlying idea
in inheritance of property is the desire to keep the wealth of
" the house," *i.e.*, estate, together, and if it were allowed to pass
into the hands of weak people, like women and young children,
this would not be done. Another strong argument against
the theory that it arises from the doubtful relationship of the
son, is that certain ju-ju always go to the son of the chief
wife, if he is old enough, at the time of the father's death, even
in those tribes where the wealth goes elsewhere.

Certain tribes acknowledge the right of the women and
children to share in the dead man's wealth, given that these

are legally married wives, or the children of legally married wives; it is so in Cameroons, for example. An esteemed friend of mine who helps to manage things for the Fatherland down there was trying a palaver the other day with a patience peculiar to him, and that intelligent and elaborate care I should think only a mind trained on the methods of German metaphysicians could impart into that most wearisome of proceedings, wherein every one says the same thing over fourteen different times at least, with a similar voice and gesture, the only variation being in the statements regarding the important points, and the facts of the case, these varying with each individual. This palaver was made by a son claiming to inherit part of his father's property; at last, to the astonishment, and, of course, the horror, of the learned judge, the defendant, the wicked uncle, pleaded through the interpreter, "This man cannot inherit his father's property, because his parents married for love." There is no encouragement to foolishness of this kind in Cameroon, where legal marriage consists in purchase.

In Bonny River and in Opobo the inheritance of "the house" is settled primarily by a vote of the free men of the house; when the chief dies, their choice has to be ratified by the other chiefs of houses; but in Bonny and Opobo the white traders have had immense influence for a long time, so one cannot now find out how far this custom is purely native in idea.

Among the Fans the uncle is, as I have before said, an important person although the father has more rights than among the Igalwa, and here I came across a peculiar custom regarding widows. M. Jacot cited to me a similar case or so, one of which I must remark was in an Ajumba town. The widows were inside the dead husband's hut, as usual; the Fan huts are stoutly built of sheets of flattened bark, firmly secured together with bark rope, and thatched— they never build them in any other way except when they are in the bush rubber-collecting or elephant-hunting, when they make them of the branches of trees. Well, round the bark hut, with the widows inside, there was erected a hut made of branches, and when this was nearly completed, the Fans com-

menced pulling down the inner bark hut, and finally cleared
it right out, thatch and all, and the materials of which it had
been made were burnt. I was struck with the performance
because the Fans, though surrounded by intensely superstitious tribes, are remarkably free from superstition [1] themselves, taking little or no interest in speculative matters, except to get charms to make them invisible to elephants, to keep
their feet in the path, to enable them to see things in the forest,
and practical things of that sort, and these charms they frequently gave me to assist and guard me in my wanderings.

The M'pongwe and Igalwa have a peculiar funeral custom,
but it is not confined in its operation to widows, all the near
relatives sharing in it. The mourning relations are seated on
the floor of the house, and some friend—Dr. Nassau told me he
was called in in this capacity—comes in and "lifts them up,"
bringing to them a small present, a factor of which is always
a piece of soap. This custom is now getting into the survival form in Libreville and Glass. Nowadays the relatives
do not thus sit, unwashed and unkempt, keenly requiring
the soap. Among the bush Igalwa, I am told, the soap is
much wanted.

It is not only the widows that remain, either theoretically
or practically unwashed ; all the mourners do. The Ibibios
seem to me to wear the deepest crape in the form of
accumulated dirt, and all the African tribes I have met have
peculiar forms of hair cutting—shaving the entire head, not
shaving it at all, shaving half of it &c.—when in mourning.

The period of the duration of wearing mourning is, I believe,
in all West Coast tribes that which elapses between the
death and the burial of the soul. I believe a more thorough
knowledge would show us that there is among the Bantu also
a fixed time for the lingering of the soul on earth after death,
but we have not got sufficient evidence on the point yet. The
only thing we know is that it is not proper for the widow to
re-marry while his soul is still in her vicinity.

Among the Calabar tribes the burial of the spirit liberates

[1] In speaking of native ideas I should prefer to use the good Yorkshire
term of " overthrowing " in place of " superstition," but as the latter is the
accepted word for such matters I feel bound to employ it.

the woman. Among the Tschwi she requires special ceremonies on her own account. In Togoland, among the Ewe
people, I know the period is between five and six weeks,
during which time the widow remains in the hut, armed with
a good stout stick, as a precaution against the ghost of her
husband, so as to ward off attacks should he be ill-tempered.
After these six weeks the widow can come out of the hut, but
as his ghost has not permanently gone hence, and is apt to
revisit the neighbourhood for the next six months, she has to
be taken care of during this period. Then, after certain ceremonies, she is free to marry again. So I conclude the period
of mourning, in all tribes, is that period during which the soul
remains round its old possessions, whether these tribes have a
definite soul-burial or devil-making or not.

The ideas connected with the under-world to which the
ghost goes are exceedingly interesting. The Negroes and
Bantus are at one on these subjects in one particular only,
and that is that no marriages take place there. The Tschwis
say that this under-world, Srahmandazi, is just the same as this
world in all other particulars, save that it is dimmer, a veritable
shadow-land where men have not the joys of life, but only the
shadow of the joy. Hence, says the Tschwi proverb, " One
day in this world is worth a year in Srahmandazi." The
Tschwis, with their usual definiteness in this sort of detail,
know all about their Srahmandazi. Its entrance is just east
of the middle Volta, and the way down is difficult to follow,
and when the sun sets on this world it rises on Srahmandazi.
The Bantus are vague on this important and interesting point.
The Benga, for example, although holding the absence of
marriage there, do not take steps to meet the case as
the Tschwis do, and kill a supply of wives to take down with
them. This reason for killing wives at a funeral is another
instance that, however strange and cruel a custom may be here
in West Africa, however much it may at first appear to be the
flower of a rootless superstition, you will find on close investigation that it has some root in a religious idea, and a common-
sense element. The common-sense element in the killing of
wives and slaves among both the Tschwi and the Calabar tribes
consists in the fact that it discourages poisoning. A Calabar

chief elaborately explained to me that the rigorous putting down
of killing at funerals that was being carried on by the Government not only landed a man in the next world as a wretched
pauper, but added an additional chance to his going there
prematurely, for his wives and slaves, no longer restrained by
the prospect of being killed at his death and sent off with
him would, on very slight aggravation, put "bush in his

VIEW ON THE MIDDLE VOLTA.

chop." It is sad to think of this thorn being added to the
rose-leaves of a West Coast chief's life, as there are $99\frac{9}{10}$
per cent. of thorns in it already.

I came across a similar case on the Gold Coast, when a
chief complained to me of the way the Government were preserving vermin, in the shape of witches, in the districts under
its surveillance. You were no longer allowed to destroy them
as of old, and therefore the vermin were destroying the game ;

for, said he, the witches here live almost entirely on the blood
they suck from children at night.   They used, in old days, to
do this furtively, and do so now where native custom is
unchecked ; but in districts where the Government says
that witchcraft is utter nonsense, and killing its proficients
utter murder which will be dealt with accordingly, the witch
flourishes exceedingly, and blackmails the fathers and mothers
of families, threatening that if they are not bought off they
will have their child's blood ; and if they are not paid, the
child dies away gradually—poison again, most likely.

I often think it must be the common-sense element in fetish
customs that enables them to survive, in the strange way they
do, in the minds of Africans who have been long under European influence and education.   In witching, for example,
every intelligent native knows there is a lot of poison in the
affair, but the explanation he gives you will not usually
display this knowledge, and it was not until I found the wide
diffusion of the idea of the advisability of administering an
emetic to the bewitched person, that I began to suspect my
black friends of sound judgment.

The good ju-juist will tell you all things act by means of
their life, which means their power, their spirit.   Dr. Nassau
tells me the efficacy of drugs is held to depend on their bene-
volent spirits, which, on being put into the body, drive away
the malevolent disease-causing spirits—a leucocytes-versus
pathogenic-bacteria sort of influence, I suppose.   On this same
idea also depends the custom of the appeal to ordeal, the
working of which is supposed to be spiritual.   Nevertheless,
the intelligent native, believing all the time in this factor,
squares the common-sense factor by bribing the witch-doctor
who makes the ordeal drink.

The feeling regarding the importance of funeral observances
is quite Greek in its intensity.   Given a duly educated
African, I am sure that he would grasp the true inwardness of
the Antigone far and away better than any European now
living can.   A pathetic story which bears on this feeling was
told me some time ago by Miss Slessor when she was
stationed at Creek Town.   An old blind slave woman was found
in the bush, and brought into the mission.   She was in a

deplorable state, utterly neglected and starving, her feet torn
by thorns and full of jiggers, and so on. Every care was
taken of her and she soon revived and began to crawl about,
but her whole mind was set on one thing with a passion that
had made her alike indifferent to her past sufferings and to
her present advantages. What she wanted was a bit, only a
little bit, of white cloth. Now, I may remark, white cloth is
anathema to the Missions, for it is used for ju-ju offerings, and
a rule has to be made against its being given to the uncon-
verted, or the missionary becomes an accessory before the fact
to pagan practices, so white cloth the old woman was told she
could not have, she had been given plenty of garments for her
own use and that was enough. The old woman, however,
kept on pleading and saying the spirit of her dead mistress
kept coming to her asking and crying for white cloth, and
white cloth she must get for her, and so at last, finding it was
not to be got at the Mission station, she stole away one day,
unobserved, and wandered off into the bush, from which she
never again reappeared, doubtless falling a victim to the many
leopards that haunted hereabouts.

To provide a proper burial for the dead relation is the great
duty of a negro's life, its only rival in his mind is the desire to
have a burial of his own. But, in a good negro, this passion
will go under before the other, and he will risk his very life
to do it. He may know, surely and well, that killing slaves and
women at a dead brother's grave means hanging for him when
their Big Consul knows of it, but in the Delta he will do it.
On the Coast, Leeward and Windward, he will spend every
penny he possesses and, on top, if need be, go and pawn himself, his wives, or his children into slavery to give a deceased
relation a proper funeral.

This killing at funerals I used to think would be more easily
done away with in the Delta than among the Tschwi tribes,
but a little more knowledge of the Delta's idea about the
future life showed me I was wrong.

Among the Tschwi the slaves and women killed are to form
for the dead a retinue, and riches wherewith to start life
in Srahmandazi, where there are markets and towns and all
things as on this earth, and so the Tschwi would have little

difficulty in replacing human beings at funerals with gold-dust, cloth, and other forms of riches, and this is already done in districts under white influence. But in the Delta there is no under-world to live in, the souls shortly after reaching the under-world being forwarded back to this, in new babies, and the wealth that is sent down with a man serves as an indication as to what class of baby the soul is to be repacked and sent up in. As wealth in the Delta consists of women and slaves I do not believe the under-world gods of the Niger would understand the status of a chief who arrived before them, let us say, with ten puncheons of palm oil, and four hundred yards of crimson figured velvet; they would say, "Oh! very good as far as it goes, but where is your real estate? The chances are you are only a trade slave boy and have stolen these things"; and in consequence of this, killing at funerals will be a custom exceedingly difficult to stamp out in these regions. Try and imagine yourself how abhorrent it must be to send down a dear and honoured relative to the danger of his being returned to this world shortly as a slave. There is no doubt a certain idea among the Negroes that some souls may get a rise in status on their next incarnation. You often hear a woman saying she will be a man next time, a slave he will be a freeman, and so on, but how or why some souls obtain promotion I have not yet sufficient evidence to show. I think a little more investigation will place this important point in my possession. I once said to a Calabar man, "But surely it would be easy for a man's friends to cheat; they could send down a chief's outfit with a man, though he was only a small man here?"

"No," said he, "the other souls would tell on him, and then he would get sent up as a dog or some beast as a punishment."

My first conception of the prevalence of the incarnation idea was also gained from a Delta negro. I said, "Why in the world do you throw away in the bush the bodies of your dead slaves? Where I have been they tie a string to the leg of a dead slave and when they bury him bring the string to the top and fix it to a peg, with the owner's name on, and then when the owner dies he has that slave again down below."

" They be fool men," said he, and he went on to explain
that the ghost of that slave would be almost immediately back
on earth again growing up ready to work for some one else,
and would not wait for its last owner's soul down below, and
out of the luxuriant jungle of information that followed I
gathered that no man's soul dallies below long, and also that
a soul returning to a family, a thing ensured by certain ju-jus,
was identified. The new babies as they arrive in the family
are shown a selection of small articles belonging to deceased
members whose souls are still absent; the thing the child
catches hold of identifies him. " Why he's Uncle John, see!
he knows his own pipe; " or " That's cousin Emma, see! she
knows her market calabash," and so on.

I remember discoursing with a very charming French official
on the difficulty of eradicating fetish customs.

" Why not take the native in the rear, Mademoiselle," said
he, " and convert the native gods ? "

I explained that his ingenious plan was not feasible,
because you cannot convert gods. Even educating gods is
hopeless work. All races of men, through countless ages,
have been attempting to make their peculiar deities understand how they are wanted to work, and what they are
wanted to do, and the result is anything but encouraging.

As I have dwelt on the repellent view of Negro funeral
custom, I must in justice to them cite their better view. There
is a custom that I missed much on going south of Calabar,
for it is a pretty one. Outside the villages in the Calabar
districts, by the sides of the most frequented roads, you
will see erections of boughs. I do not think these are
intended for huts, but for beds, for they are very like the
Calabar type of bed, only made in wood instead of clay.
Over them a roof of mats is put, to furnish a protection
against rain.

These shelters—graves or fetish huts they are wrongly
called by Europeans—are made by driving four longish stout
poles into the ground while at the height of about three feet or
so four more poles are tied so as to make a skeleton platform
which is filled in with withies and made flat. Another set of
five poles is tied above, and to these the roof is affixed. On

the platform, is placed the bedding belonging to the deceased, the undercloth, counterpane, &c., and at the head are laid the pillows, bolster-shaped and stuffed with cotton-tree fluff, or shredded palm-leaves, and covered with some gaily-coloured cotton cloth.· In every case I have seen—and they amount to hundreds, for you cannot take an hour's walk even from Duke Town without coming upon a dozen or so of these erections—the pillows are placed so that the person lying on the bed would look towards the village.

On the roof and on the bed, and underneath it on the ground, are placed the household utensils that belonged to the deceased ; the calabashes, the basins, the spoons cut out of wood, and the boughten iron ones, as we should say in Devon, and on the stakes are hung the other little possessions ; there is one I know of made for the ghost of a poor girl who died, on to the stakes of which are hung the dolls and the little pin-cushions, &c., given her by a kind missionary.

Food is set out at these places and spirit poured over them from time to time, and sometimes, though not often, pieces of new cloth are laid on them. Most of the things are deliber-ately damaged before they are put on the home for the spirit ; I do not think this is to prevent them from being stolen, because all are not damaged sufficiently to make them useless. There was a beautifully made spoon with a burnt-in pattern on one of these places when I left Calabar to go South, and on my return, some six months after, it was still there. On another there was a very handsome pair of market calabashes, also much decorated, that were only just chipped and in better repair than many in use in Calabar markets, and I make no doubt the spoon and they are still lying rotting among the *débris* of the pillows, &c. These places are only attended to during the time the spirit is awaiting burial, as they are regarded merely as a resting-place for it while it is awaiting this ceremony. The body is not buried near them, I may remark.

In spite, however, of the care that is taken to bury spirits, a considerable percentage from various causes—poverty of the relations, the deceased being a stranger in the land, accidental death in some unknown part of the forest or the surf—remain unburied, and hang about to the common danger of the village they may choose to haunt. Many devices are resorted to, to purify the villages from these spirits. One which was in use in Creek Town, Calabar, to within a few years ago, and which I am informed is still customary in some interior villages, was very ingenious, and believed to work well by those who employed it.

In the houses were set up Nbakim,—large, grotesque images carved of wood and hung about with cloth strips and gew-gaws. Every November in Creek Town (I was told by some authorities it was every second November) there was a sort of festival held. Offerings of food and spirits were placed before these images ; a band of people accompanied by the rest of the population used to make a thorough round of the town, up and down each street and round every house, dancing, singing, screaming and tom-toming, in fact making all the noise they knew how to—and a Calabar Effik is very gifted in the power of making noise. After this had been done for what was regarded as a sufficient time, the images were taken out of the houses, the crowd still making a terrific row and were then thrown into the river, and the town was regarded as being cleared of spirits.

The rationale of the affair is this. The wandering spirits are attracted by the images, and take shelter among their rags, like earwigs or something of that kind. The *charivari* is to drive any of the spirits who might be away from their shelters back into them. The shouting of the mob is to keep the spirits from venturing out again while they are being carried to the river. The throwing of the images, rags and all, into the river, is to destroy the spirits or at least send them elsewhere. They did not go and pour boiling water on their earwig-traps, as wicked white men do, but they meant the same thing, and when this was over they made and set up new images for fresh spirits who might come into the town, and these were kept and tended as before, until the next N'dok ceremony came round.

It is owing to the spiritual view which the African takes of existence at large that ceremonial observances form the greater part of even his common-law procedure.

There is, both among the Negro and Bantu, a recognised

code of law, founded on principles of true but merciless justice. It is not often employed, because of the difficulty and the danger to the individual who appeals to it, should that individual be unbacked by power, but nevertheless the code exists.

The African is particularly hard on theft ; he by no means "compounds for sins he is inclined to by damning those he has no mind to," for theft is a thing he revels in.

Persons are tried for theft on circumstantial evidence, direct testimony, and ordeal. Laws relating to mortgage are practically the same among Negroes and Bantu and Europeans. Torts are not recognised ; unless the following case from Cameroon points to a vague realisation of them. A. let his canoe out to B., in good order, so that B. could go up river, and fetch down some trade. B. did not go himself, but let C., who was not his slave, but another free man who also wanted to go up for trade, have the canoe on the understanding that in payment for the loan of the said canoe C. should bring down B's. trade.

A. was not told about this arrangement at all. B. says A. was, only A. was so blind drunk at the time he did not understand. Well, up river C. goes in the canoe, and fetches up on a floating stump in the river, and staves a hole you could put your head in, in the bow of the said canoe. C. returns it to B. in this condition. B. returns it to A. in this condition. A. sues B. before native chief, saying he lent his canoe to B. on the understanding, always implied in African loans, that it was to be returned in the same state as when lent, fair wear and tear alone expected. B. tries first to get C. to pay for the canoe, and for the rent of the canoe on top, as a compensation for the delay in bringing down his, B's. trade. C. calls B. the illegitimate offspring of a green house-lizard, and pleads further that the floating log was a *force majeure*—an act of God, and denies liability on all counts. B. then pleads this as his own defence in the case of A. and B. (authorities cited in support of this view) ; he also pleads he is not liable, because C. is a free man, and not his slave.

The case went on for a week ; the judge was drunk for five days in his attempt to get his head clear. The decision finally was that B. was to pay A. full compensation. B. *v.* C. is still pending.

The laws against adultery are, theoretically, exceedingly severe. The punishment is death, and this is sometimes carried out. The other day King Bell in Cameroon flogged one of his wives to death, and the German Government have deposed and deported him, for you cannot do that sort of thing with impunity within a stone's throw of a. Government head-quarters. But as a general rule all along the Coast the death penalty for murder or adultery is commuted to a fine, or you can send a substitute to be killed for you, if you are rich. This is frequently done, because it is cheaper, if you have a seedy slave, to give him to be killed in your stead than to pay a fine which is often enormous.

The adultery itself is often only a matter of laying your hand, even in self-defence from a virago, on a woman—or brushing against her in the path. These accusations of adultery are, next to witchcraft, the great social danger to the West Coast native, and they are often made merely from motives of extortion or spite, and without an atom of truth in them.

It is customary for a chief to put his wives frequently to ordeal on this point, and this is almost always done after there has been a big devil-making, or a dance, which his family have been gracing with their presence. The usual method of applying the ordeal is by boiling palm-oil—a pot is nearly filled with the oil, which is brought to the boil over a fire ; when it is seething, the woman to be tried is brought out in front of it. She first dips her hands into water, and then has administered to her the M'biam oath saying or having said for her that long elaborate formula, in a form adjusted to meet the case. Then she plunges her hand into the boiling oil for an instant, and shakes the oil off with all possible rapidity, and the next woman comes forward and goes through the same per- formance, and so on. Next day, the hands of the women are examined, and those found blistered are adjudged guilty, and punished. In order to escape heavy punishment the woman will accuse some man of having hustled against her, or sat down on a bench beside her, and so on, and the accused man has to pay up. If he does not, in the Calabar district, Egbo will come and "eat the adultery," and there won't be much of that man's earthly goods left. Sometimes the accusation is volunteered by the woman, and frequently the husband and wife conspire together and cook up a case against a man for the sake of getting the damages. There is nothing that ensures a man an unblemished character in West Africa, save the possession of sufficient power to make it risky work for people to cast slurs on it.

The ownership of children is a great source of palaver. The law among Negroes and Bantus is that the children of a free woman belong to her. In the case of tribes believing in the high importance of uncles considerable powers are vested in that relative, while in other tribes certain powers are vested in the father.

The children of slave wives are the only children the father has absolute power over if he is the legal owner of the slave woman. If, as is frequently the case, a free man marries a slave woman who belongs to another man, all her children are the absolute property of her owner, not her husband ; and the owner of the woman can take them and sell them, or do whatsoever he chooses with them, unless the free man father redeems them, as he usually does, although the woman may still remain the absolute property of the owner, recallable by him at any time.

This law is the cause of the most brain-spraining palavers that come before the white authorities. There is naturally no statute of limitations in West Africa, because the African does not care a row of pins about time. The wily A. will let his slave woman live with B. without claiming the redemption fees as they become due—letting them stand over, as it were, at compound interest. All the male as well as the female children of the first generation are A.'s property, and all the female children of these children are his property even unto the second and third generation and away into eternity. A. may die before he puts in his claim, in which case the ownership passes on into the hands of his heir or assignees, who may foreclose at once, on entering into heir heritage, or may again let things accumulate for their heirs. Anyhow, sooner or later the foreclosure comes and then there is trouble. X., Y., Z., &c., free men, have married some of the original A.'s slave woman's descendants. They have either bought them right out, or kept on conscientiously redeeming children of theirs as they arrived. Of course A., or his heirs, contend that X., Y., Z., &c. have been wasting time and money by so doing, because the people X., Y., Z. have paid the money to had no legal title to the women. Of course X., Y., Z. contend that their particular woman, or her ancestress, was duly redeemed from the legal owner.

Remember there is no documentary evidence available, and squads of equally reliable and oldest inhabitants are swearing hard-all both ways. Just realise this, and that your Government says that whenever native law is not blood-stained it must be supported, and you may be able to realise the giddy mazes of a native palaver, which if you continuously attempt to follow with the determination that justice shall be duly administered, will for certain lay you low with an attack of fever.

The law of ownership is not all in favour of the owner, masters being responsible for damage done by their slaves, and this law falls very heavily and expensively on the owner of a bad slave. Indeed, when one lives out here and sees the surrounding conditions of this state of culture, the conviction grows on you that, morally speaking, the African is far from being the brutal fiend he is often painted, a creature that loves cruelty and blood for their own sake. The African does not ; and though his culture does not contain our institutions, lunatic asylums, prisons, workhouses, hospitals, &c., he has to deal with the same classes of people who require these things So with them he deals by means of his equivalent institutions, slavery, the lash, and death. You have just as much right, my logical friend, to call the West Coast Chief hard names for his habit of using brass bars, heads of tobacco, and so on, in place of sixpenny pieces, as you have to abuse him for clubbing an inveterate thief. It's deplorably low of him, I own, but by what alternative plan of government his can be replaced I do not quite see, under existing conditions. In religious affairs, the affairs which lead him into the majority of his iniquities, his real sin consists in believing too much. In his witchcraft, the sin is the same. Toleration means indifference, I believe, among all men. The African is not indifferent on the subject of witchcraft, and I do not see how one can expect him to be. Put yourself in his place and imagine you have got hold of a man or woman who has been placing a live crocodile or a catawumpus of some kind into your own or a valued relative's, or fellow-townsman's inside, so that it may eat up valuable viscera, and cause you or your friend suffering and death. How would you feel ? A little like lynching your captive, I fancy.

I confess that the more I know of the West Coast Africans the more I like them. I own I think them fools of the first water for their power of believing in things ; but I fancy I have analogous feelings towards even my fellow-countrymen when they go and violently believe in something that I cannot quite swallow.

CHAPTER XXII

FETISH—(*Continued*)

In which the Voyager complains of the inconveniences arising from the method of African thought, and discourses on apparitions and Deities.

HOWEVER much some of the African's mental attributes get under-rated, I am sure there are others of them for which he gets more credit than he deserves. One of these is his imagination. It strikes the new-comer with awe, and frequently fills him with rage, when he first meets it ; but as he matures and gets used to the African, he sees the string. For the African fancy is not the "aërial fancy flying free," mentioned by our poets, but merely the aërial of the theatre suspended by a wire or cord. The wire that supports the African's fancy may be a very thin, small fact indeed, or in some cases merely his incapacity to distinguish between animate and inanimate objects, which give rise to his idea that everything is possessed of a soul. Everything has a soul to him, and to make confusion worse confounded, he usually believes in the existence of matter apart from its soul. But there is little he won't believe in, if it comes to that ; and I have a feeling of thankfulness that Buddhism, Theosophy, and above all Atheism, which chases its tail and proves that nothing can be proved, have not yet been given the African to believe in. He would believe the whole lot if he had the chance, and his mind is in a pretty muddle as it is. I dare say I speak with irritation, but I have suffered much from the African's mind muddle.

The African's want of making it clear in his language whether he is referring to an animate or inanimate thing, has landed me in many a dilemma, and his foolishness in not having a male and female gender in his languages amounts to a nuisance, and has nearly, at one fell swoop, turned my hairs gray, and brought them in sorrow to the grave.   For example, I am a most lady-like old person and yet get constantly called " Sir."   I hasten to assure you I never even wear a masculine collar and tie, and as for encasing the more earthward extremities of my anatomy in—you know what I mean—well, I would rather perish on a public scaffold.   The other day, circumstances having got beyond my control during the afternoon, I arrived in the evening in a saturated condition at a white settlement, and wishing to get accommodation for myself and my men, I made my way to the factory of a firm from whose representatives I have always received great and most courteous help.   The agent in charge was not at home, and his steward-boy said, " Massa live for Mr. B.'s house."   " Go tell him I live for come from," &c., said I, and " I fit for want place for my men."   I had nothing to write on, or with, and I thought the steward-boy could carry this little message to its destination without dropping any of it, as Mr. B.'s house was close by ; but I was wrong.   Off he went, and soon returned with the note I here give a copy of :—

" DEAR OLD MAN,

         " You must be in a deuce of a mess after the tornado. Just help yourself to a set of my dry things.   The shirts are in the bottom drawer, the trousers are in the box under the bed, and then come over here to the sing-song.   My leg is dickey or I'd come across.—Yours," &c.

Had there been any smelling salts or sal volatile in this subdivision of the Ethiopian region I should have forthwith fainted on reading this, but I well knew there was not, so I blushed until the steam from my soaking clothes (for I truly was " in a deuce of a mess ") went up in a cloud and then, just as I was, I went " across " and appeared before the author of that awful note.   When he came round, he said it had taken seven years' growth out of him, and was intensely apologetic. I remarked it had very nearly taken thirty years' growth out of me, and he said the steward boy had merely informed him that "White man live for come from X," a place where he knew there was another factory belonging to his firm, and he naturally thought it was the agent from X who had come across. He offered to commit suicide, and kill the boy ; but I thought that, under the circumstances, I had no right to avail myself of the first part of his offer, and as my chief pride in West Africa is that I have never raised hand nor caused hand to be raised against a native, I did not like to have the boy killed. So after seeing my men safe for the night I settled down and had supper.

You rarely, indeed I believe never, find an African with a gift for picturesque descriptions of scenery. The nearest approach to it I ever got was from my cook when we were on Mungo mah Lobeh. He proudly boasted he had been on a mountain, up Cameroon River, with a German officer, and on that mountain, " If you fall down one side you die, if you fall down other side you die."

Graphic and vivid descriptions of incidents you often get, but it is not Art. The effect is produced entirely by a bald brutality of statement, the African having no artistic reticence whatsoever. One fine touch, however, which does not come in under this class was told me by my lamented friend Mr. Harris of Calabar. Some years ago he had out a consignment of Dutch clocks with hanging weights, as is natural to the Dutch clock. They were immensely popular among the chiefs, and were soon disposed of save one, which had seen trouble on the voyage out and lost one of its weights. Mr. Harris, who was a man of great energy and resource, melted up some metal spoons and made a new weight and hung it on the clock. The day he finished this a chief came in, anxious for a Dutch clock, and Mr. Harris forthwith sold him the repaired one. About a week elapsed, and then the chief turned up at the factory again with a rueful countenance, followed by a boy carrying something swathed in a cloth. It was the clock.

" You do me bad too much, Mr. Harris," said the chief.

Mr. Harris denied this on the spot with the vehemence of injured innocence. The chief shook his head and spat profusely and sorrowfully.

"You no sabe him clock you done sell me?" said he. "When I look him clock it no be to-day, it be to-morrow." Mr. Harris took the clock back, to see what was the cause of this strange state of affairs. Of course it arose from his having been too liberal in the amount of spoon in the weight, and this being altered, the chief was not hurried onward to his grave at such a rattling pace; "but," said Mr. Harris, "that clock was a flyer to the last."

Phrases in the native languages often point to a power of imagery; for example the Effik word for both stars and fire-flies is Ntan-ta fiong, and if one takes the translation some authorities give of this, namely "moon dust," it is pretty, but other authorities say it means "made of the same stuff as the moon," which reduces it to simple idiocy. The name for butterflies, meaning "the cloth of the spirit," has no detractors; nor has that for the pretty little gecko lizard that haunts the houses and is now learning to walk on ceilings, "the spirit of the child," and so on. But I will not go into the subject of African languages here, but only remark of them that although they are elaborate enough to produce, for their users, nearly every shade of erroneous statement, they are not, save perhaps M'pongwe, elaborate enough to enable a native to state his exact thought. Some of them are very dependent on gesture. When I was with the Fans they frequently said, "We will go to the fire so that we can see what they say," when any question had to be decided after dark, and the inhabitants of Fernando Po, the Bubis, are quite unable to converse with each other unless they have sufficient light to see the accompanying gestures of the conversation. In all cases I feel sure the African's intelligence is far ahead of his language.

The African is usually great at dreams, and has them very noisily; but he does not seem to me to attach immense import- ance to them, certainly not so much as the Red Indian does. I doubt whether there is much real ground for supposing that from dreams came man's first conception of the spirit world, and I think the origin of man's religious belief lies in man's misfortunes.

There can be little doubt that the very earliest human beings found, as their descendants still find, their plans frustrated, let them plan ever so wisely and carefully ; they must have seen their companions overtaken by death and disaster, arising both from things they could see and from things they could not see. The distinction between these two classes of phenomena is not so definitely recognised by savages or animals as it is by the more cultured races of humanity. I doubt whether a savage depends on his five senses alone to teach him what the world is made of, any more than a Fellow of the Royal Society does. From this method of viewing nature I feel sure that the general idea arose—which you find in all early cultures—that death was always the consequence of the action of some malignant spirit, and that there is no accidental or natural death, as we call it ; and death is, after all, the most impressive attribute of life.

If a man were knocked on the head with a club, or shot with an arrow, the cause of death is clearly the malignancy of the person using these weapons ; and so it is easy to think that a man killed by a fallen tree, or by the upsetting of a canoe in the surf, or in an eddy in the river, is also the victim of some being using these things as weapons.

A man having thus gained a belief that there are more than human actors in life's tragedy, the idea that disease is also a manifestation of some invisible being's wrath and power seems to me natural and easy ; and he knows you can get another man for a consideration to kill or harm a third party, and so he thinks that, for a consideration, you can also get one of these superhuman beings, which we call gods or devils, but which the African regards in another light, to do so.

A certain set of men and women then specialise off to study how these spirits can be managed, and so arises a priesthood ; and the priests, or medicine men as they are called in their earliest forms, gradually, for their own ends, elaborate and wrap round their profession with ritual and mystery.

The savage is also conscious of another great set of phenomena which, he soon learns, take no interest in human affairs. The sun which rises and sets, the moon which changes, the tides which come and go :—what do they care ? Nothing ; and what is more, sacrifice to them what you may, you cannot get them to care about you and your affairs, and so the savage turns his attention to those other spirits that do take only too much interest, as is proved by those unexpected catastrophes ; and, as their actions show, these spirits are all malignant, so he deals with them just as he would deal with a bad man whom he was desirous of managing. He flatters and fees them, he deprives himself of riches to give to them as sacrifices, believing they will relish it all the more because it gives him pain of some sort to give it to them. He holds that they think it will be advisable for them to encourage him to continue the giving by occasionally doing what he asks them. Naturally he never feels sure of them ; he sees that you may sacrifice to a god for years, you may wrap him up —or more properly speaking, the object in which he resides— in your only cloth on chilly nights while you shiver yourself ; you and your children, and your mother, and your sister and her children, may go hungry that food may rot upon his shrine ; and yet, in some hour of dire necessity, the power will not come and save you—because he has been lured away by some richer gifts than yours.

You white men will say, " Why go on believing in him then ? " but that is an idea that does not enter the African mind. I might just as well say " Why do you go on believing in the existence of hansom cabs," because one hansom cab driver malignantly fails to take you where you want to go, or fails to arrive in time to catch a train you wished to catch.

The African fully knows the liability of his fetish to fail, but he equally fully knows its power. One, to me, grandly tragic instance of this I learnt at Opobo. There was a very great Fetish doctor there, universally admired and trusted, who lived out on the land at the mouth of the Great River. One day he himself fell sick, and he made ju-ju against the sickness ; but it held on, and he grew worse. He made more ju-ju of greater power, but again in vain, and then he made the greatest ju-ju man can make, and it availed nought, and he knew he was dying ; and so, with his remaining strength, he broke up and dishonoured and destroyed all the Fetishes in which the spirits lived, and cast them out into the surf and died like a man.

Then horror came upon the people when they knew he had done this, and they burnt his house and all things belonging to him, and cried upon the spirits not to forsake them, not to lay this one man's deadly sin at their doors. I rather doubt whether those spirits have come round yet, for Dr. Tompstone wrote to me that last November, just when their yearly plays were in full swing, to make sure of having fine weather for them, Opobo "called in a noted consultant from up river and," says the Doctor with a gracious sympathy for a fellow medical man, "it has rained in torrents ever since. It is very rough on him, as I believe he did his best and sacrificed large numbers of fowls."

In connection with the gods of West Africa I may remark that in almost all the series of native tradition there, you will find accounts of a time when there was direct intercourse between the gods or spirits that live in the sky, and men. That intercourse is always said to have been cut off by some human error ; for example, the Fernando Po people say that once upon a time there was no trouble or serious disturbance upon earth because there was a ladder, made like the one you get palm-nuts with, "only long, long ;" and this ladder reached from earth to heaven so the gods could go up and down it and attend personally to mundane affairs. But one day a cripple boy started to go up the ladder, and he had got a long way up when his mother saw him, and went up in pursuit. The gods, horrified at the prospect of having boys and women invading heaven, threw down the ladder, and have since left humanity severely alone. The Timneh people, north-east of Sierra Leone, say that in old times God was very friendly with men, and when He thought a man had lived long enough on earth, He sent a messenger to him telling him to come up into the sky, and stay with Him ; but once there was a man who, when the messenger of God came, did not want to leave his wives, his slaves, and his riches, and so the messenger had to go back without him ; and God was very cross and sent another messenger for him, who was called Disease, but the man would not come for him either, and so Disease sent back word to God that he must have help to bring the man ; and so God sent another messenger whose name was Death ; and Disease and Death together got hold of the man, and took him to God ; and God said in future He would always send these messengers to fetch men.

The Fernando Po legend may be taken as fairly pure African, but the Timneh, I expect, is a transmogrified Arabic story—though I do not know of anything like it among Arabic stories ; but they are infinite in quantity, and there is a certain ring about it I recognise, and these Timnehs are much in contact with the Mohammedan, Mandingoes, &c. In none of the African stories is there given anything like the importance to dreams that there is given to attempts to account for accidents and death ; and surely it must have been more impressive and important to a man to have got his leg or arm snapped off by a crocodile in the river, or by a shark in the surf, or to have got half killed, or have seen a friend killed by a falling tree in the forest in the day time, than to have experienced the most wonderful of dreams. He sees that however terrific his dream-experiences may have been, he was not much the worse for them. Not so in the other case, a limb gone or a life gone is more impressive, and more necessary to account for.

No trace of sun-worship have I ever found. The firmament is, I believe, always the great indifferent and neglected god, the Nyan Kupon of the Tschwi, and the Anzambe, Nzam, &c., of the Bantu races. The African thinks this god has great power if he would only exert it, and when things go very badly with him, when the river rises higher than usual and sweeps away his home and his plantations ; when the smallpox stalks through the land, and day and night the corpses float down the river past him, and he finds them jammed among his canoes that are tied to the beach, and choking up his fish traps ; and then when at last the death-wail over its victims goes up night and day from his own village, he will rise up and call upon this great god in the terror maddened by despair, that he may hear and restrain the evil workings of these lesser devils ; but he evidently finds, as Peer Gynt says, "Nein, er hört nicht. Er ist taub wie gewöhnlich " for there is no organised cult for Anzam.

Accounts of apparitions abound in all the West Coast
districts, and although the African holds them all in high
horror and terror, he does not see anything supernatural in
his "Duppy." It is a horrid thing to happen on, but there
is nothing strange about it, and he is ten thousand times more
frightened than puzzled over the affair. He does not want to
"investigate" to see whether there is anything in it. He wants
to get clear away, and make ju-ju against it, "one time."

These apparitions have a great variety of form, for, firstly,
there are all the true spirits, nature spirits ; secondly, the spirits
of human beings—these human spirits are held to exist before
as well as during and after bodily life ; thirdly, the spirits of
things. Probably the most horrid of class one is the Tschwi's
Sasabonsum. Whether Sasabonsum is an individual or a class
is not quite clear, but I believe he is a class of spirits, each
individual of which has the same characteristics, the same
manner of showing anger, the same personal appearance, and
the same kind of residence. I am a devoted student of his
cult and I am always coming across equivalent forms of him
in other tribes as well as the Tschwi, and I think he is very
early. I see no reason why gorillas should not believe in
Sasabonsum, only unfortunately Dr. Garner has not given us
that grammar and dictionary of Gorillese, so I cannot question
these interesting people on the point. As the Tschwi have
got their religious notions in a most tidy and definite state,
we will take their version of Sasabonsum.

He lives in the forest, in or under those great silk-cotton
trees around the roots of which the earth is red. This
coloured earth identifies a silk-cotton tree as being the residence
of a Sasabonsum, as its colour is held to arise from the
blood it whips off him as he goes down to his under-world
home after a night's carnage. All silk-cotton trees are suspected because they are held to be the roosts for Duppies.
But the red earth ones are feared with a great fear, and no one
makes a path by them, or a camp near them at night.

Sasabonsum is a friend of witches. He is of enormous
size, and of a red colour. He wears his hair straight and he
waylays unprotected wayfarers in the forest at night, and in
all districts except that of Apollonia he eats them. Round

Apollonia he only sucks their blood. Natives of this district after meeting him have crawled home and given an account of his appearance, and then expired.

Ellis says he is believed to be implacable, and when angered can never be mollified or propitiated, but it is certain that human victims are constantly sacrificed to him in districts beyond white control; in districts under it, the equivalent value of a human sacrifice in sheep and goats is offered to him. In Ashantee he has priests, and of course human sacrifice. Away among the Dahomeyan tribes—where he has kept his habits but got another name, and seems to have crystallised from a class into an individual—the usual way in which a god develops—he has priests and priestesses, and they are holy terrors; but among the Tschwi, Sasabonsum is mainly dealt with by witches, and people desirous of possessing the power of becoming witches. They derive their power from him in a remarkable way. I put myself to great personal inconvenience (fever risk, mosquito certainty, high leopard and snake palaver probability, and grave personal alarm and apprehension) to verify Colonel Ellis's account of the methods witches employ in this case, and finding his account correct I quote it, because it is more concise than mine is likely to be.

Ellis says, " A person who wishes to obtain a suhman (tutelary deity) proceeds to the dark and gloomy recesses of the forest, wherein, among the Bombaces a local Sasabonsum resides. There, having first poured a small quantity of rum upon the earth as a propitiatory offering, he adopts one of the following courses.

" 1. He cuts from a tree a moderately thick branch which he carves into a rude resemblance of the human figure ; usually these figures are simply cylindrical pieces of wood, from ten to fourteen inches in length and from three to four in diameter. Two or three inches from one end, which may be called the top, the stick is notched so as to roughly resemble a neck, and the top is then rounded to bear some rough distant resemblance to a head.

" 2. He takes the root of a plant or bush growing there, scrapes it, and grinds it into a paste with the blood of a fowl.

" 3. He takes some red earth from the spot and mixes it

into a paste with blood or rum. In the second and third cases the preparation is kept in a small brass pan, and the red tail-feathers of a parrot are commonly stuck in the paste. A suhman prepared in one of the last three modes is frequently kept covered in Shea butter, but a wooden figure never.

"Having adopted one of these courses, the individual in quest of a suhman then calls upon the spirit of Sasabonsum to enter the object which he has prepared, promising to reverence it and give it offerings. According to most natives he then picks certain leaves, the juice of which he squeezes upon the object, saying, 'eat this and speak.' Then, if a spirit has entered the object—in other words if the latter has become a suhman—a low hissing noise is heard. Being thus assured that the spirit is there, the man then puts a number of questions—ought he, the suhman, to be kept in a box, or left unenclosed? should he be anointed with Shea butter, or left dry? and those questions to which a low hissing sound is heard in reply are believed to be answered in the affirmative."

In the two cases in which I saw a suhman procured, the methods employed were Nos. 1 and 3. I have seen ehsuhman in the possession of individuals, answering all the particulars in appearance of the other kinds.

The chief use of a suhman is the power it gives its owner to procure the death of other people, not necessarily his own enemies, for he will sell charms made by the agency of his suhman to another person whose nerves have not been equal to facing Sasabonsum on his own account. He can also provide by its agency other charms, such as those that protect houses from fire, and things and individuals from accidents on the road, or in canoes, and the home circle from good-looking but unprincipled young men, and so on.

The quantity of charms among the Negroes, as among the Bantu, verges on infinity. Most of them are procured from suhman holders, but not all. I fancy a suhman wears himself out in making charms, for you will sometimes come across "dead" ones that you may buy. These dead ones are ehsuhman (pl.) who have failed several times to work because the spirit has left them; whereas a live charm is treasured, and treated as a sentient thing. A man I know had a bundle of feathers with a porcupine tail in their midst, and he used always to squirt out of his mouth a little rum over it when he was drinking.

As a rule the person who has a suhman keeps the fact pretty quiet, for the possession of such an article would lead half the catastrophes in his district, from the decease of pigs, fowls, and babies, to fires, &c., to be accredited to him, which would lead to his neighbours making "witch palaver" over him, and he would have to undergo poison-ordeal and other unpleasantness to clear his character. He, however, always keeps a special day in his suhman's honour, and should he be powerful, as a king or big chief, he will keep this day openly. King Kwoffi Karri Kari, whom we fought with in 1874, used to make a big day for his suhman, which was kept in a box covered with gold plates, and he sacrificed a human victim to it every Tuesday, with general festivities and dances in its honour.

I should remark that Sasabonsum is married. His wife, or more properly speaking his female form, is called Sha-mantin. She is far less malignant than the male form. Her name comes from Srahman—ghost or spirit ; the termination "tin" is an abbreviation of tsintsin—tall. She is of immense height, and white ; perhaps this idea is derived from the white stem of the silk-cotton trees wherein she invariably abides. Her method of dealing with the solitary wayfarer is no doubt inconvenient to him, but it is kinder than her husband's ways, for she does not kill and eat him, as Sasabonsum does, but merely detains him some months while she teaches him all about the forest : what herbs are good to eat, or to cure disease ; where the game come to drink, and what they say to each other, and so forth. I often wish I knew this lady, for the grim, grand African forests are like a great library, in which, so far, I can do little more than look at the pictures, although I am now busily learning the alphabet of their language, so that I may some day read what these pictures mean.

Do not go away with the idea, I beg, that goddesses as a general rule, are better than gods. They are not. There are stories about them which I could—I mean I could not—tell you. There is one belonging also to the Tschwi. She lives

at Moree, a village five miles from Cape Coast. She is, as is
usual with deities, human in shape and colossal in size, and as is
not usual with deities, she is covered with hair from head to
foot,—short white hair like a goat.   Her abode is on the path
to surf-cursed Anamabu near the sea-beach, and her name is
Aynfwa ; a worshipper of hers has only got to mention the
name of a person he wishes dead when passing her abode
and Aynfwa does the rest.   She is the goddess of all albinoes,
who are said to be more frequent in occurrence round Moree
than elsewhere.   Ellis says that in 1886, when he was there,
they were 1 per cent. of the entire population.   These albinoes
are, *ipso facto*, her priests and priestesses, and in old days an
albino had only to name anywhere a person Aynfwa wished
for, and that person was forthwith killed.

I think I may safely say that every dangerous place in
West Africa is regarded as the residence of a god—rocks
and whirlpools in the rivers—swamps " no man fit to pass "—
and naturally, the surf.   Along the Gold Coast, at every place
where you have to land through the surf, it fairly swarms
with gods.   A little experience with the said surf inclines you
to think, as the dabblers in spiritualism say, " that there is
something in it."   I will back this West Coast surf—" the
Calemma," as we call it down South, against any other malevolent abomination, barring only the English climate.   Its ways
of dealing with human beings are cunning and deceitful.   In its
most ferocious moods it seizes a boat, straightway swamps it,
and feeds its pet sharks with the boat's occupants.   If the
surf is merely sky-larking it lets your boat's nose just smell
the sand, and then says " Thought you were all right this time,
did you though," and drags the boat back again under the
incoming wave, or catches it under the stern and gaily
throws it upside down over you and yours on the beach.
Variety, they say, is charming.   Let those who say it, and
those who believe it, just do a course of surf-work, and I'll
warrant they will change their minds ; and above all let men
who have to do with the demon-possessed surf of the West
African sea-board take care not to get their minds entirely
filled with the terror of getting drowned or eaten by sharks,
for these are minor dangers in the affair, though they occur.

The danger is your own boat, for it is not given to every man to do like my gigantic friend, Captain Heldt, and swim ashore and crawl up the beach, with three ribs broken, and his legs temporarily paralysed, by having a heavy surf-boat hurled by a wave on to his back, while engaged in an independent venture to reach the shore, after a catastrophe on the outer breakers. And let me add that when you are advised in a yell to jump into the surf by the black bo'sn of the windward coast, or the equally black Padrone of the S.W. Coast, do so " one time.' Never mind those sharks, but mind and jump out on the windward side of the boat, the side that the surf is breaking against, the side that looks the worst, for by this means you may keep clear of the boat. I do not advise you to take a white man's advice as to jumping until you have gone through his genealogy and ascertained that beyond doubt he is a direct descendant of George Washington. There was a nice young doctor once on a S.W. Coast boat, who did not pursue this plan, and did not know that in this nineteenth century it is every man's duty to keep his powers of belief for religious purposes; so this doctor frittered his powers away on old coasters and sea-captains, most excellent people, but supremely human. I am one myself now, so I speak with authority ; only the information we lavish on the new-comer is often too strong for him, and it was so in this doctor's case. They had told him about the surf; how you had to jump and swim the last breakers of it as soon as you heard the shout, and so on ; so when going ashore at Batanga, the gallant boat-boys gave the rousing war-yell with which it is their custom to greet their enemy, "with that stern joy a warrior feels," over the side the doctor went like a shot, to the horror of the remorse-smitten sea-captain, who was in the boat. He got through all right, however. Now and again, I own, the new-comer scores. There was one who came out for the Government to Accra, where the surf is notorious. The boat got upset in the first line of breakers, and there was as bad a surf on that day as Accra ever rose. When he got ashore, the old coasters thought he would be impressed and terrified ; but no. He just remarked it was lucky he had such a

good day for landing, " for he'd only had to swim the last
fifty yards."

And finally, as the preacher says, remember it is highly
advisable to have your conscience clear, at any rate regarding
your past treatment of your Kru or Accra boat-boys, before
you trust yourself to them to take you through a surf. There
was a bad man once on the Gold Coast who had ill-used his men
and when they took him out through the surf to go aboard
the ship that was to take him home, there was the usual catastrophe, which no one thought much of, only saying " It was
hard on B. just as he was going home," until the body of B.
came ashore, and then, in the clothes, were found three iron
shark hooks, with lots of line attached, wherewith the men had
held B. back from shore, and played him like a fish, until the
surf beat the life out of him.

Forgive this digression on surf, but a coaster cannot help
going on like this as soon as his pet enemy is mentioned, and
I humbly return to African apparitions. There is one thing
about the surf that I do not understand, and that is why
witches always walk stark naked along the beach by it
at night, and eat sea crabs the while. That such is a
confirmed habit of theirs is certain ; and they tell me that
while doing this the witches emit a bright light, and also that
there is a certain medicine, which, if you have it with you, you
can throw over the witch, and then he, or she, will remain
blazing until morning time, running to and fro, crying out
wildly, in front of the white, breaking, thundering surf wall,
and when the dawn comes the fire burns the witch right
up, leaving only a grey ash—and palaver set in this world
and the next for that witch.

A highly-esteemed native minister told me when I was at
Cape Coast last, that a fortnight before, he had been away in
the Apollonia district on mission work. One evening he and
a friend were walking along the beach and the night was dark,
so that you could see only the surf. It is never too dark to
see that, it seems to have light in itself. They saw a flame
coming towards them, and after a moment's doubt they knew
it was a witch, and feeling frightened, hid themselves among
the bushes that edge the sandy shore. As they watched, it

came straight on and passed them, and they saw it disappear in the distance. My informant laughed at himself, and very wisely said, "One has not got to believe those things here, one has in Apollonia."

To the surf and its spirits the sea-board-dwelling Tschwis bring women who have had children and widows, both after a period of eight days from the birth of the child, or the death of the husband.

A widow remains in the house until this period has elapsed, neglecting her person, eating little food, and sitting on the bare floor in the attitude of mourning. On the Gold Coast they bury very quickly, as they are always telling you, usually on the day after death, rarely later than the third day, even among the natives; and the spirit, or Srah, of the dead man is supposed to hang about his wives and his house until the ceremony of purification is carried out. This is done, needless to say, with uproar. The relations of each wife go to her house with musical instruments—I mean tom-toms and that sort of thing—and they take a quantity of mint, which grows wild in this country, with them. This mint they burn, some of it in the house, the rest they place upon pans of live coals and carry round the widow as she goes in their midst down to the surf, her relatives singing aloud to the Srah of the departed husband, telling him that now he is dead and has done with the lady he must leave her. This singing serves to warn all the women who are not relations to get out of the way, which of course they always carefully do, because if they were to see the widow their own husbands would die within the year.

When the party has arrived at the shore, they strip every rag off the widow, and throw it into the surf ; and a thoughtful female relative having brought a suit of dark blue baft with her for the occasion, the widow is clothed in this and returns home, where a suitable festival is held, after which she may marry again ; but if she were to marry before this ceremony, the Srah of the husband would play the mischief with husband number two or three, and so on, as the case might be.

In the inland Gold Coast districts the widows remain in

a state of mourning for several months, and a selection
of them, a quantity of slaves, and one or two free men are
killed to escort the dead man to Srahmandazi ; and as well as
these, and in order to provide him with merchandise to keep
up his house and state in the under-world, quantities of gold
dust, rolls of rich velvets, silks, satins, &c., are thrown into the
grave.

Among the dwellers in Cameroon, when you are across the
Bantu border-line, velvets, &c., are buried with a big man or
woman; but I am told it is only done for the glorification of
his living relatives, so that the world may say, "So and so
must be rich, look what a lot of trade he threw away at that
funeral of his wife," or his father, or his son, as the case may
be ; but I doubt whether this is the true explanation.   If it is,
I should recommend my German friends, if they wish to
intervene, to introduce the income tax into Cameroon—that
would eliminate this custom.

The Tschwis hold that there is a definite earthly existence
belonging to each soul of a human kind.   Let us say, for example, a soul has a thirty years' bodily existence belonging
to it.   Well, suppose that soul's body gets killed off at twenty-
five, its remaining five years it has to spend, if it is left alone,
in knocking about its old haunts, homes, and wives.   In
this state it is called a Sisa, and is a nuisance.   It will cause
sickness.   It will throw stones.   It will pull off roofs, and it
will play the very mischief with its wives' subsequent husbands,
all because, not having reached its full term of life, it has not
learnt its way down the dark and difficult path to
Srahmandazi, the entrance to which is across the Volta
River to the N.E.   This knowledge of the path to Srahmandazi
is a thing that grows gradually on a man's immortal soul (the
other three souls are not immortal), and naturally not having
been allowed to complete his life, his knowledge is imperfect.
A man's soul, however, can be taught the way, if necessary, in
the funeral "custom" made by his relatives and the priests ;
but in a case of an incompletelifeonearthsoul, as a German
would say, when it does arrive in the land of Insrah (pl.) it is
in a weak and feeble state from the difficulties of its journey,
whereas a soul that has lived out its allotted span of life goes

straightway off to Srahmandazi as soon as its " custom " or
" devil " is made and gives its surviving relatives no further
trouble. Still there is great difference of opinion among all
the Tschwis and Ga men I have come across on this point,
and Ellis likewise remarks on this difference of opinion.
Some informants say that a soul that has been sent hence
before its time, although it is exhausted by the hardships it
has suffered on its journey down, yet recovers health in a
month or so; while a soul that has run its allotted span on earth
is as feeble as a new-born babe on arriving in Srahmandazi,
and takes years to pull round. Other informants say they
have no knowledge of these details, and state that all the
difference they know of between the souls of men who have
been killed and the men who have died, is that the former can
always come back, and that really the safest way of disposing of
this class of soul is, by suitable spells and incantations, to get it to
enter into the body of a new-born baby, where it can live out the
remainder of its life. This method is not difficult to carry out,
because a Sisa is always on the look-out for a body, and causes
a great deal of harm by whipping itself into the bodies of
sleeping persons whose own dream-Srah is temporarily absent.
But getting a Sisa into a new baby is a mean thing to do,
because, as I have said before, it is held that some of these
Insisa become wanderer-souls and are a trial to the baby
owners.

Before closing these observations on Srahmandazi I will
give the best account of that land that I am at present able
to. Some day perhaps I may share the fate of the Oxford
Professor in *In the Wrong Paradise* and go there myself, but so
far my information is second-hand. It is like this world. There
are towns and villages, rivers, mountains, bush, plantations,
and markets. When the sun rises here it sets in Srahmandazi.
It has its pleasures and its pains, not necessarily retributive
or rewarding, but dim. All souls in it grow forward or
backward into the prime of life and remain there, some
informants say; others say that each inhabitant remains there
at the same age as he was when he quitted the world above.
This latter view is most like the South West one. The former
is possibly only an attempt to make Srahmandazi into a

heaven in conformation with Christian teaching, which it is not, any more than it is a hell.

I have much curious information regarding its flora and fauna. A great deal of both is seemingly indigenous, and then there are the souls of great human beings, the Asrahmanfw, and the souls of all the human beings, animals, and things sent down with them. I have had great and highly abstruse controversies with Ethiopian theologians on the question of what happens to the soul of the soul of things, when the Asrahmanfo kills these for his support in Srahmandazi. But as nothing since the Middle Ages has approached these controversies in confusion of idea and worthlessness of ultimate deductions arrived at, I will not inflict them on you here. The ghosts do not' seem to leave off their interest in mundane affairs, for they not only have local palavers, but try palavers left over from their earthly existence ; and when there is an outbreak of sickness in a Fantee town or village, and several inhabitants die off, the opinion is often held that there is a big palaver going on down in Srahmandazi and that the spirits are sending up on earth for witnesses, subpœnaing them as it were. Medicine men or priests are called in to find out what particular earthly grievance can be the subject of the ghost palaver, and when they have ascertained this, they take the evidence of every one in the town on this affair, as it were on commission, and transmit the information to the court sitting in Srahmandazi. This prevents the living being incommoded by personal journeys down below and although the priests have their fee, it is cheaper in the end, because the witnesses funeral expenses would fall heavier still.

Although far more elaborated and thought out than any other African under-world I have ever come across, the Tschwi Srahmandazi may be taken as a type of all the African underworlds. The Bantu's idea of a future life is a life spent in much such a place. As far as I can make out there is no definite idea of eternity. I have even come across cases in which doubt was thrown on the present existence of the Creating God, but I think this has arisen from attempts having been made to introduce concise conceptions into the African mind, conceptions that are quite foreign to its true

nature and which alarm and worry it. You never get the
strange idea of the difference between time and eternity—the
idea I mean, that they are different things—in the African
that one frequently gets in cultured Europeans; and as for
the human soul, the African always believes "that still
the spirit is whole, and life and death but shadows of the
soul."

CHAPTER XXIII

FETISH—(*Concluded*)

In which the discourse on apparitions is continued, with some observations on secret societies, both tribal and murder, and the kindred subject of leopards.

APPARITIONS are by no means always of human soul origin. All the Tschwis and the Ewe gods, for example, have the habit of appearing pretty regularly to their priests, and occasionally to the laity, like Sasabonsum; but it is only to priests that these appearances are harmless or beneficial. The effect of Sasabonsum's appearance to the layman I have cited above, and I could give many other examples of the bad effects of those of other gods, but will only now mention Tando, the Hater, the chief god of the Northern Tschwis, the Ashantees, &c. He is terribly malicious, human in shape, and though not quite white, is decidedly lighter in complexion than the chief god of the Southern Tschwis, Bobowissi. His hair is lank, and he carries a native sword and wears a long robe. His well-selected messengers are those awful driver ants (Inkran) which it is not orthodox to molest in Tando's territories. He uses as his weapons lightning, tempest, and disease, but the last is the most favourite one.

There is absolutely no trick too mean or venomous for Tando. For example, he has a way of appearing near a village he has a grudge against in the form of a male child, and wanders about crying bitterly, until some kind-hearted, unsuspecting villager comes and takes him in and feeds him. Then he develops a contagious disease that clears that village out.

This form of appearance and subsequent conduct is, unhappily, not rigidly confined to Tando, but is used by many spirits as a method of collecting arrears in taxes in the way of sacrifices. I have found traces of it among Bantu gods or spirits, and it gives rise to a general hesitation in West Africa to take care of waifs and strays of unexplained origin.

Other things beside gods and human spirits have the habit of becoming incarnate. Once I had to sit waiting a long time at an apparently perfectly clear bush path, because in front of us a spear's ghost used to fly across the path about that time in the afternoon, and if any one was struck by it they died. A certain spring I know of is haunted by the ghost of a pitcher. Many ladies when they have gone alone to fill their pitchers in the evening time at this forest spring have noticed a very fine pitcher standing there ready filled, and thinking exchange is no robbery, or at any rate they would risk it if it were, have left their own pitcher and taken the better looking one ; but always as soon as they have come within sight of the village huts, the new pitcher has crumbled into dust, and the water in it been spilt on the ground ; and the worst of it is, when they have returned to fetch their own discarded pitcher, they find it also shattered into pieces.

There is also another class of apparition, of which I have met with two instances, one among pure Negroes (Okÿon) ; the other among pure Bantu (Kangwe). I will give the Bantu version of the affair, because at Okÿon the incident had happened a good time before the details were told me, and in the Bantu case they had happened the previous evening. But there was very little difference in the main facts of the case, and it was an important thing because in both cases the underlying idea was sacrificial.

The woman who told me was an exceedingly intelligent, shrewd, reliable person. She had been to the factory with some trade, and had got a good price for it, and so was in a good temper on her return home in the evening. She got out of her canoe and leaving her slave boy to bring up the things, walked to her house, which was the ordinary house of a prosperous Igalwa native, having two distinct rooms in it, and a separate cook-house close by in a clean, sandy yard. She

trod on some nastiness in the yard, and going into the cook-
house found the slave girls round a very small and inefficient
fire, trying to cook the evening meal. She blew them up for
not having a proper fire ; they said the wood was wet, and
would not burn. She said they lied, and she would see to
them later, and she went into the chamber she used for a
sleeping apartment, and trod on something more on the
floor in the dark ; those good-for-nothing hussies of slaves had
not lit her palm-oil lamp, and mentally forming the opinion
that they had been out flirting during her absence, and resolving to teach them well the iniquity of such conduct, she
sat down on her bed into a lot of messy stuff of a clammy,
damp nature. Now this fairly roused her, for she is a notable
housewife, who keeps her house and slaves in exceedingly
good order. So dismissing from her mind the commercial
consideration she had intended to gloat over when she came
into her room, she called Ingremina and others in a tone that
brought those young ladies on the spot. She asked them how
they dared forget to light her lamp ; they said they had not,
but the lamp in the room must have gone out like the other
lamps had, after burning dim and spluttering. They further
said they had not been out, but had been sitting round the fire
trying to make it burn properly. She duly whacked and pulled
the ears of all within reach. I say within reach for she is not very
active, weighing, I am sure, upwards of eighteen stone. Then
she went back into her room and got out her beautiful English
paraffin lamp, which she keeps in a box, and taking it into the
cook-house, picked up a bit of wood from the hissing, spluttering fire, and lit it. When she picked up the wood she noticed
that it was covered with the same sticky abomination she had
met before that evening, and it smelt of the same faint smell
she had noticed as soon as she had reached her house, and
by now the whole air seemed oppressive with it.

As soon as the lamp was alight she saw what the stuff
was, namely, blood. Blood was everywhere, the rest of the
sticks in the fire had it on them, it sizzled at the burning ends,
and ran off the other in rills. There were pools of it about
her clean, sandy yard. Her own room was reeking, the bed,
the stools, the floor ; it trickled down the door-post ; coagu-

lated on the lintel. She herself was smeared with it from the things she had come in contact with in the dark, and the slaves seemed to have been sitting in pools of it. The things she picked up off the table and shelf left rims of it behind them ; there was more in the skillets, and the oil in the open palm-oil lamps had a film of it floating on the oil. Investigation showed that the whole of the rest of her house was in a similar mess. The good lady gave a complete catalogue of the household furniture and its condition, which I need not give here. The slave girls when the light came were terrified at what they saw, and she called in the aristocracy of the village, and asked them their opinion on the blood palaver. They said they could make nothing of it at first, but subsequently formed the opinion that it meant something was going to happen, and suggested with the kind, helpful cheerfulness of relatives and friends, that they should not wonder if it were a prophecy of her own death. This view irritated the already tried lady, and she sent them about their business, and started the slaves on house-cleaning. The blood cleaned up all right when you were about it, but kept on turning up in other places, and in the one you had just cleaned as soon as you left off and went elsewhere ; and the morning came and found things in much the same state until "before suntime," say about 10 o'clock, when it faded away.

I cautiously tried to get my stately, touchy dowager duchess to explain how it was that there was such a lot of blood, and how it was it got into the house. She just said " it had to go somewhere," and refused to give rational explanations as *Chambers's Journal* does after telling a good ghost story. I found afterwards that it was quite decided it was a case of " blood come before," and at Okÿon, Miss Slessor told me, in regard to the similar case there, that this was the opinion held regarding the phenomenon. It is always held uncanny in Africa if a person dies without shedding blood. You see, the blood is the life, and if you see it come out, you know the going of the thing, as it were. If you do not, it is mysterious. At Okÿon, a few days after the blood appeared, a nephew of the person whose house it came into was killed while felling a tree in the forest ; a bough struck him and broke his neck, without shedding a drop of blood, and this bore out the theory, for the blood having "to go somewhere" came before. In the Bantu case I did not hear of such a supporting incident happening.

Certain African ideas about blood puzzle me. I was told by a Batanga friend, a resident white trader, that a short time previously a man was convicted of theft by the natives of a village close to him. The hands and feet of the criminal were tied together, and he was flung into the river. He got himself free, and swam to the other bank, and went for bush. He was recaptured, and a stone tied to his neck, and in again he was thrown. The second time he got free and ashore, and was recaptured, and the chief then, most regretfully, ordered that he was to be knocked on the head before being thrown in for a third time. This time palaver set, but the chief knew that he would die himself, by spitting the blood he had spilt, from his own lungs, before the year was out. I inquired about the chief when I passed this place, more than eighteen months after, and learnt from a native that the chief was dead, and that he had died in this way. The objection thus was not to shedding blood in a general way, but to the shedding in the course of judicial execution. There may be some idea of this kind underlying the ingenious and awful ways the negroes have of killing thieves, by tying them to stakes in the rivers, or down on to paths for the driver ants to kill and eat, but this is only conjecture ; I have not had a chance yet to work this subject up ; and getting reliable information about underlying ideas is very difficult in Africa. The natives will say "Yes" to any mortal thing, if they think you want them to ; and the variety of their languages is another great hindrance. Were it not for the prevalence of Kru English or trade English, investigation would be almost impossible ; but, fortunately, this quaint language is prevalent, and the natives of different tribes communicate with each other in it, and so round a fire, in the evening, if you listen to the gossip, you can pick up all sorts of strange information, and gain strange and often awful lights on your absent white friends' characters, and your present companions' religion. For example, the other day I had a set of porters composed of four

Bassa boys, two Wei Weis, one Dualla, and two Yorubas. None of their languages fitted, so they talked trade English, and pretty lively talk some of it was, but of that anon.

I cannot close this brief notice of native ideas without mentioning the secret societies; but to go fully into this branch of the subject would require volumes, for every tribe has its secret society. The Poorah of Sierra Leone, the Oru of Lagos, the Egbo of Calabar, the Yasi of the Igalwa, the Ukuku of the M'pongwe, the Ikun of the Bakele, and the Lukuku of the Bachilangi, Baluba, are some of the most powerful secret societies on the West African Coast.

These secret societies are not essentially religious, their action is mainly judicial, and their particularly presiding spirit is not a god or devil in our sense of the word. The ritual differs for each in its detail, but there are broad lines of agreement between them. There are societies both for men and for women, but no mixed societies for both sexes. Those that I have mentioned above are all male, and women are utterly forbidden to participate in the rites or become acquainted with their secrets, for one of the chief duties of these societies is to keep the women in order ; and besides this reason it is undoubtedly held that women are bad for certain forms of ju-ju, even when these forms are not directly connected, as far as I can find out, with the secret society. For example, the other day a chief up the Mungo River deliberately destroyed his ju-ju by showing it to his women. It was a great ju-ju, but expensive to keep up, requiring sacrifices of slaves and goats, so what with trade being bad, fall in the price of oil and ivory and so on, he felt he could not afford that ju-ju, and so destroyed its power, so as to prevent its harming him when he neglected it. Probably the destructive action of women is not only the idea of their inferiority—for had inferiority been the point, that chief would have laid his ju-ju with dogs, or pigs—but arises from the undoubted fact that women are notably deficient in real reverence for authority, as is demonstrated by the way they continually treat that of their husbands.

The general rule with these secret societies is to admit the young free people at an age of about eight to ten years, the

boys entering the male, the girls the female society. Both
societies are rigidly kept apart. A man who attempts to penetrate the female mysteries would be as surely killed as a woman
who might attempt to investigate the male mysteries ; still I
came, in 1893, across an amusing case which demonstrates the
inextinguishable thirst for knowledge, so long as that knowledge
is forbidden, which characterises our sex. Alas ! had only this
Forschungschwärmerei filled us for other classes of knowledge,
we might have been the discoverers of the electric telegraph,
and a thing or so more of that order.

It was in the district just south of Big Batanga. The male
society had been very hard on the ladies for some time, and
one day one star-like intellect among the latter told her next-
door neighbour, in strict confidence, that she did not believe
Ikun was a spirit at all, but only old So-and-so dressed up in
leaves. This rank heresy spread rapidly, in strict confidence,
among the ladies at large, and they used to assemble together
in the house of the foundress of the theory, secretly of course,
because husbands down there are hasty with the cutlass and
the kassengo, and they talked the matter over. Somehow or
other, this came to the ears of the men. Whether the ladies
got too emancipated and winked when Ikun was mentioned,
or asked how Mr. So-and-so was this morning, in a pointed
way, after an Ikun manifestation, I do not know ; some people
told me this was so, but others, who, I fear, were right, considering the acknowledged slowness of men in putting two
and two together, and the treachery of women towards
each other, said that a woman had told a man that she had
heard some of the other women were going on in this
heretical way. Anyhow, the men knew, and were much
alarmed ; scepticism had spread by now to such an extent
that nothing short of burning or drowning all the women
could stamp it out and reintroduce the proper sense of awe
into the female side of society, and after a good deal of consideration the men saw, for men are undoubtedly more gifted
in foresight than our sex, that it was no particular use re-
introducing this awe if there was no female half of society to
be impressed by it. It was a brain-spraining problem for the
men all round, for it is clear society cannot be kept together

without some superhuman aid to help to keep the feminine portion of it within bounds.

Grave councils were held, and it was decided that the woman at whose house these treasonable meetings were held should be sent away early one morning on a trading mission to the nearest factory, a job she readily undertook ; and while the other women were away in the plantation or at the spring, certain men entered her house secretly and dug a big chamber out in the floor of the hut, and one of them, dressed as Ikun, and provided with refreshments for the day, got into this chamber, and the whole affair was covered over carefully and the floor re-sanded. That afternoon there was a big manifestation of Ikun. He came in the most terrible form, his howls were awful, and he finally went dancing away into the bush as the night came down. The ladies had just taken the common-sense precaution of removing all goats, sheep, fowls, &c., into enclosed premises, for, like all his kind, he seizes and holds any property he may come across in the street, but there was evidently no emotional thrill in the female mind regarding him, and when the leading lady returned home in the evening the other ladies strolled into their leader's hut to hear about what new cotton prints, beads, and things Mr.—— had got at his factory by the last steamer from Europe, and interesting kindred subjects bearing on Mr.——. When they had threshed these matters out, the conversation turned on to religion, and what fools those men had been making of themselves all the afternoon with their Ikun. No sooner was his name uttered than a venomous howl, terminating in squeals of rage and impatience, came from the ground beneath them. They stared at each other for one second, and then, feeling that something was tearing its way up through the floor, they left for the interior of Africa with one accord. Ikun gave chase as soon as he got free, but what with being half-stifled and a bit cramped in the legs, and much encumbered with his vegetable decorations, the ladies got clear away and no arrests were made—but society was saved. Scepticism became in the twinkling of an eye a thing of the past ; and, although no names were taken, the men observed that certain ladies were particularly anxious, and regardless of expense, in buying immunity from Ikun, and they fancied that these ladies were probably in that hut on that particular evening, but they took no further action against them, save making Ikun particularly expensive. There ought to be a moral to an improving tale of this order, I know, but the only one I can think of just now is that it takes a priest to get round a woman; and I always feel inclined to jump on to the table myself when I think of those poor dear creatures sitting on the floor and feeling that awful thing clapper-clawing its way up right under them.

Ikun has the peculiar habit of coming in from the sea in a canoe. The heads of his society always see him first, and go out to meet him in their canoes, and bring him in his Jack-in-the-Green dress ashore; meanwhile all the women dash about driving into enclosures ducks, chickens, children, sheep, and goats, and then conceal themselves. He is the only member of his class I have ever heard of that comes in from the sea; they usually come out of the bush like Egbo and Yasi, and his dress is bush anyhow. There is another peculiarity of Ikun, which is that he has a peculiar way of taking payment for a thing which all his fellow secret societies and spirits also supply, namely, the power of becoming rich.

For example, a man desires this power, so he goes to some one known to possess Ikun, and inquires of him if he will let him have a certain quantity of his power, say, enough to ensure his becoming a thousand-pound-a-yearer. The man who possesses the power says that for this quantity of the power the applicant must pay the lives of fifty of his blood relations. All these lives the man must take himself, from time to time, secretly, as occasion offers; and the spirits of the murdered go to Ikun in the under-world and work for him as slaves, and as they go down, so every undertaking of the murderer turns out profitably, and he gradually grows richer and richer.

It is a dangerous practice in this world, because when your neighbours notice how your relatives are going off, and how you are getting on, they are apt to say you are making Ikun; whereupon they descend on you and kill you, and collar your hard-earned wealth, and have a dance in the evening; but I am assured that if you succeed in killing off your relations, unnoticed, up to the proper amount, there is no eternal unpleasantness awaiting you personally as there would be in Europe if you made a deal with the devil. Whether this arises from a lack of moral perception of the iniquity of this sort of thing in the African, or from the difficulty of imagining —with only the African's allowance of imagination—a greater hell than existence in a West African village under native law, I must leave to psychologists.

LADY OF OBAMBO, OGOWÉ, SHOWING CICATRISATION.

Tattooing on the West Coast is comparatively rare, and I think I may say never used with decorative intent only. The skin decorations are either paint or cicatrices—in the former case the pattern is not kept always the same by the individual. A peculiar form of it you find in the Rivers, where a pattern is painted on the skin, and then when the paint is dry, a wash is applied which makes the unpainted skin rise up in between the painted pattern. The cicatrices are sometimes tribal marks, but sometimes decorative. They are made by cutting the skin and then placing in the wound the fluff of the silk cotton tree.

The great point of agreement between all these West African secret societies lies in the methods of initiation.

The boy, if he belongs to a tribe that goes in for tattooing, is tattooed, and is handed over to instructors in the societies' secrets and formulæ. He lives, with the other boys of his tribe undergoing initiation, usually under the rule of several instructors, and for the space of one year. He lives always in the forest, and is naked and smeared with clay.

The boys are exercised so as to become inured to hardship; in some districts, they make raids so as to perfect themselves in this useful accomplishment. They always take a new name, and are supposed by the initiation process to become new beings in the magic wood, and on their return to their village at the end of their course, they pretend to have entirely forgotten their life before they entered the wood; but this pretence is not kept up beyond the period of festivities given to welcome them home. They all learn, to a certain extent, a new language, a secret language only understood by the initiated.

The same removal from home and instruction from initiated members is also observed with the girls. However, in their case, it is not always a forest-grove they are secluded in, sometimes it is done in huts. Among the Grain Coast tribes, however, the girls go into a magic wood until they are married. Should they have to leave the wood for any temporary reason, they must smear themselves with white clay. A similar custom holds good in Okÿon, Calabar district, where, should a girl have to leave the fattening-house, she must be covered with white clay. I believe this fattening-house custom in Calabar is not only for fattening up the women to improve their appearance, but an initiatory custom as well, although the main intention is now, undoubtedly, fattening, and the girl is constantly fed with fat-producing foods, such as fou-fou soaked in palm oil. I am told, but I think wrongly, that the white clay with which a Calabar girl is kept covered while in the fattening-house, putting on an extra coating of it should she come outside, is to assist in the fattening process by preventing perspiration.

The duration of the period of seclusion varies somewhat. San Salvador boys are six months in the wood. Cameroon boys are twelve months. In most districts the girls are betrothed in infancy, and they go into the wood or initiatory hut for a few months before marriage. In this case the time seems to vary with the circumstances of the individual ; not so with the boys, for whom each tribal society has a duly appointed course terminating at a duly appointed time ; but sometimes, as among some of the Yoruba tribes, the boy has to remain under the rule of the presiding elders of the society, painted white, and wearing only a bit of grass cloth, if he wears anything, until he has killed a man. Then he is held to have attained man's estate by having demonstrated his courage and also by having secured for himself the soul of the man he has killed as a spirit slave.

The initiation of boys into a few of the elementary dogmas of the secret society by no means composes the entire work of the society. All of them are judicial, and taken on the whole they do an immense amount of good. The methods are frequently a little quaint. Rushing about the streets disguised under masks and drapery, with an imitation tail swinging behind you, while you lash out at every one you meet with a whip or cutlass, is not a European way of keeping the peace, or perhaps I should say maintaining the dignity of the law. But discipline must be maintained, and this is the West African way of doing it.

The Egbo of Calabar is a fine type of the secret society. It is exceedingly well developed in its details, not sketchy like Yasi, nor so red-handed as Poorah. Unfortunately, however, I cannot speak with the same amount of knowledge of Egbo as I could of Poorah.

Egbo has the most grades of initiation, except perhaps Poorah, and it exercises jurisdiction over all classes of crime except witchcraft. Any Effik man who desires to become an influential person in the tribe must buy himself into as high a grade of Egbo as he can afford, and these grades are expensive, £1,500 or £1,000 English being required for the higher steps, I am informed. But it is worth it to a great trader, as an influential Effik necessarily is, for he can call out his own class

of Egbo and send it against those of his debtors who may be
of lower grades, and as the Egbo methods of delivering its
orders to pay up consist in placing Egbo at a man's doorway.
and until it removes itself from that doorway the man dare
not venture outside his house, it is most successful.

Of course the higher a man is in Egbo rank, the greater his
power and security, for lower grades cannot proceed against
higher ones. Indeed, when a man meets the paraphernalia of
a higher grade of Egbo than that to which he belongs, he has
to act as if he were lame, and limp along past it humbly, as if
the sight of it had taken all the strength out of him, and,
needless to remark, higher grade debtors flip their fingers at
lower grade creditors.

After talking so much about the secret society spirits, it may
be as well to say what they are. They are, one and all, a kind
of a sort of a something that usually (the exception is Ikun)
lives in the bush. Last February I was making my way back
toward Duke Town—late, as usual; I was just by a town on
the Qwa River. As I was hurrying onward I heard a terrific
uproar accompanied by drums in the thick bush into which,
after a brief interval of open ground, the path turned. I
became cautious and alarmed, and hid in some dense bush as
the men making the noise approached. I saw it was some
ju-ju affair. They had a sort of box which they carried on
poles, and their dresses were peculiar, and abnormally ample
over the upper part of their body. They were prancing about
in an ecstatic way round the box, which had one end open, beating their drums and shouting. They were fairly close to me,
but fortunately turned their attention to another bit of undergrowth, or that evening they would have landed another kind
of thing to what they were after. The bushes they selected
they surrounded, and evidently did their best to induce something to come out of them and go into their box arrangement.
I was every bit as anxious as they were that they should succeed, and succeed rapidly, for you know there are a nasty lot
of snakes and things in general, not to mention driver ants,
about that Calabar bush, that do not make it at all pleasant
to go sitting about in. However, presently they got this
something into their box and rejoiced exceedingly, and

departed staggering under the weight. I gave them a good start, and then made the best of my way home; and all that night Duke Town howled, and sang, and thumped its tom-toms unceasingly; for I was told Egbo had come into the town. Egbo is very coy, even for a secret society spirit, and seems to loathe publicity; but when he is ensconced in this ark he utters sententious observations on the subject of current politics, and his word is law. The voice that comes out of the ark is very strange, and unlike a human voice. I heard it shortly after Egbo had been secured. I expect, from what I saw, that there was some person in that ark all the time, but I do not know. It is more than I can do to understand my ju-ju details at present, let alone explain them on rational lines. I hear that there is a tribe on the slave coast who have been proved to keep a small child in the drum that is the residence of their chief spirit, and that when the child grows too large to go in it is killed, and another one that has in the meantime been trained by the priests takes the place of the dead one, until it, in its turn, grows too big and is killed, and so on. I expect this killing of the children is not sacrificial, but arises entirely from the fact that as ex-kings are dangerous to the body politic, therefore still more dangerous would ex-gods be.

Very little is known by outsiders regarding Egbo compared to what there must be to be known, owing to a want of interest or to a sense of inability on the part of most white people to make head or tail out of what seems to them a horrid pagan practice or a farrago of nonsense.

It is still a great power, although its officials in Duke or Creek Town are no longer allowed to go chopping and whipping promiscuous-like, because the Consul-General has a prejudice against this sort of thing, and the Effik is learning that it is nearly as unhealthy to go against his Consul-General as against his ju-ju. So I do not believe you will ever get the truth about it in Duke Town, or Creek Town. If you want to get hold of the underlying idea of these societies you must go round out-of-the-way corners where the natives are not yet afraid of being laughed at or punished. I subjoin a fragment from my Duke Town diaries to demonstrate that I did endeavour to do what I could in the interests of science.

"They are at it down in Duke Town to-night, not only rubbing the drum, but singing one of the big tunes. I'll just go down and see to it, though it's inky dark, and Calabar has not risen to the cultured level of oil street-lamps ; still there's lots of sheet lightning. Two and a half hours later. It's a perfect scandal they do not keep those Duke Town paths in a better state. They are nothing in this world but drains, and precious bad at that. There ought to be one fixed light at Mr. Fynn's Ditch, or by the bridge, and *then* you would know which was which before you were waist-high in water."

Of the South-West Coast secret societies the Ukuku seems the most powerful. The Yasi belonging to those indolent Igalwas, and M'pongwe is now little more than a play. You pretty frequently come upon Yasi dances just round Libreville. You will see stretched across the little street in a cluster of houses, a line from which branches are suspended, making a sort of screen. The women and children keep one side of this screen, the men dancing on the other side to the peculiar monotonous Yasi tune. Poorah I have spoken of elsewhere, but one thing I may remark regarding it which struck me as peculiar. I was in the forest at the back of Victoria, Cameroons. I recognised in a piece of forest a peculiar look about a portion of it. The branches were bent, and the tendrils were tied together in a way I had seen elsewhere, but which I had never noticed among Bantu tribes. I was puzzled, and after having passed this place a couple of hundred yards or so I turned back to look at it again, telling the men to go on. I examined the place closely for some minutes, and then rejoined my men, and said nothing.

Presently said one of my Wei Weis, "How you sabe them thing, ma?"

"What thing?" said I, not wishing to give him the lead.

"You look them thing, ma, when you pass him then you go look him again, you sabe Poorah, ma?" in a tone of accusation.

"Well," said I, "what is it doing here?"

"Them Sa lone (Sierra Leone) boys done bring him, ma," was the answer.

Until this I did not know that secret societies were exported from their own districts.

I believe that these secret societies are always distinct from the leopard societies. I have pretty nearly enough evidence to prove that it is so in some districts, but not in all. So far my evidence only goes to prove the distinction of the two among the negroes, not among the Bantu, and in all cases you will find some men belonging to both. Some men, in fact, go in for all the societies in their district, but not all the men ; and in all districts, if you look close, you will find several societies apart from the regular youth-initiating one.

These other societies are practically murder societies, and their practices usually include cannibalism, which is not an essential part of the rites of the great tribal societies, Yasi or Egbo. In the Calabar district I was informed by natives that there was a society of which the last entered member has to provide, for the entertainment of the other members, the body of a relative of his own, and sacrificial cannibalism is always breaking out, or perhaps I should say being discovered, by the white authorities in the Niger Delta. There was the great outburst of it at Brass, early last year, and the one chronicled in the *Liverpool Mercury* for August 13th, 1895, as occurring at Sierra Leone. This account is worth quoting. It describes the hanging by the authorities of three murderers, and states the incidents, which took place in the Imperi country behind Free Town.

One of the chief murderers was a man named Jowe, who had formerly been a Sunday-school teacher in Sierra Leone. He pleaded in extenuation of his offence that he had been compelled to join the society. The others said they committed the murders in order to obtain certain parts of the body for ju-ju purposes, the leg, the hand, the heart, &c. The *Mercury* goes on to give the statement of the Reverend Father Bomy, of the Roman Catholic Mission. " He said he was at Bromtu, where the St. Joseph Mission has a station, when a man was brought down from the Imperi country in a boat. The poor fellow was in a dreadful state, and was brought to the station for medical treatment. He said he was working on his farm, when he was suddenly pounced upon from behind. A number of sharp instruments were driven into the back of his neck. He presented a fearful sight, having wounds all over his body supposed to have been inflicted by the claws of the leopard, but in reality they were stabs from sharp-pointed knives. The native, who was a powerfully-built man, called out, and his cries attracting the attention of his relations, the leopards made off. The poor fellow died at Bromtu from the injuries. It was only his splendid physique that kept him alive until his arrival at the Mission." The *Mercury* goes on to quote from the *Pall Mall*, and I too go on quoting to show that these things are known and acknowledged to have taken place in a colony like Sierra Leone, which has had unequalled opportunities of becoming christianised for more than one hundred years, and now has more than one hundred and thirty places of Christian worship in it. "Some twenty years ago there was a war between this tribe Taima and the Paramas. The Paramas sent some of their war boys to be ambushed in the intervening country, the Imperi, but the Imperi delivered these war boys to the enemy. In revenge, the Paramas sent the Fetish Boofima into the Imperi country. This Fetish had up to that time been kept active and working by the sacrifice of goats, but the medicine men of the Paramas who introduced it into the Imperi country decreed at the same time that human sacrifices would be required to keep it alive, thereby working their vengeance on the Imperi by leading them to exterminate themselves in sacrifice to the Fetish. The country for years has been terrorised by this secret worship of Boofima and at one time the Imperi started the Tonga dances, at which the medicine men pointed out the supposed worshippers of Boofima—the so-called Human Leopards, because when seizing their victims for sacrifice they covered themselves with leopard skins, and imitating the roars of the leopard, they sprang upon their victim, plunging at the same time two three-pronged forks into each side of the throat. The Government some years ago forbade the Tonga dances, and are now striving to suppress the human leopards. There are also human alligators who, disguised as alligators, swim in the creeks upon the canoes and carry off the crew. Some of them have been brought for trial but no complete case has been made out against them!" In comment upon this account, which is evidently written by some one well versed in the affair, I will only remark that sometimes, instead of the three-pronged forks, there are fixed in the paws of the leopard skin sharp-pointed cutting knives, the skin being made into a sort of glove into which the hand of the human leopard fits. In one skin I saw down south this was most ingeniously done. The knives were shaped like the leopard's claws, curved, sharp-pointed, and with cutting edges underneath, and I am told the American Mendi Mission, which works in the Sierra Leone districts, have got a similar skin in their possession. In Calabar and Libreville, these murders used to be very common right in close to the white settlements; but in Calabar white jurisdiction is now too much feared for them to be carried on near it, and in Libreville the making of the "Boulevard" between that town and Glass has cleared the custom out from its great haunt along by the swamp path that was formerly there. But before the existence of the Boulevard, when the narrow track was intercepted by patches of swamp, and ran between dense bush, it was notoriously unsafe even for a white man to go along it after dark. In the districts I know where human leopardism occurs (from Bonny to Congo Belge) the victims are killed to provide human flesh for certain secret societies who eat it as one of their rites. Sometimes it is used by a man playing a lone hand to kill an enemy.

The human alligator mentioned, is our old friend the witch crocodile—the spirit of the man in the crocodile. I never myself came across a case of a man in his corporeal body swimming about in a crocodile skin, and I doubt whether any native would chance himself inside a crocodile skin and swim about in the river among the genuine articles for fear of their penetrating his disguise mentally and physically.

In Calabar witch crocodiles are still flourishing. There is an immense old brute that sporting Vice-Consuls periodically go after, which is known to contain the spirit of a Duke Town chief who shall be nameless, because they are getting on at such a pace just round Duke Town that haply I might be had up for libel. When I was in Calabar once, a peculiarly energetic officer had hit that crocodile and the chief was forthwith laid up by a wound in his leg. He said a dog had bit him. They, the chief and the crocodile, are quite well again now, and I will say this in favour of that chief, that nothing on earth would persuade me to believe that he went fooling about in the Calabar River in his corporeal body, either in his own skin or a crocodile's.

The introduction of the Fetish Boofima into the country of the Imperi is an interesting point as it shows that these different tribes have the same big ju-ju. Similarly, Calabar Egbo can go into Okÿon, and will be respected in some of the New Calabar districts, but not at Brass, where the secret society is a distinct cult. Often a neighbouring district will send into Calabar, or Brass, where the big ju-ju is, and ask to have one sent up into their district to keep order, but Egbo will occasionally be sent into a district without that district in the least wanting it ; but, as in the Imperi case, when it is there it is supreme. But say, for example, you were to send Egbo round from Calabar to Cameroon. Cameroon might be barely civil to it, but would pay it no homage, for Cameroon has got no end of a ju-ju of its own. It can rise up as high as the Peak, 13,760 feet. I never saw the Cameroon ju-ju do this, but I saw it start up from four feet to quite twelve feet in the twinkling of an eye, and I was assured that it was only modest reticence on its part that made it leave the other 13,748 feet out of the performance.

Cameroon also has its murder societies, but I have never been resident sufficiently long in Cameroon River to speak with any authority regarding them, but when I was in there in May, 1895, the natives of Bell Town were in a state of great anxiety about their children. A week before, two little girls and a boy belonging to one family had gone down among a host of other children to the river-beach by Bell Town, to fill the pots and calabashes for the evening. It was broad daylight at the time, and the place they went to is not a lonely place but right on the beach before the town and plenty of people about in all directions. The children filled the pots and then, after playing about as is usual, the little girls went home with their vessels of water, with a nice piece of palm leaf put on the top of the water to prevent it splashing as they went up the hill side of the bluff on which the town stands. " Where is your brother ? " said the mother, and they said they did not know ; they thought he was playing with the other children. As the dusk came down and he did not return, the mother went down to the riverside and found all the other children had gone home. She made inquiries but no one knew of him save that he had been playing on the beach. A thorough search was started, but it was five long days before the boy was found, and then his body, decorated with palm leaves, suddenly appeared lying on the beach. It was slit all over longitudinally with long cuts on the face, head, legs, and arms. The crime could not be traced by means convincing to white man's law, but had the witch doctors had the affair in their hands a near relative of the dead boy would have been killed. Those natives who did not share the opinion of this man's guilt said it was the people in the water who had done the thing. These people in the water are much thought of in Cameroon. " They are just the same as people on land, only they live in water."

Doctor Nassau seems to think that the tribal society of the Corisco regions is identical with the leopard societies. He has had considerable experience of the workings of the Ukuku, particularly when he was pioneering in the Benito regions, when it came very near killing him. I will not quote the grand account he gave me of his adventures with it, because I should wish every one to read for themselves the biography he wrote of his first wife, *Crowned in Palm Land*, for they will find there a series of graphic descriptions of what life really is in the Corisco region, and certainly one of the most powerful and tragic bits of writing in any literature— the description of his wife's death in an open boat out at sea, when he was trying to take her to Gaboon for medical aid.

In reference to Ukuku, he says the name signifies a departed spirit. " It is a secret society into which all the males are initiated at puberty, whose procedure may not be seen by females, nor its laws disobeyed by any one under pain of death, a penalty which is sometimes commuted to a fine, a heavy fine. Its discussions are uttered as an oracle from any secluded spot by some man appointed for the purpose.

"On trivial occasions any initiated man may personate Ukuku or issue commands for the family. On other occasions, as in Shiku, to raise prices, the society lays its commands on foreign traders."

Some cases of Ukuku proceedings against white traders have come under my own observation. A friend of mine, a trader in the Batanga district, in some way incurred the animosity of the society's local branch. He had, as is usual in the South-West Coast trade, several sub-factories in the bush. He found himself under taboo ; no native came in to his yard to buy or sell at the store, not even to sell food. He took no notice and awaited developments. One evening when he was sitting on his verandah, smoking and reading, he thought he heard some one singing softly under the house, this, like most European buildings hereabouts, being elevated just above the earth. He was attracted to the song and listened : it was evidently one of the natives singing, not one of his own Kruboys, and so, knowing the language, and having nothing else particular to do, he attended to the affair.

It was the same thing sung softly over and over again, so softly that he could hardly make out the words. But at last, catching his native name among them, he listened more intently than ever, down at a knot-hole in the wooden floor. The song was—" They are going to attack your factory at . . . to-morrow. They are going to attack your factory at . . . to-morrow," over and over again, until it ceased ; and then he thought he saw something darker than the darkness round it creep across the yard and disappear in the bush. Very early in the morning he, with his Kruboys and some guns, went and established themselves in that threatened factory in force. The Ukuku Society turned up in the evening, and reconnoitred the situation, and finding there was more in it than they had expected, withdrew.

In the course of the next twenty-four hours he succeeded in talking the palaver successfully with them. He never knew who his singing friend was, but suspected it was a man whom he had known to be grateful for some kindness he had done him. Indeed there were, and are, many natives who have cause to be grateful to him, for he is deservedly popular among his local tribes, but the man who sang to him that night deserves much honour, for he did it at a terrific risk.

Sometimes representatives of the Ukuku fraternity from several tribes meet together and discuss intertribal difficulties, thereby avoiding war.

Dr. Nassau distinctly says that the Bantu region leopard society is identical with the Ukuku, and he says that although the eopards are not very numerous here they are very daring, made so by immunity from punishment by man. "The superstition is that on any man who kills a leopard will fall a curse or evil disease, curable only by ruinously expensive process of three weeks' duration under the direction of Ukuku. So the natives allow the greatest depredations and ravages until their sheep, goats, and dogs are swept away, and are roused to self-defence only when a human being becomes the victim of the daring beast. With this superstition is united another similar to the werewolf of Germany, viz., a belief in the power of human metamorphosis into a leopard. A person so metamorphosed is called 'Uvengwa.' At one time in Benito an intense excitement prevailed in the community. Doors and shutters were rattled at the dead of night, marks of leopard claws were scratched on door-posts. Then tracks lay on every path. Women and children in lonely places saw their flitting forms, or in the dusk were knocked down by their spring, or heard their growl in the thickets. It is difficult to decide in many of these reports whether it is a real leopard or only an Uvengwa—to native fears they are practically the same,—we were certain this time the Uvengwa was the thief disguised in leopard's skin, as theft is always heard of about such times."

When I was in Gaboon in September, 1895, there was great Ukuku excitement in a district just across the other side of the estuary, mainly at a village that enjoyed the spacious and resounding name of Rumpochembo, from a celebrated chief, and all these phenomena were rife there. Again, when

I was in a village up the Calabar there were fourteen goats and five slaves killed in eight days by leopards, the genuine things, I am sure, in this case ; but here, as down South, there was a strong objection to proceed against the leopard, and no action was being taken save making the goat-houses stronger. In Okyon, when a leopard is killed, its body is treated with great respect and brought into the killer's village. Messages are then sent to the neighbouring villages, and they send representatives to the village and the gall-bladder is most carefully removed from the leopard and burnt *coram publico*, each person whipping their hands down their arms to disavow any guilt in the affair. This burning of the gall, however, is not ju-ju, it is done merely to destroy it, and to demonstrate to all men that it is destroyed, because it is believed to be a deadly poison, and if any is found in a man's possession the punishment is death, unless he is a great chief—a few of these are allowed to keep leopards' gall in their possession. John Bailey tells me that if a great chief commits a great crime and is adjudged by a conclave of his fellow chiefs to die, it is not considered right he should die in a common way, and he is given leopards' gall. A precisely similar idea regarding the poisonous quality of crocodiles' gall holds good down South.

The ju-ju parts of the leopard are the whiskers. You cannot get a skin from a native with them on, and gay, reckless young hunters wear them stuck in their hair and swagger tremendously while the elders shake their heads and keep a keen eye on their subsequent conduct.

I must say the African leopard is an audacious animal, although it is ungrateful of me to say a word against him, after the way he has let me off personally, and I will speak of his extreme beauty as compensation for my ingratitude. I really think, taken as a whole, he is the most lovely animal I have ever seen ; only seeing him, in the one way you can gain a full idea of his beauty, namely in his native forest, is not an unmixed joy to a person, like myself, of a nervous disposition. I may remark that my nervousness regarding the big game of Africa is of a rather peculiar kind. I can confidently say I am not afraid of any wild animal—until I see it—and then—well I will yield to nobody in terror ; fortunately as I say my terror is a special variety ; fortunately because no one can manage their own terror. You can suppress alarm, excitement, fear, fright, and all those small-fry emotions, but the real terror is as dependent on the inner make of you as the colour of your eyes, or the shape of your nose ; and when terror ascends its throne in my mind I become preternaturally artful, and intelligent to an extent utterly foreign to my true nature, and save, in the case of close quarters with bad big animals, a feeling of rage against some unknown person that such things as leopards, elephants, crocodiles, &c., should be allowed out loose in that disgracefully dangerous way, I do not think much about it at the time. Whenever I have come across an awful animal in the forest and I know it has seen me I take Jerome's advice, and instead of relying on the power of the human eye rely upon that of the human leg, and effect a masterly retreat in the face of the enemy. If I know it has not seen me I sink in my tracks and keep an eye on it, hoping that it will go away soon. Thus I once came upon a leopard. I had got caught in a tornado in a dense forest. The massive, mighty trees were waving like a wheat-field in an autumn gale in England, and I dare say a field mouse in a wheat-field in a gale would have heard much the same uproar. The tornado shrieked like ten thousand vengeful demons. The great trees creaked and groaned and strained against it and their bush-rope cables groaned and smacked like whips, and ever and anon a thundering crash with snaps like pistol shots told that they and their mighty tree had strained and struggled in vain. The fierce rain came in a roar, tearing to shreds the leaves and blossoms and deluging everything. I was making bad weather of it, and climbing up over a lot of rocks out of a gully bottom where I had been half drowned in a stream, and on getting my head to the level of a block of rock I observed right in front of my eyes, broadside on, maybe a yard off, certainly not more, a big leopard. He was crouching on the ground, with his magnificent head thrown back and his eyes shut. His fore-paws were spread out in front of him and he lashed the ground with his tail, and I grieve to say, in face of that awful danger—I don't mean me, but the tornado—that

depraved creature swore, softly, but repeatedly and profoundly.
I did not get all these facts up in one glance, for no sooner did
I see him than I ducked under the rocks, and remembered
thankfully that leopards are said to have no power of smell.
But I heard his observation on the weather, and the flip-flap
of his tail on the ground. Every now and then I cautiously
took a look at him with one eye round a rock-edge, and he
remained in the same position. My feelings tell me he
remained there twelve months, but my calmer judgment puts
the time down at twenty minutes ; and at last, on taking
another cautious peep, I saw he was gone. At the time I
wished I knew exactly where, but I do not care about that
detail now, for I saw no more of him. He had moved off in
one of those weird lulls which you get in a tornado, when for
a few seconds the wild herd of hurrying winds seem to have
lost themselves, and wander round crying and wailing like
lost souls, until their common rage seizes them again and they
rush back to their work of destruction. It was an immense
pleasure to have seen the great creature like that. He was
so evidently enraged and baffled by the uproar and dazzled
by the floods of lightning that swept down into the deepest
recesses of the forest, showing at one second every detail of
twig, leaf, branch, and stone round you, and then leaving you
in a sort of swirling dark until the next flash came ; this,
and the great conglomerate roar of the wind, rain and thunder,
was enough to bewilder any living thing.

I have never hurt a leopard intentionally ; I am habitually
kind to animals, and besides I do not think it is ladylike to
go shooting things with a gun. Twice, however, I have been in
collision with them. On one occasion a big leopard had
attacked a dog, who, with her family, was occupying a broken-
down hut next to mine. The dog was a half-bred boarhound,
and a savage brute on her own account. I, being roused by
the uproar, rushed out into the feeble moonlight, thinking she
was having one of her habitual turns-up with other dogs, and
I saw a whirling mass of animal matter within a yard of me.
I fired two mushroom-shaped native stools in rapid succession into the brown of it, and the meeting broke up into a
leopard and a dog. The leopard crouched, I think to spring

on me. I can see its great, beautiful, lambent eyes still, and I seized an earthen water-cooler and flung it straight at them. It was a noble shot ; it burst on the leopard's head like a shell and the leopard went for bush one time. Twenty minutes after people began to drop in cautiously and inquire if anything was the matter, and I civilly asked them to go and ask the leopard in the bush, but they firmly refused. We found the dog had got her shoulder slit open as if by a blow from a cutlass, and the leopard had evidently seized the dog by the scruff of her neck, but owing to the loose folds of skin no bones were broken and she got round all right after much ointment from me, which she paid me for with several bites. Do not mistake this for a sporting adventure. I no more thought it was a leopard than that it was a lotus when I joined the fight. My other leopard was also after a dog. Leopards always come after dogs, because once upon a time the leopard and the dog were great friends, and the leopard went out one day and left her whelps in charge of the dog, and the dog went out flirting, and a snake came and killed the whelps, so there is ill-feeling to this day between the two. For the benefit of sporting readers whose interest may have been excited by the mention of big game, I may remark that the largest leopard skin I ever measured myself was, tail included, 9 feet 7 inches. It was a dried skin, and every man who saw it said, " It was the largest skin he had ever seen, except one that he had seen somewhere else."

The largest crocodile I ever measured was 22 feet 3 inches, the largest gorilla 5 feet 7 inches. I am assured by the missionaries in Calabar, that there was a python brought into Creek Town in the Rev. Mr. Goldie's time, that extended the whole length of the Creek Town mission-house verandah and to spare. This python must have been over 40 feet. I have not a shadow of doubt it was. Stay-at-home people will always discredit great measurements, but experienced bushmen do not, and after all, if it amuses the stay-at-homes to do so, by all means let them ; they have dull lives of it and it don't hurt you, for you know how exceedingly difficult it is to preserve really big things to bring home, and how, half the time, they fall into the hands of people who would not bother

their heads to preserve them in a rotting climate like West
Africa.

The largest python skin I ever measured was a damaged one,
which was 26 feet.   There is an immense one hung in front
of a house in San Paul de Loanda which you can go and
measure yourself with comparative safety any day, and which is,
I think, over 20 feet.   I never measured this one.   The common run of pythons is 10–15 feet, or rather I should say this is
about the sized one you find with painful frequency in your
chicken-house.

Of the Lubuku secret society I can speak with no personal
knowledge.   I had a great deal of curious information regarding it from a Bakele woman, who had her information second-
hand, but it bears out what Captain Latrobe Bateman says
about it in his most excellent book *The First Ascent of the
Kasai* (George Phillip, 1889), and to his account in Note J
of the Appendix, I beg to refer the ethnologist.   My information also went to show what he calls "a dark inference as to
its true nature," a nature not universally common by any
means to the African tribal secret society.

In addition to the secret society and the leopard society,
there are in the Delta some ju-jus held only by a few great
chiefs.   The one in Bonny has a complete language to itself,
and there is one in Duke Town so powerful that should you
desire the death of any person you have only to go and name
him before it.   "These ju-jus are very swift and sure."   I
would rather drink than fight with any of them—yes, far.

CHAPTER XXIV

ASCENT OF THE GREAT PEAK OF CAMEROONS

Setting forth how the Voyager is minded to ascend the mountain called
Mungo Mah Lobeh, or the Throne of Thunder, and in due course
reaches Buea, situate thereon.

AFTER returning from Corisco I remained a few weeks in
Gaboon, and then regretfully left on the *Niger*. My regrets,
I should say, arose from leaving the charms and interests of
Congo Français, and had nothing whatever to do with taking
passage on one of the most comfortable ships of all those
which call on the Coast.

The *Niger* was homeward-bound when I joined her, and in
due course arrived in Cameroon River, and I was once again
under the dominion of Germany. It would be a very interesting thing to compare the various forms of European government in Africa—English, French, German, Portuguese, and
Spanish ; but to do so with any justice would occupy more
space than I have at my disposal, for the subject is extremely
intricate. Each of these forms of government have their good
points and their bad. Each of them are dealing with bits
of Africa differing from each other—in the nature of their
inhabitants and their formation, and so on—so I will not enter
into any comparison of them here, but merely remark that, on
the whole, German colonial methods in Africa are more akin
to English than to French, and that Germany has one of
the main English faults in an emphasised state—namely, a
want of due appreciation of the work of the men who serve
her in Africa. Time after time I have come across cases of
German officers in Cameroon who have done their country

good and noble service, and who yet, on their return to the Fatherland they have loved so well, have found, not only a want of due reward, but worse. When the flush of enthusiasm for colonial enterprise dies out in Germany—as it may die out in the face of the want of profit from her colonies, arising from a too heavy expenditure of money on them —the sin of her ingratitude to those men who have served her in Cameroon will find her out, and no longer will her best and bravest sons risk their honour in her service. The worst case of German ingratitude to Germans is the last, that of the late Vice-Governor of Cameroon, Herr von Lucke, of whom I shall later have occasion to speak. This fine young officer, full of enthusiasm for his country and devoted to his Emperor, was driven to suicide from a vile lie to the effect that he had spoken disrespectfully of his Emperor—a lie told by I know not whom, but I presume by some of those in Germany who seem to make it their special mission in life to run down her greatest colony, Cameroon. A more devoted subject, or a truer gentleman and soldier than Herr von Lucke, no country and no ruler ever possessed. I also see in German newspapers that Governor von Puttkamer has been accused of severity to natives in Cameroon, and I and those Englishmen who know him have no hesitation in saying this accusation is also ill-founded ; but I hope Germany in carpet slippers and in barracks has by this time realised that it is not fitted to judge Germany in Africa. I will say no more, however, on this subject (for I am devoted through good and ill report to my first-cousins, the German and the Dane), but will return to my own trivial experiences.

From the deck of the *Niger* I found myself again confronted with my great temptation—the magnificent Mungo Mah Lobeh—the Throne of Thunder. Now it is none of my business to go up mountains. There's next to no fish on them in West Africa, and precious little good rank fetish, as the population on them is sparse—the African, like myself, abhorring cool air. Nevertheless, I feel quite sure that no white man has ever looked on the great Peak of Cameroon without a desire arising in his mind to ascend it and know in detail the highest point on the western side of the

continent, and indeed one of the highest points in all
Africa. Do not, however, imagine that the ascent is a
common incident in a coaster's life; far from it. The
coaster as a rule resists the temptation of Mungo firmly,
being stronger minded than I am; moreover, he is busy and
only too often fever-stricken in the bargain. But I am the
exception, I own, and I have given in to the temptation and am
the third Englishman to ascend the Peak and the first to
have ascended it from the south-east face. The first man to
reach the summit was Sir Richard Burton, accompanied by
the great botanist, Gustav Mann. He went up, as did the
succeeding twenty-five (mostly Germans) from Babundi; a
place on the seashore to the west. The first expedition to
reach the summit from the side I tackled it was composed
of the first lieutenant and doctor of the German man-of-war
Hyæna. These gentlemen had accomplished this feat a few
weeks before I landed at Victoria to make my attempt. I go
into these details so as to excuse myself for subsequently
giving you a detailed account of the south-east face of Mungo
mah Lobeh.

So great is the majesty and charm of this mountain that
the temptation of it is as great to me to-day as it was on
the first day I saw it, when I was feeling my way down the
West Coast of Africa on the s.s. *Lagos* in 1893, and it revealed
itself by good chance from its surf-washed plinth to its sky-
scraping summit. Certainly it is most striking when you see
it first, as I first saw it, after coasting for weeks along the low
shores and mangrove-fringed rivers of the Niger Delta. Suddenly, right up out of the sea, rises the great mountain to
its 13,760 feet, while close at hand, to westward, towers the
lovely island mass of Fernando Po to 10,190 feet. But every
time you pass it by its beauty grows on you with greater and
greater force, though it is never twice the same. Sometimes
it is wreathed with indigo-black tornado clouds, sometimes
crested with snow, sometimes softly gorgeous with gold,
green, and rose-coloured vapours tinted by the setting sun,
sometimes completely swathed in dense cloud so that you
cannot see it at all; but when you once know it is there it
is all the same, and you bow down and worship.

There are only two distinct peaks to this glorious thing that geologists brutally call the volcanic intrusive mass of the Cameroon Mountains, viz., Big Cameroon and Little Cameroon. The latter, Mungo Mah Etindeh, has not yet been scaled, although it is only 5,820 feet. One reason for this is doubtless that the few people in fever-stricken, over-worked West Africa who are able to go up mountains, naturally try for the adjacent

PEAK OF CAMEROONS FROM THE NORTH-WEST.

Big Cameroon; the other reason is that Mungo Mah Etindeh, to which Burton refers as "the awful form of Little Cameroon," is mostly sheer cliff, and is from foot to summit clothed in an almost impenetrable forest. Behind these two mountains of volcanic origin, which cover an area on an isolated base of between 700 and 800 square miles in extent, there are distinctly visible from the coast two chains of mountains, or I should think one chain deflected, the so-called Rumby and Omon ranges. These are no relations of Mungo, being of very different structure and conformation ; the geological specimens I have brought from them and from the Cameroons being identified by geologists as respectively schistose grit and vesicular lava.

After spending a few pleasant days in Cameroon River in the society of Frau Plehn, my poor friend Mrs. Duggan having, I ought to say, departed for England on the death of her husband, I went round to Victoria, Ambas Bay, on the *Niger*, and in spite of being advised solemnly by Captain Davies to " chuck it as it was not a picnic," I started to attempt the Peak of Cameroons as follows.

September 20th, 1895.—Left Victoria at 7.30, weather fine. Herr von Lucke, though sadly convinced, by a series of experiments he has been carrying on ever since I landed, and I expect before, that you cannot be in three places at one time, is still trying to do so ; or more properly speaking he starts an experiment series for four places, man-like, instead of getting ill as I should under the circumstances, and he kindly comes with me as far as the bridge across the lovely cascading Lukole River, and then goes back at about seven miles an hour to look after Victoria and his sick subordinates in detail.

I, with my crew, keep on up the grand new road the Government is making, which when finished is to go from Ambas Bay to Buea, 3,000 feet up on the mountain's side. This road is quite the most magnificent of roads, as regards breadth and general intention, that I have seen anywhere in West Africa, and it runs through a superbly beautiful country, It is, I should say, as broad as Oxford Street ; on either side of it are deep drains to carry off the surface waters, with banks of varied beautiful tropical shrubs and ferns, behind which rise, 100 to 200 feet high, walls of grand forest, the column-like tree-stems either hung with flowering, climbing plants and ferns, or showing soft red and soft grey shafts sixty to seventy feet high without an interrupting branch. Behind this again rise the lovely foot hills of Mungo, high up against the sky, coloured the most perfect soft dark blue.

The whole scheme of colour is indescribably rich and full in

tone. The very earth is a velvety red brown, and the butterflies—which abound—show themselves off in the sunlight, in
their canary-coloured, crimson, and peacock-blue liveries, to
perfection. After five minutes' experience of the road I envy
those butterflies. I do not believe there is a more lovely
road in this world, and besides, it's a noble and enterprising thing of a Government to go and make it, considering
the climate and the country ; but to get any genuine pleasure
out of it, it is requisite to hover in a bird- or butterfly-like
way, for of all the truly awful things to walk on, that road,
when I was on it, was the worst.

Of course this arose from its not being finished, not having
its top on in fact : the bit that was finished, and had got its
top on, for half a mile beyond the bridge, you could go over
in a Bath chair. The rest of it made you fit for one for the
rest of your natural life, for it was one mass of broken lava
rock, and here and there leviathan tree-stumps that had been
partially blown up with gunpowder.

When we near the forest end of the road, it comes on to
rain heavily, and I see a little house on the left-hand side,
and a European engineer superintending a group of very
cheerful natives felling timber. He most kindly invites me
to take shelter, saying it cannot rain as heavily as this for
long. My men also announce a desire for water, and so I sit
down and chat with the engineer under the shelter of his
verandah, while the men go to the water-hole, some twenty
minutes off.

The engineer is an Alsatian, and has been engaged on the
Congo Free State Railway, which he abandoned because they
put him up at the end station, on those awful Palaballa
mountains. Four men who were at the station died of fever
and he got it himself, and applied for leave to go down to
Matadi to see a doctor. His request was peremptorily
refused, and he was told he must remain at his post until
another engineer came up to take over charge. He stayed
for some days waiting, but no one came or gave signs of
coming, and he found the company had given all their employés orders that he was not to be allowed on a train, so he
walked down to Matadi. How he did it, knowing that

country, I cannot think, but he was exceedingly ill when he got there, as may easily be imagined, and as soon as he had sufficiently recovered, he came up to Cameroons, and obtained his present appointment, after having been kept and nursed up in the hospital there, to his considerable surprise after his Congo experiences. He was not hopeful about the future of that Congo railroad, or of that of its directors. He quoted as one of the reasons for his leaving it the doubt that it would ever be finished. Inexplicable is man! Why he should have cared whether it was finished or not as long as it kept on paying him £1 a day, I do not know. He had kept a diary of the accidents, which averaged two a day, and usually took the form of something going off the line, because the railway engines used were so light as to be flighty, and not really powerful enough to take up more than two trucks at a time, though always expected to do so. The wages of the natives employed were from 1s. to 1s. 6d. a day; very high pay. The Chinamen imported as navvies were an awful nuisance, always making palaver. The Senegal men are dangerous, because the French officials on the line always support them against other white men, Senegalese being Frenchmen, just as Kruboys are Englishmen.

While I am getting this last news from Congo, the rain keeps on pouring down. I presently see one of my men sitting right in the middle of the road on a rock, totally unsheltered, and a feeling of shame comes over me in the face of this black man's aquatic courage. Besides, Herr von Lucke had said I was sure to get half-drowned and catch an awful cold, so there is no use delaying. Into the rain I go, and off we start. I may remark I subsequently found that my aquatic underling was drunk. I conscientiously attempt to keep dry, by holding up an umbrella, knowing that though hopeless it is the proper thing to do.

We leave the road about fifty yards above the hut, turning into the unbroken forest on the right-hand side, and following a narrow, slippery, muddy, root-beset bush-path that was a comfort after the road. Presently we come to a lovely mountain torrent flying down over red-brown rocks in white foam;

exquisitely lovely, and only a shade damper than the rest of things. Seeing this I solemnly fold up my umbrella and give it to Kefalla. My relations, nay, even Mrs. Roy, who is blind to a large percentage of my imperfections, say the most scathing things about my behaviour with regard to water. But really my conduct is founded on sound principles. I know from a series of carefully conducted experiments, carried out on the Devonshire Lynn, that I cannot go across a river on slippery stepping-stones ; therefore, knowing that attempts to keep my feet out of water only end in my placing the rest of my anatomy violently in, I take charge of Fate and wade.

This particular stream, too, requires careful wading, the rocks over which it flows being arranged in picturesque, but perilous confusion ; however all goes well, and getting to the other side I decide to " chuck it," as Captain Davis would say, as to keeping dry, for the rain comes down heavier than ever.

Now we are evidently dealing with a foot-hillside, but the rain is too thick for one to see two yards in any direction, and we seem to be in a ghost-land forest, for the great palms and red-woods rise up in the mist before us, and fade out in the mist behind, as we pass on. The rocks which edge and strew the path at our feet are covered with exquisite ferns and mosses—all the most delicate shades of green imaginable, and here and there of absolute gold colour, looking as if some ray of sunshine had lingered too long playing on the earth, and had got shut off from heaven by the mist, and so lay nestling among the rocks until it might rejoin the sun.

The path now becomes an absolute torrent, with mud-thickened water, which cascades round one's ankles in a sportive way, and round one's knees in the hollows in the path. Five seconds after abandoning the umbrella I am wet through, but it is not uncomfortable at this temperature, something like that of a cucumber frame with the lights on, if you can clear your mind of all prejudice, as Dr. Johnson says, and forget the risk of fever which saturation entails.

On we go, the path underneath the water seems a pretty

equal mixture of rock and mud, but they are not evenly distributed. Plantations full of weeds show up on either side of us, and we are evidently now on the top of a foot-hill. I suspect a fine view of the sea could be obtained from here, if you have an atmosphere that is less than 99¾ per cent. of water. As it is, a white sheet—or more properly speaking, considering its soft, stuffy woolliness, a white blanket—is stretched across the landscape to the south-west, where the sea would show.

We go down-hill now, the water rushing into the back of my shoes for a change. The path is fringed by high, sugar-cane-like grass which hangs across it in a lackadaisical way, swishing you in the face and cutting like a knife whenever you catch its edge, and pouring continually insidious rills of water down one's neck. It does not matter. The whole Atlantic could not get more water on to me than I have already got. Ever and again I stop and wring out some of it from my skirts, for it is weighty. One would not imagine that anything could come down in the way of water thicker than the rain, but it can. When one is on the top of the hills, a cold breeze comes through the mist chilling one to the bone, and bending the heads of the palm trees, sends down from them water by the bucketful with a slap; hitting or missing you as the case may be.

Both myself and my men are by now getting anxious for our " chop," and they tell me, " We look them big hut soon." Soon we do look them big hut, but with faces of undisguised horror, for the big hut consists of a few charred roof-mats, &c., lying on the ground. There has been a fire in that simple savage home.. Our path here is cut by one that goes east and west, and after a consultation between my men and the Bakwiri, we take the path going east, down a steep slope between weedy plantations, and shortly on the left shows a steep little hill-side with a long low hut on the top. We go up to it and I find it is the habitation of a Basel Mission black Bible-reader. He comes out and speaks English well, and I tell him I want a house for myself and my men, and he says we had better come and stay in this one. It is divided into two chambers, one in which the children who attend the mission-school stay, and wherein there is a fire, and one evidently the abode of the teacher. I thank the Bible-reader and say that I will pay him for the house, and I and the men go in streaming, and my teeth chatter with cold as the breeze chills my saturated garment while I give out the rations of beef, rum, blankets, and tobacco to the men. Then I clear my apartment out and attempt to get dry, operations which are interrupted by Kefalla coming for tobacco to buy firewood off the mission teacher to cook our food by.

Presently my excellent little cook brings in my food, and in with it come two mission teachers—our first acquaintance, the one with a white jacket, and another with a blue. They lounge about and spit in all directions, and then chiefs commence to arrive with their families complete, and they sidle into the apartment and ostentatiously ogle the demijohn of rum.

They are, as usual, a nuisance, sitting about on everything. No sooner have I taken an unclean-looking chief off the wood sofa, than I observe another one has silently seated himself in the middle of my open portmanteau. Removing him and shutting it up, I see another one has settled on the men's beef and rice sack.

It is now about three o'clock and I am still chilled to the bone in spite of tea. The weather is as bad as ever. The men say that the rest of the road to Buea is far worse than that which we have so far come along, and that we should never get there before dark, and " for sure " should not get there afterwards, because by the time the dark came down we should be in " bad place too much." Therefore, to their great relief, I say I will stay at this place—Buana—for the night, and go on in the morning time up to Buea ; and just for the present I think I will wrap myself up in a blanket and try and get the chill out of me, so I give the chiefs a glass of rum each, plenty of head tobacco, and my best thanks for their kind call, and then turn them and the expectorating mission teachers out. I have not been lying down five minutes on the plank that serves for a sofa by day and a bed by night, when Charles comes knocking at the door. He wants tobacco. " Missionary man no fit to let we have firewood unless we buy em." Give Charles a head and shut him out again, and drop off to sleep again for a quarter of an hour, then am aroused by some enterprising sightseers pushing open the window-shutters ; when I look round there are a mass of black heads sticking through the window-hole.   I tell them respectfully that the circus is closed for repairs, and fasten up the shutters, but sleep is impossible, so I turn out and go and see what those men of mine are after.   They are comfortable enough round their fire, with their clothes suspended on strings in the smoke above them, and I envy them that fire.   I then stroll round to see if there is anything to be seen, but the scenery is much like that you would enjoy if you were inside a blancmange.   So as it is now growing dark I return to my room and light candles, and read Dr. Günther on Fishes.   If this sort of weather goes on I expect I shall specialise fins and gills myself.   Room becomes full of blacks.   Unless you watch the door, you do not see how it is done.   You look at a corner one minute and it is empty, and the next time you look that way it is full of rows of white teeth and watching eyes.   The two mission teachers come in and make a show of teaching a child to read the Bible.   I, having decided that it does not matter much what kind of fins you wear as they all work well, write up my log.   About seven I get cook to make me some more tea, and shortly after find myself confronted with difficulties as to the disposal of the two mission teachers for the night.   This class of man has no resource in him, and I think worse of the effects of mission-teaching than usual as I prepare to try and get a sleep ; not an elaborate affair, I assure you, for I only want to wrap myself round in a blanket and lie on that plank, but the rain has got into the blankets and horror ! there is no pillow.   The mission men have cleared their bed paraphernalia right out.   Now you can do without a good many things, but not without a pillow, so hunt round to find something to make one with ;   find the Bible in English, the Bible in German, and two hymn-books, and a candle-stick. These seem all the small articles in the room—no, there is a parcel behind the books—mission teachers' Sunday trousers— make delightful arrangement of books bound round with trousers and the whole affair wrapped in one of my towels. Never saw till now advantage of Africans having trousers.

Civilisation has its points after all. But it is no use
trying to get any sleep until those men are quieter. The
partition which separates my apartment from theirs is a bamboo and mat affair, straight at the top so leaving under the
roof a triangular space above common to both rooms. Also
common to both rooms are the smoke of the fire and the conversation. Kefalla is holding forth in a dogmatic way, and
some of the others are snoring. There is a new idea in decoration along the separating wall. Mr. Morris might have made
something out of it for a dado. It is composed of an arrangement in line of stretched out singlets. Vaseline the revolver.
Wish those men would leave off chattering. Kefalla seems
to know the worst about most of the people, black and
white, down in Ambas Bay, but I do not believe those last
two stories. Evidently great jokes in next room now ; Kefalla
has thrown himself, still talking, in the dark, on to the top of
one of the mission teachers. The women of the village outside have been keeping up, this hour and more, a most
melancholy coo-ōoing. Those foolish creatures are evidently
worrying about their husbands who have gone down to market
in Ambas Bay, and who, they think, are lost in the bush. I have
not a shadow of a doubt that those husbands who are not home
by now are safely drunk in town, or reposing on the grand new
road the kindly Government have provided for them, either in
one of the side drains, or tucked in among the lava rock.

September 21st.—Coo-ōoing went on all-night. I was aroused
about 9.30 P.M., by uproar in adjacent hut : one husband had
returned in a bellicose condition and whacked his wives, and
their squarks and squalls, instead of acting as a warning to
the other ladies, stimulate the silly things to go on coo-ōoing
louder and more entreatingly than ever, so that their husbands
might come home and whack them too, I suppose, and whenever
the unmitigated hardness of my plank rouses me I hear them
still coo-ōoing.

No watchman is required to wake you in the morning
on the top of a Cameroon foot-hill by 5.30, because about
4 A.M. the dank chill that comes before the dawn does so most
effectively. One old chief turned up early out of the mist
and dashed me a bottle of palm wine ; he says he wants to

dash me a fowl, but I decline, and accept two eggs, and give him four heads of tobacco.

The whole place is swathed in thick white mist through which my audience arrive. But I am firm with them, and shut up the doors and windows and disregard their bangings on them while I am dressing, or rather redressing. The mission teachers get in with my tea, and sit and smoke and spit while I have my breakfast. Give me cannibal Fans! I do not believe Blue Jacket is a teacher at all, but a horrible Frankenstein parasite thing on White Jacket. He takes everything away from White Jacket as soon as I give it him : White Jacket feebly remonstrating. I see as we leave that he is taking the money I gave the latter *vi et armis* out of his pocket.

It is pouring with rain again now, and we go down the steep hillock to the path we came along yesterday, keep it until we come to where the old path cuts it, and then turn up to the right following the old path's course and leave Buana without a pang of regret. Our road goes N.E. Oh, the mud of it! Not the clearish cascades of yesterday but sticky, slippery mud, intensely sticky, and intensely slippery. The narrow path which is filled by this, is V-shaped underneath from wear, and I soon find the safest way is right through the deepest mud in the middle.

The white mist shuts off all details beyond ten yards in any direction. All we can see, as we first turn up the path, is a patch of kokos of tremendous size on our right. After this comes weedy plantation, and stretches of sword grass hanging across the road. The country is not so level as—or rather, I should say, more acutely unlevel than—-that we came over yesterday. On we go, patiently doing our mud pulling through the valleys ; toiling up a hillside among lumps of rock and stretches of forest, for we are now beyond Buana's plantations; and skirting the summit of the hill only to descend into another valley. Evidently this is a succession of foot-hills of the great mountain and we are not on its true face yet. As we go on they become more and more abrupt in form, the valleys mere narrow ravines. Evidently in the wet season (this is only the tornado season) each of these valleys is occupied by a raging torrent from the look of the confused water-worn boulders. Now among the rocks there are only isolated pools, for the weather for a fortnight before I left Victoria had been fairly dry, and this rich porous soil soaks up an immense amount of water. It strikes me as strange that when we are either going up or down the hills, the ground is less muddy than when we are skirting their summits, but as my brother would say, " it is perfectly simple, if you think about it," because on the inclines the rush of water clears the soil away down to the bed rock. There is an outcrop of clay down by Buana, but though that was slippery, it is nothing to the slipperiness of this fine, soft, red-brown earth that is the soil higher up, and also round Ambas Bay. This gets churned up into a sort of batter where there is enough water lying on it, and, when there is not, an ice slide is an infant to it.

My men and I flounder about ; thrice one of them, load and all, goes down with a squidge and a crash into the side grass, and says "damn !" with quite the European accent ; as a rule, however, we go on in single file, my shoes giving out a mellifluous squidge, and their naked feet a squish, squash. The men take it very good temperedly, and sing in between accidents ; I do not feel much like singing myself, particularly at one awful spot, which was the exception to the rule that ground at acute angles forms the best going. This exception was a long slippery slide down into a ravine with a long, perfectly glassy slope up out of it. I remember one of my tutors saying, " Always when on a long march assume the attitude you feel most inclined to, as it is less tiring." There could not be the least shadow of a doubt about your inclinations as to attitude here, nor to giving way to them, so we arrive at the bottom of that ravine in a fine confused heap. As for going up out of it, it was not mere inclination—it was passion that possessed you. What you wanted to do was to plant your nose against the hill-side and wave your normally earthward extremities in the air, particularly when you were near the middle of the slope, or close to the top. Two of the boys gave way to this impulse ; I, of course, did not, but when I felt it coming on like a sort of fit, flung myself sideways into the dense bush that edges the path, and when it had passed off, scrambled out and had another try at the slide.

After this we have a stretch of rocky forest, and pass by a widening in the path which I am told is a place where men blow, *i.e.*, rest, and then pass through another a little further on, which is Buea's bush market. Then through an opening in the great war-hedge of Buea, a growing stockade some fifteen feet high, the lower part of it wattled. Close by is a cross put up to mark the spot where that gallant young German officer fell last January twelvemonth, when on the first expedition to open up this side of the mountain.

At the sides of the path here grow banks of bergamot and balsam, returning good for evil and smiling sweetly as we crush them. Thank goodness we are in forest now, and we seem to have done with the sword-grass. The rocks are covered with moss and ferns, and the mist curling and wandering about among the stems is very lovely. I have to pause in life's pleasures because I want to measure one of the large earthworms, which, with smaller sealing-wax-red worms, are crawling about the path. He was eleven inches and three-quarters. He detained me some time getting this information, because he was so nervous during the operation.

In our next ravine there is a succession of pools, part of a mountain torrent of greater magnitude evidently than those we have passed, and in these pools there are things swimming. Spend more time catching them, with the assistance of Bum. I do not value Kefalla's advice, ample though it is, as being of any real value in the affair. Bag some water-spiders and two small fish. The heat is less oppressive than yesterday. All yesterday one was being alternately smothered in the valley and chilled on the hill-tops. To-day it is a more level temperature, about 70°, I fancy.

The soil up here, about 2,500 feet above sea-level, though rock-laden is exceedingly rich, and the higher we go there is more bergamot, native indigo, with its under-leaf dark blue, and lovely coleuses with red markings on their upper leaves, and crimson linings. I, as an ichthyologist, am in the wrong paradise. What a region this would be for a botanist! The country is gloriously lovely if one could only see it for

the rain and mist ; but one only gets dim hints of its beauty
when some cold draughts of wind come down from the great
mountains and seem to push open the mist-veil as with spirit
hands, and then in a minute let it fall together again.   I do
not expect to reach Buea within regulation time, but at 11.30
my men say " we close in," and then, coming along a forested
hill and down a ravine, we find ourselves facing a rushing
river, wherein a squad of black soldiers are washing clothes,
with the assistance of a squad of black ladies, with much uproar and sky-larking.   I hesitate on the bank.   I am in an
awful mess—mud-caked skirts, and blood-stained hands and
face.   Shall I make an exhibition of myself and wash here, or
make an exhibition of myself by going unwashed to that unknown German officer who is in charge of the station ?
Naturally I wash here, standing in the river and swishing the
mud out of my skirts ; and then wading across to the other
bank, I wring out my skirts, but what is life without a towel ?
The ground on the further side of the river is cleared of bush,
and only bears a heavy crop of balsam ; a few steps onwards
bring me in view of a corrugated iron-roofed, plank-sided
house, in front of which, towards the great mountain which
now towers up into the mist, is a low clearing with a quadrangle of native huts—the barracks.

I receive a most kindly welcome from a fair, grey-eyed
German gentleman, only unfortunately I see my efforts to
appear before him clean and tidy have been quite unavailing,
for he views my appearance with unmixed horror, and suggests
an instant hot bath.   I decline.   Men can be trying !   How in
the world is any one going to take a bath in a house with no
doors, and only very sketchy wooden window-shutters ?

The German officer is building the house quickly, as Ollen-
dorff would say, but he has not yet got to such luxuries
as doors, and so uses army blankets strung across the doorway ; and he has got up temporary wooden shutters to keep the
worst of the rain out, and across his own room's window he
has a frame covered with greased paper.   Thank goodness he
has made a table, and a bench, and a washhand-stand out of
planks for his spare room, which he kindly places at my
disposal ; and the Fatherland has evidently stood him an iron

bedstead and a mattress for it. But the Fatherland is not spoiling or cosseting this man to an extent that will enervate him in the least.

I get the loads brought into my room, where they steam and distil rills of water on to the bare floor, and then, barricading the door-blankets and the window-shutters, I dispossess myself of the German territory I have acquired during the last twenty-four hours, and my portmanteau having kept fairly watertight, I appear as a reasonable being before society—*i.e.*, Herr Liebert, the German officer—and hunt up my boys to get me tea. This being done, I go out on the verandah and discourse.

Society has got a dreadfully bad foot ; weeks ago he injured it on the road, and then in cleaning out a bad sore on one of the men some of the purulent matter got into the wound, and consequently he has nearly lost his leg, or more properly speaking his life, for he lay thirteen days in bed, and there was no doctor even down in Victoria to take the leg off, if it had turned to gangrene, as it seemed likely to do. He makes nothing of it, and hops about in a most energetic way, looking after seventy black soldiers and their wives and children, giving them out their rations, drilling them, doctoring them, and everything else, and hankering to do more. Many of the soldiers are down with bad feet, in consequence of the badness of the roads hereabouts. These soldiers are an assortment of Wei-Weis and Su-Su from Sierra Leone, and some Yorubas. They are smart men and well cared for, and their uniforms far more reasonable and military than the absurd uniforms we put our Haussas into in Calabar, only the Fatherland ordains that they shall wear braces, and these unnecessary articles for an African are worn flowing free, except by those men actually on duty.

The mist clears off in the evening about five, and the surrounding scenery is at last visible. Fronting the house there is the cleared quadrangle, facing which on the other three sides are the lines of very dilapidated huts, and behind these the ground rises steeply, the great S.E. face of Mungo Mah Lobeh. It looks awfully steep when you know you have got to go up it. This station at Buea is 3,000 feet above sea-level, which explains the hills we have had to come up. The moun-

tain wall when viewed from Buea is very grand, although it
lacks snow-cap or glacier, and the highest summits of Mungo
are not visible because we are too close under them, but its enormous bulk and its isolation make it highly impressive. The
forest runs up it in a great band above Buea, then sends up
great tongues into the grass belt above. But what may be
above this grass belt I know not yet, for our view ends at the
top of the wall of the great S.E. crater. My men say there are
devils and gold up beyond, but the German authorities do not
support this view. Those Germans are so sceptical. This
station is evidently on a ledge, for behind it the ground falls
steeply, and you get an uninterrupted panoramic view of the
Cameroon estuary and the great stretches of low swamp lands
with the Mungo and the Bimbia rivers, and their many creeks
and channels, and far away east the strange abrupt forms
of the Rumby Mountains. Herr Liebert says you can see
Cameroon Government buildings from here, if only the day
is clear, though they are some forty miles away. This
view of them is, save a missionary of the Basel mission, the
only white society available at Buea. Society here says the
intercourse, though better than none, is slow. I suggest he
should pay calls and indulge in conversation by means of a
code of fireworks. " Ha ! " says he, " you're like the Calabar
major." " Which one ? " say I, for there are majors and majors.
" The one who came here last dry season," he said, " and who
went up on to the wall and set the grass on fire to show how he
was going on, and had to run down for his life." I know that
man, and a very excellent man he is, but he is not in Calabar,
nor is he a major ; but society everywhere makes mistakes in
technical things.

I hear more details about the death of poor Freiherr von
Gravenreuth, whose fine monument of a seated lion I saw in
the Government House grounds in Cameroons the other day.
Bush fighting in these West African forests is dreadfully
dangerous work. Hemmed in by bush, in a narrow path
along which you must pass slowly in single file, you are a
target for all and any natives invisibly hidden in the undergrowth ; and the war-hedge of Buea must have made an
additional danger and difficulty here for the attacking party.

The lieutenant and his small band of black soldiers had, after a stiff fight, succeeded in forcing the entrance to this, when their ammunition gave out, and they had to fall back. The Bueans, regarding this as their victory, rallied, and a chance shot killed the lieutenant instantly. A further expedition was promptly sent up from Victoria and it wiped the error out of the Buean mind and several Bueans with it. But it was a very necessary expedition. These natives were a constant source of danger to the more peaceful trading tribes, whom they would not permit to traverse their territory. The Bueans have been dealt with mercifully by the Germans, for their big villages, like Sapa, are still standing, and a continual stream of natives come into the barrack-yard, selling produce, or carrying it on down to Victoria markets, in a perfectly content and cheerful way. I met this morning a big burly chief with his insignia of office—a great stick. He, I am told, is the chief or Sapa whom Herr von Lucke has called to talk some palaver with down in Victoria.

At last I leave Herr Liebert, because everything I say to him causes him to hop, flying somewhere to show me something, and I am sure it is bad for his foot. I go and see that my men are safely quartered. Kefalla is laying down the law in a most didactic way to the soldiers. Herr Liebert has christened him " the Professor," and I adopt the name for him, but I fear " Windbag " would fit him better.

At 7.30 a heavy tornado comes rolling down upon us. Masses of indigo cloud with livid lightning flashing in the van, roll out from over the wall of the great crater above ; then with that malevolence peculiar to the tornado it sees all the soldiers and their wives and children sitting happily in the barrack yard, howling in a minor key and beating their beloved tom-toms, so it comes and sits flump down on them with deluges of water, and sends its lightning running over the ground in livid streams of living death. Oh they are nice things are tornadoes ! I wonder what they will be like when we are up in their home ; up atop of that precious wall ? I had no idea Mungo was so steep. If I had —well, I am in for it now !

CHAPTER XXV

ASCENT OF THE GREAT PEAK OF CAMEROONS—(*Continued*)

Wherein is recounted how the Voyager sets out from Buea, and goes up through the forest belt to the top of the S.E. crater of Mungo Mah Lobeh, with many dilemmas and disasters that befell on the way.

September 22nd.—Wake at 5. Fine morning. Fine view towards Cameroon River. The broad stretch of forest below, and the water-eaten mangrove swamps below that, are all a glorious indigo flushed with rose colour from "the death of the night," as Kiva used to call the dawn. No one stirring till six, when people come out of the huts, and stretch themselves and proceed to begin the day, in the African's usual perfunctory, listless way. I am not stating this as a peculiar trait arising from his cerebral development; it is merely the natural sequence of the nights he goes in for so cheerily : *Katzenjammer*, is, I believe, the technical term.

My crew are worse than the rest. I go and hunt cook out. He props open one eye, with difficulty, and yawns a yawn that nearly cuts his head in two. I wake him up with a shock, by saying I mean to go on up to-day, and want my chop, and to start one time. He goes off and announces my horrible intention to the others. Kefalla soon arrives upon the scene full of argument, "You no sabe this be Sunday, Ma?" says he in a tone that tells he considers this settles the matter. I "sabe" unconcernedly ; Kefalla scratches his head for other argument, but he has opened with his heavy artillery ; which being repulsed throws his rear lines into confusion. Bum, the head man, then turns up, sound asleep inside, but quite ready to come. Bum, I find, is always ready to do what he is told, but has no more original ideas in his head than there are in a chair leg. Kefalla, however, by scratching other parts of his anatomy diligently, has now another argument ready, the two Bakwiris are sick with abdominal trouble, that requires rum and rest, and one of the other boys has hot foot.

Herr Liebert now appears upon the scene, and says I can have some of his labourers, who are now more or less idle, because he cannot get about much with his bad foot to direct them, so I give the Bakwiris and the two hot foot cases " books " to take down to Herr von Lucke who will pay them off for me, and seeing that they have each a good day's rations of rice, beef, &c., eliminate them from the party.

In addition to the labourers, I am to have as a guide Sasu, a black sergeant, who went up the Peak with the officers of the *Hyæna*, and I get my breakfast, and then hang about watching my men getting ready very slowly to start. They spin some plausible yarns about getting food cooked, in case they cannot get a fire when we reach the top of the forest belt, where we are to camp. I never saw a forest yet in Africa where you could not get a fire, but knowing that my previous experiences have never been beyond 5,000 feet in elevation, I let them have their way. Off we get about 8, and start with all good wishes, and grim prophecies, from Herr Liebert.

Led by Sasu, and accompanied by " To-morrow," a man who has come to Buea from some interior unknown district, and who speaks no known language, and whose business it is to help to cut a way through the bush, we go down the path we came and cross the river again. This river seems to separate the final mass of the mountain from the foot-hills on this side. Immediately after crossing it we turn up into the forest on the right hand side, and " To-morrow " cuts through an overgrown track for about half-an-hour, and then leaves us.

Everything is reeking wet, and we swish through thick undergrowth and then enter a darker forest where the earth is rocky and richly decorated with ferns and moss. For the first time in my life I see tree-ferns growing wild in luxuriant profusion. What glorious creations they are! Then we get out into the middle of a koko plantation. Next to sweet-

potatoes, the premier abomination to walk through, give me
kokos for good· all-round tryingness, particularly when they
are wet, as, is very much the case now.   These gigantic arums
poise in their broad leaves little reservoirs of water, which you
upset over yourself as you pass through.   The big round
roots are excellent things to fall over.   They project above
the earth, and you can jam your foot against them and pitch
forward, or you can step on one of them and fall backwards
or sideways.   The entertainment they afford the wayfarer is
not monotonous, but it is exasperating.   Getting through
these we meet the war hedge again, and after a conscientious
struggle with various forms of vegetation in a muddled, tangled
state, Sasu says, "No good, path done got stopped up," so we
turn and retrace our steps all the way, cross the river,
and horrify Herr Liebert by invading his house again.   We
explain the situation.   Grave headshaking between him and
Sasu about the practicability of any other route, because there
is no other path.   I do not like to say "so much the better,"
because it would have sounded ungrateful, but I knew from
my Ogowé experiences that a forest that looks from afar a
dense black mat is all right underneath, and there is a short
path recently cut by Herr Liebert that goes straight up
towards the forest above us.   It had been made to go to a
clearing, where ambitious agricultural operations were being
inaugurated, when Herr Liebert hurt his foot.   Up this we
go, it is semi-vertical while it lasts, and it ends in a scrubby
patch that is to be a plantation ; this crossed we are in the
Urwald, and it is more exquisite than words can describe,
but not good going, particularly at one spot where a gigantic
tree has fallen down across a little rocky ravine, and has to be
crawled under.   It occurs to me that this is a highly likely
place for snakes, and an absolutely sure find for scorpions, and
when we have passed it three of these latter interesting
creatures are observed on the load of blankets which is
fastened on to the back of Kefalla.   We inform Kefalla of the
fact on the spot.   A volcanic eruption of entreaty, advice,
and admonition results, but we still hesitate.   However, the
gallant cook tackles them in a sort of tip-cat way with a stick,
and we proceed into a patch of long grass, beyond which there

is a reach of amomums. The winged amomum I see here in Africa for the first time. Horrid slippery things amomum sticks to walk on, when they are lying on the ground ; and there is a lot of my old enemy the calamus about.

On each side are deep forested dells and ravines, and rocks show up through the ground in every direction, and things in general are slippery, and I wonder now and again, as I assume with unnecessary violence a recumbent position, why I came to Africa ; but patches of satin-leaved begonias and clumps of lovely tree-ferns reconcile me to my lot. Cook does not feel these forest charms, and gives me notice after an hour's experience of mountain forest-belt work ; what cook would not ?

As we get higher we have to edge and squeeze every few minutes through the aërial roots of some tremendous kind of tree, plentiful hereabouts. One of them we passed through I am sure would have run any Indian banyan hard for extent of ground covered, if it were measured. In the region where these trees are frequent, the undergrowth is less dense than it is lower down.

Imagine a vast, seemingly limitless cathedral with its countless columns covered, nay, composed of the most exquisite dark-green, large-fronded moss, with here and there a delicate fern embedded in it as an extra decoration. The white, gauze-like mist comes down from the upper mountain towards us : creeping, twining round, and streaming through the moss-covered tree columns—long bands of it reaching along sinuous, but evenly, for fifty and sixty feet or more, and then ending in a puff like the smoke of a gun. Soon, however, all the mist-streams coalesce and make the atmosphere all their own, wrapping us round in a clammy, chill embrace ; it is not that wool-blanket, smothering affair that we were wrapped in down by Buana, but exquisitely delicate. The difference it makes to the beauty of the forest is just the same difference you would get if you put a delicate veil over a pretty woman's face or a sack over her head. In fact, the mist here was exceedingly becoming to the forest's beauty. Now and again growls of thunder roll out from, and quiver in the earth beneath our feet. Mungo is making a big tornado, and is stirring and simmering it softly so as to make it strong. I only hope he will not overdo it, as he does six times in seven, and make it too heavy to get out on to the Atlantic, where all tornadoes ought to go. If he does the thing will go and burst on us in this forest to-night.

The forest now grows less luxuriant though still close—we have left the begonias and the tree-ferns, and are in another zone. The trees now, instead of being clothed in rich, dark-green moss, are heavily festooned with long, greenish-white lichen. It pours with rain.

At last we reach the place where the sergeant says we ought to camp for the night. I have been feeling the time for camping was very ripe for the past hour, and Kefalla openly said as much an hour and a half ago, but he got such scathing things said to him about civilians' legs by the sergeant that I did not air my own opinion.

We are now right at the very edge of the timber belt. My head man and three boys are done to a turn. If I had had a bull behind me or Mr. Fildes in front, I might have done another five or seven miles, but not more.

The rain comes down with extra virulence as soon as we set to work to start the fire and open the loads. I and Peter have great times getting out the military camp-bed from its tight, bolster-like case, while Kefalla gives advice, until, being irritated by the bed's behaviour, I blow up Kefalla and send him to chop firewood. However, we get the thing out and put up after cutting a place clear to set it on: owing to the world being on a stiff slant hereabouts, it takes time to make it stand straight. I get four stakes cut, and drive them in at the four corners of the bed, and then stretch over it Herr von Lucke's waterproof ground-sheet, guy the ends out. to pegs with string, feel profoundly grateful to both Herr Liebert for the bed and Herr von Lucke for the sheet, and place the baggage under the protection of the German Government's two belongings. Then I find the boys have not got a fire with all their fuss, and I have to demonstrate to them the lessons I have learnt among the Fans regarding fire-making. We build a fire-house and then all goes well. I notice they do not make a fire Fan fashion, but build it in a circle.

Evidently one of the labourers from Buea, named Xenia, is a good man. Equally evidently some of my other men are only fit to carry sandwich-boards for Day and Martin's blacking. I dine luxuriously off tinned fat pork and hot tea, and then feeling still hungry go on to tinned herring. Excellent thing tinned herring, but I have to hurry because I know I must go up through the edge of the forest on to the grass land, and see how the country is made during the brief period of clearness that almost always comes just before nightfall. So leaving my boys comfortably seated round the fire having their evening chop, I pass up through the heavily lichen-tasselled fringe of the forest-belt into deep jungle grass, and up a steep and slippery mound.

In front the mountain-face rises like a wall from behind a set of hillocks, similar to the one I am at present on. The face of the wall to the right and left has two dark clefts in it. The peak itself is not visible from where I am ; it rises behind and beyond the wall. I stay taking compass bearings and look for an easy way up for to-morrow. My men, by now, have missed their " ma " and are yelling for her dismally, and the night comes down with great rapidity for we are in the shadow of the great mountain mass, so I go back into camp. Alas ! how vain are often our most energetic efforts to remove our fellow creatures from temptation. I knew a Sunday down among the soldiers would be bad for my men, and so came up here, and now, if you please, these men have been at the rum, because Bum, the head man, has been too done up to do anything but lie in his blanket and feed. Kefalla is laying down the law with great detail and unction. Cook who has been very low in his mind all day, is now weirdly cheerful, and sings incoherently. The other boys, who want to go to sleep, threaten to " burst him " if he " no finish." It's no good—cook carols on, and soon succumbing to the irresistible charm of music, the other men have to join in the choruses. The performance goes on for an hour, growing woollier and woollier in tone, and then dying out in sleep.

I write by the light of an insect-haunted lantern, sitting on the bed, which is tucked in among the trees some twenty

yards away from the boys' fire. There is a bird whistling
in a deep rich note that I have never heard before.

September 23rd.—Morning gloriously fine. Rout the boys
out, and start at seven, with Sasu, Head man, Xenia, Black
boy, Kefalla and Cook.

The great south-east wall of the mountain in front of us
is quite unflecked by cloud, and in the forest are thousands
of bees. We notice that the tongues of forest go up the
mountain in some places a hundred yards or more above the
true line of the belt. These tongues of forest get more
and more heavily hung with lichen, and the trees thinner
and more stunted, towards their ends. I think that these
tongues are always in places where the wind does not
get full play. All those near our camping place on this
south-east face are so. It is evidently not a matter of soil, for
there is ample soil on this side above where the trees are,
and then again on the western side of the mountain—the side
facing the sea—the timber line is far higher up than on this.
Nor, again, is it a matter of angle that makes the timber line
here so low, for those forests on the Sierra del Cristal were
growing luxuriantly over far steeper grades. There is some
peculiar local condition just here evidently, or the forest
would be up to the bottom of the wall of the crater. I am
not unreasonable enough to expect it to grow on that, but its
conduct in staying where it does requires explanation.

We clamber up into the long jungle grass region and go
on our way across a series of steep-sided, rounded grass
hillocks, each of which is separated from the others by dry,
rocky watercourses. The effects produced by the seed-ears
of the long grass round us are very beautiful ; they look a
golden brown, and each ear and leaf is gemmed with dewdrops, and those of the grass on the sides of the hillocks at a
little distance off show a soft brown-pink.

After half an hour's climb, when we are close at the base
of the wall, I observe the men ahead halting, and coming up
with them find Monrovia Boy down a hole ; a little deep
blow-hole, in which, I am informed, water is supposed to be.
But Monrovia soon reports " No live."

I now find we have not a drop of water, either with us or in camp, and now this hole has proved dry. There is, says the sergeant, no chance of getting any more water on this side of the mountain, save down at the river at Buea.

This means failure unless tackled, and it is evidently a trick played on me by the boys, who intentionally failed to let me know of this want of water before leaving Buea, where it seems they have all learnt it. Had I known, of course I should have brought up a sufficient supply. Now they evidently think that there is nothing to be done but to return to Buea, and go down to Victoria, and get their pay, and live happily ever after, without having to face the horror of the upper regions of the mountain. They have worked their oracle with other white folk, I find, for they quote the other white folk's docile conduct as an example to me. I express my opinion of them and of their victims in four words—send Monrovia boy, who I know is to be trusted, back to Buea with a scribbled note to Herr Liebert asking him to send me up two demijohns of water. I send cook with him as far as the cámp in the forest we have just left with orders to bring up three bottles of soda water I have left there, and to instruct the men there that as soon as the water arrives from Buea they are to bring it on up to the camp I mean to make at the top of the wall.

The men are sulky, and Sasu, Peter, Kefalla, and head man say they will wait and come on as soon as cook brings the soda water, and I go on, and presently see Xenia and Black boy are following me. We get on to the intervening hillocks and commence to ascend the face of the wall.

The angle of this wall is great, and its appearance from below is impressive from its enormous breadth, and its abrupt rise without bend or droop for a good 2,000 feet into the air. It is covered with short, yellowish grass through which the burnt-up, scoriaceous lava rock protrudes in rough masses.

I got on up the wall, which when you are on it is not so perpendicular as it looks from below, my desire being to see what sort of country there was on the top of it, between it and the final peak. Sasu had reported to Herr Liebert that it was a wilderness of rock, in which it would be impossible to fix a tent, and spoke vaguely of caves. Here and there on

the way up I come to holes, similar to the one my men had
been down for water. I suppose these holes have been caused
by gases from an under hot layer of lava bursting up through
the upper cool layer. As I get higher, the grass becomes
shorter and more sparse, and the rocks more ostentatiously
displayed. Here and there among them are sadly tried
bushes, bearing a beautiful yellow flower, like a large yellow
wild rose, only scentless. It is not a rose at all, I may remark.
The ground, where there is any basin made by the rocks,
grows a great sedum, with a grand head of whity-pink flower,
also a tall herb, with soft downy leaves silver grey in colour,
and having a very pleasant aromatic scent, and here and there
patches of good honest parsley. Bright blue, flannelly-looking
flowers stud the grass in sheltered places and a very pretty
large green orchid is plentiful. Above us is a bright
blue sky with white cloud rushing hurriedly across it to the
N.E. and a fierce sun. When I am about half-way up, I
think of those boys, and, wanting rest, sit down by an
inviting-looking rock grotto, with a patch of the yellow flowered
shrub growing on its top. Inside it grow little ferns and
mosses, all damp ; but alas ! no water pool, and very badly I
want water by this time.

Below me a belt of white cloud had now formed, so that I
could see neither the foot-hillocks nor the forest, and presently
out of this mist came Xenia toiling up, carrying my black
bag. " Where them Black boy live ? " said I. " Black boy say
him foot be tire too much," said Xenia, as he threw himself
down in the little shade the rock could give. I took a cupful
of sour claret out of the bottle in the bag, and told Xenia to
come on up as soon as he was rested, and meanwhile to yell to
the others down below and tell them to come on. Xenia did,
but sadly observed, " softly softly still hurts the snail," and I
left him and went on up the mountain.

When I had got to the top of the rock under which I had
sheltered from the blazing sun, the mist opened a little, and I
saw my men looking like as many little dolls. They were
still sitting on the hillock where I had left them. Buea
showed from this elevation well. The guard house and the
mission house, like little houses in a picture, and the make of

the ground on which Buea station stands, came out distinctly
as a ledge or terrace, extending for miles N.N.E. and S.S.W.
This ledge is a strange-looking piece of country, covered
with low bush, out of which rise great, isolated, white-
stemmed cotton trees.   Below, and beyond this is a denser
band of high forest, and again below this stretches the
vast mangrove-swamp fringing the estuary of the Cameroons,
Mungo, and Bimbia rivers.   It is a very noble view, giving
one an example of the peculiar beauty one oft-times gets
in this West African scenery, namely colossal sweeps of
colour.   The mangrove-swamps looked to-day like a vast
damson-coloured carpet threaded with silver where the
waterways ran.   It reminded me of a scene I saw once near
Cabinda, when on climbing to the top of a hill I suddenly
found myself looking down on a sheet of violet pink more
than a mile long and half a mile wide.   This was caused by
a climbing plant having taken possession of a valley full
of trees, whose tops it had reached and then spread and
interlaced itself over them, to burst into profuse glorious
laburnum-shaped bunches of flowers.

After taking some careful compass bearings for future use
regarding the Rumby and Omon range of mountains, which
were clearly visible and which look fascinatingly like my
beloved Sierra del Cristal, I turned my face to the wall of
Mungo, and continued the ascent.   The sun, which was blazing,
was reflected back from the rocks in scorching rays.   But
it was more bearable now, because its heat was tempered by a
bitter wind.

The slope becoming steeper, I gradually made my way
towards the left until I came to a great lane, as neatly walled
with rock as if it had been made with human hands.   It runs
down the mountain face, nearly vertically in places and at stiff
angles always, but it was easier going up this lane than on
the outside rough rock, because the rocks in it had been
smoothed by mountain torrents during thousands of wet
seasons, and the walls protected one from the biting wind, a
wind that went through me, for I had been stewing for nine
months and more in tropic and equatorial swamps.

Up this lane I went to the very top of the mountain wall,

and then, to my surprise, found myself facing a great, hillocky,
rock-encumbered plain, across the other side of which rose the
mass of the peak itself, not as a single cone, but as a wall
surmounted by several, three being evidently the highest
among them.

I started along the ridge of my wall, and went to its
highest part, that to the S.W., intending to see what I could
of the view towards the sea, and then to choose a place for
camping in for the night.

When I reached the S.W. end, looking westwards I saw
the South Atlantic down below, like a plain of frosted
silver. Out of it, barely twenty miles away, rose Fernando
Po to its 10,190 feet with that majestic grace peculiar to a
volcanic island. Immediately below me, some 10,000 feet
or so, lay Victoria with the forested foot-hills of Mungo Mah
Lobeh encircling it as a diadem, and Ambas Bay gemmed with
rocky islands lying before it. On my left away S.E. was the
glorious stretch of the Cameroon estuary, with a line of white
cloud lying very neatly along the course of Cameroon River.

In one of the chasms of the mountain wall that I had come
up—in the one furthest to the north—there was a thunderstorm
brewing, seemingly hanging on to, or streaming out of the
mountain side, a soft billowy mass of dense cream-coloured
cloud, with flashes of golden lightnings playing about in it
with soft growls of thunder. Surely Mungo Mah Lobeh himself, of all the thousands he annually turns out, never made
one more lovely than this. Soon the white mists rose from
the mangrove-swamp, and grew rose-colour in the light of
the setting sun, as they swept upwards over the now purple
high forests. In the heavens, to the north, there was a rain-
bow, vivid in colour, one arch of it going behind the peak,
the other sinking into the mist sea below, and this mist sea
rose and rose towards me, turning from pale rose-colour to
lavender, and where the shadow of the Mungo lay across it, to
a dull leaden grey. It was soon at my feet, blotting the under-
world out, and soon came flowing over the wall top at its
lowest parts, stretching in great spreading rivers over the
crater plain, and then these coalescing everything was shut
out save the two summits : that of Cameroon close to

me, and that of Clarence away on Fernando Po. These two stood out alone, like great island masses made of iron rising from a formless, silken sea.

The space around seemed boundless, and there was in it neither sound nor colour, nor anything with form, save those two terrific things. It was like a vision, and it held me spellbound, as I stood shivering on the rocks with the white mist round my knees until into my wool-gathering mind came the memory of those anything but sublime men of mine; and I turned and scuttled off along the rocks like an agitated ant left alone in a dead universe.

I soon found the place where I had come up into the crater plain and went down over the wall, descending with twice the rapidity, but ten times the scratches and grazes, of the ascent.

I picked up the place where I had left Xenia, but no Xenia was there, nor came there any answer to my bush call for him, so on I went down towards the place where, hours ago, I had left the men. The mist was denser down below, but to my joy it was warmer than on the summit of the wind-swept wall.

I had nearly reached the foot of this wall and made my mind up to turn in for the night under a rock, when I heard a melancholy croak away in the mist to the left. I went towards it and found Xenia lost on his own account, and distinctly quaint in manner, and then I recollected that I had been warned Xenia is slightly crazy. Nice situation this: a madman on a mountain in the mist. Xenia, I found, had no longer got my black bag, but in its place a lid of a saucepan and an empty lantern. To put it mildly, this is not the sort of outfit the R.G.S. *Hints to Travellers* would recommend for African exploration. Xenia reported that he gave the bag to Black boy, who shortly afterwards disappeared, and that he had neither seen him nor any of the others since, and didn't expect to this side of Srahmandazi. In a homicidal state of mind, I made tracks for the missing ones followed by Xenia. I thought mayhap they had grown on to the rocks they had sat upon so long, but presently, just before it became quite dark, we picked up the place we had left them in and found there only an empty soda-water bottle. Xenia poured out a muddled mass of observations to the effect that "they got fright too much about them water palaver."

I did not linger to raise a monument to them, but I said I wished they were in a condition to require one, and we went on over our hillocks with more confidence now that we knew we had stuck well to our unmarked track.

> " The moving Moon went up the sky,
> And nowhere did abide :
> Softly she was going up,
> And a star or two beside."

Only she was a young and inefficient moon, and although we were below the thickest of the mist band, it was dark.

Finding our own particular hole in the forest wall was about as easy as finding " our particular rabbit hole in an unknown hay-field in the dark," and the attempt to do so afforded us a great deal of varied exercise. I am obliged to be guarded in my language, because my feelings now are only down to one degree below boiling point. The rain now began to fall, thank goodness, and I drew the thick ears of grass through my parched lips as I stumbled along over the rugged lumps of rock hidden under the now waist-high jungle grass.

Our camp hole was pretty easily distinguishable by daylight, for it was on the left-hand side of one of the forest tongues, the grass land running down like a lane between two tongues here, and just over the entrance three conspicuously high trees showed. But we could not see these "picking-up" points in the darkness, so I had to keep getting Xenia to strike matches, and hold them in his hat while I looked at the compass. Presently we came full tilt up against a belt of trees which I knew from these compass observations was our tongue of forest belt, and I fired a couple of revolver shots into it, whereabouts I judged our camp to be.

This was instantly answered by a yell from human voices in chorus, and towards that yell in a slightly amiable—a very slightly amiable—state of mind I went.

I will draw a veil over the scene, particularly over my observations to those men. They did not attempt to deny their desertion, but they attempted to explain it, each one saying that it was not he but the other boy who " got fright too much."

As the black sergeant was nominally our guide, I asked him for his views on the situation. He said that when he got back to the camp the boys were drunk, which I daresay was true, but left the explanation of why he went back out of the affair. I pointed this out, and Bum, the Head man, charged into the gap with the statement that Black boy had got " sick in him tummick, he done got fever bad bad too much," and so he and the rest had to escort Black boy back to camp. This statement, though a contribution to the knowledge of the reason of the return, was manifestly untrue; because Black boy, who did not know English, sat laughing and talking at the fire during this moving recital of his woes. Those men should have rehearsed their explanations, and then Black boy could have done a good rousing writhe to support poor Bum's statement.

I closed the palaver promptly with a brief but lurid sketch of my opinion on the situation, and ordered food, for not having had a thing save that cup of sour claret since 6.30 A.M., and it being now 11 P.M., I felt sinkings. Then arose another beautiful situation before me. It seems when Cook and Monrovia got back into camp this morning Master Cook was seized with one of those attacks of a desire to manage things that produce such awful results in the African servant, and sent all the beef and rice down to Buea to be cooked, because there was no water here to cook it. Therefore the men have got nothing to eat. I had a few tins of my own food and so gave them some, and they became as happy as kings in a few minutes, listening and shouting over the terrible adventures of Xenia, who is posing as the Hero of the Great Cameroon. I get some soda-water from the two bottles left and some tinned herring, and then write out two notes to Herr Liebert asking him to send me three more demijohns of water, and some beef and rice from the store, promising faithfully to pay for them on my return.

I would not prevent those men of mine from going up that peak above me after their touching conduct to-day. Oh! no; not for worlds, dear things.

CHAPTER XXVI

THE GREAT PEAK OF CAMEROONS—(*Continued*)

Setting forth how the Voyager for a second time reaches the S.E. crater
with some account of the pleasures incidental to camping out in the
said crater.

September 24th.—Lovely morning, the grey-white mist in the
forest makes it like a dream of Fairyland, each moss-grown tree
stem heavily gemmed with dewdrops. At 5.30 I stir the boys,
for Sasu, the sergeant, says he must go back to his military
duties. The men think we are all going back with him as he is
our only guide, but I send three of them down with orders to go
back to Victoria—two being of the original set I started with.
They are surprised and disgusted at being sent home, but they
have got "hot foot," and something wrong in the usual seat
of African internal disturbances, their "tummicks," and I am
not thinking of starting a sanatorium for abdominally-
afflicted Africans in that crater plain above. Black boy is
the other boy returned, I do not want another of his attacks.

They go, and this leaves me in the forest camp with Kefalla,
Xenia, and Cook, and we start expecting the water sent for
by Monrovia boy yesterday forenoon. There are an abominable lot of bees about ; they do not give one a moment's peace,
getting beneath the waterproof sheets over the bed, and pretending they can't get out and forthwith losing their tempers,
which is imbecile, because the whole four sides of the affair
are broad open.

The ground, bestrewn with leaves and dried wood, is a mass
of large flies rather like our common house-fly, but both butterflies and beetles seem scarce ; but I confess I do not feel up

to hunting much after yesterday's work, and deem it advisable to rest.

My face and particularly my lips are a misery to me, having been blistered all over by yesterday's sun, and last night I inadvertently whipped the skin all off one cheek with the blanket, and it keeps on bleeding, and, horror of horrors, there is no tea until that water comes.

I wish I had got the mountaineering spirit, for then I could say, " I'll never come to this sort of place again, for you can get all you want in the Alps." I have been told this by my mountaineering friends—I have never been there—and that you can go and do all sorts of stupendous things all day, and come back in the evening to *table d'hôte* at an hotel ; but as I have not got the mountaineering spirit, I suppose I shall come fooling into some such place as this as soon as I get the next chance.

About 8.30, to our delight, the gallant Monrovia boy comes through the bush with a demijohn of water, and I get my tea, and give the men the only half-pound of rice I have and a tin of meat, and they eat, become merry, and chat over their absent companions in a scornful, scandalous way. Who cares for hotels now ? When one is in a delightful place like this, one must work, so off I go to the north into the forest, after giving the rest of the demijohn of water into the Monrovia boy's charge with strict orders it is not to be opened till my return. Quantities of beetles.

A little after two o'clock I return to camp, after having wandered about in the forest and found three very deep holes, down which I heaved rocks and in no case heard a splash. In one I did not hear the rocks strike, owing to the great depth. I hate holes, and especially do I hate these African ones, for I am frequently falling, more or less, into them, and they will be my end. So far I have never fallen down a West Coast native gold mine, but I know people who have ; but all the other sorts I have tried, having pitched by day and night into those, from three to twelve feet deep, made by industrious indigenous ones, as Mrs. Gault calls them, digging out sand and earth to make the " swish " walls of their simple savage homes ; and also into those from twenty to thirty feet deep

with pointed stakes at the bottom, artfully disposed to impale
the elephant and leopard of the South-West Coast. But
my worst fall was into a disused Portuguese well of unknown depth at Cabinda. I "feel the place in frosty weather
still," though I did not go down all the way, my descent being
arrested by a collection of brushwood and rubbish, which had
been cast into it, and which had hitched far down in the shaft.
When I struck this subterranean wood raft, I thought—Saved !
The next minute it struck me that raft was sinking, and so it
was, slowly and jerkily, but sinking all the same. I clapper-
clawed round in the stuffy dark for something at the side to
hang on to, and got some tough bush rope, just as I was convinced that my fate was an inglorious and inverted case of
Elijah, and I was being carried off, alive, to Shiöl.

The other demijohns of water have not arrived yet, and
we are getting anxious again because the men's food has
not come up, and they have been so exceedingly thirsty that
they have drunk most of the water—not, however, since it has
been in Monrovia's charge ; but at 3.15 another boy comes
through the bush with another demijohn of water. We
receive him gladly, and ask him about the chop. He knows
nothing about it. At 3.45 another boy comes through the
bush with another demijohn of water ; we receive him kindly ;
he does not know anything about the chop. At 4.10 another
boy comes through the bush with another demijohn of water,
and knowing nothing about the chop, we are civil to him, and
that's all.

A terrific tornado which has been lurking growling about
then sits down in the forest and bursts, wrapping us up in a
lively kind of fog, with its thunder, lightning, and rain. It
was impossible to hear, or make one's self heard at the distance
of even a few paces, because of the shrill squeal of the wind,
the roar of the thunder, and the rush of the rain on the trees
round us. It was not like having a storm burst over you in
the least ; you felt you were in the middle of its engine-room
when it had broken down badly. After half an hour or so the
thunder seemed to lift itself off the ground, and the lightning
came in sheets, instead of in great forks that flew like flights of
spears among the forest trees. The thunder, however, had not

settled things amicably with the mountain ; it roared its rage at Mungo, and Mungo answered back, quivering with a rage as great, under our feet. One feels here as if one were constantly dropping, unasked and unregarded, among painful and violent discussions between the elemental powers of the universe. Mungo growls and swears in thunder at the sky, and sulks in white mist all the morning, and then the sky answers back, hurling down lightnings and rivers of water, with total disregard of Mungo's visitors. The way the water rushes down from the mountain wall through the watercourses in the jungle just above, and then at the edge of the forest spreads out into a sheet of water that is an inch deep, and that flies on past us in miniature cascades, trying the while to put out our fire, and so on, is—quite interesting. (I exhausted my vocabulary on those boys yesterday.)

As soon as we saw what we were in for, we had thrown dry wood on to the fire, and it blazed just as the rain came down, so with our assistance it fought a good fight with its fellow elements, spitting and hissing like a wild cat. It could have managed the water fairly well, but the wind came, very nearly putting an end to it by carrying away its protecting bough house, which settled on " Professor " Kefalla, who burst out in a lecture on the foolishness of mountaineering and the quantity of devils in this region. Just in the midst of these joys another boy came through the bush with another demijohn of water. We did not receive him even civilly ; I burst out laughing, and the boys went off in a roar, and we shouted at him, " Where them chop ? " " He live for come," said the boy, and we then gave him a hearty welcome and a tot of rum, and an hour afterwards two more boys appear, one carrying a sack of rice and beef for the men, and the other a box for me from Herr Liebert, containing a luxurious supply of biscuits, candles, tinned meats, and a bottle of wine and one of beer.

We are now all happy, though exceeding damp, and the boys sit round the fire, with their big iron pot full of beef and rice, busy cooking while they talk. Wonderful accounts of our prodigies of valour I hear given by Xenia, and terrible accounts of what they have lived through from the others, and the men who have brought up the demijohns and the chop recount the last news from Buea. James's wife has run away again.

I have taken possession of two demijohns of water and the rum demijohn, arranging them round the head of my bed. The worst of it is those tiresome bees, as soon as the rain is over, come in hundreds after the rum, and frighten me continually. The worthless wretches get intoxicated on what they can suck from round the cork, and then they stagger about on the ground buzzing malevolently. When the boys have had the chop and a good smoke, we turn to and make up the loads for to-morrow's start up the mountain, and then, after more hot tea, I turn in on my camp bed—listening to the soft sweet murmur of the trees and the pleasant, laughing chatter of the men.

September 25th.—Rolled off the bed twice last night into the bush. The rain has washed the ground away from under its off legs, so that it tilts ; and there were quantities of large longicorn beetles about during the night—the sort with spiny backs ; they kept on getting themselves hitched on to my blankets and when I wanted civilly to remove them they made a horrid fizzing noise and showed fight—cocking their horns in a defiant way. I awake finally about 5 a.m. soaked through to the skin. The waterproof sheet has had a label sewn to it, so is not waterproof, and it has been raining softly but amply for hours. I wish the camp bed had had a ticket sewn on, and nothing but my profound admiration for Kaiser Wilhelm, Emperor of Germany, its owner, prevents me from making holes in it, for it sags in the middle, and constitutes an excellent rain-water cistern. I have been saying things to it, during the night, about this habit, but the bed is so imbued with the military spirit that it says, " My orders are to be waterproof, and waterproof I'll be " : so I decide to leave it behind, carefully drying it and protecting it as much as possible.

About seven we are off again, with Xenia, head man, cook, Monrovia boy and a labourer from Buea—the water-carriers have gone home after having had their morning chop.

We make for the face of the wall by a route to the left of that I took on Monday, and when we are clambering up it, some 600 feet above the hillocks, swish comes a terrific rain-storm at us accompanied by a squealing, bitter cold wind. We can hear the roar of the rain on the forest below, and hoping to get above it we keep on ; hoping, however, is vain. The dense mist that comes with it prevents our seeing more than two yards in front, and we get too far to the left. I am behind the band to-day, severely bringing up the rear, and about 1 o'clock I hear shouts from the vanguard and when I get up to them I find them sitting on the edge of one of the clefts or scars in the mountain face.

I do not know how these quarry-like chasms have been formed. They both look alike from below—the mountain wall comes down vertically into them—and the bottom of this one slopes forward, so that if we had had the misfortune when a little lower down to have gone a little further to the left, we should have got on to the bottom of it, and should have found ourselves walled in on three sides, and had to retrace our steps ; as it is we have just struck its right-hand edge. And fortunately, the mist, thick as it is, has not been sufficiently thick to lead the men to walk over it ; for had they done so they would have got killed, as the cliff arches in under so that we look straight into the bottom of the scar some 200 or 300 feet below, when there is a split in the mist. The sides and bottom are made of, and strewn with, white, moss-grown masses of volcanic cinder rock, and sparsely shrubbed with gnarled trees which have evidently been under fire—one of my boys tells me from the burning of this face of the mountain by "the Major from Calabar" during the previous dry season.

We keep on up a steep grass-covered slope, and finally reach the top of the wall. The immense old crater floor before us is to-day the site of a seething storm, and the peak itself quite invisible. My boys are quite demoralised by the cold. I find most of them have sold the blankets I gave them out at Buana ; and those who have not sold them have left them behind at Buea, from laziness perhaps, but more possibly from a confidence in their powers to prevent us getting so far.

I believe if I had collapsed too—the cold tempted me to do

so as nothing else can—they would have lain down and died in the cold sleety rain.

I sight a clump of gnarled sparsely-foliaged trees be-draped heavily with lichen, growing in a hollow among the rocks ; thither I urge the men for shelter and they go like storm-bewildered sheep. My bones are shaking in my skin and my teeth in my head, for after the experience I had had of the heat here on Monday I dared not clothe myself heavily.

The men stand helpless under the trees, and I hastily take the load of blankets Herr Liebert lent us off a boy's back and undo it, throwing one blanket round each man, and opening my umbrella and spreading it over the other blankets. Then I give them a tot of rum apiece, as they sit huddled in their blankets, and tear up a lot of the brittle, rotten wood from the trees and shrubs, getting horrid thorns into my hands the while, and set to work getting a fire with it and the driest of the moss from beneath the rocks. By the aid of it and Xenia, who soon revived, and a carefully scraped up candle and a box of matches, the fire soon blazes, Xenia hold-ing a blanket to shelter it, while I, with a cutlass, chop stakes to fix the blankets on, so as to make a fire tent.

The other boys now revive, and I hustle them about to make more fires, no easy work in the drenching rain, but work that has got to be done. We soon get three well alight, and then I clutch a blanket—a wringing wet blanket, but a comfort—and wrapping myself round in it, issue orders for wood to be gathered and stored round each fire to dry, and then stand over cook while he makes the men's already cooked chop hot over our first fire, when this is done getting him to make me tea, or as it more truly should be called, soup, for it contains bits of rice and beef, and the general taste of the affair is wood smoke.

Kefalla by this time is in lecturing form again, so my mind is relieved about him, although he says, " Oh ma ! It be cold, cold too much. Too much cold kill we black man, all same for one as too much sun kill you white man. Oh ma ! . . . ," &c. I tell him they have only got them-selves to blame ; if they had come up with me on Monday we should have been hot enough, and missed this storm of rain.

When the boys have had their chop, and are curling themselves up comfortably round their now blazing fires, Xenia must needs start a theory that there is a better place than this to camp in ; he saw it when he was with an unsuccessful expedition that got as far as this. Kefalla is fool enough to go off with him to find this place ; but they soon return, chilled through again, and unsuccessful in their quest. I gather that they have been to find caves. I wish they had found caves, for I am not thinking of taking out a patent for our present camp site.

The bitter wind and swishing rain keep on. We are to a certain extent sheltered from the former, but the latter is of that insinuating sort that nothing but a granite wall would keep off.

Just at sundown, however, as is usual in this country, the rain ceases for a while, and I take this opportunity to get out my seaman's jersey, and retire up over the rocks to have my fight into it unobserved. It is a mighty fight to get that thing on, or off, at the best of times, but to-day it is worse than usual, because I have to get it on over my saturated cotton blouse, and verily at one time I fear I shall have to shout for assistance or be suffocated, so firmly does it get jammed over my head. But I fight my way unaided into it, and then turn to survey our position, and find I have been carrying on my battle on the brink of an abysmal hole whose mouth is concealed among the rocks and scraggly shrubs just above our camp. I heave rocks down it, as we in Fanland would offer rocks to an Ombwiri, and hear them go " knickity-knock, like a pebble in Carisbrook well." I think I detect a far away splash, but it was an awesome way down. This mountain seems set with these man-traps, and " some day some gentleman's nigger " will get killed down one.

The mist has now cleared away from the peak, but lies all over the lower world, and I take bearings of the three highest cones or peaks carefully. Then I go away over the rocky ground southwards, and as I stand looking round, the mist

sea below is cleft in twain for a few minutes by some fierce
down-draught of wind from the peak, and I get a strange,
clear, sudden view right down to Ambas Bay. It is just
like looking down from one world into another. I think
how Odin hung and looked down into Nifelheim, and then of
how hot, how deliciously hot, it was away down there, and
then the mist closes over it. I shiver and go back to
camp, for night is coming on, and I know my men will
require intellectual support in the matter of procuring
firewood.

The men are now quite happy ; over each fire they have
made a tent with four sticks with a blanket on, a blanket that
is too wet to burn, though I have to make them brace the
blankets to windward for fear of their scorching.

The wood from the shrubs here is of an aromatic and a
resinous nature, which sounds nice, but it isn't ; for the volumes
of smoke it gives off when burning are suffocating, and the boys,
who sit almost on the fire, are every few moments scrambling
to their feet and going apart to cough out smoke, like so many
novices in training for the profession of fire eaters. However,
they soon find that if they roll themselves in their blankets,
and lie on the ground to windward they escape most of the
smoke. They have divided up into three parties : Kefalla
and Xenia, who have struck up a great friendship, take the
lower, the most exposed fire. Head man, Cook, and Monrovia
Boy have the upper fire, and the labourer has the middle one
—he being an outcast for medical reasons. They are all
steaming away and smoking comfortably.

I form the noble resolution to keep awake, and rouse up any
gentleman who may catch on fire during the night, a catastrophe which is inevitable, and see to wood being put on the
fires, so elaborately settle myself on my wooden chop-box,
wherein I have got all the lucifers which are not in the
soap-box. The very address on that chop-box, ought to
keep its inside dry and up to duty, for it is "An den
Hochwohlgebornen Freiherrn von Stettin," &c. Owing to there
not being a piece of ground the size of a sixpenny piece level
in this place, the arrangement of my box camp takes time, but
at last it is done to my complete satisfaction, close to a tree

trunk, and I think, as I wrap myself up in my two wet blankets and lean against my tree, what a good thing it is to know how to make one's self comfortable in a place like this. This tree stem is perfection, just the right angle to be restful to one's back, and one can rely all the time on Nature hereabouts not to let one get thoroughly effete from luxurious comfort, so I lazily watch and listen to Xenia and Kefalla at their fire hard by.

They commence talking to each other on their different tribal societies; Kefalla is a Vey, Xenia a Liberian, so in the interests of science I give them two heads of tobacco to stimulate their conversation. They receive them with tragic grief, having no pipe, so in the interests of science I undo my blankets and give them two out of my portmanteau; then do myself up again and pretend to be asleep. I am rewarded by getting some interesting details, and form the opinion that both these worthies, in their pursuit of their particular ju-jus, have come into contact with white prejudices, and are now fugitives from religious persecution. I also observe they have both their own ideas of happiness. Kefalla holds it lies in a warm shirt; Xenia that it abides in warm trousers; and every half-hour the former takes his shirt off, and holds it in the fire smoke, and then puts it hastily on; and Xenia, who is the one and only trouser wearer in our band, spends fifty per cent. of the night on one leg struggling to get the other in or out of these garments, when they are either coming off to be warmed, or going on after warming. Those trousers of Xenia's have something wrong about them; I don't pretend to understand the garment, never having gone in for that sort of thing myself, but it is my belief he slings them too high, with those braces, which *more Alemanni* he wears. Anyhow, in season and out, they want taking off. Three mortal times to-day when on that wind- and rain-swept wall, the whole of us have been brought to a standstill by Xenia having to stand on one leg and do something to his peculiar vestments. It's a mercy he did not kill himself when he fell over while engaged in these operations among the rocks this afternoon—as it is, I see he has smashed the lantern glass again, so that I have to keep it under my blankets to prevent the candle getting blown out by this everlasting N.E. wind.

There seem but few insects here. I have only got two moths to-night—one pretty one with white wings with little red spots on, like an old-fashioned petticoat such as an early Victorian-age lady would have worn—the other a sweet thing in silver.

Then a horrid smell of burning negro interrupts my writing and I have to get up and hunt it down. After some trouble I find it is a spark in cook's hair, he sleeping the while sweetly. I rouse him, *via* his shins, and tell him to put himself out, and he is grateful.

My face is a misery to me, as soon as it dries it sets into a mask, and when I move it, it splits and bleeds.

(Later, *i.e.*, 2.15 A.M.). I have been asleep against that abominable vegetable of a tree. It had its trunk covered with a soft cushion of moss, and pretended to be a comfort—a right angle to lean against, and a softly padded protection to the spine from wind, and all that sort of thing; whereas the whole mortal time it was nothing in this wretched world but a water-pipe, to conduct an extra supply of water down my back. The water has simply streamed down it, and formed a nice little pool in a rocky hollow where I keep my feet, and I am chilled to the innermost bone, so have to scramble up and drag my box to the side of Kefalla and Xenia's fire, feeling sure I have contracted a fatal chill this time. I scrape the ashes out of the fire into a heap, and put my sodden boots into them, and they hiss merrily, and I resolve not to go to sleep again. 5 A.M.— Have been to sleep twice, and have fallen off my box bodily into the fire in my wet blankets, and should for sure have put it out like a bucket of cold water had not Xenia and Kefalla been roused up by the smother I occasioned and rescued me—or the fire. It is not raining now, but it is bitter cold and cook is getting my tea. I give the boys a lot of hot tea with a big handful of sugar in, and they then get their own food hot.

CHAPTER XXVII

THE GREAT PEAK OF CAMEROONS—(*Continued*)

Setting forth how the Voyager attains the summit of Mungo Mah Lobeh, and descends therefrom to Victoria, to which is added some remarks on the natural history of the West Coast porter, and the native methods of making fire.

September 26th.—The weather is undecided and so am I, for I feel doubtful about going on in this weather, but I do not like to give up the peak after going through so much for it. The boys being dry and warm with the fires have forgotten their troubles. However, I settle in my mind to keep on, and ask for volunteers to come with me, and Bum, the head man, and Xenia announce their willingness. I put two tins of meat and a bottle of Herr Liebert's beer into the little wooden box, and insist on both men taking a blanket apiece, much to their disgust, and before six o'clock we are off over the crater plain. It is a broken bit of country with rock mounds sparsely overgrown with tufts of grass, and here and there are patches of boggy land, not real bog, but damp places where grow little clumps of rushes, and here and there among the rocks sorely-afflicted shrubs of broom, and the yellow-flowered shrub I have mentioned before, and quantities of very sticky heather, feeling when you catch hold of it as if it had been covered with syrup. One might fancy the entire race of shrubs was dying out; for one you see partially alive there are twenty skeletons which fall to pieces as you brush past them.

It· is downhill the first part of the way, that is to say, the trend of the land is downhill, for be it down or up, the details

of it are rugged mounds and masses of burnt-out lava rock.
It is evil going, but perhaps not quite so evil as the lower
hillocks of the great wall where the rocks are hidden beneath
long slippery grass.   We wind our way in between the
mounds, or clamber over them, or scramble along their sides
impartially.   The general level is then flat, and then comes a
rise towards the peak wall, so we steer N.N.E. until we
strike the face of the peak, and then commence a stiff
rough climb.   We are all short of breath, but I do not think
from the altitude; my shortness arises from a cold I have got,
and my men's from too much breakfast, I fancy.

We keep as straight as we can, but get driven at an angle
by the strange ribs of rock which come straight down.   These
are most tiresome to deal with, getting worse the higher we
go, and so rotten and weather-eaten are they that they crumble
into dust and fragments under our feet.   Head man gets half
a dozen falls, and when we are about three parts of the way
up Xenia gives in.   The cold and the climbing are too much
for him, so I make him wrap himself up in his blanket, which
he is glad enough of now, and shelter in a depression under
one of the many rock ridges, and head man and I go
on.   When we are some 600 feet higher the iron-grey mist
comes curling and waving round the rocks above us, like some
savage monster defending them from intruders, and I again
debate whether I was justified in risking the men, for it is a
risk for them at this low temperature, with the evil weather I
know, and they do not know, is coming on.   But still we
have food and blankets with us enough for them, and the
camp in the plain below they can reach all right, if the worst
comes to the worst; and for myself—well—that's my own
affair, and no one will be a ha'porth the worse if I am dead in
an hour.   So I hitch myself on to the rocks, and take bearings,
particularly bearings of Xenia's position, who, I should say,
has got a tin of meat and a flask of rum with him, and then
turn and face the threatening mist.   It rises and falls, and sends
out arm-like streams towards us, and then Bum, the head man,
decides to fail for the third time to reach the peak, and I
leave him wrapped in his blanket with the bag of provisions,
and go on alone into the wild, grey, shifting, whirling mist

above, and soon find myself at the head of a rock ridge in a narrowish depression, walled by massive black walls which show fitfully but firmly through the mist.

I can see three distinctly high cones before me, and then the mist, finding it cannot drive me back easily, proceeds to desperate methods, and lashes out with a burst of bitter wind, and a sheet of blinding, stinging rain. I make my way up through it towards a peak which I soon see through a tear in the mist is not the highest, so I angle off and go up the one to the left, and after a desperate fight reach the cairn—only, alas! to find a hurricane raging and a fog in full possession, and not a ten yards' view to be had in any direction. Near the cairn on the ground are several bottles, some of which the energetic German officers, I suppose, had emptied in honour of their achievement, an achievement I bow down before, for their pluck and strength had taken them here in a shorter time by far than mine. I do not meddle with anything, save to take a few specimens and to put a few more rocks on the cairn, and to put in among them my card, merely as a civility to Mungo, a civility his Majesty will soon turn into pulp. Not that it matters—what is done is done.

The weather grows worse every minute, and no sign of any clearing shows in the indigo sky or the wind-reft mist. The rain lashes so fiercely I cannot turn my face to it and breathe, the wind is all I can do to stand up against.

Verily I am no mountaineer, for there is in me no exultation, but only a deep disgust because the weather has robbed me of my main object in coming here, namely to get a good view and an idea of the way the unexplored mountain range behind Calabar trends.

No doubt had the weather been clear I should have been able to do this well, for the whole Omon range must be visible from this great summit of Cameroons, which rises at right angles to it. For when I was in Okyon close to this Rumby or Omon range, Mungo's great mass was perfectly visible looking seawards. My only consolation is that my failure to do this bit of work is not my own fault, save as regards my coming here at the wrong season, which matter was also beyond my control. Moreover there was just the chance, as this is the tornado season, and not the real wet, that I might have had a clear day on the peak. I took my chance and it failed, so there's nothing to complain about.

Comforting myself with these reflections, I start down to find Bum, and do so neatly, and then together we scramble down carefully among the rotten black rocks, intent on finding Xenia. The scene is very grand. At one minute we can see nothing save the black rocks and cinders under foot ; the next the wind-torn mist separates now in one direction, now in another, showing us always the same wild scene of great black cliffs, rising in jagged peaks and walls around and above us. I think this walled cauldron we had just left is really the highest crater on Mungo.[1]

We soon become anxious about Xenia, for this is a fearfully easy place to lose a man in such weather, but just as we get below the thickest part of the pall of mist, I observe a doll-sized figure, standing on one leg taking on or off its trousers— our lost Xenia, beyond a shadow of a doubt, and we go down direct to him.

When we reach him we halt, and I give the two men one of the tins of meat, and take another and the bottle of beer myself, and then make a hasty sketch of the great crater plain below us. At the further edge of the plain a great white cloud

[1] Since my return to England I have read Sir Richard Burton's account of his first successful attempt to reach the summit of the Great Cameroons in 1862. His companions were Herr Mann, the botanist, and Señor Calvo. Herr Mann claimed to have ascended the summit a few days before the two others joined him, but Burton seems to doubt this. The account he himself gives of the summit is : " Victòria mountain now proved to be a shell of a huge double crater opening to the south-eastward, where a tremendous torrent of fire had broken down the weaker wall, the whole interior and its accessible breach now lay before me plunging down in vertical cliff. The depth of the bowl may be 360 feet. The total diameter of the two, which are separated by a rough partition of lava, 1,000 feet. . . . Not a blade of grass, not a thread of moss, breaks the gloom of this Plutonic pit, which is as black as Erebus, except where the fire has painted it red or yellow." This ascent was made from the west face. I got into the " Plutonic pit " through the S.E. break in its wall, and was the first English person to reach it from the S.E., the third of my nation, all told, to ascend the peak, and the twenty-eighth ascender according to my well-informed German friends.

is coming up from below, which argues badly for our trip down the great wall to the forest camp, which I am anxious to reach before nightfall after our experience of the accommodation afforded by our camp in the crater plain last night.

While I am sitting waiting for the men to finish their meal, I feel a chill at my back, as if some cold thing had settled there, and turning round, see the mist from the summit above coming in a wall down towards us. These mists up here, as far as my experience goes, are always preceded by a strange breath of ice-cold air—not necessarily a wind.

Bum then draws my attention to a strange funnel-shaped thing coming down from the clouds to the north. A big waterspout, I presume : it seems to be moving rapidly N.E., and I profoundly hope it will hold that course, for we have quite as much as we can manage with the ordinary rain-water supply on this mountain, without having waterspouts to deal with.

We start off down the mountain as rapidly as we can. Xenia is very done up, and Head man comes perilously near breaking his neck by frequent falls among the rocks ; my unlucky boots are cut through and through by the latter. When we get down towards the big crater plain, it is a race between us and the pursuing mist as to who shall reach the camp first, and the mist wins, but we have just time to make out the camp's exact position before it closes round us, so we reach it without any real difficulty. When we get there, about one o'clock, I find the men have kept the fires alight and Cook is asleep before one of them with another conflagration smouldering in his hair. I get him to make me tea, while the others pack up as quickly as possible, and by two we are all off on our way down to the forest camp.

The boys are nervous in their way of going down over the mountain wall. The misadventures of Cook alone would fill volumes. Monrovia boy is out and away the best man at this work. Just as we reach the high jungle grass, down comes the rain and up comes the mist, and we have the worst time we have had during our whole trip, in our endeavours to find the hole in the forest that leads to our old camp.

Unfortunately, I must needs go in for acrobatic performances

on the top of one of the highest, rockiest hillocks. Poising
myself on one leg I take a rapid slide sideways, ending in a
very showy leap backwards which lands me on the top of the
lantern I am carrying to-day, among miscellaneous rocks.
There being fifteen feet or so of jungle grass above me, all the
dash and beauty of my performance are as much thrown away
as I am, for my boys are too busy on their own accounts in
the mist to miss me. After resting some little time as I fell,
and making and unmaking the idea in my mind that I am
killed, I get up, clamber elaborately to the top of the next
hillock, and shout for the boys, and " Ma," " ma," comes
back from my flock from various points out of the fog. I
find Bum and Monrovia boy, and learn that during my absence
Xenia, who always fancies himself as a path-finder, has taken
the lead, and gone off somewhere with the rest. We shout
and the others answer, and we join them, and it soon becomes
evident to the meanest intelligence that Xenia had better have
spent his time attending to those things of his instead of
going in for guiding, for we are now right off the track we
made through the grass on our up journey, and we proceed
to have a cheerful hour or so in the wet jungle, ploughing
hither and thither, trying to find our way.

At last we pick up the top of a tongue of forest that we all
feel is ours, but we—that is to say, Xenia and I, for the others go
like lambs to the slaughter wherever they are led—disagree as
to the path. He wants to go down one side of the tongue, I to
go down the other, and I have my way, and we wade along,
skirting the bushes that fringe it, trying to find our hole. I
own I soon begin to feel shaky about having been right in
the affair, but soon Xenia, who is leading, shouts he has got
it, and we limp in, our feet sore with rugged rocks, and everything we have on, or in the loads, wringing wet, save the
matches, which providentially I had put into my soap-box.

Anything more dismal than the look of that desired camp
when we reach it, I never saw. Pools of water everywhere.
The fire-house a limp ruin, the camp bed I have been thinking
fondly of for the past hour a water cistern. I tilt the water
out of it, and say a few words to it regarding its hide-bound
idiocy in obeying its military instructions to be waterproof;

and then, while the others are putting up the fire-house, head man and I get out the hidden demijohn of rum, and the beef and rice, and I serve out a tot of rum each to the boys, who are shivering dreadfully, waiting for cook to get the fire. He soon does this, and then I have my hot tea and the men their hot food, for now we have returned to the luxury of two cooking pots.

Their education in bush is evidently progressing, for they make themselves a big screen with boughs and spare blankets, between the wind and the fire-house, and I get Xenia to cut some branches, and place them on the top of my waterproof sheet shelter, and we are fairly comfortable again, and the boys quite merry and very well satisfied with themselves.

Unfortunately the subject of their nightly debating society is human conduct, a subject ever fraught with dangerous elements of differences of opinion. They are busy discussing, with their mouths full of rice and beef, the conduct of an absent friend, who it seems is generally regarded by them as a spendthrift. " He gets plenty money, but he no have none no time." " He go frow it away on woman, and drink." " He no buy clothes." This last is evidently a very heavy accusation, but Kefalla says, " What can a man buy with money better than them thing he like best ? "

This philosophic outburst from Kefalla is followed by a wordy war on the innate worthlessness of woman and drink, the details of which I will not give, but presently there is an extra row, and Cook rushes to me, holding in one hand the cooking pot, into which I find I am expected to shove my nose, and then to sniff at his abominably dirty singlet. Kefalla comes hurrying after him talking sixteen to the dozen. It seems that during the discussion of a particularly knotty point on practical ethics, Kefalla fell out with Cook, and seizing his rum and water, threw it at him, and what has not gone over Cook has gone into his supper in the pot. Cook displays a lively horror of the smell of rum in his rice, which is, coming from him, a bit comic. I call up head man, who is as usual not attending to his duty of keeping the others in order, and we two talk the palaver and decide, in spite of Kefalla's specious arguments, that he is to pay Cook for both

the rice and the rum, and the latter goes off content, vowing
he'll have their value to the last farthing out of Kefalla. The
men then gradually go off to sleep, breaking out now and
again spasmodically into little rows over a pipe, and so on,
until at last all is peace.

There is a very peculiar look on the rotten wood on the
ground round here ; to-night it has patches and flecks of
iridescence like one sees on herrings or mackerel that have
been kept too long. The appearance of this strange eerie
light in among the bush is very weird and charming. I have
seen it before in dark forests at night, but never so much of it.

September 27th.—Fine morning. It's a blessing my Pappenheimers have not recognised what this means for the afternoon.
We take things very leisurely. I know it's no good hurrying,
we are dead sure of getting a ducking before we reach Buea
anyhow, so we may as well enjoy ourselves while we can.

I ask my boys how they would " make fire suppose no
matches live." Not one of them thinks it possible to do so,
" it pass man to do them thing suppose he no got live stick or
matches." They are coast boys, all of them, and therefore
used to luxury, but it is really remarkable how widely diffused
matches are inland, and how very dependent on them these
natives are. When I have been away in districts where
they have not penetrated, it is exceedingly rarely that the
making of fire has to be resorted to. I think I may say that in
most African villages it has not had to be done for years and
years, because when a woman's fire has gone out, owing to
her having been out at work all day, she just runs into some
neighbour's hut where there is a fire burning, and gives compliments, and picks up a burning stick from the fire and runs
home. From this comes the compliment, equivalent to our
" Oh ! don't go away yet," of " You come to fetch fire." This
will be said to you all the way from Sierra Leone to Loanda,
as far as I know, if you have been making yourself agreeable
in an African home, even if the process may have extended
over a day or so. The hunters, like the Fans, have to make
fire, and do it now with a flint and steel ; but in districts where
their tutor in this method—the flint-lock gun—is not available,
they will do it with two sticks, not always like the American

Indians' fire-sticks. One stick is placed horizontally on the ground and the other twirled rapidly between the palms of the hands, but sometimes two bits of palm stick are worked in a hole in a bigger bit of wood, the hole stuffed round with the pith of a tree or with silk. cotton fluff, and the two sticks rotated vigorously. Again, on one occasion I saw a Bakele woman make fire by means of a slip of rafia palm drawn very rapidly, to and fro, across a notch in another piece of rafia wood. In most domesticated tribes, like the Effiks or the Igalwa, if they are going out to their plantation, they will enclose a live stick in a hollow piece of a certain sort of wood, which has a lining of its interior pith left in it, and they will carry this " fire box" with them. Or if they are going on a long canoe journey, there is always the fire in the bow of the canoe put into a calabash full of sand, or failing that, into a bed of clay with a sand rim round it.

By 10 o'clock we are off down to Buea. At 10.15 it pours as it can here ; by 10.17 we are all in our normal condition of bedraggled saturation, and plodding down carefully and cheerfully among the rocks and roots of the forest, following the path we have beaten and cut for ourselves on our way up. It is dangerously slippery, particularly that part of it through the amomums, and stumps of the cut amomums are very likely to spike your legs badly—and, my friend, never, never, step on one of the amomum stems lying straight in front of you, particularly when they are soaking wet. Ice slides are nothing to them, and when you fall, as you inevitably must, because all the things you grab hold of are either rotten, or as brittle as Salviati glass-ware vases, you hurt yourself in no end of places on those aforesaid cut amomum stumps. I am speaking from sad experiences of my own, amplified by observations on the experiences of my men.

The path, when we get down again into the tree-fern region is inches deep in mud and water, and several places where we have a drop of five feet or so over lumps of rock are worse work going down than we found them going up, especially when we have to drop down on to amomum stems. One abominable place, a V-shaped hollow, mud-lined, and with an immense tree right across it—a tree one of our tornadoes has thrown down since we passed—bothers the men badly, as they slip and scramble down, and then crawl under the tree and slip and scramble up with their loads. I say nothing about myself. I just take a flying slide of twenty feet or so and shoot flump under the tree on my back, and then deliberate whether it is worth while getting up again to go on with such a world ; but vanity forbids my dying like a dog in a ditch, and I scramble up, rejoining the others where they are standing on a cross-path : our path going S.E. by E., the other S.S.W. Two men have already gone down the S.W. one, which I feel sure is the upper end of the path Sasu had led us to and wasted time on our first day's march ; the middle regions of which were, as we had found from its lower end, impassable with vegetation. So after futile attempts to call the other two back, we go on down the S.E. one, and get shortly into a plantation of giant kokos mid-leg deep in most excellent fine mould—the sort of stuff you pay 6s. a load for in England to start a conservatory bed with. Upon my word, the quantities of things there are left loose in Africa, that ought to be kept in menageries and greenhouses and not let go wild about the country, are enough to try a saint.

We then pass through a clump of those lovely great tree-ferns. The way their young fronds come up with a graceful curl, like the top of a bishop's staff, is a poem ; but being at present fractious, I will observe that they are covered with horrid spines, as most young vegetables are in Africa. But talking about spines, I should remark that nothing save that precious climbing palm—I never like to say what I feel about climbing palms, because one once saved my life—equals the strong bush rope which abounds here. It is covered with short, strong, curved thorns. It creeps along concealed by decorative vegetation, and you get your legs twined in it, and of course injured. It festoons itself from tree to tree, and when your mind is set on other things, catches you under the chin, and gives you the appearance of having made a determined but ineffectual attempt to cut your throat with a saw. It whisks your hat off and grabs your clothes, and commits other iniquities too numerous to catalogue here. Years and years that bush rope will wait for a man's blood, and when he comes within reach it will have it.

We are well down now among the tree-stems grown over with rich soft green moss and delicate filmy-ferns. I should think that for a botanist these south-eastern slopes of Mungo Mah Lobeh would be the happiest hunting grounds in all West Africa.

The vegetation here is at the point of its supreme luxuriance, owing to the richness of the soil; the leaves of trees and plants I recognise as having seen elsewhere are here far larger, and the undergrowth particularly is more rich and varied, far and away. Ferns seem to find here a veritable paradise. Everything, in fact, is growing at its best. I dare say a friend of mine who told me that near Victoria he had stuck his umbrella into the ground one evening, and found in the morning it was growing leaves all up its stick, was overstating the facts of the case; still, if the incident could happen anywhere it would be in this region.

We come to another fallen tree over another hole; this tree we recognise as an old acquaintance near Buea, and I feel disgusted, for I had put on a clean blouse, and washed my hands in a tea-cupful of water in a cooking pot before leaving the forest camp, so as to look presentable on reaching Buea, and not give Herr Liebert the same trouble he had to recognise the white from the black members of the party that he said he had with the members of the first expedition to the peak; and all I have got to show for my exertion that is clean or anything like dry is one cuff over which I have been carrying a shawl.

We double round a corner by the stockade of the station's plantation, and are at the top of the mud glissade—the new Government path, I should say—that leads down into the barrack-yard.

In the wild exhilaration the view of the barrack-yard and the official residence gives me, I feel mightily inclined to toboggan down it, but I observe what I imagine to be Society on his verandah, and so forbear. But I find when I reach the verandah I might have done it, for Society was superintending making a back drain for surface water and it

was only Society's washing that was drying from the wash
that had alarmed me.

Our arrival brings Herr Liebert promptly on the scene,
as kindly helpful and energetic as ever, and again anxious
for me to have a bath. The men bring our saturated loads
into my room, and after giving them their food and plenty of
tobacco, I get my hot tea and change into the clothes I had
left behind at Buea, and feeling once more fit for polite
society, go out and find his Imperial and Royal Majesty's
representative making a door, tightening the boards up with
wedges in a very artful and professional way. We discourse
on things in general and the mountain in particular. The
great south-east face is now showing clear before us, the
clearness that usually comes before nightfall. It looks again
a vast wall, and I wish I were going up it again to-morrow.
When "the Calabar major" set it on fire in the dry season it
must have been a noble sight, and it is small wonder
Cameroons thought "die grosse Kolonie" was going to be
Pompeied by an awful eruption from "der grossen Kolonie
am grössten feuerspeienden Berg."

The north-eastern edge of the slope of the mountain seems
to me unbroken up to the peak. The great crater we went
and camped in must be a very early one in the history of the
mountain, and out of it the present summit seems to have
been thrown up. From the sea face, the western, I am told the
slope is continuous on the whole, although there are several
craters on that side ; seventy craters all told are so far known
on Mungo.

The last reported eruption was in 1852, when signs of
volcanic activity were observed by a captain who was passing
at sea. The lava from this eruption must have gone down
the western side, for I have come across no fresh lava beds in my
wanderings on the other face. Herr Liebert has no confidence
in the mountain whatsoever, and announces his intention of
leaving Buea with the army on the first symptom of renewed
volcanic activity. I attempt to discourage him from this
energetic plan, pointing out to him the beauty of that Roman
soldier at Pompeii who was found, centuries after that
eruption, still at his post ; and if he regards that as merely

mechanical virtue, why not pursue the plan of the elder Pliny ? Herr Liebert planes away at his door, and says it's not in his orders to make scientific observations on volcanoes in a state of eruption. When it is he'll do so—until it is, he most decidedly will not. He adds Pliny was an admiral and sailors are always as curious as cats.

Buea seems a sporting place for weather even without volcanic eruptions, during the whole tornado season (there are two a year), over-charged tornadoes burst in the barrack yard. From the 14th of June till the 27th of August you never see the sun, because of the terrific and continuous wet season downpour. At the beginning and end of this cheerful period occurs a month's tornado season, and the rest of the year is dry, hot by day and cold by night.

They are talking of making Buea into a sanatorium for the fever-stricken. I do not fancy somehow that it's a suitable place for a man who has got all the skin off his nerves with fever and quinine, and is very liable to chill ; but all Governments on the Coast, English, German, or French, are stark mad on the subject of sanatoriums in high places, though the experience they have had of them has clearly pointed out that they are valueless in West Africa, and a man's one chance is to get out to sea on a ship that will take him outside the three-mile-deep fever-belt of the coast. I hear grand accounts of other people who have gone up the peak, or tried to ; I gather most of the failures have been on account of the porters. Herr Leist went up once from Babundi, and once this side. This side he failed because the three boys he had with him nearly died from the cold, and would have done so entirely if he and Herr Yost, who was with him, had not taken a world of trouble to wrap them in blankets, and rub them, and then, on the boys' account, return down. My Head man, Bum, was with Herr Leist when he tried the sea face side from Babundi and he says they turned back then because it was too steep. I am sure the boys collapsed on that side too, if the truth were known. The only point I congratulate myself on is having got my men up so high, and back again, undamaged ; but, as they said, I was a Father and a Mother to them, and a very stern though kind set of parents I have been.

I cannot help thinking how very perfectly Kipling's observations on the 'Oont fit the African carrier, for like the
commissariat camel

> 'E's a devil an' an ostrich an' an orphan child in one.

also

> 'E'll gall and chafe and lame and fight,
> 'E smells most awful vile,
> 'E'll lose hisself for ever, if you let him stray a mile.
> 'E's game to graze the 'ole day long
> And 'owl the ole night through ;
> An' when he comes to greasy ground
> He splits hisself in two.

Volumes upon volumes all illustrated with instantaneous
photographs, and stiff with statistics, couldn't give you a truer
account of him.   For instance there are those two who strayed
down that other path this afternoon, just coming down the
slide in front of us, thank goodness ! for I was making up my
mind it was my pater-maternal duty to go and find them.

Herr Liebert gives me some interesting details about the first
establishment of the station here and a bother he had with the
plantations.   Only a short time ago the soldiers brought him
in some black wood spikes, which they had found with their
feet, set into the path leading to the station's koko plantations, to the end of laming the men.   On further investigation there were also found pits, carefully concealed with
sticks and leaves, and the bottoms lined with bad thorns, also
with malicious intent.   The local Bakwiri chiefs were called in
and asked to explain these phenomena existing in a country
where peace had been concluded, and the chiefs said it was
quite a mistake, those things had not been put there to kill
soldiers, but only to attract their attention, to kill and injure
their own fellow-tribesmen who had been stealing from plantations latterly.   That's the West African's way entirely all
along the Coast ; the " child-like " native will turn out and shoot
you with a gun to attract your attention to the fact that a tribe
you never heard of has been and stolen one of his ladies, whom
you never saw.   It's the sweet infant's way of " rousing up
popular opinion," but I do not admire or approve of it.   If I

am to be shot for a crime, for goodness sake let me commit the crime first.

September 28*th.*—Down to Victoria in one day, having no desire to renew and amplify my acquaintance with the mission station at Buana.   It poured torrentially all the day through. I wonder what it is like here in the wet season ; something rather like the climate of the bed of the Atlantic, I presume.

My boots are a dreadful nuisance to-day.   I got them dried last night for the first time since I left Victoria, and they are like boards.   Xenia brought them to me this morning and I congratulated him on being able to do without boots, but he proudly pointed to his distorted toe-joints, and informed me that once he always wore boots, better boots than mine, and boots that were " all shiny."   I am sure Xenia has had a chequered past ; he is from the Republic of Liberia.   I wonder whether he is a fugitive president or a defaulting bank mana- ger ?   They have copies of all the high points of American culture there, l am told.

The old chief at Buana was very nice to-day when we were coming through his territory.   He came out to meet us with some of his wives.   Both men and women among these Bakwiri are tattooed, or rather painted, on the body, face and arms, but as far as I have seen not on the legs.   The patterns are handsome, and more elaborate than any such that I have seen.   One man who came with the party had two figures of men tattooed on the region where his waistcoat should have been.   I gave the chief some tobacco though he never begged for anything.   He accepted it thankfully, and handing it to his wives preceded us on our path for about a mile and a half and then having reached the end of his district, we shook hands and parted.

After all the rain we have had, the road was of course worse than ever, and as we were going through the forest towards the war hedge, I noticed a strange sound, a dull roar which made the light friable earth quiver under our feet, and I remembered with alarm the accounts Herr Liebert has given me of the strange ways of rivers on this mountain ; how by Buea, about 200 metres below where you cross it, the river goes bodily down a hole.   How there is a waterfall on the south face of the mountain that falls right into another hole, and is never seen again, any more than the Buea River is. How there are in certain places underground rivers, which though never seen can be heard roaring, and felt in the quivering earth under foot in the wet season, and so on. So I judged our present roar arose from some such phenomenon, and with feminine nervousness began to fear that the rotten water-logged earth we were on might give way, and engulf the whole of us, and we should never be seen again. But when we got down into our next ravine, the one where I got the fish and water-spiders on our way up, things explained themselves. The bed of this ravine was occupied by a raging torrent of great beauty, but alarming appearance to a person desirous of getting across to the other side of it. On our right hand was a waterfall of tons of water thirty feet high or so. The brown water wreathed with foam dashed down into the swirling pool we faced, and at the other edge of the pool, striking a ridge of higher rock, it flew up in a lovely flange some twelve feet or so high, before making another and a deeper spring to form a second water-fall. My men shouted to me above the roar that it was "a bad place." They never give me half the credit I deserve for seeing danger, and they said, "Water all go for hole down there, we fit to go too suppose we fall." "Don't fall," I yelled which was the only good advice I could think of to give them just then.

Each small load had to be carried across by two men along a submerged ridge in the pool, where the water was only breast high. I had all I could do to get through it, though assisted by my invaluable Bakwiri staff. But no harm befell. Indeed we were all the better for it, or at all events cleaner. We met five torrents that had to be waded during the day ; none so bad as the first, but all superbly beautiful.

When we turned our faces westwards just above the wood we had to pass through before getting into the great road, the view of Victoria, among its hills, and fronted by its bay, was divinely lovely and glorious with colour. I left the boys here, as they wanted to rest, and to hunt up water, &c., among the little cluster of huts that are here on the right-hand side of the path, and I went on alone down through the wood, and out on to the road, where I found my friend, the Alsatian engineer, still flourishing and busy with his cheery gang of wood-cutters. I made a brief halt here, getting some soda water. I was not anxious to reach Victoria before nightfall, but yet to reach it before dinner, and while I was chatting, my boys came through the wood and the engineer most kindly gave them a tot of brandy apiece, to which I owe their arrival in Victoria. I left them again resting, fearing I had overdone my arrangements for arriving just after nightfall and went on down that road which was more terrible than ever now to my bruised, weary feet, but even more lovely than ever in the dying light of the crimson sunset, with all its dark shadows among the trees begemmed with countless fire-flies—and so safe into Victoria —sneaking up the Government House hill by the private path through the Botanical Gardens.

Idabea, the steward, turned up, and I asked him to let me have some tea and bread and butter, for I was dreadfully hungry. He rushed off, and I heard tremendous operations going on the room above. In a few seconds water poured freely down through the dining-room ceiling. It was bath palaver again. The excellent Idabea evidently thought it was severely wanted, more wanted than such vanities as tea. Fortunately, Herr von Lucke was away down in town, looking after duty as usual, so I was tidy before he returned to dinner. When he returned he had the satisfaction a prophet should feel. I had got half-drowned, and I had got an awful cold, the most awful cold in the head of modern times, I believe, but he was not artistically exultant over my afflictions.

My men having all reported themselves safe I went to my comfortable rooms, but could not turn in, so fascinating was the warmth and beauty down here ; and as I sat on the verandah overlooking Victoria and the sea, in the dim soft light of the stars, with the fire-flies round me, and the lights of Victoria away below, and heard the soft rush of the Lukola River, and the sound of the sea-surf on the rocks, and the tom-tomming and singing of the natives, all matching and mingling together, " Why did I come to Africa ? " thought I. Why ! who would not come to its twin brother hell itself for all the beauty and the charm of it !

CHAPTER XXVIII

THE ISLANDS IN THE BAY OF AMBOISES

Setting forth how the Voyager abandons a noble project, and luxuriates in a port on account of the goodwill of the Viceroy of the Emperor of Germany, with some account of this port, and its islands, and of its foundation, and the futility of sanatoriums in this country, and divers other matters ; ending in the safe return of the Voyager to England.

IT had been my intention when I landed at Victoria either to procure a canoe and go round into that black mud mangrove-swamp-fringed river the Rio del Rey, or to get the Ambas Bay Trading Company to run me round to their trading station in that river on their little steamer. Once in the Rio del Rey I knew I could get a canoe to paddle me through the creek into the Akwayafe river, a fourteen hours' paddle. And then I expected to be able to get up in a canoe to that remarkable gentleman, Mr. Holmes, who, I was confident, would send me round somehow into the Calabar, if I could only make him hear that I wanted to go there.

Had the desire to get myself killed, with which I am constantly being taxed, been my real and only motive for going to West Africa, I should have rigidly adhered to this fine variegated plan, all the more so, because Herr von Lucke said it was highly dangerous during the tornado season to go in the open and deep sea round from Victoria to Rio del Rey in a canoe, because of the violent storms that sweep down suddenly from the mountain and the unhandiness of the native craft. He, with his abiding accuracy regarding statistics and detail, said two in six native canoes so going, got lost with all hands, and he added it would be better for me to go round to Calabar

in the *Nachtigal*, a powerful little guard-ship which acts as the
Governor of Cameroons' yacht. " True, O King ! " I replied,
" but I am not the Governor of Cameroons."   He bowed and
said he knew that, but the *Nachtigal* was in a few days coming
into Victoria on her way to Calabar with Herr von Besser,
who was the German representative on the Calabar-Cameroon
Delimitation Commission, and that he was sure Governor von
Puttkamer would allow me to go round in her.   Previous
experience of the kindness and courtesy of Governor von
Puttkamer made me feel Herr von Lucke was right, and
I gladly accepted this generous offer and proceeded to wait
for the *Nachtigal*, and a very pleasant process this was.

The first day after my return from the mountain, Herr von
Lucke suggested what he called a walk, and what I knew
meant an affair of fourteen miles or so, taken at a good five
miles an hour.   And I, being as stiff as a table-leg, declined.
Then he suggested going to see the islands in the bay in a
boat, and I did not decline, and off we went.

This Bay of Amboises, commonly called Ambas Bay, is
without doubt both the most lovely and the most fertile spot
on the whole of the western side of the continent of Africa ;
and experienced mariners who have wandered far and wide
say that it has few rivals in either quality in any other region
of the world.   To me with my experience of the world strictly
limited to England and West Africa, it is an unthinkable thing
that there can be any place more perfect in loveliness, majesty,
colour and charm, with its circumambient mountains to land-
ward—mountains that rise out of its dark, clear waters to
heights from 3,000 to 13,760 feet.   At their feet is just one
narrow strip of flat shore, on which, nestling among the mango
trees, is the pretty, long, ribbon-like town of Victoria—a soft
brown native town, here and there speckled with a few white
European buildings, while in the bay itself are three islands—
Ambas, Mondoleh and Bobia—and several pinnacle rocks
with energetic acrobats of trees growing in among their clefts
and crevices.

Ambas and Bobia Islands are perfect gems of beauty.
Mondoleh I cannot say I admire.   It always looks to me
exactly like one of those flower-stands full of ferns and plants

—the sort that you come across in drawing-rooms at home,
with wire-work legs. I do not mean that Mondoleh has wire-
work legs under water, but it looks as if it might have. It is
a bunch of crammed-together vegetation, half a mile long,
200 feet high, with rocky but rich soil made of a combination of decomposed rock and decomposed vegetation.
On Mondoleh there is a very nice house, built, I believe, by
that indefatigable consul Sir H. H. Johnston, once of Calabar,
now of East Africa. As long as ever we have held Calabar
it has been regarded as an unhealthy place to live in, so
unhealthy that it was also regarded as a certainty that anywhere else must necessarily be better. At first when consuls
were established there, they and the missionaries used to
think it advisable to leave it during the wet season and go on
to Fernando Po, which island we held up to 1858 as a naval
depot for the suppression of the slave trade. Then Fernando
Po, by means of several epidemics of yellow fever, demonstrated that it could not be regarded as a health resort, and
Mondoleh was selected as a more suitable site for a consular
residence. This house was then built nearly at its summit on the
seaward side of the island, and was used until the Niger Coast
Protectorate was formed under the governorship of Sir Claude
MacDonald. This energetic officer soon recognised that let
the healthiness of Mondoleh be what it might, it was an
inconvenient spot for a consul to have as his chief residence ;
because, for one thing, it was a difficult place to get on to, and
for another a difficult place to get off from, as the only means
of doing either of these things was to wait for a man-of-war
coming along, or to go knocking about this very draughty bit
of rocky Atlantic in an open gig. Also there was not enough
room on it for the enlarged staff and the Haussa troops. So
Sir Claude built the present fine Government head-quarters
in Old Calabar, and not being a man who would leave his
staff to live or die in a place where he would not do so himself, he
disposed of the house at Mondoleh to the German Governor,
who was most anxious to possess it, for it was the only piece
of British territory left in Cameroon, and its acquisition as it
were rounded off the German Empire. It is not now used as
a residence for any one but a black caretaker and his family,

Governor von Puttkamer having a belief in the healthiness of residences open to sea breezes—a belief I do not share. Nor, evidently, did the builder of the residence on Mondoleh, for they are carefully excluded by a dense plantation of gigantic bamboos and heavily-latticed, deep verandahs, making the interior of the house very dark. The landing at Mondoleh also is bad, the water round being deep and the island's sides precipitous and rocky. From the little landing-place there is the most awful sort of staircase made carefully with logs and stone up the steep hill-side to the residence. I shall never forget either going up or coming down those stairs. There is every convenience for taking a headlong dive into the deep Atlantic on one side of it and dense bush on the other, and not two of those steps are either the same height or the same distance apart. A friend of mine who had once tried them assured me it was "exactly like going up the Tower of London when you were drunk." He may have been right, for certainly the steps gave one, in the blazing heat, a feeling of bewilderment after the first dozen or so. When I was there last, the heavy tornado rains had caused a landslip from the top of the island to the bottom, which now shows as a yellow scar, and which nearly swept the staircase clean away.

Ambas Island is the outermost island in the bay. It is smaller and lower than Mondoleh and but little forested. Indeed most of it is only covered with brushwood and grass, for there is not much soil among its rocks. It now belongs to an officer of the *Hyæna*, who won it in a raffle for 500 marks. But although Ambas Island is very beautiful, and so on, I do not think the returns on the invested capital will be high for some years to come. It has no human habitation or inhabitants yet on it, and its population consists of goats and pigs. The most noticeable thing about Ambas Island is the fact that both the English and the Germans have got it arranged wrong on their charts. Bobia is the most interesting of all the three islands. It is on a line with the Pirate rocks. Indeed it is really one of them, only slightly bigger than its neighbours, and it is called sometimes Pirate Island. Its sides are strictly perpendicular, and you can get to the top by a projecting rock ridge which runs up the cliff on the northern

side. I did not go up, for the day I was taken round it the
weather was too rough for us to get to the ledge of rock on
which you land. Strangely enough, this rocky and least fertile
of all the islands in Ambas Bay is densely inhabited by a
quantity of fisher-folk and their wives, families, pigs, and
goats, all living together in a village on the top, facing
seawards. Facing landwards they have made on the top of a
sheer cliff a long bench, on which the fishermen sit in a row
most of the day, watching Victoria, while their wives look
after the rest of the inhabitants and do odd jobs generally,
and I should imagine these good ladies must lead anxious
lives for fear of either the children or the live stock falling
out of the village into the sea. At night Ambas Bay is
dotted all over with the torches of these fishermen, as they
seem to do most of their fishing by spearing, and they are
obliged to be industrious at their profession because among
other inconveniences Bobia has no water, and all the water
has to be bought and brought from the mainland and there is
no room for a plantation. Besides, the pig population is too
heavy to allow of agriculture. I deeply regret not having
been able to bring home a Bobia pig. One would have caused
a profound sensation at the Royal Agricultural Show. These
interesting animals are black in colour, as indeed is common in
African pigs, two-thirds head, and after a very small and very
flat bit of body, end in an inordinately long tail. Their
mental dispositions are lively, frolicsome and extremely
nomadic and predatory. The Chief of Bobia, in a burst of
affection, gave Herr von Lucke one just before I arrived in
Victoria, and a good deal of my time while waiting to start up
Mungo, was spent in assisting Idabea and the steward boys
in chivying this pig. Herr von Lucke had given strict orders
it was to be kept tied up, and solemnly warned his retainers
they were responsible for its safe keeping. But somehow or
another it was always slipping its cable and getting away, and
I used to meet it away in the Botanical Gardens, and in fact
in so many unexpected places that I should not have been
surprised to have met it anywhere. After my first few days' experience of it, whenever I met it I used first to try and secure
it, and then failing brilliantly, post off uphill and report its

iniquities.   All household work would be suspended for the
next hour or so, and finally, after giving good sport, the pig
would be brought back squealing by triumphant and heated
stewards.

When I got back to Victoria one of my first inquiries was
after that Bobia pig.   I instantly saw I had aroused sad
memories, and learnt that the cook—its most responsible custodian—was under arrest, though out on bail—on its behalf. It
seems it got adrift as usual, and when the hunt was started no
pig was to be found, so cook, fearing the ire of Germany, posts
off into the town and gets hold of the first pig there he can
lay hands on.   Now this pig was the property of a lady—a
woman of spirit, and she clouted cook and swore cook
clouted her.   But anyhow cook bore off his prize, and tied it
up in place of the Bobia pig, trusting that his busy master
would not notice the difference in the two pigs, and would not
hear of his raid.   His hopes were vain.   Herr von Lucke saw
that this succulent little porker was not the offering from
Bobia, and with a truly Roman sense of duty, handed his own
cook over to be tried by the native court, presided over by
the Baptist minister and two local chiefs.   The case took
nearly all day, and all the Government House staff had to be
absent from their work, giving evidence as to the character of
the cook, and the pig, and so on.   The case went against cook
in the end, and he had to pay damages to the injured lady and
return his capture.   What became of the original Bobia pig
I do not know, for it had not been found up to the time of
my leaving Victoria.

The problem why so many people choose to reside on this
isolated rock is quite as great as the problem of the whereabouts
of that pig.   Their own explanation is that the people on the
mainland were too bad for respectable people to live among ;
in short, as Mr. Micawber would say, they were driven on to
the island ; but then you can very rarely believe what people
say about themselves in West Africa.   Then the people on
the mainland say that they, the mainlanders, are injured inno-
cents, and that the men of Bobia live on that island so as to
carry on to greater advantage piratical practices : hence the
name Pirate Island that Bobia bears, and that—but then again

you can hardly ever believe what people say about each other in West Africa, so the problem is unsolved.

The Pirate rocks extend S.W. from Bobia Island, and are quite uninhabited. It is possible, at certain states of the tide, in calm weather, to get from Bobia to the nearest one, on which there are a few trees. The next rock has a remarkable hole in it through which the water flies in a great jet, and as the weather was rough the day we were round it, this showed grandly. The others that are above water are mere rocky pinnacles.

These rocks are by no means all the rocks in Ambas Bay, which, like Corisco Bay, though to a far less extent, is not half so good a harbour as it looks on a map.

In 1858 the Spanish Government decided definitely to retake possession of Fernando Po, which had been lent to the English for the purpose of forming a naval depot for suppressing the slave trade, and in May of that year, the Spanish man-of-war *Vasco Nuñez de Balboa* came into Clarence and issued a lengthy proclamation, one article of which was :—" The religion of this colony is that of the Roman Catholic Church, as the only one of the kingdom of Spain, with the exclusion of any other, and no other religious profession is tolerated or allowed but that made by the missionaries of the aforesaid Catholic religion, and no school allowed."

This proclamation, says Mr. Hutchinson, who was then the English consul for the Bights, fell like a bombshell amongst the inhabitants of Clarence, who had been since 1843 under the religious superintendence of the Baptist missionaries, and who, since their first settlement there under Captain Owen in 1827, had considered themselves to be safely under the protection of the British Government, and therefore entitled to perfect liberty of religious worship. A remonstrance was at once made by the Baptists against this proclamation as being contrary " to that liberty of worship decreed and allowed by Don J. O. de Lorena, captain of the Spanish Navy and commander of the brig *Nervion*, in the year 1844, and confirmed by the Spanish Consul-General (the Chevalier Guillemard) in the year 1846." This remonstrance further

entreated that the execution of the foregoing decree should be
delayed until a final appeal could be made to the Queen of
Spain. The commander of the *Balboa*, Don Carlos Chacon,
courteously expressed his readiness to forward this memorial
to his Queen, and this was done ; but things still proving most
unsatisfactory to the Baptists, they decided to leave Clarence
and make a settlement at the foot of Cameroon Mountain, in
Ambas Bay, which was then regarded as British property, and
this settlement they called Victoria. The Baptist missionary
at Clarence in those days was a Mr. Saker, to whom we are
indebted for a great deal of valuable scientific information
about this region, and whose name is still held in great reverence among the native Baptists on the West Coast. This
gentleman with his family and two or three families of the
native members of his church, went to Victoria, acquired a
large stretch of land there—a possession which has been
honourably acknowledged by the present German Government—and built their new church and schools, and to this day
they are the dominant party in Victoria, under the leadership
of Mr. Wilson, who came over when a boy with Mr. Saker.
Mr. Wilson has been appointed as magistrate, and presides
over a bench whose other members are two chiefs ; and before
this bench come all the minor offences of the native population. The Baptists of Victoria have no white minister among
them, but seem a very well-ordered and prosperous body.
They cherish a feeling of grievance against the English for the
way they were first abandoned to the Spaniards and then
handed over to the Germans, but they still profess a sentimental attachment to the English. However, as far as I had
opportunities of judging, they have little to complain of in the
way the German Government have treated them—a very
different line of action to that of the Spanish Government
for the Spaniards virtually confiscated the extensive property which the Baptists had received from the West African
Company at Clarence. The Spanish version of this affair is
that the real criminals were the West African Company, who
had no rights whatsoever to make over the land to the Baptists,
as the land was not theirs to dispose of.

Mr. Saker, when he settled in Ambas Bay, formed a very

high opinion of its value as a harbour, and the high lands
above it as a site for a sanatorium. Mr. MacGregor Laird
communicated to Earl Grey in 1856 a lengthy statement
founded on Mr. Saker's information. Read by the light of
after years this memorandum is highly interesting, although
almost all the asseverations in it have now been proved
fallacious ; for example, Ambas Bay is described as "being
capable of being made a most complete naval station."
Further on as "a good open harbour, accessible at all times to
ships of the largest class and easily descended."

Mr. Saker made a communication to Consul Hutchinson in
June, 1858, in which the advantages of Ambas Bay as a
harbour were set down in detail, but a survey of the bay, made
in 1859 by Commodore Wise, R.N., in H.M.S. *Vesuvius*, did
not prove it to correspond to the description given of it by
the enthusiastic missionaries. One important point in the
bay described in the Reverend Mr. Saker's chart as having
four to six fathoms of water, was found by Mr. Brown,
Master R.N., who had charge of the soundings, to have only
from six to nine feet. And from that day to this people have
gone on discovering pinnacle and shoal rocks in the bay.

I have been now five times into Ambas Bay, and with those
very sporting vessels, the British and African, and the Royal
African steamers, and I have never seen one of them
nestle right up in Morton Cove, as the inner part is
called ; and as for men-o'-war, although their official organ,
the *West Coast Pilot*, says, "the anchorage is excellent
in all parts of Ambas Bay with good holding ground, and a
depth of six to seven fathoms," I have never seen a man-o'-
war such a fool as to act on this statement and come well inside. The *West Coast Pilot* certainly does go on to say, " It
forms a lee shore, and there is an incessant swell," and then
"that the prevalent wind is S.W. to which the bay is quite
open." These later observations may be the things that deter
men-o'-war from coming well inside, and as for the merchant-
men, although they have a sort of genial affection for the
Pilot, they do not trust it, unless its statements agree with
their own personal knowledge.

The *Pilot*, goes on to say, referring to the climate, "From the peculiarity of its situation and from local circumstances, Ambas Bay will probably be found to be one of the most healthy situations on the West Coast of Africa." Now this statement is utterly unsupported by facts, and there are no healthy places on the West Coast of Africa at all, so it cannot be more healthy than others, but it might be less unhealthy, and it is not even that; Ambas Bay, Cameroon River, and Gaboon being the three deadliest spots between Calabar and the Congo.

This idea that Ambas Bay and the mountain-sides of Mungo might give to the fever-smitten West Coast a reliable sanatorium, I have no doubt first arose from Mr. Saker's reports on it, and it is a theory that lives on, floating in air, as it were, after its foundations have been removed by experience, just as that other notion that there are no sharks south of the Congo ; and it is hopeless work to attempt to destroy an idea of this kind. Any amount of sharks may display themselves ostentatiously south of Congo, and any amount of fever occur in Ambas Bay, but the statements survive. I have never been in Ambas Bay without finding severe cases of fever, and during my stay there this last time, the wife of the Basle missionary died of fever, and every one except Herr von Lucke, the head agent of the Ambas Bay Company, and myself, had fever more or less severely. This is reasonable enough when you look at the subject with the light of personal experience of the place. It is exceedingly hot, and exceedingly damp, and the cold winds from the mountains, and the sea-breezes that come into it in the mornings, are conducive to that main pre-disposing cause of an attack of fever—chill.

The idea that a sanatorium might be built high on the mountain, above the so-called fever line—a line that is merely an imaginative figment, for local conditions alter it in every separate place—at first seemed reasonable, but a closer know-ledge of the peculiar meteorological conditions of the great mountain has proved this idea also to be an erroneous one.

A very noble and devoted Scotch gentleman named Thomson, possessed of considerable wealth and anxious to do what he could to aid the mission work of the United Presbyterians in Calabar, came out and did his best to establish a sanatorium where the fever-stricken missionaries from Calabar could come and recruit their health without having to make the voyage home to England.[1] The station he established upon the mountain at the elevation of 3,000 feet is now occupied by a Roman Catholic mission, and their health has been little, if at all, better than that of other Roman Catholics at a lower level. I say other Roman Catholics advisedly, because these missionaries live, as a rule, in a more healthy way than members of other missions in West Africa. The reasons why the upper slopes of Mungo do not afford the healthiness expected of them are many. Chief among them is the exceedingly heavy rainfall. At Babundi, I am told, there was a panic a short time ago among the natives because there was no rain for an entire week, and this extraordinary phenomenon gave rise to the idea that something serious had gone wrong with Nature and that something was going to happen, but a calm business man told me this story must be without foundation, because it has never been dry for a week at Babundi.

The reason of the heavy rainfall and drenching mists which fall on the mountain is that it is surrounded by enormous steaming swamps : to the north by those of the Rio del Rey and Calabar, to the south by those of the Cameroon, Mungo, and Bimbia Rivers, while its superior height catches the heavy, water-laden clouds floating in from the Atlantic. In addition to this, the cold air rushes down its sides in draughts that condense the water in the hot overladen lower layers of the atmosphere.

One hears a great deal in West Africa of the 3,000 feet line as being the limit of the region of malarial fever, but I do not think this is anything more than a theoretical idea, and indeed there are few situations in West Africa besides Mungo, where the theory could be put to the test. Buea, and De Buncha, Mr. Thomson's sanatorium site, are at about this elevation. Buea has not yet had sufficient trial as a health resort to speak of it finally, but the great prevalence there of phagedænic ulcers does not lead one to regard the air

[1] Mr. George Thomson died at Victoria, while engaged on this work, in 1871.

as healthy. Of its climate I have spoken already. Buea, however, has this advantage over De Buncha, that it has a fine water-supply, the finest, indeed as far as is at present known, the only considerable water supply above 2,000 feet on the mountain. When one is in Victoria, particularly in the evening of a hot rainless day, you can see a great band of white mist girdling the mountain where the water-laden hot air rising from the forest and swamps meets the cold air of the upper mountain, which condensing, must cause it to deposit, not only the water, but the exhalations from the swamp lands, and every morning and evening you see great whiffs of mist coming up one of the forests on the foot-hills round Victoria, making the whole district look as if it were ·a great smouldering fire. The difficulty of getting a sick man up to either Buea or De Buncha would at present be great, but granting these difficulties removed, as one will be when the road to Buea is completed, I do not think that when a fever patient got up above the 3,000 feet level he would find much benefit, and he would run great risk of chill and dysentery. I regard this idea of the possibility of finding an elevated situation in West Africa suitable for a sanatorium, as one of the most dangerous the governmental authorities suffer from, for it induces them to build houses in out-of-the-way places, and send men suffering from fever to them to die, robbing the sick man of his great chance of recovery, namely, getting out to sea. The true sanatorium for the Coast would be a hospital vessel attached to each district, but as this is practically impossible, the next best thing would be for the indefatigable Mr. A. L. Jones and Messrs. Elder Dempster to have a special hospital cabin on every one of their vessels. The drawback to this is that getting out to a vessel through the Gold Coast surf would be risky work for a sick man, and in the Rivers the mail steamers have to go from one mangrove swamp river to another, and into places like Forcados, where, owing to Lagos Bar's iniquities, vessels are detained for days, lying idle in the sweltering heat waiting for cargo. Below the Rivers, on the South West-Coast, these objections would only hold to a lesser extent, but then the South-West Coast is by no means so much in need of sanatoriums, and the

white men living there are fewer and more scattered than on
the West Coast or in the Rivers. There is another plan which
might work well for Lagos and the Oil Rivers, and that is to
have hospital hulks anchored outside. The experience of
the French guard-ship *Minerve* seems to show that this would
be a repaying plan, particularly if it were not combined with
the French therapeutic methods,' which have an immense
amount of dash and go in them, and I dare say if a man were
in rude health he might undergo them with little permanent
injury to his constitution.

The next excitement after cruising in the bay was the
arrival of the *Nachtigal* early in the morning. Of course I
packed furiously, and when I was quite ready found her
arrival had nothing to do with going to Calabar ; she had
brought round the Governor from Cameroons, he having been,
I am sorry to say, nearly dead with fever. With him came
my old friend Doctor Plehn, and I heard sad news of the
numbers of bad fever cases in Cameroon River since I had left
it, and the Doctor, who had been anxiously expected here for
some time, flew hither and thither and rapidly repaired the
health of Victoria.

Herr von Puttkamer kindly asked me to breakfast on board
the *Nachtigal*, and confirmed Herr von Lucke's statement
about my being welcome to go round in her to Calabar. He
said as soon as he got back to Cameroons he should be sending her round with the Commissioner.

I had a very pleasant afternoon, and got a good deal of
material for a work on the Natural History of Governors
which I do not intend to publish, but I will just state that all the
West.Coast Governors, whatever may be the nation they
represent, are exceedingly good society. The Governor of
Cameroons I consider the best ; he is the most experienced,
for one thing. He was Governor in Togo before he came to
Cameroons, and also was for some time in Lagos and on the
Niger ; but that is another story, and although a highly diverting one, we will not go into it here. But for fear there should be
a rush of people out from home to enjoy the charms of the
society of West African Governors, I will remark that they
have their faults. They are awfully bad for your clothes. It

is this way : after being in West Africa some little time, particularly if you have been away in the bush, your wardrobe is always in a rarefied state. For example, when in Cameroons I had one dress, and one only, that I regarded as fit to support the dignity of a representative of England, so of course when going to call on the representative of another Power I had to put that dress on, and then go out in open boats to war-ships or for bush walks in it, and equally of course down came tornadoes and rain by the ton. I did not care for the thunder, lightning, or wind. What worried me was the conviction that that precious rain would take the colour out of my costume.

Governor von Puttkamer has a peculiarity not shared by any other Governor on the Coast. He likes the sea, so during breakfast the *Nachtigal* was ordered to steam about the bay, which she energetically did. Fortunately, I like the sea too, or—well ! as it was, the only inconvenience we suffered was getting a heavy shock in the middle of the meal. We thought we had discovered a new rock, but found we had only struck a sleeping whale. What the whale thought I do not know, but it made a considerable fuss and left the bay without a word of apology to the Governor.

The *Nachtigal* left Victoria the next day, it being held too unhealthy a place for the Governor to stay in after his severe illness, and went round to Man-o'-War Bay. And the day after Herr von Lucke took me round to the plantation in Man-o'-War Bay, whereat the Governor was staying for a few days.

Man-o'-War Bay is a very peculiar and charming bay to the south of Ambas, having a narrower inlet and not quite so great a depth as the latter, from which it is separated by a high rocky promontory of hills. I do not think it has been carefully sounded, but there is deep water close alongside its shores, which rise very steeply in densely wooded mountains. The main peculiarity of it is that through a rock wall at its eastern end there is a natural tunnel in the rock, and you can row through this in a boat and then find yourself on another sheet of water which has no other inlet or outlet, and is, if possible, more beautiful than Man-o'-War Bay itself, though much smaller. It would be an exquisite place for smuggling.

On the southern shore of Man-o'-War Bay is a beautiful little quay and landing-place for the grand plantation colloquially known as Frederickshafen, after its energetic custodian. This plantation is the property of a syndicate, the main shareholders being Messrs. Woermann, and its magnificent condition and grand output ought to do much to heal that firm's feelings regarding their great losses over their Gaboon plantation. The house belonging to it is the finest house I know in West Africa. It is built of brick and wood and has the customary deep verandah running round it, but with this important difference, that this verandah is closed in with glazed windows, which prevent the inner rooms from being too dark to work in, and also prevents the verandah from being draughty. On the West Coast these are two dreadful faults in the European-built houses. You cannot imagine what an intolerable gloom and discomfort arises from the usual English sort of house here. The abominable structure is made of corrugated iron, roof and all, with just its skeleton and floors made of wood. Sometimes the under part of the house is closed in and used for stores and offices ; sometimes it is left open, but always the living rooms are on the first floor and open out on to a verandah. The sides of this verandah are usually closed in by venetian shutters with windows at intervals. During the tornado seasons these shutters and windows have to be closed up on an average twice a day. During the wet season they are kept closed most of the six months' spell. Consequently you have to live on the verandah, for the inner rooms are then " as dark as ignorance," and the venetians only keep out a percentage of the rain, and divide the fierce tornado winds into strips which cut into you and give you your death of fever, and send all your papers flying ; while the tornado, or the wet season rain plays like fifty thousand demons on the tom-tom of your corrugated iron roof. Now these things were avoided in the house at Frederickshafen, for when the windows round the verandah were shut, they, being glazed, kept out the wind and let in the light, and the roof was a roof of tiles and not a horrid tin tom-tom affair.

Herr Fredericksky most kindly showed me all over his plantation. When it was first started the cautious planter then in charge planted coffee and oil-palms so as to have something to fall back on should the coffee fail, and to a considerable extent coffee has failed throughout Victoria. It gets afflicted with a sort of blight analogous to honey-dew, and on this honey-dew grows a large black mildew which mats the coffee-berries together and ruins them, although it does not seem to injure the health of the tree much. But cacao flourishes exceedingly in the Victoria district, and has so far got no disease. And so the coffee in this plantation, and in the native plantations round Ambas Bay, is being replaced by cacao, and to such purpose has this plan been followed, that the profit on the latter product exported by the small native growers last year amounted to £1,000 English, and this large plantation ships on an average 400 bags a month. During the two flushes which occur in the year, as many as 600 and 650 bags a month would be shipped ; during the intermediate seasons 200 to 300.

The enterprise with which capital has been expended here, and the judiciousness with which it has been employed, is very remarkable for a West Coast undertaking, wherein, as a general rule, there is usually one without the other, or a notable absence of both.

There are near to the living house large, well-built houses with the proper machinery for drying the cocoa, after it has been properly fermented and washed in another house, that is away at the further end of the plantation where the fermenting house is established, because of a suitable little river ; and wonderful to relate these two sets of houses are connected by an excellent tramway, very carefully and soundly made, and ten times pleasanter and safer to travel on than the Congo Free State Railway. The little cars on which you, or bags of cocoa, sit are pushed by energetic labourers ; a distinct improvement on West African steam-engines. After conscientiously doing the drying and the fermenting sheds, and enjoying the faint but pleasant smell of the mauve-coloured cocoa in heaps on the floors in various states of fermentation, we proceeded to seriously study cacao growing ; and I was taken by the two gigantic German gentlemen over acre after acre of plants in various stages of growth, from those just showing leaf above the ground, to those whose beautiful golden fruit were being gathered by gangs of labourers imported from the Batanga region, the Kru Coast, Sierra Leone and other places. If it had not been for driver ants, I feel sure I should have acquired enough information that afternoon to enable me to go and set up a plantation on my own account and make that plantation pay ; but as it was, I just made a mental note that it was well to cut down your forest to start a clearing with in the middle of the dry season ; then let the trees and bush-wood dry a little ; and then set them on fire. Then, just before the rains, I was to plant three cacao beans in a hole, and I learnt with pleasure that I need not bother to remove the gigantic charred tree-trunks that lay about in a glorious confusion—in fact, it was advisable to leave them, as they afforded shelter for the young plants from an excess of sun ; and also I need not bother about planting my series of three beans in one hole in tidy lines, but might just stick them in, in a general sort of way, wherever I felt disposed. This was a comfort, for how any one was to do otherwise with the ground overlaid with a confused sort of network of trees, from sixty to one hundred feet long and from three to thirty feet in circumference, I don't know. Then when these seedlings had attained a sufficient growth, they were to be carefully transplanted into a cleared piece of ground—a nursery, where they were to be planted in proper rows. Just as we reached the nursery, and my education was flowing on in a peaceful, pleasant stream, forty-eight burning hot pinchers were inserted into me and I knew " joy's short life was overpast " for that afternoon, in other words that I had got into a train of drivers. Resolving to suffer and be strong, I said nothing, and seeing that there were no more of the enemy on the ground immediately round me, I lived my tormentors down, and did my best to keep up an appearance of interest in cacao, but really the only thing that did interest me just then was whether either of my companions had got drivers on them.

They never mentioned drivers. They had a little difference of opinion over coffee disease, and a lengthy discussion on the relative value of white and blue kokos as food-supply for labourers, and one of them talked a little wildly, for him, at moments. But there was no headlong dash for water, surrounded in blue flames of bad language, such as I am accustomed to when a lord of creation gets drivers on him, and I proudly thought that to me alone belonged the glory of quietly living down driver ants, but I subsequently learnt that England had to share this honour in the field of colonial enterprise with Germany ; and so, as Mr. Pepys would say, home to Victoria, in the lovely late afternoon. There was just a doubt, however, for half-an-hour or so, whether we should succeed in rounding the rocky promontory that separates Ambas from Man-o'-War Bay, for the sea had got rough in the mysterious way seas do down here, without any weather reason, and the wind, what there was of it, was dead against us. But although my dress was nearly reduced to the dead level of my other dresses, the thing was done.

The next few days I spent expecting the *Nachtigal*. Of course I had unpacked all my things again and most of them were at the wash, when Idabea rushes into my room saying, " *Nachtigal* kommt," and I packed furiously, and stood by to go aboard, having been well educated by my chief tutor, Captain Murray, on the iniquity of detaining the ship. I hasten to say the lesson on this point I never brought down on myself. I have never robbed a church or committed a murder, so should never dream of plunging into this lowermost depth of crime without a preparatory course of capital offences. When, however, I was packed, I found that it was not the *Nachtigal* which had come in, but the *Hyæna*—the guard-ship of Cameroons River—out for an airing, and as her commander Captain Baham, kindly asked me on board to lunch, I had to unpack again. At lunch I had the honour of meeting the two officers who had first ascended the peak of Cameroon from the south-east face, and I learnt from them many things which would have been of great help to me had I had this honour before I went up, but which were none the less good to know ; and during the whole of their stay in Ambas Bay I received from the *Hyæna* an immense amount of pleasure, courtesy, and kindness, adding to the already great debt in these things I owe to Cameroons—a debt which I shall never forget, although I can never repay it.

The third announcement of the *Nachtigal* proved true, and with my dilapidated baggage I went round in her, under the charge of Herr von Besser, into Old Calabar, where I received every hospitality from Mr. Moore and Mr. Wall, for my good friends Sir Claude and Lady MacDonald had left for England some months previously—for the last time as it turned out, for shortly after his arrival in England Sir Claude was sent as British Minister to Pekin.

When I reached Calabar I found that the *Bakana*, commanded by Captain Porter and having for her chief engineer Mr. Peter Campbell, was expected to come in daily, and being a sister ship to the *Batanga* and so one of the finest boats in the service, I decided to wait for her, going up to say good-bye to Miss Slessor at Okyon during the few days at my disposal.

We had a comfortable voyage up to Sierra Leone, where a gloom fell over the whole ship from the death of the purser, Mr. Crompton. It was one of those terribly, sudden, hopeless cases of Coast fever, so common on the West Coast, where no man knows from day to day whether he or those round him will not, before a few hours are over, be in the grip of malarial fever, on his way to the grave.

APPENDICES

APPENDIX I

TRADE AND LABOUR IN WEST AFRICA

As I am under the impression that the trade of the West African Coast is its most important attribute, I hope I may be pardoned for entering into this subject. My chief excuse for so doing lies in the fact that independent travellers are rare in the Bights. The last one I remember hearing of was that unfortunate gentleman who went to the Coast for pleasure and lost a leg on Lagos Bar. Now I have not lost any portion of my anatomy anywhere on the Coast, and therefore have no personal prejudice against the place. I hold a brief for no party, and I beg the more experienced old coaster to remember that "a looker on sees the most of the game."

First of all it should be remembered that Africa does not possess ready-made riches to the extent it is in many quarters regarded as possessing. It is not an India filled with the accumulated riches of ages, waiting for the adventurer to enter and shake the pagoda tree. The pagoda tree in Africa only grows over stores of buried ivory, and even then it is a stunted specimen to that which grew over the treasure-houses of Delhi, Seringapatam, and hundreds of others as rich as they in gems and gold. Africa has lots of stuff in it; structurally more than any other continent in the world, but it is very much in the structure, and it requires hard work to get it out, particularly out of one of its richest regions, the West Coast, where the gold, silver, copper, lead, and petroleum lie protected against the miner by African fever in its deadliest form, and the produce prepared by the natives for the trader is equally fever-guarded, and requires men of a particular type to work and export it successfully—men endowed with great luck, pluck, patience, and tact.

The first things to be considered are the natural resources of the country. This subject may be divided into two sub-sections—(1) The means of working these resources as they at present stand; (2) The question of the possibility of increasing them by introducing new materials of trade-value in the shape of tea, coffee, cocoa, &c.

With regard to the first sub-division the most cheerful things that there are to say on the West Coast trade can be said; the means of transport being ahead of the trade in all districts save the Gold Coast. I know this is heresy, so I will attempt to explain the matter. First, as regards communication to Europe by sea, the West Coast is extremely well off, the two English lines of steamers managed by Messrs. Elder Dempster, the British African, and the Royal African, are most enterprisingly conducted, and their devotion to trade is absolutely pathetic. Let there be but the least vague rumour (sometimes I have thought they have not waited for the rumour, but "gone in" as an experiment) of a puncheon of oil, or a log of timber waiting for shipment at an out-of-the-world, one house port, one of these vessels will bear down on that port, and have that cargo. In addition to the English lines there is the Woermann line, equally devoted to cargo, I may almost say even more so, for it is currently reported that Woermann liners will lie off and wait for the stuff to grow. This I will not vouch for, but I know the time allowed to a Woermann captain by his owners between Cameroons and Big Batanga just round the corner is eight days.

These English and German lines, having come to a friendly understanding regarding freights, work the Bights of Benin, Biafra, and Panavia, without any rivals, save now and again the vessels chartered by the African Association to bring out a big cargo, and the four sailing vessels belonging to the Association which give an eighteenth-century look to the Rivers, and have great adventures on the bars of Opobo and Bonny.[1] The Bristol ships on the Half Jack Coast are not rivals, but a sort of floating factories, shipping their stuff home and getting it out by the regular lines of steamers. The English and German liners therefore carry the bulk of the trade from the whole Coast. Their services are complicated and frequent, but perfectly simple when you have grasped the fact that the English lines may be divided into two sub-divisions—Liverpool boats and Hamburg boats, either of which are liable when occasion demands to call at Havre. The Liverpool line is the mail line to the more important ports, the Hamburg

[1] The African Association now own two steamers. Alexander Miller Brothers and Co. also charter steamers.

line being almost entirely composed of cargo vessels calling at
the smaller ports as well as the larger.

There is another classification that must be grasped. The
English boats being divided into, firstly a line having its
terminus at Sierra Leone and calling at the Isles do Los;
secondly, a line having its terminus at Akassa ; thirdly, a line
having its terminus at Old Calabar ; fourthly, a line having
its terminus at San Paul de Loanda, and in addition, a direct
line from Antwerp to the Congo, chartered by the Congo Free
State Government. Division 4, the South-westers, are the
quickest vessels as far as Lagos, for they only call at the
Canaries, Sierra Leone, off the Kru Coast, at Accra, and off
Lagos ; then they run straight from Lagos into Cameroons,
without touching the Rivers, reaching Cameroons in twenty-
seven days from Liverpool. After Cameroons they cross to
Fernando Po and run into Victoria, and then work their way
steadily down coast to their destination. Thence up again,
doing all they know to extract cargo, but never succeeding as
they would wish, and so being hungry in the hold when they
get back to the Bight of Benin, they are liable to smell cargo
and go in after it, and therefore are not necessarily the quickest
boats home.

Two French companies run to the French possessions, subsidised by their Government (as the German line is, and as
our lines are not)—the Chargeurs Réunis and the Fraissinet.
The South-west Coast liners of these companies run to
Gaboon and then to Koutonu, up near Lagos, then back to
Gaboon, and down as far as Loango, calling on their way
home at the other ports in Congo Français. They are mainly
carriers of import goods, because they run to time, and on the
South-west Coast unless time has an ameliorating touch of
eternity in it you cannot get export goods off.

Below the Congo the rivals of the English and German
lines are the vessels of the Portuguese line, Empreza
Nacional. These run from Lisbon to the Cape Verde Islands,
thence to San Thomé and Principe, then to the ports of Angola
(Loanda, Benguella, Mossamedes, Ambrizette, &c.), and they
carry the bulk of the Angola trade at present, because of the
preferential dues on goods shipped in Portuguese bottoms.

The service of English vessels to the West Coast is weekly,
to the Rivers fortnightly, to the South-west Coast monthly ;
and it is the chief thing in West Coast trade enterprise that
England has to be proud of.

Any one of the English boats will go anywhere that mortal
boat can go ; and their captains' local knowledge is a thing

England at large should be proud of and the rest of the civilised world regard with awe-stricken admiration. That they leave no room for further development of ocean carriage has been several times demonstrated by the collapse of lines that have attempted to rival them—the Prince line and more recently the General Steam Navigation.

But although the West Coast trader has at his disposal these vessels, he has by no means an easy time, or cheap methods, of getting his stuff on board, save at Sierra Leone and in the Oil Rivers. Of the Gold Coast surf, and Lagos bar I have already spoken, and the Calemma as we call the South-west Coast surf is nearly, if not quite as bad as that on the Gold Coast. Indeed I hold it is worse, but then I have had more experience of it, and it has frequently to be worked in native dug-outs, and not in the well-made surf boats used on the Gold Coast. But although these surf-boats are more safe they are also more expensive than canoes, as a fine £40 or £60 surf-boat's average duration of life is only two years in the Gold Coast surf, so there is little to choose from a commercial standpoint between the two surfs when all is done.

As regards interior transport, the difficulty is greater, but in the majority of the West Coast possessions of European powers there exist great facilities for transport in the network of waterways near the coast and the great rivers running far into the interior.

These waterways are utilised by the natives, being virtually roads ; in many districts practically the only roads existing for the transport of goods in bulk, or in the present state of the trade required to exist. But there is room for more white enterprise in the matter of river navigation ; and my own opinion is that if English capital were to be employed in the direction of small suitably-built river steamers, it would be found more repaying than lines of railway. Waterways that might be developed in this manner exist in the Cross River, the Volta, and the Ancobra. I do not say that there will be any immediate dividend on these river steamboat lines, but I do not think that there will be any dividend, immediate or remote, on railways in West Africa. This question of transport is at present regarded as a burning one throughout the Continent ; and for the well-being of certain parts of the West Coast railways are essential, such as at Lagos, and on the Gold Coast. Of Lagos I do not pretend to speak. I have never been ashore there. Of the Gold Coast I have seen a little, and heard a great deal more, and I think I may safely say that railway making would not be difficult on it, for it is good hard land, not stretches of rotten swamp. The great difficulty in making railroads here will consist in landing the material through the surf. This difficulty cannot be got over, except at enormous expense by making piers, but it might be surmounted by sending the plant ashore on small bar boats that could get up the Volta or Ancobra. When up the Volta it may be said, "it would be nowhere when any one wanted it," but the cast-iron idea that goods must go ashore at places where there are government headquarters like Accra and Cape Coast, places where the surf is about at its worst, seems to me an erroneous one. The landing place at Cape Coast might be made safe and easy by the expenditure of a few thousands in "developing" that rock which at present gives shelter *when* you get round the lee side of it, but this would only make things safer for surf-boats. No other craft could work this bit of beach ; and there is plenty of room for developing the Volta, as it is a waterway which a vessel drawing six feet can ascend fifty miles from July till November, and thirty miles during the rest of the year. The worst point about the Volta is the badness of its bar —a great semicircular sweep with heavy breakers—too bad a bar for boats to cross ; but a steamer on the Lagos bar boat plan might manage it, as the *Bull Frog* reported in 1884 nineteen to twenty-one feet on it, one hour before high water. The absence of this bar boat, and the impossibility of sending goods out in surf-boats across the bar, causes the goods from Adda (Riverside), the chief town on the Volta, situated about six miles up the river from its mouth, to be carried across the spit of land to Beach Town, and then brought out through the shore surf—the worst bit of surf on the whole Gold Coast. The Ancobra is a river which penetrates the interior, through a district very rich in gold and timber and more than sus-pected of containing petroleum. It is from eighty to one hundred yards wide up as far as Akanko, and during the rains carries three and a half to four and a half fathoms, and boats are taken up to Tomento about forty miles from its mouth with goods to the Wassaw gold mines. But the bar of the Ancobra is shallow, only giving six feet, although it is firm and settled, not like that of the Volta and Lagos ; and the Portuguese, in the sixteenth century, used to get up this river, and work the country to a better profit than we do nowadays.

The other chief Gold Coast river, the Bosum Prah, that enters the sea at Chama, is no use for navigation from the sea, being obstructed with rock and rapids, and its bar only carrying two feet; but whether these rivers are used or not for the landing of railroad plant, it is certain that that plant must be landed, and the railways made, for if ever a district required them the Gold Coast does. There has been for some time much talk of the Government constructing a line, and a survey for it has been made, but I believe this survey has not given satisfaction, and a new one is in contemplation. It is to be hoped it will soon enter into the phase of construction, for it is a return to the trade (from which it draws its entire revenue) that the local government owes, and owes heavily; and if our new acquisition of Ashantee is to be developed, it must have a railway bringing it in touch with the coast trade, not necessarily running into Coomassie, but near enough to Coomassie to enable goods to be sold there at but a small advance on Coast prices.

It is an error, easily fallen into, to imagine that the natives in the interior are willing to give much higher prices than the sea-coast natives for goods. Be it granted that they are compelled now to give say on an average seventy-five per cent. higher prices to the sea-coast natives who at present act as middlemen between them and the white trader, but if the white trader goes into the interior, he has to face, first, the difficulty of getting his goods there safely; secondly, the opposition of the native traders who can, and will drive him out of the market, unless he is backed by easy and cheap means of transport. Take the case of Coomassie now. A merchant, let us say, wants to take up from the Coast to Coomassie £3,000 worth of goods to trade with. To transport this he has to employ 1,300 carriers at 1s. 3d. per day a head. The time taken is eight days there, and eight days back, = sixteen days, which figures out at £1,300, without allowing for loss and damage. In order to buy produce with these goods that will cover this, and all shipping expenses, &c., he would have to sell at a far higher figure in Coomassie than he would on the sea coast, and the native traders would easily oust him from the market. Moreover so long as a district is in the hands of native traders there is no advance made, and no development goes forward; and it would be a grave error to allow this to take place at Coomassie, now that we have at last done what we should have done in 1874 and taken actual possession, for Coomassie is a grand position that, if properly managed for a few years, will become a great interior market, attracting to itself the routes of interior trade. It is not now a great centre; because of the oppression and usury which the Kings of Ashantee have inflicted on all in their power, and which have caused Coomassie mainly to attract one form of trade, viz., slaves ; who were used in their constant human sacrifices, and for whom a higher price was procurable here than from the Mohammedan tribes to the north under French sway.   And as for the other trade stuffs, they have naturally for years drained into the markets of the French Soudan ; instead of through such a country as Ashantee, into the markets of the English Gold Coast ; and so unless we run a railroad up to encourage the white traders to go inland, and make a market that will attract these trade routes into Coomassie, we shall be a few years hence singing out " What's the good of Ashantee," and so forth, as is our foolish wont, never realising that the West Coast is not good unless it is made so by white effort.

The new *régime* on the Gold Coast is undoubtedly more active than the old—more alive to the importance of pushing inland and so forth—and a road is going to be made twenty-five feet wide all the way to Coomassie, and then beyond it, which is an excellent thing in its way.   But it will not do much for trade, because the pacification of the country, and the greater security of personal property to the native, which our rule will afford will aid him in bringing his goods to the coast, but not so greatly aid our taking our goods inland, for the carriers will require just as much for carrying goods along a road, as they do for carrying goods along a bush path, and rightly too, for it is quite as heavy work for them, and heavier, as I know from my experience of the governmental road in Cameroon. In such a country as West Africa there can be no doubt that a soft bush path with a thick coating of moss and leaves on it, and shaded from the sun above by the interlacing branches, is far and away better going than a hard, sunny wide road.   This road will be valuable for military expeditions possibly, but military expeditions are not everyday affairs on the Gold Coast ; and it cannot be of use for draught animals, because of the horse-sickness and tsetse fly which occur as soon as you get into the forest behind the littoral region : so it must not be regarded as an equivalent for steam transport, as it will only serve to bring down the little trickle of native trade, and possibly not increase that trickle much.

The question of transport of course is not confined to the Gold Coast.   Below Lagos there is the great river system, towards which the trade slowly drains through native hands to the white man's factories on the river banks, but this trade being in the hands of native traders is not a fraction of what it would become in the hands of white men ; and any mineral wealth there may be in the heavily-forested stretches of country remains unworked and unknown. The difficulty of transport here greatly hampers the exploitation of the timber wealth, it being utterly useless for the natives to fell even a fine tree, unless it is so close to a waterway that it can be floated down to the factory. This it is which causes the ebony, bar, and cam wood to be cut up by them into small billets which a man can carry. The French and Germans are both now following the plan of getting as far as possible into the interior by the waterways, and then constructing railways. The construction of these railways is fairly easy, as regards gradients, and absence of dense forest, when your waterway takes you into the great park-like plateau lands which extend, as a general rule, behind the forest belt, and the inevitable mountain range. The most important of these railways will be that of M. de Brazza up the Sanga valley in the direction of the Chad. When this railway is constructed, it will be the death of the Cameroon and Oil River trade, more particularly of the latter, for in the Cameroons the Germans have broken down the monopoly of the coast tribes, which we in our possessions under the Niger Coast Protectorate have not. The Niger Company has broken through, and taken full possession of a great interior, doing a bit of work of which every Englishman should feel proud, for it is the only thing in West Africa that places us on a level with the French and Germans in courage and enterprise in penetrating the interior, and fortunately the regions taken over by the Company are rich and not like the Senegal "made of sand and savage savages." Where in West Africa outside the Company will you find men worthy as explorers to be named in the same breath with de Brazza, Captain Binger, and Zintgraff?

Some day, I fear when it will be too late, we shall realise the foolishness of sticking down on the sea coast, tidying up our settlements, establishing schools, and drains, and we shall find our possessions in the Rivers and along the Gold Coast valueless, particularly in the Rivers, for the trade will surely drain towards the markets along the line of the French railroad behind them, for the middlemen tribe that we foster exact a toll of seventy-five per cent. on the trade that comes through their hands, and the English Government is showing great signs of an inclination to impose such duties on the only stuff the native cares much for—alcohol—that he will take his goods to the market where he can get his alcohol ; even if he pays a toll to these markets of fifty per cent.

But of this I will speak later, and we will return to the question of transport. Mr. Scott Elliot,[1] speaking on this subject as regarding East African regions, has given us a most interesting contribution based on his personal experience, and official figures. As many of his observations and figures are equally applicable to the West Coast, I hope I may be forgiven for quoting him. His criticism is in favour of the utilisation of every mile of waterway available. He says, regarding the Victoria Nyanza, that "it is possible to place on it a steamer at the cost of £12,677. Taking the cost of maintenance, fuel and working expenses at £1,200 a year (a large estimate) a capital expenditure of £53,000, (£13,000 for the steamer and £40,000 to yield three per cent. interest) would enable this steamer to convey, say thirty tons at the rate of five to ten miles an hour for £1,600 a year. This makes it possible to convey a ton at the rate of a halfpenny a mile, while it would require about £53,000 to build a railway only eighteen miles long."

The Congo Free State railway I am informed, has cost, at a rate per mile, something like eight times this. Further on Mr. Elliot says: "In America the surplus population of Europe, and the markets in the Eastern States have made railway development profitable on the whole, but in Africa, until pioneer work has been done, and the prospects of colonisation and plantation are sufficiently definite and settled to induce colonists to go out in considerable numbers, it will be ruinous to build a long railway line."

I do not quote these figures to discourage the West Coaster from his railway, but only to induce him to get his government to make it in the proper direction, namely, into the interior, where further development of trade is possible. Judging from other things in English colonies, I should expect, if left to the spirit of English (West Coast) enterprise, it would run in a line that would enable the engine drivers to keep an eye on the Atlantic Ocean instead of the direction in which it is high time our eyes should be turned. I confess I am not an enthusiast on civilising the African. My idea is that the French method of dealing with Africa is the best at present. Get as much of the continent as possible down on the map as yours, make your flag wherever you go a sacred thing to the native—a thing he dare not attack. Then, when you have done this, you may abandon the French plan, and gradually develop the trade in an English manner, but not in the English manner à la Sierra

[1] *A Naturalist in Mid Africa*, 1896.

Leone. But do your pioneer work first. There is a very excellent substratum for English pioneer work on our Coasts in the trading community, for trade is the great key to the African's heart, and everywhere the English trader and his goods stand high in West African esteem. This pioneer work must be undertaken, or subsidised by the government as it has been in the French possessions, for the West Coast does not offer those inducements to the ordinary traveller that, let us say, East Africa with its magnificent herds of big game, or the northern frontier of India, with its mountains and its interesting forms, relics, and monuments of a high culture, offer. Travel in West Africa is very hard work, and very unhealthy. There are many men who would not hesitate for a moment to go there, were the dangers of the native savagery the chief drawback ; but they hesitate before a trip which means, in all probability, month after month of tramping through wet gloomy forests with a swamp here and there for a change,[1] and which will, the chances are 100 to 1, end in their dying ignominiously of fever in some wretched squalid village.

Reckless expenditure of money in attempts to open up the country is to be deprecated, for this hampers its future terribly, even if attended with partial success, the mortgage being too heavy for the estate, as the Congo Free State finances show ; and if it is attended with failure it discourages further efforts. What we want at present in West Africa are three or four Bingers and Zintgraffs to extend our possessions northwards, eastwards, and south-eastwards, until they command the interior trade routes. And there is no reason that these men should enter from the West Coast, getting themselves killed, or half killed, with fever, before they reach their work. Uganda, if half one hears of it is true, would be a very suitable base for them to start from, and then travelling west they might come down to the present limit of our West Coast possessions. This belt of territory across the continent would give us control of, and place us in touch with, the whole of the interior trade. A belt from north to south in Africa— thanks to our supineness and folly—we can now never have.

I will now briefly deal with the second sub-division I spoke of some pages back—the possibility of introducing new trade exports by means of cultivating plantations. The soil of

[1] The accounts given by the various members of the Stanley Emin Relief Expedition well describe the usual sort of West African hinterland work, but the forests of the Congo are less relieved by open park-like country than those of the rivers to the north or south. Still the Congo, in spite of this disadvantage, has greater facilities for transport in the way of waterways than is found east of the Cross or Cameroon.

West Africa is extremely rich in places, but by no means so in all, for vast tracts of it are mangrove swamps, and other vast tracts of it are miserably poor, sour, sandy clay.   It is impossible in the space at my disposal to enter into a full description of the localities where these unprofitable districts occur, but you will find them here and there all along the Coast after leaving Sierra Leone.   The sour clay seems to be new soil recently promoted into the mainland from dried-up mangrove swamps, and a good rough rule is, do not start a plantation on soil that is not growing hard-wood forest.   Considerable areas on the Gold Coast, even though the soil is good, are now useless for cultivation, on account of their having been deforested by the natives' wasteful way of making their farms, coupled with the Harmattan and the long dry season.

The regions of richest soil are not in our possessions, but in those of Germany, France, Spain, and Portugal, namely, the Cameroons and its volcanic island series, Fernando Po, Principe, and San Thomé.

The rich volcanic earths of these places will enable them to compete in the matter of plantations with any part of the known world.   Cameroons is undoubtedly the best of these, because of its superior river supply, and although not in the region of the double seasons it is just on the northern limit of them, and the height of the Peak—13,760 feet—condenses the water-laden air from its surrounding swamps and the Atlantic, so that rain is pretty frequent throughout the year.   When within the region of the double seasons just south of Cameroons you have a rainfall no heavier than that of the Rivers, yet better distributed, an essential point for the prosperity of such plantations as those of tea and tobacco, which require showers once a month.   To the north of Cameroons there is no prospect of either of these well-paying articles being produced in a quantity, or quality, that would compete with South America, India, or the Malayan regions, and they will have to depend in the matter of plantations on coffee and cacao. Below Cameroons, Congo Français possesses the richest soil and an excellently arranged climate.   The lower Congo soil is bad and poor close to the river.   Kacongo, the bit of Portuguese territory to the north of the Congo banks, and that part of Angola as far as the River Bingo, are pretty much the same make of country as Congo Français, only less heavily forested.   The whole of Angola is an immensely rich region, save just round Loanda where the land is sand-logged for about fifty square miles, and those regions to the extreme south and south-east, which are in the Kalahari desert regions.

Coffee grows wild throughout Angola in those districts removed from the dry coast-lands—in the districts of Golongo Alto and Cassengo in great profusion, and you can go through utterly uncultivated stretches of it, thirty miles of it at a time. The natives, now the merchants have taught them its value, are collecting this wild berry and bringing it in in quantities, and in addition the English firm of Newton and Carnegie have started plantations up at Cassengo. The greater part of these plantations consist of clearing and taking care of the wild coffee, but in addition regularly planting and cultivating young trees, as it is found that the yield per tree is immensely increased by cultivation.

Six hundred to eight hundred bags a month were shipped from Ambrizette alone when I was there in 1893, and the amount has since increased and will still further increase when that leisurely, but very worthy little railroad line, which proudly calls itself the Royal Trans-African, shall have got its sections made up into the coffee district. It was about thirty miles off at Ambaca when I was in Angola, but by now it may have got further. However, I do not think it is very likely to have gone far, and I have a persuasion that that railroad will not become trans-African in my day; still it has an "immediate future" compared with that which any other West Coast railway can expect; for besides the coffee, Angola is rich in malachite and gum of high quality, and its superior government will attract the rubber from the Kassai region of the Congo Free State.

In our own possessions the making of plantations is being carried on with much energy by Messrs. Miller Brothers on the Gold Coast,[1] by several private capitalists, including Mr. A. L. Jones of Liverpool, at Lagos ; by the Royal Niger Company in their territory, and by several head Agents in the Niger Coast Protectorate. Sir Claude MacDonald offered every inducement to this trade development, and gave great material help by founding a botanical station at Old Calabar, where plants could be obtained. He did his utmost to try and get the natives to embark on plantation-making, ably seconded by Mr. Billington, the botanist in charge of the botanical station,

---

[1] Export of coffee from the Gold Coast, 1894, given in the Colonial Report on that year published in 1896, was of the value of £1,265 3s. 4d. ; cocoa, £546 17s. 4d. The greater part of this coffee goes to Germany.

Export of coffee from Lagos, given in Colonial Report for 1892, published in 1893, was of the value of £12. No figures on this subject are given in the 1894 report, published in 1896, but I cite these figures to show the delay in publishing these reports by the Colonial Office and the difficulty of getting reliable statistics on West African trade.

who wrote an essay in Effik on coffee growing and cultivation at large for their special help and guidance.   A few
chiefs, to oblige, took coffee plants, but they are not enthusiastic, for the slaves that would be required to tend coffee and
keep it clean, in this vigorous forest region, are more profitably
employed now in preparing palm oil.

Of the coffee plantation at Man o' War Bay I have already
spoken, and of those in Congo Français, which, although not
at present shipping like the German plantation, will soon be
doing so.   In addition to coffee and cacao attempts are
being made in Congo Français to introduce the Para rubber
tree, a large plantation of which I frequently visited near
Libreville, and found to be doing well.   This would be an
excellent tree to plant in among coffee, for it is very clean and
tidy, and seems as if it would take to West Africa like a duck
to water, but it is not a quick cropper, and I am informed
must be left at least three or four years before it is tapped at
all, so, as the gardening books would say, it should be planted
early.

It is very possible many other trees producing tropical
products valuble in commerce might be introduced successfully into West Africa.   The cultivation of cloves and nutmegs
would repay here well, for allied species of trees and shrubs are
indigenous, but the first of these trees takes a long time before
coming into bearing and the cultivation of the second is a
speculative affair.   Allspice I have found growing wild in several
districts, but in no large quantity.   Cotton with a fine long staple
grows wild in quantities wherever there is open ground, but it
is not cultivated by the natives ; and when attempts have been
made to get them to collect it they do so, but bring it in very
dirty, and the traders having no machinery to compress it like
that used in America, it does not pay to ship.   Indigo is
common everywhere along the Coast and used by the natives for
dyeing, as is also a teazle, which gives a very fine permanent
maroon ; and besides these there are many other dyes and
drugs used by them—colocynth, datura soap bark, cardam-
mom, ginger, peppers, strophanthus, nux vomica, &c., &c., but
the difficulty of getting these things brought in to the traders
in sufficient quantities prevents their being exported to any
considerable extent.   Tea has not been tried, and is barely
worth trying, though there is little doubt it would grow in
Cameroons and Congo Français where it would have an
excellent climate and pretty nearly any elevation it liked.
But I believe tea has of late years been discovered to be
like coffee, not such a stickler for elevation as it used to

be thought, merely requiring not to have its roots in standing water.

Vanilla grows with great luxuriance in Cameroons. In Victoria a grove of gigantic cacao trees is heavily overgrown with this lovely orchid in a most perfect way. It does not seem to injure the cacaos in the least, and there are other kinds of trees it will take equally well to. I saw it growing happily and luxuriantly under the direction of the Roman Catholic Mission at Landana ; but it requires a continuously damp climate. Vanilla when once started gives little or no trouble, and its pods do not require any very careful manipulation before sending to Europe, and this is a very important point, for a great hindrance—*the* great hindrance to plantation enterprise on the Coast—is the difficulty of getting neat-handed labourers. I had once the pleasure of meeting a Dutch gentleman—a plantation expert, who had been sent down the West Coast by a firm trading there, and also in the Malay Archipelago—prospecting, at a heavy fee, to see whether it would pay the firm to open up plantations there better than in Malaysia. I believe his final judgment was adverse to the West African plan, because of the difficulty of getting skilful natives to tend young plants, and prepare the products. Tea he regarded as quite hopeless from this difficulty, and he said he did not think you would ever get Africans at as cheap a rate, or so deftly fingered to roll tea, as you can get Asiatics. No one knows until they have tried it the trouble it is to get an African to do things carefully ; but it is a trouble, not an impossibility. If you don't go off with fever from sheer worry and vexation the thing can be done, but in the meantime he is maddening. I have had many a day's work on plantations instructing cheerful, willing, apparently intelligent Ethiopians of various sexes and sizes on the mortal crime of hoeing up young coffee plants. They have quite seen it. " Oh, Lor ! massa, I no fit to do dem thing." Aren't they ! You go along to-morrow morning, and you'll find your most promising pupils laying around them with their hoes, talking about the disgraceful way their dearest friends go on, and destroying young coffee right and left. They are just as bad, if not slightly worse, particularly the ladies, when it comes to picking coffee. As soon as your eye is off them, the bough is off the tree. I know one planter who leads the life of the Surprise Captain in W. H. S. Gilbert's ballad, lurking among his groves, and suddenly appearing among his pickers. This, he says, has given them a feeling of uncertainty as to when and where he may appear, kassengo and all, that has done much to preserve his plantation ; but it is a wearying life, not what he expected from his book on coffee-plantations, which had a frontispiece depicting a planter seated in his verandah, with a tumblerful of something cool at his right hand, and a pipe in his mouth, contemplating a large plantation full of industrious natives picking berries into baskets on all sides.

LABOUR.—The labour problem is one that must be studied and solved before West Africa can advance much further than its present culture condition, because the climate is such that the country cannot be worked by white labourers; and that this state of affairs will remain as it is until some true specific is discovered for malaria, something important happens to the angle of the earth's axis, or some radical change takes place in the nature of the sun, is the opinion of all acquainted with the region. The West African climate shows no signs of improving whatsoever. If it shows any sign of alteration it is for the worse, for of late years two extremely deadly forms of fever have come into notice here, malarial typhoid and blackwater. The malarial typhoid seems confined to districts where a good deal of European attention has been given to drainage systems, which is in itself discouraging.

The labour problem has been imported with European civilisation. The civilisation has not got on to any considerable extent, but the labour problem has ; for, being a malignant nuisance, it has taken to West Africa as a duck to water, and it is now flourishing. It has not yet, however, attained its zenith ; it is just waiting for the abolition of domestic slavery for that— and then ! Meanwhile it grows with the demand for hands to carry on plantation work, and public works. On the West Coast —that is to say, from Sierra Leone to Cameroon—it is worse than on the South West Coast from Cameroon to Benguella.

The Kruman, the Accra, and the Sierra Leonian are at present on the West Coast the only solution available. The first is as fine a ship-and-beach-man as you could reasonably wish for, but no good for plantation work. The second is, thanks to the practical training he has received from the Basle Mission, a very fair artisan, cook, or clerk, but also no good for plantation work, except as an overseer. The third is a poor artisan, an excellent clerk, or subordinate official, but so unreliable in the matter of honesty as to be nearly reliable to swindle any employer. Lagos turns out a large quantity of educated natives, but owing to the growing prosperity of the colony, these are nearly all engaged in Lagos itself.

An important but somewhat neglected factor in the problem is the nature of the West African native, and as I think a calm and unbiassed study of this factor would give us the satisfactory solution to the problem, I venture to give my own observations on it.

The Kruboys, as the natives of the Grain Coast are called, irrespective of the age of the individual, by the white men— the Menekussi as the Effiks call them—are the most important people of West Africa ; for without their help the working of the Coast would cost more lives than it already does, and would be in fact practically impossible. Ever since vessels have regularly frequented the Bights, the Kruman has had the helpful habit of shipping himself off on board, and doing all the heavy work. Their first tutors were the slavers, who initiated them into the habit, and instructed them in ship's work, that they might have the benefit of their services in working their vessels along the Slave Coast. And in order to prevent any Kruboy being carried off as a slave by mistake, which would have prejudiced these useful allies, the slavers persuaded them always to tattoo a band of basket-work pattern down their foreheads and out on to the tip of their broad noses : this is the most extensive bit of real tattoo that I know of in West Africa, and the Kruboys still keep the fashion. Their next tutors were the traders, who have taught and still teach them beach work ; how to handle cargo, try oil, and make themselves generally useful in a factory, —" learn sense," as the Kruboy himself puts it. To religious teaching the Kruboy seems for an African singularly impervious, but the two lessons he has learnt—ship and shore work—are the best that the white has so far taught the black, because unattended with the evil consequences that have followed the other lessons. Unfortunately, the Kruman of the Grain Coast and the Cabinda of the South West Coast, are the only two tribes that have had the benefit of this kind of education, but there are many other tribes who, had circumstances led the trader and the slaver to turn their attention to them, would have done their tutors quite as much credit. But circumstances did not, and so nowadays, just as a hundred years ago, you must get the Kruboy to help you if you are going to do any work, missionary or mercantile, from Sierra Leone to Cameroon. Below Cameroon the Kruboy does not like to go, except to the beach of an English house, for he has suffered much from the Congo Free State, and from Spaniards and Portuguese, who have not respected his feelings in the matter of wanting to return every year, or every two years at the most, to his own country, and his rooted aversion to agricultural work and carrying loads about the bush.

The pay of the Kruboy averages £1 a month. There are modifications in the way in which this sum is reached ; for example, some missionaries pay each man £20 a year, but then he has to find his own chop. Some South West Coast traders pay £8 a year, but they find their boys entirely, and well, in food, and give them a cloth a week. English men-of-war on the West African Station have, like other vessels, to take them on to save the white crew, and they pay the Kruboys the same as they pay the white men, *i.e.*, £4 10*s.* a month with rations. Needless to say, men-of-war are popular, although service on board them cuts our friend off from almost every chance of stealing chickens and other things of which I may not speak, as Herodotus would say. I do not know the manner in which men-of-war pay off the Kruboy, but I think in hard cash. In the circles of society I most mix with on the Coast—the mercantile marine and the trading—he is always paid in goods, in cloth, gin, guns, tobacco, gunpowder, &c., with little concessions to his individual fancy in the matter, for each of these articles has a known value, and just as one of our coins can be changed, so you can get here change for a gun or any other trade article.

The Kruboy much prefers being paid off in goods. I well remember an exquisite scene between Captain —— and King Koffee of the Kru Coast when the subject of engaging boys was being shouted over one voyage out. The Captain at that time thought I was a W.W.T.A.A. and ostentatiously wanted Koffee to let him pay off the boys he was engaging to work the ship in money, and not in gin and gunpowder. King Koffee's face was a study. If Captain ——, whom he knew of old, had stood on his head and turned bright blue all over with yellow spots, before his eyes, it would not have been anything like such a shock to his Majesty. "What for good him ting, Cappy ?" he said, interrogation and astonishment ringing in every word. "What for good him ting for we country, Cappy ? I suppose you gib gin, tobacco, gun he be fit for trade, but money——" Here his Majesty's feelings flew ahead of the Royal command of language, great as that was, and he expectorated with profound feeling and expression. Captain ——'s expressive countenance was the battle ground of despair and grief at being thus forced to have anything to do with a traffic unpopular in missionary circles. He however controlled his feelings sufficiently to carefully arrange the due amount of each article to be paid, and the affair was settled.

The somewhat cumbrous wage the Kruboy gets at the end of his term of service, minus those things he has had on account and plus those things he has "found," is certainly a source of great worry to our friend. He obtains a box from the carpenter of the factory, or buys a tin one, and puts therein his tobacco and small things, and then he buys a padlock and locks his box of treasure up, hanging the key with his other ju-jus round his neck, and then he has peace regarding this section of his belongings. Peace at present, for the day must some time dawn when an experimental genius shall arise among his fellow countrymen, who will try and see if one key will not open two locks. When this possibility becomes known I can foresee nothing for the Kruboy but nervous breakdown ; for even now, with his mind at rest regarding the things in his box, he lives in a state of constant anxiety about those out of it, which have to lie on the deck during the return voyage to his home. He has to keep a vigilant eye on them by day, and sleep spread out over them by night, for fear of his companions stealing them. Why he should take all this trouble about his things on his voyage home I can't make out, if what is currently reported is true, that all the wages earned by the working boys become the property of the elders of his tribe when he returns to them. I myself rather doubt if this is the case, but expect there is a very heavy tax levied on them, for your Kruboy is very much a married man, and the elders of his tribe have to support and protect his wives and families when he is away at work, and I should not wonder if the law was that these said wives and families " revert to the State " if the boy fails to return within something like his appointed time. There must be something besides nostalgia to account for the dreadful worry and apprehension shown by a detained Kruboy. I am sure the tax is heavily taken in cloth, for the boys told me that if it were made up into garments for themselves they did not have to part with it on their return. Needless to say, this makes our friend turn his attention to needlework during his return voyage, and many a time I have seen the main deck looking as if it had been taken possession of by a demoniacal Dorcas working party.

Strangely little is known of the laws and language of these Krumen, considering how close the association is between them and the whites. This arises, I think, not from the difficulty of learning their language, but from the ease and fluency

with which they speak their version of our own—Kru-English,
or "trade English," as it is called, and it is therefore unnecessary for a hot and wearied white man to learn "Kru mouth."
What particularly makes me think this is the case is, that I
have picked up a little of it, and I found that I could make a
Kruman understand what I was driving at with this and my
small stock of Bassa mouth and Timneh, on occasions when I
wished to say something to him I did not want generally
understood. But the main points regarding Krumen are well
enough known by old coasters—their willingness to work if
well fed, and their habit of engaging for twelve-month terms
of work and then returning to "we country." A trader who
is satisfied with a boy gives him, when he leaves, a bit of
paper telling the captain of any vessel that he will pay the
boy's passage to his factory again, when he is willing to come.
The period that a boy remains in his beloved "we country"
seems to be until his allowance of his own earnings is expended. One can picture to one's self some sad partings in
that far-away dark land. "My loves," says the Kruboy to
his families, his voice heavy with tears, "I must go. There
is no more cloth, I have nothing between me and an easily-
shocked world but this decayed filament of cotton." And
then his families weep with him, or, what is more likely, but
not so literary, expectorate with emotion, and he tears
himself away from them and comes on board the passing
steamer in the uniform of Gunga Din—nothing much before
and rather less than half of that behind, and goes down Coast
on the strength of the little bit of paper from his white master
which he has carefully treasured, and works like a nigger in the
good sense of the term for another spell, to earn more goods
for his home-folk.

Those boys who are first starting on travelling to work, and
those without books, have no difficulty in getting passages on
the steamers, for a captain is glad to get as many on board as
he can, being sure to get their passage money and a premium
for them, so great is the demand for Kru labour. But even
this help to working the West Coast has been much interfered
with of late years by the action of the French Government in
imposing a tax per head on all labourers leaving their ports on
the Ivory Coast. This tax, I believe, is now removed or much
reduced ; but as for the Liberian Republic, it simply gets its
revenue in an utterly unjustifiable way out of taxing the
Krumen who ship as labourers. The Krumen are no property
of theirs, and they dare not interfere with them on shore ; but
owing to that little transaction in the celebrated Rubber

Monopoly, the Liberians became possessed of some ready cash, which, with great foresight, they invested in two little gun-boats which enabled them to enforce their tax on the Krumen in their small canoes. I do not feel so sympathetic with the Krumen or their employers in this matter as I should, for the Krumen are silly hens not to go and wipe out Liberia on shore, and the white men are silly hens not to——but I had better leave that opinion unexpressed.

The power of managing Kruboys is a great accomplishment for any one working the West Coast. One man will get 20 per cent. more work out of his staff, and always have them cheerful, fit, and ready ; while another will get very little out of the same set of men except vexation to himself, and accidents to his goods ; but this very necessary and important factor in trade is not to be taught with ink. Some men fall into the proper way of managing the boys very quickly, others may have years of experience and yet fail to learn it. The rule is, make them respect you, and make them like you, and then the thing is done ; but first dealing with the Kruboy, with all his good points, is very trying work, and they give the new hand an awful time of it while they are experimenting on him to see how far they can do him. They do this very cleverly, but shortsightedly, *more Africano*, for they spoil the tempers of half the white men whom they have to deal with. It is not necessary to treat them brutally, in fact it does not pay to do so, but it is necessary to treat them severely, to keep a steady hand over them. Never let them become familiar, never let them see you have made a mistake. When you make a mistake in giving them an order let it be understood that that way of doing a thing is a peculiarly artful dodge of your own, and if it fails, that it is their fault. They will quite realise this if it is properly managed. I speak from experience ; for example, once, owing to the superior sex being on its back with fever and sending its temperature up with worrying about getting some ebony logs off to a bothering wretch of a river steamer that must needs come yelling along for cargo just then, I said, "You leave it to me, I'll get it shipped all right," and proceeded, with the help of three Kruboys, to raft that ebony off. I saw as soon as I had embarked on the affair, from the Kruboys' manner, I was down the wrong path, but how, or why, I did not see until a neat arrangement of ebony billets tied together with tie-tie was in the water. Then I saw that I had constructed an excellent sounding apparatus for finding out the depth of water in the river ; and that ebony had an affinity for the bottom of water, not for the top. The situation was a trying one and the way the captain of the vessel kept dancing about his deck saying things in a foreign tongue, but quite comprehensible, was distracting ; but I did not devote myself to giving him the information he asked for, as to what particular kind of idiot I was, because he was neither a mad doctor nor an ethnologist and had no right to the information ; but I put a raft on the line of a very light wood we had a big store of, and this held up the ebony, and the current carried it down to the steamer all right. Then we hauled the line home and sent him some more on the patent plan, but, just to hurry up, you understand, and not delay the ship, a deadly crime, *some* of that ebony went off in a canoe and all ended happily, and the Kruboys regarded themselves as having been the spectators of another manifestation of white intelligence. In defence of the captain's observations, I must say he could not see me because I was deploying behind a woodstack ; nevertheless, I do not mean to say this method of shipping ebony is a good one. I shall not try it again in a hurry, and the situation cannot be pulled through unless you have, as Allah gave me, a very swift current ; and although, *when* the thing went well, I *did* say things from behind the woodstack to the captain, I did not feel justified in accepting his apologetic invitation to come on board and have a drink.

My experiences with Kruboys would, if written in full, make an excellent manual for a new-comer, but they are too lengthy for this appendix. My first experience with them on a small bush journey aged me very much ; and ever since I have shirked chaperoning Kruboys about the West African bush among ticklish-tempered native gentlemen and their forward hussies of wives.

I have always admired men for their strength, their courage, their enterprise, their unceasing struggle for the beyond—the something else, but not until I had to deal with Krumen did I realise the vastness to which this latter characteristic of theirs could attain. One might have been excused for thinking that a man without rates and taxes, without pockets, and without the manifold, want-creating culture of modern European civilisation and education would necessarily have been bounded, to some extent, in his desires. But one would have been wrong, profoundly wrong, in so thinking, for the Kruman yearns after, and duns for, as many things for his body as the lamented Faustus did for his soul, and away among the apes this interesting creature would have to go, at once, if the wanting of little were a crucial test for the determination of the family termed by the scientific world the Hominidæ. Later, when I got to know the Krumen well, I learnt that they desired not only the vast majority of the articles that they saw, but did more—obtained them—at all events some of them, without asking me for them ; such commodities, for example, as fowls, palm wine, old tins and bottles, and other gentlemen's wives were never safe. One of that first gang of boys showed self-help to such a remarkable degree that I christened him Smiles. His name—You-be-d——d—being both protracted and improper, called for change of some sort, but even this brought no comfort to one still hampered with conventional ideas regarding property, and frequent roll-calls were found necessary, so that the crimes of my friend Smiles and his fellows might not accumulate to an unmanageable extent.

This used to be the sort of thing—" Where them Nettlerash lib ? " " He lib for drunk, Massa." " Where them Smiles ? " " He lib for town, for steal, Massa." " Where them Black Man Misery ? " But I draw a veil over the confessional, for there is simply no artistic reticence about your Kruman when he is telling the truth, or otherwise, regarding a fellow creature.

After accumulating with this gang enough experience to fill a hat (remembering always " one of the worst things you can do in West Africa is to worry yourself ") I bethought me of the advice I had received from my cousin Rose Kingsley, who had successfully ridden through Mexico when Mexico was having a rather worse revolution than usual, " to always preserve a firm manner." I thought I would try this on those Kruboys and said " NO " in place of " I wish you would not do that, please." I can't say it was an immediate success. During this period we came across a trader's lonely store wherein he had a consignment of red parasols. After these appalling objects the souls of my Krumen hungered with a great desire. " NO," said I, in my severest tone, and after buying other things, we passed on. Imagine my horror, therefore, hours afterwards and miles away, to find my precious crew had got a red parasol apiece. Previous experience quite justified me in thinking that these had been stolen ; and I pictured to myself my Portuguese friends, whose territory I was then in, commenting upon the incident, and reviling me as another instance of how the brutal English go looting through the land. I found, however, I was wrong, for the parasols had been " dashed " my rapacious rascals " for top," and the last one connected with the affair who deserved pity was the trader from whom I had believed them stolen. It was I, not he, who suffered, for it was the wet season in West Africa and those red parasols ran. To this day my scientific soul has never been able to account for the vast body of crimson dye those miserable cotton things poured out, plentifully drenching myself and their owners, the Kruboys, and everything we associated with that day. I am quite prepared to hear that some subsequent wanderer has found a red trail in Africa itself like that one so often sees upon the maps. When they do, I hereby claim that real red trail as mine.

I confess I like the African on the whole, a thing I never expected to do when I went to the Coast with the idea that he was a degraded, savage, cruel brute ; but that is a trifling error you soon get rid of when you know him. The Kruboy is decidedly the most likeable of all Africans that I know. Wherein his charm lies is difficult to describe, and you certainly want the patience of Job, and a conscience made of stretching leather to deal with the Kruboy in the African climate, and live. In his better manifestations he reminds me of that charming personality, the Irish peasant, for though he lacks the sparkle, he is full of humour, and is the laziest and the most industrious of mankind. He lies and tells the truth in such a hopelessly uncertain manner that you cannot rely on him for either. He is ungrateful and faithful to the death, honest and thievish, all in one and the same specimen of him.

Ingratitude is a crime laid very frequently to the score of all Africans, but I think unfairly ; certainly I have never had to complain of it, and the Krumen often show gratitude for good treatment in a grand way. The way those Kruboys of gallant Captain Lane helped him work Lagos Bar and save lives by the dozen from the stranded ships on it and hauled their " Massa " out from among the sharkey foam every time he went into it, on the lifeboat upsetting, would have done credit to Deal or Norfolk lifeboat men, but the secret of their devotion is their personal attachment. They do not save people out of surf on abstract moral principles. The African at large is not an enthusiast on moral principles, and one and all they'll let nature take its course if they don't feel keen on a man surviving.

Half the African's ingratitude, although it may look very bad on paper, is really not so very bad ; for half the time you have been asking him to be grateful to you for doing to, or giving him things he does not care a row of pins about. I have quite his feelings, for example, for half the things in civilised countries I am expected to be glad to get. " Oh, how nice it must be to be able to get about in cars, omnibuses and railway trains again !" Is it? Well I don't think so, and I do not feel glad over it. Similarly, we will take an African case of ingratitude. A white friend of mine put himself to an awful lot of trouble to save the life of one of his sub-traders who had had an accident, and succeeded. It had been the custom of the man's wife to bring the trader little presents of fowls, etc., from time to time, and some time after the accident he met the lady and told her he had noticed a falling off in her offerings and he thought her very ungrateful after what he had done for her husband. She grunted and the next morning she brings in as a present the most forlorn, skinny, one-and-a-half-feathered chicken you ever laid eye on, and in answer to the trader's comments she said : " Massa, fo sure them der chicken no be 'ticularly good chicken, but fo sure dem der man no be 'ticularly good man. They go " (they match each other).

I have referred at great length to the Krumen because of their importance, and also because they are the natives the white men have more to do with as servants than any other ; but methods of getting on with them are not necessarily applicable to dealing with other forms of African labourers, such as plantation hands in the Congo Français, Angola, and Cameroon. In Cameroon the Germans are now using largely the Batanga natives on the plantations ; the Duallas, the great trading tribe in Cameroon River, being too lazy to do any heavy work ; and they have also tried to import labourers from Togo Land, but this attempt was not a success, ending in the revolt of 1894, which lost several white lives. The public work is carried on, as it is in our own colonies, by the criminals in the chain-gang. The Germans have had many accusations hurled against them by people of their own nationality, but on the whole these " atrocities " have been much exaggerated and only half understood ; and certainly have not amounted to anything like the things that have gone on in the " philan-thropic " Congo Free State. The food given out by the German Government is the best Government rations given on the whole West Coast. When they have allowed me to have some of their native employés, as when I was up Cameroon Mountain, for example, I bought rations from the Government stores for them, and was much struck by the soundness and good quality of both rice and beef, and the rations they gave out to those Dahomeyans or Togolanders who revolted was so much more than they could, or cared to eat, that they used to sell much of it to the Duallas in Bell Town. This is not open to the criticism that the stuff was too bad for the Togolanders to eat, as was once said to me by a philanthropic German who had never been to the Coast, because the Duallas are a rich tribe, perfectly free traders in the matter, able to go to the river factories and buy provisions there had they wished to, and so would not have bought the Government rations unless they were worth having. The great point that has brought the Germans into disrepute with the natives employed by them is their military spirit, which gives rise to a desire to regulate everything; and that other attribute of the military spirit, nagging. You should never nag an African, it only makes him bothered and then sulky, and when he's sulky he'll lie down and die to spite you. But in spite of the Germans being over-given to this unpleasant habit of military regularity and so on, the natives from the Kru Coast and from Bassa and the French Ivory Coast return to them time after time for spells of work, so there must be grave exaggeration regarding their bad treatment, for these natives are perfectly free in the matter.

The French use Loango boys for factory hands and these people are very bright and intelligent, but as a M'pongwe, who knew them well, said: "They are much too likely to be devils to be good too much" and are undoubtedly given to poisoning, which is an unpleasant habit in a house servant. Their military force are composed of Senegalese Laptot, very fine, fierce fellows, superior, I believe, as fighting men to our Hausas, and very devoted to, and well treated by, their French officers.

That the Frenchman does not know how to push trade in his possessions, the trade returns, with the balance all on the wrong side, clearly show; still he does know how to get possession of Africa better than we do, and this means he knows how to deal with the natives. The building up of Congo Français for example, has not cost one-third of the human lives, black or white, that an equivalent quantity of Congo Belge has, nor one-third of the expense of Uganda or Sierra Leone. It is customary in England to dwell on the commercial failure, and deduce from it the erroneous conclusion that France will soon leave it off when she finds it does not pay. This is an error, because commercial success— the making the thing pay—is not the French ideal in the affair. It is our own, and I am the last person to say our ideal is wrong; but it is not the French ideal, and I am the last person to say France is wrong either. There may exist half a hundred or more right reasons for doing anything, and the reasons France has for her energetic policy in Africa are sound ones ; for they are the employment of her martial spirits where their activity will not endanger the State, the stowing of these spirits in Paris having been found to be about as advisable as stowing over-proof spirits and gunpowder in a living-room with plenty of lighted lucifers blazing round ; and her other reason is the opportunity African enterprise affords for sound military training. You will often hear in England regarding French annexation in Africa, " Oh ! let her have the deadly hole, and much good may it do her." France knows very well what good it will do her, and she will cheerfully take all she is allowed to get quietly, as a sop for her quietness regarding Egypt, and she will cheerfully fight you for the rest —small blame to her. She knows Africa is a superb training ground for her officers. Sham fights and autumn manœuvres have a certain value in the formation of a fighting army, but the whole of these parlour-games, put together in a ten-year lump, are not to be compared to one month's work at real war, to fit an army for its real work, and France knows well the real work will come some day—not far off—for her army. How soon it comes she little cares, for she has no ideal of Peace before her, never has had, never will have, and the next time she tries conclusions with one of us Teutonic nations, she will be armed with men who have learned their trade well on the burning sands of Senegal, and they will take a lot of beating. We do not require Africa as a training ground for our army ; India is as magnificent a military academy as any nation requires ; but we do require all the Africa we can get, West, East, and South, for a market, and it is here we clash with France ; for France not only does not develop the trade of her colonies for her own profit, but stamps trade at large out by her preferential tariffs, &c. ; so that we cannot go into her colonies and trade freely as she and Germany *can* come into ours. We can go into her colonies and do business with French goods, and this is done ; but French goods are not so suitable, from their make, nor capable of being sold at a sufficient profit to make a big trade. But France throws few obstacles, if any, in the matter of plantation enterprise. Still this enterprise being so hampered by the dearth of good labour is not at the present time highly remunerative in Africa.

FOREIGN LABOUR.—Several important authorities have advocated the importation of foreign labour into Africa. This seems to me to be a fatal error, for several reasons. For one thing, experience has by now fully demonstrated that the West Coast climate is bad for men not native to it, whether those

men be white, black, or yellow. The United Presbyterian
Mission who work in Old Calabar was founded with the intention of inaugurating a mission which, after the white men had
established it, was to be carried on by educated Christian
blacks from Jamaica, where this mission had long been established and flourished. But it was found that these men,
although primarily Africans, had by their deportation from
Africa in the course, in some cases, of only one generation, lost
the power of resistance to the deadly malarial climate their
forefathers possessed, and so the mission is now carried on by
whites ; not that these good people have a greater resistance
to the fever than the Jamaica Christians, but because they are
more devoted to the evangelisation of the African ; and what
black assistance they receive comes with the exception of
Mrs. Fuller, from a few educated Effiks of Calabar.

The Congo Free State have imported as labourers both
West Indian negroes—principally Barbadians—and Chinamen. In both cases the mortality has been terrible—more
than the white mortality, which competent authorities put
down for the Congo at 77 per cent., and the experiment has
therefore failed. It may be said that much of this mortality
has arisen from the way in which these labourers have been
treated in the Free State, but that this is not entirely the
case is demonstrated by the case of the Annamese in Congo
Français, who are well treated. These Annamese are the
political prisoners arising from the French occupation of
Tong-kin ; and the mortality among one gang of 100 of them
who were employed to make the path through swampy
ground from Glass to Libreville—a distance of two and a half
miles—was seventy, and this although the swamp was nothing
particularly bad as swamps go, and was swept by sea-air the
whole way.

Even had the experiment of imported labour been successful for the time being, I hold it would be a grave error
to import labour into Africa. For this reason, that Africa
possesses in herself the most magnificent mass of labour
material in the whole world, and surely if her children could
build up, as they have, the prosperity and trade of the
Americas, she should, under proper guidance and good
management, be able to build up her own. But good guidance and proper management are the things that are
wanted—and are wanting. It is impossible to go into this
complicated question fully here, and I will merely ask unprejudiced people who do not agree with me, whether they
do not think that as so much has been done with one African

tribe, the Krumen—a tribe possessing no material difference in make of mind or body from hundreds of other tribes, but which have merely been trained by white men in a different way from other tribes—that there is room for great hope in the native labour supply? And would not a very hopeful outlook for West Africa regarding the labour question

BRINGING IN RUBBER—CONGO.

be possible, if a *régime* of common sense were substituted for our present one?

This is of course the missionary question—a question which I feel it is hopeless to attempt to speak of without being gravely misunderstood, and which I therefore would willingly shirk mentioning, but I am convinced that the future of Africa is not to be dissociated from the future of its natives by the importation of yellow races or Hindoos ; and the missionary question is not to be dissociated from the future of the African natives ; and so the subject must be touched on ; and I preface my remarks by stating that I have a profound personal esteem for several missionaries, naturally, for it is impossible to know such men and women as Mr. and Mrs. Dennis Kemp, of the Gold Coast, Mme. and M. Jacot, and Mme. and M. Forget, and M. Gacon, and Dr. Nassau, of Gaboon, and many others without recognising at once the beauty of their natures, and the nobility of their intentions. Indeed, taken as a whole, the missionaries must be regarded as superbly brave, noble-minded men who go and risk their own lives, and often those of their wives and children, and definitely sacrifice their personal comfort and safety to do what, from their point of view, is their simple duty ; but it is their methods of working that have produced in West Africa the results which all truly interested in West Africa must deplore ; and one is bound to make an admission that goes against one's insular prejudice— that the Protestant English missionaries have had most to do with rendering the African useless.

The bad effects that have arisen from their teaching have come primarily from the failure of the missionary to recognise the difference between the African and themselves as being a difference not of degree but of kind. I am aware that they are supported in this idea by several eminent ethnologists ; but still there are a large number of anatomical facts that point the other way, and a far larger number still relating to mental attributes, and I feel certain that a black man is no more an undeveloped white man than a rabbit is an undeveloped hare ; and the mental difference between the two races is very similar to that between men and women among ourselves. A great woman, either mentally or physically, will excel an indifferent man, but no woman ever equals a really great man. The missionary to the African has done what my father found them doing to the Polynesians—"regarding the native minds as so many jugs only requiring to be emptied of the stuff which is in them and refilled with the particular form of dogma he is engaged in teaching, in order to make them the equals of the white races." This form of procedure works in very various ways. It eliminates those parts of the native fetish that were a wholesome restraint on the African. The children in the mission school are, be it granted, better than the children outside it in some ways; they display great aptitude for learning anything that comes in their way—but there is a great difference between white and black children. The black child is a very solemn thing. It comes into the world in large quantities and looks upon it with its great sad eyes as if it were weighing carefully the question whether or no it is a fit place for a respectable soul to abide in. Four times in ten it decides that it is not, and dies. If, however, it decides to stay, it passes between two and three years in a grim and profound study — occasionally emitting howls which end suddenly in a sob—whine it never does. At the end of this period it takes to spoon food, walks about and makes itself handy to its mother or goes into the mission school. If it remains in the native state it has no toys of a frivolous nature, a little hoe or a little calabash are considered better training ; if it goes into the school, it picks up, with astonishing rapidity, the lessons taught it there—giving rise to hopes for its future which are only too frequently disappointed in a few years' time. It is not until he reaches years of indiscretion that the African becomes joyful ; but, when he attains this age he always does cheer up considerably, and then, whatever his previous training may have been, he takes to what Mr. Kipling calls " boot" with great avidity—and of this he consumes an enormous quantity. For the next sixteen years, barring accidents, he "rips" ; he rips carefully, terrified by his many fetish restrictions, if he is a pagan ; but if he is in that partially converted state you usually find him in when trouble has been taken with his soul—then he rips unrestrained.

It is most unfair to describe Africans in this state as "converted," either in missionary reports or in attacks on them. They are not converted in the least. A really converted African is a very beautiful form of Christian ; but those Africans who are the chief mainstay of missionary reports and who afford such material for the scoffer thereat, have merely had the restraint of fear removed from their minds in the mission school without the greater restraint of love being put in its place.

The missionary-made man is the curse of the Coast, and you find him in European clothes and without, all the way down from Sierra Leone to Loanda. The pagans despise him, the whites hate him, still he thinks enough of himself to keep him comfortable. His conceit is marvellous, nothing equals it except perhaps that of the individual rife among us which the *Saturday Review* once aptly described as " the suburban agnostic " ; and the missionary man is very much like the suburban agnostic in his religious method. After a period of mission-school life he returns to his country-fashion, and deals with the fetish connected with it very much in the same way as the suburban agnostic deals with his religion, *i.e.*, he removes from it all the inconvenient portions. " Shouldn't wonder if there might be something in the idea of the immortality of the soul, and a future Heaven, you know—but as for Hell, my dear sir, that's rank superstition, no one believes in it now, and as for Sabbath-keeping and food-restrictions—what utter rubbish for enlightened people ! "   So the backsliding African deals with his country-fashion ideas : he eliminates from them the idea of immediate retribution, &c., and keeps the polygamy and the dances, and all the lazy, hazy-minded native ways. The education he has received at the mission school in reading and writing fits him for a commercial career, and as every African is a born trader he embarks on it, and there are pretty goings on !   On the West Coast he frequently sets up in business for himself ; on the South West Coast he usually becomes a sub-trader to one of the great English, French, or German firms.   On both Coasts he gets himself disliked, and brings down opprobrium on all black traders, expressed in language more powerful than select.   This wholesale denunciation of black traders is unfair, because there are many perfectly straight trading natives ; still the majority are recruited from missionary school failures, and are utterly bad.

" *Post hoc non propter hoc* " is an excellent maxim, but one that never seems to enter the missionary head down here. Highly disgusted and pained at his pupils' goings-on, but absolutely convinced of the excellence of his own methods of instruction, and the spiritual equality, irrespective of colour, of Christians ; the missionary rises up, and says things one can understand him saying about the bad influence of the white traders ; stating that they lure the pupils from the fold to destruction.   These things are nevertheless not true.   Then the white trader hears them, and gets his back up and says things about the effect of missionary training on the African, which are true, but harsh, because it is not the missionaries' intent to turn out skilful forgers, and unmitigated liars, although they practically do so.   My share when I drop in on this state of mutual recrimination is to get myself into hot water with both parties.   The missionary thinks me misguided for regarding the African's goings-on as part of the make of the man, and the trader regards me as a soft-headed idiot when I state that it is not the missionary's individual blame that a lamb recently acquired from the fold has gone down the primrose path with the trust, or the rum. Shade of Sir John Falstaff! what a life this is!

The two things to which the missionary himself ascribes his want of success are polygamy, and the liquor traffic. Now polygamy is, like most other subjects, a difficult thing to form a just opinion on, if before forming the opinion you make a careful study of the facts bearing on the case. It is therefore advisable, if you wish to produce an opinion generally acceptable in civilised circles, to follow the usual recipe for making opinions—just take a prejudice of your own, and fix it up with the so-called opinion of that class of people who go in for that sort of prejudice too. I have got myself so entangled with facts that I cannot follow this plan, and therefore am compelled to think polygamy for the African is not an unmixed evil ; and that at the present culture-level of the African it is not to be eradicated. This arises from two reasons ; the first is that it is perfectly impossible for one African woman to do the work of the house, prepare the food, fetch water, cultivate the plantations, and look after the children attributive to one man. She might do it if she had the work in her of an English or Irish charwoman, but she has not, and a whole villageful of African women do not do the work in a week that one of these will do in a day. Then, too, the African lady is quite indifferent as to what extent her good man may flirt with other ladies so long only as he does not go and give them more cloth and beads than he gives her ; and the second reason for polygamy lies in the custom well-known to ethnologists, and so widely diffused that one might say it was constant throughout all African tribes, only there are so many of them whose domestic relationships have not been carefully observed.

As regards the drink traffic—no one seems inclined to speak the truth about it in West Africa ; and what I say I must be understood to say only about West Africa, because I do not like to form opinions without having had opportunities for personal observation, and the only part of Africa I have had these opportunities in has been from Sierra Leone to Angola ; and the reports from South Africa show that an entirely different, and a most unhealthy state of affairs exist there from its invasion by mixed European nationalities, with individuals of a low type, greedy for wealth. West African conditions are no more like South African conditions than they are like Indian. The missionary party on the whole have gravely exaggerated both the evil and the extent of the liquor traffic in West Africa. I make an exception in favour of the late superintendent of the Wesleyan mission on the Gold Coast, the Rev. Dennis Kemp, who had enough courage and truth in him to stand up at a public meeting in Liverpool, on July 2nd, 1896, and record it as his opinion that, "the natives of the Gold Coast were remarkably abstemious; but spirits were, 'he believed,' of no benefit to the natives, and they would be better without them." I have quoted the whole of the remark, as it is never fair to quote half a man says on any subject, but I do not agree with the latter half of it, and the Gold Coast natives are not any more abstemious, if so much so, as other tribes on the Coast. I have elsewhere[1] attempted to show that the drink-traffic is by no means the most important factor in the mission failure on the West Coast, but that it has been used in an unjustifiable way by the missionary party, because they know the cry against alcohol is at present a popular one in England, and it has also the advantage of making the subscribers at home regard the African as an innocent creature who is led away by bad white men, and therefore still more interesting and more worthy, and in more need of subscriptions than ever. I should rather like to see the African lady or gentleman who could be "led away"—all the leading away I have seen on the Coast has been the other way about.

I do not say every missionary on the West Coast who makes untrue statements on this subject is an original liar; he is usually only following his leaders and repeating their observations without going into the evidence around him; and the missionary public in England and Scotland are largely to blame for their perpetual thirst for thrilling details of the amount of Baptisms and Experiences among the people they pay other people to risk their lives to convert, or for thrilling details of the difficulties these said emissaries have to contend with. As for the general public who swallow the statements, I think they are prone, from the evidence of the evils they see round them directly arising from drink, to accept as true—without bothering themselves with calm investigation—statements of a like effect regarding other people. I have no hesitation in saying that in the whole of West Africa, in one week, there is not one-quarter the amount of drunkenness you can see any Saturday night you choose in a couple of hours in the Vauxhall Road; and you will not find in a whole year's investigation on the Coast, one seventieth part of the evil, degradation, and premature decay you

[1] "The Development of Dodos." *National Review*, March, 1896.

can see any afternoon you choose to take a walk in the more densely-populated parts of any of our own towns. I own the whole affair is no business of mine ; for I have no financial interest in the liquor traffic whatsoever. But I hate the preying upon emotional sympathy by misrepresentation, and I grieve to see thousands of pounds wasted that are bitterly needed by our own cold, starving poor. I do not regard the money as wasted because it goes to the African, but because such an immense percentage of it does no good and much harm to him.

It is customary to refer to the spirit sent out to West Africa as " poisonous " and as raw alcohol. It is neither. I give an analysis of a bottle of Van Huytemer's trade-gin, which I obtained to satisfy my own curiosity on the point.

" ANALYSIS OF SAMPLE OF TRADE-GIN.

" With reference to the bottle of the above I have the honour to report as follows :—

It contains—	Per cent.
Absolute alcohol	39·35
Acidity expressed as acetic acid . .	0·0068
Ethers expressed as acetic acid . .	0·021
Aldehydes . . . Present in small quantity.	
Furfural . . . Ditto ditto	
Higher alcohols . . Ditto ditto	

" The only alcohol that can be estimated quantitively is Ethyl Alcohol.

" There is no methyl, and the higher alcohols, as shown by Savalie's method, only exist in traces. The spirit is flavoured by more than one essential oil, and apparently oil of juniper is one of these oils.

" The liquid contains no sugar, and leaves but a small extract. In my opinion the liquid essentially consists of a pure distilled spirit flavoured with essential oils.

" Of course no attempt to identify these oils in the quantity sent, viz., 632 c.c. (one bottle) was made. The ethers are returned as ethyl acetate, but from fractional distillation amyl acetate was found to be present.

" I have the honour to be, &c.,
(Signed) " G. H. ROBERTSON.
" Fellow of the Chemical Society,
" Associate of the Institute of Chemistry."

In a subsequent letter Mr. Robertson observed that he had been "assisted in making the above analysis by an expert in the chemistry of alcohols, who said that the present sample differed in no material particulars from, and was neither more nor less deleterious to health than, gin purchased in different parts of London and submitted to analysis."

In addition to this analysis I have also one of Messrs. Peters' gin, equally satisfactory, and as Van Huytemers and Peters are the two great suppliers of the gin that goes to West Africa, I think the above is an answer to the "poison" statements, and should be sufficient evidence against it for all people who are not themselves absolute teetotalers. Absolute teetotalers are definite-minded people, and one respects them more than one does those who do not hold with teetotalism for themselves, but think it a good thing for other people, and moreover it is of no use arguing with them because they say all alcohol is poison, and won't appreciate any evidence to the contrary, so "palaver done set"; but a large majority of those who attack, or believe in the rectitude of the attack on, the African liquor traffic are not teetotalers and so should be capable of forming a just opinion.

My personal knowledge of the district where most of the liquor goes in—the Oil Rivers—has been gained in Duke Town, Old Calabar. I have been there four separate times, and last year stayed there continuously for some months during a period in which if Duke Town had felt inclined to go on the bust, it certainly could have done so; for the police and most of the Government officials were away at Brass in consequence of the Akassa palaver, and those few who were left behind and the white traders were down with an epidemic of malarial typhoid. But Duke Town did nothing of the kind. I used to be down in the heart of the town, at Eyambas market by Prince Archebongs's house, night after night alone, watching the devil-makings that were going on there, and the amount of drunkenness I saw was exceedingly small. I did the same thing at the adjacent town of Qwa. My knowledge of Bonny, Bell, and Akkwa towns, Libreville, Lembarene, Kabinda, Boma, Banana, Nkoi, Loanda, &c., is extensive and peculiar, and I have spent hours in them when the whole of the missionary and Government people have been safe in their distant houses; so had the evils of the liquor traffic been anything like half what it is made out to be I must have come across it in appalling forms, and I have not.

The figures of the case I will not here quote because they are easily obtainable from Government reports by any one interested in the matter.   I regard their value as being small unless combined with a knowledge of the West Coast trade. The liquor goes in at a few ports on the West Coast, and into the hands of those tribes who act as middlemen between the white trader and the interior trade-stuff-producing tribes ; and is thereby diffused over an enormous extent of thickly inhabited country.   We English are directly in touch with none of the interior trade—save in the territory of the Royal Niger Company, and the Delta tribes with whom we deal in the Oil Rivers subsist on this trade between the interior and the Coast, and they prefer to use spirits as a buying medium because they get the highest percentage of profit from it, and the lowest percentage of loss by damage when dealing with it.   It does not get spoilt by damp, like tobacco and cloth do ; indeed, in addition to the amount of moisture supplied by their reeking climate, they superadd a large quantity of river water to the spirit before it leaves their hands, while with the other articles of trade it is one perpetual grind to keep them free from moisture and mildew.   In their coast towns there are immense stores of gin in cases, which they would as soon think of drinking themselves as we, if we were butchers, would think of eating up the stock in the shop.   A certain percentage of spirit is consumed in the Delta, and if spirits are wanted any-where they are wanted in the Niger Delta region ; and about one-eighth part of that used here is used for fetish-worship, poured out on the ground and mixed with other things to hang in bottles over fish-traps, and so on to make residences for guardian spirits who are expected to come and take up their abode in them.   Spirits to the spirits, on the sweets to the sweet principle is universal in West Africa ; and those photo-graphs you are often shown of dead chiefs' graves with bottles on them merely demonstrate that the deceased was taking down with him a little liquor for his own use in the under world—which he holds to be possessed of a chilly and damp climate—and a little over to give a propitiatory peg to one of the ruling authorities there—or any old friend he may come across in the Elysian fields.   This is possibly a misguided heathen thing of him to do, and it is generally held in European circles that the under-world such an individual as he will go to is neither damp, nor chilly.   But granting this, no one can contest but that the world he spends his life here in is damp, and that the natives of the Niger Delta live in a saturated forest swamp region that reeks with malaria.   Their damp mud-walled houses frequently flooded, they themselves spend the greater part of their time dabbling about in the stinking mangrove swamps, and then, for five months in the year, they are wrapped in the almost continuous torrential downpour of the West African wet season, followed in the Delta by the so-called " dry " season, with its thick morning and evening mists, and the air rarely above dew-point. Then their food is of poor quality and insufficient quantity, and in districts near the coast noticeably deficient in meat of any kind. I think the desire for spirits and tobacco, given these conditions, is quite reasonable, and that when they are taken in moderation, as they usually are, they are anything but deleterious. The African himself has not a shadow of a doubt on the point, and some form of alcohol he will have. When he cannot get white man's spirit—*min makara*, as he calls it in Calabar—he takes black man's spirit *min effik*. This is palm wine, and although it has escaped the abuse heaped on rum and gin, it is worse for the native than either of these, for he has to drink a disgusting quantity of it, because from the palm wine he does not get the stimulating effect quickly as from gin or rum, and the enormous quantity consumed at one sitting will distribute its effects over a week. You can always tell whether a native has had a glass too much rum, or half a gallon or so too much palm wine ; the first he soon recovers from, while the palm wine keeps him a disgusting nuisance for days, and the constitutional effects of it are worse, for it produces a definite type of renal disease which, if it does not cut short the life of the sufferer in a paroxysm, kills him gradually with dropsy. There is another native drink which works a bitter woe on the African in the form of intoxication combined with a brilliant bilious attack. It is made from honey flavoured with the bark of a certain tree, and as it is very popular I had better not spread it further by giving the recipe. The imported gin keeps the African off these abominations which he has to derange his internal works with before he gets the stimulus that enables him to resist this vile climate ; particularly will it keep him from his worst intoxicant lhiamba (*Cannabis sativa*), a plant which grows wild on the South-West Coast and on the West for all I know, as well as the African or bowstring hemp (*Sanseviera guiniensis*). The plant that produces the lhiamba is a nettle-like plant growing six to ten feet high, and the natives collect the tops of the stems, with the seed on, in little bundles and dry them. It is evidently the seeds which are regarded by them as being the important part, although they do not collect these separately ; but you hear great rows among them when buying and selling a little bundle, on the point of the seeds being shaken out, "Chi! Chi! Chi!" says A., "this is worthless, there are no seeds." "Ai, Ai," says B., "never were there so many seeds in a bunch of lhiamba," &c. It is used smoked, like the *ganja* of India, not like the preparation *bhang*, and the way the Africans in the Congo used it was a very quaint one. They would hollow out a little hole in the ground, making a little dome over it ; then in went a few hemp-tops, and on to them a few stones made red hot in a fire. Then the dome was closed up and a reed stuck through it. Then one man after another would go and draw up into his lungs as much smoke as he could with one prolonged deep inspiration ; and then go apart and cough in a hard, hacking distressing way for ten minutes at a time, and then back to the reed for another pull. In addition to the worry of hearing their coughs, the lhiamba gives you trouble with the men, for it spoils their tempers, making them moody and fractious, and prone to quarrel with each other ; and when they get an excessive dose of it their society is more terrifying than tolerable. I once came across three men who had got into this state and a fourth man who had not, but was of the party. They fought with him, and broke his head, and then we proceeded on our way, one gentleman taking flying leaps at some places, climbing up trees now and again, and embedding himself in the bush alongside the path " because of the pools of moving blood on it." ("If it had not kept moving," he said as he sat where he fell—" he could have managed it ")—the others having grand times with various creatures, which, judging from their description of them, I was truly thankful were not there. The men's state of mind, however, soon cleared ; and I must say this was the only time I came across this lhiamba giving such strong effects ; usually the men just cough with that racking cough that lets you know what they have been up to, and quarrel for a short time. When, however, a whiff of lhiamba is taken by them in the morning before starting on a march, the effect seems to be good, enabling them to get over the ground easily and to endure a long march without being exhausted. But a small tot of rum is better for them by far. Many other intoxicants made from bush are known to and used by the witch doctors.

You may say :—Well ! if it is not the polygamy and not the drink that makes the West African as useless as he now is as a developer, or a means of developing the country, what is it ? In my opinion, it is the sort of instruction he has received, not that this instruction is necessarily bad in itself, but bad from being unsuited to the sort of man to whom it has been given. It has the tendency to develop his emotionalism, his sloth, and his vanity, and it has no tendency to develop those parts of his character which are in a rudimentary state and much want it ; thereby throwing the whole character of the man out of gear.

The great inferiority of the African to the European lies in the matter of mechanical idea. I own I regard not only the African, but all coloured races, as inferior—inferior in kind not in degree—to the white races, although I know it is unscientific to lump all Africans together and then generalise over them, because the difference between various tribes is very great. But nevertheless there are certain constant quantities in their character, let the tribe be what it may, that enable us to do this for practical purposes, making merely the distinction between Negroes and Bantu, and on the subject of this division I may remark that the Negro is superior to the Bantu. He is both physically and intellectually the more powerful man, and although he does not christianise well, he does often civilise well. The native officials cited by Mr. Hodgson in his letter to the *Times* of January 4, 1895, as having satisfactorily carried on all the postal and the governmental printing work of the Gold Coast Colony, as well as all the subordinate custom-house officials in the Niger Coast Protectorate—in fact I may say all of them in the whole of the British possessions on the West Coast—are educated Negroes. I am aware that all sea-captains regard this latter class as poisonous nuisances, but then every properly constituted sea-captain regards custom-house officials, let their colour be what it may, as poisonous nuisances anywhere. In addition to these, you will find, notably in Lagos, excellent pure-blooded negroes in European clothes, and with European culture. The best men among these are lawyers, doctors, and merchants, and I have known many ladies of Africa who have risen to an equal culture-level with their lords. On the West African seaboard you do not find the Bantu equally advanced, except among the M'pongwe, and I am persuaded that this tribe is not pure Bantu but of Negro origin. The educated blacks that are not M'pongwe on the Bantu coast (from Cameroons to Benguela), you will find are Negroes, who have gone down there to make money, but this class of African is the clerk class, and we are now concerned with the labourer. The African's own way of doing anything mechanical is the simplest way, not the easiest, certainly not the quickest : he has all the chuckle-headedness of that overrated creature the ant, for his head never saves his heels.

Watch a gang of boat-boys getting a surf-boat down a sandy beach. They turn it broadside on to the direction in which they wish it to go, and then turn it bodily over and over, with structure-straining bumps to the boat, and any amount of advice and recriminatory observations to each other. Unless under white direction they will not make a slip, nor will they put rollers under her. Watch again a gang of natives trying to get a log of timber down into the river from the bank, and you will see the same sort of thing—no idea of a lever, or any thing of that sort—and remember that, unless under white direction, the African has never made an even fourteenth-rate piece of cloth or pottery, or a machine, tool, picture, sculpture, and that he has never even risen to the level of picture-writing. I am aware of his ingenious devices for transmitting messages, such as the cowrie shells, strung diversely on strings, in use among the Yoruba, but even these do not equal the picture-writing of the South American Indians, nor the picture the Red Indian does on a raw elk hide; they are far and away inferior to the graphic sporting sketches left us of mammoth hunts by the prehistoric cave men.

This absence of mechanical aptitude is very interesting, though it most likely has the very simple underlying reason that the conditions under which the African has been living have been such as to make no call for a higher mechanical culture. In his native state he does not want to get heavy surf-boats into the sea; his own light dug-out is easily slid down, he does not want to cut down heavy timber trees, and get them into the river, and so on; but this state is now getting disturbed by the influx of white enterprise, and not only disturbed, but destroyed, and so he must alter his ways or there will be grave trouble; but it is encouraging to remark that the African is almost as teachable and as willing to learn handicrafts as he is to assimilate other things, provided his mind has not been poisoned by fallacious ideas, and the results already obtained from the Krumen and the Accras are good. The Accras are not such good workmen as they might be, because they are to a certain extent spoilt by getting, owing to the dearth of labour, higher wages and more toleration for indifferent bits of work than they deserve, or their work is worth; but they have not yet fallen under that deadly spell worked by so many of the white men on so many of the black—the idea that it is the correct and proper thing not to work with your own hands but to get some underling to do all that sort of thing for you, while you read and write. This false ideal formed by the native from his empirical observations of some of the white men around him, has been the cause of great mischief. He sees the white man is his ruling man, rich, powerful, and honoured, and so he imitates him, and goes to the mission-school classes to read and write, and as soon as an African learns to read and write he turns into a clerk. Now there is no immediate use for clerks in Africa, certainly no room for further development in this line of goods. What Africa wants at present, and will want for the next 200 years at least, are workers, planters, plantation hands, miners, and seamen ; and there are no schools in Africa to teach these things or the doctrine of the nobility of labour save the technical mission-schools. Almost every mission on the Coast has now a technical school just started or having collections made at home to start one ; but in the majority of these crafts such as bookbinding, printing, tailoring, &c., are being taught which are not at present wanted. Still any technical school is better than none, and apart from lay considerations, is of great religious value to the mission indirectly, for there are many instances in mission annals of a missionary receiving great encouragement from the natives when he first starts in a district. At first the converts flock in, get baptised in batches, go to church, attend school, and adopt European clothes with an alacrity and enthusiasm that frequently turns their devoted pastor's head, but after the lapse of a few months their conduct is enough to break his heart. Dressing up in European clothes amuses the ladies and some of the young men for a long time, in some cases permanently, but the older men and the bolder youths soon get bored, and when an African is bored—and he easily is so—he goes utterly to the bad. It is in these places that an industrial mission would be so valuable to the spiritual cause, for by employing and amusing the largely preponderating lower faculties of the African's mind, it would give the higher faculties time to develop. I have frequently been told when advocating technical instruction, that there are objections against it from spiritual standpoints, which, as my own views do not enable me to understand them, I will not enter into. Also several authorities, not mission authorities alone, state with ethnologists that the African is incapable of learning, except during the period of childhood.

Prof. A. H. Keane says—" their inherent mental inferiority, almost more marked than their physical characters, depends on physiological causes by which the intellectual faculties seem to be arrested before attaining their normal development ";

and further on, " We must necessarily infer that the development of the negro and white proceeds on different lines. While with the latter the volume of the brain grows with the expansion of the brain-pan ; in the former the growth of the brain is on the contrary arrested by the premature closing of the cranial sutures, and lateral pressure of the frontal bone." [1] You will frequently meet with the statement that the negro child is as intelligent, or more so, than the white child, but that as soon as it passes beyond childhood it makes no further mental advance. Burton says : " His mental development is arrested, and thenceforth he grows backwards instead of forwards." Now it is nervous work contradicting these statements, but with all due respect to the makers of them I must do so, and I have the comfort of knowing that many men with a larger personal experience of the African than these authorities have, agree with me, although at the same time we utterly disclaim holding the opinion that the African is a man and a brother. A man he is, but not of the same species ; and his cranial sutures do, I agree, close early ; indeed I have seen them almost obliterated in skulls of men who have died quite young ; but I think most anthropologists are nowadays beginning to see that the immense value they a few years since set upon skull measurements and cranial capacity, &c., has been excessive and not to have so great a bearing on the intelligence as they thought. There has been an enormous amount of material carefully collected, mainly by Frenchmen, on craniology, which is exceedingly interesting, but full of difficulty, and giving very diverse indications. Take the weights of brain given by Topinard :—

1	Annamite	. .	1233	grammes
7	African negroes	. .	1238	„
8	African negroes	. .	1289	„
1	Hottentot	. .	1417	„

and I think you will see for practical purposes such considerations as weight of brain, or closure of sutures, &c., are negligible, and so we need not get paralysed with respect for " physiological causes." Moreover I may remark that the top-weight, the Hottentot, was a lady, and that M. Broca weighed one negro's brain which scaled 1,500 grammes, while 105 English and Scotchmen only gave an average of 1,427.

So I think we may make our minds easy on the safety of sticking to outside facts, and say that after all it does not much affect the question of capacity for industrial training in

[1] *Ethnology*, p. 266. A. H. Keane, Cambridge, 1896.

the African if he does choose to close up the top of his head early, and that the whole attempt to make out that the African is a child-form, " an arrested development," is—well, not supported by facts. The very comparison between white and black children's intelligence to the disadvantage of the former is all wrong. The white child is not his inferior ; he is not so quick in picking up parlour tricks ; but then where are either of the children at that alongside a French poodle? What happens to the African from my observations is just what happens to the European, namely, when he passes out of childhood, he goes into a period of hobbledehoyhood. During this period, his skull might just as well be filled inside with wool as covered outside with it. But after a time, during which he has succeeded in distracting and discouraging the white men who hoped so much of him when he was a child, his mind clears up again and goes ahead all right. It is utter rubbish to say "You cannot teach an adult African," and that " he grows backwards " ; for even without white interference he gets more and more cunning as the time goes on. Does any one who knows them feel inclined to tell me that those old palm-oil chiefs have not learnt a thing or two during their lives ? or that a well-matured bush trader has not ? Go down to West Africa yourself, if you doubt this, and carry on a series of experiments with them in subjects they know of—trade subjects—try and get the best of a whole series of matured adults, male or female, and I can promise you you will return a wiser and a poorer man, but with a joyful heart regarding the capacity of the African to grow up. Whether he does this by adding convolutions or piling up his gray matter we will leave for the present. All that I wish to urge regarding the African at large is that he has been mismanaged of late years by the white races. The study of this question is a very interesting one, but I have no space to enter into it here in detail. In my opinion—I say my own, I beg you to remark, only when I am uttering heresy—this mismanagement has been a by-product of the wave of hysterical emotionalism that has run through white culture and for which I have an instinctive hatred.

I have elsewhere briefly pointed out the evil worked by mis directed missionary effort on the native mind,[1] but it is not the missionary alone that is doing harm. The government does nearly as much. Whether it does this because of the fear of Exeter Hall as representing a big voting interest, or whether just from the tendency to get everything into the hands of a

[1] "Development of Dodos," *National Review*, March, 1896.

council, or an office, to be everlastingly nagging and legislating and inspecting, matters little ; the result is bad, and it fills me with the greatest admiration for my country to see how in spite of this she keeps the lead. That she will always keep it I believe, because I believe that it is impossible that this phase of emotionalism—no, it is not hypocrisy, my French friends, it is only a sort of fit—will last, and we shall soon be back in our clear senses again and say to the world, "We do this thing because we think it is right ; because we think it is best for those we do it to and for ourselves, not because of the wickedness of war, the brotherhood of man, or any other notion bred of fear."

The way in which the present ideas acting through the government do harm in Africa are many. English government officials have very little and very poor encouragement given them if they push inland and attempt to enlarge the sphere of influence, which their knowledge of local conditions teaches them requires enlarging, because the authorities at home are afraid other nations will say we are rapacious land-grabbers. Well, we always have been, and they will say it anyhow ; and where after all is the harm in it ? We have acted in unison with the nations who for good sound reasons of their own have cut down Portuguese possessions in Africa because we were afraid of being thought to support a nation who went in for slavery. I always admire a good move in a game or a brilliant bit of strategy, and that was a beauty ; and on our head now lie the affairs of the Congo Free State, while France and Germany smile sweetly, knowing that these affairs will soon be such that they will be able to step in and divide that territory up between themselves without a stain on their character—in the interests of humanity—the whole of that rich region, which by the name of Livingstone, Speke, Grant, Burton, and Cameron, should now be ours.

Then again in commercial competition our attitude seems to me very lacking in dignity. We are now just beginning to know it is a fight, and this commercial war has been going on since 1880—since, in fact, France and Germany have recovered from their war of 1870.

And if we are to carry on this commercial war with any hope of success, we must abandon our "Oh! that's not fair ; I wont play" attitude—and above all we must have no more government restrictions on our foreign trade. In West Africa governmental restriction settles, like dew in autumn, on the liquor traffic. It is a case of give a dog a bad name and

hang him. Moreover, raising the import dues on liquor
may bring into the government a good revenue ; but it is a
short-sighted policy—for the liquor is the thing there is
the best market for in West Africa. The natives have no
enthusiasm about cotton-goods, as they seem from some
accounts to have in East Central, and the supply of them
they now get, and get cheap and good, is as much as they
require. And if the question of the abstract morality of
introducing clothes, or introducing liquor, to native races,
were fairly gone into, the results would be interesting—for
clothing native races in European clothes works badly for them
and kills them off. Indeed the whole of this question of trade
with the lower races is full of curious and unexpected points.
Speaking at large, the introduction of European culture—
governmental, religious, or mercantile—has a destructive
action on all the lower races ; many of them the governmental
and religious sections have stamped right out ; but trade has
never stamped a race out when disassociated from the other
two, and it certainly has had no bad effect in tropical Africa.
With regard to the liquor traffic, try and put yourself in the
West African's place. Imagine, for example, that you want a
pair of boots. You go into a shop, prepared to pay for them,
but the man who keeps the shop says, " My good friend, you
must not have boots, they are immoral. You can have a tin of
sardines, or a pocket-handkerchief, they are much better for
you." Would you take the sardines or the pocket-handkerchiefs ? more particularly would you feel inclined to take
them instead of your desired boots if you knew there was a
shop in a neighbouring street where boots are to be had ?
And there is a neighbouring shop-street to all our West
Coast possessions which is in the hands of either France or
Germany.

I do not for a moment deny that the liquor traffic requires
regulation, but it requires more regulation in Europe than it
does in Africa, because Europe is more given to intoxication.
In Africa all that is wanted is that the spirit sent in should
be wholesome, and not sold at a strength over 45° below
proof. These requirements are fairly well fulfilled already on
the West Coast, and I can see no reason for any further
restriction or additional impost. If further restrictions in the
sale of it are wanted, it is not for interior trade where the
natives are not given to excess, but in the larger coast towns,
where there is a body of natives who are the *débris* of
the disintegrating process of white culture. But even in
those towns like Sierra Leone and Lagos these men are

a very small percentage of the population.[1]   If things are even made no worse for him than they are at present, the English trader may be trusted to hold the greater part of the trade of West Africa for the benefit of the English manufacturers ; if he is more heavily hampered, the English trade will die out, the English trader remain, because he is the best trader with the natives ; but it will be small profit to the English manufacturers because the trader will be dealing in foreign-made stuff, as he is now in the possessions of France and Germany.   English manufacturers, I may remark, have succeeded in turning out the cloth goods best suited for the African markets, but there has of late years been an increase in the quantity of other goods made by foreigners used in the West Coast trade.   The imports from France and Germany and the United States to the Gold Coast for 1894 (published 1896) were £217,388 0s. 1d., the exports £212,320 1s. 3d. ; and the Consular Report (158) for the Gold Coast says that while the trade with the United Kingdom has increased from £1,054,336 17s. 6d. in 1893 to £1,190,532 1s. 3d. in 1894, or roughly 13 per cent., the trade with foreign countries has increased upwards of 22 per cent., namely, from £350,387 3s. 5d. to £429,708 1s. 4d.   In the Lagos Consular Report (No. 150) similar comparative statistics are not given, but the increase at that place is probably greater than on the Gold Coast, as a heavy percentage of the Lagos trade goes through the hands of two German firms ; but this increase in foreign trade in our colonies seems to be even greater in other parts of Africa, for in a Foreign Office Report from Mozambique it is stated, regarding Cape Colony, that "while British imports show an otherwise satisfactory increase, German trade has more than trebled." [2]

There is a certain school of philanthropists in Europe who say that it is not advisable to spread white trade in Africa, that the native is provided by the Bountiful Earth with all that he really requires, and that therefore he should be allowed to live his simple life, and not be compelled or urged to work for the white man's gain.   I have a sneaking sympathy with these good

---

[1] Lagos Annual Consular Report (150, p. 6), 1894 : "There were only three cases of drunkenness. Considering that in the Island of Lagos alone the population is over 33,300, this clearly proves that drunkenness in this part of Africa is uncommon, and that there is insufficient evidence for the contention which is advanced that the native is being ruined by what is so often spoken of as the heinous gin traffic ; it is a well-known fact by those in a position best able to judge by long residence that the inhabitants of this country have a natural repugnance to intemperance."

[2] *Board of Trade Journal*, August 1896.

people, because I like the African in his bush state best ; and one can understand any truly human being being horrified at the extinction of native races in the Polynesian, Melanesian, and American regions.   But still their view is full of error as regards Africa, for one thing I am glad to say the African does not die off as do those weaker races under white control, but increases ; and herein lies the impossibility of accepting this plan as within the sphere of practical politics, most certainly in regard to all districts under white control, for the Bountiful Earth does not amount to much in Africa with native methods of agriculture.   It sufficed when a percentage of the population were shipped to America as slaves ; now it suffices only to help to keep the natives in their low state of culture—a state that is only kept up even to its present level by trade.   The condition of the African native will be a very dreadful one if this trade is not maintained ; indeed, I may say if it is not increased proportionately to the increase of white government control—for this governmental control does many things that are good in themselves, and glorious on paper.   It prevents the export slave trade ; it suppresses human sacrifice ; it stops internecine war among the natives—in short, it does everything save suppress the terrible infant mortality (why it does not do this I need not discuss) to increase the native population, without in itself doing anything to increase the means of supporting this population ; nay, it even wants to decrease these by importing Asiatics to do its work, in making roads, &c.

It may be said there is no fear of the trade, which keeps the native, disappearing from the West Coast, but it is well to remember that the stuff that this trade is dependent on, the stuff brought into the traders' factory by the native, is mainly —indeed, save for the South-West Coast coffee and cacao, we may say, entirely—bush stuff, uncultivated, merely collected and roughly prepared, and it is so wastefully collected by the native that it cannot last indefinitely.   Take rubber, for example, one of the main exports.   Owing to the wasteful methods employed in its collection it gets stamped out of districts.   The trade in it starts on a bit of coast ; for some years so rich is the supply, that it can be collected almost at the native's back door, but owing to his cutting down the vine, he clears it off, and every year he has to go further and further afield for a load.   But his ability to go further than a certain point is prevented by the savage interior tribes not under white control ; and also on its paying him to go on these long journeys, for the price at home takes little notice of his difficulties, because of the more carefully collected supply of rubber sent into the home markets by

South America and India; therefore the native loses, and when he has cleared the districts reachable by him, the trade is finished there, and he has no longer the wherewithal to buy those things which in the days of his prosperity he has acquired a taste for. The Oil Rivers, which send out the greatest quantity of trade on the West Coast possessions, subsist entirely on palm oil for it. Were anything to happen to the oil palms in the way of blight, or were a cheap substitute to be found for palm oil at home, the population of the Oil Rivers, even at its present density, would starve. The development of trade is a necessary condition for the existence of the natives, and the discovery of products in the forests that will be marketable in Europe, and the making of plantations whose products will help to take the place of those he so recklessly now destroys, will give him a safer future than can any amount of abolitions of domestic slavery, or institutions of trial by jury, &c. If white control advances and plantations are not made and trade with the interior is not expanded, the condition of the West African will be a very wretched one, far worse than it was before the export slave-trade was suppressed. In the more healthy districts the population will increase to a state of congestion and will starve. The coast region's malaria will always keep the black, as well as the white, population thinned down, but if deserted by the trader, and left to the government official and the missionary, without any longer the incentive of trade to make the native exert himself, or the resulting comforts which assist him in resisting the climate, which the trade now enables him to procure, the Coast native will sink, *via* vice and degradation, to extinction, and most likely have this process made all the more rapid and unpleasant for him by incursions of the wild tribes from the congested interior.

I do not cite this as an immediate future for the West African, but "a little more and how much it is, a little less and how far away." Remember human beings are under the same rule as other creatures; if you destroy the things that prey on them, they are liable to overswarm the food-producing power of their locality. It may be said this is not the case; look at the Polynesians, the South American Indians, and so on. You may look at them as much as you choose, but what you see there will not enable you to judge the African. The African does not fade away like a flower before the white man—not in the least. Look at the increase of the native in the Cape territory; look at what he has stood on the West Coast. Christopher Columbus visited him before he discovered the

American Indians.   Whaling captains, and seamen of all sorts
and nationalities have dropped in on him " frequent and free."
He has absorbed all sorts of doctrine from religious sects ;
cotton goods, patent medicines, foreign spirits, and—as the
man who draws up the Lagos Annual Colonial Report
poetically observes—twine, whisky, wine, and woollen goods.
Yet the West Coast African is here with us by the million—
playing on his tom-tom, paddling his dug-out canoe, living
in his palm leaf or mud hut, ready and able to stand more
" white man stuff." Save for an occasional habit of going
raving or melancholy mad when educated for the ministry,
and dying when he, and more particularly she, is shut up in
the broiling hot, corrugated-iron school-room with too many
clothes on, and too much headwork to do, he survives in a
way which I think you will own is interesting, and which
commands my admiration and respect.   But there is nowadays a new factor in his relationship with the white races—the
factor of domestic control.   I do not think the African will
survive this and flourish, if it is to be of the nature that the
present white ideas aim to make it.   But, on the other hand, I
do not believe that he will be called upon to try, for under the
present conditions white control will not become very thorough ;
and in the event of a European war, governmental attention will
be distracted from West Africa, and the African will then do
what he has done several times before when the white eye has
been off him for a decade or so,—sink back to his old level as he
has in Kacongo after the Jesuits tidied him up, and as he must
have done after his intercourse with the Phœnicians and
Egyptians.   The travellers of a remote future will find him,
I think, still with his tom-tom in his dug-out canoe—just as
willing to sell as " big curios " the *débris* of our importations
to his ancestors at a high price.   Exactly how much he will
ask for a Devos patent paraffin oil tin or a Morton's tin, I
cannot imagine, but it will be something stiff—like he asks
nowadays for the Phœnician " Aggry " beads.   There will
be then as there is now, and as there was in the past,
individual Africans who will rise to a high level of culture,
but that will be all for a very long period.   To say that the
African race will never advance beyond its present culture-
level, is saying too much, in spite of the mass of evidence
supporting this view, but I am certain he will never advance
above it in the line of European culture.   The country he
lives in is unfitted for it, and the nature of the man himself is all against it—the truth is the West Coast mind
has got a great deal too much superstition about it, and too

little of anything else. Our own methods of instruction have not been of any real help to the African, because what he wants teaching is how to work. Bishop Ingram would have been able to write a more cheerful and hopeful book than his *Sierra Leone after* 100 *Years*, if the Sierra Leonians had had a thorough grounding in technical culture, suited to the requirements of their country, instead of the ruinous instruction they have been given, at the cost of millions of money, and hundreds of good, if ill-advised, white men's lives. For it is possible for a West African native to be made by European culture into a very good sort of man, not the same sort of man that a white man is, but a man a white man can shake hands with and associate with without any loss of self-respect. It is by no means necessary, however, that the African should have any white culture at all to become a decent member of society at large. Quite the other way about, for the percentage of honourable and reliable men among the bushmen is higher than among the educated men.

I do not believe that the white race will ever drag the black up to their own particular summit in the mountain range of civilisation. Both polygamy and slavery are, for divers reasons, essential to the well-being of Africa—at any rate for those vast regions of it which are agricultural, and these two institutions will necessitate the African having a summit to himself. Only—alas! for the energetic reformer—the African is not keen on mountaineering in the civilisation range. He prefers remaining down below and being comfortable. He is not conceited about this; he admires the higher culture very much, and the people who inconvenience themselves by going in for it—but do it himself? NO. And if he is dragged up into the higher regions of a self-abnegatory religion, six times in ten he falls back damaged, a morally maimed man, into his old swampy country fashion valley.

APPENDIX II

DISEASE IN WEST AFRICA

GREAT as is the delay and difficulty placed in the way
of the development of the immense natural resources of
West Africa by the labour problem, there is another cause
of delay to this development greater and more terrible by far
—namely, the deadliness of the climate. " Nothing hinders
a man, Miss Kingsley, half so much as dying," a friend said to
me the other day, after nearly putting his opinion to a practical
test. Other parts of the world have more sensational outbreaks of death from epidemics of yellow fever and cholera,
but there is no other region in the world that can match West
Africa for the steady kill, kill, kill that its malaria works on the
white men who come under its influence.

Malaria you will hear glibly talked of ; but what malaria
means and consists of you will find few men ready to attempt to
tell you, and these few by no means of a tale. It is very strange
that this terrible form of disease has not attracted more
scientific investigators, considering the enormous mortality
it causes throughout the tropics and sub-tropics. A few years
since, when the peculiar microbes of everything from measles
to miracles were being " isolated," several bacteriologists
isolated the malarial microbe, only unfortunately they did not all
isolate the same one. A *résumé* of the various claims of these
microbes is impossible here, and whether one of them was the
true cause, or whether they all have an equal claim to this
position, is not yet clear ; for malaria, as far as I have seen or
read of it seems to be not so much one distinct form of fever
as a group of fevers—a genus, not a species. Many things
point to this being the case ; particularly the different forms
so called malarial poisoning takes in different localities. This
subject may be also subdivided and complicated by going
into the controversy as to whether yellow fever is endemic on
the West Coast or not. That it has occurred there from time

to time there can be no question: at Fernando Po in 1862 and 1866, in Senegal pretty frequently, and at least one epidemic at Bonny was true yellow fever. But in the case of each of these outbreaks it is said to have been imported from South America, into Fernando Po, by ships from Havana, and into Bonny by a ship which had on her previous run been down the South American ports with a cargo of mules. The litter belonging to this mule cargo was not cleared out of her until she got into Bonny, when it was thrown overside into the river, and then the yellow fever broke out. But, on the other hand, South America taxes West Africa—the Guinea Coast—with having first sent out yellow fever in the cargoes of slaves. This certainly is a strange statement, because the African native rarely has malarial fever severely—he has it, and you are often informed So-and-so has got yellow fever, but So-and-so does not often die of it, merely is truly wretched and sick for a day or so, and then recovers.

Regarding the hæmaturia there is also controversy. A very experienced and excellent authority doubts whether this is entirely a malarial fever, or whether it is not, in some cases at any rate, brought on by over-doses of quinine, and Dr. Plehn asserts, and his assertions are heavily backed up by his great success in treating this fever, that quinine has a very bad influence when the characteristic symptoms have declared themselves, and that it should not be given. I hesitate to advise this, because I fear to induce any one to abandon quinine, which is the great weapon against malaria, and not from any want of faith in Dr. Plehn, for he has studied malarial fevers in Cameroon with the greatest energy and devotion, bringing to bear on the subject a sound German mind trained in a German way, and than this, for such subjects, no better thing exists. His brother, also a doctor, was stationed in Cameroon before him, and is now in the German East African possessions, similarly working hard, and when these two shall publish the result of their conjoint investigations, we shall have the most important contribution to our knowledge of malaria that has ever appeared. It is impossible to over-rate the importance of such work as this to West Africa, for the man who will make West Africa pay will be the scientific man who gives us something more powerful against malaria than quinine. It is too much to hope that medical men out at work on the Coast, doctoring day and night, and not only obliged to doctor, but to nurse their white patients, with the balance of their time taken up by giving bills of health to steamers, wrestling with the varied and awful sanitary problems presented by the native town,

&c., can have sufficient time or life left in them to carry on series of experiments and series of cultures, but they can and do supply to the man in the laboratory at home grand material for him to carry the thing through ; meanwhile we wait that man and do the best we can.

The net results of laboratory investigation, according to the French doctors, is that the mycetozoic malarial bacillus, the microbe of paludism, is amœboid in its movements, acting on the red corpuscles, leaving nothing of them but the dark pigment found in the skin and organs of malarial subjects.[1] The German doctors make a practice of making microscopic examinations of the blood of a patient, saying that the microbes appear at the commencement of an attack of fever, increase in quantity as the fever increases, and decrease as it decreases, and from these investigations they are able to judge fairly accurately how many remissions may be expected ; in fact to judge of the severity of the case which, taken with the knowledge that quinine only affects malarial microbes at a certain stage of their existence, is helpful in treatment.

There is, I may remark, a very peculiar point regarding hæmaturic disease, the most deadly form of West Coast fever. This disease, so far as we know, has always been present on the South-West Coast, at Loando, the Lower Congo and Gaboon, but it is said not to have appeared in the Rivers until 1881, and then to have spread along the West Coast. My learned friend, Dr. Plehn, doubts this, and says people were less observant in those days, but the symptoms of this fever are so distinct, that I must think it also totally impossible for it not to have been differentiated from the usual remittent or intermittent by the old West Coasters if it had occurred there in former times with anything like the frequency it does now ; but we will leave these theoretical and technical considerations and turn to the practical side of the question.

You will always find lots of people ready to give advice on

---

[1] See also Klebs and Tommasi Crudeli, *Arch. f. exp. Path.*, xi. ; Ceci, *ibid*, xv.; Tommasi Crudeli, *La malaria de Rome*, Paris, 1881 ; *Nuovi studj sulla natura della Malaria*, Rome, 1881 ; " Malaria and the Ancient Drainage of the Roman Hills," *Practitioner*, ii., 1881 ; *Instituzioni de anat. Path.*, vol. i., Turin, 1882 ; Marchiafava e Cuboni *Nuovi studj sulla natura della Malaria*, *Acad. dei Lincei*, Jan. 2, 1881; Marchand,*Virch. Arch.*, vol. lxxxviii. ; Laveran, *Nature parasitaire des accidents d'impaludisme*, Paris, 1881 ; Richard, *Comptes Rendus*, 1881 ; Steinberg, *Rep. Nat. Board of Health (U.S.)*, 1881. *Malaria-krankheiten*, K. Schwalbe ; Berlin, 1890 ; Parkes, *On the Issue of a Spirit Ration in the Ashantee Campaign*, Churchill, 1875 ; Zumsden, *Cyclopædia of Medicine* ; *Ague*, Dr. M. D. O'Connell, Calcutta, 1885.

fever, particularly how to avoid getting it, and you will find the most dogmatic of these are people who have been singularly unlucky in the matter, or people who know nothing of local conditions. These latter are the most trying of all to deal with. They tell you, truly enough no doubt, that the malaria is in the air, in the exhalations from the ground, which are greatest about sunrise and sunset, and in the drinking water, and that you must avoid chill, excessive mental and bodily exertion, that you must never get anxious, or excited, or lose your temper. Now there is only one—the drinking water—of this list that you can avoid, for, owing to the great variety and rapid growth of bacteria encouraged by the tropical temperature, and the aqueous saturation of the atmosphere from the heavy rainfall, and the great extent of swamp, &c., it is practically impossible to destroy them in the air to a satisfactory extent. I was presented by scientific friends, when I first went to the West Coast, with two devices supposed to do this. One was a lamp which you burnt some chemical in; it certainly made a smell that nothing could live with—but then I am not nothing, and there are enough smells on the Coast now. I gave it up after the first half-hour. The other device was a muzzle, a respirator, I should say. Well! all I have got to say about that is that you need be a better-looking person than I am to wear a thing like that without causing panic in a district. Then orders to avoid the night air are still more difficult to obey—may I ask how you are to do without air from 6.30 P.M. to 6.30 A.M.? or what other air there is but night air, heavy with malarious exhalations, available then?

The drinking water you have a better chance with, as I will presently state; chill you cannot avoid. When you are at work on the Coast, even with the greatest care, the sudden fall of temperature that occurs after a tornado coming at the end of a stewing-hot day, is sure to tell on any one, and as for the orders regarding temper neither the natives, nor the country, nor the trade, help you in the least. But still you must remember that although it is impossible to fully carry out these orders, you can do a good deal towards doing so, and preventive measures are the great thing, for it is better to escape fever altogether, or to get off with a light touch of it, than to make a sensational recovery from Yellow Jack himself.

There is little doubt that a certain make of man has the best chance of surviving the Coast climate—an energetic, spare, nervous but light-hearted creature, capable of enjoying whatever there may be to enjoy, and incapable of dwelling on discomforts or worries. It is quite possible for a person of this sort to live, and work hard on the Coast for a considerable period, possibly with better health than he would have in England. The full-blooded, corpulent and vigorous should avoid West Africa like the plague. One after another, men and women, who looked, as the saying goes, as if you could take a lease of their lives, I have seen come out and die, and it gives one a sense of horror when they arrive at your West Coast station, for you feel a sort of accessory before the fact to murder, but what can you do except get yourself laughed at as a croaker, and attend the funeral?

The best ways of avoiding the danger of the night air are—to have your evening meal about 6.30 or 7,—8 is too late ; sleep under a mosquito curtain whether there are mosquitoes in your district or not, and have a meal before starting out in the morning, a good hot cup of tea or coffee and bread and butter, if you can get it, if not, something left from last night's supper or even *aguma*. Regarding meals, of course we come to the vexed question of stimulants—all the evidence is in favour of alcohol, of a proper sort, taken at proper times, and in proper quantities, being extremely valuable. Take the case of the missionaries, who are almost all teetotalers, they are young men and women who have to pass a medical examination before coming out, and whose lives on the Coast are far easier than those of other classes of white men, yet the mortality among them is far heavier than in any other class.

Mr. Stanley says that wine is the best form of stimulant, but that it should not be taken before the evening meal. Certainly on the South-West Coast, where a heavy, but sound, red wine imported from Portugal is the common drink, the mortality is less than on the West Coast. Beer has had what one might call a thorough trial in Cameroon since the German occupation and is held by authorities to be the cause in part of the number of cases of hæmaturic fever in that river being greater than in other districts. But this subject requires scientific comparative observation on various parts of the Coast, for Cameroons is at the beginning of the South-West Coast, whereon the percentage of cases of hæmaturic to those of intermittent and remittent fevers is far higher than on the West Coast.

A comparative study of the diseases of the western division of the continent would, I should say, repay a scientific doctor, if he survived. The material he would have to deal with would be

enormous, and in addition to the history of hæmaturic he
would be confronted with the problem of the form of fever
which seems to be a recent addition to West African afflictions,
the so-called typhoid malaria, which of late years has come
into the Rivers, and apparently come to stay. This fever is,
I may remark, practically unknown at present in the South-
West Coast regions where the "sun for garbage" plan is
adhered to. At present the treatment of all white man's
diseases on the Coast practically consists in the treatment of
malaria, because whatever disease a person gets hold of
takes on a malarial type which masks its true nature. Why,
I knew a gentleman who had as fine an attack of the
smallpox as any one would not wish to have, and who for
days behaved as if he had remittent, and then burst out
into the characteristic eruption ; and only got all his earthly
possessions burnt, and no end of carbolic acid dressings for
his pains.

I do not suppose this does much harm, as the malaria is
the main thing that wants curing ; unless Dr. Plehn is right
and quinine is bad in hæmaturia. His success in dealing with
this fever seems to support his opinion ; and the French doctors
on the Coast, who dose it heavily with quinine, have certainly
a very heavy percentage of mortality among their patients
with the hæmaturic, although in the other forms of malarial
fever they very rarely lose a patient.

But to return to those preventive measures, and having
done what we can with the air, we will turn our attention to
the drinking water, for in addition to malarial microbes the
drinking and washing water of West Africa is liable to contain
dermazoic and entozoic organisms, and if you don't take care
you will get from it into your anatomy Tinea versicolor, Tinea
decalvans, Tinea circinata, Tinea sycosis, Tinea favosa, or some
other member of that wretched family, let alone being nearly
certain to import Trichocephalus dispar, Ascaris lumbricoides,
Oxyuris vermicularis, and eight varieties of nematodes, each
of them with an awful name of its own, and unpleasant consequences to you, and, lastly, a peculiar abomination, a filaria.
This is not, what its euphonious name may lead you to suppose,
a fern, but it is a worm which gets into the white of the eye and
leads there a lively existence, causing distressing itching,
throbbing and pricking sensations, not affecting the sight
until it happens to set up inflammation. I have seen the eyes
of natives simply swarming with these filariæ. A curious thing
about the disease is that it usually commences in one eye, and
when that becomes over-populated an emigration society sets

out for the other eye, travelling thither under the skin of the
bridge of the nose, looking while in transit like the bridge of
a pair of spectacles. A similar, but not identical, worm is
fairly common on the Ogowé, and is liable to get under the
epidermis of any part of the body. Like the one affecting the
eye it is very active in its movements, passing rapidly about
under the skin and producing terrible pricking and itching,
but very trifling inflammation in those cases which I have
seen. The treatment consists of getting the thing out, and
the thing to be careful of is to get it out whole, for if any part
of it is left in, suppuration sets in, so even if you are personally convinced you have got it out successfully it is just
as well to wash out the wound with carbolic or Condy's fluid.
The most frequent sufferers from these filariæ are the natives,
but white people do get them. I hear there is an account in
the *Lancet*, October 17th, 1894, of one that was extracted
from the eye of a European. This case came from Calabar,
but the disease is more frequent on the South-West Coast.

Do not confuse this filaria with the Guinea worm, Filaria
medinensis, which runs up to ten and twelve feet in length, and
whose habits are different. It is more sedentary, but it is in
the drinking water inside small crustacea (cyclops). It appears
commonly in its human host's leg, and rapidly grows, curled
round and round like a watch-spring, showing raised under
the skin. The native treatment of this pest is very cautiously to
open the skin over the head of the worm and secure it between
a little cleft bit of bamboo and then gradually wind the rest
of the affair out. Only a small portion can be wound out at
a time, as the wound is very liable to inflame, and should the
worm break, it is certain to inflame badly, and a terrible wound
will result. You cannot wind it out by the tail because you
are then, so to speak, turning its fur the wrong way, and it
catches in the wound.

I should, I may remark, strongly advise any one who likes to
start early on a canoe journey to see that no native member
of the party has a Filaria medinensis on hand ; for winding
it up is always reserved for a morning job and as many other
jobs are similarly reserved it makes for delay.

I know, my friends, that you one and all say that the drinking
water at your particular place is of singular beauty and purity,
and that you always tell the boys to filter it ; but I am convinced that that water is no more to be trusted than the boys,
and I am lost in amazement at people of your intelligence
trusting the trio of water, boys, and filter, in the way you do.
One favourite haunt of mine gets its drinking water from a

cemented hole in the back yard into which drains a very strong-smelling black little swamp, which is surrounded by a ridge of sandy ground, on which are situated several groups of native houses, whose inhabitants enhance their fortunes and their drainage by taking in washing. At Fernando Po the other day I was assured as usual that the water was perfection, " beautiful spring coming down from the mountain," &c. In the course of the afternoon affairs took me up the mountain to Basile, for the first part of the way along the course of the said stream. The first objects of interest I observed in the drinking-water supply were four natives washing themselves and their clothes ; the next was the bloated body of a dead goat reposing in a pellucid pool. The path then left the course of the stream, but on arriving in the region of its source I found an interesting little colony of Spanish families which had been imported out whole, children and all, by the Government. They had a nice, neat little cemetery attached, which his excellency the doctor told me was " stocked mostly with children, who were always dying off from worms." Good, so far, for the drinking water ! and as to what that beautiful stream was soaking up when it was round corners—I did not see it so I do not know—but I will be bound it was some abomination or another. But it's no use talking, it's the same all along, Sierra Leone, Grain Coast, Ivory Coast, Gold Coast, Lagos, Rivers, Cameroon, Congo Français, Kacongo, Congo Belge, and Angola. When you ask your white friends how they can be so reckless about the water, which, as they know, is a decoction of the malarious earth, exposed night and day to the malarious air, they all up and say theirs is not ; they have " got an awfully good filter, and they tell the boys," &c., and that they themselves often put wine or spirit in the water to kill the microbes. Vanity, vanity ! At each and every place I know, men have died and worms have eaten them. The safest way of dealing with water I know is to boil it hard for ten minutes at least, and then instantly pour it into a jar with a narrow neck, which plug up with a wad of fresh cotton-wool—not a cork ; and should you object to the flat taste of boiled water, plunge into it a bit of red-hot iron, which will make it more agreeable in taste. *Before* boiling the water you can carefully filter it if you like. A good filter is a very fine thing for clearing drinking water of hippopotami, crocodiles, water snakes, catfish, &c., and I daresay it will stop back sixty per cent. of the live or dead African natives that may be in it ; but if you think it is going to stop back the microbe of marsh fever—my good sir, you are mistaken. And remember that you must give up cold water, boiled or unboiled, altogether ; for if you take the boiled or filtered water and put it into one of those water-coolers, and leave it hanging exposed to night air or day on the verandah, you might just as well save yourself the trouble of boiling it at all.

Next in danger to the diseases come the remedies for them. Let the new-comer remember, in dealing with quinine, calomel, arsenic, and spirits, that they are not castor sugar nor he a glass bottle, but let him use them all—the two first fairly frequently—not waiting for an attack of fever and then ladle-ing them into himself with a spoon. The third, arsenic—a drug much thought of by the French, who hold that if you establish an arsenic cachexia you do not get a malarial one—should not be taken except under a doctor's orders. Spirit is undoubtedly extremely valuable when, from causes beyond your control, you have got a chill. Remember always your life hangs on quinine, and that it is most important to keep the system sensitive to it, which you do not do if you keep on pouring in heavy doses of it for nothing and you make yourself deaf into the bargain. I have known people take sixty grains of quinine in a day for a bilious attack and turn it into a disease they only got through by the skin of their teeth ; but the prophylactic action of quinine is its great one, as it only has power over malarial microbes at a certain state of their development,—the fully matured microbe it does not affect to any great degree—and therefore by taking it when in a malarious district, say, in a dose of five grains a day, you keep down the malaria which you are bound, even with every care, to get into your system. When you have got very chilled or over-tired, take an extra five grains with a little wine or spirit at any time, and when you know, by reason of aching head and limbs and a sensation of a stream of cold water down your back and an awful temper, that you are in for a fever, send for a doctor if you can. If, as generally happens, there is no doctor near to send for, take a compound calomel and colocynth pill, fifteen grains of quinine and a grain of opium, and go to bed wrapped up in the best blanket available. When safely there take lashings of hot tea or, what is better, a hot drink made from fresh lime-juice, strong and without sugar—fresh limes are almost always to be had—if not, bottled lime-juice does well. Then, in the hot stage, don't go fanning about, nor in the perspiring stage, for if you get a chill then you may turn a mild dose of fever into a fatal one. If, however, you keep conscientiously rolled in your blanket until the perspiring stage is well over, and stay in bed till the next morning, the chances are you will be all right, though a little shaky about the legs. You should continue the quinine, taking it in five-grain doses, up to fifteen to twenty grains a day for a week after any attack of fever, but you must omit the opium pill. The great thing in West Africa is to keep up your health to a good level; that will enable you to resist fever, and it is exceedingly difficult for most people to do this, because of the difficulty of getting exercise and good food. But do what you may it is almost certain you will get fever during a residence of more than six months on the Coast, and the chances are two to one on the Gold Coast that you will die of it. But, without precautions, you will probably have it within a fortnight of first landing, and your chances of surviving are almost *nil*. With precautions, in the Rivers and on the S.W. Coast your touch of fever may be a thing inferior in danger and discomfort to a bad cold in England.

Yet remember, before you elect to cast your lot in with the West Coasters, that 85 per cent. of them die of fever or return home with their health permanently wrecked. Also remember that there is no getting acclimatised to the Coast. There are, it is true, a few men out there who, although they have been resident in West Africa for years, have never had fever, but you can count them up on the fingers of one hand. There is another class who have been out for twelve months at a time, and have not had a touch of fever; these you want the fingers of your two hands to count, but no more. By far the largest class is the third, which is made up of those who have a slight dose of fever once a fortnight, and some day, apparently for no extra reason, get a heavy dose and die of it. A very considerable class is the fourth—those who die within a fortnight to a month of going ashore.

The fate of a man depends solely on his power of resisting the so-called malaria, not in his system becoming inured to it. The first class of men that I have cited have some unknown element in their constitutions that renders them immune. With the second class the power of resistance is great, and can be renewed from time to time by a spell home in a European climate. In the third class the state is that of cumulative poisoning; in the fourth of acute poisoning.

Let the new-comer who goes to the Coast take the most cheerful view of these statements and let him regard himself as preordained to be one of the two most favoured classes. Let him take every care short of getting frightened, which is as deadly as taking no care at all, and he may—I sincerely

hope he will—survive; for a man who has got the grit in him
to go and fight in West Africa for those things worth fighting
for—duty, honour and gold—is a man whose death is a dead
loss to his country.

The cargoes from West Africa truly may " wives and mithers
maist despairing ca' them lives o' men." Yet grievous as is the
price England pays for her West African possessions, to us who
know the men who risk their lives and die for them, England
gets a good equivalent value for it; for she is the greatest
manufacturing country in the world, and as such requires
markets. Nowadays she requires them more than new colonies.
A colony drains annually thousands of the most enterprising
and energetic of her children from her, leaving behind them
their aged and incapable relations. Moreover, a colony
gradually becomes a rival manufacturing centre to the mother
country, whereas West Africa will remain for hundreds of
years a region that will supply the manufacturer with his
raw material, and take in exchange for it his manufactured
articles, giving him a good margin of profit. And the holding
of our West African markets drains annually a few score of
men only—only too often for ever—but the trade they carry
on and develop there—a trade, according to Sir George Baden-
Powell, of the annual value of nine millions sterling—enables
thousands of men, women and children to remain safely in
England, in comfort and pleasure, owing to the wages and
profits arising from the manufacture and export of the articles
used in that trade.

So I trust that those at home in England will give all honour
to the men still working in West Africa, or rotting in the
weed-grown, snake-infested cemeteries and the forest swamps
—men whose battles have been fought out on lonely beaches far
away from home and friends and often from another white
man's help, sometimes with savages, but more often with a
more deadly foe, with none of the anodyne to death and
danger given by the companionship of hundreds of fellow
soldiers in a fight with a foe you can see, but with a foe you
can see only incarnate in the dreams of your delirium, which
runs as a poison in burning veins and aching brain—the
dread West Coast fever. And may England never again dream
of forfeiting, or playing with, the conquests won for her by
those heroes of commerce, the West Coast traders; for of
them, as well as of such men as Sir Gerald Portal, truly it
may be said—of such is the Kingdom of England.

APPENDIX III

DR. A. GÜNTHER ON REPTILES AND FISHES[1]

Report on a Collection of Reptiles and Fishes made by Miss M. H. Kingsley during her travels on the Ogowé River and in Old Calabar. By Dr. A. GÜNTHER, F.R.S.

MISS MARY H. KINGSLEY, on returning from her first visit to the West Coast of Africa in 1894, brought with her a miscellaneous collection of zoological specimens, sufficiently large to show the interest she took in the fauna of the countries visited by her. Last year she started again from England, with the object of extending her travels in the interior of the Gaboon country; and as she intended to follow during a part of this expedition the course of the Ogowé River, she readily fell in with my view that an opportunity of collecting the fishes of this mighty river should not be lost. The means of preserving and transporting the specimens were naturally limited, as Miss Kingsley travelled alone with a native crew; besides, whilst traversing the region of the rapids, which extends over some hundred of miles, the upsetting of her canoe was a matter of frequent occurrence. Nevertheless she succeeded in bringing home in excellent condition a collection of eighteen species of Reptiles and about sixty-five species of Fishes, which will be enumerated or described in this paper, besides a number of other, especially entomological, specimens.

During a temporary stay at Old Calabar and a visit to the island of Corisco some freshwater fishes were added to the main collection from the Ogowé River. These will be also embodied in the present paper, whilst the marine species, being all well known, are omitted.

[1] Reprinted by permission from the *Annals and Magazine of Natural History*, 6th series, No. 100. April, 1896.

Thirty years ago scarcely anything but the name was known of the Ogowé River ; but between 1860 and 1870 French officials and traders began to trace its course inland, discovering a long stretch of rapids in its middle course which render navigation dangerous and, at places, impossible to any vessel larger than a boat.   Among those earlier explorers an Englishman, Mr. R. B. N. Walker, took a prominent part,[1] making two expeditions in 1866 and 1873, and penetrating to Lopé, in the Okanda country.   The survey of the upper parts of the river was completed by Messrs. de Brazza and Balay.

All that was known before the year 1860 of the reptiles and fishes of the Gaboon country has been collected by Aug. Duméril in his memoir " Reptiles et Poissons de l'Afrique Occidentale," in Arch. Mus. vol. x.   I find that in the list at the end of his memoir he mentions eight freshwater fishes from Gaboon, all being from the littoral portion of the country. In 1867[2] I described the collection made by Walker on the Ogowé, adding seventeen species to its fauna, ten of which were new.   This list was increased by six others found by Buchholz and determined by Peters (MB. Berlin Akad. 1876, p. 244).   Two years later M. Sauvage commenced to publish the results of his examination of the materials that had accumulated in the Paris Museum (Bull. Soc. Philom. 1878, pp. 90-103), giving a complete account of the then knowledge of this fish-fauna in his memoir " Étude sur la Faune ichthyologique de l'Ogôoué," in N. Arch. Mus. iii. 1880.   In it he enumerates thirty-seven species, a part of which, however, he knew only from the papers of his predecessors.   This number has been increased by him in a last supplementary list to forty-six (Bull. Soc. Zool. France, ix. 1884).

In the present paper I have added to the Gaboon fauna from Miss Kingsley's collection the following sixteen species :—

Gobius æneofuscus, Gthr.
Eleotris senegalensis, Stdchr.
Ophiocephalus obscurus, Gthr.
Ctenopoma gabonense, sp. n. (? = *Ct. multispine*, Sauv., nec Ptrs.).
—— *nanum*, sp. n.
—— *Kingsleyæ*, sp. n. (? = *Ct. Petherici*, Sauv., nec Gthr.).

[1] Bull. Soc. Géogr. Paris, 1879, p. 114.
[2] Ann. & Mag. Nat. Hist. 1867, xx. p. 109.   In this paper the name of the river is misspelt Ogome.

Chromis ogowensis, sp. n. (? = *Ch. microcephalus*, Sauv., nec Blkr.).
Cynoglossus senegalensis, Kaup.
Clarias Walkeri, sp. n.
Eutropius liberiensis, Hubrecht.
Chrysichthys Büttikoferi, Stdchr. (= *Ch. macrops*, Sauv., nec Gthr.).
Barilius bibie, Joannis.
Alestes longipinnis, Gthr.
—— *Kingsleyæ*, sp. n.
Mormyrus amblystoma, sp. n.
Notopterus nigri, Gthr.

Deducting from M. Sauvage's list three species which I consider merely synonyms, and allowing for four others which I believe to figure in my and M. Sauvage's lists under different names, I compute the total number of species known at present from this river to be fifty-one, a number which may be expected to be doubled by future investigations. The fish-fauna of the Nile consists of about ninety species.

The localities which will be mentioned in this report are the following :

Warri, on the Forcados River (mouth of the Niger).
Azuminé Creek, freshwater, running into the Cpobo River, with a swift current, 25 miles from the sea (Niger delta region).
Egwanga, on the Opobo River (Niger delta region).[1]
Corisco Island, off the Gaboon Coast.
Lambarene,[1] Ogowé River.
Talagouga, about 180 miles from the mouth of the Ogowé.
Kondo-Kondo, an island in the Alemba Rapids of the Ogowé.

REPTILES AND BATRACHIANS.

The Reptiles were collected at Lambarene, and belong to the following species :—

1. *Cycloderma Aubryi*, D. B.—A young specimen well agreeing with one figured by Peters (MB. Berl. Akad. 1876, p. 117).

---

[1] = Lembarene Island, sometimes also spelt Lambarenie Island.

2. *Monitor niloticus.* L.
3. *Poromera Fordii*, Hallow.
4. *Mabouia Raddonii*, Gray.
5. *Gymnodactylus fasciatus*, D. B.
6. *Polemon Barthii*, Jan.
7. *Coronella fuliginoides*, Gthr.
8. *Grayia Smythii*, Leach.
9. *Hydræthiops melanogaster*, Gthr.
10. *Hapsidophrys lineatus*, Fisch.
11. *Philothamnus nitidus*, Gthr.
12. *Lycophidium irroratum*, Leach.
13. *Dipsadoboa assimilis*, Matschie.
14. *Naja melanoleuca*, Hallow.
15. *Vipera nasicornis*, Shaw.
16. *Atheris anisolepis*, Mocq.
17. *Cornufer Johnstonii*, Blgr.
18. *Rana crassipes*, Ptrs.

Before passing on to the Fishes I offer remarks on a few of these species.

POROMERA.

Poromera, Boul. Liz. iii. p. 6.

Nostril between two nasals and the suture between rostral and first labial. Lower eyelid scaly. Collar present. Back covered with scales larger than those of the tail, and strongly keeled, the keels forming continuous longitudinal ridges; sides with much smaller scales; ventral scales rather large, imbricate, keeled, the keels again forming continuous series. Fingers and toes slender, with a double series of smooth, very small scutes beneath. Femoral pores; no inguinal pores. Tail long, cylindrical.

Poromera Fordii.

Tachydromus Fordii, Hallow. Proc. Ac. Nat. Sci. Philad. 1857, p. 48.
Poromera Fordii, Boul. *l. c.*

General aspect of a *Tachydromus.*
The scutes on the upper side of the head show longitudinal ridges either along the middle or concentric with their margins. The anterior nasal meets its fellow in the median line behind the rostral. Anterior frontal longer than broad; an unpaired small scute between the posterior frontals. Vertical bell-shaped, twice as long as broad; a pair of anterior occipitals,

half the size of the posterior, between which a central occipital. The posterior occipitals are fringed by some smaller marginal scutes. Two large supraoculars on each side. Seven or eight narrow upper labials, of which the penultimate is the largest. Four chin-shields on one side, five on the other. Temporal scales small, strongly keeled.

Ear very open, vertically long. Collar more distinct in front of the shoulder-joint, and nearly obsolete across the chest. Dorsal scales in eight, ventral in ten, longitudinal series. Præanal region covered by keeled scales, in size and shape scarcely differing from those preceding them. About twelve femoral pores. All the caudal scales strongly keeled.

The fore limb pressed backwards does not reach the groin ; the hind limb carried forwards extends to the ear. Thigh finely granular behind.

The upper parts are brown, or, after the removal of the epidermis, green iridescent. Back anteriorly with a black longitudinal band of each side of the median line, the two bands coalescent further behind. An indistinct greenish band along each side of the neck. Lower parts whitish.

	millim.
Distance of snout from vent	45
Length of tail	110
Distance of snout from ear	12
Length of fore limb	20
Length of hind limb	30
Length of fourth toe (measured from its junction with the fifth)	12

I have given a full description of this lizard, as the specimen found by Miss Kingsley at Lambarene seems to be only the second known to exist in collections. Its specific identity with *Tachydromus Fordii* of Hallowell might be questioned, as this author has described the specimen in the museum of the Philadelphia Academy as possessing only six rows of ventral scales ; also the scutellation of the præanal region is differently described. However, as there is a great agreement in other respects between the two specimens, and the locality (Gaboon) as given by Hallowell points likewise to a specific identity, I adopt the name given by the latter author.

Dipsadoboa assimilis.

Dipsadoboa assimilis, Matschie, SB. Ges. naturf. Fr. Berl. 1893, p. 173 (Togoland) ; Bocage, Jorn. Sc. Lisb. iv. 1895, p. 17.

The specimen obtained at Lambarene agrees better with *D. assimilis* than with *D. unicolor* with regard to the number and disposition of the labial shields.

Professor Bocage refers his specimens from Fernando Po also to *D. assimilis*, whilst, singularly enough, I have now some evidence that the type of *D. unicolor* came from the same island, as I received some years ago a specimen from Fernando ·Po which is identical with *D. unicolor*. Therefore, as far as our present experience goes, both *D. unicolor* and *assimilis* (if they are really distinct) would seem to occur in Fernando Po, while the former does not extend on to the mainland.

Atheris anisolepis.

Atheris anisolepis, Mocquard, Bull. Soc. Philom. 1887, p. 90.
Atheris læviceps, Boettger, Zool. Anz. x. p. 651 ; Ber. Senckenb. Ges. 1888, p. 92, tab. ii. fig. 7 (head).

An adult specimen from Lambarene. The specimens from which Boettger took his description came from Banana (Congo delta). The principal distinctive characters of this species are, in my opinion, the number and size of scales and the two series of suboculars, rather than the degree of carination of some of the scales on the crown of the head, which depends on age.

Thanks to the kindness of Professor L. Vaillant and Dr. Jentink I have been able, by a re-examination of the typical specimens described by Schlegel and Mocquard, to form a definite opinion as to the species of *Atheris* which deserve recognition. They are the following :—

1. *A. squamigera*, Hallowell, = *A. subocularis*, Fisch., probably = *A. Burtonii*, Gthr. With 17 (in *A. Burtonii* with 19) series of scales ; only one row of minute subocular scales (exceptionally partly confluent with upper labials).

2. *A. anisolepis*, Mocquard 1887), = *A. læviceps*, Boettger (1887), = *A. chloroechis*, Boettg., part. With 22–25 series of scales ; two rows of minute suboculars, the lower row sometimes incomplete, but always indicated by several scales.

3. *A. chloroechis*, Schleg., = *A. polylepis*, Ptrs. With 31–36 series of scales and with a double row of suboculars.

4. *A. ceratophora*, Werner.

Rana crassipes, Buchh. & Ptrs.

One young specimen from Glass, Gaboon estuary.

This specimen, as well as an adult in the British Museum, has no vomerine teeth, whilst two short groups are present in the second of the British Museum specimens, which is intermediate in size between the two former.

FRESHWATER FISHES.

Gobius æneofuscus.

Gobius æneofuscus, Peters, MB. Berl. Akad. 1852, p. 681, and Reise n. Mossamb., Flussf. p. 18, Taf. iii. fig. 1 ; Günth. Fish. iii. p. 61.
Gobius æneofuscus, var. *guineensis*, Peters, MB. Berlin. Akad. 1876, p. 248.
Gobius tajasica, Steind. Not. Leyd. Mus. xvi. p. 25 (not synom.).

A Goby which seems to be very common in the freshwaters of Liberia and the Cameroon River, and is abundant in the Ogowé River, where numerous examples were obtained by Miss Kingsley at Kondo-Kondo, is identical with the species discovered by Peters in the Zambeze, but not, as Dr. Steindachner thinks, with the West-Indian *G. banana*, which has considerably smaller scales on the tail. *G. æneofuscus*, therefore, belongs to the freshwater fauna of Tropical Africa extending right across the continent.

Gobius lateristriga, A. Dum. Arch. Mus. x. p. 247, pl. xxi. fig 1, if not identical with this species, is, at any rate, closely allied to it ; unfortunately the author has omitted to describe the scales, dentition, and other important characters.

Periophthalmus Koelreuteri, var. papilio, Bl. Schn.

Common on the West Coast, and attracting the notice of every traveller by its semiterrestrial habits and by the astonishing rapidity with which it leaps, frog-like, over the mud-flats of the littoral.

Island of Corisco (Steindachner, SB. Wien. Akad. 1869, lx. p. 945).

Eleotris senegalensis.

Eleotris (Culius) senegalensis, Steind. SB. Wien. Akad. 1869, lx. p. 949, Taf. ii. figs. 1, 2.

Ascends the Ogowé River, specimens having been obtained at Kondo-Kondo.

Mastacembelus cryptacanthus.

Mastacembelus cryptacanthus, Günth. P. Z. S. 1867, p. 102 ; Ann. & Mag. Nat. Hist. 1867, xx. p. 110.
Mastacembelus Marchei, Sauv. Bull. Soc. Philom. 1876, p. 94, and N. Arch. Mus. iii. 1880, p. 36, pl. i. fig. 1 ; Steind. Not. Leyd. Mus. xvi. p. 31 ; Denkschr. Wien. Ak. 1879, xli., "Ueber einige neue . . . Fisch.," p. 16.

Lambarene.

Mugil falcipinnis, C. V.

Warri (Niger delta).

Ophiocephalus obscurus, Gthr.

Lambarene and Kondo-Kondo.
Figured in Petherick's "Travels," 1869, ii. pl. ii. fig. B.

CTENOPOMA, Ptrs.

From an examination of a much greater number of specimens than were at my disposal some years ago I have come to the conclusion that the variation in the characters of the species is of a limited extent, and that a greater number of species exist than I was formerly inclined to admit. Neither is the distinction of this genus from *Spirobranchus* so sharp as was supposed, the armature of the opercles not being equally developed in all species, and very young Ctenopomas apparently lacking it. At present I divide the specimens before me under the following specific names :—

I. A very distinct space between anal and caudal fins.
  A. Large scales on the back, above the lateral line.
    1. Maxillary extending below the centre of the eye.
      D. $\frac{17-18}{9}$. A. $\frac{9}{9}$. Subopercular armature strong . . . . 1. *multispine,* Ptrs.

2. Maxillary extending to below the centre
of the eye.

    D. $\frac{20}{9-10}$.   A. $\frac{9-11}{9}$. Subopercular arma-
ture strong . . . . 2. *gabonense*, sp. n.

3. Maxillary not extending to below centre
of the eye.

    a. D. $\frac{15-16}{9}$. A. $\frac{8}{9-10}$.   Suboperculum
not serrated . . . . 3. *nanum*, sp. n.

    b. D. $\frac{17}{8}$. A. $\frac{11}{10}$.   Suboperculum ser-
rated . . . . 4. *congicum*, Blgr.[1]

B. Small scales on the back, above the lateral
line . . . . 5. *microlepidotum*, Gthr.

II. Anal and caudal fins nearly continuous.

    A. D. $\frac{15-17\,(18)}{7-10}$. A. $\frac{10\,(9)}{9-11}$. Depth of body $\frac{2}{5}$
of length in adult, $\frac{1}{3}$ in young . . . 6. *Petherici*, Gthr.

    B. D. $\frac{16-17}{9}$. A. $\frac{9-10}{9-10}$. Depth of body $\frac{1}{2}$ of
length in adult, $\frac{2}{7}$ in young . . . . 7. *Kingsleyæ*, Gthr.

Ctenopoma gabonense, sp. n.   (Pl. I. fig. C.)

Ctenopoma multispine, var., Günth. Ann. & Mag. Nat. Hist. 1867, xx.
p. 110.

    D. $\frac{20}{9-10}$. A. $\frac{9-11}{9}$. L. lat. 32. L. transv. $2\frac{1}{2}/9$.

Body almost as oblong as in *Ct. multispine*, to which this
species is closely allied. The height of the body is two
sevenths, or less than one third, of the total length (without
caudal), the length of the head two sevenths or rather more
than two sevenths. The snout equals the diameter of the
eye, which is one fifth of the length of the head ; interorbital
space nearly flat, much wider than the orbit. Mouth moderately wide, the maxillary not extending beyond the vertical
from the centre of the eye. The entire margin of the suboperculum is armed with prominent spines ; also part of the
interopercular margin is spiny. The space between anal and
caudal fins is equal to, or even longer than, the diameter of
the eye. Ventral fin not reaching the vent. Pores on the
head rather small, inconspicuous. Coloration uniform.

Of this species there are two specimens in the British
Museum, 140 and 153 millim. long, both from the Gaboon.
One was obtained by Mr. R. B. N. Walker, and therefore most probably came from the Ogowé River. Both
have twenty dorsal spines, which number does not seem to
have been ever observed in *Ct. multispine ;* from the latter

---

[1] Ann. & Mag. Nat. Hist. 1887, xix. p. 148.

species the present differs besides in a rather smaller mouth and much stronger subopercular armature. Vomerine and palatine teeth present.

Ctenopoma nanum, sp. n.   (Pl. I. fig. B.)

D. $\frac{15-16}{9}$.   A. $\frac{8}{9-10}$.   L. lat. 27.   L. transv. $2\frac{1}{2}/9$.

Body stouter than in *Ct. multispine* or *Ct. gabonense*, its greatest depth being contained $2\frac{3}{4}$ in the total length (without caudal) and nearly equal to the length of the head. The snout equals the diameter of the eye, which is contained $4\frac{3}{4}$ in the length of the head ; interorbital space rather convex, not wider than the orbit. Mouth rather narrow, the maxillary not extending to the vertical from the centre of the eye. Opercular armature weak ; there are only a few spinous teeth above and below the opercular notch, and none at all on the sub- and interoperculum. The space between anal and caudal fins is equal to a diameter of the eye. Pores on the head entirely covered by scales. Five series of scales on the cheek, the lowermost covering the præopercular margin. Ventral fins reaching beyond the origin of the anal, the two outer rays being prolonged into filaments. Body with darker cross-band ; an indistinct oblique irregular dark band from the eye towards the root of the pectoral.

Two specimens from the Gaboon 67 millim. long, are in the British Museum : they were collected with specimens of *Ct. Petherici*.

This species does not possess palatine teeth, and I am unable to see any teeth on the vomer, the head of which, however, is visible and not covered by the mucous membrane. Of course the possibility of these specimens being the young of one of the other species has been considered ; but beside agreeing among themselves and differing from the other species in the number of spines, the comparative size of the eye and width of the interorbital space clearly point to their being either mature or not far removed from maturity.

Ctenopoma Petherici.

Ctenopoma Petherici, Günth. Ann. & Mag. Nat. Hist. 1864, xiii. p. 211, and 1867, xx. p. 110 (part.) ; and in Petherick's " Travels," ii. 1869, p. 208, pl. i. fig. A.

The British Museum contains a specimen the exact habitat of which is not known, but which was bought with other

West-African fishes. Although this specimen differs from typical *Ct. Petherici* in the fin-formula, which is D. $\frac{18}{10}$, A. $\frac{9}{11}$, I refer it for the present to the Nilotic species.

In young specimens, 60 millim. long, the opercular armature and the vomerine and palatine teeth are well developed ; but these specimens have the body still lower than the adult, viz., one third of the total (without caudal) ; in the adult it is a little less than two fifths. The ornamental colours are prettier than in the adult, the diffuse blackish spot on the tail of the latter being a complete white-edged ocellus in the young.

Ctenopoma Kingsleyæ, sp. n. (Pl. I. fig. A.)

Ctenopoma Petherici, part., Günth. Ann. & Mag. Nat. Hist. 1867, xx. p. 110 (part.).

This species is allied to *Ct. Petherici*, but has a deeper body, and especially the young differs much from that of the Nilotic species.

D. $\frac{16-17}{9}$. A. $\frac{9-10}{9-10}$. L. lat. 25. L. transv. $2\frac{1}{2}/9$.

The depth of the body is scarcely less than one half of the total length (without caudal), the length of the head a little less than one third. The snout is nearly equal to the diameter of the eye, which is two ninths of the length of the head ; interorbital space rather convex, wider than the orbit. Mouth narrow, the maxillary extending somewhat beyond the front margin of the orbit. Vomerine teeth ; palatine teeth in a very narrow linear band. A series of short spinous teeth above and below the opercular notch ; subopercular and part of the interopercular margin finely and equally serrated. Tail very short, the anal terminating immediately before, or subcontinuous with, the caudal. Pores on the head entirely covered by scales. Five or six rows of scales on the cheek, the scales near the eye being much smaller than the others. Ventral fins not prolonged, reaching the vent. Soft parts of the vertical fins scaly. Blackish, a diffuse large black spot on the end of the tail, in front of the root of the caudal.

This diagnosis is taken from an adult specimen 150 millim. long ; two young ones, 60 millim. long, differ in the following points :—

Their body is somewhat less elevated (though much more than in young *Ct. Petherici*), its depth being contained $2\frac{1}{3}$ times in the total length (without caudal). Interorbital space as wide as the diameter of the eye, which is one fourth of the length of the head. Two or three spines above and one below the opercular notch; suboperculum partly and indistinctly, interoperculum not serrated. Vomerine teeth developed, only traces of palatine teeth in front of the bone. Coloration as in the adult.

All three specimens from Kondo-Kondo.

Chromis latus, Gthr.

Warri.

The typical specimen was most likely from the same locality, the late Mr. Fraser being known to have collected in, or to have received collections from, the Niger delta.

Chromis ogowensis, sp. n.

? *Chromis microcephalus*, Sauvage, Bull, Soc. Zool. France, ix. 1884, p. 196 (nec Bleek.).

D. $\frac{14}{11}$. A. $\frac{3}{8}$. P. 13. L. lat. 27. L. transv. 3/11.

Scales on the cheek in three series. Twenty-eight notched teeth on each side of the upper jaw. The maxillary terminates some distance in advance of the vertical from the eye. The depth of the body is a little less than one half of the total length (without caudal), the length of the head a little less than one third. Eye two ninths of the length of the head, much less than the length of the snout and than the width of the interorbital space. Pectoral fin with the third and fourth rays produced and extending to the first anal spine. Caudal fin truncated, scaly. Body with indistinct cross-bands. Vertical fins blackish, the dorsal with black longitudinal stripes, longitudinal on the spinous portion, oblique on the soft; a large oval black spot behind the last dorsal spine. Ventrals black. A black opercular spot.

	millim.
Total length	170
, ,, without caudal	143
Length of the head	47
Diameter of the eye	10
Length of the eighth dorsal spine	19

Ogowé River (Lambarene)

Hemichromis fasciatus, Ptrs.

Azuminé Creek ; Ogowé River.

Hemichromis bimaculatus.

Hemichromis bimaculatus, Gill. Proc. Philad, Ac. 1862, p. 137 ; Steind. Notes Leyd. Mus. xvi. p. 49.
Hemichromis auritus, Gill, *l. c.* p. 135.

Allied to *H. guttatus* and *H. subocellatus*, but with the body deeper and the spinous dorsal higher.

D. $\frac{14}{10}$. A. $\frac{3}{8}$. L. lat. 24. L. transv. 3/10.

The height of the body is contained $2\frac{1}{2}$ in the total length (without caudal), the length of the head $2\frac{3}{4}$. Length of the snout equal to the diameter of the eye, which is one fourth of the length of the head and equal to the width of the interorbital space. Teeth conical, brown, equal in size. Four series of scales on the cheek. Cleft of the mouth rather narrow, slightly oblique, with the lower jaw slightly projecting and with the maxillary not quite reaching the vertical from the front margin of the orbit. The length of the eighth dorsal spine is two fifths of that of the head. In the adult the soft dorsal and anal and the ventral fin are produced into points. Brownish above, a deep black spot on the end of the operculum and another in the middle of the body ; three or four series of round bluish spots on the cheek and gill-cover. Fins without spots.

	millim.
Total length	78
„ „ without caudal	60
Depth of the body	25
Length of the head	22
Diameter of the eye	6

From the middle course of the Ogowé River.

Hemichromis Schwebischi.

? *Hemichromis Schwebischi*, Sauvage, Bull. Soc. Zool. France, ix. 1884, p. 198, pl. v. fig. 2.

D. $\frac{15-16}{11}$. A. $\frac{3}{8}$. L. lat. 28. L. transv. 3/10.

The height of the body is contained $2\frac{2}{5}$ times in the total length (without caudal), the length of the head $2\frac{2}{5}$ times. Snout produced, with the upper jaw slightly the longer, longer than the postorbital portion of the head. Mouth of moderate width, very slightly oblique, the maxillary reaching but little beyond the vertical from the nostril. Teeth small, subequal, with brown pointed tips. The eye is a little less than one-half of the length of the snout and contained 4⅖ times in that of the head ; its diameter does not equal the width of the interorbital space in the largest specimen. Præorbital as wide as the eye. Præoperculum with a broad scaleless inferior limb, but its width is much narrower than the cheek, on which the scales are arranged in four series. The dorsal fin commences above the root of the pectoral fin ; its spines are of moderate strength, the middle ones being much longer than the eye. Caudal fin slightly emarginate.

Specimens from Azuminé Creek have sixteen dorsal spines and the pectoral fin reaches nearly the vent. Two faint broad longitudinal bands on the upper half of the body are crossed by five or six transverse bands, equally faint, the parts crossed being of a darker tint. These markings are more distinct in young examples than in the adult. An opercular spot.

Specimens from Kondo-Kondo have fifteen dorsal spines and a rather shorter pectoral. None of the markings are present beside the opercular spot.

		millim.
Total length		148
„ „ without caudal	. .	125
Length of the head		45
Diameter of the eye		10
Length of the ninth dorsal spine		15

The specimen described by Sauvage was considerably larger than ours ; to this circumstance I am inclined to ascribe the discrepancies between the two descriptions.

Cynoglossus senegalensis, Kaup.

Lambarene.

Clarias Walkeri, sp. n.

D. 77.   A. 56.   P. 1/8.

Vomerine teeth villiform, forming a rather narrow band, without posterior projection, and as broad as the intermaxillary band ; each half of the latter is twice as wide as broad, and both the intermaxillary and vomerine bands have the same lateral extent. Head covered above with smooth thin skin, scarcely any granulation being visible. The occipital process projects as an isosceles triangle, the hind margin of the head forming an open crescent on each side of the process. The fontanelle is elongate, slightly encroaching upon the base of the triangular process. The length of the head (measured to the end of the process) is two-ninths of the total (without caudal); the width of the interorbital space is one-half of the length of the head. Barbels moderately long, that of the nostril not reaching the gill-opening, and that of the maxillary extending to the origin of the dorsal fin, which is opposite to the end of the pectoral. Anal fin not low. Vertical fins separated from each other by a small interspace. Coloration uniform blackish brown.

	millim.
Total length	171
,, ,, without caudal	150
Length of upperside of head	35
Width of interorbital space	18
Diameter of the eye	2·7

Ogowé River.

Clarias gabonensis.

Clarias gabonensis, Günth, Ann. & Mag. Nat. Hist. 1867, xx. p. 110.

D. 76–78. A. 56–60. P. 1/10.

Vomerine teeth villiform, forming a band which is a little broader than the intermaxillary band, without posterior projection; each half of the intermaxillary band is twice as wide as it is broad, and laterally scarcely extends so far as the vomerine band. Head naked above, finely granular and striated. The occipital process triangular, with rounded end, its base being a little longer than its sides. The fontanelle is ovate, and does not encroach upon the base of the triangular process. Length of the head one-fourth of the total (without caudal); snout contracted, the width of the interorbital space being less than one-half of the length of the head. Barbels moderately long, that of the nostril reaching to the root of the pectoral fin and that of the maxillary to the origin of the dorsal, which is nearly opposite to the end of the pectoral. Anal fin not low. Vertical fins separated from each other by a small interspace. Coloration uniform blackish brown.

	millim.
Total length	168
,, ,, without caudal	148
Length of upperside of the head	38
Width of interorbital space	15
Diameter of the eye	3

This species inhabits also the Ogowé River. To facilitate comparison with the other species here described, I have given a fuller diagnosis than my former one.

Clarias buthupogon.

? *Clarias læviceps*, Gill, Proc. Ac. Nat. Sci. Philad, 1862, p. 139.
Clarias buthupogon, Sauvage, Bull. Soc. Philom. 1878, p. 96.
Clarias gabonensis (Clarias megapogon), Sauvage, N. Arch. Mus. iii. 1880, p. 39, pl. i. fig. 2 (not Günth.).

D. 84–87. A. 65–67. P. 1/8.

Vomerine teeth villiform, forming a rather broad band, without posterior projection, and as broad as the intermaxillary band ; each half of the latter is twice as wide as broad, and both the intermaxillary and vomerine bands have the same lateral extent. Head covered above with a very thin skin and finely and rather sparsely granular. The occipital process projects as an isosceles triangle, the hind margin of the head being deeply notched on each side of the process. The fontanelle is of an oval shape, its greater portion lying in advance of the base of the process. The length of the head (measured to the end of the process) is two-sevenths or one-fourth of the total (without caudal) ; the width of the interorbital space is somewhat less than one-half of the length of the head. All the barbels very long, the nasal reaching beyond the head and the maxillary beyond the origin of the anal. Pectoral fin extending to the vertical from the first dorsal ray. Anal fin low ; both the dorsal and anal extend to the root of the caudal. Sides of the head and neck with whitish specks.

	millim.
Total length	225
„ „ without caudal	195
Length of upperside of head	48
Width of interorbital space	21
Diameter of the eye	4·5

The specimens were obtained at Kondo-Kondo and in Corisco Island. The original description of *C. læviceps* runs as follows :—" Height at anus a tenth of length ; head (laterally) a sixth, its breadth an eighth ; the surface smooth ; maxillary barbels twice as long as head. D. 86, A. 61,"— and is quite insufficient for exact determination of specimens. The typical specimen came probably from Liberia.

Schilbe mystus, Cuv. Val.

Old Calabar.

Schilbe dispila, Gthr.

Azuminé Creek (Opobo River).
I believe that the specimens so named should be reunited
with *Schilbe mystus*.

Eutropius liberiensis.

Eutropius liberiensis Hubrecht, Notes Leyd. Mus. iii. p. 69 ; Steind.
ibid. xvi. p. 59.

D. 47–50.

Lambarene.

Eutropius congensis, Gthr.

Warri.

Chrysichthys Büttikoferi.

Chrysichthys Büttikoferi, Steindachner, Notes Leyd. Mus. xvi. p. 60.

This is a species clearly distinct from *Ch. macrops*, having
the adipose fin much shorter and further distant from the
dorsal fin.   In this respect it agrees with *Ch. nigrodigitatus*,
which, as a rule, has a more contracted snout and narrower
mouth.   However, I have examined large specimens which
it is difficult to refer to either of these two species with certainty.   And the difficulty is increased, as I find that there
are specimens with eleven and with thirteen anal rays in
both the narrow-snouted form (*Ch. nigrodigitatus*) and the
broad-snouted (*Ch. Büttikoferi*).   Possibly more than these
two species should be distinguished.   Miss Kingsley found
Ch. Büttikoferi at Kondo-Kondo and in Corisco Island.

Synodontis serratus, Rüpp.

Old Calabar.

Malapterurus beninensis, Murr.

Old Calabar ; Ogowé River.

Labeo coubie, Rüpp.

Old Calabar.

Barbus Kessleri, Steind.

Specimens from the Ogowé River have the barbels rather longer and the base of the dorsal fin at a steeper slope than specimens from Angola.

Barilius bibie. (Pl. II. fig. C.)

? *Leuciscus bibie*, De Joannis, Guérin, Mag. Zool. 1835, Pisc. pl. iv. ; Günth. Fish. vii. p. 293.

D. 10. A. 18. V. 9. L. lat. 54. L. transv. 8/4.

Body compressed, its depth being two-ninths, the length of the head one-fourth, of the total length (without caudal). Head oblong, with pointed snout, which is equal to the diameter of the eye or two-sevenths of the length of the head. Width of the interorbital space equal to the diameter of the eye. Mouth wide, oblique, the narrow maxillary extending to below the middle of the eye, its extremity being hidden below the suborbital, when the mouth is shut. Præorbital about half the area of the orbit ; the first suborbital is narrow, much narrower than the second and third, which nearly entirely cover the cheek, leaving only a space uncovered about equal to the size of the first suborbital. The origin of the dorsal fin is rather nearer to the caudal than to the occiput ; origin of the anal fin below the middle of the dorsal. Caudal fin deeply forked. Pectoral fin shorter than the head, not reaching the much shorter ventral. Scales thin, with very distinct radiating striæ ; lateral line sweeping down in a curve towards the abdomen, and, following the lower profile, terminates below the centre of the caudal fin. Silvery, with twelve bluish vertical bars along the middle of the side, and with a large blackish spot at the root of the caudal.

	millim.
Total length	110
„ „ without caudal	95
Length of the head	22
Diameter of the eye	6

Ogowé River.

This is one of the most interesting fishes in the collection. Originally described and figured in a very rude manner from a small specimen from the Nile, *L. bibie* has remained undiscovered in that river up to the present time. De Joannis does not mention the bluish cross-bars, which, however, are very faint. It is most desirable that specimens from the Nile should be directly compared with West African ones.

I am unable to arrive at a definite conclusion as to whether *Barilius senegalensis*, Steindachner (SB. Wien. Akad. 1870, lxi. p. 564, Taf. v. fig. 2), from the Senegal, should be referred to this species. Lat. l. 59–63 ; maxillary extending to behind the centre of the eye.

I am equally uncertain with regard to *Opsaridium Buchholzi*, Peters (MB. Berl. Akad. 1876, p. 251, fig. 4). It also comes from the Ogowé River ; but, to judge from the diagnosis and figure, Peters's fish has fewer scales in the lateral line (46), a smaller eye and longer snout (the specimens are of about the same size), and a longer maxillary, which reaches behind the middle of the eye. Peters represents his fish without any colour-markings.

Assuming that there are two distinct species of *Barilius* in West Africa, from a geographical point of view *B. senegalensis* would probably prove to be identical with the Nile fish, whilst the Ogowé specimens described by Peters and myself might prove to be the second species ; but this assumption is not confirmed by the description of the various authors. Thus, as not one of the descriptions extant fully agrees with our specimen, I apply at present the oldest name to it.

Alestes macrophthalmus.

Alestes macrophthalmus, Günth, Ann. & Mag. Nat. Hist. 1867, xx. p. 112.

Talagouga.

Alestes macrolepidotus, C. V.

Old Calabar.

Alestes leuciscus.

Alestes leuciscus, Günth. Ann. & Mag. Nat. Hist. 1867, xx. p. 113.

Egwanga, on the Opobo River.

Alestes longipinnis.

Brachyalestes longipinnis, Günth, Fish. v. p. 315.

Azuminé Creek and Ogowé River.

Alestes Kingsleyæ, sp. n.   (Pl. II. fig. B.)

D. 10.   A. 15–16.   L. lat. 23–24.   L. transv. 4/3½.

The height of the body is one-third of the total length (without caudal), the length of the head one-fourth. Eye two-sevenths of the length of the head, equal to that of the snout; but less than the width of the interorbital space. Origin of the dorsal fin a little behind that of the ventrals. None of the fin-rays elongate. A deep black band commences abruptly in the middle of the tail, opposite to the origin of the anal fin, and runs to the end of the central caudal rays; it is broader at its commencement than at its end. A more or less distinct dark spot above the commencement of the lateral line.

	millim.
Total length	115
„ „ without caudal	95
Length of the head	26
Diameter of the eye	8

Ogowé River.

Sarcodaces odoë, Bl.

Old Calabar; Ogowé River.

Distichodus notospilus.

Distichodus notospilus, Günth. Ann. & Mag. Nat. Hist. 1867, xx. p. 114.

Lambarene.

Xenocharax spilurus.

Xenocharax spilurus, Günth. Ann. & Mag. Nat. Hist. 1867, xx. p. 113, pl. iii. fig. B.

Talagouga.

Mormyrus zanclirostris.

Mormyrus zanclirostris, Günth, Ann. & Mag. Nat. Hist. 1867, xx. p. 114, pl. ii. fig. B.

Common at Talagouga.

Mormyrus microcephalus.

Mormyrus microcephalus, Günth. Ann. & Mag. Nat. Hist. 1867, xx p. 114.

Common at Talagouga.

Mormyrus lepturus.

Mormyrus lepturus, Günth. P.Z.S. 1871, p. 670, pl. lxix. fig. B.
? *Mormyrus grandisquamis*, Peters, MB. Berl. Akad. 1876, p. 250.

I described this species from two young specimens 3 inches long. Miss Kingsley has rediscovered it at Talagouga, and collected specimens apparently adult and up to 190 millim. in length. Thus I am enabled to amend my original diagnosis in several points.

D. 20–24. A. 25–29. L. lat. 42–44.

Snout obtuse, with the mouth terminal and, with age, with the lower lip thickened into a short adipose protuberance. The upper profile is somewhat more curved than the lower. Eye small, shorter than (in adult specimens only half as long as) the snout, situated in the anterior half of the head. Teeth of moderate size, notched, few in number. The height of the body is two-sevenths of the total length (without caudal) the length of the head two-ninths. The caudal peduncle is slender, about as long as the head, its depth being one-third of its length. Origin of the dorsal fin a little behind that of the anal, midway between the root of the caudal and the head. Pectoral a little shorter than the head, extending to the middle of the ventral, which is only half as long and terminates a long way from the vent. The scales of the anterior part of the trunk are of moderate size ; they gradually increase in size towards behind, and are largest on the hinder part of the tail and on the caudal peduncle, on the side of which they stand in three series. Brownish or silvery, darker on the head. Two black vertical bands descend from the anterior and hindmost dorsal rays to the anal, spreading more or less over that fin.

Mormyrus sphecodes.

Mormyrops sphekodes, Sauvage, Bull. Soc. Philom. 1878, p. 101 ; N. Arch. Mus. iii. 1880, p. 55, pl. ii. fig. 4.

D. 22. A. 26. L. lat. 65.

The teeth on the palate and tongue are well developed. Sauvage's description is fairly applicable to a specimen from Talagouga, 138 millim. long, but I count only 65 transverse series of scales, whilst Sauvage states 82. The diameter of the eye is only one-eighth of the length of the head in our specimen. These differences could be accounted for by a somewhat less perfect state of preservation of Sauvage's specimen.

Mormyrus Kingsleyæ, sp. n.   (Pl. II. fig. A.)

D. 17.   A. 22.   L. lat. 56.

Snout short, rounded, parabolic, with the small mouth antero-inferior. Five notched teeth above and six below. The eye is small, half the length of the snout and scarcely one-seventh of that of the head. Body rather elongate, its greatest depth being contained 4⅓ times, the length of the head 4⅘ times in the total (without caudal). Caudal peduncle compressed, moderately long, shorter than the head, its depth being one-half of its length. Origin of the dorsal fin behind that of the anal and twice as distant from the end of the snout as from the root of the caudal. The length of the base of the anal equals that of the head. Pectoral fin shorter than the head, nearly reaching the ventral. Ventral fin more than half as long as the pectoral, and half as long as the distance of its root from the vent. Scales rather small ; there are eight in an oblique series running from the first anal ray to the lateral line, and five longitudinal series on the side of the caudal peduncle. Uniform brown.

	millim.
Total length	106
„ „ without caudal	93
Length of the head	19
Diameter of the eye	2·4
Height of the body	20
Length of the caudal peduncle	15

A single specimen was obtained in Old Calabar. This species is nearest to *M. liberiensis* (Steind.), but readily distinguished by a shorter anal fin, with a smaller number of rays.

Mormyrus amblystoma, sp. n.

D. 24.   A. 30.   L. lat. 40.

Snout short, obtuse, as long as the eye, with the mouth at the lower side. The mouth is very broad, twice as broad as the eye, armed above with twenty-two and below with thirty notched teeth ; its corner is beyond the vertical from the front margin of the eye. The upper profile of the head is somewhat more curved than the lower and steadily ascends to the dorsal fin. Eye small, one-fifth of the length of the head. The height of the body is contained $2\frac{3}{5}$ times in the total length (without caudal), the length of the head $3\frac{3}{4}$ times ; the caudal peduncle is slender, much shorter than the head, its depth being two-fifths of its length. The origin of the dorsal fin is behind that of the anal and nearer to the root of the caudal than to the head. The anal extends also further backwards than the dorsal. Pectoral shorter than the head, reaching to the middle of the ventral. Ventral very short, only half as long as the pectoral or as the distance of its root from the vent. Scales rather large ; there are eight in an oblique series running from the first anal ray to the lateral line, and three and two half longitudinal series on the side of the peduncle of the tail. Silvery brownish above ; a deep black spot on the root of the caudal, and another high up on the side below the origin of the dorsal fin.

		millim.
Total length		155
„ „ without caudal		133
Length of the head		35
Diameter of the eye		7
Width of the mouth		14
Length of the pectoral fin		25
„ „ ventral fin		12
„ „ caudal peduncle		23
Height of the body		49

One specimen from Talagouga.

Mormyrus simus.

Mormyrus (Petrocephalus) simus, Sauvage, Bull. Soc. Philom. 1878, p. 100 ; Nouv. Arch. Mus. iii. 1880, p. 51, pl. ii. fig. 3 (fig. mediocr.).
Mormyrus tenuicauda, Steind. Notes Leyd. Mus. xvi. 1894, p. 69, pl. iv. fig. 1.

D. 26–28. A. 31—33. L. lat. 48.[1]

Snout short, obtuse, a little shorter than the eye, with the mouth at its lower side. The mouth is narrow, not wider than the eye, armed above with twelve and below with twenty-two teeth ; its corner lies beyond the vertical from the front margin of the eye. The upper profile of the head is a little more curved than the lower, and steadily ascends to the origin of the dorsal fin. Eye one-fourth of the length of

[1] This is the number of transverse series above the lateral line, which is composed of larger scales, only forty in number.

the head.   The height of the body is contained 2⅘ times in
the total length (without caudal), the length of the head four
times.   Caudal peduncle slender, much shorter than the head
(measured from the last anal ray), its depth being contained
2⅘ times in its length.   The origin of the dorsal fin is behind
that of the anal and midway between the root of the caudal
and end of the opercle.   The anal extends also further backwards than the dorsal.   Pectoral fin shorter than the head,
reaching rather beyond the middle of the ventral.   Ventral
fin only half as long as the pectoral or as the distance of its
root from the vent.   Scales of moderate size ; there are twelve
or thirteen in an oblique series running from the first anal ray
to the lateral line, and three and two half longitudinal series
on the side of the caudal peduncle.   Silvery, brownish above ;
anterior part of the dorsal blackish.

	millim.
Total length	130
„ „ without caudal	106
Length of the head	25
Diameter of the eye	6
Width of the mouth	5·5
Height of the body	41
Length of the caudal peduncle	20

There are some slight discrepancies between this and
Sauvage's descriptions, which are quite within the limits of
individual variation.   Besides, our specimens from Talagouga belong to the same district as Sauvage's, which came
from Doumé (Ogowé).   Steindachner's description is more
precise and his figure more accurate ; he compared the species
with *M. Sauvagii* (Blgr.), which, however, has a much wider
mouth.   The specimens described by Steindachner came
from Liberia.   Thanks to Dr. Jentink's kindness I have been
able to compare the latter with those collected by Miss
Kingsley.

Mormyrus Sauvagii.

Mormyrus (*Petrocephalus*) *Sauvagii*, Boulenger, Ann. & Mag. Nat.
    Hist. 1887, xix. p. 149.

Warri.

Mormyrus affinis.

Petrocephalus affinis, Sauvage, Bull. Soc. Philm. 1878, p. 101.
Mormyrus (*Petrocephalus*) *affinis*, Sauvage, N. Arch. Mus. iii. 1880,
    p. 52, pl. ii. fig. 2.

I refer a young specimen, 86 millim. long, from Talagouga

to this species, although it shows some discrepancies from the typical specimen (from Doumé) ; it has D. 20, A. 25, L. lat. 58 ; there are eight notched teeth in the upper as well as lower jaw. Five longitudinal series of scales along each side of the caudal peduncle.

Mormyrus Marchei.

? *Petrocephalus Marchei*, Sauvage, Bull. Soc. Philom. 1878, p. 100.
? *Mormyrus (Petrocephalus) Marchei*, Sauvage, N. Arch. Mus. iii. 1880, p. 50, pl, ii. fig. 5.

D. 22. A. 30. L. lat. 63.

Snout short, obtuse, but rather longer than the eye, with the mouth at its lower side. Mouth narrow, a little wider than the eye, armed above and below with six notched teeth ; its corner lies a little in advance of the vertical from the front margin of the orbit. The upper profile of the head is somewhat more convex than the lower and ascends slightly towards the origin of the dorsal. Eye one-fifth of the length of the head. The height of the body is contained $3\frac{3}{4}$ times in the total length (without caudal), the length of the head $5\frac{1}{2}$ times. Caudal peduncle extremely slender, longer than the head (measured from the last anal ray), its depth being only two-ninths of its length. The origin of the dorsal fin is behind that of the anal and midway between the root of the caudal and the end of the opercle. The anal extends also further backwards than the dorsal. Pectoral fin as long as the head, reaching beyond the middle of the ventral ; ventral fin half as long as the pectoral or as the distance of its root from the vent. Abdomen behind the ventral fin compressed into a ridge. Scales of moderate size ; there are nine in an oblique series running from the vent to the lateral line and three and two half longitudinal series cover the side of the caudal peduncle. Silvery, light brownish above.

	millim.
Total length	175
„ „ without caudal	150
Length of the head	27
Diameter of the eye	5
Width of the mouth	5˙5
Height of the body	38
Length of caudal peduncle	33

One specimen from Talagouga.

Pellonula vorax, Gthr.

Old Calabar.

Notopterus afer, Gthr.

Old Calabar.

Notopterus nigri, Gthr.

Kondo-Kondo.

Tetrodon pustulatus, Murr.

Old Calabar.

EXPLANATION OF THE PLATES.

PLATE I.

Fig. A. *Ctenopoma Kingsleyæ.*
Fig. B. —— *nanum.*
Fig. C. —— *gabonense.*

PLATE II.

Fig. A. *Mormyrus Kingsleyæ.*
Fig. B. *Alestes Kingsleyæ.*
Fig. C. *Barilius bibie.*

*** The specimens mentioned in this paper as from the Azuminé Creek and Warri were kindly given to me by W. H. Hamilton, Esq., and D. Bleasby, Esq., respectively.—M. H K.

APPENDIX IV

ORTHOPTERA, HYMENOPTERA, AND HEMIPTERA

A List of the Orthoptera, Hymenoptera, and Hemiptera collected by Miss Kingsley on the River Ogowé, with Descriptions of some new Genera and Species. By W. F. KIRBY, F.L.S., F.E.S., &c., Assistant in Zoological Department, British Museum (Natural History).

The collection formed by Miss Kingsley, though small,[1] contained several species of considerable interest, in addition to the novelties ; and hence I have thought it worth while to prepare a complete list. Eight species in all are here described as new, for two of which it has been necessary to establish new genera. It is, however, to be regretted that in most cases only single specimens were received, and several of them were immature, or the number of new species might have been larger.

Order ORTHOPTERA.

Family **Blattidæ**.

Subfamily *PANCHLORINÆ*.

TRICHOMERA, gen. nov.

Female.—Apterous : front of head rounded, projecting beyond the prothorax ; face hardly oblique ; antennæ thickened at base and tapering to tips ; prothorax moderately arched, the hinder angles rounded off, those of the meso- and metathorax less rounded and more produced backwards ; tibiæ

---

[1] This collection is entirely from Lembarene (River Ogowé). I have no lists of collection of insects from Calabar.—M. H. K.

strongly spined above, but femora with no spines, but only clothed with fine hair ; abdomen very broad, supra-anal plate triangularly emarginate at the extremity to nearly half its length ; cerci very broad, pointed at the end, and a little shorter than the supra-anal lamina.

The unarmed femora place this genus in the Panchlorinæ, but in shape it resembles the females of some of the Blattinæ. The male is probably winged.

Trichomera insignata, sp. n.

Long. corp. 20–21 millim., lat. 13 millim.

Female.—Blackish, with testaceous markings ; face nearly smooth, shining black below the vertex, the sides, mouth, and a band within the eyes and antennæ testaceous ; vertex testaceous in front, with blackish streaks projecting into it from behind ; head and thorax clothed with fine down ; prothorax and sides of meso- and metathorax finely punctured, middle of meso- and metathorax and abdomen rather coarsely granulated ; mesothorax testaceous, somewhat speckled with reddish brown, the centre filled up with a large blackish blotch, with two projecting angles on each side in front and behind, the two innermost of the hinder projections extending to the hinder margin of the prothorax, and the second of the front projections connected with a large oblong black patch bordering part of the sides of the prothorax ; meso- and metathorax bordered on the sides with reddish brown and with several irregular testaceous markings ; on the abdomen these are continued more regularly, forming a central and nearly parallel series, and two outer series, the first of which is nearly straight and the second connected with the testaceous border below the lateral angles of the segments ; supra-anal plate black, with a broad testaceous band on each side ; cerci black ; antennæ reddish, shading into brown ; pectus testaceous ; abdomen brown beneath.

Two specimens obtained.

Family **Mantidæ.**

Subfamily *MANTINÆ.*

HIERODULA, Burm.

A single immature specimen of this genus, remarkable for the very heavy black band on the front femora and tibiæ and for the black spines of the latter.

Family **Phasmidæ**.

Subfamily *PALOPHINÆ*.

Palophus centaurus.

Palophus centaurus, Westw. Cat. Phasm. p. 91, n. 233, pl. xxxi. fig. 1 (1859); Brogn. Nouv. Arch. Mus. Paris, (3) iii. p. 195, pl. viii., pl. ix. figs. 1-4 (1892).

One of the largest winged African Phasmidæ. A single female specimen was in the collection.

Subfamily *PHASMINÆ*.

BATHYCHARAX, gen. nov.

Female.—Apterous, rather stout, granulated; antennæ rather shorter than the front femora, 23-jointed, with most of the joints long and cylindrical; scape flattened, about twice as long as broad, second joint also longer than broad and considerably longer than the following joints; front legs much longer and front femora much thicker than in the last two pairs of legs.

Readily distinguished from *Phasma* (*Bacillus* auct.) by the granulated body and the cylindrical joints of the antennæ.

Bathycharax granulatus, sp. n.

Uniform brown, except that the face is varied above with black and below with yellow. Head with a row of four raised tubercles behind; pronotum with three imperfectly formed grooves and a transverse one dividing it nearly equally; there is also a distinct carina on each side; mesonotum thickly granulated and with three central carinæ, the lateral ones not extending to its extremity, but a central one continued along the metanotum and abdomen; abdomen with segments 2–8 (counting the median segment as 1) gradually diminishing in length; ninth short and transverse; tenth three times as long as broad, gradually tapering, and extending for half its length beyond the operculum; cerci very short, rather broad and rounded, just projecting on each side at the base of the tenth segment. Under surface of the body carinated throughout on the central line behind the propectus, which is carinated on the sides; most of the hinder part of the body is carinated on the sides both above and below the middle. Legs carinated and sulcated; first joint of front tarsi about as long as all the remaining joints together ; first joint of four hinder legs about as long as the terminal joint, the second and third being each about twice as long as the fourth, which is the shortest.

Dimensions.

		millim.
Long.	corporis	100
„	antennarum	18
„	capitis	6
„	pronoti	5
„	mesonoti	22
„	metanoti, cum segmento medio	17
„	segmenti medii	4
„	„ terminali	9
„	femorum anticorum	24
„	„ mediorum	19
„	„ posteriorum	22
„	tibiarum anticarum	26
„	„ mediarum	15
„	„ posteriarum	22

In many particulars this species agrees with the description of *Bacillus Buchholzi*, Gerstaecker, from the Cameroons (Mitth. naturw. Ver. Neu-Vorpommern und Rügen, xiv. p. 99, 1883), but it is much larger, and the structure of the abdomen appears to be very dissimilar in the two insects.

Family **Achetidæ**.

Subfamily *GRYLLOTALPINÆ*.

Gryllotalpa africana.

Gryllotalpa africana, Palisot de Beauvois, Ins. Afr. Amér. p. 229, Orth pl. iii. *c*. fig. 6 (1805 ?).

An abundant species throughout the warmer parts of the world.

Family **Phasgonuridæ**.

Subfamily *HETRODINÆ*.

Cosmoderus Kingsleyæ, sp. n.

Long. 21–25 millim.
Rufo-testaceous, abdomen inclining to cupreous, especially in the female ; face yellowish, slightly varied with red, and with a black spot on each side at the base of the clypeus ;

antennæ reddish on the basal half, shading into blackish, at
least 40-jointed, the scape and second joint thickened, the scape
half as long again as broad, the second joint hardly longer than
broad, the third joint twice as long as the fourth, the rest tapering and gradually decreasing in length to beyond the middle,
when they become longer and more cylindrical; vertex and
thorax closely punctured, the latter more coarsely ; thorax
with two strong spines at the frontal angles, a strong spine on
each side, between which runs a raised ridge, and a row of
eight large spines behind.   There is one more large spine on
each side slightly before the others ; on the yellow lower ridge
of the thorax most of the spines are red, tipped with black ;
those on the legs are described in characterising the genus,
The dividing ridge of the thorax is brownish ; before it are
two pairs of shallow brownish depressions, and behind it a
row of five on each side, curving outwards, and two or three
additional pairs in the middle.   Abdomen smooth, more or
less cupreous, with some scattered punctures towards the end
of the segments.

Much resembles *C. erinaceus*, Fairmaire, from the Gaboon,
but only half the size.   Described from two males and one
female, which hardly differ in structure, thus making it prob-
able that the insect alluded to by Dr. Karsch as the female of
Cosmoderus erinaceus (Berl. ent. Zeitschr. xxxi. p. 59) belongs
to a different genus, and not improbably to *Aprophantia*, described below.

The curious wingless insects belonging to the family Hetro-
didæ must be very numerous in the warmer parts of Africa.
Almost every collection from these regions, however small,
furnishes one or more new species if it contains any Orthoptera.   I take the opportunity of adding the description of a
new genus and species, which appears to have been confounded
with *Cosmoderus erinaceus*, in a footnote.[1]

---

[1] APROPHANTIA, gen. nov.

Allied to *Cosmoderus*, but with longer and more slender legs, the hind
tibiæ especially being considerably longer than the others.   All the tibiæ
sulcated, front tibiæ with conspicuously open foramina.   Femora above
with a strong pair of terminal spines ; femora and tibia otherwise unarmed above, but with a double row of very strong spines beneath.
Frontal spine very strong ; front coxæ spined, and a spine in front of the
middle tarsi.
Abdomen smooth ; mesothorax raised in the middle, its front angles
armed with a large double spine, from which a strong carina runs to the
sides of the ridge, where the carina rises into another large spine ; the
hinder part of the mesothorax is armed with a row of nine or ten more

Subfamily *CONOCEPHALINÆ.*

Pseudorhynchus sicarius.

Pseudorhynchus sicarius, Serville, Hist. Nat. Ins., Orth. p. 310 (1839).

One specimen.

Subfamily *MECOPODINÆ.*

Macroscirtes kanguroo. .

Macroscirtes kanguroo, Pictet, Mém. Soc. Genève, xxxi. (6) p. 14, pl. iii. fig. 38 (1888).

One specimen of this curious long-legged insect.

Family Locustidæ.

PŒCILOCERA, Serv.

A single immature specimen probably belonging to this genus.

Cyrtacanthacris ruficornis.

Gryllus ruficornis, Fabr. Ent. Syst. ii. p. 54, n. 28 (1793).

One of the great migratory locusts of Africa. The description of Fabricius seems to have been taken from an unusually dark specimen.

strong spines, extending on each side nearly to the level of the front coxæ.

Aprophantia maculata, sp. n.

Long. corp. 38–48 millim.

Testaceous yellow (probably green during life) ; the tips of the spines, a double row of spots more or less complete on both sides of the femora, and a patch over the foramina on the front tibiæ black. Antennæ testaceous, with five long black bands increasing in length, the last terminal. Male with some obsolete brown markings on the face, two running up from above the frontal horn, and one on each side beyond, angulated outwards. The male also has some obsolete depressed brown marks on the front and sides of the thorax above, nearly as in the species of true *Cosmoderus.* In the female these markings are wanting, and the colour is darker, especially at the sides of the thorax, the front and back of the abdomen, and towards the extremities of the tibiæ, and along their carinæ. The male has three pairs of spines on the femora beneath and two additional spines on the outer carina of the hind femora, and six pairs of spines on the four front tibiæ, and eight or nine rows of spines (not all paired) on the hind tibiæ. The female differs in having five pairs of spines on the hind femora, but the legs are otherwise spined nearly as in the male.

Described from a single pair (♂ and ♀) from the Cameroons.

Order HYMENOPTERA.

Section TEREBRANTIA.

Subsection Entomophaga.

Family **Braconidæ**.

Bracon plumosus, sp. n.

Long. corp. 11 millim.; long. ovip. 10 millim.

Female.—Head, antennæ, and abdomen (including the petiole) black above; head beneath and mouth-parts fulvous; mandibles bidentate and tipped with black; thorax wholly rufous. Front legs: coxæ and base of femora rufous, the rest wanting; middle legs rufous, tarsi and tibiæ above black; hind legs black, a white spot at the end of the coxæ above and the second joint of the trochanters rufous. Abdomen below white, with a row of five long black dashes on each side, the first bifid in front. Ovipositor rufous, partly black towards the extremity; above it are two long and rather stout black setæ, densely plumose beyond the middle, the apical third of the cilia being white; the extreme tip of the setæ is spatulate and whitish beneath. Wings smoky, the transverse nervures bordered with subhyaline.

Probably allied to *B. semiflavus*, Brullé.

Family **Ichneumonidæ**.

Subfamily *PIMPLINÆ*.

Pimpla nigricornis, sp. n.

Long. corp. cum ovip. 15 millim.; ovip. 3 millim.; exp. al. 23 millim.

Female.—Yellow, antennæ and ovipositor black; vertex with a black band covering the ocelli, which is pointed in front and on each side of the frontal ocellus; mesothorax with a large oval black spot on each side, a triangular reddish patch in front, the hinder angle of which is black, and a transverse black patch in front of the raised scutellum; abdomen yellow on the first two segments and shading into light reddish beyond; a large black spot on each side of segments 3–5; the first segment has a slight impression on each side, the five following ones have a deep groove before the extremity; the front of the body is nearly smooth, but the third segment of the abdomen is sparingly, and segments 4–6 heavily, punctured. Legs slightly suffused with reddish ; middle femora slightly, and hind femora considerably, thickened ; hind legs much longer than the others and hind tarsi clothed with a blackish pubescence.

One specimen.

Allied to the Indian *P. punctata*, Fabr.

Subfamily OPHIONINÆ·

Ophion latipenne, sp. n.

Long. corp. 26 millim.; exp. al. 53 millim. ; lat. al. ant. 9 millim.

Female.—Rufo-testaceous, slightly pubescent ; occiput, antennæ, legs, and especially the sides of the face, slightly more yellowish ; eyes slightly emarginate in front just above the antennæ, below the antennæ they are nearly parallel, or very slightly incurved. Antennæ pubescent, about 50-jointed joints three and four annular, joint five the longest, the remainder cylindrical, hardly longer than broad in the middle, and gradually tapering and lengthening towards the extremity, the last conical ; tips of mandibles black ; ocelli very large, filling up the space between the eyes on the vertex, black, except extreme front of the frontal ocellus beneath, and the outer sides of the two hinder ocelli. Thorax and abdomen very finely and closely punctured ; mesothorax with two converging lines slightly yellower than the ground-colour, but only carinated at the lateral borders ; metathorax also with a middle carina. Abdomen very large, raised, and somewhat compressed laterally. Hind legs longer than the others ; all the tibia armed with a pair of terminal spines. Wings rather broad, yellowish hyaline, more strongly tinged with yellow at the base and along the costal area of the hind wings, and towards the tip a little smoky, especially on the hind wings. Nervures rufous along the costa and towards the inner margin ; otherwise blackish. Anterior wings with three bullæ— one on the lower curve of the cell near its extremity, one on the recurrent nervule, and the third on the cross-nervule running upwards from the extremity of the internal nervule.

The Ophionidæ of Africa are rather numerous, but very few have yet been described.

Family **Evaniidæ**.

Evania lævigata.

Evania lævigata, Latr. Gen. Crust. Ins. iii. p. 251 (1807).

The species of this curious genus, though rare in England, are common in many countries, and are believed to be parasitic on cockroaches.

Section ACULEATA.

Subsection HETEROGYNA.

Family **Formicidæ**.

Subfamily *FORMICINÆ*

Camponotus maculatus.

Formica maculata, Fabr. Spec. Ins. i. p. 491, n. 15 (1781).

A common African species.

Œcophylla virescens.

Formica virescens, Fabr. Syst. Ent. p. 392, n. 9 (1775).

These green ants are found throughout the tropics of the Old World, and form their nests of leaves on trees.

Subfamily *PONERINÆ*.

Anomura molesta.

Anomura molesta, Gerst. Mon. Akad. Wiss. Berl. 1858, p. 262 ; Peters's Reise Mossamb., Zool. v. p. 562, pl. xii. fig. 2 (1862).

A species originally described from Mozambique.

Subsection FOSSORES.

Pelopæus spirifex.

Sphex spirifex, Linn. Syst. Nat. (ed. x.) i. p. 570, n. 8 (1758).

A widely distributed species in South Europe and Africa.

Subsection DIPLOPTERA.

Family **Eumenidæ.**

Eumenes decipiens, sp. n.

Eumenes melanosoma, Smith, MS., nec. Sauss.

Long. corp. 15–17 millim. ; exp. al. 25–27 millim.

Head black above, the points of the angles within the eyes
yellowish ; antennæ ferruginous, black above ; face ferruginous, very long, beak-like, sometimes yellow, only the
mandibles and a space at the base of the clypeus remaining
ferruginous. Prothorax red, with a large triangular black
spot nearly filling up the hinder angles on each side ; mesothorax black ; tegulæ large, black, bordered outside with
reddish ; scutellum black, a short yellow dash running from
its extremity between the base of the wings ; postscutellum
black, with a yellow dot on each side ; metathorax black,
deeply sulcated in the middle, and forming two long triangles,
the points reddish, into which runs an oblique lateral yellow
line. Pectus black, red towards the sutures. Petiole and
abdomen black, shining, and much more finely punctured
than the thorax ; petiole rufous beneath and bordered behind
above with a pale yellow line. First segment of abdomen
bordered behind above with a yellow line, widely interrupted
in the middle. Legs rufous, front (and sometimes middle)
tibiæ lined with yellowish ; tarsi clothed with greyish pubescence, and the four hinder legs more or less blackish above.
Wings iridescent purplish subhyaline.

Agrees very closely with the description and figure of the
Javan *E. melanosoma,* Sauss., but appears to be distinct.
Specimens in the British Museum from Sierra Leone were
labelled *E. melanosoma* by the late F. Smith. The species
belongs to the group of *E. æthiopica,* Sauss.

Synagris dentata.

Synagris dentata, Sauss. Études Fam. Vesp. i. p. 80, p. xiii. fig. 3
(1852).

A common African species.

Subsection ANTHOPHILA.

Family **Apidæ**.

Subfamily *MEGACHILINÆ*.

Euaspis abdominalis.

Thynnus abdominalis, Fabr. Ent. Syst. ii. p. 245, n. 3 (1793).

A single specimen.

Subfamily *XYLOCOPINÆ*.

Xylocopa imitator.

Xylocopa imitator, Smith, Cat. Hym. Ins. Brit. Mus. ii. p. 351, n. 35 (1854).

One specimen.

Order HEMIPTERA.

Suborder HETEROPTERA.

Family **Scutelleridæ**.

Subfamily *ARTHIOPTERINÆ*.

Plataspis punctata.

Canopus punctatus, Leach, Bowdich, Mis. Ashantee, App. p. 496 (1819); Gray, Griffith's Anim. Kingd. xv. p. 233, pl. xcii. fig. 2 (1832).

A very pretty species.

Brachyplatys pallipes.

Cimex pallipes, Fabr. Spec. Ins. ii. p. 343, n. 26 (1781).

One specimen.

Coptosoma Murrayi (?).

Coptosoma Murrayi, Sign., Thomson, Arch. Ent. ii. p. 271, pl. ii. fig. 2 (1858) ; Stål, Hem. Afr. i. p. 9 (1864).
Coptosoma hirtella, Stål, Œfv. Vet.-Akad. Förh. 1858, p. 433.

One specimen only.

Subfamily *SCUTELLERINÆ*.

Sphærocoris ocellatus.

Tetyra ocellata, Klug, Symb. Phys. v. pl. xliii. figs. 1-3 (1834).

A common species in most parts of Africa.

Family **Pentatomidæ.**

Subfamily *PENTATOMINÆ.*

Gen. ——?

An undetermined species of Pentatomidæ, superficially resembling *Dolycoris baccarum*, Linn., but with longer and more slender antennæ.

Atelocera serrata.

Halys serrata, Fabr. Syst. Rhyng. p. 181, n. 2 (1803).

One specimen.

Aspongopus, Lap., sp.

An immature specimen, apparently allied to *A. femoralis*, Stål; black, with the tegmina, borders of the abdomen, and femora greenish cupreous, and the last joint of the antennæ rufo-testaceous, except at the base.

Subfamily *TESSERATOMINÆ.*

Piezosternum mucronatum.

Pentatoma mucronata, Pal. de Beauvois, Ins. Afr. Amér. p. 46, Hémipt. pl. vi. fig. 5 (1805 ?).

One specimen, considerably smaller than *P. calidum*, Fabr., and agreeing fairly with Palisot de Beauvois's figure quoted above, which I have no doubt was taken from an African specimen, though it has latterly been referred to the American *P. subulatum.* This small form may or may not prove to be distinct from *P. calidum*, for a series would be required to compare the characters; and I therefore provisionally retain Palisot's name for it.

Subfamily *PHYLLOCEPHALINÆ.*

Gen. ——?

An immature specimen, apparently belonging to a new genus near *Macrina*, Amyot.

Family **Coreidæ.**

Subfamily *COREINÆ.*

Mygdonia tuberculosa.

Mictis tuberculosa, Sign. Rev. Zool. 1851, p. 447, pl. xv. g. 5.

A common West-African species.

Mictis tristator.

Lygæus tristator, Fabr. Ryng. p. 266, n. 13 (1803).
Two specimens obtained.

Family **Pyrrhocoridæ.**

Subfamily *PYRRHOCORINÆ.*

Antilochus submaculatus, sp. n.

Long. corp. 16 millim.

Head red, occiput and vertex black nearly as far as the
base of the antennæ, but upper orbits red ; the lower part of
the head under the proboscis is blackish, except behind ;
head with a central groove and rugose-punctate ; close to the
back is a waved line, the narrow part behind which is finely
punctured. Antennæ black, the terminal joint testaceous,
brown towards the tip. Scape curved, thicker than the
remaining joints, and a little shorter than the second and
fourth joints, which are of equal length ; third joint rather
shorter than the scape. Rostrum extending as far as the
hind coxæ ; the basal joint grooved. Thorax black, bordered
all round with testaceous ; the inner edge of the border and
the hinder lobe marked with large punctures ; front lobe with
a central groove and not punctured, except on a narrow
triangular space in front. Scutellum and clavus sparingly
punctured, corium more thickly ; scutellum and tegmina
black, clavus bordered with a narrow red line at the base and
on the inside ; corium rather broadly bordered with rufo-
testaceous on the outside, the stripe then crossing to the end
of the clavus, and then curving outwards again, leaving the
greater part of the centre and the apex black, as is also the
membrane. Legs black ; coxæ, trochanters, base and under
surface of femora coral-red ; tarsi, except the basal joint,
yellowish grey below. Pleura black, bordered with testaceous
above and in the sutures, and with red below ; abdomen coral-

red, the first five segments beneath with a long black band on
the sides behind.

Allied to *A. bærhaviæ*, Fabr., but very distinct.

Family **Reduviidæ.**

Subfamily *REDUVIINÆ.*

Reduvius, Fabr., sp.

An immature specimen.

Family **Belostomatidæ.**

Hydrocyrius herculeus (?).

Ilyotrephes herculeus, Stål, Œfv. Vet.-Akad. Förh. 1855, p. 46.
Hydrocyrius herculeus, Stål, Hemipt. Afr. iii. p. 181 (1865).

From Lembarene.
Agrees fairly with Stål's description, taken from Caffrarian
specimens.

List of Arachnida and Myriapoda sent by Miss Kingsley to the British Museum.[1]

A. Ticks. —Red velvety Tick from Ambaca—Trom-
bidium tinctorium, Linn.
Elephant Tick from Old Calabar—
Ixodes sp. ?

B. Spiders. —1. Nephila femoralis, Luc. ⎧ The two
2. Nephila lucasii, Sim. ⎪ species that
Gold Coast and Old ⎬ spin the great
Calabar. ⎪ webs of which
⎪ the natives
⎩ use the silk.

3. Heteropoda venatoria, Linn. Old
Calabar. Large, long-legged, flattish
House Spider.

4. Ctenus guineensis, Luc. Old Calabar.
Large Spider.

C. Pedipalp. —Titanodamon johnstonii, Poc. Old
Calabar. Okyon, Talagonga.

D. Millipede.—Oxydermus vittatus, Cook. Old Calabar.

[1] All these insects were collected during the dry season.—M. H. K.

List of Shells, etc. Collected at Corisco, Gaboon Estuary.

Conus prometheus.
Terebra cingula, Kiener.
Malongena morio, Lamarck.
Oliva acuminata, Lamarck.
Purpura coronata, Lamarck.
Cypræa starcororia, Linn.
Cypræa lurida, Linn.
Cypræa zonata, Chamintz.
Strombus bubonius, Lamarck.   (Fernando Po.)
Cassis spinosus, Gronovius.
Littorina ahenea, Reeve.
Pachymalania Byroni, Gray.   (Old Calabar R.)
Tympanolomus fuscatus, Linn.
Tympanolomus radula, Linn.
Achatina marginata, Swainson.
Achatina balteata, Reeve.
Pseudachatina Downesi, Gray.
Cardium costatune, Linn.
Dosinia africana, Gray.
Cardita lacunosa, Reeve.
Macoma nymphalis, Lamarck.
Schizodesma nitida, Schreetar.
Schizodesma largillierti, Philippi.
Standella silicula, Deshayes.
Donose rugosus, Linn.
Ungulina alba, Kang.

Two Gorgonias.

Leptogorgia pinnata.
Antillia sp.

Plants Collected in the Cameroons and Ogowé Districts.

C = from the bundle labelled " Cameroons."
O ,, ,, ,, " Ogowé."

Triumfetta semitriloba, O.
Adenocarpus Mannii, Hook. f.   C.
Crassula abyssinica, A. Rich.   C.
Cuviera acutiflora, D. C.

Morinda citrifolia, O.
Psychotria sp. O.
Helichrysum Mannii, Hook. f. C.
Helichrysum globosum, Schpr. C.
Senecio Burtoni, Hook. f. C.
Senecio clarenceana, Hook. f. C.
Lactuca capensis, Thunb. O.
Ericinella Mannii, Hook. f. C.
Lippia sp. near L. asperifolia, A. Rich. C.
Stachys? C.
Habenaria, 3 species. C.
Renealmia africana, Benth. C
Commelinacea sp. O.
Cyperus diffusus, Vahl. O.
Gleichenia dichotoma, Hook. O.
Pteris aquilina, O.
Pteris quadriaurita, Retz. C.
Asplenium Brachypteron, Kze. C.
Nephrodium cicutarium, Baker. C.
Nephrodium Filix mas, Rich? C.
Dalbergia? O.
Usnea barbata, Fr. O.
Usnea barbata, var. O.
Physcia leucomela, Mich. O.

Fasicated stem of Dracanea from Rembwe Swamps.

List of Grasses Collected in West Tropical Africa.

Trichopteryx near T. elegans.
Trichopteryx flammida, Benth.
Pennisetum setosum, Rich.
Setaria sp. near S. aurea.
Panicum ovalifolium, Beauv.?
Panicum plicatum, Lam.?
Paspalum paniculatum, L.
Sporobolus elongatus, R. Br.

APPENDIX V

THE INVENTION OF THE CLOTH LOOM

This story is taken down from an Eboe, but practically the same story can be found among all the cloth-making tribes in West Africa.

IN the old times there was a man who was a great hunter ; but he had a bad wife, and when he made medicine to put on his spear, she made medicine against his spear, but he knew nothing of this thing and went out after bush cow.

By and by he found a big bush cow, and threw his spear at it, but the bush cow came on, and drove its horns through his thigh, so the man crept home, and lay in his house very sick, and the witch doctor found out which of his wives had witched the spear, and they killed her, and for many days the man could not go out hunting. But he was a great hunter, and his liver grew hot in him for the bush, so he dragged himself to the bush, and lay there every day. One day, as he lay, he saw a big spider making a net on a bush and he watched him. By and by he saw how the spider caught his game, and that the spider was a great hunter, and the man said :—" If I had hunted as this spider hunts, if I had made a trap like that and put it in the bush and then gone aside and let the game get into it and weary itself to death quickly,—quicker and safer than they do in pitfalls—that bush cow would not have gored me." And so after a time he tried to make a net like the spider's, out of bush rope, and he did this thing and put his net into the forest, and caught bush deer (gazelles) and earth-pig (pangolins) and porcupines, and he made more nets, and every net he made was better, and he grew well, and became a greater hunter than before. One day he made a very fine net, and his wife said "This is a cloth, it is better than our cloth (bark cloth) because when the rain gets to it, it does not shrivel. Make me a cloth like this and then I will beat it with the mallet and wear it." And the man tried to do this thing, but he could not get it a good shape and he said, " Yet the spider gets a shape in his cloth. I will go and ask him again about this thing." And he went to the spider, and took him offering, and said: " Oh, my lord, teach me more things." And he sat and watched him for many days.

LOOM AT EQUETTA.

By and by he saw more (his eyes were opened) and he saw the spider made his net on sticks, and so he went home and got fine bush rope that he had collected, and taken there, to make his game nets with, and he brought them to the bush near the spider, and fixing the strings on to the bush he made a new net and he got shape into it, and he made more nets this way, and every net he made was better. And his wife was pleased and gave him sons, and by and by the man saw that he did not want all the sticks of a bush to make his net on, only some of them ; and so he took these home and put them up in his house, and made his nets there, and after a time his wife said : "Why do you make the stuff for me with that bush rope? Why do you not make it with something finer?" And he went into the bush and took offerings to the spider and said : "Oh, my lord, teach me more things!" And he sat and watched the spider, but the spider only went on making stuff out of his belly. And the man said : "Oh, my lord, you pass me. I cannot do this thing." And as he went home he thought and saw that there are trees, and there are bush ropes, thick bush rope and thin bush rope, and then there is grass which was thinner still, and he took the grass, and tried to make a net with it, and did this thing and made more nets and every net he made was better. And his wife was pleased and said "This is good cloth." And the man lived to be very old and was a great chief and a great hunter. For it is good for a man to be a great hunter, and it is good for a man to please women. This is the origin of the cloth loom.

It was in the old time, and men have got now thread on spools from the white man, for the white man is a great spider ; but this is how the black man learnt to make cloth.

INDEX

MARY HENRIETTA KINGSLEY (1862–1900) was born in Islington, London, the daughter of George Henry Kingsley, physician, naturalist and travel writer, and niece of the novelist Charles Kingsley. She educated herself at home, becoming interested in natural history and ethnology, but was given lessons in German to enable her to assist her father in his work. In the 1880s the family moved to Cambridge, where Mary Kingsley became acquainted with the work of Charles Darwin and T.H. Huxley. Until their deaths in 1892 she looked after and nursed her parents; shortly after this, her brother went to Burma, and Mary Kingsley at last had some time to herself.

In 1893 she set out on her first journey to West Africa; in 1894 she returned there to collect fishes and insects, and to investigate tribal customs and fetish. It was as a result of this second journey that *Travels in West Africa* (1897), for which she became famous, was written.

After her return to England, Mary Kingsley wrote articles and lectured all over the country on tropical Africa. *West African Studies*, an amplification of her ethnological work, which included a proposal for an alternative system of governing British territory in West Africa, was published in 1899. In March 1900, she went to South Africa to nurse Boer prisoners of war at Simonstown. There she caught enteric fever and died; by her own wish she was buried at sea. Her edition of her father's writings, *Notes on Sport and Travel*, and her *Story of West Africa*, were both published the year of her death. The Mary Kingsley Society of West Africa, later the African Society, was established in her memory.